THE TIMES

Good University Guide

2013

John O'Leary

with
Patrick Kennedy
Dr Nicki Horseman

TIMES BOOKS

Published in 2012 by Times Books

HarperCollins Publishers
77–85 Fulham Palace Road
Hammersmith
London W6 8JB

www.harpercollins.co.uk

First published in 1993 by Times Books. Nineteenth edition 2012

ISBN 978-0-00-746434-0

Patrick Kennedy and Dr Nicki Horseman have been lead consultants for Exeter Enterprises Limited, which has compiled the main university league table and the individual subject tables for this guide on behalf of *The Times* and HarperCollins.

Please see chapters 4 and 5 for a full explanation of the sources of data used in the ranking tables. The data providers do not necessarily agree with the data aggregations or manipulations appearing in this book and are also not responsible for any inference or conclusions thereby derived.

Project editor: Christopher Riches
Design, editorial and additional research: Edenside Computing Services Ltd

Printed and bound in Great Britain by Clays Ltd, St Ives plc.

MIX
Paper from
responsible sources
FSC www.fsc.org **FSC™ C007454**

FSC™ is a non-profit international organisation established to promote the responsible management of the world's forests. Products carrying the FSC label are independently certified to assure consumers that they come from forests that are managed to meet the social, economic and ecological needs of present and future generations, and other controlled sources.

Find out more about HarperCollins and the environment at
www.harpercollins.co.uk/green

Contents

About the Author

John O'Leary is a freelance journalist and education consultant. He was the Editor of *The Times Higher Education Supplement* from 2002 to 2007 and was previously Education Editor of *The Times*, having joined the paper in 1990 as Higher Education Correspondent. He has been writing on higher education for more than 30 years and is a member of the executive board of the QS World University Rankings. He is the author of *Higher Education in England*, published in 2009 by the Higher Education Funding Council for England. He has a degree in politics from the University of Sheffield.

Acknowledgements

We would like to thank the many individuals who have helped with this edition of *The Times Good University Guide*, particularly Greg Hurst, Education Editor of *The Times*, and Patrick Kennedy and Dr Nicki Horseman, the lead consultants for Exeter Enterprises Limited, which has compiled the main university league table and the individual subject tables for this *Guide* on behalf of *The Times* and HarperCollins Publishers; to the members of *The Times Good University Guide* Advisory Group for their time and expertise: Josie Lewis-Gibbs, Planning Officer, Imperial College, London; Jim Galbraith, Senior Strategic Planner, University of Edinburgh; Sue Hybart, Director of Planning, Cardiff University; Tom Wale, Senior Planning Officer at Loughborough University; Christine Couper, Head of Planning and Statistics, University of Greenwich; Lucy Hodson, Director of Strategic Planning, De Montfort University; and Alison Hartley, Head of Planning, the School of Oriental and African Studies; James McLaren and Jonathan Waller of HESA for their technical advice; Martin Ince, Kaya Burgess, Alice Hancock and Adam O'Leary for their contributions to the book.

We also wish to thank the publishers of the QS World University Rankings, the Academic Ranking of World Universities and *Times Higher Education* for permission to reproduce some of their main league tables, and all the university staff who assisted in providing information for this edition.

How to Use This Book

The *Times Good University Guide 2013* will help you to select the subject and university of your choice and to guide you through the whole process of getting to university. The answers to the questions below will help you to get the most out of the information we offer.

How do I choose a course?
» The first half of chapter 1 provides advice on what you should consider when choosing a subject area and relevant courses within that subject.
» The tables near the beginning of chapter 2 give details of the employment prospects for all major subjects.
» Chapter 5 provides details for 62 different subject areas (as listed on page 64).
» For each subject there is a league table that provides our assessment of the ranking of all universities offering courses in the particular subject area.
» For each subject we also provide some background information, details of employment prospects and selected websites where you can find out more about the subject.
» Specific advice for international students is given in chapter 12.

How do I choose a university?
» The second half of chapter 1 provides advice on choosing a university.
» If you are considering studying abroad, chapter 3 provides guidance and practical information.
» Central is the main *Times* League Table on pages 57–61. This ranks the universities by assessing their quality not just according to student satisfaction (drawn from the National Student Survey) but also through seven other factors, including research quality, the spending on services and facilities, and graduate employment prospects. This table gives an indication of the overall performance of each university.
» The second half of the book contains two pages on each university, giving a general overview of the institution as well as data on student numbers, how to contact the university, the accommodation provided by the university, and the fees and financial support for 2012–13. Note that details for support for 2013–14 had not been released when this book went to print in spring 2012.
» In addition, chapter 10 provides information on sport and sporting facilities across all the universities.
» For those considering Oxford or Cambridge, details of admission processes and of all the colleges can be found in chapter 13.
» Specific advice for international students is given in chapter 12.

How do I apply?
» Chapter 6 outlines the application procedure for university entry.
» It starts by advising you on how to complete the UCAS application, and then takes you through the process that we hope will lead to your university place for autumn 2013.
» Specific information about applying to Oxford and Cambridge is given in chapter 13.

Can I afford it?

» Chapters 7 and 8 outline the costs of studying at university (including the payment of fees) as well as sources of funds (including student loans, grants and bursaries).
» Chapter 9 provides advice on where to live while you are there.
» Accommodation charges for each university are given in the university profiles in chapter 14.

How will university enhance my career?

» The employment prospects and average starting salaries for the main subject groups are given in chapter 2.
» Universities are now doing more to increase the employability of their graduates. Some examples are given in chapter 2 – and check whether your chosen universities provide similar services.

How do I find out more?

» In each university profile (chapter 14) contact details are given (including email addresses and websites), so you can obtain more information on any university you are interested in.
» At the end of each chapter, a selection of useful websites is given.
» A further listing (pages 540–41) provides contact details for higher education institutes and university colleges that are not covered elsewhere within the book.
» *The Times Good University Guide* website **www.thetimes.co.uk/gug** will keep you up to date with developments throughout the year and contains further information and online tables.

Introduction

The impact of higher fees

The relationship between universities and their students has changed forever with the introduction of fees of up to £9,000 a year. Although no payment is required upfront, for the first time the individual, rather than the state, will meet most of the costs of a degree. Both universities and ministers expect students to demand more as a result.

Of course, the changes are not just about expectations and nor will the new system have settled down by the time prospective students make their applications for courses beginning in 2013. Universities are still adjusting – and, in many cases, reducing – the variety of subjects they offer at degree level, as well as rethinking their fees and student support packages. They are also required to make more information available to guide potential applicants this year and may have to make further changes to the number of places they provide.

Anyone hoping to embark on a degree in 2013 will need to tread carefully and muster as much comparative information as possible before making their choices. This *Guide* is intended as a starting point, a tool to help navigate the statistical minefield that will face applicants, as universities present their performance in the best possible light. There is a new chapter on the impact of the fee changes, as well as one focusing on all-important employment issues and the usual ranking of universities and more than 60 individual subject tables.

The first round of applications under the new fee arrangements suggests that the university system is weathering this shock, as it has so many others in the past. But first impressions can be deceptive. If the two previous fee landmarks, in 1998 and 2006, are anything to go by, competition for places will grow in 2013. The pattern then, following the introduction of the first fees of £1,000 and again with their subsequent trebling, was an initial sharp decline in demand, followed by an immediate recovery. This is because, as in 2011, there tends to be a boom year before fees rise, as those mature students who can, advance their plans. School-leavers, by contrast, do not choose when to take A levels and are less likely to be deterred by rising fees, particularly if their career aspirations lie in one of the ever-increasing number of occupations that require a degree.

By April 2012, the number of British 18-year-olds applying to universities and colleges had dropped by less than 9,000, or 3.4 per cent, some of which was the result of a fall in the size of the age group. In the context of nearly 500,000 admissions, it was a much less serious decline than many had predicted. Mature students accounted for the bulk of the overall decline of 9 per cent among UK applicants.

The question in 2013 will be whether the impact of recession and abnormally high graduate unemployment will be to delay a return to recent levels of demand from mature students and to deter more of those who are leaving school. Although the labour market for young people is at a low ebb, a growing number of employers have stepped up their recruitment of 18-year-olds, conscious of an opportunity to attract bright candidates who would rather not build up tens of thousands of pounds of debt at university. It is an understandable temptation, but one which may hamper future promotion prospects unless the scheme includes the option of higher education at some stage.

Expensive though the new fees may be – among the most expensive in the world – the right degree should still pay off in financial terms, as well as offering a life-enhancing experience. International comparisons consistently show the salary premium enjoyed by British graduates to be among the biggest in the world, even if it has been coming down in recent years. No one can predict the eventual impact of the downturn on the jobs market, but few good judges expect the outcome to be an economy in which a degree is less of an advantage than it has been in recent years.

However, the new fees surely will encourage prospective students and their parents or advisers to look more closely than ever at the likely benefits of degrees by subject and individual university. There are big differences in the immediate employment prospects and earnings of graduates in different subjects, as the tables in chapter 2 confirm, and these can be multiplied in subsequent years. The contrast between different universities is just as marked, although the subject tables in chapter 5 demonstrate that it pays to examine strengths and weaknesses at departmental level.

The institutions are already experiencing closer scrutiny at open days and in other inquiries from prospective applicants. Their prospectuses and access agreements are full of promises of employment-related schemes and an improved "student experience". This *Guide* may be one of the weapons in the students' armoury in testing those claims.

The outlook for applicants

The 2012 applications season was still unfolding when this *Guide* went to press. The number of applicants may have come as a pleasant surprise for ministers and most universities, but it is enrolments, not applications, that determine the health of institutions and their departments. A few universities were 20 per cent down on the record applications of the previous year; others knew that however great the demand for places, they would be compelled to take fewer students than in 2011. Still others were likely to find that applications did not translate into as many enrolments as they had hoped because high-achievers were able to go to more prestigious universities, while lower fees or more generous support packages might lure others away in the end.

In short, it is too soon to gauge the full impact of higher fees in 2012, let along further ahead. One study has even suggested that 15 universities will go bankrupt in the next few years, although there is absolutely no sign of this at present. Not only has there never been a university closure in modern times, but most are running healthy surpluses, having planned for more serious cuts than they have actually faced. Indeed, there will be increases in teaching income where universities are able to recruit to their target numbers.

Even where enrolments slump in 2012, most universities will be well able to survive one poor year because two larger, state-funded year groups will still be there to cushion the blow, along with postgraduates and overseas students. But that does not mean they will stand idly by in 2013. With further Government intervention likely to bring more unintended – and certainly unpredictable – consequences, there may well be course closures and fee changes at a number of universities. The University and College Union estimates that the number of undergraduate courses at UK universities has dropped by 27 per cent since 2006. This figure may rise in 2013, reducing the options available to applicants, as universities become even less patient with those that fail to pay their way.

Thus far, the changes could hardly have been introduced in a way more calculated to create instability. Universities have had to set fees without knowing the conditions that might affect their ability to recruit. Although the new system is intended to produce a market of sorts, in which student choice rules, there has been constant intervention. First, fees were limited and then places removed and redistributed.

The dominant theme in this *Guide* and in most discussions of higher education is the new fee regime for home and European Union undergraduates in England. Across the whole of the UK, however, the picture is much more confused. About one undergraduate in five across the UK will be paying more than £9,000 – and many already were before 2012–13 – because they come from outside the EU. Their fees are unaffected by the Coalition's university funding revolution, but some face an increase in any case. Other students are paying much less than £9,000 – nothing at all if they live and study in Scotland, or if they come from another EU country to a Scottish university. There are savings, too for Welsh and Northern Irish students, which are outlined in Chapter 7, but for students from England will find themselves paying between £7,000 and £9,000 for university degree courses, wherever they go in the UK.

That is not going to change in 2013, although it would be rash to assume that individual universities will charge the same – or offer the same scholarships and bursaries – as they did in 2012. They learnt the hard way that the Government may move the goalposts after they have agreed their pricing plan if they act too soon. That happened in 2011 when universities were told, after many had set their fees, of complicated new restrictions on how many students they could recruit, with different rules for the best-qualified students and the lowest fees.

The changes may have sounded technical, but they had a measurable impact on the opportunities available to different types of student. Previously, universities were told how many undergraduates they could enrol. Now they could recruit as many students as they liked who achieved at least AAB at A level, or its equivalent, opening the way for the top universities to mop up all the best candidates at the expense of the rest. Some, like Oxford and Cambridge, do not want to expand, but elsewhere there will be more places available on many of the most popular courses for those with the magic AAB grades. The question is what happens to the rest, since the overall number of places is set to fall by at least 10,000, and another 20,000 places are being redistributed to universities and colleges charging less than £7,500 a year.

In 2013, restrictions will also be lifted for those achieving ABB or the equivalent – a much more sizeable group. Some of the top universities will not be subject to any restrictions on the numbers they can recruit because their entire intake normally achieves more than three Bs, while the rest will face further uncertainty. With about a third of the available places either falling into this category or reserved for universities with low fees, candidates with lower grades may find their options limited. It will never have been so important to judge applications correctly and then to get the right grades.

Applicants should not assume that if they achieve ABB or above, they will necessarily have their pick of the top degrees. There will still be more qualified candidates than places on the most popular courses and it may be even more important to make the right "insurance" choice. Growing numbers of well-qualified students have been left without a place in recent years because they have applied only to high-demand courses, and then not been interested in the options available in Clearing. It saves a wasted year and a considerable amount of money to secure an offer from a university with lower entrance requirements than your first-choice institutions.

If your predicted grades are three Bs or less, it is will be even more important to be realistic about your choices in 2013. There may be fewer places available at universities in the top half of the main League Table, especially in the most popular subjects. The entry grades quoted in the subject tables are a good guide to levels of competition, but they include AS levels and multiple entries at A level, so most candidates with AAB at A level will score considerably more than 320 points overall.

For those who do misjudge their applications, there will be further options in the UCAS Extra system that operates from the beginning of June and in the Clearing period that follows A-level results day in late August. Although Clearing will soon be replaced by a new system, it will operate in 2013, and may include more of the leading universities than in previous years since they will still be able to recruit as many of the best-qualified students as they choose. However, it is likely to become a two-tier exercise, as those with lower grades are restricted to an even smaller range of universities.

Candidates with better grades than they expected may also find more options available in the Adjustment Period that runs for five days after results have been published. Although only 552 students found places this way in 2011, the lifting of recruitment restrictions should help to free up more places in 2013. Universities at the very top of the table may still be full, but there should be more opportunities to "trade up" if your grades are better than your highest offer.

Finding a place

Previous editions of this *Guide* have asserted confidently that there would be a place somewhere in higher education for every qualified applicant who wanted one. Although tens of thousands of candidates have always failed to secure a place, most either did not achieve the necessary entrance qualifications or changed their mind about going to university. Recent years have been different. The fact that thousands of last year's candidates reapplied in 2012, in spite of the fees hike, demonstrates that the shortage of places was real.

There were 1.3 applications per place in full-time higher education throughout the first decade of the 21st century. In 2011, it was still not far above 1.4 per place. Levels of competition have increased, particularly at the leading universities, but these are still far from impossible odds. More than 90 per cent of those with two A-level passes go on to higher education each year, and most of the remainder choose a different career path, rather than being rejected.

Commentators on higher education distinguish between "selecting universities" and "recruiting universities", but these labels underestimate the complexity of the choices facing today's applicants. Even now, there are very few universities where all the courses are heavily selective – there are simply not enough well-qualified candidates to go around in some subjects – and most so-called recruiting universities have areas in which they excel and can attract a strong field of applicants. This *Guide* uses the ratings of academics and students, plus entry standards and graduate employment rates, to differentiate between universities in 62 different subject areas.

When *The Times Good University Guide* first appeared, it helped to explode the myth that any British degree was as good as any other. Since then, the statistics behind the tables have confirmed significant variations in performance within British higher education. Employers distinguish between universities as well as individuals. The need to know the standing of a university, both as an institution and in the various subjects it offers, can only become more important as time goes on.

Changing patterns of demand

The number of applications may have dropped in 2012, but the demand for degree places remains close to the record levels seen in the first years of this decade. What higher fees may bring, however, is a lasting change in the pattern of demand for different subjects and types of course. Many vocational courses have seen a predictable surge in popularity, but applicants appear to be making their own judgments about the prospects for different areas of employment. Building courses are still struggling, for example, while computer science is enjoying a new lease of life.

Not surprisingly, given the economic picture, one discernible pattern appears to be continued growth in home-based study. The longstanding British preference for studying away from home had begun to reassert itself among those who can afford it, after a move in the opposite direction when top-up fees were introduced in 2006. Now, it may be that a change of culture will become established. Several (but not all) of the big post-1992 universities have seen considerable growth in applications continue in 2012.

There is no consistent pattern of subject choices, however. For several years, students have been more conscious of the need for a marketable qualification to service growing levels of debt among graduates. But the initial rush away from pure academic subjects towards the vocational did not persist in the years following the introduction of £3,000 fees. While some job-related degrees, including most branches of engineering, continue to prove attractive, a few subjects such as anthropology, with no direct link to employment, increased their popularity in 2012. Some subjects obviously have been affected by the recession, but prospective students seem to recognise that the majority of graduate jobs are open to any discipline.

One significant development will almost certainly be a rise in the popularity of part-time courses, encouraged by the introduction of the first proper system of student support. Although fees have risen, part-time education has become much more affordable through the provision of loans on courses that occupy at least 25 per cent of the time taken on an equivalent full-time course. Ministers expect many more students to take the option of spreading out their studies, where possible working at the same time.

What will not change, in all likelihood, is the growing tendency for UK students to remain within national borders. More Scots have applied to Scottish universities, where they no longer pay the graduate endowment; more Welsh are applying to study in Wales, although they do not have to do so to enjoy the advantage of reduced fees; and most English students continue to chase places at universities in England, with fewer looking further afield. There has been much speculation about increased interest in American and Continental universities as a consequence of higher fees in England, but it appears that there was no more than marginal growth in the take-up of places in 2012. Foreign universities are on the radar of sixth-formers, particularly at independent schools, to a much greater extent than in previous years. But it may take time for this to translate into action.

The other imponderable about the new fee levels has been their impact on working-class participation in higher education, which has been rising – although far less than successive Governments would have liked. Previous fee changes were not all bad news for students of any background: the requirement to pay upfront was scrapped and grants, bursaries and scholarships made available to bring down the cost for those from poor backgrounds. This is still the case under the new system and the extra financial support for students and higher threshold on the repayment of loans appear to have had an effect. Applications from the lowest socio-economic groups held steady at the start of 2012, while the decline came from more prosperous homes. The institutional profiles in this year's *Guide* include a section detailing the (sometimes complex) arrangements at each university.

This year's tables

Unlike most of the rankings that have sprung up in recent years, *The Times Good University Guide* has maintained as much consistency as possible in the methods used to compare universities. The indicators and weightings used in the overall ranking of universities are the same as last year. One marginal change in the main table is another reweighting of the grades awarded in the 2008 Research Assessment Exercise to give universities extra credit for work considered to be world-leading. The previous scores mirrored the official system used to allocate research funds to universities in England and the new ones follow a change in that procedure.

Another minor change has been to use only the most recent ratings of student satisfaction, one of the two most highly-weighted measures in the main league table. In the early years of the National Student Survey, it was thought prudent to average two years' scores to allow for possible instability and to ensure that as many universities as possible were included. Initially, some failed to reach the 50 per cent threshold for the publication of results. Now that the survey is fully established and attracts a substantial response from final-year undergraduates, the review group that meets annually to consider the methodology used to compile the tables felt there was no reason to use anything but the most recent results. This change is largely responsible for greater volatility in this year's table than in most recent editions.

There is one more university in this year's *Times* League Table, although only its name is completely new to the ranking. West London University appeared many times as Thames Valley, but chose not to submit data last year while it was affecting the transition to a new identity. As in previous years, there is no distinction made between public and private institutions, but only full universities with a range of faculties are included. There is no room, therefore, for the most expensive institution in the UK: the New College of the Humanities, which launched in 2012 with fees of £18,000 a year. In any case, it takes several years for a new institution to build up the data that enables it to be assessed in a league table.

The top of the main table has a familiar look, with Oxford and Cambridge extending their lead over the London School of Economics and Imperial College London. But the two ancient rivals are closer together than at any time in the past decade – ten points out of 1,000 across a range of indicators is almost the equivalent of a dead heat. And while Oxford leads in the main table, Cambridge is again dominant in the 62 subject tables, leading in more than half of them.

Scores are close in many other parts of the main table, emphasising how competitive the modern higher education system has become. Three points cover 18th to 21st places, for example, and the bottom three universities are within a single point of each other. Where scores are so close, there is little or no statistical significance in the relative placings.

In Scotland, St Andrews remains the leading university, in sixth place overall, but Glasgow is now within a point of Edinburgh. Cardiff retains a clear lead over Aberystwyth in Wales, while Queen's, Belfast is the long-established leader in Northern Ireland. Robert Gordon is again the highest-placed post-1992 university, just outside the top 50, but Lincoln has joined Oxford Brookes in a tie for that distinction in England.

Largely because of the switch to a single year's student satisfaction data, there have been some spectacular rises – and falls – in the latest table. Coventry and the University of the Arts London have made the most progress, jumping 22 places, while Bedfordshire and Derby are both up 18 places. Buckingham, however, has been a victim of its own success. It has dropped 20 places after re-entering the table last year close to the top 20 because staffing levels and spending on facilities did not keep pace with the extraordinary growth in the number of students.

Universities and league tables

League tables are seldom popular with those being measured. But the rankings at the heart of this *Guide* have stood the test of time, after 19 years of publication, and are quoted frequently by those with an interest in higher education, both at home and abroad. They are even used by governments in the allocation of scholarships and, in rare cases, in immigration decisions, although their prime function remains to help prospective students choose courses. Favourable results invariably appear prominently on universities' websites. Professor David Eastwood, now the Vice-Chancellor of Birmingham University, who was chief executive of the Higher Education Funding Council for England at the time of its review of university rankings, reminded universities at a conference to discuss its findings that they often "deplore league tables one day and deploy them the next". He said the tables had become part of the higher education landscape and one of the sources to which prospective students would refer when choosing where and what to study.

Only three universities have refused to release information for this and other league tables this year: Liverpool Hope, Wolverhampton and Swansea Metropolitan. Wolverhampton says on its website that measures of its quality are available elsewhere – as they are, if you know where to look. But the way in which it quotes existing measures may help to explain why readers value the independent nature of guides such as this. Wolverhampton says, quite accurately, that it is among the top universities in the National Student Survey for the quality of its learning resources and access to specialist equipment, but it neglects to mention that it was barely in the top 100 universities in the 2011 survey for overall satisfaction.

In any case, this *Guide* contains far more than league tables. There are chapters on choosing a course and a university, the application process, managing your money as a student, where to live and what to expect in terms of sport. There are chapters, too, on employment and on going abroad to study. There are also special sections for overseas applicants and for parents, as well as profiles of every university and Oxbridge college.

Why university?

Particularly in an economic downturn, some will be tempted, once the cost of living has been added to the growing fees burden and the attractions of university life balanced against loss of potential earnings, to write off higher education. There are plenty of self-made millionaires who still swear by the University of Life as the only training ground for success. Yet even by narrow financial criteria it would be rash to dismiss higher education. With so many more competing for jobs, a degree will never again be an automatic passport to a fast-track career. But graduates' financial prospects remain much brighter than school leavers', as are their prospects in other important areas, such as health.

Even for those who cannot or do not wish to afford three or more years of full-time education after leaving school, university remains a possibility. The modular courses adopted by most universities enable students to work through a degree at their own pace, dropping out for a time if necessary, or switching to part-time attendance. Distance learning is another option, and advances in information technology now mean that some nominally full-time courses are delivered mainly online.

For many – perhaps most – students, the university experience is not what it was in their parents' day. There is more assessment, more crowding, more pressure to get the best possible degree while also finding gainful employment for at least part of the year. The proportion of students achieving first-class degrees has risen significantly, while an upper second (rather than the previously ubiquitous 2:2) has become the norm. Research shows that the classification has a real impact in the labour market.

Most graduates do not regret their decision to go to university, however. Students from all over the world flock to British universities, and they offer a valuable resource for those on their doorstep. No league table can determine which is the right university for any candidate, but this *Guide* should provide some of the information necessary to draw up a shortlist for further investigation.

1 What and Where to Study

All over the world, career prospects are uppermost in the mind of most people considering a higher education course, but your choice of course and university must be about more than money: these are life-shaping decisions. The outcome will help determine the direction of your career and personal life far beyond the next three or four years (and they are important enough). Many graduates end up living and working near their university; they may make their closest friends in their student days and may even meet their future partner there. So finding the right university demands serious thought and research, and this *Guide* may play an important part.

Is higher education for you?

Before you start, there is one important question to ask yourself: what do you want out of higher education? The answer will make it easier to choose where (and if) to be a student. With more than a third of school-leavers going on to university, it is easy to drift that way without much thought, opting for the subject in which you expect the best grades, and looking for a university with a reasonable reputation and a good social life. Your career will look after itself – you hope.

With graduate debt soaring, however, and job prospects varying widely between subjects, now is the time to look at your own motivation. One apparent benefit of England's higher fees is that more prospective students are doing just this. Some – though not as many as predicted – are opting out of higher education as a result, while others appear to be rethinking their choice of course.

Love of a subject is an excellent reason for taking a degree, and one that allows you to focus almost exclusively on the search for a course that corresponds with your passions. If, however, higher education is a means to an end, you need to think about career ambitions and look carefully at employment rates for any courses you might consider. These are examined in more detail in chapter 2.

Many graduates look back on their student days as the best years of their lives, and there is nothing wrong with wanting to have a good time. Remember, though, that you will be paying for it later (literally) and there will be more studying than partying. If you have not enjoyed sixth-form or college courses, you may be better off in a job and possibly becoming one of the hundreds of thousands each year who return to education later in life.

Setting your priorities

With graduate unemployment at a 17-year high and the cost of going to university growing dramatically, economic considerations are sure to become even more dominant. Yet there are good reasons to believe that the right degree will still be a good investment.

No one knows which subjects will be in demand when the downturn ends, but graduates will almost certainly be in a stronger position than those who choose not to invest in better qualifications. The majority of graduate jobs are not subject-specific – employers value the transferable skills that higher education confers. Rightly or wrongly, however, most employers are influenced by which university a graduate attended, so the choice of institution remains as important as ever.

Some students may cut their costs by taking a part-time course; others by enrolling on a two-year Foundation degree, which can be converted into an honours degree later. But, at a time of low employment generally, logic suggests that it would be a false economy to dismiss higher education entirely.

Those who want to add value to their degree in the jobs market will find that growing numbers of universities are offering employment-related schemes that are considered in more detail in chapter 2. In many cases, this will involve work experience or extra activities organised by the careers service. Some universities, such as Leicester, now run certificated employability programmes, while others, such as Liverpool John Moores, have built such skills into degree programmes. Such programmes are also highlighted in chapter 2 and in the institutional profiles in chapter 13.

Key reasons for going to university

To improve job opportunities	**74%**
To improve knowledge in an area of interest	**64%**
To improve salary prospects	**62%**
To obtain an additional qualification	**58%**
To specialise in a certain subject / area	**57%**
To become more independent	**48%**
Essential for my chosen profession	**47%**
To meet new people	**45%**
It's the obvious next step, it's just what you do	**40%**
To experience a different way of life	**37%**
To have a good social life	**26%**
My parents expected me to	**26%**
I didn't want to get a job straightaway	**24%**
I didn't know what else to do	**18%**
All my friends were going	**13%**
Can live at home and still go to university	**10%**

Sodexo University Lifestyle Survey 2012

Narrowing down the field

Once you have decided that higher education is for you, the good news is that, as long as you start early enough, finding the right university can be relatively straightforward. Media attention focuses on the scramble for places on a relatively small proportion of courses where competition is intense, but there are plenty of places at good universities for candidates with the basic qualifications – it's just a matter of finding the one that suits you best. For older applicants, relevant work experience and demonstrable interest in a subject may be enough to win a place.

If anything, the problem is that of too much choice, although universities have reduced the number of degree combinations in anticipation of tougher financial conditions. Students prepared to move away from home will still have more than 100 universities and numerous specialist colleges to consider, most with hundreds – even thousands – of course combinations on offer. Institutions come in all shapes and sizes, so there is work to do at the outset narrowing down your options.

Deciding what you want to study may reduce the field considerably – there are only seven institutions offering veterinary medicine for example, although the total is around 100 in subjects such as law and English. By the time you have factored in personal preferences about the type or location of your ideal university, the list of possibilities may already be reduced to manageable proportions.

After that, you can take a closer look at what the courses contain and what life is really like for students. Prospectuses and university websites will give you an accurate account of course combinations, and important facts like the accommodation available to new students, but it is their job to sell the university. To get a true picture, you need more – preferably a visit not just to the university, but to the department where you would be studying. If that is not possible, there are plenty of other sources of objective information, such as the National Student Survey (which is available online, with a range of additional data about each institution, at **http://unistats.direct.gov.uk**).

Many students' unions publish alternative prospectuses, giving a "warts and all" view of the university, and those that do not provide this service may be able to arrange a brief discussion with a current student, either by phone or email. Your school or college may put you in contact with someone who went to a university that you are considering. Guides and collections of statistics may give you valuable information about a course or a university, but there is no substitute for personal experience.

What to study?

Most people seeking a place in higher education start by choosing a subject and a course, rather than a university. If you take a degree, you are going to spend at least three years immersed in your subject. It has to be one you will enjoy and can master – not to mention one that you are qualified to study. Many economics degrees require maths, for example, while some medical schools demand chemistry or biology. The UCAS website (**www.ucas. com**) contains course profiles, including entrance requirements, which is a good starting point, while universities' own sites contain more detailed information. In chapter 5, we describe 62 subject areas and provide league tables for each of them.

Your school subjects and the UCAS tariff

The official yardstick by which your results will be judged is the UCAS tariff (see page 18), which gives a score for each grade of most UK qualifications considered relevant for university entrance, as well as for the International Baccalaureate (IB). This tariff has become controversial as more subjects and types of qualifications have been included in it. Top scores in the new vocational diplomas developed under the Labour government, for example, attract more points than a full set of A grades at A level, while the most successful IB students already earn considerably more points.

While the majority of universities use the tariff to make offers of places, many of the leading universities prefer to stipulate the grades that they require. This allows them to specify the subjects in which particular grades must be achieved, as well as to determine which vocational qualifications are relevant to different degrees. In certain universities, some departments, but not others, will use the tariff to set offers. There may well be changes in the tariff from 2014, following a review of vocational qualifications which recommended that many should be downgraded. Indeed, there has been debate within UCAS about scrapping the tariff altogether, but it will still be in place for applications for courses beginning in 2013. Course profiles on the UCAS website and/or universities' own sites should show whether

The UCAS tariff

Tariff points for selected qualifications are given below. The full range of acceptable qualifications and their tariff values are given on the UCAS website.

GCE/VCE Qualifications					Points	Scottish Qualifications	
GCE AS/AS VCE	GCE AS Double Award	GCE A level/A VCE	A level with additional AS (9 units)	GCE/AVCE Double Award		Advanced Higher	Higher
				A*A*	280		
				A*A	260		
				AA	240		
				AB	220		
		A*A		BB	200		
		AA		BC	180		
		AB			170		
				CC	160		
			BB		150		
		A*	BC	CD	140		
					130	A	
	AA	A	CC	DD	120		
	AB		CD		110	B	
	BB	B		DE	100		
	BC		DD		90	C	
	CC	C	DE	EE	80		A
					72	D	
	CD				70		
					65		B
A	DD	D	EE		60		
B	DE				50		C
C	EE	E			40		
					36		D
D						30	
E					20		

UCAS tariff for the International Baccalaureate

Points for the International Baccalaureate (IB) are awarded to candidates who achieve the IB Diploma.

IB Dip.	Points	IB Dip.	Points	IB Dip.	Points	IB Dip.	Points	IB Dip.	Points
45	720	40	611	35	501	30	392	25	282
44	698	39	589	34	479	29	370	24	260
43	676	38	567	33	457	28	348		
42	654	37	545	32	435	27	326		
41	632	36	523	31	413	26	304		

offers are framed in terms of grades or tariff points. It is important to find out which, especially if you are relying on points from qualifications other than A level or Scottish Highers.

"Soft subjects"

There is a related issue for some of the top universities about the subjects studied at A level. The variety of A-level courses now available includes many subjects that they do not consider on a par with traditional academic subjects. For many years a minority of universities have refused to accept General Studies as a full A level for entrance purposes (although even some leading universities do). The growth of supposedly "soft" subjects, such as media studies and photography, has prompted a few universities to produce lists of subjects that will only be accepted as a third, or fourth, A level.

The Russell Group of 24 leading universities has published an extremely useful report, called *Informed Choices*, on the post-16 qualifications preferred by its members for a wide range of degrees. Although it names media studies, art and design, photography and business studies among the vocational subjects that would normally be given this label, it does not subscribe to the notion of a single list of "soft" subjects. The report suggests you choose at most a single vocational course and primarily select from a list of "facilitating subjects", which are required for many degrees and welcomed generally at Russell Group universities. The list comprises *maths, further maths, English, physics, biology, chemistry, geography, languages (classical and modern) and history*. In addition their guide indicates the "essential" and "useful" A-level subjects for 60 different subject areas studied at Russell Group universities.

For most courses at most universities, there are no such restrictions, as long as your main subjects or qualifications are relevant to the degree you hope to take. Nevertheless, when choosing A levels it would be wise to bear the Russell Group lists in mind if you are likely to apply to one or more of the leading universities. At the very least, it is an indication of the subjects that admissions tutors may take less seriously than the rest. Although only the London School of Economics identifies those subjects publicly (see below), others may adopt less formal weightings.

"Soft Subjects"

The London School of Economics would prefer to see only one subject from this list in your mix of A-level subjects.

- » Accounting
- » Art and design
- » Business studies (especially when combined with Economics)
- » Communication studies
- » Dance
- » Design and technology
- » Drama/theatre studies (some departments)
- » Home economics
- » Information and communication technology
- » Law
- » Media studies
- » Music technology (music is acceptable)
- » Sports studies
- » Travel and tourism

Those studying either accounting or law "should not be put off applying to the LSE, as, depending on their overall academic profile, they may be made an offer". General studies and critical thinking A levels will only be considered as fourth A-level subjects.

Admissions tests

Some of the most competitive courses now have additional entrance tests. The most significant tests are listed below. A few others may also require tests, so check the course details on the UCAS website.

Law

Law National Admissions Test (LNAT): for entry to law courses at Birmingham, Bristol, Durham, Glasgow, King's College London, Manchester, Nottingham, Oxford, University College, London.

For 2011, registration opened 2 August 2011; closing date 5 October 2011 (for Oxford), 15 January 2012 (other universities).

> www.lnat.ac.uk

Mathematics

Sixth Term Examination Papers (STEP): for entry to mathematics at Cambridge and Warwick (also encouraged by Bristol, Bath, Imperial College, London, and Oxford).

Standard closing date for 2012 entry was 30 April 2012. Date for 2013 entry to be announced in September 2012.

> www.admissionstests.cambridgeassessment.org.uk/adt/step

Medical subjects

BioMedical Admissions Test (BMAT): for entry to medicine and veterinary medicine at Cambridge, Imperial College London, Oxford, Royal Veterinary College, University College London.

Standard closing date for 2013 admissions is 1 October 2012.

> www.admissionstests.cambridgeassessment.org.uk/adt/bmat

Graduate Medical School Admissions Test (GAMSAT): for graduate entry to medicine and dentistry at Keele, Nottingham, Peninsula College of Medicine and Dentistry, St. George's, University of London, Swansea. Closing date for registration is 10 August 2012.

> www.gamsatuk.org

Health Professions Admissions Test (HPAT–Ulster): for certain medical courses at Ulster.

Closing date for 2013 registration not confirmed. For 2012 admissions it was 11 January 2012, with test on 28 January 2012.

> www.hpat.org.uk

UK Clinical Aptitude Test (UKCAT): for entry to medical and dental schools at Aberdeen, Brighton and Sussex Medical School, Barts and the London School of Medicine and Dentistry, Cardiff, Dundee, Durham, East Anglia, Edinburgh, Glasgow, Hull York Medical School, Imperial College London (graduate entry), Keele, King's College London, Leeds, Leicester, Manchester, Newcastle, Nottingham, Oxford (graduate entry), Peninsula College of Medicine and Dentistry, Queen's University Belfast, Sheffield, Southampton, St Andrews, St George's, University of London, Warwick (graduate entry).

Registration for 2013 entry from 1 May to 21 September 2012; tests from 3 July to 5 October 2012.

> www.ukcat.ac.uk

Cambridge University

Modern and Medieval Languages Test (MML): for entry to modern and medieval languages at Cambridge, taken at Cambridge during interview process.

> www.cam.ac.uk/admissions/undergraduate/courses/mml/tests.html

Thinking Skills Assessment (TSA) Cambridge: mainly for computer science, economics, engineering, land economy and politics, natural sciences, psychology and sociology at most colleges, taken during interview process. See also Mathematics and Medical subjects.

> www.admissionstests.cambridgeassessment.org.uk/adt/tsacambridge

Oxford University

Oxford administers its own tests for: any course including classics, computer science, economics, geography (under review), history, joint courses including history, mathematics, joint courses including mathematics, modern languages (including all courses where a language is

Vocational qualifications

The Education Department has announced that many vocational qualifications will be downgraded in school league tables from 2014. This can only add to the confusion surrounding the value placed on diplomas and other qualifications by universities. The engineering diploma has won near-universal approval from universities (for admission to engineering courses and possibly some science degrees), but some of the other diplomas are in fields that are not on the curriculum of the most selective universities. Regardless of the points awarded under the tariff, it is essential to contact universities direct to ensure that a diploma will be an acceptable qualification for your chosen degree.

Admission tests

The growing numbers of applicants with high grades at A level have encouraged the introduction of separate admission tests for some of the most oversubscribed courses. There are national tests in medicine and law that are used by some of the leading universities, while Oxford and Cambridge have their own in a number of subjects. The details are listed opposite and below. In all cases, the tests are used as an extra selection tool, not as a replacement for A level or other general qualifications.

Making a choice

Your A levels or Scottish Highers may have chosen themselves, but the range of subjects across the whole university system is vast. Even subjects that you have studied at school may be quite different at degree level – some academic economists actually prefer their undergraduates not to have taken A-level economics because they approach the subject so differently. Other students are disappointed because they appear to be going over old ground when they continue with a subject that they enjoyed at school. Universities now publish quite detailed syllabuses, and it is a matter of going through the fine print.

---

combined with another subject). Test taken on 7 November 2012, usually at candidate's educational institution. The following tests are also specific for Oxford, but require separate registration. See also sections on Law, Mathematics and Medical subjects above.

www.ox.ac.uk/admissions/undergraduate_courses/how_to_apply/tests

English Literature Admissions Test (ELAT): for entry to English. Closing date for 2013 entry is 15 October 2012; test 7 November 2012.

www.admissionstests.cambridgeassessment.org.uk/adt/elat

History Aptitude test (HAT): for entry to all Oxford courses in history and history joint courses. Closing date for 2013 entry is 15 October 2012; test taken 7 November 2012.

www.admissionstests.cambridgeassessment.org.uk/adt/hat

Physics Aptitude Test (PAT): for entry to all Oxford courses in physics and engineering. Closing date for 2013 entry is 15 October 2012; test taken 7 November 2012.

www.admissionstests.cambridgeassessment.org.uk/adt/pat

Thinking Skills Assessment (TSA) Oxford: for economics and management, experimental psychology, philosophy, politics and economics (PPE), psychology, philosophy and linguistics, and theology (under review). Closing date for 2013 entry is 15 October 2012; test taken 7 November 2012.

www.admissionstests.cambridgeassessment.org.uk/adt/tsaoxford

University College London

Thinking Skills Assessment (TSA) UCL: for entry to European social and political studies at University College London; the test is arranged in the interview process.

www.admissionstests.cambridgeassessment.org.uk/adt/tsaucl

The greater difficulty comes in judging your suitability for the many subjects that are not on the school or college curriculum. Philosophy and psychology sound fascinating (and are), but you may have no idea what degrees in either subject entail – for example, the level of statistics that may be required. Forensic science may look exciting on television – more glamorous than plain chemistry – but it opens fewer doors, as the type of work portrayed in *Silent Witness* or *Raising the Dead* is very hard to find.

Academic or vocational?

There is frequent and often misleading debate about the differences between academic and vocational education. It is usually about the relative value of talking a degree, as opposed to a directly work-related qualification. But it also extends to higher education itself, with jibes about so-called "Mickey Mouse" degrees in areas that were not part of the higher education curriculum when most of the critics were students.

Such attitudes ignore the fact that medicine and law are both vocational subjects, as are architecture, engineering and education. They are not seen as any less academic than geography or sociology, but for some reason social work or nursing, let alone media studies and sports science, are often looked down upon. The test of a degree should be whether it is challenging and a good preparation for working life. Both general academic and vocational degrees can do this.

Nevertheless, it would be surprising if the prospect of much higher graduate debt did not encourage more students into job-related subjects, rather than traditional academic disciplines, in the hope of improving their employment prospects. This is understandable and, if you are sure of your future career path, possibly also sensible. But much depends on what that career is – and whether you are ready to make such a long-term commitment. Some of the programmes that have attracted public ridicule, such as surf science or golf course management, may narrow graduates' options to a worrying extent, but often boast strong employment records.

As you would expect, many vocational courses are tailored to particular professions. If you choose one of these, make sure that the degree is recognised by the relevant professional body (such as the Engineering Council or one of the institutes) or you may not be able to use the skills that you acquire. Most universities are only too keen to make such recognition

The ten most popular subjects by applications in 2012		The ten most popular subjects by acceptances in 2011	
1 Nursing	182,792	1 Nursing	24,587
2 Law	89,362	2 Design studies	19,701
3 Psychology	85,840	3 Law	19,168
4 Medicine	81,721	4 Psychology	16,709
5 Design studies	81,069	5 Computer science	13,299
6 Combinations within business and admin studies	63,485	6 Business studies	13,232
7 Management studies	60,453	7 Management studies	13,076
8 Computer science	51,676	8 Combinations within business and admin studies	11,377
9 English studies	50,704	9 Social work	11,334
10 Training teachers	49,355	10 Sports science	11,097

UCAS 2012 (number of applicants to 20 February 2012)   UCAS 2011

clear in their prospectus; if no such guarantee is published, contact the university department running the course and seek assurances.

Even where a course has professional recognition, bear in mind that a further qualification may be required to practise. Both law and medicine, for example, demand additional training to become a fully qualified solicitor, barrister or doctor. Nor is either degree an automatic passport to a job: only about half of all law graduates go into the profession and the UK is now training more medical students than the National Health Service can afford. Both law and medicine also provide a route into the profession for graduates who have taken other subjects. Law conversion courses, though not cheap, are increasingly popular, and there are a growing number of graduate-entry medical degrees.

One way to ensure that a degree is job-related is to take a "sandwich" course, which involves up to a year in business or industry. Students often end up working for the organisation which provided the placement, while others gain valuable insights into a field of employment – even if only to discount it. The drawback with such courses is that, like the year abroad that is part of most language degrees, the period away from university inevitably disrupts living arrangements and friendship groups. But most of those who take this route find that the career benefits make this a worthwhile sacrifice.

Employers' organisations calculate that more than half of all graduate jobs are open to applicants from any subject, and recruiters for the most competitive graduate training schemes often prefer traditional academic subjects to apparently relevant vocational degrees. Newspapers, for example, often prefer a history graduate to one with a media studies degree; computing firms take a disproportionate number of classicists. A good degree classification and the right work experience are more important than the subject for most non-technical jobs. But it is hard to achieve a good result on a course that you do not enjoy, so scour prospectuses, and email or phone university departments to ensure that you know what you are letting yourself in for. Their reaction to your approach will also give you an idea of how responsive they are to their students.

If you are not sure whether you will be suited to a particular subject, you can take an online aptitude test through the UCAS website. The "Choosing courses" section gives you access to the Stamford Test, which uses an online questionnaire to match your interests and strengths to possible courses and careers.

Total number of students by subject area 2010–2011

Business and administrative studies	358,295
Subjects allied to medicine	299,800
Education	223,730
Social studies	218,135
Biological sciences	190,035
Creative arts and design	176,700
Engineering and technology	160,885
Languages	134,720
Combined subjects	105,955
Computer science	99,025
Historical and philosophical studies	96,760
Physical sciences	93,580
Law	92,950
Medicine and dentistry	66,840
Architecture, building and planning	62,780
Mass communications	53,680
Mathematical sciences	41,110
Agriculture and related subjects	20,790
Veterinary science	5,540
All subjects	2,501,295

HESA 2012

Studying more than one subject

You may find that more than one subject appeals, in which case you could consider Joint Honours – degrees that combine two subjects – or even Combined Honours, which will cover several related subjects. Such courses obviously allow you to extend the scope of your studies, but they should be approached with caution. Even if the number of credits suggests a similar workload to Single Honours, covering more than one subject inevitably involves extra reading and often more essays or project work.

However, there are advantages. Many students choose a "dual" to add a vocational element to make themselves more employable – business studies with languages or engineering, for example, or media studies with English. Others want to take their studies in a particular direction, perhaps by combining history with politics, or statistics with maths. Some simply want to add a completely unrelated interest to their main subject, such as environmental science and music, or archaeology and event management – both combinations that are available at UK universities.

At most universities, however, it is not necessary to take a degree in more than one subject in order to broaden your studies. The spread of modular programmes ensures that you can take courses in related subjects without changing the basic structure of your degree. You may not be able to take an event management module in a single-honours archaeology degree, but it should be possible to study some history or a language. The number and scope of the combinations offered at many of the larger universities is extraordinary. Indeed, it has been criticised by academics who believe that "mix-and-match" degrees can leave a graduate without a rounded view of a subject. But for those who seek breadth and variety, close scrutiny of university prospectuses is a vital part of the selection process.

What type of course?

Once you have a subject, you must decide on the level and type of course. Most readers of this *Guide* will be looking for full-time degree courses, but higher education is much broader than that. You may not be able to afford the time or the money needed for a full-time commitment of three or four years at this point in your life.

Part-time courses

Tens of thousands of people each year opt for a part-time course – usually while holding down a job – to continue learning and improve their career prospects. With little or no financial support available from the Government, the numbers have dropped recently, but that may well change in 2012 both because of the high fees for full-time courses and the introduction of a much more generous system of student support for part-time students.

Under these arrangements, loans are available for students whose courses occupy between a quarter and three-quarters of the time expected on a full-time course. Repayments will be on the same conditions as those for full-time courses, except that repayments will begin after three years of study even if the course has not been completed by then. The downside is that universities may increase their fees in the knowledge that part-time students will be able to take out student loans to cover fees, but the change should still be beneficial. At Birkbeck, University of London, for example, full-time fees will be up to £9,000, with part-timers paying in proportion to the number of credits they take. Now, for the first time, students need pay nothing upfront if they take out income-contingent loans.

Part-time study can be exhausting unless your employer gives you time off, but if you have the stamina for a course that will usually take twice as long as the full-time equivalent, this route should still make a degree more affordable. Part-time students tend to be highly committed to their subject, and many claim that the quality of the social life associated with their course makes up for the quantity of leisure time enjoyed by full-timers.

Distance learning

If you are confident that you can manage without regular face-to-face contact with teachers and fellow students, distance learning is an option. Courses are delivered mainly or entirely online or through correspondence, although some programmes offer a certain amount of local tuition. The process might sound daunting and impersonal, but students of the Open University (OU), all of whom are educated in this way, are among the most satisfied in the country, according to the results of the annual National Student Survey. Attending lectures or oversized seminars at a conventional university can be less personal than regular contact with your tutor at a distance. Of course, not all universities are as good at communicating with their distance-learning students as the OU, or offer such high-quality course materials, but this mode of study does give students ultimate flexibility to determine when and where they study. Distance learning is becoming increasingly popular for the delivery of professional courses, which are often needed to supplement degrees. The OU now takes students of all ages, including a growing number of school-leavers, not just mature students.

Foundation degrees

Even if you are set on a full-time course, you might not want to commit yourself for three or more years. Two-year vocational Foundation degrees have become a popular route into higher education in recent years. Many other students take longer-established two-year courses, such as Higher National Diplomas or other diplomas tailored to the needs of industry or parts of the health service. Those who do well on such courses usually have the option of converting their qualification into a full degree with further study, although many are satisfied without immediately staying on for the further two or more years that completing a BA or BSc will require.

Other short courses

A number of universities are experimenting with two-year degrees, squeezing more work into an extended academic year. The so-called "third semester" makes use of the summer

---

Subjects with highest ratio of applications to acceptances 2011		**Universities with the highest application to place ratio 2011**	
1 Medicine	10.8	1 Brighton and Sussex Medical School	16.2
2 Dentistry	10.6	2 London School of Economics	13.9
3 Anatomy, physiology and pathology	9.2	3 Stirling	12.7
4 Nursing	8.9	4 Bristol	10.7
5 Veterinary medicine	8.7	5 St George's, London (medical school)	10.2
6 Medical technology	8.1	6 King's College London	9.8
7 Training teachers	7.9	7 University College London	9.5
8 Social work	7.2	8 Edinburgh	9.0
9 Pharmacology, toxicology and pharmacy	7.2	9 Keele	8.9
10 Drama	7.2	10 City	8.8
UCAS 2011		UCAS 2011	

vacation for extra teaching, so that mature students, in particular, can reduce the length of their career break. Several universities are offering accelerated degrees as part of a pilot project initiated under the last Government. But the pattern has really only caught on at the University of Buckingham, the UK's only established private university, where it has had a small but enthusiastic following for more than 30 years.

Other short courses – usually lasting a year – are designed for students who do not have the necessary qualifications to start a degree in their chosen subject. Foundation courses in art and design have been common for many years, and are the chosen preparation for a degree at leading departments, even for many students whose A levels would win them a degree place elsewhere. Access courses perform the same function in a wider range of subjects for students without A levels, or for those whose grades are either too low or in the wrong subjects to gain admission to a particular course. Entry requirements are modest, but students have to reach the same standard as regular entrants if they are to progress to a degree.

Yet more choice

No single guide can allow for personal preferences in choosing a course. You may want one of the many degrees that incorporate a year at a partner university abroad, or to try a six-month exchange on the Continent through the European Union's Erasmus Programme. Either might prove a valuable experience and add to your employability. You might prefer a January or February start to the traditional autumn start – there are plenty of opportunities for this, mainly at post-1992 universities.

In some subjects – particularly engineering and the sciences – the leading degrees may be Masters courses, taking four years rather than three (in England). In Scotland, most degree courses take four years, although those who come with A levels may apply to go straight into the second year.

Job prospects

Even before the recession, job prospects were the key element in choosing a subject for many (probably most) students. Chapter 2 examines this topic in detail, providing information on employment prospects by subject and initial starting salaries by subject, as well as giving advice on how to enhance your chances in the jobs market.

Where to study

Once you have decided what to study, there are still several factors that might influence your choice of university or college. Obviously, you need to have a reasonable chance of getting in, you may want reassurance about the university's reputation, and its location will probably also be important to you. On top of that, most applicants have views about the type of institution they are looking for – big or small, old or new, urban or rural, specialist or comprehensive. You may surprise yourself by choosing somewhere that does not conform to your initial criteria, but working through your preferences is another way of narrowing down your options.

Entry standards

Unless you are a mature student or have taken a gap year, your passport to your chosen university will be a conditional offer based on your predicted grades, previous exam performance, personal statement, and school or college reference. A lucky few may get an offer that is so low that success is a foregone conclusion – because the university considers them outstanding and needs no further evidence of their potential. But only those who already have their grades receive unconditional offers.

Supply and demand dictate whether you will receive an offer – whatever the reaction to the second year of higher fees in England, large numbers will still apply. Beyond the national picture, your chances will be affected both by the university and the subject you choose. A few universities (but not many) at the top of the league tables are heavily oversubscribed in every subject; others will have areas in which they excel, but may make relatively modest demands for entry to other courses. Even in many of the leading universities, the number of applicants for each place in languages or engineering is still not high. Conversely, three As at A level will not guarantee a place on one of the top English or law degrees, but there are enough universities running courses to ensure that three Cs will put you in with a chance somewhere. The difference in recent years has been that the pressure on places in popular subjects is greater than before at the more lowly ranked universities.

University prospectuses and the UCAS website will give you the "standard offer" for each course, but in some cases this is pitched deliberately low in order to leave admissions staff extra flexibility. The standard A-level offer for medicine, for example, is often two As and a B, but nearly all successful applicants have three As or more.

The average entry scores in our subject tables give the actual points obtained by successful applicants – many of which are far above the offer made by the university,

Non-academic factors considered when choosing a university

Good impression from open days	**53%**
Friendly atmosphere	**43%**
Geographic location	**43%**
Attractive university environment	**37%**
Campus university	**34%**
Close to transport links	**32%**
Living away from home, but sufficiently close if support needed	**29%**
Active social life and good social facilities	**28%**
Internet research favourable to university	**27%**
Quality of accommodation	**23%**
City centre university	**22%**
Recommendation from friends	**22%**
Close to home/able to live at home	**22%**
Low cost of living	**17%**
Cost of accommodation	**15%**
Advice from teachers	**14%**
Advice from parents	**12%**
Good sporting facilities	**12%**
Opportunities for part-time jobs	**9%**

Sodexo University Lifestyle Survey 2012

but which give an indication of the pecking order at entry. The subject tables (in chapter 5) are, naturally, a better guide than the main table (in chapter 4), where average entry scores are influenced by the range of subjects available at each university.

Location

The most obvious starting point is the country you study in. Most degrees in Scotland take four years, rather than the UK norm of three. It is possible, but not normal, for A-level candidates to go straight into the second year of a Scottish degree course. Fewer applicants than might be expected, given the savings, take this option, perhaps partly because they do not wish to join a year group where friendships are already well established. It goes without saying that four years cost more than three, especially given the loss of the year's salary you might have been earning after graduation. A later chapter will go into the details of the system, but suffice to say that students from Scotland pay no fees, while those from the rest of the UK do. Nevertheless, Edinburgh and St Andrews remain particularly popular with English students, despite charging them £9,000 a year for the full four years of a degree. More than 1,000 students from Northern Ireland entered Scottish universities in 2011, but applications were down substantially at the start of 2012 with the prospect of higher fees.

Close to home

Far from crossing national boundaries, however, growing numbers of students choose to study near home, whether or not they continue to live with their family. This is understandable for Scots, who will save themselves tens of thousands of pounds by studying at their own fees-free universities. But many others are choosing to study close to home either to cut costs or for personal reasons, such as family circumstances, a girlfriend or boyfriend, continuing employment, or religion. Some simply want to stick with what they know.

The trend for full-time students who do go away to study, is to choose a university within about two hours' travelling time. The assumption is that this is far enough to discourage parents from making unannounced visits, but close enough to allow for occasional trips home to get the washing done and have a decent meal. The leading universities recruit from all over the world, but most still have a regional core.

University or college?

This *Guide* is primarily concerned with universities, the destination of choice for the vast majority of higher education students. But there are other options – and not just for those searching for lower fees. A number of specialist higher education colleges offer a similar, or sometimes superior, quality of course in their particular fields. The subject tables in chapter 5 chart the successes of various colleges in art, agriculture, music and teacher training in particular. Some colleges of higher education are not so different from the newer universities and may acquire that status themselves in future years.

The second group of colleges offering degrees are further education colleges. These are often large institutions with a wide range of courses, from A levels to vocational subjects at different levels, up to degrees in some cases. Although their numbers of higher education students have been falling in recent years, the new fee structure presents them with a fresh

Largest percentage decreases in applications 2012 over 2011		The ten most popular universities by degree applications	
1 University for the Creative Arts	−29.7%	1 Nottingham	48,584
2 Roehampton	−27.5%	2 Manchester	46,730
3 Goldsmiths, University of London	−22.0%	3 Leeds	45,684
4 Aston	−20.5%	4 Edinburgh	43,811
5 Surrey	−20.3%	5 Manchester Metropolitan	43,341
6 Derby	−19.5%	6 Birmingham	35,718
7 Chichester	−19.1%	7 Leeds Metropolitan	35,473
8 University of the Arts London	−17.4%	8 Sheffield Hallam	35,465
9 Nottingham Trent	−17.3%	9 Bristol	35,059
10 Bath Spa	−16.7%	10 Nottingham Trent	32,576

UCAS applications to 15 January 2012

UCAS applications to 15 January 2012

opportunity because they tend not to bear all the costs of a university campus. For that reason, too, they may not offer a broad student experience of the type that universities pride themselves on, but the best colleges respond well to the local labour market and offer small teaching groups and effective personal support. FE colleges are a local resource and tend to attract mature students who cannot or do not want to travel to university. Many of their higher education students apply nowhere else. But, as competition for university places has increased, they have become more of an option for school-leavers, and for their own students, to continue their studies, as they always have done in Scotland. Ministers hope that they will now also become more attractive by virtue of price.

Both further and higher education colleges are audited by the Quality Assurance Agency and appear in the National Student Survey, where their results usually show wide variation. Some demonstrate higher levels of satisfaction among their students than most universities.

The final group of colleges that present an alternative to university has been insignificant in terms of size until now, but may also prosper under the new fee regime. This is the private sector, seen mainly in business and law but also in some other specialist fields. The best-known currently is BPP University College, which was given that title in 2010 and offers degrees, as well as shorter courses, in both law and business subjects. Like Buckingham, BPP runs two-year degrees with short vacations to maximise teaching time – a model that other private providers are likely to follow. Fees were £6,000 for a two-year degree and £5,000 for a three-year course in 2012.

At the other end of the cost spectrum, the New College of the Humanities will be taking its first students in autumn 2012. Offering economics, English, history, law and philosophy, the college will be charging £18,000 a year for guaranteed small-group teaching and some big-name visiting lecturers. Up to 30 per cent of students will be offered bursaries for degree courses validated by the University of London.

City universities

The most popular universities, in terms of total applications, are nearly all in big cities – generally with other major centres of population within that two-hour travelling window. For those looking for the best nightclubs, top sporting events, high-quality shopping or a varied cultural life – in other words, most young people, and especially those who live in cities already – city universities are a magnet. The big universities also, by definition, offer the widest range of subjects, although that does not mean that they necessarily have the particular course that is right for you. Nor does it mean that you will actually use the array of nightlife and shopping that looks so alluring in the prospectus, either because you cannot afford to, because student life is focused on the university, or even because you are too busy working.

Campus universities

City universities are the right choice for many young people, but it is worth bearing in mind that the National Student Survey shows that the highest satisfaction levels tend to be at smaller universities, often those with their own self-contained campuses. It seems that students identify more closely with institutions where there is a close-knit community and the social life is based around the students' union rather than the local nightclubs.

Few UK universities are in genuinely rural locations, but some – particularly among the newly promoted – are in relatively small towns. Several longer-established institutions in Wales and Scotland also share this type of setting, where the university dominates the town.

Importance of Open Days

The only way to be certain if this, or any other type of university, is for you is to visit. Schools often restrict the number of open days that sixth-formers can attend in term-time, but some universities offer a weekend alternative. The full calendar of events is available at **www.opendays.com** and on universities' own websites. Bear in mind, if you only attend one or two, that the event has to be badly mismanaged for a university not to seem an exciting place to someone who spends his or her days at school, or even college. Try to get a flavour of several institutions before you make your choice.

How many universities to pick?

When that time comes, of course, you will not be making one choice but five; four if you are applying for medicine, dentistry or veterinary science. (Full details of the application process are given in chapter 6.) Tens of thousands of students each year eventually go to a university that did not start out as their first choice, either because they did not get the right offer or because they changed their mind along the way. UCAS rules are such that applicants do not list universities in order of preference anyway – indeed, universities are not allowed to know where else you have applied. So do not pin all your hopes on one course; take just as much care choosing the other universities on your list.

The value of an "insurance" choice

Until recently, nearly all applicants included at least one "insurance" choice on that list – a university or college where entry grades were significantly lower than at their preferred institutions. This practice has been in decline, presumably because candidates expecting high grades think they can pick up a lower offer either in Clearing or through UCAS Extra, the service that allows applicants rejected by their original choices to apply to courses that still have vacancies after the first round of offers. However, it is easy to miscalculate and leave yourself without a place that you want. You may not like the look of the options in Clearing, leaving yourself with an unwelcome and potentially expensive year off at a time when jobs are thin on the ground.

If you are at all uncertain about your grades, including an insurance choice remains a sensible course of action – especially since entry requirements have risen in response to increased demand for places. Indeed, even if you are sure that you will match the standard

The top universities for student satisfaction in the 2013 *Times* table		The top universities for students going into graduate-level jobs or studying in the 2013 *Times* table	
=1 Oxford	87%	1 London School of Economics	87.8%
=1 Cambridge	87%	2 Imperial College	87.1%
=1 Buckingham	87%	3 Cambridge	84.4%
=4 Bath	84%	4 University College London	79.9%
=4 Loughborough	84%	5 Oxford	79.8%
=4 Leicester	84%	6 King's College London	79.6%
=7 Durham	83%	7 Bristol	79.2%
=7 St Andrews	83%	8 Bath	79.1%
=7 Glasgow	83%	9 Durham	78.5%
=7 Keele	83%	10 Robert Gordon	78.4%
=7 Aberystwyth	83%		

offers of your chosen universities, there is no guarantee that they will make you an offer. Particularly for degrees demanding three As at A level, there may simply be too many highly qualified applicants to offer places to all of them – UCAS estimates that the odds against winning a place on one of the top ten English degrees for those who made no other choices was 10:1 in 2009. The main proviso for insurance choices, as with all others, is that you must be prepared to take up that place. If not, you might as well go for broke with courses with higher standard offers and take your chances in Clearing, or even retake exams if you drop grades. Thousands of applicants each year end up rejecting their only offer when they could have had a second, insurance, choice.

Reputation

The reputation of a university is something intangible, usually built up over a long period and sometimes outlasting reality. Before universities were subject to external assessment and the publication of copious statistics, reputation was rooted in the past. League tables are partly responsible for changing that, although employers are often still influenced by what they remember as the university pecking order when they were students.

The fragmentation of the British university system into groups of institutions is another factor: the Russell Group represents 24 research-intensive universities, nearly all with medical schools; the 1994 Group, a similar number of smaller research universities; and the Million+ Group containing many of the former polytechnics and newer universities. To these have been added the University Alliance, which provides a home for 23 universities, both old and new, that did not fit into the other categories. In addition there is GuildHE, an organisation mainly for specialist colleges, but including five of the newest universities, and the Cathedrals Group: an affiliation of church-based universities and colleges. The university profiles in chapter 14 give the affiliation of each university.

Many of today's applicants will barely have heard of a polytechnic, let alone be able to identify which of today's universities had that heritage, but most will know which of two universities in the same city has the higher status. While that should matter far less than the quality of a course, it would be naïve to ignore institutional reputation entirely if that is going to carry weight with a future employer. Some big firms restrict their recruitment efforts to a small group of universities (see chapter 2), and, however shortsighted that might be, it is something to bear in mind if a career in the City or a big law firm is your ambition.

Cost

Quite apart from the level of fees, the cost of studying in different parts of the UK inevitably varies. Some cities – notably London – are notoriously expensive for students and non-students alike. But even these comparisons can be complicated by the availability of part-time employment – an important factor for a growing number of students today. The 2010 NatWest survey rated London as the cheapest place in the UK to study once earning opportunities are taken into account. If you intend to take part-time employment while studying, check that your chosen university has a "job shop", or some other organisation to help students find reasonably paid work.

Accommodation costs listed alongside the university profiles in this *Guide* are probably the nearest proxy for a cost-of-living indicator. The *Guide* also includes a summary of the bursaries available at each university. The size of bursaries varies enormously, as do the rules governing eligibility. Scholarships are awarded for other achievements, regardless of family income.

Facilities

Universities compete for the best students not only through their courses but, increasingly, also through non-academic facilities. Accommodation is the main selling point for those living away from home, but sports facilities, libraries and computing equipment also play an important part. Even campus nightclubs have become part of the facilities race that has coincided with the introduction of top-up fees.

Many universities guarantee first-year students accommodation in halls of residence or university-owned flats. But it is as well to know what happens after that. Are there enough places for second or third-year students who want them, and if not, what is the private market like? Rents for student houses vary quite widely across the country and there have been tensions with local residents in some cities. All universities offer specialist accommodation for disabled students – and are better at providing other facilities than most public institutions. Their websites give basic information on what is provided, as well as contact points for more detailed inquiries.

Special-interest clubs and recreational facilities, as well as political activity, tend to be based in the students' union – sometimes knows as the guild of students. In some universities, the union is the focal point of social activity, while in others the attractions of the city seem to overshadow the union to the point where facilities are underused. Students' union websites are included with the information found in the university profiles (chapter 13).

Sources of information

With nearly 120 universities to choose from, the Unistats and UCAS websites, as well as guides such as this one, are the obvious places to start your search for the right course. But once you have narrowed down the list of candidates, you will want to go through undergraduate prospectuses. Most are available online, where you can select the relevant sections rather than waiting for an account of every course to arrive in the post. Beware of generalised claims about the standing of the university, the quality of courses, friendly atmosphere and legendary social life. Stick, if you can, to the factual information.

If the material that the universities publish about their own qualities is less than objective, much of what you will find on the internet is equally unreliable, for different reasons. A simple search on the name of a university will turn up spurious comparisons of everything from the standard of lecturing to the attractiveness of the students. These can be seriously misleading and are usually based on anecdotal evidence, at best. Make sure that any

---

Checklist

Choosing a subject and a place to study is a major decision. Make sure you can answer these questions:

Choosing a course

» What do I want out of higher education?
» Which subjects do I enjoy studying at school?
» Which subject or subjects do I want to study?
» Do I have the right qualifications?
» What are my career plans and does the subject and course fit these?
» Do I want to study full-time or part-time?
» Do I want to study at a university or a college?

Choosing a university

» What type of university do I wish to go to: campus, city or smaller town?
» How far is the university from home?
» Is it large or small?
» Is it specialist or general?
» Does it offer the right course?
» How much will it cost?
» Have I arranged to visit the university?

information you may take into account comes from a reputable source and, if it conflicts with your impression, try to cross-check it with this *Guide* and the institution's own material.

Useful websites

The following websites will help you find out more about the topics discussed in this chapter. The best starting point is the UCAS website (**www.ucas.com** or **www.ucas.ac.uk**). On the site there's lots of information on courses, universities and the whole process of applying to university. In addition UCAS has an official presence on Facebook (**www.facebook.com/ucasonline**) and Twitter (**@UCAS_online**) and now also has a series of video guides (**www.ucas.tv**) on the process of applying, UCAS resources and comments from other students on higher education.

Within the UCAS site, useful but not immediately obvious pages include:
The Stamford Test
www.ucas.com/students/choosingcourses/choosingcourse//stamfordtest
The UCAS tariff (and especially its use with vocational qualifications)
www.ucas.com/students/ucas_tariff/tarifftables

For statistical information which allows limited comparison between universities (and for full details of the National Student Survey), visit: **http://unistats.direct.gov.uk**

For an official listing of recognised degrees and recognised higher education institutions:
www.bis.gov.uk/policies/higher-education/recognised-uk-degrees

UK Course Finder: **www.ukcoursefinder.com**

For a full calendar of university and college open days: **www.opendays.com**

Students with disabilities: Disability Alliance: **www.disabilityalliance.org/skill.htm**

University groupings

1994 Group, a group of medium and small research-intensive universities:
www.1994group.ac.uk
GuildHE, a group of higher education colleges, specialist institutions and some universities: **www.guildhe.ac.uk**
Million+ Group, a group of newer universities: **www.millionplus.ac.uk**
Russell Group: a group of large research-intensive universities: **www.russellgroup.ac.uk**
The University Alliance, a group of old and new universities: **www.university-alliance.ac.uk**
The Cathedrals Group: an affiliation of church-based universities and colleges:
www.cathedralsgroup.org.uk

2 Graduate Employment Prospects

Every set of employment figures seems to bring more bad news for young people, whether or not they have been to university. Early in 2012, unemployment among recent graduates was said to be running at almost 20 per cent – the worst rate since the recession of the early 1990s and far in excess the official figures quoted in this *Guide*, which date from the end of 2010. But every report also shows that a degree continues to confer substantial advantages in the labour market. Indeed, the salary premium enjoyed by graduates over those who do not go to university remains higher in the UK than in almost any other part of the world.

Inevitably, such figures average out the experiences of millions of people. This chapter will begin to tease out the often contrasting employment prospects of graduates in different subjects and different types of university. Choosing a degree is about much more than future earning power – most students taking theology or fine art have never expected to match the likely salaries of those in the medical school. But, with tuition fee debt alone soon to exceed £25,000 on many courses, it is important to know what you may be letting yourself in for. The latest estimates by the Office for National Statistics (ONS) suggest that a mathematician or engineer is likely to earn 50 per cent more over a working life than an arts graduate. Another survey suggested that a graduate from the Million+ group of universities was twice as likely to be unemployed three and a half years after graduation than one from a university in the Russell Group.

Perhaps the greatest threat for recent graduates, however, has not been unemployment but underemployment. Even in the current climate of job scarcity, the proportion out of work drops from 19 per cent in the two years immediately after graduation to 6.7 per cent in the two years after that, and 4.4 per cent between four and six years into a career. But the ONS also found that more than a third of recent graduates were in low-skilled jobs at the end of 2011, compared with little more than a quarter ten years previously. Its figures differ from those quoted in this *Guide* not only because of the timing of the surveys but also because the official statistics for universities measure activity only six months after graduation. Figures for the proportion of graduates in "non-graduate" jobs are given in every subject table in chapter 5, and are at least as significant as those for unemployment. In some subjects – particularly the performing arts, but also in areas such as media studies – a period of freelancing or relatively low-level employment is a long-established entry route to graduates' careers of choice.

Whatever methods are used to calculate the figures, however, every survey confirms that the economic downturn has been especially tough for new graduates. No one can predict the changes that may take place in the three or four years before those starting a degree in 2013 begin their careers. But those choosing a course now will want to know what they can do to insulate themselves against the possibility of unemployment or underemployment after they leave university.

There are at least signs of a recovery in the private sector, although it is too soon to gauge the impact of the Coalition's austerity measures on the important public sector labour market for graduates. Although the same may not be true of smaller firms, the biggest companies actually increased their recruitment in 2011. *The Graduate Market 2012* report by High Fliers found that there had been a 2.8 per cent increase in graduate recruitment by leading employers, with the same firms planning a further 6.2 per cent rise in 2012. The report was even optimistic about the public sector, suggesting a significant increase in vacancies in spite of recruitment freezes in central and much of local government. A more recent report by Incomes Data Services forecast a 9 per cent increase in vacancies, although it warned that nine out of ten employers intended to freeze graduate starting salaries.

Nevertheless, the UK may never return to the days of plentiful, well-paid graduate jobs that it enjoyed only a few years ago. With the numbers emerging from universities still growing year on year, graduates will need to do all they can to make themselves attractive to employers. Whatever the economic conditions, they will still be in a much better position than young people without higher education, but there are going to be a lot of graduates chasing a more limited number of opportunities than in the past.

Universities targeted by the largest number of top employers in 2011–12

1	(3)	Manchester
2	(4)	London
3	(1)	Cambridge
4	(6)	Nottingham
5	(5)	Oxford
6	(7)	Bristol
7	(2)	Warwick
8	(9)	Durham
9	(12)	Birmingham
10	(8)	Bath
11	(10)	Leeds
12	(14)	Sheffield
13	(11)	Edinburgh
14	(13)	Loughborough
15	(15)	Southampton
16	(19)	Newcastle
17	(17)	Aston
18	-	Liverpool
19	(16)	Cardiff
20	(20)	Exeter

Last year's position in brackets
Source: The Graduate Market in 2012

Subject choice and career opportunities

The tables on pages 36–37 and 40–41 will help you assess whether your prospective course will pay off in career terms, at least to start with. They date from 2009–10, but there is no reason to believe that the pattern of success rates in different subjects will have changed. The Higher Education Statistics Agency (HESA) collects data on what graduates do straight after graduation (sometimes called graduate destinations) and on their average salaries. Because they represent only the first six months of a graduate's career – not even that if he or she has gone on to postgraduate study – the results are to be treated with caution. They make no allowances for the variety of entry routes into different areas of employment.

What graduates do by subject studied

The Times Subject Area ranked by the total of the first four columns on the right	Employed in graduate job	Employed in graduate job and studying	Studying and not employed	Employed in non-graduate job and studying	Employed in non-graduate job	Unemployed
1 Dentistry	92%	8%	0%	0%	0%	0%
2 Medicine	91%	3%	5%	0%	0%	0%
3 Nursing	90%	5%	1%	0%	2%	2%
4 Veterinary Medicine	86%	3%	4%	0%	5%	3%
5 Pharmacology and Pharmacy	62%	20%	9%	1%	6%	3%
6 Chemical Engineering	52%	4%	21%	1%	8%	13%
7 Mechanical Engineering	58%	4%	15%	1%	13%	10%
8 General Engineering	54%	6%	15%	1%	14%	9%
9 Physics and Astronomy	29%	6%	40%	1%	12%	11%
10 Chemistry	31%	5%	39%	2%	14%	9%
11 Education	59%	4%	10%	2%	20%	4%
12 Other Subjects Allied to Medicine	60%	6%	8%	2%	17%	8%
13 Mathematics	33%	11%	26%	3%	17%	10%
14 Russian	40%	6%	24%	4%	19%	8%
15 Economics	43%	11%	17%	2%	18%	9%
16 Anatomy and Physiology	23%	4%	42%	4%	21%	6%
17 Civil Engineering	52%	5%	15%	1%	14%	13%
18 Social Work	59%	6%	5%	2%	18%	10%
19 Town and Country Planning and Landscape	45%	6%	19%	2%	18%	10%
20 French	43%	4%	22%	3%	23%	6%
21 Architecture	48%	8%	13%	2%	17%	12%
22 Celtic Studies	16%	4%	46%	5%	24%	5%
23 Law	21%	5%	38%	7%	23%	7%
24 Theology and Religious Studies	30%	4%	32%	4%	24%	6%
25 German	42%	6%	20%	3%	24%	6%
26 Electrical and Electronic Engineering	50%	4%	14%	2%	18%	12%
27 Middle Eastern and African Studies	45%	5%	16%	3%	18%	13%
28 Aeronautical and Manufacturing Engineering	45%	3%	18%	2%	21%	11%
29 Iberian Languages	42%	3%	21%	3%	24%	8%
30 Land and Property Management	58%	3%	5%	2%	21%	12%
31 Materials Technology	52%	2%	11%	2%	24%	8%
32 Geology	32%	3%	30%	3%	23%	10%
33 Classics and Ancient History	28%	2%	31%	5%	23%	10%
34 Italian	41%	2%	21%	3%	26%	8%
35 Food Science	49%	3%	11%	2%	26%	8%

The Times Subject Area ranked by the total of the first four columns on the right	Employed in graduate job	Employed in graduate job and studying	Studying and not employed	Employed in non-graduate job and studying	Employed in non-graduate job	Unemployed
36 Computer Science	50%	3%	11%	2%	20%	14%
37 Politics	34%	4%	23%	4%	26%	9%
38 Biological Sciences	25%	4%	32%	3%	25%	10%
39 East and South Asian Studies	39%	4%	20%	1%	16%	19%
40 Building	54%	4%	5%	1%	23%	13%
41 Music	36%	5%	21%	3%	26%	9%
42 Anthropology	34%	3%	21%	5%	25%	11%
43 Philosophy	31%	5%	24%	4%	27%	10%
44 Accounting and Finance	30%	17%	10%	5%	26%	11%
45 History of Art, Architecture and Design	32%	3%	22%	5%	32%	7%
46 Geography and Environmental Sciences	31%	4%	23%	4%	30%	8%
47 Business Studies	45%	5%	8%	2%	29%	10%
48 Agriculture and Forestry	38%	9%	9%	4%	33%	7%
49 History	27%	3%	25%	4%	32%	9%
50 English	29%	3%	22%	5%	33%	8%
51 Sports Science	35%	4%	15%	4%	36%	6%
52 Linguistics	29%	5%	20%	4%	34%	9%
53 American Studies	31%	4%	18%	3%	35%	9%
54 Librarianship and Information Management	41%	6%	6%	4%	30%	14%
55 Archaeology	26%	3%	22%	4%	33%	12%
56 Art and Design	42%	3%	6%	3%	34%	12%
57 Psychology	27%	4%	16%	6%	38%	8%
58 Social Policy	31%	4%	13%	4%	39%	9%
59 Drama, Dance and Cinematics	36%	3%	8%	4%	39%	10%
60 Hospitality, Leisure, Recreation, and Tourism	39%	2%	6%	3%	42%	8%
61 Sociology	30%	3%	13%	4%	42%	9%
62 Communication and Media Studies	38%	2%	7%	2%	39%	13%
Overall	**43%**	**5%**	**15%**	**3%**	**25%**	**9%**

Source: HESA 2009/10 DLHE return
Data shown rounded to the nearest percentage point.

Degrees in social work, for example, can sometimes involve a placement after final exams, so graduates of these courses can seem to be unemployed when they might in fact have reasonable job prospects.

We use classifications developed at the universities of Warwick and the West of England to distinguish between "graduate-level" work and jobs that do not normally require a degree. Subjects are ranked on "positive destinations" which include postgraduate study and other forms of training, whether or not they are combined with a job. Some similar tables – often quoted on university websites – do not make a distinction between different types of job. These tend to give the impression that all universities and subjects have uniformly high employment rates.

The employment table in this *Guide* contains some unexpected results, such as unemployment of over 12 per cent for graduates in computer science and various branches of engineering. By contrast, it shows that a course in education is the most certain route to a job apart from various branches of medicine, with 4 per cent unemployment. The table also shows that some subjects, especially sciences such as physics and chemistry, have a higher expectation than others that their graduates will undertake further study, often for a doctorate.

The second table, on pages 40–41, gives average earnings six months after graduation. It contains interesting – and in some cases surprising – information about early career pay levels. Few would have placed social work or geology in the top ten fields for graduate pay, while business studies and accounting appear in 20th and 21st place respectively. Those positions underline the differences between starting salaries and long-term prospects in different jobs. The ONS survey of pay between the ages of 21 and 64, puts business graduates ahead of those who took education degrees, although both were found to earn more than the £15.18-an-hour average for all graduates in 2011. Arts graduates were at the bottom of the pay league, on £12.08 an hour – still comfortably more than the £8.92 earned by non-graduates.

Average wage for graduates aged 21–64 by degree subject studied (average hourly earnings, 2010–11)

Medicine and dentistry	£21.29
Mathematical sciences, engineering, technology and architecture	£18.92
Physical or environmental sciences	£17.74
Business	£17.30
Education	£16.97
Law	£16.95
Social studies	£16.33
Biological and agricultural sciences	£15.83
Librarianship and languages	£14.85
Medical related subjects	£14.65
Humanities	£14.63
Arts	£12.06
All graduates	**£15.18**
Non-graduates	**£8.92**

Source: Office for National Statistics Labour Force Survey

Enhancing your employability

Universities are well aware of the difficulties in the graduate employment market and have been introducing all manner of schemes to try to give their graduates an advantage in the labour market. Many have incorporated specially designed employability modules into degree courses; some are certificating extra-curricular activities to improve their graduates' CVs; others are stepping up their efforts to provide work experience to complement degrees.

Opinion is divided on the value of such schemes. Some of the biggest employers restrict their recruitment activities to a small number of universities, believing that these institutions attract the brightest minds, and that trawling more widely is not cost-effective. The High Fliers report, which focuses on *The Times* top 100 graduate employers, names Manchester and the various colleges of the University of London as the institutions most often targeted for recruitment in 2011. These companies, often big payers from the City of London and including some of the top law firms, are not likely to change their ways at a time when they are more anxious than ever to control costs. Widening the pool of universities from which they recruit is costly, and unnecessary in a buyers' market like the one we see today. As before, they will expect to pick up outstanding candidates who went to other universities later in their careers.

However, most graduates do not work in the City, and most students do not go to universities at the top of the league tables. The best advice for those looking to maximise their employment opportunities (and who isn't?) must be to go for the best university you can.

University schemes

If a university offers extra help towards employment, it is worth considering whether its scheme is likely to work for you. Some are too new to show results in the labour market, but they may have been endorsed by big employers or introduced at an institution whose graduates already have a record of success in the jobs market. In time, these extras may turn into mandatory parts of degree study, complete with course credit.

At Liverpool John Moores University, for example, the World of Work (WoW) programme was devised with the help of the CBI, Shell, Sony, and Marks and Spencer. Taken by students in all subjects, including postgraduates, it offers classes in CV writing, interview skills, finance, entrepreneurship and negotiation skills, among many other topics. There are guest lectures and demonstrations related to the eight employment-related skills that WoW is intended to develop, and employers carry out mock interviews to assess students' strengths and weaknesses.

Hertfordshire is another university to have demonstrated a sustained focus on its students' job prospects. It was arguably the first of many universities to describe itself as "business-facing". Employer groups are consulted on the curriculum, and often supply guest lecturers on degree courses. Like some other universities, such as Derby, it offers career development support to graduates throughout their working life.

Other universities, such as Exeter, have taken a different tack and are helping students make the most of their voluntary and extra-curricular activities by certificating them. The Exeter Award gives credit for attendance at skills sessions and training courses, active participation in sporting and musical activities, engagement in work experience and voluntary work. The university already claimed to have more students than any other involved in voluntary activities. It believes that the award will encourage employers to take more notice of them.

The York Award is another well-established example of this type of scheme that has the involvement of organisations from the public, private and voluntary sectors. The university has found that employers value a combination of academic study, work experience and leisure interests. The scheme offers York students a framework to gain recognition for activities that are not formally recognised through the degree programme. Among the subjects on an extensive list of courses are networking, time management, counselling and understanding different cultures.

What graduates earn by subject studied

	Subject	Graduate employment or self employment	Non-graduate employment or self employment
1	Dentistry	£30,293	..
2	Medicine	£29,141	..
3	Chemical Engineering	£27,195	£16,571
4	General Engineering	£26,542	£17,781
5	Economics	£25,722	£16,237
6	Veterinary Medicine	£2,3875	£18,273
7	Geology	£24,766	£14,437
8	Mechanical Engineering	£24,726	£16,621
9	Social Work	£24,290	£14,346
10	Mathematics	£24,259	£15,582
11	Russian	£23,967	..
12	Physics and Astronomy	£23,675	£14,966
13	Civil Engineering	£23,667	£15,503
14	Aeronautical and Manufacturing Engineering	£23,268	£15,946
15	Electrical and Electronic Engineering	£23,233	£15,205
16	Nursing	£22,484	£17,203
17	Computer Science	£22,325	£15,370
18	Building	£21,695	£15,339
19	Politics	£21,582	£15,127
20	Business Studies	£21,341	£15,658
21	Accounting and Finance	£21,327	£16,207
22	Philosophy	£21,096	£14,512
23	Education	£21,061	£14,070
24	German	£21,032	£15,213
25	Other Subjects Allied to Medicine	£20,741	£14,771
26	Law	£20,719	£14,786
27	Chemistry	£20,712	£15,651
28	Middle Eastern and African Studies	£20,537	£15,872
29	Librarianship and Information Management	£20,518	£16,679
30	Materials Technology	£20,371	£15,243
31	Food Science	£20,336	£15,269
32	Pharmacology and Pharmacy	£20,236	£15,222
33	Geography and Environmental Sciences	£20,215	£14,341
34	French	£20,178	£15,494
35	Classics and Ancient History	£20,073	£15,374
36	Theology and Religious Studies	£20,068	£14,099
37	Town and Country Planning and Landscape	£19,976	£16,176
38	Italian	£19,957	£15,890
39	History	£19,869	£14,279
40	Sociology	£19,639	£14,210
41	Iberian Languages	£19,617	£16,198
42	Social Policy	£19,540	£14,410

	Subject	Graduate employment or self employment	Non-graduate employment or self employment
43	Land and Property Management	£19,497	£14,690
44	American Studies	£19,440	£13,979
45	Biological Sciences	£19,373	£14,036
46	Anatomy and Physiology	£19,291	£14,177
47	East and South Asian Studies	£19,278	£14,408
48	Anthropology	£18,780	£15,894
49	History of Art, Architecture and Design	£18,588	£14,659
50	Sports Science	£18,527	£14,304
51	Music	£18,493	£13,809
52	English	£18,486	£14,230
53	Agriculture and Forestry	£18,282	£15,295
54	Psychology	£18,119	£14,094
55	Architecture	£18,041	£14,645
56	Linguistics	£17,968	£14,706
57	Archaeology	£17,819	£14,284
58	Hospitality, Leisure, Recreation and Tourism	£17,814	£15,573
59	Art and Design	£17,676	£13,932
60	Drama, Dance and Cinematics	£17,631	£14,017
61	Communication and Media Studies	£17,272	£14,205
62	Celtic Studies	£17,191	£14,693
	Average	**£21,589**	**£14,735**

NOTE: ".." Indicates a suppressed mean salary based on 7 or less graduates
Source: HESA 2009/10 DLHE return

The value of work experience

As the table earlier in this chapter showed, there are big differences in the average employment prospects for different subjects. But the majority of graduate jobs are open to applicants from any discipline. For those general positions, employers tend to be more impressed by a good degree from what they consider a prestigious university than by an apparently relevant qualification. Here numeracy, literacy and communications – the arts needed to function effectively in any organisation – are of vital importance.

Specialist jobs – for example in engineering or design – are a different matter. Employers may be much more knowledgeable about the quality of individual courses and less influenced by a university's overall position in league tables when the job relies directly on knowledge and skills acquired as a student. That goes for the likes of medicine and architecture as well as the new vocational areas such as computer games design or environmental management.

In either case, however, work experience has become increasingly important. More than half of the employers in the latest High Fliers survey said that graduates who had no work experience stood little chance of getting onto their graduate training programmes. Many had employed graduates who had already worked for them in holiday jobs, internships, placements or during sponsored degrees. Sandwich degrees, extended programmes that include up to a year at work, have always boosted employment prospects. Graduates often end up working where they undertook their placement. And while a sandwich year will make your course longer, it will not be subject to a full year's fees.

Many conventional degrees now include shorter work placements that should offer some advantages in the labour market. Not all are arranged by the university so, unless you have an opening that you would like to pursue, that is something to establish and weigh in the balance when choosing a course. The majority of big graduate employers offer some provision of this nature, although access to it can be competitive.

If your chosen course does not include a work placement, you may still want to consider the possibilities for arranging your own part-time or temporary employment. The majority of supposedly full-time students now take jobs during term time, as well as in vacations, to make ends meet. But such jobs can also boost your CV – even working in a bar or a shop shows some experience of dealing with the public and coping with the disciplines of the workplace. Inevitably, the more prosperous cities are likely to offer more employment opportunities than rural areas or conurbations that have been hard hit in the recession.

Of course, the ultimate work-related degree is one sponsored by an employer or even taken in the workplace – something that Government ministers have encouraged recently. Middlesex University provides tailored programmes for Dell and Marks and Spencer, among other organisations, and has more than 1,000 students taking courses run by its Institute of Work-Based Learning. Most such courses are provided for people already employed by the companies concerned, rather than as a route into the company. But they may become an alternative to entering full-time higher education straight from school or college.

Consider part-time degrees

Another option favoured by ministers is part-time study. The level of financial support has improved, with a tuition fee loan for most university degrees, and numbers are expected to rise considerably in 2013. Part-time study requires a high degree of commitment – knuckling down to an essay or an assignment after a hard day at work is not easy – but it does reduce the cost of higher education for those in work. Bear in mind, however, that most part-time courses take twice as long to complete as the full-time equivalent. If your earning power is linked to the qualification, it will take that much longer for you to enjoy the benefits.

Plan early for your career

Whatever type of course you choose, it is sensible to start thinking about your future career early in your time at university. There has been a growing tendency in recent years for students to convince themselves that there would be plenty of time to apply for jobs after graduation, and that they were better off focusing entirely on their degree while at university. In the current employment market, all but the most obviously brilliant graduates need to offer more than just a degree, whether it be work experience, leadership qualities demonstrated through clubs and societies, or commitment to voluntary activities. Many students finish a degree without knowing what they want to do, but a blank CV will not impress a prospective employer.

Useful websites

Prospects, the UK's official graduate careers website: **www.prospects.ac.uk**
For information on internships and graduate schemes: **www.milkround.com**

3 Going Abroad to University

As university fees rise and the graduate labour market becomes increasingly international, many more young people have begun to consider the possibility of taking a degree abroad. As yet, relatively few of them take up the option in the end, although – particularly at independent schools – it has become a natural part of the decision-making process for those choosing universities.

There is good reason for applicants to spread the university net more widely. Research by QS, publishers of the World University Rankings, found that 60 per cent of employers worldwide – and 42 per cent of those in the UK – gave extra weight to an international student experience when recruiting graduates. Of course, everything will depend on what and where that experience was. Harvard is going to carry more weight than the University of Lapland, which has been trying to attract British students recently. But leaving the UK to study certainly need not hold back your career or provide an inferior education.

The question is how to judge a university that may be thousands of miles from home against more familiar names in the UK. This chapter will make some suggestions, including the use of the growing number of global rankings that are available online or in print.

It is possible to have your academic cake and eat it by going on an international exchange or work placement organised by a UK university, or even to attend a British university in another country. Nottingham University has campuses in China and Malaysia; Middlesex can offer Dubai or Mauritius, where students registered in the UK can take part or all of their degree. Other universities, such as Liverpool, also have joint ventures with overseas institutions which offer an international experience (in China, in Liverpool's case) and degrees from both universities.

In most cases, however, an overseas study experience means a foreign university. Until recently, this was usually for a postgraduate degree – and there are still strong arguments for spending your undergraduate years in the UK before going abroad for more advanced study. Older students taking more specialised programmes may get more out of an extended period overseas than those who go at 18 and, since first degrees in the UK are shorter than elsewhere, it may also be the more cost-effective option.

Nevertheless, many believe that rising fees will turn the turn the trickle of undergraduates leaving the UK to study into a torrent. There are no fees in some Continental countries, after all, and even many American universities are not so much more expensive than staying at home now. The logic of the argument is impeccable, but there are several reasons for thinking that the torrent is still some way off. Where Europe is concerned, the main issue concerns the language barrier. Although there are now thousands of postgraduate courses taught in English at Continental universities, first degree programmes are much thinner on the ground. A few universities, like Maastricht, in the Netherlands, have made a serious pitch for business from the UK and are offering a wide range of subjects in English at a fraction of the cost of a UK degree. But most European universities teach undergraduates in the host language – and, up to now, that has always deterred UK students.

The obvious alternative lies in US, Australian and Canadian universities, all of which are keen to attract more international students. Here, cost and distance are the main obstacles. Four-year courses add considerably to the cost of affordable-looking fees, while the state of the pound has been another serious disadvantage. Add in the natural reluctance of most 18-year-olds to commit to life on the other side of the world (or even just the Atlantic), and the prospect of a dramatic increase in student emigration lessens considerably.

It is too soon to tell how these conflicting pressures will balance out, although it will be surprising if there is not at least a gradual increase international mobility. There is remarkably little official monitoring of the numbers going abroad at the moment. A recent report commissioned by the Department for Business, Innovation and Skills (BIS) put the total at about 23,000 in 2009, while the UK International Higher Education Unit's estimate is nearly 10,000 higher. Both include further education students and postgraduates, so it can be assumed that the number of undergraduates studying abroad is below 15,000 – much less than one student in 100.

Where students go to?

For all the economic advantages of studying in Continental Europe, the USA remains by far the most popular student destination. The BIS report includes the scarcely credible finding, culled from OECD statistics, that New Zealand is next on the list, with almost 14 per cent of those studying abroad (more than 3,000 students) going there. Previous surveys have put Canada, France and Germany (in that order) as the biggest attractions outside the USA. A few British students find their way to unexpected locations, like South Korea or Slovakia, but usually for family reasons or to study the language. The figures suggest that British students are more attracted to countries that are familiar or close at hand, and where they can speak English. Many are doubtless planning to stay in their adopted country after they graduate, although visa regulations may make this difficult.

Studying in Europe

Particularly with fees rising so steeply in most of the UK, you may be able to save considerable sums by studying abroad, especially in another EU nation. You are entitled to study there for the same fees as a local resident. This will be much lower for most undergraduates than in the UK, or may even be zero for some courses. In the EU, you will also be able get a job while studying. Farther afield, your student visa might not allow you to take on paid work.

Undergraduates can study at a French university for £150 a year but, not surprisingly, nearly all first degrees are taught in French. Only 45 of the 700 Licence (Bachelors equivalent) programmes listed on the Campus France website (**www.campusfrance.org/en**) are taught in English – and 13 of them have some teaching in French.

Germany is much the same, despite attracting large numbers of international students.

The DAAD website (**www.daad.de/en**) lists 102 undergraduate programmes taught wholly or mainly in English, but many are at private universities like Jacobs University in Bremen, which charges more than £16,000 a year. Some, such as the BSc in mechanical engineering at the Karlsruhe Institute of Technology are worth considering on grounds of quality, but not to save money: the fees are about £10,000 a year.

Any potential saving has to be considered with care. Despite the Bologna process – an inter-governmental agreement which means that degrees across Europe are becoming more similar in content and duration – many Continental courses are longer than their UK equivalents, adding to the cost and to your lost earnings from attending university. And, of course, you will have higher travel costs. It is harder to generalise about the cost of living. It can be lower than the UK in southern Europe, but eyewateringly high in Scandinavia.

You can cut down the cost of an international experience and hedge your bets about committing yourself to a full course overseas by opting instead for an exchange scheme. UK universities have exchange partners all over the world, providing opportunities for everything from a summer school of less than a month to a full year abroad.

The most common offering is the EU's Erasmus scheme, which funds exchanges of between three months and a year, the work counting towards your degree. More than 2 million students throughout Europe have used the scheme, and there are 2,000 universities to choose from in 30 countries. Applications, which are made through universities' international offices, must be approved by the UK university as well as by the Erasmus administrators. Erasmus students do not pay any extra fees and they are eligible for grants to cover the extra expense of travelling and living in another country.

Studying in America

American universities remain the first choice of British students going abroad to take a degree, just as the UK is the first choice for Americans. Regardless of any special relationship, this is not surprising since international rankings consistently show US and UK universities to be the best in the world (as well as teaching in English).

Nearly 9,000 British students took courses in the USA during the academic year 2010–11, around half of them undergraduates. Already by far the most popular student destination, its attractions have multiplied since fees in England hit £9,000. The Fulbright Commission, which promotes American higher education, has seen a 30 per cent increase in the number

Top 10 European countries, as destinations for UK students, 2009		Top 10 student cities in the world	
1 France	2,580	1 Paris	France
2 Ireland	2,184	2 London	United Kingdom
3 Germany	1,260	3 Boston	United States
4 Spain	634	4 Melbourne	Australia
5 Czech Republic	402	5 Vienna	Austria
6 Norway	318	6 Sydney	Australia
7 Switzerland	290	7 Zurich	Switzerland
8 Austria	258	8 Berlin	Germany
9 Italy*	247	8 Dublin	Ireland
10 Netherlands	208	10 Montreal	Canada

Source: UNESCO Institute for Statistics. * 2008 data

Source: QS Best Student Cities in the World 2012

of Britons taking US university entrance exams. The top universities, in particular, have seen demand shoot up: Harvard received 41 per cent more applications from the UK in 2010–11, Yale 23 per cent and Pennsylvania 50 per cent more.

The sheer depth of the US university system means that if you are thinking of studying abroad, the USA is almost bound to be on the list of possibilities. Outside the Ivy League, the fee gap has been narrowing, although fees at many state universities have shot up in the last two years as politicians have tried to balance the books. At Texas A&M University, for example, ranked in the top 200 in the world, international students still only paid $11,000 a year, about £7,000 at the time of writing. Fees are lower than that at the State University of New York, although the university puts the total cost for those living on campus at $30,000.

The individual systems of state universities and private universities means that there is a great variation in the financial support given to international students. Fulbright advises students considering a US degree to assess and negotiate a funding package at the same time as pursuing their application. Otherwise, they may end up with a place they cannot afford, losing valuable time in the quest for a more suitable one.

Which countries are best?

Anyone going abroad to study will be in search of a memorable all-round experience, not just a good course. In 2010 the British Council completed a detailed analysis of how well countries around the world work to attract foreign students, as well as how well-regarded the degrees they award are internationally.

The report shows that, relative to their student population, smaller countries send the most people abroad to study. Almost 11 per cent of Moroccan students are outside Morocco, and 10 per cent of Irish students are outside Ireland. The equivalent for the UK would be about 0.7 per cent, although that figure may grow. The proportion in China may be similarly low but, as it is the world's most populous country, it is much the biggest exporter of students.

The British Council report, prepared by the Economist Intelligence Unit, went on to look in detail at which countries have the most developed approach to welcoming international students. No doubt to the British Council's relief, Britain comes third in the world as a destination for international students. The top place goes to Germany, with Australia second. China is in fourth place, while Malaysia, the USA, Japan, Russia, Nigeria, Brazil and India (these two in joint tenth place) complete the top eleven.

The report says that Germany is one of the few nations that does not allow public universities to increase fees for foreign students, and a German student visa lasts until a year after graduation, to help you look for a permanent job there. In Australia, universities can charge foreign students big fees, but other aspects of its system are highly rated. The quality of Australian degrees is generally regarded as high, and despite the high cost of getting there and the strength of the Australian dollar, life there costs less than in the UK once you arrive.

Many Asian countries are looking to recruit more foreign students, both as part of a broader internationalisation agenda and to compensate for falling numbers of potential students at home. Japan is a case in point. The high cost of living may put off many potential students, as may the unfamiliarity of its language, but more support is being offered to attract foreign students and more courses are being taught in English. However, as with any non-English speaking country, the language of instruction is only part of the story. You will need to know enough of the local language to manage the shops and the transport system, and, of course, to make friends and get the most out of being there.

Another option of growing interest is China. While you may not believe the whole of the story that China is about to take over the world, it has already grown massively in importance. Its university system is growing in quality, especially at the C9 group of international institutions, which have become known as the Chinese Ivy League. Familiarity with China is unlikely to be a career disadvantage for anyone in the 21st century. Some see Hong Kong, which has several world-ranked universities and a familiar feel for Britons, as the perfect alternative to mainland Chinese universities.

Will my degree be recognised?

Even in the era of globalisation, you need to bear in mind that not all degrees are equal. At one extreme is the MBA, which has an international system for accrediting courses, and a global admissions standard. But with many professional courses, study abroad is a potential hazard. To work as a doctor, engineer or lawyer in the UK, you need a qualification which the relevant professional body will recognise. It is understandable that to practise law in England, you need to have studied the English legal system. For other subjects, the issues are more to do with the quality and content of courses outside UK control.

There are ways of researching this issue in advance. One is to contact NARIC, the National Recognition Centre for the UK (**www.naric.org.uk**). NARIC exists to examine the compatibility and acceptability of qualifications from around the world. The other approach is to ask the UK professional body in question – maybe an engineering institution, the Law Society or the General Teaching, Medical or Dental Councils – about the qualification you propose to study for.

The British Council report suggests that Australian and German degrees are the most internationally acceptable from its Top 11 countries, with Brazil at the bottom. The USA comes fifth. While it is home to the world's top universities, the USA also has many less prestigious institutions whose qualifications are less likely to be welcomed around the world.

Which are the best universities?

Going abroad to study is a big and expensive decision, and you want to get it right. But a 2009 survey of UK students who were studying abroad or planning to do so suggested that excitement, adventure and glamour were more important in their choice than career positioning. Many have family money and have been privately educated. Their approach contrasts with that of international students coming to the UK, most of whom are highly tactical and career-minded about the choice they are making. But let's assume that you are more thoughtful in your approach than this survey suggests. Especially if you plan to study abroad to establish yourself as an internationally mobile high-flyer, you will want to know that the university you are going to is taken seriously around the world.

At the moment there are three main systems for ranking universities on a world scale. One is run by QS (Quacquarelli Symonds), an educational research company based in London (**www.topuniversities.com**). Another is by Shanghai Ranking Consultancy, a company set up by Shanghai Jiao Tong University in China and is called the Academic Ranking of World Universities (ARWU) (**www.arwu.org**). These two have been joined by *Times Higher Education* (**www.timeshighereducation.co.uk**), a weekly magazine with no connection to *The Times*, which produced its own ranking for the first time in 2010, having previously published the QS version.

The QS system uses a number of measures including academic opinion, employer opinion, international orientation, research impact and staff/student ratio to create its listing, while the ARWU uses measures such as Nobel Prizes and highly cited papers, which are more related to excellence in scientific research. *The Times Higher* has added a number of measures to the QS model, including research income and a controversial global survey of teaching quality. Despite these different approaches, many universities appear in all three rankings. If you go to a university that features highly on any of the tables, you will be at a place that is well-regarded around the world. After all, even the 200th university on any of these rankings is an elite institution in a world with more than 4,000 universities. The top 50 universities in all three rankings are listed on the following pages.

These systems tend to favour universities which are good at science and medicine. Places that specialise in the humanities and the social sciences, such as the London School of Economics, can appear in deceptively modest positions. In addition, the rankings tend to look at universities in the round, and contain only limited information on specific subjects. QS published the first 26 global subject rankings in 2011.

One advantage of the QS ranking system is that 10 per cent of a university's possible score comes from a global survey of recruiters. So you can look at this column of the table for an idea about where the major employers like to hire. Note that the author of this *Guide* has a role in developing the QS Rankings.

Other options for overseas studies

If you decide that studying abroad for a complete degree is too much, a number of options remain open. A language degree will typically involve a year abroad, and a look at the UCAS website will show many options for studying another subject alongside your language of choice. UK universities offer degrees in information technology, science, business and even journalism with a major language such as Chinese.

Many universities offer a year abroad, either studying or in a work placement, even to those who are not taking a language. At Aston University, for example, 70 per cent of students do a year's work placement and a growing number do so abroad. China and Chile have been among recent destinations. Other universities offer the opportunity to take credit-bearing courses with partner institutions overseas. American universities are again the most popular choice. The best approach is to decide what you want to study and then see if there is a UK university that offers it as a joint degree or with a placement abroad. Be aware that employers and academics alike sometimes look askance at joint degrees. Make sure that all the universities involved are well-regarded, for example by looking at their rankings on one or other of the websites mentioned at the end of the table.

Useful websites

Prospects: studying abroad: **www.prospects.ac.uk/studying_abroad.htm**
Association of Commonwealth Universities: **www.acu.ac.uk**
Campus France: **www.campusfrance.org/en**
College Board (USA): **www.collegeboard.org**
DAAD (for Germany): **www.daad.de/en**
Education Ireland: **www.educationireland.ie**
Erasmus Programme (EU): **www.britishcouncil.org/erasmus**
Finaid (USA): **www.finaid.org**
Fulbright Commission: **www.fulbright.co.uk**
Study in Australia: **www.studyinaustralia.gov.au**
Study in Canada: **www.studyincanada.com**
Study Overseas: **www.studyoverseas.com**

The top 50 universities in the world in 2010 according to QS World University Ranking (QS), the Academic Ranking of World Universities (ARWU) and Times Higher Education (THE)

QS Rank	Institution	Country	ARWU Rank	Institution	Country	THE Rank	Institution	Country
1	University of Cambridge	UK	1	Harvard University	USA	1	California Institute of Technology	USA
2	Harvard University	USA	2	Stanford University	USA	=2	Harvard University	USA
3	Massachusetts Institute of Technology	USA	3	Massachusetts Institute of Technology	USA	=2	Stanford University	USA
4	Yale University	USA	4	University of California, Berkeley	USA	4	University of Oxford	UK
5	University of Oxford	UK	5	University of Cambridge	UK	5	Princeton University	USA
6	Imperial College London	UK	6	California Institute of Technology	USA	6	University of Cambridge	UK
7	University College London	UK	7	Princeton University	USA	7	Massachusetts Institute of Technology	USA
8	University of Chicago	USA	8	Columbia University	USA	8	Imperial College London	UK
9	University of Pennsylvania	USA	9	University of Chicago	USA	9	University of Chicago	USA
10	Columbia University	USA	10	University of Oxford	UK	10	University of California, Berkeley	USA
11	Stanford University	USA	11	Yale University	USA	11	Yale University	USA
12	California Institute of Technology	USA	12	University of California, Los Angeles	USA	12	Columbia University	USA
13	Princeton University	USA	13	Cornell University	USA	13	University of California, Los Angeles	USA
14	University of Michigan	USA	14	University of Pennsylvania	USA	14	Johns Hopkins University	USA
15	Cornell University	USA	15	University of California, San Diego	USA	15	ETH Zurich (Swiss Federal Institute of Technology)	Switzerland
16	Johns Hopkins University	USA	16	University of Washington	USA	16	University of Pennsylvania	USA
17	McGill University	Canada	17	University of California, San Francisco	USA	17	University College London	UK
18	ETH Zurich (Swiss Federal Institute of Technology)	Switzerland	18	Johns Hopkins University	USA	18	University of Michigan	USA
19	Duke University	USA	19	University of Wisconsin, Madison	USA	19	University of Toronto	Canada
20	University of Edinburgh	UK	20	University College London	UK	20	Cornell University	USA

The top 50 universities in the world in 2010 according to QS World University Ranking (QS), the Academic Ranking of World Universities (ARWU) and Times Higher Education (THE)

QS Rank	Institution	Country	ARWU Rank	Institution	Country	THE Rank	Institution	Country
21	University of California, Berkeley	USA	21	University of Tokyo	Japan	21	Carnegie Mellon University	USA
22	University of Hong Kong	Hong Kong	22	University of Michigan, Ann Arbor	USA	=22	University of British Columbia	Canada
23	University of Toronto	Canada	23	ETH Zurich (Swiss Federal Institute of Technology)	Switzerland	=22	Duke University	USA
24	Northwestern University	USA	24	Imperial College London	UK	24	Georgia Institute of Technology	USA
25	University of Tokyo	Japan	25	University of Illinois, Urbana-Champaign	USA	25	University of Washington	USA
26	Australian National University	Australia	26	University of Toronto	Canada	26	Northwestern University	USA
27	King's College London	UK	27	Kyoto University	Japan	27	University of Wisconsin-Madison	USA
28	National University of Singapore	Singapore	28	University of Minnesota, Twin Cities	USA	28	McGill University	Canada
29	University of Manchester	UK	29	New York University	USA	29	University of Texas at Austin	USA
30	University of Bristol	UK	30	Northwestern University	USA	30	University of Tokyo	Japan
31	University of Melbourne	Australia	31	Washington University in St Louis	USA	31	University of Illinois, Urbana-Champaign	USA
32	Kyoto University	Japan	32	University of Colorado at Boulder	USA	32	Karolinska Institute	Sweden
33	Ecole Normale Supérieure, Paris	France	=33	Rockefeller University	USA	33	University of California, San Diego	USA
34	University of California, Los Angeles	USA	=33	University of California, Santa Barbara	USA	34	University of Hong Kong	Hong Kong
35	Ecole Polytechnique Fédérale de Lausanne	Switzerland	=35	Duke University	USA	35	University of California, Santa Barbara	USA
36	Ecole Polytechnique ParisTech	France	=35	University of Texas at Austin	USA	36	University of Edinburgh	UK

Rank	University	Country
37	Chinese University of Hong Kong (CUHK)	Hong Kong
38	University of Sydney	Australia
39	Brown University	USA
40	Hong Kong University of Science and Technology	Hong Kong
41	University of Wisconsin, Madison	USA
42	Seoul National University	South Korea
43	Carnegie Mellon University	USA
44	New York University	USA
45	Osaka University	Japan
46	Peking University	China
47	Tsinghua University	China
48	University of Queensland	Australia
49	University of New South Wales	Australia
50	University of Warwick	UK

Rank	University	Country
37	University of British Columbia	Canada
=38	University of Manchester	UK
=38	University of Maryland, College Park	USA
40	University of Paris Sud, Paris 11	France
41	Pierre and Marie Curie University, Paris 6	France
42	University of North Carolina, Chapel Hill	USA
43	University of Copenhagen	Denmark
44	Karolinska Institute	Sweden
45	Pennsylvania State University, University Park	USA
46	University of Southern California	USA
47	Technical University, Munich	Germany
=48	University of California, Davis	Australia
=48	University of California, Irvine	Australia
=48	Utrecht University	UK

Rank	University	Country
37	University of Melbourne	Australia
=38	Australian National University	Australia
=38	University of California, Davis	USA
40	National University of Singapore	Singapore
41	Washington University, St Louis	USA
42	University of Minnesota	USA
43	University of North Carolina, Chapel Hill	USA
44	New York University	USA
45	Ludwig-Maximilians-Universität, Munich	Germany
46	École Polytechnique Fédérale de Lausanne	Switzerland
47	London School of Economics and Political Science	UK
48	University of Manchester	UK
=49	Peking University	China
=49	Brown University	USA

We gratefully acknowledge permission to reproduce these three rankings. The full QS World University Rankings 2010 can be consulted at **www.topuniversities. com** and the full Academic Ranking of World Universities 2010 at **www.arwu.org**. The full *Times Higher Education* rankings can be viewed at **www. timeshighereducation.co.uk.**

For information on the recognition in the UK of international degrees, visit the National Recognition Centre for the UK (NARIC): **www.naric.org.uk**.

4 The Top Universities

The editor of a rival guide insists that there is no such thing as a top university, just the best one for each individual. Nothing could be further from the truth. Of course not everyone would find the top universities to their taste, even if they were able to secure a place. But that does not mean that there are not important differences in the quality of universities and the courses they offer. These, in turn, can have a crucial bearing on future employment prospects.

But what distinguishes a top university? And who is to say that one course is better than another – especially when the university system is so reluctant to make any such comparison? Higher education publishes copious statistics, but resists combining them in a way that might answer applicants' questions. Critics of league tables insist that this is because every university has different priorities, and every course different ways of approaching a subject. Students must choose the one that suits them best. So they must. However, the sheer range of universities and courses is such that most applicants need some help paring down the options to create a shortlist for their five application choices. For 19 years, *The Times Good University Guide* has been assisting students and their parents with that process, using the statistics that universities themselves employ to measure their own performance.

Every element of the table in this chapter has been chosen for the light it shines on the undergraduate experience and a student's future prospects. The selection of these eight measures and the way in which they are combined give a particular view of universities' overall strengths, and it is one that has stood the test of time. Unlike some others, *The Times Good University Guide* has placed a premium on consistency, confident that the measures are the best available for the task. Some changes have been forced upon us. Universities stopped assessing teaching quality by subject, when this was the most heavily weighted measure in the table, for example. There have been new developments, too, such as the National Student Survey, which was first used in the table six years ago.

The basic information that applicants need, however, in order to judge universities and their courses does not change. A university's entry standards, staffing levels, completion rates, degree classifications and graduate employment rates are all vital pieces of intelligence for anyone deciding where to study. Research grades, while not directly involving undergraduates, bring with them considerable funds and enable a university to attract top academics.

Any of these measures can be discounted by an individual, but the package has struck a chord with readers. The ranking is the most-quoted of its type both in Britain and overseas, and has built a reputation as the most authoritative arbiter of changing fortunes in higher education. The measures used are kept under review by a group of university administrators and statisticians, which meets annually. The raw data that go into the table in this chapter and the subject tables in chapter 5 are all in the public domain and are sent to universities for checking before any scores are calculated.

Indeed, while the various official bodies concerned with higher education do not publish league tables, several produce system-wide statistics in a format that invites comparisons. The Higher Education Funding Councils' Research Assessment Exercise was one early example of this. The Higher Education Statistics Agency (HESA), which supplies most of the figures used in our tables, also publishes annual "performance indicators" on everything from completion rates to research output at each university.

Any scrutiny of league table positions is best carried out in conjunction with an examination of the relevant subject table – it is the course, after all, that will dominate your under-graduate years and influence your subsequent career.

How *The Times* League Table works

The table is presented in a format that displays the raw data, wherever possible. In building the table, scores for student satisfaction and research quality were weighted by 1.5; all other measures were weighted by 1. The indicators were combined using a common statistical technique known as Z-scores, to ensure that no indicator has a disproportionate effect on the overall total for each university, and the totals were transformed to a scale with 1000 for the top score.

For entry standards, student–staff ratio, good honours and graduate prospects, the score was adjusted for subject mix. For example, it is accepted that engineering, law and medicine graduates will tend to have better graduate prospects than their peers from English, psychology and sociology courses. Comparing results in the main subject groupings helps to iron out differences attributable simply to the range of degrees on offer. This subject-mix adjustment means that it is not possible to replicate the scores in the table from the published indicators because the calculation requires access to the entire dataset.

The Z-score technique makes it impossible to compare universities' total scores from one year to the next, although their relative positions in the table are comparable. Individual scores are dependent on the top performer: a university might drop from 60 per cent of the top score to 58 per cent but still have improved, if the leading university had done better still.

Only where data are not available from HESA are figures sourced directly from universities. Where this is not possible – for example, in the case of those Scottish universities that are not part of the National Student Survey – scores are generated according to a university's average performance on other indicators.

The organisations providing the raw data for the tables are not involved in the process of aggregation, so are not responsible for any inferences or conclusions we have made. Every care has been taken to ensure the accuracy of the tables and accompanying information, but no responsibility can be taken for errors or omissions.

The Times League Table uses eight important measures of university activity, based on the most recent data available at the time of compilation:

- » Student satisfaction
- » Research quality
- » Entry standards
- » Student–staff ratio
- » Services and facilities spend
- » Completion
- » Good honours
- » Graduate prospects

Student satisfaction

This is a measure of students' views of the quality of their courses. The National Student Survey (NSS) was the source of this data. The NSS is an initiative undertaken by the Funding Councils for England, Northern Ireland and Wales. It is designed, as an element of the quality assurance for higher education, to inform prospective students and their advisers in choosing what and where to study. The survey encompasses the views of final-year students on the quality of their courses. Data from the survey published in 2011 were used.

» The National Student Survey covers six aspects of a course: teaching, assessment and feedback, academic support, organisation and management, learning resources and personal development, with an additional question gauging overall satisfaction. Students answer on a scale from 1 (bottom) to 5 (top) and the measure is the percentage of positive responses (4 and 5) in each section, averaged to produce the final score.

» The survey is based on the opinion of final-year students rather than directly assessing teaching quality. Most undergraduates have no experience of other universities, or different courses, to inform their judgements. Although all the questions relate to courses, rather than the broader student experience, some types of university – notably medium-sized campus universities – tend to do better than others.

» Scottish universities were not automatically included in the survey, although 13 out of 15 have so far opted in.

Research quality

This is a measure of the quality of the research undertaken in each university. The information was sourced from the 2008 Research Assessment Exercise (RAE), a peer-review exercise used to evaluate the quality of research in UK higher education institutions undertaken by the UK Higher Education funding bodies. Additionally, academic staffing data for 2007–08 from the Higher Education Statistics Agency have been used.

» A research quality profile was given to every university department that took part. This profile used the following categories: 4* world-leading; 3* internationally excellent; 2* internationally recognised; 1* nationally recognised; and unclassified. The Funding Bodies decided to direct more funds to the very best research by applying weightings. The English, Scottish and Welsh funding councils have slightly different weightings. Those adopted by HEFCE (the funding council for England) for funding in 2012–13 are used in the tables: 4* is weighted by a factor of 3, 3* is weighted by a factor of 1. Outputs of 2* and 1* carry zero weight. This results in a maximum score of 3 in the table.

» Universities could choose which staff to include in the RAE, so, to factor in the depth of the research quality, each quality profile score has been multiplied by the number of staff returned in the RAE as a proportion of all eligible staff.

» Estimations of the eligible staff for each university were made drawing from publicly available data that have been quality assured by universities themselves. The eligible staff data include all staff directly responsible for teaching and research (excluding those on part-time contracts of less than 20 per cent of a full-time position as they were not eligible), with an adjustment made to remove more junior staff on research-only contracts.

An adjustment has also been made to reflect patterns of staffing in those institutions which carry out further education as well as higher education. The calculations were checked against the figures published by a number of universities that declared the proportion of eligible staff entered for assessment.

Estimation was necessary because, as you will see from the note on page 56, HESA decided not to publish data on numbers of staff in university departments who were eligible to be submitted in the RAE. The proportion of staff entered by each university had been considered sufficiently important to be included in the grades used in every previous RAE to give an indication of the ethos and overall quality of departments. The methodology used in *The Times* League Table attempts to replicate that process as accurately as possible, given the restrictions imposed by HESA.

Entry standards

This is the average score, using the UCAS tariff (see page 18), of new students under the age of 21 who took A and AS Levels, Scottish Highers and Advanced Highers and other equivalent qualifications (eg, International Baccalaureate). It measures what new students actually achieved rather than the entry requirements suggested by the universities. The data comes from HESA for 2010–11. The original sources of data for this measure are data returns made by the universities themselves to HESA.

» Using the UCAS tariff, each student's examination results were converted to a numerical score. HESA then calculated an average for all students at the university. The results have then been adjusted to take account of the subject mix at the university.

» A score of 360 represents three As at A level. Although all of the top 33 universities in the table have entry standards of at least 360, it does not mean that everyone achieved such results – let alone that this was the standard offer. Courses will not demand more than three subjects at A level and offers are pitched accordingly. You will need to reach the entry requirements set by the university, rather than the scores represented here.

Student–staff ratio

This is a measure of the average number of students to each member of the academic staff, apart from those purely engaged in research. In this measure a low score is better than a high score. The data comes from HESA for 2010–11. The original sources of data for this measure are data returns made by the universities themselves to HESA.

» The figures, as calculated by HESA, allow for variation in employment patterns at different universities. A low value means that there are a small number of students for each academic member of staff, but this does not, of course, ensure good teaching quality or contact time with academics.

» Student–staff ratios vary by subject, for example the ratio is usually low for medicine. In building the table, the score is adjusted for the subject mix taught by each university.

Services and facilities spend

The expenditure per student on staff and student facilities, including library and computing facilities. The data comes from HESA for 2009–10 and 2010–11. The original data sources for this measure are data returns made by the universities to HESA.

» This is a measure calculated by taking the expenditure on student facilities (sports, grants to student societies, careers services, health services, counselling, etc.) and library and computing facilities (books, journals, staff, central computers and computer networks, but not buildings) and dividing this by the number of full-time-equivalent students. Expenditure is averaged over two years to even out the figures (for example, a computer upgrade undertaken in a single year).

Completion

This measure gives the percentage of students expected to complete their studies (or transfer to another institution) for each university. The data comes from the HESA performance indicators, based on data for 2010–11 and earlier years.

» This measure is a projection, liable to statistical fluctuations.

Good honours

This measure is the percentage of graduates achieving a first or upper second class degree. The results have been adjusted to take account of the subject mix at the university. The data comes from HESA for 2010–11. The original sources of data for this measure are data returns made by the universities themselves to HESA.

» Four-year first degrees, such as an MChem, are treated as equivalent to a first or upper second.

» Scottish Ordinary degrees (awarded after three years of study) are excluded.

» Universities control degree classification, with some oversight from external examiners. There have been suggestions that since universities have increased the numbers of good honours degrees they award, this measure may not be as objective as it should be. However, it remains the key measure of a student's success and employability.

Graduate prospects

This measure is the percentage of the total number of graduates who take up graduate-level employment or further study. The results have been adjusted for subject mix. The data come from HESA for 2010 graduates.

» HESA surveys graduates six months after graduation to find out what they are doing and the data are based on this survey.

Statement from the Higher Education Statistics Agency (HESA) regarding the use of staffing data in looking at Research Assessment Exercise performance:

This analysis of the results of the Research Assessment Exercise 2008 makes use of contextual data supplied under contract by the Higher Education Statistics Agency (HESA). It is a contractual condition that this statement should be published in conjunction with the analysis.

HESA holds no data specifying which or how many staff have been regarded by each institution as eligible for inclusion in RAE 2008, and no data on the assignment to Units of Assessment of those eligible staff not included. Further, the data that HESA does hold is not an adequate alternative basis on which to estimate eligible staff numbers, whether for an institution as a whole, or disaggregated by Units of Assessment, or by some broader subject-based grouping.

	Student satisfaction (%)	Research quality	Entry standards	Student–staff ratio	Services and facilities spend per student (£)	Completion (%)	Good honours (%)	Graduate prospects (%)	Total
1 Oxford	87	1.33	574	11.1	3298	98.1	90.9	79.8	1000
2 Cambridge	87	1.35	596	11.8	2994	98.8	87.4	84.4	990
3 London School of Economics	79	1.16	527	11.8	2625	96.5	80.9	87.8	911
4 Imperial College	78	0.99	556	11.6	3588	95.9	81.7	87.1	835
5 Durham	83	0.89	503	15.3	2281	96.2	81.8	78.5	834
6 St Andrews	83	0.84	519	13.6	2308	97.4	82.9	74.1	814
7 University College London	79	0.99	498	10.1	2197	93.9	81.0	79.9	811
8 Warwick	81	0.87	496	14.5	2053	96.5	80.8	77.6	789
9 Bath	84	0.70	461	17.1	1742	96.4	81.1	79.1	767
10 Exeter	82	0.84	459	18.5	2017	96.1	82.8	73.0	764
11 Bristol	81	0.89	478	14.3	1992	96.4	83.2	79.2	762
12 Lancaster	82	0.85	410	14.8	1795	93.4	73.4	73.6	759
13 York	81	0.87	453	15.6	2025	94.5	74.7	70.6	749
14 Edinburgh	76	0.98	476	13.9	1989	92.3	82.8	74.5	735
15 Glasgow	83	0.73	465	15.3	2186	88.3	74.1	77.0	734
16 Loughborough	84	0.74	393	16.7	1768	93.2	70.1	72.1	727
17 Leicester	84	0.60	409	13.7	2175	92.5	70.4	65.1	724
=18 Southampton	79	0.69	441	13.4	1947	92.7	76.4	72.0	717
=18 Sussex	81	0.77	385	16.6	1663	92.4	79.2	71.1	717
20 Nottingham	80	0.72	436	14.0	1656	94.9	74.9	76.0	715
21 Sheffield	82	0.82	445	15.4	1551	94.0	73.9	72.7	714
22 King's College London	78	0.70	458	11.7	1938	92.3	78.7	79.6	710

	Student satisfaction (%)	Research quality	Entry standards	Student–staff ratio	Services and facilities spend per student (£)	Completion (%)	Good honours (%)	Graduate prospects (%)	Total
23 Newcastle	82	0.65	427	15.3	1773	93.8	74.6	76.5	702
=24 Birmingham	78	0.72	435	15.5	2036	94.4	76.1	74.0	690
=24 Reading	81	0.68	377	14.9	1454	92.3	73.4	69.3	690
26 Surrey	81	0.61	399	17.9	2081	89.6	67.6	72.5	688
27 Royal Holloway	78	0.83	399	15.6	1512	92.2	71.8	66.1	680
28 East Anglia	82	0.63	396	13.9	1689	88.4	69.6	62.8	675
29 Liverpool	79	0.60	409	13.0	2041	92.7	72.7	71.0	673
30 Leeds	81	0.68	413	15.7	1216	90.9	77.3	73.0	672
31 School of Oriental and African Studies	72	0.65	419	11.3	1867	84.8	75.4	64.5	662
32 Cardiff	79	0.63	437	14.4	1307	92.9	71.7	76.1	661
33 Manchester	76	0.86	425	15.2	1732	93.0	71.8	70.5	660
34 Kent	80	0.51	352	14.6	1341	89.7	67.8	69.6	657
35 Queen's, Belfast	79	0.56	387	15.3	1933	91.9	73.4	71.9	653
=36 Aston	80	0.40	383	17.0	1564	89.7	67.8	75.7	646
=36 Strathclyde	79	0.50	440	17.9	1635	84.2	76.0	72.0	646
38 Queen Mary, London	80	0.69	396	12.8	1614	87.8	62.7	71.1	638
39 Aberdeen	81	0.62	401	16.2	1428	81.6	68.7	71.5	630
40 Essex	81	0.68	331	15.9	1536	87.6	62.5	53.7	620
41 Buckingham	87	:	276	10.7	1396	79.3	42.2	76.4	618
42 Heriot-Watt	81	0.54	384	18.8	1341	81.8	68.8	71.5	613
43 Brunel	81	0.51	343	18.0	1680	86.1	63.1	61.3	612
44 Dundee	80	0.47	382	14.2	1299	81.6	71.2	68.2	609

Rank	University									
45	Keele	83	0.38	339	16.0	1205	86.9	66.0	71.8	607
46	City	75	0.43	372	16.6	1865	85.7	69.0	71.7	597
47	Aberystwyth	83	0.61	307	19.1	1307	85.9	59.2	52.1	576
48	Goldsmiths College	76	0.74	347	17.7	946	81.3	70.1	52.2	561
49	Hull	81	0.33	329	19.9	1313	84.5	53.9	67.8	558
50	Stirling	80	0.41	342	20.5	1209	84.3	64.2	60.5	556
51	Robert Gordon	80	0.16	335	19.1	1252	78.3	60.6	78.4	555
=52	Lincoln	78	0.15	316	18.8	1272	85.7	58.6	67.0	549
=52	Oxford Brookes	76	0.17	333	16.7	1332	86.0	67.6	64.1	549
=52	Swansea	74	0.48	343	16.4	1279	89.0	61.4	66.3	549
55	Coventry	81	0.07	287	15.4	1205	78.0	61.2	66.8	548
56	Bangor	81	0.48	295	19.1	1106	79.7	60.2	61.9	544
57	Huddersfield	81	0.06	305	17.9	1398	77.7	55.7	69.3	540
58	Northumbria	78	0.08	318	17.4	1329	87.7	59.5	63.6	538
59	Chester	79	0.03	283	16.6	1364	78.6	60.0	67.1	527
60	University of the Arts, London	70	0.61	307	17.4	1216	88.3	65.0	55.5	524
61	Chichester	81	0.05	295	18.4	1147	89.0	59.0	53.5	522
62	West of England	78	0.14	299	20.8	1409	77.6	63.9	65.1	510
63	Portsmouth	79	0.16	289	19.8	1267	85.1	54.2	61.9	509
64	Plymouth	75	0.20	303	16.5	1301	84.5	61.1	62.4	508
=65	Gloucestershire	78	0.06	293	21.4	1213	83.9	68.7	53.3	506
=65	Ulster	77	0.33	282	16.5	1490	78.5	63.4	49.9	506
67	Bradford	78	0.30	279	17.6	1411	80.4	50.8	69.0	504
68	Hertfordshire	78	0.10	300	19.8	1636	78.2	61.8	60.7	500
69	Brighton	78	0.29	292	18.6	948	84.8	62.0	52.7	499
70	Bath Spa	78	0.09	304	21.6	821	87.7	67.0	53.7	497
71	Central Lancashire	78	0.11	297	18.5	1639	74.3	52.3	57.7	492
72	De Montfort	79	0.18	288	18.1	1084	81.7	52.8	56.0	488

Rank	University	Student satisfaction (%)	Research quality (%)	Entry standards	Student–staff ratio	Services and facilities spend per student (£)	Completion (%)	Good honours (%)	Graduate prospects (%)	Total
=73	Edge Hill	81	0.02	266	18.5	1005	79.1	56.4	62.0	487
=73	Sheffield Hallam	76	0.12	305	19.6	1067	84.5	61.8	57.6	487
=75	Birmingham City	78	0.07	283	21.1	1516	77.8	59.2	61.9	486
=75	Winchester	76	0.12	293	18.5	1070	85.6	62.4	51.0	486
77	Sunderland	79	0.14	278	16.9	1294	79.6	50.5	50.2	482
=78	Cardiff Metropolitan	78	0.10	272	19.9	1263	82.9	54.6	52.2	478
=78	Nottingham Trent	73	0.13	302	19.0	1470	83.9	55.9	59.6	478
80	York St John	79	0.03	282	21.4	1150	84.3	58.7	53.1	475
=81	Bournemouth	69	0.13	328	20.4	1335	85.0	64.8	65.1	474
=81	Glasgow Caledonian	76	0.09	338	20.9	1405	76.0	66.8	55.5	474
83	Queen Margaret Edinburgh	73	0.10	336	20.6	1177	80.3	71.7	56.8	470
84	Edinburgh Napier	78	0.09	300	23.6	1071	75.4	64.4	65.4	468
85	Canterbury Christ Church	75	0.05	258	17.6	1098	85.0	59.0	62.9	467
86	Roehampton	75	0.23	260	20.8	1372	77.0	54.8	60.1	463
87	Teesside	79	0.05	295	19.5	1315	73.0	52.8	58.6	461
88	Bedfordshire	77	0.05	206	19.4	2004	74.1	53.6	57.4	458
89	Derby	78	0.03	278	18.1	1326	76.1	52.0	52.2	456
90	Middlesex	75	0.15	218	21.9	2401	70.0	54.7	55.5	453
=91	Greenwich	80	0.09	257	22.1	1444	74.2	51.5	55.1	452
=91	Salford	74	0.28	286	16.2	964	75.1	57.1	56.4	452
=93	Liverpool John Moores	76	0.11	277	21.0	1214	83.5	60.6	51.8	451
=93	Worcester	78	0.01	288	21.5	1006	81.9	55.3	56.2	451

Rank	University								
=95	Glamorgan	77	0.13	289	20.5	1377	72.2	58.7	54.9	447
=95	Westminster	71	0.15	292	18.4	1302	78.3	58.3	59.3	447
=97	Cumbria	72	0.01	268	17.2	1174	81.1	61.1	60.4	446
=97	Glyndŵr	76	0.04	220	21.0	1654	73.7	54.4	66.9	446
99	Northampton	76	0.04	240	20.6	1489	80.0	57.2	50.4	438
100	Staffordshire	78	0.03	248	21.6	1161	75.8	50.6	58.9	437
101	Kingston	73	0.10	281	19.8	1154	80.2	61.0	56.6	435
102	Manchester Metropolitan	72	0.13	293	18.9	1116	77.3	58.5	58.1	434
103	University for Creative Arts	73	0.15	262	19.3	1539	80.5	48.9	49.5	430
104	Leeds Metropolitan	75	0.06	263	19.5	936	80.9	54.5	53.6	429
105	Trinity St David	75	0.27	245	18.8	1281	75.6	48.3	51.1	428
106	Buckinghamshire New	74	0.02	231	23.3	1923	83.2	47.2	48.7	413
107	Anglia Ruskin	74	0.05	241	19.1	1064	79.2	55.6	54.8	410
108	Newport, University of Wales	75	0.10	259	24.8	1012	78.0	51.4	50.0	392
109	West of Scotland	76	0.14	271	22.2	1196	69.3	47.9	58.2	387
110	West London	73	0.06	235	21.0	1497	68.2	47.7	53.8	380
111	London South Bank	73	0.08	212	22.4	1062	76.1	55.1	61.0	378
112	Abertay	..	0.09	280	25.2	1208	67.7	51.3	48.8	366
113	Southampton Solent	72	0.02	268	21.2	1160	74.9	48.1	41.9	363
114	Highlands and Islands	..	0.06	269	..	760	57.5	77.0	39.4	357
115	Bolton	75	0.06	234	19.6	679	62.4	48.6	41.4	328
=116	East London	76	0.12	205	23.7	852	61.1	43.9	48.6	327
=116	London Metropolitan	69	0.10	228	19.2	630	71.3	50.1	47.9	327

Last year's figure for Completion have been used for London South Bank; Glasgow Caledonian have provided a replacement figure. The Student Satisfaction and SSR figures have been suppressed for Highlands and Islands. Derby and Edinburgh provided replacement Good Honours. Exeter, Glamorgan, Loughborough, Manchester Metropolitan, Northumbria, Nottingham, Nottingham Trent, Plymouth provided amended student data. Queen Mary supplied replacement Spend information.

5 The Top Universities by Subject

Knowing where a university stands in the pecking order of higher education is a vital piece of information for any prospective student, but the quality of the course is what matters most. As the latest Research Assessment Exercise (RAE) in 2008 confirmed, the most modest institution may have a centre of specialist excellence, and even famous universities have mediocre departments. This section offers some pointers to the leading universities in a wide range of subjects. With a number of universities reviewing the courses they will offer in the future, it is possible that not all institutions listed in a particular subject area will be running courses in 2013.

The subject tables in this *Guide* also include scores from the National Student Survey (NSS). These distil the views of final-year undergraduates on several aspects of their course, including teaching quality, assessment and feedback, and the quality of learning resources. The three other measures used are research quality, students' entry qualifications and graduate employment prospects. None of the measures are weighted.

The tables include the research grades drawn from the deliberations of expert assessors in the 2008 RAE. No data have been released on the proportion of academics entered for assessment, for example, so it has not been possible to mirror the approach adopted in the main institutional ranking (see pages 57–61). Data supplied by the Higher Education Statistics Agency (HESA) are used to calculate average entry qualifications and the employment prospects of graduates. The prospects information draws a distinction between different types of employment: graduate employment, where a degree is normally required, and non-graduate employment. The tables give the percentage of "positive destinations" by adding those undertaking further study to the total in graduate employment.

Many subjects, such as dentistry or sociology, have their own table, but others are grouped together in broader categories, such as subjects allied to medicine, which includes such specialisms as physiotherapy and radiology. Not all universities in Scotland participate in the National Student Survey, so to qualify for inclusion in the table a university has to have data for at least two of the other measures. Scores are not published where the number of students is too small for the outcome to be statistically reliable. In the NSS, a 50 per cent response rate is required from a minimum of 30 students.

Cambridge is again the most successful university. It tops 32 of the 62 tables. Oxford has the next highest number of top places with 12, while 9 other universities also gain top spots.

The subject rankings demonstrate that there are "horses for courses" in higher education. Thus the London School of Economics is more than a match for its rivals in social policy, while Loughborough remains a force in sports science and librarianship, and this year retains a top spot in building. In their own fields, table-toppers such as Warwick in American studies, drama, and communication and media studies, Durham in theology, Nottingham in agriculture and veterinary medicine, and Surrey in hospitality, are equally well-known. But the tables contain less obvious success stories, such as Edinburgh in nursing and Bath in social work.

Research quality

This is a measure of the quality of the research undertaken in the subject area. The information was sourced from the 2008 Research Assessment Exercise (RAE), a peer-review exercise used to evaluate the quality of research in UK higher education institutions, undertaken by the UK Higher Education Funding Bodies.

For each subject, a research quality profile was given to those university departments that took part, showing how much of their research was in various quality categories. These categories were: 4* world-leading; 3* internationally excellent; 2* internationally recognised; 1* nationally recognised; and unclassified. The funding bodies decided to direct more funds to the very best research by applying weightings. The English, Scottish and Welsh funding councils have slightly different weightings. Those adopted by HEFCE (the funding council for England) for funding in 2012–13 are used in the tables: 4* is weighted by a factor of 3, 3* is weighted by a factor of 1. Outputs of 2* and 1* carry zero weight.

Staffing data to show how many of a department's academics were submitted in the RAE are not currently available. Some research ratings shown could relate to a relatively low proportion of the academic staff in the department.

Entry standards

This is the average UCAS tariff score for new students under the age of 21, based on A and AS Levels and Scottish Highers and Advanced Highers and other equivalent qualifications (including the International Baccalaureate), taken from HESA data for 2010–11. Each student's examination grades were converted to a numerical score using the UCAS tariff (see page 18 for details) and added up to give a total score. HESA then calculated an average score for each university.

Student satisfaction

This measure is taken from the National Student Survey results published in 2010 and 2011. A single year's figures are used when that is all that is available, but an average of the two years' results is used in all other cases. The score for each university represents the percentage of final-year undergraduates declaring themselves satisfied or very satisfied with their course, averaged over the seven sections of the survey (teaching, assessment and feedback, academic support, organisation and management, learning resources, personal development and overall satisfaction).

Graduate prospects

This is the percentage of graduates undertaking further study or in a graduate job, in the annual survey by HESA six months after graduation. Two years of data (2009 and 2010 graduates) are aggregated to make the data more reliable. A low score on this measure does not necessarily indicate unemployment – some graduates may have taken jobs that are not categorised as graduate work. The averages for each subject are given close by the relevant subject table in this chapter and in a table in chapter 2 (see pages 36–37).

The Education table uses a fifth measure: teaching quality, as measured by the outcomes of Ofsted inspections of teacher training courses.

The subjects listed below are covered in the tables in this chapter:

Accounting and Finance
Aeronautical and Manufacturing
   Engineering
Agriculture and Forestry
American Studies
Anatomy and Physiology
Anthropology
Archaeology
Architecture
Art and Design
Biological Sciences
Building
Business Studies
Celtic Studies
Chemical Engineering
Chemistry
Civil Engineering
Classics and Ancient History
Communication and Media Studies
Computer Science
Dentistry
Drama, Dance and Cinematics
East and South Asian Studies
Economics
Education
Electrical and Electronic Engineering
English
Food Science
French
General Engineering
Geography and Environmental Sciences
Geology
German

History
History of Art, Architecture and Design
Hospitality, Leisure, Recreation and
   Tourism
Iberian Languages
Italian
Land and Property Management
Law
Librarianship and Information Management
Linguistics
Materials Technology
Mathematics
Mechanical Engineering
Medicine
Middle Eastern and African Studies
Music
Nursing
Other Subjects Allied to Medicine
   (see page 163 for included subjects)
Pharmacology and Pharmacy
Philosophy
Physics and Astronomy
Politics
Psychology
Russian and East European Languages
Social Policy
Social Work
Sociology
Sports Science
Theology and Religious Studies
Town and Country Planning and Landscape
Veterinary Medicine

Accounting and Finance

While universities have cut many courses in anticipation of higher fees, accounting and finance have continued to grow. Eight institutions have joined this table since the 2011 *Guide*, some of which offered the subject in previous years but did not have enough students to qualify. Applications were stable in accounting and up in finance in 2012, when most subjects saw a decline. The demand for places has been growing over several years, despite the fact that the early career prospects for graduates are surprisingly meagre. While those who found graduate jobs in 2010 were just outside the top 20 for graduate salaries, averaging £21,300, the subjects were in the bottom 20 in the employment table. Some universities managed a healthy employment rate, but two saw fewer than one leaver in five go straight into a graduate job or onto a postgraduate course.

Bath, a previous leader in accounting and finance, takes over at the top of the table, although it does not lead on any single measure. Warwick, last year's leader, has dropped two places and Lancaster, its nearest challenger, is now only seventh. Strathclyde's high entry grades – bettered only by the London School of Economics – help it move up to second and leave it well clear of its rivals in Scotland.

Good scores are dotted around the table. Lincoln, for example, has the most satisfied students, despite being only 33rd overall. For the fifth year in a row, Robert Gordon is both the top post-1992 university and the best for graduate prospects. Cardiff, the leader in Wales, had the best grade in the 2008 Research Assessment Exercise, but is again restricted to eighth place because more than a quarter of its graduates were without a graduate-level job or a training place six months after completing their degrees.

As in many of the subject tables, higher entry scores and research grades make the difference for the old universities. Entry grades have risen again since the 2011 *Guide*: 23 universities (rather than 19) averaged at least 400 points at A level, although five had averages below 200 points, one more than last year.

In the latest survey, 17 per cent were continuing to study while in a graduate job six months after leaving university – a proportion exceeded by only one other subject. This reflects the professional structure of accountancy and shows that a high proportion of graduates are going on to practise accountancy. However, more than a quarter of all leavers start work in a non-graduate job and the 11 per cent unemployment rate is above average for all subjects.

Employed in graduate job:	30%	Employed in non-graduate job and studying:	5%
Employed in graduate job and studying:	17%	Employed in non-graduate job:	26%
Studying:	10%	Unemployed:	11%
Average starting graduate salary:	£21,327	Average starting non-graduate salary:	£16,207

Accounting and Finance	Research quality	Entry standards	Student satisfaction %	Graduate prospects %	Overall rating
1 Bath	1.3	476	87	87	100.0
2 Strathclyde	1.2	498	89	77	98.3
3 Warwick	1.3	484	86	79	97.7
4 Loughborough	0.9	452	90	86	97.0

Accounting and Finance cont

	Research quality	Entry standards	Student satisfaction %	Graduate prospects %	Overall rating
5 London School of Economics	1.3	509	78	86	95.5
6 Glasgow	0.7	488	89	82	94.2
7 Lancaster	1.3	380	83	86	93.3
8 Cardiff	1.4	430	80	73	92.3
9 Leeds	1.1	438	81	79	91.7
=10 Exeter	0.8	464	82	80	89.7
=10 City	0.9	426	84	75	89.7
12 Newcastle	0.7	443	82	83	89.1
13 Bristol	0.8	435	84	74	89.0
14 Nottingham	1.1	403	78	79	88.6
=15 Edinburgh	0.7	453	79	78	86.9
=15 Robert Gordon	0.3	368	87	91	86.9
17 Durham	0.9	402	78	80	86.0
18 Southampton	0.9	441	77	70	84.7
19 Queen's, Belfast	0.9	421	76	74	84.5
20 Kent	0.8	373	80	71	84.4
21 Manchester	1.2	424	74	64	84.3
22 Reading	0.7	400	78	75	83.7
23 Birmingham	1.0	409	77	62	83.2
=24 Stirling	0.5	384	86	64	83.1
=24 Brunel	0.7	336	84	67	83.1
26 Sheffield	0.9	400	77	61	82.0
27 Queen Mary, London	0.9	403	79	56	81.8
28 East Anglia	0.7	359	83	60	81.4
29 Heriot-Watt	0.7	355	79	69	80.8
30 De Montfort	0.6	289	87	57	80.1
=31 Dundee	0.5	348	82	61	79.4
=31 Portsmouth	0.5	296	86	61	79.4
33 Lincoln		302	94	57	79.3
34 Aberdeen	0.6	389	75	67	78.7
=35 Hull	0.6	334	83	54	78.5
=35 Essex	0.8	330	78	59	78.5
=37 Bangor	1.0	314	80	44	78.0
=37 Aberystwyth	0.4	264	90	50	78.0
=37 Bradford	0.8	286	81	57	78.0
=40 Brighton	0.9	265	80	53	77.1
=40 Salford	0.4	265	89	47	77.1
42 Ulster	0.5	302	83	57	76.9
=43 Northumbria	0.2	322	82	66	76.8
=43 West of England	0.6	283	79	64	76.8
=43 Bournemouth	0.4	298	83	59	76.8
46 Surrey	0.7	403	78	37	76.3
47 Sheffield Hallam	0.4	292	82	62	76.0

48	Swansea	0.6	327	74	64	75.7
49	Keele	0.7	305	76	61	75.6
50	Glamorgan	0.3	255	86	59	75.4
51	Edinburgh Napier	0.2	292	82	67	75.1
52	Greenwich	0.3	254	86	53	75.0
53	Huddersfield	0.3	309	78	67	74.9
54	Central Lancashire	0.4	314	80	49	73.7
55	Oxford Brookes		323	83	57	73.4
56	Manchester Metropolitan	0.5	281	76	62	73.2
57	Liverpool	0.7		75	48	72.4
58	Plymouth	0.4	282	77	55	72.2
59	Birmingham City	0.4	272	77	59	72.0
60	Hertfordshire	0.5	283	79	47	71.9
61	Glasgow Caledonian	0.2	362	78	49	71.8
=62	Nottingham Trent	0.4	294	73	58	70.4
=62	Leeds Metropolitan		252	84	52	70.4
64	Kingston		322	81	47	70.2
65	Coventry		276	80	58	70.0
66	Gloucestershire		298	79	54	69.6
67	Southampton Solent		231	85	46	69.0
68	Northampton		218	82	54	68.5
=69	London South Bank	0.3	186	81	38	66.7
=69	Derby		272	78	46	66.7
71	Liverpool John Moores	0.1	279	77	47	66.6
72	Staffordshire		226	76	61	66.5
73	East London		187	80	52	66.0
74	Newport		223	82	39	65.6
75	Cardiff Metropolitan		253	80	37	65.3
76	Middlesex		210	82	39	65.2
77	West of Scotland	0.4	304	75	18	64.2
78	West London		199	80	37	63.3
79	Bolton	0.1	204	80	24	61.5
80	London Metropolitan		206	73	37	59.0
81	Canterbury Christ Church		201	70	45	58.6
=82	Edge Hill		244	76	18	58.4
=82	Buckinghamshire New	0.2	150	64	62	58.4
84	Anglia Ruskin		212	62	57	56.6
85	Bedfordshire		172	74	21	55.6

» Actuarial Profession: **www.actuaries.org.uk**
» Association of Chartered Certified Accountants: **www.accaglobal.com**
» Careers in accounting: **www.careers-in-accounting.com**
» Chartered Institute of Public Finance and Accountancy: **www.cipfa.org.uk**
» Institute of Chartered Accountants: **www.icaew.co.uk**
» Institute of Chartered Accountants of Scotland: **www.icas.org.uk**
» Institute of Financial Services: **www.ifslearning.ac.uk**

Aeronautical and Manufacturing Engineering

Aeronautical and manufacturing engineering have recovered some of the ground they lost in last year's employment ranking, moving back into the top half of the table for graduate prospects. The unemployment rate is still higher than average for all subjects, but the proportion in graduate jobs shows significant improvement. Starting salaries in graduate jobs are slightly down on last year, at £23,268, but this is still close to the top ten.

Most of the courses in this ranking focus on aeronautical or manufacturing engineering, but it includes some with a mechanical title. To add to the confusion, manufacturing degrees often go under the rubric of production engineering (*see* General Engineering and Mechanical Engineering). The number of institutions in the table has grown significantly for the first time in several years, reflecting larger intakes rather than new universities making the considerable investment required to introduce the subject.

Cambridge has increased its lead over Bristol and Sheffield this year. It has by far the highest entry grades and easily the best performance in the latest Research Assessment Exercise (RAE), when some of the university's work in this field was submitted in other engineering categories. Only Surrey and Bath have more satisfied students, while only Newcastle, in seventh place, has a better score for graduate prospects.

Bath makes the most progress at the top of the table, moving up four places with much higher entry grades and more satisfied students than last year. Further down, the University of the West of England has risen five places to become the leading post-1992 institution and the only one in the top 20. Swansea is the clear leader in Wales, but Glasgow is only just ahead of Strathclyde in Scotland.

Applications for degrees in aerospace engineering were down in March 2012, but the 1.5 per cent decline was much less than in most subjects and followed three years of big increases. The smaller area of manufacturing and production engineering saw a much steeper decline. Entry grades are high at the leading universities, with Cambridge averaging more than 600 points and Bristol, Imperial and Bath more than 500. But three Bs at A level has been enough secure a place at most universities outside the top 20.

Many graduates go on to further study or training to meet professional requirements. Eight universities saw fewer than half of their graduates find graduate-level work or training places, but the success rate was over 90 per cent at both Cambridge and Newcastle.

Employed in graduate job:	45%	Employed in non-graduate job and studying:	2%
Employed in graduate job and studying:	3%	Employed in non-graduate job:	21%
Studying:	18%	Unemployed:	11%
Average starting graduate salary:	£23,268	Average starting non-graduate salary:	£15,946

Aeronautical and Manufacturing Engineering	Research quality	Entry standards	Student satisfaction %	Graduate prospects %	Overall rating
1 Cambridge	1.8	615	87	94	100.0
2 Bristol	1.3	529	83	85	89.1
3 Sheffield	1.4	436	83	87	87.1
4 Bath	0.8	516	89	84	86.3
5 Surrey	1.1	427	90	78	86.2

6	Imperial College	1.4	563	72	77	83.6
7	Newcastle	1.0		79	96	83.3
8	Loughborough	1.1	414	83	80	82.7
9	Nottingham	1.3	397	78	85	82.0
10	Leeds	1.2	399	87	64	81.9
11	Southampton	0.9	493	79	75	80.1
12	Manchester	1.1	430	71	77	76.3
13	Liverpool	1.1	409	73	72	75.1
14	Glasgow	0.7	465	76	73	74.9
15	Swansea	0.7	356	78	79	73.5
16	Strathclyde	0.8	444	78	56	73.1
17	Queen's, Belfast	1.0	369	70	70	71.1
18	Aston	0.6	367	78	67	70.9
19	West of England	0.8	349	72	76	70.5
20	Queen Mary, London	0.7	345	79	60	70.2
21	De Montfort	0.6		72	82	69.9
22	Brighton	0.8	348	74		69.8
23	Brunel	0.7	362	76	57	69.4
24	Sussex		360	85	63	68.4
25	Portsmouth	0.6	255	83	51	66.9
26	Salford	0.7	298	75	51	65.6
27	Coventry	0.2	269	75	75	64.2
28	Hertfordshire	0.8	290	67	62	63.9
29	Liverpool John Moores	1.0	195	71	52	63.0
30	Glamorgan	0.7	246	70	43	59.7
=31	Plymouth	0.3	230	72	61	59.6
=31	Glyndŵr	0.5	205		60	59.6
33	City	0.7	330	68	36	59.5
=34	Sheffield Hallam	0.5	267	73	43	59.4
=34	Kingston	0.4	272	71	51	59.4
36	London South Bank	0.7	218	74	30	58.2
37	West of Scotland		264	77	42	57.3
38	Cardiff Metropolitan		301	67	63	57.0
39	Ulster		225	75	53	56.9
40	Manchester Metropolitan	0.4	268	69	43	56.3
41	Glasgow Caledonian		312	68	44	54.3
42	Northampton		191		26	45.4

» Manufacturing Institute: **www.makeit.org.uk**
» Royal Aeronautical Society: **www.aerosociety.com**
» Why Aeronautical Engineering?:
  www.science-engineering.net/aeronautical_engineering.htm

Agriculture and Forestry

Nottingham remains the clear leader in agriculture and forestry, with a good research record and the highest entry grades. Reading, which shared top place two years ago, has closed the gap slightly but stays in second place. Harper Adams University College, the agricultural specialist in Shropshire, has dropped two places to fifth, but still boasts the top employment score and ties with Aberystwyth for the most satisfied students. Aberystwyth, however, has been overtaken by Bangor as the top university in Wales for these subjects. Aberdeen, in fourth, has the best research score. The Scottish Agricultural College, which does not qualify for this table, is now the only place to take a full degree in agriculture north of the border, but Aberdeen offers forestry and plant and soil science, while Highlands and Islands provides a number of forestry courses.

Small intakes in some of the 19 institutions in the table leave more statistical gaps than in most subjects and make for greater volatility. The most striking change is the entry of Oxford Brookes in sixth place, while another new entrant, Kent, also makes the top ten. There are generally low scores on all measures in these subjects: no university averages 400 points at entry or satisfies 90 per cent of final-year undergraduates. But it is the employment scores that cause the most concern. The 7 per cent success rate at the Highlands and Islands may be

Agriculture and Forestry	Research quality	Entry standards	Student satisfaction %	Graduate prospects %	Overall rating
1 Nottingham	0.9	376	82	57	100.0
2 Reading	0.7	358	83	70	97.6
3 Newcastle	0.6	324	84	73	93.6
4 Aberdeen	1.0			37	90.6
5 Harper Adams	0.3	315	86	78	90.4
6 Oxford Brookes		358		64	88.7
7 Bangor	0.6	322		42	83.8
8 Kent		352	67	73	82.5
9 West of England	0.6	297		48	81.8
10 Lincoln	0.2	320	70	60	80.0
=11 Queen's, Belfast	0.4	313	55	77	79.5
=11 Aberystwyth	0.7	250	86	36	79.5
13 Plymouth	0.1	322	79	40	78.4
14 Greenwich	0.4			42	78.1
15 Royal Agricultural College	0.2	284	77	55	77.1
16 Worcester		275		70	76.4
17 Nottingham Trent		287	73	43	71.1
18 Cumbria	0.0	282			65.3
19 Highlands and Islands	0.1			7	54.5

Employed in graduate job:	38%	Employed in non-graduate job and studying:		4%
Employed in graduate job and studying:	9%	Employed in non-graduate job:		33%
Studying:	9%	Unemployed:		7%
Average starting graduate salary:	£18,282	Average starting non-graduate salary:		£15,295

a statistical blip caused by small numbers and dispersed nature of the university, but nowhere did eight out of ten leavers find graduate-level jobs or go into further training within six months of completing their course. The definition of a graduate job does no favours to agriculture or forestry in the employment statistics, however, and the unemployment rate of 7 per cent was lower than the average for all subjects. More than a third of graduates start in lower-level jobs and the average starting salary for those who do find graduate-level employment is in the bottom ten for all subjects, at less than £18,300.

Applications for degree courses in agriculture had dropped by 6 per cent in March 2012, but there had been a compensating rise in the demand for Foundation degrees. Forestry is a much smaller area, with little more than 100 applications by the same date. A quarter of those enrolling for degrees in agriculture and more than a third in forestry do so without A levels, often coming with relevant work experience. About one in seven arrives through the Clearing system. Entry grades have been rising from a low base: no university now averages less than 250 points.

» Institute of Chartered Foresters: **www.charteredforesters.org**
» Royal Agricultural Society of England: **www.rase.org.uk**
» Royal Forestry Society: **www.rfs.org.uk**
» Royal Scottish Forestry Society: **www.rsfs.org**
» Sector Skills Council for Land-Based and Environmental Industries (LANTRA): **www.lantra.co.uk**

American Studies

American studies had suffered one of the biggest falls in applications of any subject in March 2012. The surge in popularity that followed the election of Barack Obama was sustained until higher fees were introduced. But a 19 per cent drop in the latest statistics confirmed fears that many potential candidates would switch to subjects with better employment prospects. American studies is among the bottom ten subjects for the proportion of graduates going straight into graduate-level work or further study. Salary levels have improved, however, for those who do find graduate jobs: the £19,440 average this year is only just inside the bottom 20 for all subjects.

Warwick remains well clear of the field, sharing the lead for research quality and boasting much the highest entry standards. Only Essex, in tenth place, had a better employment record – still only seven out of ten leavers going straight into graduate-level jobs or continuing their studies. Manchester was the other research star in the 2008 assessments, while the most satisfied students are at second-placed Leicester. Satisfaction levels are high throughout the table: none of the 21 universities failed to satisfy at least three quarters of their final-year undergraduates.

Kent has made the most progress in the upper reaches of the table, taking fifth place, behind East Anglia and Birmingham, thanks to improved graduate employment levels. Portsmouth is the top-rated new university and the only one to enter the last Research Assessment Exercise. Dundee and Swansea are the only universities from outside England.

Entry scores are more bunched than in many subjects, with only five universities averaging more than 400 points and none slipping below 250. Nine out of ten students taking American Studies have A levels or equivalent qualifications and there is an impressive level of firsts and 2:1s.

American Studies cont

Employed in graduate job:	31%	Employed in non-graduate job and studying:	3%
Employed in graduate job and studying:	4%	Employed in non-graduate job:	35%
Studying:	18%	Unemployed:	9%
Average starting graduate salary:	£19,440	Average starting non-graduate salary:	£13,979

American Studies	Research quality	Entry standards	Student satisfaction %	Graduate prospects %	Overall rating
1 Warwick	1.4	480	83	69	100.0
2 Leicester	0.9	397	90	62	95.7
3 East Anglia	0.9	385	88	57	92.4
4 Birmingham	0.9	421	84	61	91.9
5 Kent	1.3	341	86	50	90.9
6 Nottingham	1.0	408	79	68	90.8
7 Lancaster	1.3		86	36	89.9
8 Sussex	1.2	408	78	55	89.4
9 Manchester	1.4	414	75	53	88.8
10 Essex	0.8	348	80	70	87.2
11 Keele	0.7	339	83	53	84.8
12 Hull	0.8	339	85	46	84.6
13 Liverpool	0.7	336	81	58	83.8
14 Swansea	0.5	345	75	56	78.4
15 Portsmouth	0.8	293	82	33	77.9
16 Dundee		377	85	35	77.2
17 Goldsmiths College		374	76	62	76.9
18 Lincoln		255	84	38	72.1
19 Derby		271	81	43	71.9
20 Canterbury Christ Church		255	79	44	70.3
21 Winchester		291	81	29	69.8

» British Association for American Studies: **www.baas.ac.uk**

Anatomy and Physiology

Anatomy, physiology and pathology are only just outside the 20 most popular subjects, and the demand for places has remained stable since higher fees were introduced. This ranking covers degrees in cell biology, neurosciences and pathology, as well as anatomy and physiology. Universities often demand at least two science subjects – usually biology and chemistry, although some new universities will accept just one science. More than 30,000 applications had been received by March 2012.

It is a highly competitive field, with nine applications for every place, although average entry scores at some of the universities towards the bottom of the table remain around 300 points. At top-placed Oxford, the average is close to 600 points, while second-placed Cambridge's score is well over that mark. Grades are boosted by the fact that the subjects are often a fall-back for candidates whose real target was medical school.

Oxford, which achieved much the best grades in the 2008 Research Assessment Exercise, has regained the lead it last held six years ago, moving up from third place. But it cannot match the 94 per cent satisfaction rate at Huddersfield, which remains the leading post-1992 university despite slipping out of the top 20. Scores in the 2011 National Student Survey were generally high, with only two universities satisfying less than 75 per cent of the final-year undergraduates.

Anatomy and Physiology	Research quality	Entry standards	Student satisfaction %	Graduate prospects %	Overall rating
1 Oxford	1.4	580	85	80	100.0
2 Cambridge	1.0	630	87	83	99.2
3 Cardiff	0.9		90	100	97.9
4 Dundee	1.2	460	91	57	89.7
5 Loughborough	1.0	387	93	69	88.9
=6 Sussex	1.0	390	85	83	88.4
=6 University College London	1.1	494	78	77	88.4
8 Newcastle	0.9	421	91	69	88.3
9 Manchester	1.1	427	85	70	87.8
10 Edinburgh	0.9		91	63	86.6
=11 Nottingham	0.5	443	90	77	86.4
=11 Bristol	0.9	436	82	79	86.4
13 King's College London	1.0	436	79	73	84.5
14 Glasgow	0.9	454	83	66	84.4
15 Liverpool	0.8	408	89	65	84.2
=16 Aberdeen	0.5	424	87	73	83.5
=16 Queen's, Belfast	0.9	390	80	77	83.5
18 Huddersfield		360	94	91	83.1
19 Leeds	0.9	417	82	61	81.9
20 Reading	0.5	375	85	68	78.5
21 East London	0.5		72	89	77.8
22 Oxford Brookes	0.5	355	83	62	76.0
23 Leicester		410	86	69	75.7
24 Keele		356	90	64	74.2
25 Plymouth	0.2	337	85		72.0
26 Manchester Metropolitan	0.5	309	81		71.4
27 Nottingham Trent	0.9		77	40	70.4
28 Ulster		319	69	71	64.2
29 Westminster		288	78	51	62.4

Employed in graduate job:	23%	Employed in non-graduate job and studying:	4%
Employed in graduate job and studying:	4%	Employed in non-graduate job:	21%
Studying:	42%	Unemployed:	6%
Average starting graduate salary:	£19,291	Average starting non-graduate salary:	£14,177

Anatomy and Physiology cont

Despite slipping to third place, Cardiff again had by far the best employment record. Every leaver had a graduate-level job or a place on a postgraduate course within six months of graduating. Dundee remains the top university in Scotland, while Cardiff is the only provider of these subjects in Wales.

Anatomy and physiology are among the top 20 subjects for employment prospects, with one of the lowest unemployment rates, at 6 per cent. More than four out of ten students go on to full-time postgraduate training – one of the highest proportions for any group of subjects. However, there was a drop of more than £1,000 in average earnings in graduate jobs, taking the subjects into the bottom 20 for salaries.

» Anatomical Society: **www.anatsoc.org.uk**
» British Association of Clinical Anatomists: **www.liv.ac.uk/HumanAnatomy/phd/baca**
» Physiological Society: **www.physoc.org**

Anthropology

Anthropology provided the big surprise of the first set of applications for £9,000-a-year degree courses – not least to anthropologists, who had feared for the future of the subject. Unnoticed by the media, applications shot up by almost 25 per cent while other arts subjects struggled. The relatively small numbers taking anthropology make for substantial swings, but this was exceptional (and unexplained). Fewer than 700 people started degree courses in 2011, so almost 5,000 applications were certain to heighten competition for places. There is no way of telling whether this was a one-off or whether the subject's popularity will be repeated in 2013.

Cambridge maintains its accustomed leadership in the new table, but the London School of Economics has overtaken Oxford to occupy second place. The LSE had the top research score in the 2008 Research Assessment Exercise, when 40 per cent of its work was judged to be world-leading, and the best employment record. But Cambridge's high entry grades and strength across the board give it a narrow lead. Oxford still has the most satisfied students and is only a fraction behind the LSE.

There are no subject-specific requirements for most degree courses, but anthropology tends to be the preserve of old universities. Liverpool John Moores is the highest-placed of a clutch of post-1992 universities at the foot this year's table. St Andrews is the top university in Scotland, despite dropping three places to sixth. Trinity St David is the only representative of Wales and would have done better with more students, if last year's table is any guide. Then it had much the best graduate employment record for anthropology and finished just outside the top ten.

Overall unemployment has fluctuated, partly because of the small numbers taking the subject. The latest rate is twice last year's figure, but only one percentage point more than in the 2011 *Guide*. Almost 30 per cent of all graduates go on to take a higher degree or some form of postgraduate training, but just as many were in non-graduate jobs when the last survey was carried out.

	Employed in graduate job:	34%	Employed in non-graduate job and studying:	5%

Employed in graduate job: 34% Employed in non-graduate job and studying: 5%
Employed in graduate job and studying: 3% Employed in non-graduate job: 25%
Studying: 21% Unemployed: 11%
Average starting graduate salary: £18,780 Average starting non-graduate salary: £15,894

Anthropology	Research quality	Entry standards	Student satisfaction %	Graduate prospects %	Overall rating
1 Cambridge	1.4	521	86	77	100.0
2 London School of Economics	1.5	453	83	78	97.0
3 Oxford	1.1	508	87	75	96.2
4 University College London	1.2	463	76	65	87.7
5 Durham	1.0	421	78	74	86.2
6 St Andrews	1.1	445	77	63	85.3
7 School of Oriental and African Studies	1.3	433	71	61	84.0
8 Edinburgh	1.1	451	75	57	83.9
9 Sussex	1.1	363	75	68	82.9
10 Manchester	0.9	390	81	49	80.9
11 Queen's, Belfast	1.3	389	76	44	80.8
12 Glasgow	0.6	471	81	46	79.9
13 Aberdeen	1.2	360	83	25	78.5
14 Goldsmiths College	1.1	338	76	48	78.0
15 Brunel	0.9	315	72	63	76.1
16 Kent	0.8	347	75	52	75.5
17 Liverpool John Moores	0.7	271	76	62	74.3
18 East London	0.6		74	50	70.9
19 Roehampton	1.1	239	70	42	69.8
20 Oxford Brookes	0.5	322	67	55	67.0
21 Trinity St David	0.8	233			66.3

» Royal Anthropological Institute: **www.therai.org.uk**

Archaeology

The number of universities offering degrees in archaeology has been growing by leaps and bounds, confounding predictions that the economic downturn would produce a flight from non-vocational subjects. But applications were down by 12 per cent when higher fees were introduced in 2012. Nevertheless, the total of 51 universities in this year's ranking is more than twice that in the 2005 *Guide*. New universities are mainly responsible, their numbers growing from three to 22 over the same period. Many of those attracted onto courses are mature students – often retired – who are studying the subject out of interest and not for career progression. Archaeology is in the bottom ten both for employment prospects and graduate salaries.

Oxford has overtaken Cambridge to top this year's table by a fraction of a point. A reversal in entry standards is largely responsible, with Oxford now top on this measure.

Archaeology cont

Third-placed University College London, which is also less than a point behind Oxford, has the most satisfied students, while fourth-placed Durham and fifth-placed Reading have the best records for research. Huddersfield, the only post-1992 university in the top 20, again has by far the best employment record. With 88 per cent of leavers going straight into graduate jobs or onto postgraduate courses, its success rate was twice that at many universities in the table and 10 percentage points better than its nearest challenger. Glasgow remains the top university in Scotland; Cardiff the leader in Wales.

Archaeology has produced consistently high levels of satisfaction. Only four universities in the ranking failed to satisfy at 70 per cent of their final-year undergraduates in the results published in 2011. The increase in the number of universities offering the subject has had the effect of spreading out entry scores, which now range from little more than 200 points to over 500. Applications for pure archaeology degrees lag well behind those for forensic and archaeological science.

Unemployment six months after graduation dropped in the latest survey, but remains above average for all subjects, at 12 per cent, with another 33 per cent taking non-graduate jobs. At more than 20 of the 51 universities in the table, over half of the graduates were either unemployed or in non-graduate jobs six months after completing their course.

Employed in graduate job:	26%	Employed in non-graduate job and studying:	4%
Employed in graduate job and studying:	3%	Employed in non-graduate job:	33%
Studying:	22%	Unemployed:	12%
Average starting graduate salary:	£17,819	Average starting non-graduate salary:	£14,284

Archaeology	Research quality	Entry standards	Student satisfaction %	Graduate prospects %	Overall rating
1 Oxford	1.4	526	87	72	100.0
2 Cambridge	1.2	521	86	77	99.6
3 University College London	1.2	442	93	77	99.3
4 Durham	1.5	445	83	78	97.2
5 Southampton	1.1	390	84	67	88.8
6 Exeter	1.0	430	85	63	88.4
7 Reading	1.5	354	88	51	88.3
8 Glasgow	0.7	442	89	60	88.0
9 Liverpool	1.2	371	86	60	87.5
10 York	1.1	421	91	43	87.4
11 Leicester	1.2	375	86	53	85.9
12 Newcastle	0.8	370	87	56	83.5
13 Edinburgh	1.0	413	84	45	83.1
14 Nottingham	1.0	367	83	49	81.6
15 Manchester	0.9	347	85	51	81.0
16 Cardiff	0.9	379	81	52	80.5
17 Dundee		480	88	55	80.4
18 Sheffield	1.1	391	77	46	80.0
19 Queen's, Belfast	1.1	356	89	32	79.6

20 Huddersfield		270	87	88	79.5
21 Birmingham	0.7	387	79	57	79.2
22 Aberdeen	0.7	338	83		77.9
23 Kent	0.2	337	82	70	77.2
24 Keele		323	85	71	76.2
25 Bristol	0.8	382	70	58	76.0
26 Bradford	0.9	269	77	54	74.3
27 Nottingham Trent	0.4	318	77	59	72.7
28 Robert Gordon		379	76	62	71.9
29 Central Lancashire	0.3	316	81	49	70.9
30 West of England		304	81	55	69.1
31 Hull		284	81	56	68.8
32 Staffordshire		260	86	52	68.7
33 Chester		273	84	50	67.8
34 Swansea		339	80	44	67.5
35 Derby		271	77	54	65.4
36 Lincoln		301	73	55	65.3
37 Winchester	0.2	273	83	33	65.2
38 Teesside		336	77	39	64.5
39 Bournemouth	0.6	293	65	48	64.1
40 Trinity St David	0.8	235	68	37	62.7
41 Glamorgan		300	75	38	61.5
42 London South Bank		206		54	61.2
=43 Worcester		281	76	38	61.0
=43 Glasgow Caledonian		293	75	38	61.0
45 Liverpool John Moores		231	75	46	60.7
46 Kingston		261	74	43	60.5
=47 De Montfort		276	72	42	59.8
=47 Coventry		263	75	38	59.8
49 West of Scotland		272		38	59.5
50 Anglia Ruskin		256	63	47	55.8
51 Canterbury Christ Church		220	69	36	54.2

» Council for British Archaeology: **www.britarch.ac.uk**
» TORC (Training Online Resource Centre for Archaeology): **www.torc.org.uk**

Architecture

With more than seven applications for every place, architecture is one of the most competitive of the major subjects. Entry grades at the leading universities reflect this, with 15 averaging over 400 points in the latest table. Some universities ask candidates to produce a portfolio of work if they have not taken an art or design-based A level. A drop of nearly 12 per cent in applications for degrees beginning in 2012 will bring no more than a marginal easing of the competition for places.

Bath has regained first place from Cambridge this year, with the best employment record, the most satisfied students and – more surprisingly – the highest entry grades. University College

Architecture cont

London, which leapfrogs Sheffield into third place, has the best research grades and shares the best employment score with Bath. Edinburgh is the top university in Scotland, while fifth-placed Cardiff remains the leader in Wales. Queen's, Belfast, has overtaken Ulster in Northern Ireland. New universities take up more than half the table, with Northumbria the highest-placed of eight in the top 20, although the Manchester School of Architecture, in ninth place, is a joint enterprise between Manchester and Manchester Metropolitan universities.

Training in architecture is a long haul – usually seven years, in which the first degree is but one step on the way. Until now, the graduate employment rate has been some compensation, but the recession saw unemployment shoot up to 14 per cent in the last year's *Guide*. The rate has improved, but 12 per cent is still above average for all subjects. Architecture remains outside the employment top 20 as a result. No university managed 90 per cent graduate employment this year, compared with 13 in the 2011 *Guide* and 30 the year before.

A third of all undergraduates enter architecture degrees with qualifications other than A level or Advanced Highers. Satisfaction rates are higher after graduation than during the course itself – three years into their careers, architects were among the least likely of all graduates to say that they wished they had taken a different degree or chosen a different profession. This cannot be a matter of money: architecture is in the bottom ten subjects for graduate starting salaries, averaging little more than £18,000 – a figure that has dropped more than £1,000 in two years.

Employed in graduate job:	48%	Employed in non-graduate job and studying:	2%
Employed in graduate job and studying:	8%	Employed in non-graduate job:	17%
Studying:	13%	Unemployed:	12%
Average starting graduate salary:	£18,041	Average starting non-graduate salary:	£14,645

Architecture	Research quality	Entry standards	Student satisfaction %	Graduate prospects %	Overall rating
1 Bath	1.2	534	89	92	100.0
2 Cambridge	1.4	529	85	84	98.2
3 University College London	1.5	489	70	92	91.8
4 Sheffield	1.3	491	80	72	90.1
5 Cardiff	1.1	520	80	75	89.7
6 Edinburgh	1.2	481	69	88	87.3
7 Nottingham	0.6	470	82	85	86.4
8 Liverpool	1.4	447	74	67	84.8
9 Manchester School of Architecture	0.7	425	79	79	82.6
10 Northumbria	0.6	391	88	70	82.4
11 Newcastle	1.1	476	64	75	80.7
12 Brighton	1.4	403	67	69	79.9
13 West of England	0.6	324	82	74	77.0
14 Dundee	0.5	452	77	56	75.2
15 Westminster	1.0	345	70	65	74.6
16 Sheffield Hallam	0.6	379	82	51	73.8

17	Strathclyde	0.5	447	58	87	73.6
18	Oxford Brookes		428	77	74	73.4
19	Plymouth	0.8	359	68	71	73.3
20	Huddersfield		320	81	83	72.8
21	Queen's, Belfast		385	80	71	72.6
22	Robert Gordon	0.5	376	65	79	71.9
23	Liverpool John Moores	0.9	290	78	52	71.3
24	De Montfort	1.0	298	67	69	71.2
=25	Lincoln	0.5	372	71	66	70.5
=25	Ulster	1.0	319	69	58	70.5
27	Kent		409	69	75	69.0
28	Portsmouth	0.1	316	78	66	68.3
29	Glamorgan	0.7		74	48	67.9
30	Salford	1.2	304	70	37	67.0
31	London Metropolitan	0.7	271	68	64	66.9
32	Arts University College, Bournemouth	0.1	330	77		66.2
33	Greenwich	0.6	318	69	52	65.7
34	Kingston		342	77	56	65.3
35	Derby		248	79	65	64.9
36	Central Lancashire	0.5	305	66	60	64.5
37	Glasgow Caledonian	0.9		74	28	64.0
38	Leeds Metropolitan		314	69	61	61.7
39	University for Creative Arts		261	73	60	60.9
40	Southampton Solent		229	78	55	60.7
41	Coventry		281	79	43	60.4
42	Birmingham City		310	62	67	59.5
43	London South Bank		248	72	56	59.3
44	Nottingham Trent	0.3	312	52	71	58.8
45	Bolton	0.6	202			57.3
46	East London		240	71	45	55.2
47	Cardiff Metropolitan		294	63	39	52.1

» Design Council (now incorporating CABE): **www.designcouncil.org.uk**
» Royal Institute of British Architects: **www.architecture.com**
» Royal Incorporation of Architects in Scotland: **www.rias.org.uk**

Art and Design

Taken together, art and design rank second only to nursing in terms of degree applications. But the demand for places took a serious hit when higher fees were introduced in 2012 – design was 14 per cent down and fine art 20 per cent. There had been huge increases in the two previous years, but this was largely due to changes in the admissions process. Nevertheless, the subjects remain popular despite employment rates and average starting salaries that are both in the bottom ten for all subjects. Artists and designers accept that they are likely to have a period of self-employment early in their career while they find a way to pursue their vocation, but two thirds of those surveyed three years after graduation said

Art and Design cont

they would make the same choice again. More than 40 per cent of all leavers go straight into graduate-level jobs, but only 6 per cent go on to take another full-time course – one of the lowest proportions for any subject. For the first time, no university saw 80 per cent of leavers go straight into graduate jobs or further study.

Most courses in art and design are at new universities – often in former art colleges – but the top eight places in this year's ranking are all filled by older institutions. Oxford, the oldest of them all, where fine art is taught at the Ruskin School of Drawing, retains top place. It has the best employment score highest and among the most satisfied students, although, surprisingly, Lancaster records higher entry standards this year. Glasgow has moved up to second and becomes the leader in Scotland with the next-best employment score. Third-placed University College London, where students attend the Slade School of Fine Art, has the most satisfied students and shares the best research score with Brighton, Kent, Newcastle and Reading. The final two universities have benefited from the revaluation of grades in the 2008 Research Assessment Exercise to reward world-leading submissions, mirroring the system used to allocate research grants in England. Bangor convincingly regains the lead in Wales, overtaking Aberystwyth.

The performance of the year is at Bournemouth, which has moved up six places to become the top post-1992 university, the first for four years to win a place in the top ten. Falmouth University College again makes the top 20, finishing higher than most of the former polytechnics. Low entry grades and research scores count against many of the new universities and colleges, although most artists would argue that these are of less significance than in other subjects.

Employed in graduate job:	42%	Employed in non-graduate job and studying:		3%
Employed in graduate job and studying:	3%	Employed in non-graduate job:		34%
Studying:	6%	Unemployed:		12%
Average starting graduate salary:	£17,676	Average starting non-graduate salary:		£13,932

Art and Design	Research quality	Entry standards	Student satisfaction %	Graduate prospects %	Overall rating
1 Oxford	1.3	427	87	76	100.0
2 Glasgow	1.1		86	74	95.2
3 University College London	1.4	407	89	52	93.5
4 Lancaster	1.3	467	76	58	92.2
5 Newcastle	1.4	420	86	51	91.9
6 Brunel	0.4	387	87	72	89.1
7 Reading	1.4	371	73	70	88.8
8 Edinburgh	0.9	422	76	61	87.3
9 Bournemouth	1.0	316	80	63	83.5
10 Loughborough	1.3	336	80	50	83.4
11 Goldsmiths College	1.1	339	81	51	82.9
12 Heriot-Watt	0.8	351	69	72	82.2
13 Leeds	1.1	385	68	57	81.0
14 Kent	1.4	335	63	63	79.9

15	Lincoln	0.3	324	79	63	78.3
16	Dundee	1.3	366	67	48	78.2
17	Brighton	1.4	308	78	39	77.8
18	Bangor		278	81	75	77.7
19	West of England	0.8	288	76	57	76.9
20	Falmouth	0.4	293	82	57	76.8
21	University of the Arts, London	1.0	310	68	55	75.4
22	Westminster	1.2	295	66	56	75.1
23	Birmingham City	1.2	316	69	45	74.8
24	Kingston	0.3	338	74	56	74.7
25	Norwich University College of the Arts	0.5	300	78	53	74.4
26	Nottingham Trent	0.5	315	71	60	74.3
27	Arts University College, Bournemouth	0.1	281	79	63	74.1
=28	Northumbria	0.8	315	68	56	74.0
=28	Huddersfield		314	76	63	74.0
30	Cardiff Metropolitan	0.9	293	79	39	73.8
31	Robert Gordon	0.6	339	69	54	73.6
32	Aberystwyth		305	80	55	72.9
33	Teesside		332	79	48	72.3
34	Manchester Metropolitan	0.7	322	69	49	72.1
35	Coventry	0.5	299	72	52	71.9
36	Sheffield Hallam	0.9	311	67	46	71.7
37	Manchester		355	76	45	71.3
=38	Ulster	0.9	291	72	42	71.1
=38	Hertfordshire	0.8	267	72	49	71.1
40	Chester	0.1	308	74	56	71.0
41	Derby	0.4	300	76	46	70.9
42	Plymouth	0.8	288	69	50	70.8
=43	Canterbury Christ Church		264	74	65	70.6
=43	Newport	0.9	299	67	45	70.6
45	Central Lancashire	0.2	271	77	52	69.9
46	Edinburgh Napier	0.3	337	66	54	69.7
=47	Oxford Brookes	0.6	289	76	37	69.4
=47	De Montfort	0.6	284	71	47	69.4
49	Bath Spa	0.3	298	72	48	69.2
50	Southampton	0.4	385	64	41	69.1
51	Gloucestershire	0.2	307	78	37	68.5
52	Greenwich		270	79	46	67.6
=53	Portsmouth	0.1	271	77	43	67.0
=53	Chichester		328	75	39	67.0
=53	Sunderland	0.5	257	74	42	67.0
=56	Glamorgan		286	75	47	66.8
=56	Buckinghamshire New	0.4	269	70	48	66.8
58	Essex		241	76	53	66.6
59	University for Creative Arts	0.4	258	70	49	66.5
60	Staffordshire	0.1	272	76	43	66.3
61	Leeds Metropolitan	0.3	233	82	37	65.7

Art and Design cont	Research Quality	Entry Standards	Student satisfaction %	Graduate prospects %	Overall rating
62 Salford	0.3	254	74	42	65.5
63 Middlesex	0.4	248	69	50	65.4
64 Anglia Ruskin	0.4	260	73	37	64.5
65 Hull		301	79	26	63.6
66 York St John		289	67	46	62.9
67 Bolton	0.0	256	79	33	62.8
68 East London	0.6	190	67	46	61.7
69 Glyndŵr	0.1	242	66	48	60.5
70 Glasgow Caledonian		344	66	28	60.4
71 West London	0.2	234	66	42	59.7
=72 Worcester		313	66	29	59.2
=72 Northampton	0.1	238	68	41	59.2
74 Southampton Solent	0.3	261	62	37	58.9
75 Liverpool John Moores	0.4	218	63	36	56.7
76 Cumbria	0.1	308	55	36	56.3
77 Bedfordshire		190	72	35	56.1
78 London Metropolitan	0.1	268	54	44	56.0
79 London South Bank		205	61	41	53.5

» Design Council: **www.designcouncil.org.u**k
» National Society for Education in Art and Design: **www.nsead.org**
» Creative Skillset: **www.creativeskillset.org**

Biological Sciences

While other science subjects have struggled to attract applicants in recent years, biological subjects have thrived. The various elements all registered increases in applications at the start of 2012 – nearly 3 per cent in the case of biology itself, which remained well ahead of chemistry and physics in the demand for places. Molecular biology and biochemistry experienced even stronger growth, while the much smaller field of biotechnology was the star recruiter, with a 15 per cent increase in applications. Two thirds of all entrants arrive with A levels or their equivalent, and almost four in ten go on to take postgraduate courses, either full or part-time.

The top two in the table are unchanged for the eighth successive year. Cambridge has extended its lead with some of the highest entry grades in any subject and the best graduate employment record. Despite averaging more than 550 points on the UCAS tariff, even Oxford's entrants are 65 points behind Cambridge's score. York has overtaken Sheffield to take third place, sharing the distinction of having the most satisfied students with the University of East Anglia, in 16th. Manchester and Dundee achieved the best grades in the 2008 Research Assessment Exercise, but Dundee has lost its position as the top university in Scotland and slipped out of the top 20 after a poor year for graduate employment. Glasgow is now the leader north of the border, while Cardiff remains well clear of the competition in Wales. Nottingham Trent is the highest-placed post-1992 university and the only one in the top 30, joined by West of England and Huddersfield in the top 40.

Entry standards have been rising: in addition to Oxford and Cambridge, another 23 universities average at least 400 points – ten more than two years ago. For the first time, no university has an average below 200 points, even though a relatively high proportion of the entrants (11 per cent in 2009) win places through Clearing. Graduate employment prospects nationally are slightly below average for all subjects. Starting salaries are in the bottom 20 and are particularly low for those who fail to find a graduate-level job.

Employed in graduate job:	25%	Employed in non-graduate job and studying:	3%
Employed in graduate job and studying:	4%	Employed in non-graduate job:	25%
Studying:	32%	Unemployed:	10%
Average starting graduate salary:	£19,373	Average starting non-graduate salary:	£14.036

Biological Sciences

	Research quality	Entry standards	Student satisfaction %	Graduate prospects %	Overall rating
1 Cambridge	1.0	630	87	83	100.0
2 Oxford	1.1	565	85	79	96.7
3 York	1.1	474	89	69	92.2
4 Sheffield	1.1	460	87	71	91.5
5 Imperial College	1.1	526	73	82	90.0
6 University College London	1.1	499	78	76	89.2
7 Bristol	0.9	468	86	68	88.3
8 Lancaster	1.0	403	84	74	88.2
9 Manchester	1.2	440	83	66	87.8
=10 Glasgow	0.9	440	88	62	86.5
=10 Bath	0.7	443	85	72	86.5
12 Durham	0.7	490	79	76	86.1
13 Leicester	0.7	439	86	70	85.7
14 Edinburgh	0.9	481	79	68	85.1
15 King's College London	1.1	442	78	66	84.6
16 East Anglia	0.7	406	89	64	84.5
=17 Exeter	0.7	429	84	68	84.4
=17 Surrey	1.0	399	77	74	84.4
=19 Nottingham	0.8	416	81	70	84.1
=19 Birmingham	0.7	432	84	68	84.1
21 Sussex	0.7	393	82	73	84.0
22 Cardiff	0.9	435	83	63	83.9
23 St Andrews	0.7	499	79	66	83.6
24 Leeds	0.9	391	81	66	82.6
=25 Southampton	0.7	413	80	70	82.2
=25 Liverpool	0.6	403	84	67	82.2
27 Newcastle	0.9	389	78	68	81.9
28 Dundee	1.2	400	81	54	81.7
=29 Nottingham Trent	0.9	277	77	81	81.6
=29 Strathclyde	0.9	399	82	61	81.6

Biological Sciences cont

	Research quality	Entry standards	Student satisfaction %	Graduate prospects %	Overall rating
31 Warwick	0.7	423	76	69	80.4
32 Heriot-Watt	0.5	368	84	67	80.0
33 Royal Holloway	1.0	349	77	64	79.5
34 Brunel	0.5	328	84	70	79.1
=35 Aberdeen	0.9	376	85	50	78.7
=35 Aston	0.8	340	82	61	78.7
37 Queen Mary, London	0.5	392	77	70	78.0
=38 West of England	0.8	305	84	56	77.8
=38 Queen's, Belfast	0.4	358	79	73	77.8
40 Huddersfield	0.3	264	87	71	76.8
41 Portsmouth	0.8	289	82	60	76.6
42 Bradford	0.5	290	81	69	76.5
43 Reading	0.5	377	80	62	76.4
44 Abertay	0.7	279		67	75.7
45 Teesside		301	83	75	75.1
=46 Hull	0.3	336	83	62	74.9
=46 Keele	0.2	331	84	65	74.9
48 Kent	0.5	338	79	63	74.7
49 Glasgow Caledonian	0.4	391	79	53	73.2
50 Plymouth	0.4	331	79	58	73.1
51 Stirling	0.6	356	76	57	73.0
52 Essex	0.5	298	81	56	72.9
53 Swansea	0.2	357	83	56	72.8
54 Staffordshire		243	88	64	72.3
55 Oxford Brookes	0.3	343	78	59	72.2
56 Chester	0.2	283	79	69	72.1
57 Sheffield Hallam	0.3	306	80	62	71.9
58 Ulster		304	83	64	71.6
59 Edge Hill		270	81	70	71.5
60 Brighton	0.6	286	80	52	71.2
61 Canterbury Christ Church		255	78	75	70.9
62 Coventry		292	82	62	70.5
63 Hertfordshire	0.5	327	78	51	70.2
64 Northumbria	0.4	329	70	62	69.1
65 Northampton		247	77	70	68.6
66 Manchester Metropolitan	0.5	288	75	55	68.5
67 Sunderland		223	75	75	68.3
=68 Edinburgh Napier	0.2	298	78	55	68.2
=68 Greenwich		255	86	52	68.2
70 Kingston	0.4	249	76	59	67.9
71 Cardiff Metropolitan	0.3	287	68	70	67.7
72 Roehampton	0.1	253	78	63	67.5
73 Derby	0.2	276	77	57	67.3

74 Bath Spa	0.0	287	77	58	66.7
75 Central Lancashire		318	74	59	66.5
76 Aberystwyth		298	85	43	66.0
77 Bolton		235	73	69	65.9
=78 Glamorgan	0.1	302	77	49	64.9
=78 Liverpool John Moores	0.4	290	73	47	64.9
80 Bangor	0.4	321	71	48	64.8
81 Worcester		281	76	54	64.7
82 Robert Gordon		333	70	59	64.6
83 Salford	0.5	246	76	42	63.9
84 Gloucestershire		281	79	43	62.7
85 Westminster		275	73	50	61.7
86 Leeds Metropolitan		232	72	55	61.1
87 Anglia Ruskin		244	70	49	58.6
88 East London		240	73	44	58.2
89 Bedfordshire	0.3	200	68		58.1
90 Bournemouth		269	51	48	49.8

» Biochemical Society: **www.biochemistry.org**
» British Society for Cell Biology: **www.bscb.org**
» Society of Biology: **www.societyofbiology.org**
» Society for Experimental Biology: **www.sebiology.org**

Building

As might be expected during the economic downturn, the unemployment rate among building graduates is among the highest in this year's *Guide*, at 13 per cent. But more than half of the 2009 and 2010 graduates went straight into graduate-level jobs, one of the highest proportions outside the medical professions. Average starting salaries are still in the top 20 for all subjects, although £3,000 lower than they were in the 2010 *Guide*. The decline is reflected in individual universities' employment scores: while only two universities slipped below 70 per cent positive destinations two years ago, 19 are in that position in the latest table.

Applications were down by more than 20 per cent early in 2012, following further declines in the three previous years. Entry standards have always been comparatively modest, but a gradual decline in average grades has been arrested in the latest table. Although only third-placed Nottingham averages more than 400 points, 11 of the 33 universities reach 300 points, compared with eight last year.

Loughborough has maintained its lead at the top of the table, and it still has by far the most satisfied students and among the best employment prospects. University College London, still in second place, recorded the best grades in the 2008 Research Assessment Exercise. Oxford Brookes, in 16th place, recorded a creditable 93 per cent of graduates in graduate-level jobs or further training after six months. Robert Gordon is now the leading university in Scotland for building. Westminster is the top post-1992 university and is joined by Plymouth, Glasgow Caledonian and Robert Gordon in the top ten. Glamorgan is the only representative of Wales.

Building has been one of the best prospects for a place in Clearing and may be so again in 2013. Almost half of all building students come with qualifications other than A level.

Building cont

Employed in graduate job:	54%
Employed in graduate job and studying:	4%
Studying:	5%
Average starting graduate salary:	£21,695

Employed in non-graduate job and studying:	1%
Employed in non-graduate job:	23%
Unemployed:	13%
Average starting non-graduate salary:	£15,339

Building	Research quality	Entry standards	Student satisfaction %	Graduate prospects %	Overall rating
1 Loughborough	1.3	345	88	87	100.0
2 University College London	1.5	398	70	89	96.7
3 Nottingham	0.6	412	80		90.5
4 Reading	1.2	352	72	79	89.4
5 Manchester	1.0		71	82	85.5
6 Westminster	1.0	293	77	72	84.7
7 Robert Gordon	0.5	312	76	91	84.2
8 Heriot-Watt	0.8	388	75	58	83.5
9 Glasgow Caledonian	0.9	325	74	61	81.5
10 Plymouth	0.8	267	83	57	79.5
=11 Northumbria	0.6	285	73	74	78.5
=11 Salford	1.2	287	66	64	78.5
13 Glamorgan	0.7	248	74	78	78.4
14 West of England	0.6	260	73	76	76.4
15 Sheffield Hallam	0.6	303	74	62	76.2
16 Oxford Brookes		315	70	93	75.9
17 Aston	0.6	320	73	56	75.5
18 Liverpool John Moores	0.9	248	70	58	74.1
19 Edinburgh Napier	0.5	307	70	63	73.4
20 Brighton	0.4	247	76	62	72.3
21 Portsmouth		244	76	72	70.1
22 Nottingham Trent	0.3	270	66	73	70.0
=23 Ulster	1.0	215	64	55	69.1
=23 Central Lancashire	0.5	256	69	58	69.1
25 Coventry		275	79	54	68.8
26 Greenwich	0.6	213	67	63	68.3
27 Kingston		287	70	63	67.0
28 Anglia Ruskin		253	73	60	66.0
29 London South Bank		248	66	71	64.7
30 Leeds Metropolitan		242	67	60	62.5
31 Bolton	0.6	161		27	52.9
32 Birmingham City		245	51	49	51.9
33 Southampton Solent		165	59	44	50.1

» Chartered Institute of Building: **www.ciob.org.uk**

Business Studies

The various branches of business and management are among the most popular subjects in higher education. Even without the many dual or combined honours degrees that are common for both of the main areas, there were more than 110,000 applications by March 2012. But a run of increases in applications had turned into a decline with the introduction of higher fees, albeit smaller than the average for all subjects. Management courses were down by 4.6 per cent and business studies by nearly 8 per cent. The subjects are the biggest recruiters in many of the new universities, although some of the most famous business schools are absent from this ranking because they do not offer undergraduate courses. Manchester Business School provides Manchester's courses.

Cambridge takes over from Oxford at the top of this year's table, but the universities can only be compared on two measures because Cambridge undergraduates did not respond to the National Student Survey in sufficient numbers to produce a student satisfaction score and there are no separate entry scores for Cambridge. Neither Oxford's Said Business School nor Cambridge's Judge School of Management qualify for the table, being exclusively postgraduate institutions, so both universities are assessed on courses offered by other faculties. Cambridge has the best scores in the ranking for both employment, jointly with the LSE, and research. Imperial College actually produced the best grades in the 2008 assessments, but has dropped out of the table this year. Loughborough, in sixth place, again has the most satisfied students.

Even before the recession, employment scores were surprisingly varied. Overall, the subjects are in the bottom half of the employment table, although half of those completing courses go straight into graduate-level jobs. Three years after graduation, this proportion rises to nearly three-quarters. Average starting salaries in graduate jobs are in the top 20 for all subjects, at £21,341. St Andrews has maintained its position as the top Scottish university, while Cardiff remains the clear the leader in Wales. More than half of the institutions are new universities, but only Robert Gordon and Lincoln appear in this year's top 40.

Up to now, about 10 per cent of those securing places in business and management have done so through Clearing. Entrance qualifications vary widely, with 22 universities averaging 400 points or more and six less than 200. Satisfaction levels have been improving in the National Student Survey: 25 universities managed to satisfy at least 80 per cent of final-year undergraduates, nearly twice as many as last year. They are spread throughout the table, with Newport, in equal 103rd place, recording one of the top scores despite again registering the lowest employment prospects.

Employed in graduate job:	45%	Employed in non-graduate job and studying:	2%
Employed in graduate job and studying:	5%	Employed in non-graduate job:	29%
Studying:	8%	Unemployed:	10%
Average starting graduate salary:	£21,341	Average starting non-graduate salary:	£15,658

Business Studies	Research quality	Entry standards	Student satisfaction %	Graduate prospects %	Overall rating
1 Cambridge	1.5			90	100.0
2 Oxford	1.3	582	86	88	99.8

Business Studies cont

		Research quality	Entry standards	Student satisfaction %	Graduate prospects %	Overall rating
3	Bath	1.3	470	82	87	93.5
4	Warwick	1.3	482	81	82	92.2
5	London School of Economics	1.3	511	74	90	91.0
6	Loughborough	0.9	441	87	80	90.8
7	Lancaster	1.3	400	83	84	90.6
=8	Exeter	0.9	451	84	82	89.5
=8	St Andrews	0.8	521	83	76	89.5
10	King's College London	1.3	457	79	74	88.4
11	Cardiff	1.4	416	78	75	87.8
12	Strathclyde	1.2	450	83	63	87.0
13	City	0.9	447	82	72	85.5
14	Nottingham	1.1	412	77	78	84.8
15	Leeds	1.1	427	76	74	84.1
16	Durham	0.9	397	81	71	83.2
17	Aston	0.9	406	77	77	83.0
18	Glasgow	0.8	441	79	66	81.9
19	Southampton	0.9	400	78	71	81.7
20	School of Oriental and African Studies	0.5	467			81.4
21	Manchester	1.2	406	73	70	81.3
22	Sheffield	0.9	397	77	69	81.1
23	Reading	0.7	369	79	75	80.5
24	Edinburgh	0.7	444	74	66	78.7
25	Sussex	0.9	367	75	70	78.6
26	Liverpool	0.7	381	78	65	78.4
27	Birmingham	1.0	426	67	76	78.1
28	Heriot-Watt	0.7	360	78	70	77.9
29	Surrey	0.7	390	75	69	77.8
30	Newcastle	0.7	392	72	76	77.5
=31	Leicester	0.9	372	76	61	77.3
=31	Aberdeen	0.6	386	78	62	77.3
=31	Kent	0.8	326	80	63	77.3
=34	Robert Gordon	0.5	328	78	75	76.8
=34	Buckingham		280	84	87	76.8
36	University College London		413	80	69	75.6
37	York	0.7	389	70	71	75.1
38	Hull	0.6	294	78	70	75.0
39	Keele	0.7	296	76	70	74.9
=40	East Anglia	0.7	355	79	52	74.8
=40	Lincoln	0.2	301	85	64	74.8
42	Royal Holloway	0.9	384	72	57	74.7
43	Stirling	0.6	346	79	54	74.5
44	Harper Adams		288		85	74.2
45	Brunel	0.7	364	75	60	74.1

=46	Queen's, Belfast	0.9	373	76	44	73.8
=46	Bangor	1.0	297	76	54	73.8
=46	De Montfort	0.6	283	84	50	73.8
49	Essex	0.8	325	75	57	73.2
50	Queen Mary, London	0.9	375	72	51	73.0
51	Dundee		354	82	61	72.6
52	Bradford	0.8	253	79	53	72.0
53	Brighton	0.9	270	77	51	71.9
54	Oxford Brookes	0.4	316	78	60	71.8
55	Portsmouth	0.5	294	76	63	71.6
56	Northumbria	0.2	334	76	64	71.2
57	Bournemouth	0.4	333	73	62	70.3
58	Edinburgh Napier	0.2	300	76	67	70.1
59	West of England	0.3	291	75	63	69.8
60	Sheffield Hallam	0.4	299	76	58	69.6
=61	Central Lancashire	0.4	294	74	62	69.4
=61	Huddersfield	0.3	294	73	69	69.4
=63	Plymouth	0.4	286	72	66	69.1
=63	St Mary's College		236	81	67	69.1
65	Coventry	0.2	277	79	55	68.8
66	Nottingham Trent	0.4	298	69	69	68.6
67	Glamorgan	0.3	274	80	48	68.2
68	Greenwich	0.3	245	83	42	68.0
69	Bath Spa		293	80	51	67.7
70	Ulster	0.5	270	78	44	67.6
71	Salford	0.7	265	72	51	67.5
72	Staffordshire	0.5	222	76	56	67.4
=73	Kingston	0.7	272	73	46	67.0
=73	Hertfordshire	0.5	291	74	47	67.0
=73	Manchester Metropolitan	0.5	278	70	62	67.0
76	Swansea	0.6	327	68	48	66.3
77	Chester		257	74	67	66.0
=78	Westminster	0.4	296	70	55	65.9
=78	Birmingham City	0.4	271	72	56	65.9
=78	Aberystwyth	0.4	253	70	61	65.9
81	Leeds Trinity		224	80	56	65.7
82	Royal Agricultural College		277	74	61	65.6
83	Chichester		237	82	45	65.3
84	Sunderland		273	80	43	65.1
85	Glasgow Caledonian	0.3	335	75	37	65.0
86	West of Scotland	0.4	264	74	43	64.7
87	York St John		246	80	45	64.4
=88	Teesside	0.4	268	71	49	63.9
=88	University College Birmingham		231	76	58	63.9
90	Cardiff Metropolitan	0.1	267	74	50	63.7
91	London South Bank	0.3	188	79	40	63.2
=92	Abertay	0.2	272		51	63.0

Business Studies cont	Research quality	Entry standards	Student satisfaction %	Graduate prospects %	Overall rating
=92 Winchester		256	76	48	63.0
=94 Middlesex	0.4	191	76	42	62.8
=94 Glyndŵr		205		63	62.8
=94 Queen Margaret Edinburgh	0.1	286	75	43	62.8
97 Northampton	0.3	218	76	42	62.4
98 Liverpool John Moores	0.1	284	73	45	62.0
99 Gloucestershire	0.1	274	66	61	61.7
100 Southampton Solent		251	71	53	61.1
101 Roehampton		217	74	51	61.0
102 Bolton	0.1	214	76	41	60.9
=103 Canterbury Christ Church		224	72	54	60.8
=103 Newport		228	82	27	60.8
105 Worcester		289	73	39	60.6
106 Leeds Metropolitan	0.2	254	67	52	60.4
107 Edge Hill		246	71	48	59.8
108 Derby		261	70	47	59.6
109 Buckinghamshire New	0.2	201	71	47	59.5
110 West London		186	76	41	59.1
111 East London		190	73	46	58.4
112 Anglia Ruskin		213	68	53	58.0
113 Trinity St David		281	71	31	57.4
114 Bedfordshire	0.2	170	72	36	56.2
115 London Metropolitan	0.2	222	63	40	53.9
116 Cumbria		213	60	40	50.4
117 University of the Arts, London		199	54	51	49.0

» Chartered Management Institute: **www.managers.org.uk**
» Confederation of British Industry: **www.cbi.org.uk**
» Institute of Consulting: **www.iconsulting.org.uk**

Celtic Studies

Only 165 students started full-time Celtic studies degrees in 2011, making it one of the smallest categories in the *Guide*. Applications had been rising until the switch to higher fees in 2012, when there was a 12 per cent decline. With almost five applications for each place in 2011, entry grades are relatively high; only one university in the table averages less than 270 points. Students seem to enjoy their courses: only Ulster failed to satisfy at least three quarters of their final-year undergraduates.

Cambridge tops the table with entry grades 100 points ahead of its nearest rival and by far the best results in the 2008 Research Assessment Exercise, when almost half of its submission was judged to be world-leading. The university has moved up from fourth last year, when it did not have enough entrants to compile a reliable score. Aberystwyth, in second place, has the best employment record and shares the second best student satisfaction rate with third-placed Glasgow, Bangor's students being the most satisfied.

The ranking is split between four universities from Wales, which naturally major in Welsh, and the remaining six, which focus on Irish or Gaelic studies. Queen's, Belfast has regained its lead over Ulster this year as the top university in Northern Ireland. Glasgow has been joined by Aberdeen as the Scottish representatives this year, the University of the Highlands and Islands dropping out because it did not have enough students to compile a reliable score.

The small numbers in all departments play havoc with the employment data. Celtic studies is only just outside the top 20 for graduate employment, with more than half of the leavers going on to take postgraduate courses. Only 5 per cent are unemployed, although almost a quarter start their career in lower-level employment. However, Celtic studies is right at bottom of the salary table, with those in graduate-level jobs earning only £2,500 more than those in lower-level employment.

Employed in graduate job:	16%	Employed in non-graduate job and studying:	5%
Employed in graduate job and studying:	4%	Employed in non-graduate job:	24%
Studying:	46%	Unemployed:	5%
Average starting graduate salary:	£17,191	Average starting non-graduate salary:	£14,693

Celtic Studies	Research quality	Entry standards	Student satisfaction %	Graduate prospects %	Overall rating
1 Cambridge	1.7	548	89	61	100.0
2 Aberystwyth	1.2	344	90	81	94.3
3 Glasgow	0.8		90	77	93.3
4 Cardiff	0.9	447	87	71	91.6
5 Bangor	0.8	342	91	73	88.4
6 Aberdeen	0.2		83	77	81.9
7 Swansea	1.1	329	75	64	80.1
8 Queen's, Belfast	0.5	344	79	68	79.5
9 Ulster	1.5	265	65	64	76.3
10 Liverpool	0.8	343	81	47	75.0

» You can find out more about Celtic studies directly from the universities listed.

Chemical Engineering

Only medicine and dentistry produce higher starting salaries than chemical engineering. This may help to explain the continuing popularity of the subject, which has been growing for several years and had seen one of the biggest increases (11.5 per cent) in applications of any mainstream subject in April 2012. Although it is still one of the smaller branches of engineering, applications were over 12,800.

Cambridge tops the chemical engineering table for the eleventh year in a row and has a big lead over Imperial College, London. Cambridge has much the highest entry standards and shares the top research score with Imperial. Both universities had 30 per cent of

Chemical Engineering cont

their work rated as world-leading in the 2008 Research Assessment Exercise. Cambridge was ranked second only to the Massachusetts Institute of Technology in world rankings published in 2011.

Easily the most satisfied students were at Heriot Watt, which has shot up nine places to third and become the leading university in Scotland for chemical engineering. The top employment score is at sixth-placed Leeds, where 95 per cent of graduates found graduate-level work or a place on a postgraduate course within six months of completing a degree. Swansea is the only representative of Wales and London South Bank the only post-1992 university left in the ranking.

Employment prospects have dipped a little since the last *Guide*, but still almost half of the universities in the table registered "positive destinations" for at least 80 per cent of those graduating. Nationally, more than half of students go straight into graduate jobs and chemical engineering is in the top six subjects overall. However, the 13 per cent unemployment rate is still among the highest.

Degree courses normally demand chemistry and maths A levels or their equivalent and often physics as well. Four out of five chemical engineers come with A levels or equivalent qualifications, and average entry grades are the highest for any engineering subject – all but four of the 20 universities in the table average more than 400 points at entry. This helps produce engineering's largest proportion of firsts and 2:1s. Most courses offer industrial placements in the final year and lead to Chartered Engineer status.

Chemical Engineering	Research quality	Entry standards	Student satisfaction %	Graduate prospects %	Overall rating
1 Cambridge	1.5	643	87	91	100.0
2 Imperial College	1.5	573	76	86	91.6
3 Heriot-Watt	0.9	419	92	85	87.5
4 Birmingham	1.1	472	86	81	86.7
5 Newcastle	0.8	430	85	93	86.0
6 Leeds	1.2	442	70	95	84.9
=7 Loughborough	1.1	445	85	76	84.6
=7 Surrey	1.1	408	86	81	84.6
9 Bath	0.8	468	81	91	84.5
10 Manchester	1.4	483	73	76	83.3
11 Nottingham	1.3	425	73	78	81.0
12 Sheffield	0.9	465	78	76	79.8
13 Edinburgh	0.9	509	67	86	79.7
14 University College London	1.1	473	73	66	76.7
15 Strathclyde	0.5	469	80	74	76.3
16 Swansea	1.1	325	78	73	76.1
17 Aberdeen	1.0	411	72		75.8
18 Aston	0.6	336	79	72	71.2
19 Queen's, Belfast	0.6	396	70	73	70.1
20 London South Bank	0.7	287	74	59	64.8

Employed in graduate job:	52%	Employed in non-graduate job and studying:	1%
Employed in graduate job and studying:	4%	Employed in non-graduate job:	8%
Studying:	21%	Unemployed:	13%
Average starting graduate salary:	£27,195	Average starting non-graduate salary:	£16,571

» Institution of Chemical Engineers: **www.icheme.org**
» Royal Society of Chemistry: **www.rsc.org**

Chemistry

Chemistry's slide in popularity from the sixth form onwards has been reversed recently and the number of universities in this table is the largest for eight years. A series of well-publicised departmental closures prompted fears that the subject would become confined to the leading universities, but more than 50 have qualified for the latest ranking. Applications have grown by 20 per cent in five years and had not followed the general downward trend at the start of 2012. There are now more than five applications for every place. Forensic science has become an attractive alternative to the pure subject but, for many, chemistry remains the classic science. Some courses demand maths as well as chemistry and most successful candidates for the leading universities take more than one science at A level.

The top five in the table remain the same as last year, although York has joined Nottingham in equal fifth place. Oxford has narrowed the gap slightly on Cambridge at the top of the table, but Cambridge has the highest entry standards and the best research grades. Like last year, the most satisfied students are at Loughborough, where a low research grade confines the university to twentieth place.

The best employment record is at Bangor, which has jumped 11 places this year and become the leader in Wales, although it still does not make the top 20. There were good employment scores throughout most of the ranking, as chemistry moved into the top ten in the subject employment table. Almost half of all graduates continue their studies, either full or part-time. However, despite some improvement since last year's *Guide*, the subject is only just above average for graduate starting salaries.

Chemistry is old university territory, with no post-1992 institution in the top 30. Plymouth the highest-placed of 11 modern universities in the table. More than 20 of the 52 universities average 400 points or more at entry, five of them topping 500 points, while only two average less than 250 points. Nearly nine out of ten undergraduates have A levels or their equivalent, although entry requirements are not far above the average for all subjects.

Employed in graduate job:	31%	Employed in non-graduate job and studying:	2%
Employed in graduate job and studying:	5%	Employed in non-graduate job:	14%
Studying:	39%	Unemployed:	9%
Average starting graduate salary:	£20,712	Average starting non-graduate salary:	£15,651

» European Association for Chemical and Molecular Sciences: **www.euchems.org**
» Royal Society of Chemistry: **www.rsc.org**
» Society of Dyers and Colourists: **www.sdc.org.u**k

Chemistry

	Research quality	Entry standards	Student satisfaction %	Graduate prospects %	Overall rating
1 Cambridge	1.6	630	87	83	100.0
2 Oxford	1.4	578	88	87	97.6
3 Durham	1.1	564	86	86	93.6
4 St Andrews	1.3	525	85	83	92.9
=5 Nottingham	1.5	423	84	76	89.4
=5 York	1.1	474	89	73	89.4
=7 Sheffield	1.0	449	86	80	88.7
=7 Bristol	1.3	495	83	75	88.7
9 Edinburgh	1.3	482	83	69	87.8
10 Southampton	0.8	444	84	87	86.9
11 Sussex	0.7	400	88	85	86.7
12 Manchester	1.1	416	85	77	86.2
13 Strathclyde	0.9	438	86	75	86.1
14 Heriot-Watt	0.7	380	89	79	85.2
15 Liverpool	1.1	394	82	77	84.8
16 Imperial College	1.2	537	72	80	84.3
17 Hull	0.6	319	90	84	84.2
18 Bath	0.7	443	83	79	83.7
19 Surrey	1.0	376	77	89	83.5
20 Loughborough	0.3	357	93	81	83.4
21 Warwick	1.1	464	75	80	83.2
22 Leeds	1.1	414	81	71	83.1
23 Queen's, Belfast	0.6	374	87	81	83.0
24 University College London	1.0	483	77	74	82.9
25 Birmingham	0.8	403	84	74	82.7
26 Bangor	0.7	271	85	91	82.0
27 Keele	0.7	351	87	73	81.9
28 Leicester	0.5	340	91	74	81.8
29 Glasgow	0.9	464	77	75	81.7
30 Cardiff	0.8	404	79	77	80.9
31 Newcastle	0.6	395	76	80	77.2
32 Queen Mary, London	0.6	354	79	73	76.9
33 Plymouth	0.4	302	85	73	76.8
34 East Anglia	0.7	377	79	68	76.7
35 Bradford	0.9	264	76	82	76.3
36 Reading	0.3	344	82	71	74.3
=37 Kent		333	82	73	72.5
=37 Huddersfield	0.3	265	81	76	72.5
39 Aston	0.6	329		58	71.1
40 Nottingham Trent	0.9	289	74	61	71.0
41 Aberdeen	0.5	398	77	49	70.6
42 Northumbria	0.4	305	78	63	70.4
43 Sheffield Hallam	0.3	236	77	68	67.6

44 Kingston		261	78	69	67.0
45 West of Scotland		249	83	57	66.6
46 Brighton	0.6	264	75	53	66.5
47 Manchester Metropolitan	0.3	258	73	58	64.2
48 Greenwich		251		57	62.5
49 Glamorgan		276	75	52	62.1
50 Abertay		297		23	52.5

Civil Engineering

Civil engineering suffered more than other branches of the discipline from the move to higher fees in 2012. Applications were down by more than 10 per cent, following two years of significant growth. The latest figures also continue the subject's slide down the employment and salary tables. Two years ago, civil engineering was in the top ten for both, but, while average salaries have improved slightly and unemployment is down, other subjects have been recovering more strongly from the recession, when the latest survey was conducted in 2010. Considerably more than half of all leavers go straight into graduate jobs and employment figures remain good throughout most of the table.

Cambridge takes its accustomed place at the top of the civil engineering table. The university enjoys a big lead over the rest on entry standards and employment, as well as sharing the best research grades with second-placed Imperial College. For the second year in a row, however, Greenwich boasts the most satisfied students and becomes the highest-placed post-1992 university despite only just making the top 30. Bath matches it for student satisfaction in the latest edition and takes third place overall. Dundee has regained its status as the top university in Scotland and Cardiff remains the leader in Wales.

Entry scores have been rising in civil engineering, with 21 universities averaging 400 points or more, compared with 15 last year. Fewer than half of all undergraduates are admitted with A levels or equivalent qualifications, reflecting the large numbers of mature students who are upgrading their qualifications. Some of the top degrees in civil engineering are four-year courses leading to an MEng; others are sandwich courses incorporating a period at work. The leading departments will expect physics and maths A levels, or their equivalent.

Employed in graduate job:	52%	Employed in non-graduate job and studying:	1%
Employed in graduate job and studying:	5%	Employed in non-graduate job:	14%
Studying:	15%	Unemployed:	13%
Average starting graduate salary:	£23,667	Average starting non-graduate salary:	£15,503

» EngineeringUK: **www.engineeringuk.com**
» Institution of Civil Engineers: **www.ice.org.uk**
» Institution of Structural Engineers: **www.istructe.org**

Civil Engineering

	Research quality	Entry standards	Student satisfaction %	Graduate prospects %	Overall rating
1 Cambridge	1.8	615	87	94	100.0
2 Imperial College	1.8	547	80	77	90.2
3 Bath	1.2	480	89	81	89.5
=4 Sheffield	1.3	478	83	84	87.2
=4 Cardiff	1.4	459	83	81	87.2
6 Loughborough	1.0	412	88	89	86.6
7 Bristol	1.3	510	78	84	86.2
8 Southampton	1.3	469	73	86	82.9
9 Swansea	1.7	369	77	79	82.8
10 Nottingham	1.4	409	80	77	82.6
11 Surrey	1.1	385	79	91	82.5
12 Newcastle	1.3	407	77	80	81.1
13 Dundee	1.2	377	82	69	79.3
14 Warwick	1.1	439	76	73	78.8
15 Leeds	0.8	405	83	72	78.5
16 Heriot-Watt	0.7	414	87	67	78.4
17 Exeter	0.8	437	81	73	78.2
18 Durham	0.8		75	86	77.4
19 University College London	0.9	518	74	67	76.5
=20 Edinburgh	0.9	480	73	71	76.0
=20 Glasgow	0.9	457	71	77	76.0
22 Aberdeen	1.0	368	75	78	75.8
23 Salford	1.2	288	77	76	75.7
24 Liverpool	1.0	400	74	70	74.7
25 Birmingham	0.9	408	75	65	73.5
26 Queen's, Belfast	1.2	381	65	78	72.9
27 Manchester	1.1	417	65	73	72.5
28 Greenwich	0.5	248	89	60	71.2
29 Strathclyde	0.5	411	75	66	71.1
30 Northumbria	0.6		71	80	70.9
31 Plymouth	0.8	293	72	75	70.0
32 Bradford	0.7	291	73	73	69.2
33 West of Scotland		290	84	69	68.4
=34 Nottingham Trent	0.3	276	76	75	67.8
=34 Portsmouth		265	83	71	67.8
=36 City	0.7	352	69	64	66.9
=36 Coventry	0.2	295	78	68	66.9
38 Edinburgh Napier	0.4	289	73	69	66.0
=39 Brighton	0.4	288	74	60	64.6
=39 East London		269	83	58	64.6
41 Glamorgan	0.7	243	67	69	63.9
42 Glasgow Caledonian		343	68	72	63.1
43 Leeds Metropolitan		221	79	56	60.7

44 Ulster		243	75	60	60.3
45 West of England		309	72	57	60.2
46 Kingston	0.4	253	71	54	59.6
=47 Brunel		336	79	30	58.0
=47 Anglia Ruskin		226	73	57	58.0
49 Teesside		288	72	51	57.9
50 Liverpool John Moores		262	71	52	56.9
51 Abertay		291		50	56.8
52 London South Bank		220	76	46	56.7

Classics and Ancient History

There is never much between Oxford and Cambridge in classics and ancient history. Student satisfaction clinches top place for Cambridge this year, although it also had the highest grades in the 2008 Research Assessment Exercise. Another refinement of the scoring system, mirroring the one used to distribute research grants, gives extra credit for world-leading research, of which Cambridge had slightly more than Oxford. Oxford still has the highest entry standards in the table.

Satisfaction levels are generally high in classics, but employment prospects are much more mixed. Third-placed Durham was the only university to see more than 80 per cent of leavers go straight into graduate jobs or on to postgraduate courses. Classicists are often said to be favourite recruitment targets of computer companies and management consultants, but there is little sign of it in the latest results. The subject is below average for employment prospects and graduate salaries. This does not appear to have deterred applicants, however. The subjects might have appeared vulnerable when fees rose in 2012, especially given the decline of Latin in comprehensive schools. But a drop in applications of less than 4 per cent was far below the average for the whole higher education system. There were still more than five applications for every place in both classics and ancient history.

St Andrews remains the clear leader in Scotland, Swansea the better-placed of two universities in Wales, while Roehampton is the only post-1992 university in the ranking. Several universities teach the subjects as part of a modular degree scheme, but not as a degree in its own right. A-level grades in classics are among the highest for any group of subjects, but most universities offering classics teach the subject from scratch, as well as to more practised students. Almost a third of graduates opt for postgraduate courses, but the proportion going straight into graduate jobs is among the lowest in any subject.

Employed in graduate job:	28%	Employed in non-graduate job and studying:	5%
Employed in graduate job and studying:	2%	Employed in non-graduate job:	23%
Studying:	31%	Unemployed:	10%
Average starting graduate salary:	£20,073	Average starting non-graduate salary:	£15,374

Classics and Ancient History

Classics and Ancient History	Research quality	Entry standards	Student satisfaction %	Graduate prospects %	Overall rating
1 Cambridge	1.6	545	91	75	100.0
2 Oxford	1.5	568	87	79	98.5
3 Durham	1.2	500	84	81	91.8
4 Exeter	1.2	477	86	69	90.4
5 St Andrews	0.9	504	84	77	89.5
6 University College London	1.3	465	82	77	89.4
7 King's College London	1.3	472	85	61	88.1
8 Warwick	1.2	460	85	66	87.8
9 Bristol	1.0	452	82	64	84.1
10 Nottingham	0.8	415	82	68	81.7
11 Edinburgh	0.7	493	76	73	81.5
12 Glasgow	0.5	458	88	48	80.5
13 Liverpool	0.7	379	84	58	79.5
14 Manchester	1.1	408	81	46	79.0
15 Birmingham	0.9	388	80	56	78.5
16 Reading	0.7	386	87	42	78.1
17 Newcastle	0.7	408	78	59	77.0
18 Royal Holloway	0.6	383	79	58	75.5
19 Kent	0.2	350	80	71	74.5
20 Leeds	0.4	402	81	48	73.9
21 Swansea	0.4	313	78	39	66.8
22 Roehampton		281	72	29	57.2
23 Trinity St David	0.3	253	68		56.8

» Classical Association: **www.classicalassociation.org**
» Society for the Promotion of Roman Studies: **www.romansociety.org**

Communication and Media Studies

Students have flocked to degrees in these subjects, despite carping in mainstream media about their currency in the employment market. Taken together, journalism and media have been attracting more applications than mathematics. But the boom did not survive the switch to higher fees: applications for journalism were down by 19 per cent and media studies by 8.5 per cent.

The division of jobs into graduate and non-graduate fields of employment hits communication and media studies harder than most other subjects. Academics in the field argue that it is normal for students completing media courses to take "entry level" work that is not classified as a graduate job. Nevertheless, the subjects are bottom of the employment league for the second year in a row, with 13 per cent unemployment, and in the bottom two for graduate starting salaries.

Communication and media studies are mainly the preserve of the new universities, but older universities have been moving in and now fill the top 13 places. Warwick has regained top place from King's College London after surrendering it last year. The highest entry grades in the table and outstanding performance in the 2008 Research Assessment Exercise, when 60 per cent of its work in film and television studies was rated as world-class, give Warwick a healthy lead. Westminster matched Warwick's research score and is the leading post-1992 university, moving up two places to equal 14th.

Only 18 of the 92 universities and colleges satisfied 80 per cent or more of final-year undergraduates in 2011, fourth-placed Sheffield achieving the best score. Inevitably, the employment scores are even lower. Only Strathclyde, in 26th place, saw 70 per cent of their leavers go straight into graduate-level jobs or continue their studies within six months of graduation. The proportion dropped below 50 per cent in two thirds of the institutions in the table.

Cardiff remains the top university in Wales, while Stirling has overtaken Strathclyde to become the leader in Scotland. Entry grades have started to rise again: nine universities (compared with four last year) average more than 400 points, while only two drop below 200 points.

Employed in graduate job:	38%	Employed in non-graduate job and studying:	2%
Employed in graduate job and studying:	2%	Employed in non-graduate job:	39%
Studying:	7%	Unemployed:	13%
Average starting graduate salary:	£17,272	Average starting non-graduate salary:	£14,205

Communication and Media Studies

		Research quality	Entry standards	Student satisfaction %	Graduate prospects %	Overall rating
1	Warwick	2.1	457	88	50	100.0
2	King's College London	1.7	429	86	60	97.2
3	East Anglia	1.9	376	85	58	95.1
4	Exeter	1.4	450	80	64	94.1
5	Sheffield	0.7	406	89	65	92.3
6	Cardiff	1.7	431	75	57	91.1
7	Queen Mary, London	1.2	371	84	58	89.3
=8	Southampton	1.2	426	87	41	88.5
=8	Lancaster	1.3	336	86	56	88.5
10	Sussex	1.1	357	83	61	88.3
11	Newcastle	0.7	408	85		88.2
12	Loughborough	1.0	384	80	57	86.1
13	Leicester	1.4	370	77	55	85.8
=14	Royal Holloway	1.2	392	80	48	85.3
=14	Westminster	2.1	324	71	54	85.3
16	Birmingham City	1.2	324	78	60	84.6
17	Goldsmiths College	1.7	374	69	53	84.0
18	Stirling	0.9	385	80	47	82.7
19	Nottingham Trent	1.2	317		54	82.2
20	Central Lancashire	0.7	323	80	61	81.6
21	Manchester		384		61	81.5
22	Lincoln	1.0	346	74	58	81.3

Communication and Media Studies cont

	Research quality	Entry standards	Student satisfaction %	Graduate prospects %	Overall rating
23 Leeds	0.8	386	67	63	80.2
24 Liverpool		402	81	49	78.7
25 Bournemouth	0.8	369	69	57	78.4
26 Strathclyde		435	65	71	78.3
27 Hull	0.8	305	81	47	78.1
28 Robert Gordon		354	76	64	77.5
29 West of England	0.9	303	79	44	77.1
30 Keele		327	81	54	75.9
=31 City		387	66	68	75.2
=31 De Montfort	1.1	295	75	41	75.2
=33 Glasgow Caledonian	0.5	385	76	38	74.9
=33 Sunderland	1.0	285	78	41	74.9
35 Surrey	0.4	355	71	52	74.5
36 Edinburgh Napier		339	71	65	74.3
37 Queen Margaret Edinburgh	0.6	329	80	35	73.9
38 Brunel	0.6	335	74	43	73.6
39 Leeds Metropolitan	0.9	271	73	47	72.6
40 Staffordshire	0.4	262	75	54	71.9
41 Brighton	0.5	296	78	40	71.6
42 Northumbria	0.7	315	71	42	71.5
43 Ulster	1.0	272	73	39	70.9
44 Hertfordshire	0.5	306	73	43	70.6
45 Coventry	0.7	272	71	47	70.4
46 Portsmouth	0.5	281	76	40	70.2
=47 Queen's, Belfast		353	70	47	69.8
=47 Gloucestershire	0.0	294	79	42	69.8
49 Huddersfield	0.0	310	73	51	69.7
50 Kingston	0.3	293	74	44	69.5
51 West of Scotland	0.5	269	77	36	68.9
52 Oxford Brookes		327	71	48	68.6
53 University for Creative Arts		261		53	68.3
54 Salford	0.8	309	64	41	68.1
=55 Teesside		264	78	44	67.8
=55 Leeds Trinity		272	75	48	67.8
57 Bath Spa	0.4	285	76	32	67.2
58 Middlesex	0.5	224	70	51	67.1
59 Derby	0.9	261	76	22	66.4
60 Falmouth		249	73	50	66.0
61 Swansea	0.6	305	66	38	65.9
62 Winchester	0.5	302	67	39	65.8
63 Worcester		274	72	45	65.7
64 Liverpool John Moores		294	75	35	65.6
65 Roehampton	0.5	260	70	38	65.1

66 Southampton Solent		295	71	40	64.7
67 Chester		259	68	52	64.5
68 East London	1.2	196	73	25	64.3
69 London Metropolitan	0.7	242	66	39	64.1
70 St Mary's College		264	77	32	64.0
71 Bradford	0.3	239	67	46	63.6
72 Chichester		262	80	26	63.5
73 Sheffield Hallam	0.5	308	63	35	63.3
74 Greenwich	0.1	251	74	35	63.1
75 University of the Arts, London		293	60	53	63.0
=76 Bangor		216	73	45	62.7
=76 Bedfordshire	0.7	202	64	46	62.7
78 Manchester Metropolitan	0.4	289	71	25	62.6
79 Canterbury Christ Church		258	71	36	61.5
80 York St John		271	73	29	61.4
=81 London South Bank	0.7	197	70	31	61.3
=81 Marjon, Plymouth		209	74	39	61.3
83 Anglia Ruskin		231	76	29	60.8
84 Edge Hill		257	69	34	60.0
=85 Buckinghamshire New		238	66	40	58.8
=85 Cumbria		251	71	27	58.8
87 Cardiff Metropolitan		227		38	58.7
88 Glamorgan	0.5	303	57	30	58.6
89 West London	0.2	241	62	35	57.2
90 Essex		262		26	56.5
91 Northampton		234	66	24	54.2
92 Trinity St David	0.2	195		23	51.2

» Broadcast Journalism Training Council: **www.bjtc.org.uk**
» Chartered Institute of Journalists: **www.cioj.co.uk**
» National Union of Journalists: **www.nuj.org.uk**
» Creative Skillset: **www.creativeskillset.org**

Computer Science

Computer science suffered some lean years of falling applications, but began to turn the corner in 2010. A decline of 4 per cent in March 2012 was much less than the national average, leaving computer science among the ten most popular subjects. Yet a computing degree is no longer the guarantee of a lucrative career: for the third year in a row, it has the highest unemployment rate in this year's *Guide* – an unwanted distinction it shares with librarianship and information management. However, it is not all bad news in the computing world: the subject is still among the top 20 for graduate salaries and more than half of those completing degrees do go straight into graduate-level jobs.

Cambridge has extended its lead at the top of the table, with the best employment record, the highest entry standards and the best grades in the 2008 Research Assessment Exercise, when 45 per cent of the university's research was considered world-leading. Imperial College London has overtaken Oxford to snatch second place by a fraction of a point. In the 2011

Computer Science cont

National Student Survey West London, in 48th place, satisfied 91 per cent of its final year undergraduates, knocking St Andrews off the top spot for student satisfaction it held last year. St Andrews remains ahead of Glasgow in the race to be the top university in Scotland. Aberystwyth remains ahead of Swansea and Cardiff as the leader in Wales. Only four post-1992 universities, headed by Oxford Brookes, feature in the top 50. The others are Plymouth, Robert Gordon and West London. Entry standards are spread more widely than in any other subject, average scores on the UCAS tariff ranging from more than 600 points to only 150. Seventeen universities average 400 points or more, while eight have an average of less than 200, three fewer than last year. Three years after graduation, more than a quarter of computing students said they would be "very likely" to choose a different course if they had their time again – the second-highest total among 19 groups of subjects.

Employed in graduate job:	50%
Employed in graduate job and studying:	3%
Studying:	11%
Average starting graduate salary:	£22,325

Employed in non-graduate job and studying:	2%
Employed in non-graduate job:	20%
Unemployed:	14%
Average starting non-graduate salary:	£15,370

Computer Science	Research quality	Entry standards	Student satisfaction %	Graduate prospects %	Overall rating
1 Cambridge	1.8	636	89	96	100.0
2 Imperial College	1.6	564	82	95	91.9
3 Oxford	1.5	608		77	91.7
4 Bristol	1.3	493	87	84	88.3
5 St Andrews	0.9	497	90	88	88.0
6 University College London	1.5	448	83	89	87.2
7 Glasgow	1.4	456	86	82	86.9
8 Southampton	1.6	464	84	79	86.8
9 York	1.3	445	82	86	84.4
10 Edinburgh	1.6	470	78	81	83.9
11 Bath	1.3	411	82	88	83.7
12 Warwick	1.0	488	79	92	83.2
13 Exeter	1.0		84	89	82.9
14 Birmingham	1.4	402	82	84	82.8
15 Newcastle	1.1	400	83	87	82.6
16 Manchester	1.5	378	77	80	79.9
17 Durham	1.1	464	76	85	79.8
18 Liverpool	1.4	374	81	72	79.6
19 Nottingham	1.4	376	78	78	79.5
20 Sheffield	1.0	425	78	86	79.4
21 Loughborough	0.9	336	86	81	78.9
=22 Sussex	1.1	364	82	76	78.6
=22 Royal Holloway	1.2	388	73	93	78.6
=24 Leicester	1.1	345	83	77	78.4
=24 Aberdeen	1.1	366		79	78.4

26	Aberystwyth	1.2	299	80	79	76.9
=27	Strathclyde	0.8	409	80	77	76.8
=27	Dundee	1.0	383	82	70	76.8
=29	Lancaster	1.3	353	76	75	76.5
=29	Leeds	1.3	338	76	78	76.5
=29	Surrey	0.7	360	81	83	76.5
32	East Anglia	1.1	360	85	61	76.3
33	Swansea	1.2	316	76	82	75.6
34	Cardiff	1.1	369	79	68	75.5
35	King's College London	0.9	379	76	81	75.4
36	Queen's, Belfast	0.9	352	77	73	73.3
=37	Queen Mary, London	1.3	319	78	61	73.2
=37	Kent	1.0	301	74	86	73.2
39	Heriot-Watt	0.9	359	76	73	72.7
40	Reading	0.4	351	75	88	71.7
=41	Oxford Brookes	0.8	299	77	74	71.4
=41	Bangor	0.8	254	83	67	71.4
43	Hull	0.4	284	82	73	69.9
44	Essex	1.0	331	77	57	69.8
45	Robert Gordon	0.6	290	80	68	69.4
46	Aston	0.6	344	76	68	69.3
47	Plymouth	1.3	283	68	72	68.9
48	Brunel	0.9	326	74	60	68.5
49	West London	0.2	164	91	65	67.9
50	City	0.9	333	70	66	67.3
51	Lincoln	0.8	322	76	54	67.0
52	Teesside	0.8	313	77	49	66.3
53	Salford	1.0	221	75	61	66.0
54	Stirling	0.6	328		60	65.9
55	Edinburgh Napier	0.3	289	80	60	65.8
56	Goldsmiths College	1.0	289	72	56	65.7
57	West of England	0.7	281	69	73	65.4
58	De Montfort	0.7	283	76	49	64.4
59	Huddersfield	0.4	302	70	75	64.3
60	Glyndŵr	0.5	235	81	52	64.2
61	Abertay		337		63	64.0
=62	Bournemouth	0.5	298	69	72	63.8
=62	Ulster	0.8	254	73	56	63.8
64	Hertfordshire	0.8	267	71	57	63.5
65	Portsmouth	0.4	227	78	57	63.0
=66	Staffordshire	0.3	241	74	68	62.9
=66	Brighton	0.9	261	70	56	62.9
68	Northumbria		253	75	74	62.7
=69	Sheffield Hallam	0.4	262	75	59	62.3
=69	Glamorgan	0.5	299	72	54	62.3
71	Greenwich	0.2	242	82	48	62.2
72	Cardiff Metropolitan		257	83	50	62.1

		Research quality	Entry standards	Student satisfaction %	Graduate prospects %	Overall rating
73	Central Lancashire		306	76	60	62.0
=74	Keele		291	74	66	61.9
=74	Kingston	0.5	254	75	54	61.9
76	Bolton		274		65	61.5
77	Glasgow Caledonian	0.2	299	78	45	60.7
78	Chester		251	74	65	60.6
79	Derby		315	73	57	60.4
80	Sunderland	0.4	279	68	63	60.1
81	Chichester		240		65	60.0
82	Newman		250		63	59.9
=83	Nottingham Trent	0.3	258	68	64	59.5
=83	Gloucestershire		258	72	66	59.5
=83	Liverpool John Moores	0.6	204	74	47	59.5
=83	Manchester Metropolitan	0.5	255	69	56	59.5
87	Bradford	0.6	246	70	48	58.7
88	Edge Hill		243	74	58	58.6
89	Coventry	0.4	248	66	62	58.5
90	London South Bank	0.4	179	74	53	58.4
91	Newport		246	77	47	58.0
=92	Roehampton		200	77	53	57.9
=92	Southampton Solent		211	72	64	57.9
94	Leeds Metropolitan		206	77	49	57.2
95	Middlesex	0.6	167	71	47	56.4
96	Northampton		219	74	48	55.7
97	Worcester		243	68	57	55.4
98	Westminster	0.4	244	66	50	55.3
99	West of Scotland	0.3	289	68	39	55.2
100	Bedfordshire	0.3	150	70	49	53.7
101	Birmingham City		245	66	53	53.4
102	Anglia Ruskin		186	72	40	52.0
103	Canterbury Christ Church		180	67	51	51.7
=104	East London		151	72	41	51.3
=104	London Metropolitan	0.1	165	70	41	51.3
106	Buckinghamshire New		212	70	35	50.9

» BCS, The Chartered Institute for IT: **www.bcs.org**

Dentistry

Dentistry is the only subject in this year's *Guide* to command average starting salaries of more than £30,000. There is no figure for non-graduate jobs because virtually everyone who completes a degree goes on to become a dentist, so the subject also has the top overall employment rate. Only 4 of the 13 undergraduate dental schools registered less than full employment. This measure is not used to determine positions so as not to exaggerate the impact of tiny numbers delaying their entry into the profession. Even so, there had been a 7 per cent drop in applications in March 2012 to follow a smaller decline in the previous year. Most degrees last five years, although several universities offer a six-year option for those without the necessary scientific qualifications. The number of places has been increased in recent years to tackle shortages in the profession, but there are still over ten applications to the place – more than in any subject except medicine. Entry standards are correspondingly high: none of the schools averages less than 450 points. Most demand chemistry and many give preference to candidates who also have biology; some also demand maths or physics. Scores in the subject are so close that the ranking changes frequently. Glasgow is back in the top position that it occupied three years ago, having slipped to sixth in 2011. Newcastle, last year's leader has made exactly the opposite journey. Glasgow has the highest entry standards. Like Dundee, the other school to average more than 500 points at entry, it benefits from the upgrading of scores for Scottish Standards and Highers in the UCAS tariff.

Satisfaction levels are high throughout the table, but Queen's, Belfast, in fourth place, had the best scores in the 2011 National Student Survey. Manchester recorded the best performance in the 2008 Research Assessment Exercise. There have been no post-1992 universities in the ranking, although Plymouth was a partner with Exeter in the Peninsula Medical and Dental School which produced its first graduates in 2011. The two universities have agreed to go their own ways from 2013 and Plymouth alone will offer dentistry. It will be joined in future *Guides* by Central Lancashire, which opened a purpose-built dental school in 2007, but does not yet have sufficient data to be ranked.

Employed in graduate job:	92%	Employed in non-graduate job and studying:		0%
Employed in graduate job and studying:	8%	Employed in non-graduate job:		0%
Studying:	0%	Unemployed:		0%
Average starting graduate salary:	£30,293	Average starting non-graduate salary:		–

Dentistry	Research quality	Entry standards	Student satisfaction %	Graduate prospects %	Overall rating
1 Glasgow	0.9	532	94	100	100.0
2 King's College London	1.3	486	84	100	95.4
3 Manchester	1.4	465	88	100	95.2
4 Queen's, Belfast	0.8	482	96	100	94.3
5 Bristol	1.0	489	84	100	92.8
6 Newcastle	0.9	496	83	99	92.3
7 Dundee	0.7	509	84	99	91.8
8 Birmingham	0.8	488	86	100	91.6
9 Sheffield	1.0	464	85	100	90.7
10 Cardiff	1.0	475	83	100	90.5
11 Queen Mary, London	1.3	460	76	99	89.0
12 Liverpool	0.6	473	86	99	87.9
13 Leeds	1.0	457	76	100	86.4

» British Dental Association: **www.bda.org**

Drama, Dance and Cinematics

Drama has become one of the most popular subjects in UK higher education – consistently in the top 20 for degree applications. But it suffered nearly a 15 per cent drop in degree applications when fees rose in 2012, with an even steeper decline in Foundation degrees and other courses. The smaller area of dance and the various degrees categorised as cinematics, which include photography as well as film studies, also saw the demand for places fall by more than 15 per cent. The subjects' popularity has never been reflected in high entry grades, although 12 of the 91 universities and colleges in the table average more than 400 points at entry, compared with only six last year. For the first time, no institution slips below 200 points.

Warwick retains the top position in drama, dance and cinematics for the third year in succession, although it does not have the highest score on any single measure. Queen Mary, University of London, is only a fraction of a point behind, in second place. It had much the best results in the 2008 Research Assessment Exercise, when half of its submission was rated world-leading. Roehampton's research in dance achieved an even higher score, but it was not sustained over the whole group of subjects in this category. Third-placed Glasgow remains the leading university in Scotland and Aberystwyth is the leader in Wales.

Bristol, in fifth place, has the highest entry standards, while East Anglia boasts the most satisfied students, but did not enter the RAE in these subjects and only just makes the top 20 overall. For the fourth year in a row, by far the best graduate destinations score is at the Central School of Speech and Drama, part of the University of London, although even there a quarter of graduates did not find a graduate-level job or postgraduate course within six months of completing their course. Other employment scores remain low: even at some top-20 universities more than half of the leavers were unemployed or in low-level work six months after graduation.

There are no post-1992 universities in the top 20, although Huddersfield comes close and leads a substantial group in the top 30. This is another table where the gulf in qualifications between entrants to new and old universities is evident, although for drama and dance in particular, this is unlikely to be the main criterion for selection. Some drama courses do demand English literature A level, however.

Drama, dance and cinematics remains in the bottom four both for employment prospects and graduate salaries this year. Freelancing and periods of temporary employment are common throughout the performing arts, and less than half of all new graduates were in graduate-level jobs or still studying when the last employment survey was conducted.

Employed in graduate job:	36%	Employed in non-graduate job and studying:	4%
Employed in graduate job and studying:	3%	Employed in non-graduate job:	39%
Studying:	8%	Unemployed:	10%
Average starting graduate salary:	£17,631	Average starting non-graduate salary:	£14,017

» The Stage: **www.thestage.co.uk**
» UKP-Arts: **www.ukperformingarts.co.uk**

Drama, Dance and Cinematics	Research quality	Entry standards	Student satisfaction %	Graduate prospects %	Overall rating
1 Warwick	1.5	433	84	70	100.0
2 Queen Mary, London	1.9	401	84	65	99.7
3 Glasgow	1.7	444	88	49	97.4
4 Exeter	1.5	423	85	51	93.7
5 Bristol	1.7	481	63	66	93.4
6 Central School of Speech and Drama	0.9	357	85	75	92.9
7 Manchester	1.8	419	73	60	92.7
8 Birmingham	1.0	412	79	69	91.9
9 Royal Holloway	1.5	414	79	52	90.9
10 Lancaster	1.3	406	68	69	89.4
11 Kent	1.4	370	78	53	87.4
12 Loughborough	0.7	404	83	54	87.1
13 Leeds	1.1	367	77	61	86.7
14 Sussex		405	85	62	85.2
15 Aberdeen	1.0	376	83	42	83.4
16 Surrey	1.0	358	66	67	82.8
17 Reading	1.2	331	80	49	82.6
18 East Anglia		426	89	43	82.3
19 Nottingham	1.0	359	82	39	80.6
20 Hull	0.8	330	80	51	80.4
21 Essex	0.8	343	76	53	80.0
22 Huddersfield		308	80	71	79.8
23 Middlesex	1.0	271	75	63	79.7
24 Royal Conservatoire of Scotland		290		72	79.6
25 Coventry	0.7	301	76	54	77.1
26 Aberystwyth	1.2	272	82	38	77.0
27 Arts University College, Bournemouth	0.1	335	76	59	76.4
28 Roehampton	1.4	277	73	45	76.3
29 Plymouth	0.6	317	72	54	75.7
30 Goldsmiths College	1.1	360	65	45	75.4
=31 Oxford Brookes		343	81	49	75.0
=31 Brighton	1.4	275	70	46	75.0
33 Gloucestershire		304	88	43	74.4
34 De Montfort	0.9	299	76	40	73.8
35 Queen's, Belfast	0.9	331	72	39	73.6
36 Birmingham City		310	80	49	72.6
37 West of England		298	83	47	72.5
38 Lincoln	0.3	314	70	55	72.4
39 Glamorgan	0.4	323	69	51	72.2
40 Edge Hill		272	84	48	72.1
41 Cardiff Metropolitan		279	78	56	72.0
42 Manchester Metropolitan	0.4	307	74	46	71.9
43 Greenwich		271	81	51	71.6

Drama, Dance and Cinematics cont

	Research quality	Entry standards	Student satisfaction %	Graduate prospects %	Overall rating
44 Bishop Grosseteste		220		68	71.2
45 Chester	0.4	285	71	53	71.1
46 Brunel	0.7	327	70	37	70.9
47 Hertfordshire	0.3	306	74	46	70.8
48 West of Scotland		275	83	44	70.6
=49 Central Lancashire		303	76	50	70.5
=49 Chichester	0.4	333	75	35	70.5
=51 Northumbria		302	78	45	70.2
=51 Kingston	0.5	300	72	44	70.2
53 Queen Margaret Edinburgh	0.0	383	62	53	70.0
54 Bath Spa		306	72	49	68.8
55 Winchester	0.5	271	73	42	68.6
56 Cumbria		263	81	43	68.4
57 Liverpool John Moores		281	78	43	68.1
=58 Nottingham Trent		324	72	43	68.0
=58 University of the Arts, London		307	66	56	68.0
60 Staffordshire	0.4	253	81	35	67.9
61 Trinity St David		255	72	55	67.7
62 Portsmouth	0.1	282	71	46	66.7
63 Bedfordshire	0.7	213	75	39	66.5
64 Teesside		275	79	36	66.1
65 Worcester		319	72	38	66.0
=66 St Mary's College		286	74	38	65.0
=66 York St John	0.5	282	67	38	65.0
=68 Ulster		251	84	28	64.6
=68 Marjon, Plymouth		213	83	38	64.6
70 Westminster		275	70	43	64.3
71 London Metropolitan	0.3	230	73	40	63.8
72 University for Creative Arts		251	68	49	63.4
73 Sunderland	0.3	251	73	33	62.8
74 Falmouth		281	63	48	62.6
75 Derby		295	69	33	61.7
76 Northampton	0.3	256	73	29	61.6
77 Sheffield Hallam		313	63	38	61.4
78 Newport		277	66	39	61.1
79 Salford	0.3	269	62	38	60.4
80 Leeds Metropolitan		266	64	41	60.0
81 Anglia Ruskin		240	75	28	59.6
82 Glyndŵr		215	68	43	59.2
83 Canterbury Christ Church		284	70	26	59.1
84 Bolton		275	81	11	58.9
85 London South Bank		247	60	46	58.7
86 Norwich University College of the Arts		269	61	38	57.4

87 East London	0.5	206	59	38	56.5
88 Southampton Solent		261	62	34	56.3
89 Newman		229	68	30	55.9
90 West London		265	54	43	55.8
91 Buckinghamshire New		250	57	40	55.4

East and South Asian Studies

Degrees in these subjects attracted fewer than 500 students 2011, most taking either Japanese or Chinese. They are officially classed as "vulnerable" because of their small size and their economic and cultural importance, although the number of universities in the East and South Asian studies ranking has doubled since the subjects were placed in this category. Universities have always come in and out of the table because small student numbers mean that reliable averages cannot always be compiled, even though courses are still running.

Numbers may well grow in future years, with the clamour for more interaction with China and India. Only South Asian studies enjoyed increased applications in March 2012, when the total was still little more than 100. Japanese studies saw the biggest fall with the introduction of higher fees, applications dropping by more than a third. The demand for places to study Chinese dropped by less than 3 per cent, but the 781 applications still lagged behind the total for Japanese. The well-publicised growth in the number of schools teaching Mandarin may be beginning to have an effect on the demand for Chinese studies. The contrasting fortunes of the two main subjects may help to even out the levels of competition for places: in 2011, there were nine applications for every place in Japanese and little more than four in Chinese.

The small numbers make for exaggerated swings even in the national statistics. The latest unemployment rate of almost one in five is by far the highest of any group of subjects, whereas last year's was only marginally above average. Overall, East and South Asian studies are still not far below halfway for employment, but they have slumped 20 places in the earnings table after a £1,500 decline in average starting salaries in graduate jobs.

Cambridge remains ahead of Oxford at the top of the table, with the highest entry standards and the most satisfied students. Cardiff produced the best results in the 2008 Research Assessment Exercise, but has dropped out of the table this year, leaving the School of Oriental and African Studies with the best research score. Nottingham, in fifth place, had much the best of an extremely variable set of employment scores. Edinburgh is the only university in the ranking from outside England, while Oxford Brookes and Liverpool John Moores are the only post-1992 institutions.

Four out of five students enter with tariff scores that are above average for all subjects, so degree classifications are also high. Most learn their chosen language from scratch, although universities expect to see evidence of potential in other modern language qualifications.

Employed in graduate job:	39%	Employed in non-graduate job and studying:	1%
Employed in graduate job and studying:	4%	Employed in non-graduate job:	16%
Studying:	20%	Unemployed:	19%
Average starting graduate salary:	£19,278	Average starting non-graduate salary:	£14,408

East and South Asian Studies

	Research quality	Entry standards	Student satisfaction %	Graduate prospects %	Overall rating
1 Cambridge	0.8	555	89	69	100.0
2 Oxford	1.1	507	87	53	96.0
3 School of Oriental and African Studies	1.3	454	78	63	94.8
4 Leeds	0.6	413	75	67	81.8
5 Nottingham	0.5	379	68	81	80.1
6 Edinburgh	0.6	470	62	71	79.7
7 Sheffield	0.4	397	77	65	79.4
8 Manchester	0.6	385	69		73.8
9 Westminster	0.5	316	64		64.8
10 Liverpool John Moores		231	80	32	58.0
11 Oxford Brookes		355	64	33	56.6

» Association of South-East Asian Studies in the UK: **http://aseasuk.org.uk**
» British Association for Chinese Studies: **www.bacsuk.org.uk**
» British Association for Japanese Studies: **www.bajs.org.uk**
» British Association for Korean Studies: **www.baks.org.uk**
» British Association for South Asian Studies: **www.basas.org.uk**
» Royal Asiatic Society: **www.royalasiaticsociety.org**
» Royal Society for Asian Affairs: **www.rsaa.org.uk**

Economics

Economics is in the top five for graduate starting salaries, reflecting the value that employers place on a subject that they see combining the skills of the sciences and the arts. Although it is lower for overall employment rates, the subject is still comfortably in the top 20. Its reputation as a highly marketable degree helped economics to withstand the impact of higher fees in 2012. Applications were only slightly down on the previous year and close to the top ten in terms of popularity.

Not surprisingly, competition for places is stiff, with more than six applications for every degree place. Many prospective students underestimate the mathematical skills required for an economics degree. Most of the leading universities demand maths at A level, or its equivalent, as part of offers that are consistently high. Entry standards in this year's table reflect that, with four of the top five universities all averaging over 550 points – the equivalent of more than four As at A level and another at AS level. Another dozen have averages of at least 450 points, while only one of the 68 institutions in the ranking averages less than 200 points.

Oxford has regained the lead it lost last year to Cambridge, although the highly competitive nature of this ranking means that it does not lead on any single indicator. Cambridge has the highest entry standards and the best employment record, but an unusually low student satisfaction score (for Cambridge, at least) relegates it to fifth place this year. Both Oxford and Cambridge were eclipsed by the second-placed London School of Economics (LSE) and also by University College London, in fourth, in the 2008 Research Assessment Exercise. The most satisfied students are at Kent and Surrey, although there were good scores throughout the table. Plymouth, for example, is only two percentage points off the top score and has become the leading post-1992 university, but still does not make the top 40. Glasgow remains the leading university in Scotland, a fraction of a point ahead of Edinburgh, while Cardiff has a comfortable lead in Wales.

Almost three economists in ten continue studying after their first degree, either full or part-time. Starting salaries in graduate jobs had risen only slightly at the time of the latest survey, but the £16,237 average for other types of employment is among the highest for any subject.

Employed in graduate job:	43%	Employed in non-graduate job and studying:	2%
Employed in graduate job and studying:	11%	Employed in non-graduate job:	18%
Studying:	17%	Unemployed:	9%
Average starting graduate salary:	£25,722	Average starting non-graduate salary:	£16,237

Economics	Research quality	Entry standards	Student satisfaction %	Graduate prospects %	Overall rating
1 Oxford	1.8	596	84	83	100.0
2 London School of Economics	2.2	578	76	90	98.9
3 Warwick	1.8	551	76	89	95.0
4 University College London	2.1	546	75	84	94.9
5 Cambridge	1.4	616	73	94	94.0
6 Bristol	1.5	491	80	85	93.0
7 Durham	0.9	533	82	85	91.3
8 Nottingham	1.5	484	77	84	90.6
9 Glasgow	1.3	466	82	78	90.3
=10 Edinburgh	1.2	472	79	84	90.2
=10 Exeter	1.2	492	80	82	90.2
12 Strathclyde	1.2	444	86	69	89.2
=13 Kent	1.1	376	87	75	88.9
=13 Surrey	1.0	440	87	69	88.9
15 Bath	1.3	490	77	80	88.7
16 St Andrews	0.9	513	76	87	87.8
17 Lancaster	1.3	430	81	71	87.2
18 Queen Mary, London	1.5	428	84	58	86.6
19 Newcastle	0.7	431	84	77	86.5
20 Essex	1.8	353	85	56	86.4
21 York	1.1	474	75	81	86.1
22 Sheffield	1.0	427	83	64	84.7
23 East Anglia	1.0	398	84	65	84.6
24 Cardiff	1.4	453	74	69	83.8
25 Southampton	1.2	444	72	77	83.0
26 Heriot-Watt	0.7	370	82	74	82.9
27 Leeds	1.1	439	74	71	82.3
28 Royal Holloway	1.2	412	74	72	82.0
29 Birmingham	1.0	458	75	67	81.5

Economics cont

	Research quality	Entry standards	Student satisfaction %	Graduate prospects %	Overall rating
30 Queen's, Belfast	0.9	377	78	71	81.2
31 Leicester	1.1	402	77	64	81.1
32 Sussex	0.8	381	77	74	81.0
=33 Manchester	1.3	424	72	66	80.6
=33 Stirling	0.9	367	82	60	80.6
35 Loughborough	0.6	410	79	68	80.2
=36 Aberdeen	1.1	356	78	60	78.8
=36 Dundee	0.6	378	83	58	78.8
38 Reading	0.7	387	76	66	78.2
39 Swansea	0.9	337	78	58	77.0
40 Keele	0.7	345	78	64	76.9
41 Hull	0.6	326	77	70	76.7
42 Liverpool	0.7	383	76	62	76.6
43 Plymouth	0.4	298	85	57	76.5
44 School of Oriental and African Studies	0.6	436	71	69	76.4
45 Salford	0.4		78	67	76.0
46 Greenwich	0.3	250	86	57	75.1
47 Brighton	0.9	284	76		74.6
48 Oxford Brookes		333	80	66	74.0
49 Portsmouth	0.5	304	82	51	73.8
50 Central Lancashire	0.4	294	80	56	73.6
51 Aberystwyth	0.4	321	80	52	73.1
52 Nottingham Trent	0.4	307	78	57	72.7
53 Coventry		297	81	60	72.5
54 Hertfordshire	0.5	299	79	50	71.7
55 West of England	0.3	293	79	53	71.3
56 Brunel	0.8	322	73	50	71.2
57 Bradford	0.7	255	81	40	70.8
58 Ulster		276	80	56	70.1
59 City	0.8	406	66	52	69.5
60 Staffordshire	0.5	228	76	54	68.6
61 Birmingham City	0.4	262	75		68.4
62 London Metropolitan	0.4	245	72	52	65.5
63 Middlesex		192	69	73	65.2
64 Kingston	0.3	266	70	48	63.8
65 Liverpool John Moores	0.1	265	74	42	63.5
66 Manchester Metropolitan	0.1	284	66	55	62.6
67 East London		201	72	51	61.7
68 Leeds Metropolitan		266	67	53	61.4

» Economics, Business and Enterprise Association: **www.ebea.org.uk**
» Royal Economic Society: **www.res.org.uk**
» Why Study? Economics: **www.whystudyeconomics.ac.uk**

Education

Education is the only ranking that still contains teaching scores – because teacher training assessments are carried out by Ofsted at English universities. The new table includes the latest results, although some are no longer available on the Teaching Agency website. Sixteen universities – including two from outside the top 40, University College Birmingham and Worcester – tie for the best scores from the inspections. Cambridge and Durham, the top two overall, are among the others.

Cambridge maintains a clear lead in the table with entry standards that are over 100 points ahead of its nearest challenger and much the best research grades. West of Scotland has shot up from 15th to third place and shares the top student satisfaction score with Derby, 22 places lower. Glasgow, in fourth place, almost manages full employment, as it did last year. Eight others reach the 90 per cent mark for the proportion of graduates going straight into teaching or another graduate-level job, or on to postgraduate study. Education is just outside the top ten for employment, with more than 60 per cent of graduates going straight into schools and only 4 per cent unemployed. However, the average starting salary of £21,061 is outside the top 20 for all subjects.

Employment scores at different universities reflect to some extent the variations in demand for new staff between primary and secondary schools as well as between different parts of the UK. Universities that specialise in primary training are at an advantage at the moment because vacancies are more plentiful in primary than secondary schools. Differences are beginning to show up in the table, which includes some scores in the lower reaches that are below any in recent years.

Satisfaction levels are high generally, not only among the final-year undergraduates who complete the National Student Survey, but also in the early stage of careers. Three years after graduation, those with education degrees were among the most satisfied at work and least inclined to wish they had taken a different subject.

Some of the best-known education departments are absent from the table because they offer only the postgraduate courses that have become the normal route into secondary teaching and an increasingly popular choice for those wanting a career in primary schools. As such, they are not included in the National Student Survey for the subject and neither entry scores nor graduate destinations are comparable. The University of London's Institute of Education, which achieved the top grades in the 2008 research assessments, is one example; Oxford and King's College London, which ran it close, are others.

Low entry scores have been a concern to successive governments, but only one university averages (just) less than 200 points in the latest table, while most score more than 250. Teacher training courses have become more selective of late and there are now nearly eight applications to the place – considerably more than the average for all subjects. The economic downturn helped to encourage substantial growth in the demand for places over the past two years. Applications were down by 9 per cent in March 2012, but education was still among the ten most popular subjects.

Employed in graduate job:	59%	Employed in non-graduate job and studying:	2%
Employed in graduate job and studying:	4%	Employed in non-graduate job:	20%
Studying:	10%	Unemployed:	4%
Average starting graduate salary:	£21,061	Average starting non-graduate salary:	£14,070

Education

		Research quality	Teaching quality/5	Entry standards	Student satisfaction %	Graduate prospects %	Overall rating
1	Cambridge	1.3	4.0	512	80	86	100.0
2	Durham	1.0	4.0	408	79	91	93.7
3	West of Scotland	0.4		357	90	97	93.6
4	Glasgow	0.5		398	82	99	92.3
5	Stirling	0.9		364	80	92	91.7
6	Warwick	1.0	3.8	386	81	64	88.9
7	Edinburgh	0.8		399	71	96	88.0
8	York	0.9	4.0	359	82	57	87.3
9	Northumbria		4.0	319	88	88	86.2
=10	Leeds	1.0	3.0	353	85	70	85.9
=10	Birmingham	0.7	4.0	381	78	66	85.9
12	Keele	1.0	3.5	304	84	71	85.8
13	Dundee	0.3		343	82	89	85.7
14	Manchester Metropolitan	1.0	4.0	313	72	81	84.9
15	Manchester	1.0	4.0	330	78	53	84.2
16	Aberdeen	0.4		372	74	92	84.1
17	Reading	0.5	3.5	341	81	79	84.0
18	Brighton	0.6	4.0	308	77	79	83.7
19	Bangor	0.5		283	89	66	83.6
20	Cardiff	1.1		385	75	49	83.4
21	Bath	0.8	3.5			71	82.8
22	Birmingham City	0.4	4.0	288	79	82	82.7
23	Brunel	0.3	3.5	326		90	82.4
24	Canterbury Christ Church	0.6	4.0	310	70	87	82.2
25	Derby		4.0	298	90	62	82.1
26	Strathclyde	0.4		384	70	83	81.3
27	St Mary's College	0.1	4.0	286	77	87	80.7
28	Chichester		4.0	306	79	79	80.5
29	Oxford Brookes	0.4	3.5	324	77	74	80.2
30	Gloucestershire	0.5	3.8	302	75	75	80.0
31	Winchester	0.5	3.5	293	75	82	79.9
32	West of England	0.3	3.8	303	78	73	79.8
=33	East Anglia	0.8	4.0	359	66	58	79.7
=33	Huddersfield	0.3	3.0	324		93	79.7
=35	Plymouth	0.5	3.5	291	76	76	79.2
=35	Leeds Trinity		3.5	283	81	90	79.2
37	Edge Hill	0.1	4.0	289	75	84	79.1
38	Sunderland	0.3	3.0	330	79	85	79.0
39	Sheffield Hallam	0.4	3.5	314	74	80	78.9
=40	Newport	0.0		277	83	80	78.2
=40	Bath Spa	0.2	4.0	299	76	68	78.2
42	Worcester		4.0	307	77	70	78.1
43	Hertfordshire	0.2	3.0	308	81	81	78.0

44	Bishop Grosseteste	0.1	3.5	268	79	85	77.7
45	Aberystwyth			260	86	68	77.6
46	Ulster	0.5		267	84	52	77.0
47	Goldsmiths College	0.5	3.0	275	78	77	76.9
=48	Chester	0.2	3.8	285	74	75	76.8
=48	Hull	0.4	3.3	290	74	82	76.8
=48	Roehampton	0.4	3.5	270	74	77	76.8
=51	Northampton	0.3	3.5	259	81	67	76.7
=51	Central Lancashire	0.1		297	81	70	76.7
53	Kingston	0.3	3.0	286	81	72	76.1
54	Southampton Solent			266	88	51	75.6
55	York St John	0.0	3.0	284	80	82	75.3
56	Marjon, Plymouth	0.1	3.3	261	77	83	74.9
57	Cardiff Metropolitan	0.0		274	80	72	74.7
58	Leeds Metropolitan	0.2	3.0	278	79	71	74.4
59	University College Birmingham		4.0	220	77	68	74.0
60	Trinity St David			244	81	62	72.7
61	Middlesex		3.0	237	76	84	71.9
=62	Nottingham Trent		3.0	292	73	71	71.0
=62	Greenwich	0.2	3.3	252	71	69	71.0
64	Bedfordshire		2.7	254	77	80	70.7
65	De Montfort			278	81	42	70.6
66	Newman	0.3	3.0	251	72	69	70.3
67	Liverpool John Moores	0.2	3.0	278	72	63	70.0
68	Glyndŵr	0.1		204	78	70	69.8
69	Teesside			295	77	37	68.3
70	Cumbria	0.1	3.0	281	65	77	68.2
71	East London	0.4	3.0	196	77	42	66.9
72	Portsmouth		3.0	280		35	63.9
73	Anglia Ruskin		2.0	258	63	83	61.6
74	Glamorgan	0.2		252	73	18	61.4

» Graduate Teacher Training Registry (GTTR): **www.gttr.ac.uk**
» Get into Teaching: **www.education.gov.uk/get-into-teaching**

Electrical and Electronic Engineering

Electrical and electronic courses used to be the best recruiters of any branch of engineering until a decline set in for much of the last decade. But applications have recovered strongly over the past three years and the decline of nearly 4 per cent in 2012 was much less than the average for all subjects, leaving electrical and electronic courses within a few hundred of the total for civil engineering.

Some natural applicants have been diverted into subjects such as computer games design, but there is renewed confidence in the more general courses as well. Most of the top courses demand maths and physics at A level, or the equivalent.

Cambridge has a big lead in electrical and electronic engineering. It has by far the best

Electrical and Electronic Engineering cont

research grades and a lead of nearly 90 points on entry standards. Southampton is once again the nearest challenger since Surrey's slide from second to eighth place. Newcastle and Sussex, neither of which make the top ten, share top place for graduate destinations, with among the few 100 per cent employment records in any subject this year. The most satisfied students are at third-placed Manchester.

Glasgow has widened its lead over Edinburgh as the top university in Scotland, while Bangor remains clear of Cardiff in Wales. Huddersfield is the leading post-1992 institution, but does not make the top 30 in a subject where old universities predominate.

Employment rates have improved a little since last year's *Guide*. More than half of the top 30 saw at least 80 per cent of leavers go straight into graduate jobs or further training, and the proportion dropped below 50 per cent at only four universities in the table.

About half of the students – more in electrical engineering – come with qualifications other than A levels. Yet it is electrical engineering which has the higher proportion of firsts and 2:1s. Two thirds of the graduates in both subjects go straight into graduate jobs or continue their studies, while the 12 per cent unemployment rate is lower than in last year's *Guide*. For those who do find graduate work, the average starting salary of more than £23,000 is in the top 15 of all subjects. But there has been a £3,000 drop in the average for lower-level jobs.

Employed in graduate job:	50%	Employed in non-graduate job and studying:	2%
Employed in graduate job and studying:	4%	Employed in non-graduate job:	18%
Studying:	14%	Unemployed:	12%
Average starting graduate salary:	£23,233	Average starting non-graduate salary:	£15,205

Electrical and Electronic Engineering	Research quality	Entry standards	Student satisfaction %	Graduate prospects %	Overall rating
1 Cambridge	1.8	615	84	94	100.0
2 Southampton	1.2	493	84	94	90.2
3 Manchester	1.2	378	94	82	89.4
4 Imperial College	1.2	539	80	80	86.7
5 Sheffield	1.0	418	86	89	86.4
6 University College London	1.1	446	78	94	85.1
7 Loughborough	0.9	368	88	91	85.0
8 Surrey	1.3	398	78	90	84.6
9 Glasgow	1.1	447	83	79	84.2
10 York	0.8	397	91	79	83.8
11 Newcastle	0.9	346	83	100	83.6
=12 Bristol	0.9	465	81	86	83.4
=12 Bath	1.1	403	82	83	83.4
14 Edinburgh	0.9	485	82	74	82.0
15 Sussex	0.8	287	85	100	81.9
16 Strathclyde	0.8	455	81	78	80.9
17 Essex	1.0	345	84	74	79.5
18 Kent	0.7	277	90	81	79.1

19	Leeds	1.4	323	78	71	78.7
20	Exeter	0.8	437	81	73	78.6
=21	Nottingham	0.9	377	77	86	78.5
=21	Bangor	1.3	241		80	78.5
23	Aston	0.6	354	90	68	78.0
24	Heriot-Watt	0.8	368	79	80	76.9
25	Cardiff	0.7	405	80	69	76.2
=26	Birmingham	0.8	332	81	73	76.0
=26	Queen's, Belfast	1.0	383	72	79	76.0
28	Lancaster	0.8	379	77	78	75.8
29	Liverpool	0.9	350	77	68	74.0
30	Hull	0.4	297	84	75	72.7
31	Reading	0.5	318	79	78	72.6
32	Huddersfield	0.5	323	81	69	71.7
33	Swansea	0.5	338	76	76	71.3
34	Brunel	0.6	328	84	52	70.8
35	West of England	0.8	308	74	69	70.0
36	Robert Gordon	0.3	303	80	74	69.9
37	Salford	1.0	254	79	56	69.8
38	Queen Mary, London	0.8	321	75	60	69.7
39	Staffordshire	0.6	247	73	84	69.0
40	City	0.7	316	77	57	68.7
41	Hertfordshire	0.8	268	81	48	68.2
42	Portsmouth	0.4	245	81	70	68.1
43	Aberdeen	1.0		70	62	67.6
44	Plymouth	0.3	272	75	77	67.2
45	Northumbria	0.6	271	72	71	66.7
46	Glamorgan	0.6		72	70	66.3
47	London South Bank	0.7	232	80	48	66.0
48	Coventry	0.6	251	74	66	65.9
49	Bradford	0.1	247	78	73	65.0
50	Sheffield Hallam	0.5	250	77	57	64.7
=51	Liverpool John Moores	1.0	243	67	57	63.8
=51	Derby		287	79	61	63.8
53	De Montfort	0.5	267	73	59	63.4
54	Central Lancashire	0.3	281	76	51	62.5
55	Greenwich		268	79	53	61.5
56	Westminster	0.2	272	76	52	60.8
57	Manchester Metropolitan	0.4	243	72	55	60.2
58	Southampton Solent		227	75	63	59.9
59	Teesside		279	77	42	58.4
60	Ulster		237	70	65	57.9
61	Birmingham City		248	73	51	56.9
62	Bolton		241	65	42	50.7

» Institute of Electrical and Electronics Engineers, UK section: **http://ieee-ukri.org**

» Institution of Engineering and Technology: **www.theiet.org**

English

Applications for English were down by about the average for all subjects in March 2012, but it remained among the top ten choices for a degree. The subject's popularity has hardly been dented by the fact that it is not in the top 50 for starting salaries and barely any higher for overall employment levels. The latest dip in the demand for places follow a run of increases and there were still almost six applications for every place in 2011. High entry grades reflect this: eight universities average more than 500 points and only a handful drop below 250.

Oxford remains top in English for the third year in a row, following a series of changes of leadership in the previous decade. It has the highest entry grades, but Cambridge has more satisfied students and could not be closer overall. Chichester, down in equal-59th place, actually recorded the best scores in the 2011 National Student Survey (NSS), having been close to this achievement in 2010. Fifth-placed York produced the best results in the 2008 Research Assessment Exercise, when three quarters of its work was judged to be world-leading or internationally excellent.

Durham, the leader in 2009, is in third this year and has the best employment score. Glasgow displaces St Andrews as the top university in Scotland, while Cardiff has the same status in Wales. Leeds Trinity University College does well to finish in the top 40 for the second successive year, while Buckingham might have reached the top 30 if it had been able to enter the RAE. De Montfort is still the top post-1992 university, although it has lost its place in the top 30 after a poor year for graduate destinations. No university in the table saw eight out of ten graduates go straight into graduate-level work or further study, but ten of the 103 institutions did not manage even four out of ten.

Almost a third of English graduates continue their studies – more than go into graduate-level jobs alone. Unemployment is lower than average for all subjects, but approaching four out of ten graduates start out in lower-level jobs. However, English has produced consistently good scores in the National Student Survey. In the results published in 2011, only one university in the table failed to satisfy at least 70 per cent of the final-year undergraduates.

Employed in graduate job:	29%	Employed in non-graduate job and studying:	5%
Employed in graduate job and studying:	3%	Employed in non-graduate job:	33%
Studying:	22%	Unemployed:	8%
Average starting graduate salary:	£18,486	Average starting non-graduate salary:	£14,230

English	Research quality	Entry standards	Student satisfaction %	Graduate prospects %	Overall rating
1 Oxford	1.5	550	88	76	100.0
2 Cambridge	1.5	542	89	72	99.9
3 Durham	1.2	531	87	79	98.5
4 University College London	1.3	512	88	71	96.8
5 York	1.7	520	81	73	95.6
6 Exeter	1.6	498	84	69	95.3
7 Warwick	1.4	503	83	74	94.8
8 Leeds	1.4	460	84	70	92.8
9 Queen Mary, London	1.5	425	84	69	92.6

10	Glasgow	1.4	460	87	55	91.5
11	Nottingham	1.4	460	80	70	90.6
12	St Andrews	1.4	504	80	63	90.2
13	Loughborough	0.7	419	89	68	90.0
14	Southampton	1.2	466	84	63	89.9
15	Lancaster	1.0	440	84	68	89.7
16	Cardiff	1.3	485	82	60	89.5
17	Newcastle	1.2	464	81	67	89.2
18	Bristol	1.1	509	79	66	88.9
19	Leicester	0.9	428	85	66	88.4
20	Sussex	1.0	412	85	65	88.1
21	Liverpool	1.3	429	84	57	88.0
22	Aberdeen	1.3	379	87	54	87.4
23	Edinburgh	1.5	470	79	54	87.1
24	Kent	1.3	390	83	62	87.0
25	Sheffield	1.2	464	79	62	86.3
26	East Anglia	1.1	427	84	55	85.9
=27	Hull	0.8	366	85	62	84.2
=27	Royal Holloway	1.3	443	74	65	84.2
29	Reading	1.2	394	82	52	83.6
30	Dundee	0.7	384	86	56	83.3
31	King's College London	1.0	498	72	65	83.0
32	Birmingham	1.1	435	74	63	82.8
33	Buckingham		267	89	77	82.6
34	Stirling	0.8	380	81	59	82.0
35	Keele	0.7	346	82	62	81.8
36	De Montfort	1.4	307	86	39	81.5
37	Manchester	1.4	447	72	55	81.1
38	Queen's, Belfast	1.4	395	79	44	81.0
39	Chester	0.3	309	89	55	80.6
40	Leeds Trinity	0.4	288	84	70	80.4
41	Strathclyde	0.8	417	76	61	80.3
42	Edinburgh Napier	0.3	314	88		80.2
43	Aberystwyth	0.6	342	84	53	79.5
44	Portsmouth	0.8	321	82	52	78.6
45	Lincoln		325	86	60	78.2
46	Roehampton	0.6	285	81	62	77.8
47	Goldsmiths College	1.0	391	76	50	77.7
48	Staffordshire	0.4	271	85	58	77.5
49	Essex	0.8	340	80	48	76.9
50	Sunderland	0.6	280	85	46	76.7
51	Swansea	0.8	357	76	53	76.6
52	Glamorgan	0.7	293	83	46	76.5
53	Central Lancashire	0.2	309	83	57	76.2
54	Edge Hill	0.2	270	83	60	76.0
=55	Huddersfield	0.3	344	80	56	75.9
=55	Brunel	0.8	345	76	53	75.9

English cont	Research quality	Entry standards	Student satisfaction %	Graduate prospects %	Overall rating
57 Gloucestershire	0.5	320	82	47	75.5
58 Anglia Ruskin	0.9	249	81	47	75.3
=59 Coventry	0.2	276	82	57	75.2
=59 Chichester	0.3	290	90	36	75.2
61 Worcester	0.4	317	81	52	75.1
62 Bedfordshire	0.7	214	83	51	74.9
63 Cumbria	0.1	279		66	74.8
64 Oxford Brookes	0.5	350	77	51	74.7
=65 Teesside		307	84	52	74.6
=65 Birmingham City	0.3	296	74	70	74.6
67 Bath Spa	0.4	316	81	48	74.3
=68 Sheffield Hallam	0.4	341	82	41	74.0
=68 Newman		265	82	59	74.0
70 Plymouth	0.5	308	76	56	73.7
71 Nottingham Trent	0.8	325	77	43	73.5
72 St Mary's College	0.4	276	82	45	73.4
=73 Hertfordshire	0.7	315	79	42	73.3
=73 Northampton	0.2	248	86	47	73.3
75 Manchester Metropolitan	0.7	309	77	45	73.1
76 Northumbria	0.4	341	78	48	73.0
77 Kingston	0.6	307	78	45	72.9
78 West of England	0.4	308	81	43	72.8
79 Glyndŵr		251		62	72.6
80 Winchester		320	81	47	72.2
81 Middlesex	0.5	238	77	56	72.1
=82 Brighton	0.5	339	76	46	72.0
=82 Bishop Grosseteste	0.0	250		64	72.0
84 Derby		262	84	46	71.8
=85 Salford	0.6	269	78	46	71.7
=85 Canterbury Christ Church	0.2	275	79	53	71.7
87 Bangor	0.8	307	75	41	71.0
88 Ulster	0.5	276	82	34	70.9
=89 Aston	0.3	380	74	43	70.8
=89 Greenwich	0.3	251	82	43	70.8
91 York St John	0.1	293	83	38	70.5
92 Trinity St David	0.2	250	73	63	69.7
93 Liverpool John Moores	0.4	301	83	24	69.5
94 Cardiff Metropolitan		289	84	30	68.5
95 Falmouth		274	77	47	68.2
96 Marjon, Plymouth	0.0	276	81	37	68.0
97 Westminster	0.2	282	70	56	67.4
98 East London		238	76	48	66.5
99 Leeds Metropolitan		274	74	43	65.4

100	London Metropolitan		225	68	58	63.6
101	Newport		240		36	62.5
102	Bolton	0.1	242		32	61.7
103	Bradford	0.4	234	72	27	60.9

» Poetry Society: **www.poetrysociety.org.uk**
» Royal Society of Literature: **www.rslit.org**
» Society of Authors: **www.societyofauthors.org**
» Society for Editors and Proofreaders: **www.sfep.org.uk**
» Teaching English as a Foreign Language: **www.eflweb.com**

Food Science

The lead enjoyed by King's College London at the head of the food science table has narrowed considerably since last year, with Leeds taking over from Surrey as the nearest challenger. King's had the best grades in the 2008 Research Assessment Exercise, when two thirds of its submission in nutritional sciences was considered world-leading or internationally excellent. But a dip in student satisfaction has allowed five universities to come closer to King's than any did last year. Harper Adams University College, the leading post-1992 institution, has the top score for employment, but is restricted to seventh place by relatively low research grades and entry standards. The 94 per cent of Harper Adams graduates going straight into graduate-level jobs or further study is five percentage points higher than the rate at any university. The most satisfied students are at Leeds Metropolitan, ranked 16th overall.

The majority of the 33 institutions in the ranking are new universities, although higher entry standards and research grades ensure that their older counterparts fill the top six places. Robert Gordon has overtaken Heriot-Watt as the top university in Scotland, while Queen's, Belfast, has passed Ulster in Northern Ireland. Cardiff Metropolitan is the only university in Wales to qualify for the food science table.

Entry standards have been rising – only two universities in this year's ranking average less than 250 points – but there were still only four applications per place in 2011. Almost a third of entrants to food science courses arrive with alternative qualifications to A levels. The subjects were in the doldrums in the latter part of the last decade, but have enjoyed big increases in each of the last three years. An 18 per cent rise in 2011 was among the biggest in any subject and the move to higher fees did not prevent another big rise in 2012.

Career prospects are good, with more than half of those completing courses going straight into graduate-level jobs and only 8 per cent without work six months after graduation. Food science is mid-way in the graduate salaries league, with an average starting rate of more than £20,300.

Employed in graduate job:	49%	Employed in non-graduate job and studying:	2%
Employed in graduate job and studying:	3%	Employed in non-graduate job:	26%
Studying:	11%	Unemployed:	8%
Average starting graduate salary:	£20,336	Average starting non-graduate salary:	£15,269

Food Science

Food Science	Research quality	Entry standards	Student satisfaction %	Graduate prospects %	Overall rating
1 King's College London	1.3	452	74	80	100.0
2 Leeds	1.0	409	80	82	98.8
3 Nottingham	0.9	373	82	81	97.3
4 Surrey	1.0	392	76	85	96.2
5 Reading	0.7	353	84	80	94.4
6 Newcastle	0.6	360	84	79	94.2
7 Harper Adams	0.3	300	85	94	91.5
8 Plymouth	0.1	359	81	89	90.1
9 Coventry		338	84	87	89.2
10 Robert Gordon		423	79	78	88.8
11 Queen's, Belfast	0.4	365	80	69	87.9
12 Ulster	0.4	318	84	63	86.5
13 Heriot-Watt	0.5			69	86.4
14 Northumbria	0.3	338	81	65	85.7
15 Chester	0.2	361	72	83	83.4
16 Leeds Metropolitan		288	86	67	83.1
17 Sheffield Hallam		295	85	64	82.3
18 Greenwich	0.4	289	77	63	80.9
19 Oxford Brookes		356	81	49	80.4
20 Central Lancashire		295	80	68	80.3
21 Huddersfield		240	81	70	78.4
22 Lincoln	0.2	286	77		77.9
23 Brighton	0.6		78	33	76.5
24 Bournemouth		309	74	61	76.1
=25 St Mary's College		277	82	46	75.8
=25 Queen Margaret Edinburgh		327	72	62	75.8
27 Manchester Metropolitan	0.3	287	70	60	74.5
28 Cardiff Metropolitan	0.3	266	74	55	74.4
29 Liverpool John Moores	0.4	264	68	68	74.3
30 Roehampton		238	80	50	73.1
31 Bath Spa		295	75	48	73.0
32 London Metropolitan	0.1		70	67	72.4
33 University College Birmingham		251	79	42	71.9

» Institute of Food Science and Technology: **www.ifst.org**
» Society of Food Hygiene and Technology: **www.sofht.co.uk**

French

Until this year, French at degree level had avoided the decline in the teaching of modern languages seen in secondary schools, but the arrival of higher fees coincided with a 14 per cent drop in applications. French is still in a better position than other European (or world) languages but, with the decline continuing at A level, there is not a lot of leeway for many departments. Only 688 students started degrees in French in 2011, with another 2,700 taking broader modern language courses.

Nevertheless, entry to the top courses in particular remains competitive and there were nearly six applications to the place in 2011. Almost half of the 49 universities in the table averaged more than 400 points and none had an average of less than 250 points. Perhaps not surprisingly, nine out of ten undergraduates enter with A levels or their equivalents.

Oxford retains the slim lead over Cambridge that it established three years ago, thanks to the best performance in the 2008 Research Assessment Exercise, when 30 per cent of its submission was rated world-leading. Cambridge is ahead on all the other indicators and has the highest entry grades in the table, as well as sharing the best employment score. East Anglia, in 27th place, has the other top employment score, while Leicester, in 15th, boasts the most satisfied students in the ranking.

Southampton takes third place, but Newcastle has made the most progress in the upper reaches of the table, rising ten places to share eighth place. St Andrews remains the top university in Scotland, while Cardiff has little competition in Wales. Northumbria has overtaken Portsmouth to become the leading post-1992 university and the only one in the top 30.

French is in the top 20 subjects for employment, with seven out of ten graduates going on to graduate jobs or further study within six months. The 6 per cent unemployment rate is among the best for any subject. For the first time in recent years, not a single university dipped below the 50 per cent success mark for graduate destinations. Graduate starting salaries had improved a little in the latest survey, but remain below the average for all subjects.

Employed in graduate job:	43%	Employed in non-graduate job and studying:	3%
Employed in graduate job and studying:	4%	Employed in non-graduate job:	23%
Studying:	22%	Unemployed:	6%
Average starting graduate salary:	£20,178	Average starting non-graduate salary:	£15,494

French

	Research quality	Entry standards	Student satisfaction %	Graduate prospects %	Overall rating
1 Oxford	1.3	550	88	78	100.0
2 Cambridge	1.0	559	91	81	99.6
3 Southampton	1.2	464	90	67	92.9
4 Durham	0.8	516	84	80	92.7
5 St Andrews	0.8	501	84	80	91.9
6 Warwick	1.1	475	88	68	91.8
7 Glasgow	0.8	479	84	78	90.1
=8 Newcastle	0.8	437	87	75	89.2
=8 Bath	0.7	460	84	80	89.2
10 King's College London	1.2	461	77	74	89.0
11 Sheffield	1.0	423	80	79	88.9
12 University College London	0.8	493	81	74	88.3
13 Leeds	0.9	435	84	70	87.2

French cont

	Research quality	Entry standards	Student satisfaction %	Graduate prospects %	Overall rating
14 Exeter	0.8	479	83	66	86.5
15 Leicester	0.3	398	93	75	85.3
16 Cardiff	0.8	434	85	65	85.0
17 Birmingham	0.7	409	89	65	84.6
18 Nottingham	1.0	419	77	69	83.6
19 Bristol	0.5	447	80	76	83.4
20 Queen's, Belfast	0.6	399	82	72	83.1
21 Edinburgh	0.8	487	74	70	82.9
=22 Hull	0.8	322	83	72	82.1
=22 Aston	0.3	398	84	77	82.1
24 Liverpool	0.7	409	81	67	81.9
25 Heriot-Watt	0.5	400	80	74	81.4
26 Queen Mary, London	0.8	386	79	68	81.3
27 East Anglia		375	86	81	80.8
28 Northumbria		320	91	78	79.8
29 Manchester	0.8	409	77	62	79.6
30 Royal Holloway	0.8	396	80	60	79.5
31 Reading	0.9	368	82	55	79.1
32 Aberdeen	1.0	375	80	51	78.0
33 Stirling	0.4	357	82	66	77.1
34 Portsmouth	0.8	271	82		76.9
35 Kent	0.8	345	83	51	76.7
36 York		460	82	65	76.4
37 Chester		289	83	79	75.1
38 Lancaster	0.5	389	67	74	74.2
=39 Swansea	0.5	337	80	58	73.5
=39 Salford	0.4	349	78		73.5
41 Aberystwyth		341	87	61	73.2
42 Nottingham Trent	0.3	296	83	59	72.2
=43 Ulster	0.4	283	78	64	71.5
=43 Strathclyde		425	72	68	71.5
45 Bangor		295	85	62	71.2
46 Oxford Brookes	0.5	316	77	51	69.5
47 Sussex		359	77	61	69.0
48 Manchester Metropolitan	0.2	305	78	54	67.7
49 Westminster	0.3	283	63	59	61.7

» Alliance Française des Londres: **www.alliancefrancaise.org.uk**
» Chartered Institute of Linguists: **www.iol.org.uk**
» National Centre for Languages (CILT): **www.cilt.org.uk**
» Society for French Studies: **www.sfs.ac.uk**

General Engineering

Cambridge has extended its lead over Oxford in general engineering since last year, with the highest entry standards, by far the best employment record and the top grades in the 2008 Research Assessment Exercise (RAE), when 45 per cent of the university's work was classified as world-leading. For the second year in a row, Greenwich had the best results in the National Student Survey, remaining the leading post-1992 university and moving into the top ten. It is joined there by Nottingham Trent, which did not appear in last year's table, but is now in the top three for graduate employment. Imperial College is another new entry, joining in third place. Cardiff, in fourth place, remains the top university in Wales, while Strathclyde has overtaken Aberdeen to become the leader in Scotland.

As in the specialist branches of engineering, there is an enormous spread of entry grades, from more than 600 points at Cambridge to less than 250 at the foot of the table. Applications were down 3 per cent in March 2012 – less than average for all subjects and a better outcome than in some other branches of engineering. However, there were only four applications per place in 2011, making admissions the least competitive in the engineering disciplines.

Nationally, the subject is in the top eight for employment and the top four for starting salaries in graduate jobs, with an average of more than £26,500. Three quarters of all those completing a degree go straight into graduate jobs or further study. It is even in the top three for starting salaries in lower-level jobs. Like other engineering degrees, most of the general courses will require both maths and physics at A level, with further maths and design technology welcome additions.

Employed in graduate job:	54%	Employed in non-graduate job and studying:	1%
Employed in graduate job and studying:	6%	Employed in non-graduate job:	14%
Studying:	15%	Unemployed:	9%
Average starting graduate salary:	£26,542	Average starting non-graduate salary:	£17,781

General Engineering	Research quality	Entry standards	Student satisfaction %	Graduate prospects %	Overall rating
1 Cambridge	1.8	615	84	94	100.0
2 Oxford	1.4	588		79	92.5
3 Imperial College	1.3	509	78		87.0
4 Cardiff	1.1	374	83	88	86.0
5 Nottingham	1.3	454	78		85.4
6 Exeter	0.8	437	85	73	83.0
7 Greenwich	0.2		89	82	82.9
8 Warwick	1.1	484	76	68	81.2
9 Nottingham Trent	0.9		76	87	80.9
10 Swansea	1.1	286	78	80	79.2
11 Durham	0.8	523	76	64	78.6
12 Lancaster	0.7	418	77		77.2
13 Leicester	0.8	357	76	77	76.9
14 Strathclyde	0.9		78	61	75.5

	Research quality	Entry standards	Student satisfaction %	Graduate prospects %	Overall rating
15 Queen Mary, London	0.7	375	79	63	75.3
16 Aberdeen	1.0	386	72		74.4
17 Central Lancashire	0.3	323	80	76	74.2
18 Aston	0.6	338	78		73.7
19 Bournemouth	0.5	300		75	71.9
20 Edinburgh Napier	0.4	298	80	61	71.3
21 West of England	0.8	294	73	62	70.2
22 Liverpool John Moores	1.0	261	71		69.9
23 Bradford	0.5	291	73		67.2
24 Sheffield Hallam	0.5	258	74	58	66.4
25 Glamorgan	0.7		67	63	65.7
26 Glasgow Caledonian	0.2	295	72	57	63.9
27 De Montfort	0.4	201	72		62.1
28 Ulster	-	256	68	69	61.4
29 London South Bank	0.7	240	73	27	61.2
30 Birmingham City		232	73	50	59.7

» Engineering Council: **www.engc.org.uk**
» EngineeringUK: **www.engineeringuk.com**
» Institution of Engineering and Technology: **www.theiet.org**

Geography and Environmental Sciences

Geography and environmental sciences have been benefiting from growing interest in "green" issues among prospective students. Both fared better than the national average when higher fees arrived in 2012, with environmental science even enjoying increased applications. Physical geography was down by 5 per cent and human and social geography by only by 3 per cent in the spring of 2012, although physical remained the bigger draw. There was little between them in terms of competition for places.

Cambridge has maintained its lead over Oxford in this year's ranking, with the highest entry standards and one of the best research scores. The top four all had 30 per cent of their research rated as world-leading in the 2008 assessments. Chester, at equal 33, has become the leading post-1992 university, and has the most satisfied students, while the fifth-placed London School of Economics has by far the best of generally mediocre set of employment scores. Only nine of the 72 universities saw 70 per cent or more of leavers go straight into graduate jobs or further study and the proportion dropped below 40 per cent at five of them.

Fluctuating fortunes in the graduate employment market are the main factor behind some big changes of position in the table. Sheffield has jumped eight places to sixth, for example, while St Andrews has dropped from eighth to 25th place. Glasgow is now the leader in Scotland, a fraction of a point ahead of Edinburgh. Similarly in Wales, Cardiff is less than a point ahead of Aberystwyth.

Entry scores have risen in this year's table. Even after the introduction of A* grades, only three universities average more than 500 points, but another 18 (compared with 13 last year) top 400 points. The subjects are in the bottom half of the employment and salaries tables. In the latest survey, a third of graduates were in low-level jobs six months after completing their courses, although the 8 per cent unemployment rate was better than average for all subjects.

Employed in graduate job:	31%	Employed in non-graduate job and studying:	4%
Employed in graduate job and studying:	4%	Employed in non-graduate job:	30%
Studying:	23%	Unemployed:	8%
Average starting graduate salary:	£20,215	Average starting non-graduate salary:	£14,341

Geography and Environmental Sciences	Research quality	Entry standards	Student satisfaction %	Graduate prospects %	Overall rating
1 Cambridge	1.3	563	89	76	100.0
2 Oxford	1.3	533	85	76	96.7
3 Durham	1.3	497	82	81	95.1
4 Bristol	1.3	498	86	68	94.2
5 London School of Economics	1.1	471	78	91	92.4
6 Sheffield	1.1	438	86	70	91.7
7 Lancaster	1.0	419	85	71	89.9
8 Nottingham	1.0	437	83	73	89.5
9 East Anglia	1.2	409	84	66	88.9
10 Glasgow	0.7	445	87	67	88.1
11 Edinburgh	1.0	461	80	72	87.9
12 University College London	1.2	491	76	73	87.8
13 Queen Mary, London	1.3	375	86	58	87.6
14 Royal Holloway	1.1	378	83	69	86.8
15 Leeds	1.2	412	81	64	86.6
=16 Cardiff	1.1	393	83	62	86.5
=16 Exeter	1.0	427	83	63	86.5
18 Dundee	0.9	373	86	62	86.0
19 Aberystwyth	1.1	345	88	55	85.8
=20 King's College London	1.1	409	81	63	85.5
=20 Loughborough	0.7	381	89	58	85.5
22 Sussex	1.0	369	84	64	85.2
23 Reading	1.1	378	82	61	85.0
24 Birmingham	0.9	427	80	67	84.6
25 St Andrews	1.0	502	75	62	84.4
26 Newcastle	0.8	392	83	64	83.9
27 Manchester	1.0	411	78	64	83.2
28 Southampton	1.0	430	76	61	82.4
29 Hull	0.9	325	85	56	82.1
30 Leicester	0.6	407	82	60	81.8
31 Aberdeen	0.7	376	82	60	81.7
32 York	0.8	384	81	58	81.3
=33 Swansea	0.9	345	81	57	81.0

Geography and Environmental Sciences cont

	Research quality	Entry standards	Student satisfaction %	Graduate prospects %	Overall rating
=33 Chester	0.1	292	92	63	81.0
35 Keele		344	88	62	79.9
36 Liverpool	0.8	382	78	55	78.8
37 Strathclyde	0.2	420	82	54	78.2
38 Sheffield Hallam	0.9	325	78	52	77.1
39 West of England	0.2	306	86	54	77.0
40 Queen's, Belfast	0.7	349	79	50	76.9
41 Plymouth	0.6	297	79	59	76.8
42 Northumbria		323	85	56	76.0
43 Stirling	0.5	349	75	64	75.7
44 Portsmouth	0.4	306	85	43	75.4
45 Bournemouth	0.7	269		53	74.6
46 Staffordshire		232	87	55	73.9
47 Ulster	0.5	269	81	50	73.8
48 Coventry	0.2	298	80	58	73.6
49 Edge Hill	0.1	260	89	41	73.3
50 Manchester Metropolitan	0.5	286	79	50	73.1
51 Northampton	0.2	248	84	49	73.0
=52 Greenwich		233		68	72.8
=52 Central Lancashire		276	86	46	72.8
=52 Gloucestershire	0.2	296	85	42	72.8
55 Sunderland	0.1	271		64	72.6
56 Bradford	0.9	230		41	71.8
57 Salford	0.4	242	83	41	71.6
58 Hertfordshire		303	75	63	70.7
59 Brighton	0.4	277	80	37	69.7
=60 Bangor		303	77	53	69.5
=60 Kingston	0.4	250	73	58	69.5
62 Oxford Brookes		317	77	49	69.1
63 Glamorgan		266	81	44	68.9
=64 Nottingham Trent	0.1	276		51	68.5
=64 Bath Spa	0.2	261	79	45	68.5
66 Liverpool John Moores		275	81	35	67.2
67 Cumbria		282	75	42	64.8
68 Worcester	0.1	284		34	64.3
69 Canterbury Christ Church		257	72	40	62.0
70 Derby		250	71	41	61.2
71 Leeds Metropolitan		272		25	60.4
72 Southampton Solent		207		22	56.0

» British Cartographic Society: **www.cartography.org.uk**

» Royal Geographical Society (with the Institute of British Geographers): **www.rgs.org**

» Royal Scottish Geographical Society: **www.rsgs.org**

Geology

Starting salaries for graduate geologists have shot up by more than £3,500 since last year's *Guide*, propelling the subject into the top ten from outside the top 20, where it has generally been in the past. It is hard to believe that this news has already filtered through to sixth-formers, but geology has enjoyed a healthy increase in applications in 2012, while higher fees have depressed the demand for places in other subjects. The rise of nearly 9 per cent by March took the number of applications well past the final total in any previous year.

Cambridge remains well clear of Oxford in geology, with the best performance in the 2008 Research Assessment Exercise and has the highest entry standards in the table. Imperial College, in third place, again has clearly the best employment score. Geologists are generally satisfied with their courses, if the National Student Survey of 2011 is any guide – none more so than at Leicester, which produced the top score for the fifth year in a row. In fact, satisfaction levels were above 70 per cent for the subject across the board and only dropped below 75 per cent at one university.

All but six of the 28 institutions in this year's ranking are pre-1992 universities. Plymouth is again the highest-placed of the newer foundations, while Cardiff is the leading university in Wales, and St Andrews is the clear leader in Scotland, despite dropping five places to eighth. Manchester has made the most progress this year, breaking into the top ten after a seven-place rise.

Outside the top three, there is less contrast in entry standards in geology than in many other subjects. The average is above 250 points at all but one university in the ranking, and only seven average less than 300. Some of the leading universities expect candidates to have two, or even three, scientific or mathematical subjects at A level. Relatively few places are filled in Clearing.

Geology's mid-table position for employment prospects does not match its performance on salaries. But two thirds of geologists go on to graduate jobs or further study within six months of graduation, and the unemployment level is only just above the average for all subjects, at 10 per cent.

Employed in graduate job:	32%	Employed in non-graduate job and studying:	3%
Employed in graduate job and studying:	3%	Employed in non-graduate job:	23%
Studying:	30%	Unemployed:	10%
Average starting graduate salary:	£24,766	Average starting non-graduate salary:	£14,437

Geology	Research quality	Entry standards	Student satisfaction %	Graduate prospects %	Overall rating
1 Cambridge	1.7	630	87	83	100.0
2 Oxford	1.6	570	85	83	96.0
3 Imperial College	1.2	522	87	88	93.5
4 Durham	1.0	439	84	85	87.2
5 Leicester	0.9	417	94	64	86.3
6 Southampton	1.1	420	87	70	85.9
7 Manchester	1.1	390	89	65	85.1
8 St Andrews	1.0	454	86	67	85.0

Geology cont	Research quality	Entry standards	Student satisfaction %	Graduate prospects %	Overall rating
9 Bristol	1.3	469	78	71	83.6
10 Royal Holloway	1.1	354	85	70	82.8
11 Glasgow	0.7	404	89	70	82.4
12 Edinburgh	1.0	483	79	69	81.9
=13 East Anglia	1.2	399	81	64	81.7
=13 Leeds	1.0	401	82	70	81.7
15 Exeter	0.5	404	85	81	80.8
16 Birmingham	1.0	393	84	61	80.2
17 Aberdeen	0.8	383	77	83	79.2
18 University College London	1.3	462	72	61	78.7
19 Cardiff	1.0	398	80	57	77.8
20 Liverpool	1.1	394	76	66	77.7
21 Plymouth	0.6	290	84	63	75.2
22 Bangor	0.8	276	81	64	74.3
23 Keele		305	86	52	68.6
24 Brighton	0.4	260	78	56	66.8
25 Aberystwyth		299	82	50	65.6
26 Portsmouth	0.6	260	77	41	64.5
27 Derby		252	78	41	59.9
28 Kingston		248	78	41	59.7

» Geological Society: **www.geolsoc.org.uk**

German

The number of universities in the German ranking has stabilised after 16 dropped out in two years, reflecting a worldwide decline in the language that has been worrying the German government, as well as academic linguists. A small increase in applications in 2011 brought hope that a corner had been turned, but this year has seen a 22 per cent decline that is bound to heighten anxieties about the subject at degree level. Fewer than 300 students began degrees in German in 2011, although many more will have included the language in combination with others.

Cambridge makes it seven years in a row as the leader in German. Indeed, the top two are the same as last year, but Durham has captured third place for the first time, overtaking Southampton, which had the best results in the 2008 Research Assessment Exercise (RAE). Cambridge has the highest entry standards and shared the best score for student satisfaction with sixth-placed Warwick.

Satisfaction levels remained generally high in the 2011 National Student Survey, when only two universities failed to satisfy at least 75 per cent of final-year undergraduates.

The best employment score was at Bristol, in eighth place, the only university apart from Cambridge to see more than eight out of ten graduates go straight into graduate-level jobs or further study. Fifth-placed St Andrews remains the leading university in Scotland, while

Cardiff is now well clear of Swansea in Wales. Portsmouth is one of just three post-1992 universities left in the ranking and the only one in the top 30.

Despite the recruitment difficulties in German departments, there are still more than five applications for every place. Nine out of ten undergraduates enter with A levels or equivalent qualifications, and entry standards are relatively high, especially at the leading universities. At more than half of the universities in the table, entrants average at least 400 points.

As in other modern languages, career prospects are reasonable: two thirds of leavers go straight into graduate jobs or further study, and the 6 per cent unemployment rate is among the lowest for any subject. German has also moved up the table for starting salaries, which now average more than £21,000. Most universities in the table offer German *ab initio* as part of a languages package, as well as catering for those who took the subject at A level.

Employed in graduate job:	42%	
Employed in graduate job and studying:	6%	
Studying:	20%	
Average starting graduate salary:	£21,032	

Employed in non-graduate job and studying:	3%	
Employed in non-graduate job:	24%	
Unemployed:	6%	
Average starting non-graduate salary:	£15,213	

German	Research quality	Entry standards	Student satisfaction %	Graduate prospects %	Overall rating
1 Cambridge	1.1	559	91	81	100.0
2 Oxford	1.1	535	87	80	96.7
3 Durham	1.0	516	84	80	93.9
4 Southampton	1.2	463	87	72	93.1
5 St Andrews	1.0	511	83	78	92.6
6 Warwick	0.8	469	91	65	89.9
7 Leeds	1.0	419	86	72	89.7
8 Bristol	0.8	444	81	84	89.0
9 Edinburgh	1.0	467	83	66	88.1
10 Glasgow	0.6	490	83	76	87.4
11 Birmingham	0.9	380	88	66	86.8
12 Newcastle	0.9	452	83	66	86.1
=13 University College London	1.1	502	76	68	85.9
=13 Bath	0.7	450	82	75	85.9
15 Exeter	0.9	478	84	60	85.8
16 Nottingham	0.6	390	85	70	83.8
17 King's College London	1.1	460	78	58	83.6
18 Sheffield	0.5	437	78	80	83.5
19 Manchester	1.0	385	81	64	83.1
20 Cardiff	0.8	383	81	67	82.0
21 Heriot-Watt	0.5	400	80	74	81.6
22 Reading	0.5	358	85	65	80.7
23 Aston	0.3	397	80	68	78.2
=24 Queen Mary, London	0.5	377	78	66	77.7
=24 Kent	0.3	337	82	70	77.7
26 Portsmouth	0.8	300	82	57	77.0

	Research quality	Entry standards	Student satisfaction %	Graduate prospects %	Overall rating
27 Swansea	0.7	337	81	54	76.9
28 Aberdeen	0.3	406	80		76.2
29 Lancaster	0.5		71	79	75.9
30 Royal Holloway	1.0	397	77	43	75.6
31 Bangor		278	85	71	75.4
32 Liverpool	0.7		73	62	74.5
33 Hull		300	83	68	74.2
34 East Anglia		343	86	55	73.6
35 Nottingham Trent		296	83	59	71.3
36 Manchester Metropolitan	0.2		78	54	69.6

» Chartered Institute of Linguists: **www.iol.org.uk**
» Goethe-Institut: **www.goethe.de/enindex.htm**
» National Centre for Languages (CILT): **www.cilt.org.uk**

History

History survived the introduction of higher fees with only a small drop in applications, leaving it still close to the top ten subjects as a degree choice. The subject was already among the most competitive at entry, with almost six applications to every place in 2011. Surveys have shown a strong representation of historians among business leaders, celebrities and senior politicians, but the subject is close to the bottom ten for employment prospects and in the bottom half of the table for graduate earnings. More historians are in non-graduate jobs than those categorised as graduate occupations six months after completing a degree. Cambridge has retaken the top place in history that it lost to Durham last year, although the two remain close together. Cambridge has the highest entry standards and shares the best research score with University College London, which has dropped to seventh. In fact, Imperial College's work on the history of science won the top grade in the 2008 Research Assessment Exercise, but history is not an undergraduate subject at Imperial so it does not appear in this table.

The London School of Economics, in fourth place, once again has by far the best employment score, six percentage points ahead of its nearest rival. While the LSE saw 87 per cent of historians go straight into graduate jobs or onto postgraduate courses, the proportion was below 50 per cent at 40 of the 91 universities in the ranking.

Average entry scores at the top six universities are all over 500 points, the equivalent of more than four As at A level, with Cambridge leading the way. Other leading universities' entry standards are closer to the top six than in many other subjects: all the top ten – and another 19 universities further down the ranking – average at least 400 points.

For the second successive year, the most satisfied students are at Derby, which is not among the top 50 universities in the ranking. Satisfaction levels are high at most of the universities in the ranking: only one fails to achieve a 70 per cent approval rating. The old universities' domination of the table has increased since last year, when two post-1992 universities appeared in the top 30. Huddersfield remains the best-placed of its peers, but is restricted to a share of 33rd place this year. St Andrews remains the top university in Scotland, while Cardiff does the same in Wales.

Employed in graduate job:	27%	Employed in non-graduate job and studying:	4%
Employed in graduate job and studying:	3%	Employed in non-graduate job:	32%
Studying:	25%	Unemployed:	9%
Average starting graduate salary:	£19,869	Average starting non-graduate salary:	£14,279

History	Research quality	Entry standards	Student satisfaction %	Graduate prospects %	Overall rating
1 Cambridge	1.5	578	90	79	100.0
2 Durham	1.0	544	92	81	97.1
3 Oxford	1.4	561	86	76	96.1
4 London School of Economics	1.4	509	80	87	92.9
5 St Andrews	1.0	537	86	74	92.0
6 Warwick	1.4	507	83	68	90.5
7 University College London	1.5	475	80	76	90.4
8 King's College London	1.1	511	85	66	89.6
9 Sheffield	1.4	468	85	63	89.0
10 York	1.1	520	84	66	88.5
=11 Southampton	1.3	454	84	63	87.7
=11 Glasgow	1.1	459	89	56	87.7
=11 Exeter	1.0	475	85	68	87.7
14 Sussex	1.2	384	85	70	86.3
15 Bristol	0.9	473	82	73	85.8
16 Kent	1.4	379	86	58	85.7
17 Nottingham	0.8	453	82	75	85.4
18 Leeds	1.0	457	82	68	85.0
=19 Royal Holloway	1.0	420	82	71	84.8
=19 Liverpool	1.4	404	84	55	84.8
21 Lancaster	0.9	424	85	66	84.4
22 East Anglia	1.0	403	88	53	83.8
23 Queen Mary, London	1.2	431	80	61	83.3
24 Hull	1.0	350	90	53	82.4
25 Essex	1.4	351	86	46	82.3
26 Aberdeen	1.2	392	83	54	82.2
27 Leicester	0.9	414	86	51	81.9
28 Cardiff	0.7	443	86	55	81.4
=29 Birmingham	1.0	425	78	63	80.9
=29 Dundee	1.0	365	88	49	80.9
31 Edinburgh	1.1	456	76	59	80.7
32 School of Oriental and African Studies	1.2	419	74	65	80.4
=33 Newcastle	0.7	444	78	67	80.1
=33 Huddersfield	0.6	321	87	67	80.1

History cont

		Research quality	Entry standards	Student satisfaction %	Graduate prospects %	Overall rating
35	Keele	1.0	353	83	56	79.7
36	Reading	0.7	389	83	55	78.7
37	Manchester	1.1	426	73	59	78.3
38	Portsmouth	0.8	325	88	46	77.7
39	Teesside	0.7	293	91	45	77.4
40	Aberystwyth	0.7	320	86	54	77.3
41	Strathclyde	0.5	420	80	60	77.2
42	Oxford Brookes	1.2	342	78	52	76.6
43	Winchester	0.9	314	84	47	76.0
44	Brunel		320	92	55	75.8
45	Queen's, Belfast	0.9	376	81	43	75.5
46	Brighton	1.4	303	83	32	75.2
47	Stirling	0.8	362	81	45	75.0
48	Lincoln	0.4	312	82	62	74.7
49	Chester	0.8	304	82	51	74.5
50	Edge Hill	0.5	242	89	51	74.2
51	Central Lancashire	0.6	284	83	55	73.9
52	Hertfordshire	1.2	343	73	48	73.7
53	Bangor	0.8	290	83	45	73.4
54	Chichester	0.3	282	91	41	73.3
55	West of England	0.5	309	85	47	73.2
56	Swansea	0.8	335	78	48	72.8
57	De Montfort	0.5	286	85	48	72.7
=58	Anglia Ruskin	1.0	238	85	33	71.7
=58	Newport	0.2	259	82	65	71.7
=60	Derby		269	93	40	71.1
=60	Sunderland	0.7	264	83	42	71.1
62	Leeds Trinity	0.4	257	72	76	70.3
63	Bath Spa	0.6	310	82	38	70.0
64	Staffordshire		236	84	59	69.5
65	Northumbria	0.2	338	78	52	69.4
66	Ulster	0.9	259	81	34	69.1
67	Coventry		283	76	69	68.8
68	Sheffield Hallam	0.5	311	79	41	68.7
69	Goldsmiths College	0.5	352	74	46	68.5
=70	Roehampton	0.6	275	72	60	68.2
=70	Newman	0.0	261	84	50	68.2
72	Nottingham Trent	0.4	316	77	45	68.1
=73	Greenwich	0.6	255	78	44	67.6
=73	Canterbury Christ Church	0.3	276	81	42	67.6
75	Northampton	0.5	248	80	42	67.4
76	Plymouth	0.3	279	77	51	67.2
=77	Bradford	0.4	274		46	66.8

=77 St Mary's College		276	83	44	66.8
=79 Salford	0.4	294	76	42	65.9
=79 Glamorgan	0.7	250	79	31	65.9
=81 Cumbria	0.2			48	65.5
=81 Worcester	0.0	287	82	38	65.5
=81 Westminster	0.2	292		46	65.5
84 Liverpool John Moores	0.2	281	81	37	65.2
85 Gloucestershire	0.4	303	76	38	64.9
86 York St John		288	83	31	64.1
87 Kingston	0.4	262	70	45	62.4
88 Manchester Metropolitan	0.2	292	72	36	60.7
89 Trinity St David	0.5	256	68	41	60.4
90 Bishop Grosseteste		246		38	60.0
91 Leeds Metropolitan		233	75	38	59.3

» Historical Association: **www.history.org.uk**
» Institute of Historical Research: **www.history.ac.uk**
» Royal Historical Society: **www.royalhistoricalsociety.org**

History of Art, Architecture and Design

This table was the only one in the last edition of the *Guide* to have joint leaders. But neither London's Courtauld Institute nor Cambridge is top this year. Oxford has leapfrogged both to take a clear lead, even though employment is the only measure on which it has the highest score. Cambridge has the highest entry standards and the most satisfied students, but only saw 71 per cent of graduates in the history of art go straight into graduate jobs or onto postgraduate courses, compared with 91 per cent at Oxford.

Cambridge is also let down by an unusually low research score. Glasgow did best in the 2008 Research Assessment Exercise, which classified 85 per cent of its work as world-leading or internationally excellent.

Oxford is the only university to record "positive destinations" for more than three quarters of its graduates. The subjects are in the bottom half of the employment table, but ten places higher than last year. The 7 per cent unemployment rate is better than the average for all subjects, but more than a third of graduates go into lower-level jobs. The specialised nature of the jobs market has always made for uncertain prospects immediately after graduation, and history of art is in the bottom 20 for starting salaries.

There were good scores for most universities in the 2011 National Student Survey, however. Although only Cambridge satisfied more than nine out of ten final-year undergraduates, all 27 institutions in the ranking had satisfaction scores of 70 per cent and above. The majority of students are female. Entry standards are high, with 14 universities, compared with ten last year, averaging over 400 points and none less than 275.

Only six post-1992 universities are left in the ranking, with Brighton and Sheffield Hallam the highest-placed, just outside the top 20. Glasgow has pulled clear of St Andrews as the top university in Scotland, but Wales has lost its former representative, Aberystwyth.

History of Art, Architecture and Design cont

Employed in graduate job:	32%	Employed in non-graduate job and studying:	5%
Employed in graduate job and studying:	3%	Employed in non-graduate job:	32%
Studying:	22%	Unemployed:	7%
Average starting graduate salary:	£18,588	Average starting non-graduate salary:	£14,659

History of Art, Architecture and Design	Research quality	Entry standards	Student satisfaction %	Graduate prospects %	Overall rating
1 Oxford	1.4	527	86	91	100.0
2 Cambridge	0.8	552	91	71	94.6
3 Glasgow	1.8	442	89	54	93.3
4 Sussex	1.6	405	85	69	91.6
5 Courtauld	1.6	459	81	67	91.1
6 York	1.6	424	85	63	90.9
7 University College London	1.4	458	81	68	89.6
8 St Andrews	1.1	480	86	59	88.5
9 East Anglia	1.7	395	88	36	86.8
10 Warwick	1.0	448	83	60	85.2
11 Birmingham	1.3	414	78	66	84.8
12 Nottingham	1.2	404	82	61	84.4
13 Bristol	0.8	436	79	74	83.3
14 Leeds	1.0	385	82	64	82.3
15 Manchester	1.6	372	74	58	81.9
16 Edinburgh	0.9	445	77	63	81.7
17 Leicester	0.6	389	86	59	80.7
18 Aberdeen	1.0	411	83	40	79.2
19 School of Oriental and African Studies	1.1	383	74	62	78.8
20 Reading	0.9	365	84	46	78.6
=21 Brighton	1.4	279	84	32	75.8
=21 Sheffield Hallam	0.9		79	47	75.8
23 Plymouth	0.7	289	77	68	74.3
24 Goldsmiths College	0.9	399	74	36	72.4
25 Oxford Brookes	0.9	310	78	36	70.4
26 Kingston	0.7	280	70	41	65.0
27 Manchester Metropolitan	0.7	282	72		64.3

» Association of Art Historians: **www.aah.org.uk**
» Society of Architectural Historians of Great Britain: **www.sahgb.org.uk**

Hospitality, Leisure, Recreation and Tourism

Burgeoning demand for places over several years has taken this wide-ranging group of subjects into the top 20 for applications. But there was a 13 per cent drop in applications at degree level by March 2012, as higher fees were introduced, and an even bigger decline in the substantial cadre of Foundation degrees. The category covers a variety of courses, most directed towards management in the leisure and tourism industries.

One additional institution in this year's ranking takes the total past 50 for the first time. Most are post-1992 universities, but the two leaders are older foundations, with Surrey well ahead of Stirling at the top. Surrey's 40-year reputation in hotel and tourism management helps to give it a near six-point lead. It is one of only 12 universities with average entry grades of more than 300 points and it achieved the best of an extremely modest set of results in the 2008 Research Assessment Exercise (RAE). Fourth-placed Exeter and Birmingham, in sixth place, are 20 points ahead of most of the rest for employment prospects. Both would have been higher but did not enter the RAE in this category – only 15 of the 51 universities and colleges did. Even in the top 20, some universities saw fewer than 40 per cent of graduates going into graduate-level jobs or further study.

Exeter also has the highest entry standards, while Lincoln, in 18th place, has the most satisfied students. Satisfaction rates are generally high, most universities reaching at least 70 per cent approval in the 2011 National Student Survey. Central Lancashire, in third place, is the highest-placed post-1992 university and is joined in the top ten by Sheffield Hallam, Bournemouth, Chester, Plymouth and Brighton. Second-placed Stirling is the top university in Scotland, while Cardiff Metropolitan has that distinction in Wales.

The 8 per cent unemployment rate is better than average for all subjects, but the unusually large numbers – 45 per cent – starting their careers in lower-level jobs relegate hospitality, leisure, recreation and tourism to the bottom three of the employment table. The subjects fare a little better in terms of starting salaries in graduate jobs, and the average of £17,814 is less than £2,500 better than the average for lower-level work.

Employed in graduate job:	39%	Employed in non-graduate job and studying:	3%
Employed in graduate job and studying:	2%	Employed in non-graduate job:	42%
Studying:	6%	Unemployed:	8%
Average starting graduate salary:	£17,814	Average starting non-graduate salary:	£15,573

Hospitality, Leisure, Recreation and Tourism	Research quality	Entry standards	Student satisfaction %	Graduate prospects %	Overall rating
1 Surrey	0.7	370	83	55	100.0
2 Stirling	0.6	354	80	52	94.3
3 Central Lancashire	0.7	306	81	57	93.7
4 Exeter		451	84	82	93.3
5 Sheffield Hallam	0.6	297	78	46	85.8
6 Birmingham		359	74	79	81.6
7 Bournemouth	0.4	322	68	58	81.5
8 Chester	0.4	270	70	68	80.6
9 Plymouth	0.4	268	74	54	80.3
10 Brighton	0.6	271	73	39	80.1
11 Strathclyde		442	80	36	79.0
12 Cardiff Metropolitan	0.4	260	79	45	78.2
13 Manchester		351	79	55	77.3
14 Hertfordshire	0.5	288	78	23	76.3

	Research quality	Entry standards	Student satisfaction %	Graduate prospects %	Overall rating
15 Glamorgan		276	82	59	74.9
16 Sunderland	0.4	238	78	29	73.5
17 Manchester Metropolitan	0.5	269	57	55	73.4
18 Lincoln		269	88	45	73.3
19 Portsmouth		282	80	53	72.6
20 Oxford Brookes		309	79	46	72.3
21 Salford	0.4	229	76	30	71.9
=22 Huddersfield		284	73	62	71.7
=22 Robert Gordon		286	74	60	71.7
=24 Greenwich		272	82	47	71.3
=24 Queen Margaret Edinburgh		286	79	49	71.3
26 Edinburgh Napier		301	71	55	69.9
27 West of England	0.2	286	78	22	69.5
=28 Gloucestershire		269	71	61	69.2
=28 Arts University College, Bournemouth		249	70	68	69.2
30 Westminster		262	83	38	68.8
31 Leeds Metropolitan		250	75	55	68.5
32 Glasgow Caledonian		326	71	37	67.1
=33 Southampton Solent		267	74	42	65.7
=33 University College Birmingham		216	74	54	65.7
35 Ulster		250	81	31	65.4
36 University of the Arts, London		351	55	54	65.0
37 Bedfordshire	0.3	166	79	24	64.8
38 Coventry		266	60	60	63.7
39 Northampton		221	79	35	63.2
40 St Mary's College		241	80	27	62.8
41 West of Scotland		246	75	32	62.1
42 Derby		264	69	39	62.0
43 West London		229	75	31	60.9
44 Canterbury Christ Church		228	67	45	60.7
45 Hull		206	80	27	60.6
46 Winchester		277	61	42	59.9
47 London South Bank		210	65	44	58.1
48 Middlesex		164	75	36	57.8
49 Buckinghamshire New		233	65	27	55.0
50 Liverpool John Moores		249	66	18	54.6
51 London Metropolitan		232	53	45	53.7

» Association for Tourism in Higher Education: **www.athe.org.uk**
» Council for Hospitality Management Education: **www.chme.org.uk**
» Institute of Hospitality: **www.instituteofhospitality.org**
» Leisure Studies Association: **www.leisure-studies-association.info**

Iberian Languages

Spanish has been growing in popularity as an alternative to French in schools, and is a common choice as an element of a broader modern languages degree. It had the smallest decline of any language as higher fees arrived in 2012, but still attracted only two thirds of the applications for French. The table also includes Portuguese, which had only ten applications at degree level at the start of 2012, although it is still offered at 18 universities, at least as part of a broader languages programme.

Cambridge has maintained its lead over Oxford at the top of the table, with the highest entry standards and the most satisfied students. It also shares the best employment score with University College London, in ninth place. The two universities are the only ones in the table to see more than 80 per cent of students go straight into graduate-level jobs or further study.

Sixth-placed Nottingham and Manchester, twelfth, tied for the best performance in the 2008 Research Assessment Exercise. The 2011 National Student Survey showed high levels of satisfaction in most universities. Only the bottom two failed to satisfy at least 70 per cent of final-year undergraduates.

Entry standards have continued to rise: for the first time, more than half of the universities in the table average over 400 points and none slips below 280. All but eight of the 45 institutions in the ranking are pre-1992 universities. Northumbria is the highest-placed of the newer foundations, but has lost its place in the top 20 this year. For the fifth year in a row, Portsmouth makes the top 30.

The languages are in the top half of the employment table and the 8 per cent unemployment rate is below average. The same cannot be said of starting salaries in graduate jobs, which had fallen below £20,000 in the latest survey. Employment prospects appear to be more evenly spread between universities than in many subjects. Only one institution (compared with four last year) saw fewer than half of their leavers go into graduate jobs or further training.

Employed in graduate job:	42%	Employed in non-graduate job and studying:	3%
Employed in graduate job and studying:	3%	Employed in non-graduate job:	24%
Studying:	21%	Unemployed:	8%
Average starting graduate salary:	£19,617	Average starting non-graduate salary:	£16,198

Iberian Languages	Research quality	Entry standards	Student satisfaction %	Graduate prospects %	Overall rating
1 Cambridge	1.3	559	91	81	100.0
2 Oxford	0.9	552	89	79	94.6
3 Durham	1.1	516	84	80	92.7
4 St Andrews	0.9	497	82	75	87.8
5 Bath	0.7	459	85	79	87.1
6 Nottingham	1.4	419	77	74	86.2
7 Newcastle	0.8	446	83	75	85.6
8 Southampton	1.2	459	84	62	85.3
9 University College London	0.7	467	78	81	84.9

Iberian Languages cont	Research quality	Entry standards	Student satisfaction %	Graduate prospects %	Overall rating
=10 Leeds	1.0	427	80	72	84.6
=10 King's College London	1.1	437	81	67	84.6
12 Manchester	1.4	402	78	64	82.9
13 Bristol	0.5	449	78	80	82.8
14 Queen Mary, London	1.1	389	78	71	82.7
15 Leicester	0.6	381	87		82.1
16 Exeter	0.8	464	77	66	80.7
17 Glasgow	0.4	483	74	76	80.3
18 Heriot-Watt	0.5	400	80	74	79.9
19 Sheffield	1.1	427	73	66	79.5
20 Aberdeen	0.7	387	80	67	78.5
21 Cardiff	0.8	426	77	64	78.4
22 Aston	0.3	388	83	72	78.3
23 Birmingham	0.6	401	75	72	77.9
24 Edinburgh	0.8	508	70	60	77.3
25 Kent	0.4	341	84	69	76.9
26 Queen's, Belfast	0.9	401	75	61	76.8
27 Lancaster	0.5	407	74	71	76.2
28 Northumbria		328	89	70	76.1
29 Royal Holloway	0.8	391	73	64	75.5
30 Portsmouth	0.8	300	82	57	73.6
31 Stirling	0.4	341	82	57	72.3
32 Chester		297	83	70	72.1
33 Strathclyde	0.2	435	72	64	72.0
=34 East Anglia		343	86	57	71.3
=34 Swansea	0.7	341	72	61	71.3
36 Liverpool	0.8	404	70	52	70.9
37 Hull		308	82	67	70.8
38 Roehampton	0.4	290	79		70.5
39 Sussex		391	78	61	70.4
40 Salford	0.4	336	78	55	69.7
41 Nottingham Trent		296	83	59	68.5
42 Ulster	0.1	300	78		66.9
43 Manchester Metropolitan	0.2	290	78	54	66.1
44 Westminster		281	62	73	62.8
45 Liverpool John Moores		333	68	48	59.4

» Association for Contemporary Iberian Studies: **www.iberianstudies.net**
» Association of Hispanists of Great Britain and Ireland: **www.dur.ac.uk/hispanists**
» Instituto Cervantes: **http://londres.cervantes.es/en/default.shtm**

Italian

Two more universities have joined the Italian ranking this year, but the total is still nearly a dozen down on the 2007 *Guide*, when languages were at their peak at degree level. Applications were down by over 20 per cent in March 2012 to below 250. Only 65 students started degrees in Italian in 2011, although many more will have included it in broader language degrees. A total of 37 universities still offer Italian in some form. A relatively high proportion of the places are filled in Clearing. Most students have no previous knowledge of Italian, although they are likely to have taken another language at A level.

The low numbers can make for big swings in the annual statistics: in last year's *Guide*, for example, starting salaries had dropped by more than £1,000, but they have recovered their value in the latest edition and average almost £20,000. Cambridge, which has extended its already considerable lead over Oxford this year, has the best employment record, as well as the most satisfied students, the highest entry standards and the top grades in the 2008 Research Assessment Exercise, when 80 per cent of its submission was judged to be world-leading or internationally excellent.

Durham, in 4th place, and Strathclyde, in 17th, come close to matching Cambridge's employment successes, while Manchester, in 11th, is the nearest challenger on student satisfaction. Although there were fewer than five applications to the place in 2011, entry standards are still high. The top two average more than 500 points at entry and more than half of the 23 universities in the ranking top 400 points.

There is a high response rate and scores have generally been good in the National Student Survey. No university failed to satisfy at least seven out of ten final-year undergraduates.

St Andrews has rejoined the table this year as the top university in Scotland, while Cardiff remains ahead of Swansea in Wales. There are only three post-1992 universities left in the table, with Portsmouth the clear leader despite slipping six places.

Employed in graduate job:	41%	Employed in non-graduate job and studying:	3%
Employed in graduate job and studying:	2%	Employed in non-graduate job:	26%
Studying:	21%	Unemployed:	8%
Average starting graduate salary:	£19,957	Average starting non-graduate salary:	£15,890

Italian	Research quality	Entry standards	Student satisfaction %	Graduate prospects %	Overall rating
1 Cambridge	1.7	559	91	81	100.0
2 Oxford	1.2	542	87	66	89.9
3 Leeds	1.3	413	85	69	85.2
4 Durham	0.4	516	84	80	85.0
5 Warwick	1.2	431	86	65	84.6
6 Bristol	1.0	462	82	71	83.7
7 Bath	0.7	438	85	73	82.9
8 St Andrews	0.4	484	83		79.4
9 University College London	0.9	472	73	70	78.7
10 Exeter	0.6	473	82	60	78.5

Italian cont	Research quality	Entry standards	Student satisfaction %	Graduate prospects %	Overall rating
11 Manchester	1.0	377	90	46	77.9
=12 Glasgow	0.4		83	65	77.2
=12 Reading	1.2	373	85	48	77.2
14 Edinburgh	0.3	488	76	70	76.4
15 Birmingham	0.8		82	48	74.6
16 Cardiff	0.8	412	73	62	73.7
17 Strathclyde	0.2		72	79	72.9
18 Portsmouth	0.8	300	82	57	72.2
19 Swansea	0.4		75	60	70.1
20 Manchester Metropolitan	0.2		78	54	68.4
=21 Royal Holloway	0.5	376	77	46	67.8
=21 Nottingham Trent		296	83	59	67.8
23 Lancaster	0.5	399	71		67.4

» Chartered Institute of Linguists: **www.iol.org.uk**
» National Centre for Languages (CILT): **www.cilt.org.uk**
» Society for Italian Studies: **www.sis.ac.uk**

Land and Property Management

Despite the addition of one university in the latest *Guide*, the land and property management table is less than a third of the size it was in 2005.

The economic downturn and now fee increases have taken their toll, although the subject is still in the top half of the employment table nationally. Even that is a shadow of the position two years ago, when land and property management featured in the top 20. At that time, graduate starting salaries averaged almost £22,000, compared with less than £19,500 in the new *Guide*.

The unemployment rate is now above average, at 12 per cent, although 61 per cent of those completing courses still go straight into graduate-level jobs.

Because land and property management tend to have small intakes, it is impossible to compile reliable scores for some universities, even though they are still offering one or more of the subjects. More than 20 universities and a number of colleges advertised degrees in this field starting in 2012.

Cambridge has a predictably huge lead, despite not achieving enough responses from its final-year undergraduates for a satisfaction score to be compiled. It has entry standards that are more than 100 points higher than at second-placed Reading and 200 points above the other universities in the table. Cambridge also has by far the highest employment score and registered the best performance in the 2008 Research Assessment Exercise.

Greenwich, which has moved up to fifth this year, is a long way ahead of the rest for student satisfaction, although none of the universities registering a score slipped below 70 per cent in the 2011 National Student Survey. Sheffield Hallam is the highest-placed of four

post-1992 universities in the ranking. There are no representatives of Scotland or Wales in
the table, but Queen's, Belfast offers land use and environmental management in Northern
Ireland.

Employed in graduate job:	58%	Employed in non-graduate job and studying:	2%
Employed in graduate job and studying:	3%	Employed in non-graduate job:	21%
Studying:	5%	Unemployed:	12%
Average starting graduate salary:	£19,497	Average starting non-graduate salary:	£14,690

Land and Property Management	Research quality	Entry standards	Student satisfaction %	Graduate prospects %	Overall rating
1 Cambridge	1.4	532		95	100.0
2 Reading	1.1	414	77	90	90.3
3 Sheffield Hallam	0.9	327	77		83.4
4 Queen's, Belfast	0.5	318	76	81	80.4
5 Greenwich		269	83	47	73.8
6 Birmingham City	0.5	233	72	66	72.2
7 Westminster	0.4	239	70	74	71.2

» Chartered Institute of Housing: **www.cih.org**
» Institute of Residential Property Management: **www.irpm.org.uk**
» Royal Institution of Chartered Surveyors: **www.rics.org/uk**

Law

Only nursing had attracted more applications than law in March 2012. While other subjects
suffered from the introduction of higher fees, law managed a small increase in applications,
which totalled more than 90,000. Entry standards reflect law's popularity: only in medicine
do so many universities make such testing demands. Nine universities average more than
500 points and almost a third of the 95 universities have average entry scores of more than
400 points. For the first time, no university slips below 200 points, although the 5.5 applications
to each place in 2011 were below average for all subjects.

Oxford retains the top place it won from Cambridge two years ago, despite leading
the table on only one of the measures: entry standards. Fourth-placed University College
London ties with Strathclyde, in 12th place, for the best record for graduate destinations.
Aspiring solicitors go on to take the Legal Practice Course, while those aiming to be
barristers take the Bar Vocational Course, so it is no surprise that half of all law graduates
are engaged in postgraduate study six months after completing a degree. The unemployment
rate for law is better than average, at 7 per cent, but the subject is outside the top 20 for early
career employment prospects and there are some surprisingly low scores at the bottom of
the ranking. Average starting salaries are not as high as many might believe either, partly
because of training salaries in law firms and also because only about half of all law graduates
find their way into the profession. However, the latest figure is almost £2,000 up on the last
edition of the *Guide* and is at least in the top half of the table for all subjects.

Law cont

Once more, the most satisfied students are not at one of the top universities in the table. For the second year in a row, that distinction goes to Greenwich, in 44th place, with Newcastle, in equal 13th, again registering the next-best score. There were good performances in law throughout the 2011 National Student Survey. Only six universities – and only one of the top 50 – failed to satisfy at least 70 per cent of the undergraduates.

The London School of Economics, in third place, achieved the best grades in the 2008 Research Assessment Exercise, when three quarters of its submission was rated world-leading or internationally excellent. Edinburgh has overtaken both Glasgow and Aberdeen to become the top university in Scotland, while Cardiff is now well clear of the rest in Wales. Oxford Brookes is the leading post-1992 university.

Employed in graduate job:	21%	Employed in non-graduate job and studying:	7%
Employed in graduate job and studying:	5%	Employed in non-graduate job:	23%
Studying:	38%	Unemployed:	7%
Average starting graduate salary:	£20,719	Average starting non-graduate salary:	£14,786

Law	Research quality	Entry standards	Student satisfaction %	Graduate prospects %	Overall rating
1 Oxford	1.4	604	87	88	100.0
2 Cambridge	1.1	582		88	97.5
3 London School of Economics	1.7	551	82	87	97.4
4 University College London	1.5	534	83	89	95.7
5 Nottingham	1.3	509	88	77	93.7
6 Durham	1.3	543	83	81	93.0
7 Edinburgh	1.2	508	79	86	89.6
8 Queen Mary, London	1.0	469	88	72	88.6
9 Reading	1.0	430	83	86	88.4
10 Glasgow	0.9	517	79	87	88.3
11 Aberdeen	0.5	460	86	88	86.9
12 Strathclyde	1.0	491	74	89	86.2
=13 Newcastle	0.4	441	91	73	85.5
=13 King's College London	0.8	520	78	80	85.5
15 Warwick	0.7	498	82	78	85.3
=16 Birmingham	0.9	476	78	79	84.8
=16 Lancaster	0.6	442	83	85	84.8
18 Cardiff	1.1	448	80	71	84.3
19 Bristol	0.9	495	76	80	84.0
20 Sussex	0.7	397	85	79	83.9
21 Southampton	0.6	466	81	79	83.7
22 Exeter	0.7	467	79	81	83.6
23 Dundee	0.6	429	88	68	83.4
=24 Leeds	0.9	430	81	71	82.7
=24 Kent	1.3	373	80	70	82.7
26 Leicester	0.5	407	85	77	82.6

27	Queen's, Belfast	1.1	435	77	71	82.3
28	School of Oriental and African Studies	0.6	418	77	79	79.5
29	Manchester	0.7	452	71	80	79.0
30	Sheffield	0.8	445	74	71	78.9
31	Hull	0.6	371	80	75	78.7
32	East Anglia	0.5	423	77	75	78.4
33	Oxford Brookes	0.7	358	80	71	77.7
34	Brunel	0.6	366	77	77	77.5
35	Stirling	0.5	392	78	70	76.7
36	Buckingham		250	89	81	76.5
37	Liverpool	0.8	440	69	73	76.2
38	Edinburgh Napier	0.1	330	83	80	76.0
39	Swansea	0.6	348	79	70	75.8
=40	Hertfordshire	0.5	315	83	65	75.2
=40	Keele	0.7	348	78	64	75.2
42	Robert Gordon	0.1	339	78	85	75.1
43	West of England	0.3	327	83	66	74.6
44	Greenwich	0.1	307	92	56	74.5
45	Lincoln	0.1	325	84	67	74.0
46	Northumbria		356	83	69	73.8
=47	Surrey	0.4	399	71	75	73.1
=47	Glamorgan	0.2	298	83	68	73.1
=47	Essex	0.6	355	75	64	73.1
=50	Central Lancashire	0.2	297	81	71	72.8
=50	Coventry	0.1	311	83	69	72.8
52	Chester		310	81	72	72.3
53	Aberystwyth	0.5	308	78	65	72.2
54	Salford	0.2	369	77	65	71.8
55	Ulster	1.0	314	79	44	71.5
56	Portsmouth	0.5	325	76	64	71.2
57	Huddersfield		323	75	78	71.0
58	Glasgow Caledonian	0.2	401	78	57	70.7
59	Abertay	0.2	331		68	70.6
=60	Manchester Metropolitan	0.5	345	70	70	70.2
=60	De Montfort	0.2	282	84	56	70.2
=60	Staffordshire		273	79	74	70.2
=63	Westminster	0.4	331	70	74	70.1
=63	Bradford	0.8	284	75	57	70.1
65	Teesside		294	82	63	69.8
66	East London	0.5	213	79	65	69.7
67	City	0.5	376	65	72	69.1
68	Plymouth	0.5	310	78	53	69.0
=69	Nottingham Trent	0.1	337	72	74	68.9
=69	Sunderland	0.0	307	87	47	68.9
=71	Sheffield Hallam	0.1	320	79	62	68.8
=71	Brighton	0.9	288	69	62	68.8
73	Derby		281	84	55	68.5

	Research quality	Entry standards	Student satisfaction %	Graduate prospects %	Overall rating
74 Kingston	0.1	314	73	65	67.0
75 Birmingham City		295	70	75	66.2
76 Edge Hill		247	85	46	65.5
77 Middlesex	0.2	227	75	65	65.4
78 Bournemouth	0.0	341	67	71	65.2
79 Liverpool John Moores		294	78	53	65.1
80 St Mary's College		213	76	67	65.0
81 Leeds Metropolitan		296	71	64	64.3
82 Bangor		298	75	55	64.1
83 Buckinghamshire New		230		65	63.9
84 Bolton		219	70	72	63.2
85 Anglia Ruskin		260	75	55	62.9
86 Northampton		236	79	48	62.4
87 Gloucestershire		283	75	50	62.2
88 Southampton Solent	0.0	244	76	50	61.6
=89 West London		252	72	55	60.9
=89 London Metropolitan	0.1	226	68	64	60.9
91 Bedfordshire		205	71	63	60.8
92 London South Bank		215	68	63	59.6
93 Canterbury Christ Church		240	78	34	58.6
94 West of Scotland	0.0	270	71	27	54.2
95 Newport		229		33	51.9

» Law Society of England and Wales: **www.lawsociety.org.uk**
» Law Society of Northern Ireland: **www.lawsoc-ni.org**
» Law Society of Scotland: **www.lawscot.org.uk**

Librarianship and Information Management

There has been a drop of more than £2,500 since last year's *Guide* in the average starting salaries in graduate-level jobs following degrees in librarianship and information science. But no subject's graduates were paid as well in lower-level employment. Once again, small numbers are largely responsible for the fluctuations: only half of the eight universities in the table admitted enough entrants in 2010 for a reliable entry score to be compiled. There were only 521 applications to study information services in March 2012 – a drop of 13 per cent on the previous year.

The top two universities in the table are unchanged for the fourth year in a row, but Brighton takes third place for the first time and is the leading post-1992 university. Second-placed Sheffield has the best score for research, but Loughborough has the highest entry standards and the most satisfied students. King's College London actually produced the top results in the 2008 Research Assessment Exercise, but does not have undergraduate courses in this field so does not appear in the table.

Northumbria, in sixth place, has by far the best employment score, with 80 per cent of graduates going straight into graduate-level jobs or further study. Only Sheffield came within ten percentage points, while more than half of the universities in the table were below 50 per cent for "positive destinations" of their graduates. This contributes to an unemployment rate of 14 per cent, the second-highest in any subject.

There are five fewer universities than there were in the 2006 edition of the *Guide*. University College London, which was in third place last year, is the latest to drop out, but the arrival of Leeds ensures that numbers have not declined further. There is no representative in Scotland, and only Aberystwyth from Wales.

Employed in graduate job:	41%	Employed in non-graduate job and studying:	4%
Employed in graduate job and studying:	6%	Employed in non-graduate job:	30%
Studying:	6%	Unemployed:	14%
Average starting graduate salary:	£20,518	Average starting non-graduate salary:	£16,679

Librarianship and Information Management	Research quality	Entry standards	Student satisfaction %	Graduate prospects %	Overall rating
1 Loughborough	0.9	362	86	69	100.0
2 Sheffield	1.3	329	83	70	98.4
3 Brighton	0.6		85	36	88.2
4 Aberystwyth	0.7		80	39	86.4
5 Leeds		325	78	65	84.3
6 Northumbria	0.2	288	73	80	82.0
7 Liverpool John Moores	0.4		73	41	78.3
8 London South Bank	0.2		73	41	76.6
9 Manchester Metropolitan	0.2		71	36	74.1

» Association for Information Management: **www.aslib.com**
» Chartered Institute of Library and Information Professionals: **www.cilip.org.uk**

Linguistics

Linguistics might have looked likely to be a prime victim of the switch to higher fees, but applications were down by less than average in March 2012. Applications have fluctuated in any case over recent years, and the 5 per cent drop in 2012 was not out of the ordinary. With only 523 students beginning degrees in 2011 and only a little more than five applications to the place, the subject remains vulnerable in some universities. Entry standards remain comparatively high: no university averages less than 270 points and more than half have an average in excess of 400 points. Cambridge has retaken top place in the table, having lost it to Oxford last year. Unusually, neither of the ancient universities is in the top six for research, but Cambridge has the highest entry standards and the most satisfied students. Oxford has the top employment record and, in the absence of a score for Cambridge, was the only university to see more than three quarters of graduates find graduate-level work or a place on a postgraduate course six months after completing a degree.

Queen Mary, University of London, in sixth place, and Cardiff, just outside the top ten,

Linguistics cont

tie for the best score from a surprisingly low set of grades in the 2008 Research Assessment Exercise. Edinburgh is well ahead of Aberdeen in Scotland, while Cardiff has a similar lead over Bangor in Wales. Portsmouth is the highest-placed post-1992 university and the only one in the top ten of a ranking that is dominated by the older foundations. Hertfordshire and the West of England are the only other post-1992 universities in the top 20.

Linguistics is in bottom ten subjects for starting salaries in graduate jobs, averaging less than £18,000. Graduates' immediate employment prospects are a little better, but nearly 40 per cent start their careers in low-level jobs.

Employed in graduate job:	29%	Employed in non-graduate job and studying:	4%
Employed in graduate job and studying:	5%	Employed in non-graduate job:	34%
Studying:	20%	Unemployed:	9%
Average starting graduate salary:	£17,968	Average starting non-graduate salary:	£14,706

Linguistics	Research quality	Entry standards	Student satisfaction %	Graduate prospects %	Overall rating
1 Cambridge	0.9	574	89		100.0
2 Oxford	0.6	547	88	77	95.2
3 University College London	0.9	499	88	65	93.5
4 Lancaster	0.9	435	86	75	91.5
5 York	1.1	443	83	64	89.8
6 Queen Mary, London	1.3	405	78	62	88.0
7 Newcastle	0.7	433	81	75	87.5
8 Sheffield	1.0	442	78	63	86.6
9 Edinburgh	1.2	471	71	57	84.7
10 Portsmouth	0.8		82	59	83.9
11 Cardiff	1.3	429	75	48	83.7
12 Sussex	0.3		84	73	83.6
13 Leeds	0.6	404	79	62	80.8
14 Essex	1.1	366	76	48	79.2
15 Aberdeen		385	87	52	75.2
16 Hertfordshire	0.7	319	77	53	74.1
17 Manchester	0.8	402	69	46	73.1
18 School of Oriental and African Studies	0.6	425	75	38	72.9
19 Bangor	0.5	318	83	38	71.4
20 West of England	0.7	306	72	52	71.1
21 King's College London		412	72	61	70.8
22 Ulster	0.7	281	65	52	66.9
23 Brighton	0.1	321	76		64.7
24 York St John		285	83	28	62.2
25 Salford	0.5		67	32	59.9
26 Westminster	0.2	271	70		59.2

» British Association for Applied Linguistics: **www.baal.org.uk**
» Linguistics Association of Great Britain: **www.lagb.org.uk**

Materials Technology

Courses in this category cover three distinct areas: materials science, mining and engineering, textiles technology and printing, and marine technology. The various subjects are highly specialised and attract relatively few applicants, but have generally held their own with the onset of higher fees. The demand for places in materials technology itself, for example, had dropped less than 1 per cent in March 2012, but there were still fewer than 800 applications. The leading universities demand chemistry and sometimes also physics, maths or design technology at A level or its equivalent.

Cambridge has retained the leadership it won from Oxford four years ago, with Leeds moving up to third place from sixth last year. Cambridge has the best grades from the 2008 Research Assessment Exercise, when only 5 per cent of the university's research was considered less than world-leading or internationally excellent. It also has much the highest entry standards and shares the top score for student satisfaction with Sheffield, where, for the second year in a row, 95 per cent of graduates found graduate-level work or a place on a more advanced course within six months of leaving. Only Exeter, in tenth place, came within five percentage points of Sheffield's employment record.

Outside the top six, entry scores are tightly bunched: no university has an average of 400 points or less than 230. De Montfort is the leading post-1992 university, on the verge of the top ten. Swansea is the only university in the table from outside England.

Employment prospects are about average for all subjects: more than half of those completing a degree go straight into graduate-level work, and the unemployment rate is above the norm for all subjects. Average starting salaries for those who find graduate jobs are also firmly in mid-table, having gone up £300 since the last *Guide* appeared.

Materials Technology	Research quality	Entry standards	Student satisfaction %	Graduate prospects %	Overall rating
1 Cambridge	1.8	630	84	83	100.0
2 Oxford	1.3	570		84	93.7
3 Leeds	1.2		80	88	88.3
4 Sheffield	1.0	411	84	95	88.0
5 Imperial College	1.0	506	80	83	86.7
6 Birmingham	1.1	373	78	78	80.7
7 Loughborough	1.1	325	81	72	79.2
8 Swansea	0.9	345	76	85	78.7
9 Queen Mary, London	0.9	368	83	62	77.7
10 Exeter	0.5	386	74	90	76.9
11 De Montfort	1.7	288	74	55	75.2
12 Bolton	1.7	233	69		72.5
13 Manchester	1.2	388	62	57	69.5
14 Manchester Metropolitan	0.3	317	68	68	65.1
15 Huddersfield		321	81	46	64.2
16 Buckinghamshire New		272	74	47	59.2
17 Sheffield Hallam	0.5		66	42	56.6
18 London Metropolitan	0.0		57	44	46.2

Materials Technology cont

Employed in graduate job:	52%	Employed in non-graduate job and studying:	2%
Employed in graduate job and studying:	2%	Employed in non-graduate job:	24%
Studying:	11%	Unemployed:	8%
Average starting graduate salary:	£20,371	Average starting non-graduate salary:	£15,243

» Institute of Materials, Minerals and Mining: **www.iom3.org**
» UK Centre for Materials Education (materials science): **www.materials.ac.uk**

Mathematics

Maths has been enjoying a renaissance as a degree subject since sixth-form numbers began to recover from a slump in the last decade. Applications dropped by less than 4 per cent with the switch to higher fees, wiping out the increase in 2011. But the subject still attracted almost 15,000 more applications than it did in 2005. The number of places has grown as well – about 7,600 started degrees in 2011, after the latest in a series of increases.

Entry grades are high, even though there were only 5.5 applications to the place in 2011 – below the average for all subjects. Cambridge's average of 669 points per entrant – almost the equivalent of four A* grades and two As at AS level – is the highest there has ever been for any subject in the *Guide*. A dozen universities recorded averages of more than 500 points and more than 30 topped the 400-point mark. The totals are boosted not only by the introduction of the A*, but also by the fact that many candidates for the leading universities take two A levels in the subject, as well as two or three others.

Oxford remains in first place, largely because it outperformed Cambridge in two of the three of the subjects grouped together as mathematics in the 2008 Research Assessment Exercise. The two universities tied for the best grades in applied maths, but 90 per cent of Oxford's work in statistics and operational research was considered world-leading or internationally excellent. Imperial was top for pure mathematics.

Because of the scoring system, Oxford benefits from the fact that its final-year mathematicians again failed to respond to the 2011 National Student Survey in sufficient numbers to compile a score for student satisfaction. Sheffield Hallam, the leading post-1992 university and the only one in the top 20, had the most satisfied students, with Greenwich, in 42nd place, not far behind. Generally, mathematicians seem well satisfied with their courses: only one university fell below a 70 per cent approval rating. St Andrews, in fourth place overall, is easily the top university in Scotland, despite dropping one place this year, while Cardiff retains the lead in Wales.

Cambridge has the top employment score. Graduates' prospects are good in most universities – maths is among the top 15 subjects for positive destinations – but three universities do fall below 50 per cent on this measure in the latest table. Maths is often cited as one of the subjects most likely to lead to a lucrative career, and the earnings table seems to bear this out. Average salaries in graduate jobs are in the top 10 for any subject, topping £24,250 at the time of the latest survey.

Employed in graduate job: 33%
Employed in graduate job and studying: 11%
Studying: 26%
Average starting graduate salary: £24,259

Employed in non-graduate job and studying: 3%
Employed in non-graduate job: 17%
Unemployed: 10%
Average starting non-graduate salary: £15,582

Mathematics

	Research quality Pure Mathematics	Research quality Applied Mathematics	Research quality Statistics	Entry standards	Student satisfaction %	Graduate prospects %	Overall rating
1 Oxford	1.5	1.4	1.7	626		87	100.0
2 Cambridge	1.4	1.4	1.4	669	86	90	98.9
3 Warwick	1.5	1.2	1.2	589	81	78	90.5
4 St Andrews	0.5	1.2	0.8	589	85	80	90.0
=5 Durham	1.0	1.1	0.6	576	80	79	87.0
=5 Bath	1.1	1.1	1.0	510	80	82	87.0
7 Imperial College	1.7	1.1	1.3	591	74	79	86.9
8 Nottingham	0.8	1.1	1.1	510	82	74	85.5
9 Bristol	1.3	1.2	1.2	537	76	74	85.4
10 Lancaster	0.7		0.9	422	83	82	84.7
11 Aberdeen	1.1			380		78	84.4
12 London School of Economics	0.6		0.9	547	76	86	84.0
13 Heriot-Watt	1.2	1.0	0.7	422	81	80	83.7
14 University College London	1.0	0.7	0.7	538	78	74	82.7
15 Edinburgh	1.2	1.0	0.7	531	77	70	82.5
16 Glasgow	0.9	0.7	0.8	456	82	72	82.4
=17 Loughborough	0.8	0.7		438	82	76	82.2
=17 Surrey		1.0		442	80	72	82.2
=19 Newcastle	0.5	0.9	0.8	442	83	69	80.9
=19 King's College London	1.1	1.0		478	78	66	80.9
=19 Sheffield Hallam	0.4	0.4	0.4	290	93	73	80.9
=22 Exeter	0.8	0.8		470	82	65	80.8
=22 Manchester	1.0	1.1	1.0	460	79	65	80.8
=22 East Anglia	0.9	0.6		427	82	70	80.8
25 Keele		0.9		360	84	67	80.6
26 Sussex		0.7		375	82	76	80.5
27 Southampton	0.6	1.0	1.0	491	76	72	80.4
28 Birmingham	0.9	0.7		457	81	68	80.1
29 Kent	0.4	0.7	1.1	349	80	78	79.7
30 Sheffield	0.9	0.7	0.8	451	81	66	79.6
31 Leicester	0.7	0.6		445	85	60	79.2
32 Strathclyde		0.7	0.6	419	81	68	79.1
33 York	0.7	0.7		479	79	68	79.0
34 Reading		0.5	0.5	380	82	74	78.6
35 Leeds	0.8	0.9	1.2	450	75	71	78.5
36 Cardiff	0.5			482	77	74	78.1
37 Queen's, Belfast	0.6			413	79	73	78.0

		Research quality Pure Mathematics	Research quality Applied Mathematics	Research quality Statistics	Entry standards	Student satisfaction %	Graduate prospects %	Overall rating
38	Royal Holloway	0.3			393	81	78	77.6
39	Portsmouth		1.1		293	78	67	76.9
40	Northumbria		0.6		324	87	58	76.8
41	Liverpool	0.7	0.9	0.4	415	76	69	76.7
42	Greenwich			0.4	255	91	62	76.3
43	Edge Hill				306		86	75.8
44	Plymouth		0.3	0.3	342	84	69	75.6
45	Glamorgan		0.2		317	82	74	74.5
46	Aberystwyth	0.5			343	78	70	74.3
=47	Queen Mary, London	0.8	0.7	0.6	382	76	62	73.9
=47	London Metropolitan	0.6		0.4	208	90	58	73.9
49	Nottingham Trent	0.4	0.4	0.4	302	85	57	73.4
50	Swansea	0.5			368	72	74	72.6
51	Brunel		0.7	0.8	312	81	52	72.3
52	Chester		0.2		301		78	72.2
53	Stirling		0.5		335		63	72.0
54	Cumbria				263		80	71.7
=55	West of England		0.1		324	80	68	71.1
=55	Coventry	0.2	0.2		290	74	80	71.1
57	Manchester Metropolitan	0.6			302	76	63	71.0
58	Aston	0.6	0.6	0.6	377	66	76	70.7
59	Brighton		0.2		284	82	59	69.8
60	Hertfordshire	0.9			311	79	41	69.3
61	Glasgow Caledonian		0.2				67	69.1
=62	Essex				341	74	72	69.0
=62	Kingston				275	80	67	69.0
64	Liverpool John Moores				310		68	68.7
65	Bolton				312		67	68.4
66	Dundee		0.7		398		42	68.3
67	City		0.3		348	76	57	68.2
68	Central Lancashire				344		59	66.6
69	Oxford Brookes		0.1		338		46	61.9

» London Mathematical Society: **www.lms.ac.uk**
» Maths Careers: **www.mathscareers.org.uk**
» Royal Statistical Society: **www.rss.org.uk**

Mechanical Engineering

Mechanical engineering is among the 20 most popular subjects at degree level and attracts more applicants than any other branch of the wider discipline. The arrival of higher fees cemented this position, as applications rose by more than 6 per cent – the latest in a series of substantial rises. The number of places has also grown in recent years, allowing 6,700 students to start degrees in 2011, but six applications for every place still made it the most competitive branch of engineering. It is not hard to see why. Despite the economic downturn, mechanical engineering is among the top ten subjects both for early career prospects and starting salaries in graduate jobs, averaging more than £24,700 at the end of 2010. Most universities demand maths – preferably with a strong component of mechanics – and another science subject (usually physics) at A level or its equivalent.

Cambridge's lead in mechanical engineering has narrowed for the second year in a row, but remains considerable. Imperial College continues in second place, with Sheffield not far behind. Cambridge, which was ranked second in the world in mechanical engineering in 2011, has by far the highest entry standards, the best research grades and the top employment record. Sussex and Robert Gordon prevented a clean sweep by recording the highest scores in the 2011 National Student Survey and the latter was the highest-placed post-1992 university, despite just failing to reach the top 20. High satisfaction scores are spread through most of the table, with only ten universities failing to win the approval of at least 70 per cent of final-year undergraduates.

Entry scores vary widely. Imperial and Bristol join Cambridge with average entry scores of more than 500 points, but six universities still average less than 250 points. The large numbers of mature students upgrading their qualifications in mechanical engineering mean that more than a third of the entrants at post-1992 universities are admitted without A levels or their equivalent. Bolton is Cambridge's nearest challenger in the 2008 Research Assessment Exercise while Imperial comes closest to emulating the 94 per cent positive destinations among Cambridge graduates in 2010. Cardiff remains the top university in Wales and Strathclyde does the same in Scotland.

Employed in graduate job:	58%	Employed in non-graduate job and studying:	1%
Employed in graduate job and studying:	4%	Employed in non-graduate job:	13%
Studying:	15%	Unemployed:	10%
Average starting graduate salary:	£24,726	Average starting non-graduate salary:	£16,621

Mechanical Engineering	Research quality	Entry standards	Student satisfaction %	Graduate prospects %	Overall rating
1 Cambridge	1.8	615	84	94	100.0
2 Imperial College	1.4	568	77	91	91.1
3 Sheffield	1.4	465	83	85	88.8
4 Bristol	1.2	514	80	83	87.1
5 Loughborough	1.1	424	82	84	84.7
=6 Nottingham	1.3	427	83	75	84.2
=6 Southampton	0.9	482	80	87	84.2
8 Surrey	1.1	404	85	81	84.1
9 Bath	0.8	497	84	79	83.4
10 Cardiff	1.1	447	83	75	82.9
11 Leeds	1.2	437	79	77	82.4
12 Strathclyde	0.8	494	79	80	81.6
13 Newcastle	1.0	413	77	87	81.1

Mechanical Engineering cont

		Research quality	Entry standards	Student satisfaction %	Graduate prospects %	Overall rating
14	Liverpool	1.1	419	80	74	80.6
15	Heriot-Watt	0.8	402	83	81	80.5
=16	Exeter	0.8	437	85	73	80.3
=16	Edinburgh	0.9	490	74	83	80.3
18	Glasgow	0.7	437	85	75	80.1
19	Queen's, Belfast	1.0	379	76	81	78.2
20	Birmingham	1.1	435	77	67	78.1
21	Robert Gordon	0.3	344	86	82	76.2
22	Sussex	0.8	341	86	65	76.1
23	Aberdeen	1.0	366	68	87	75.3
=24	Swansea	0.7	351	76	83	75.1
=24	University College London	1.0	442	69	76	75.1
26	Lancaster	0.7	381	77	75	74.9
27	Queen Mary, London	0.7	359	84	64	74.6
28	Brunel	0.7	380	78	72	74.3
29	Brighton	0.8	284	77	81	73.8
30	Plymouth	0.3	300	81	89	73.7
31	Manchester	1.1	420	64	74	73.0
32	Greenwich	1.3	265	76	60	72.3
33	Warwick		420	82	73	71.8
34	West of England	0.8	298	70	77	69.9
35	Liverpool John Moores	1.0	288	74	62	69.8
36	Aston	0.6	361	70	75	69.6
37	Sunderland	0.3	291	77	78	69.4
38	Coventry	0.2	284	82	71	68.9
39	Harper Adams		308	79	81	68.8
40	Dundee		347	79	75	68.6
=41	Bolton	1.7	169	75	44	68.0
=41	Northumbria	0.6	276	76	66	68.0
43	Portsmouth	0.6	269	69	77	66.5
44	Bradford	0.6	247	74	67	66.1
45	Hull	0.4	313	77	56	65.2
46	Huddersfield	0.5	268	68	77	64.9
47	City	0.7	352	78	35	64.3
48	Glamorgan	0.7	215	72		63.8
49	Hertfordshire	0.8	298	68	55	63.7
=50	Central Lancashire		258	80	64	63.4
=50	Staffordshire	0.6	262	74	53	63.4
52	Glyndŵr	0.5			62	62.6
53	Sheffield Hallam	0.5	262	69	63	62.1
54	Manchester Metropolitan	0.4	278	70	60	61.3
55	Birmingham City		228	74	71	61.2
56	De Montfort	0.6	246	70	55	61.0

57 Ulster		229	70	74	60.2
58 Oxford Brookes		330	68	64	59.8
59 Kingston	0.4	272	66	52	57.4
60 London South Bank	0.7		58	39	49.7

» Engineering UK: **www.engineeringuk.com**
» Institution of Mechanical Engineers: **www.imeche.org**

Medicine

The introduction of A* grades at A level has produced another step change in the already fearsome entry grades at UK medical schools. Entrants at 20 of the 30 schools average more than 500 points in the latest table, compared with nine last year, and none comes close to dropping below 450 points. No other subject has such high standards. Yet only four subjects attract more applications, even though candidates are restricted to four medical schools, and a decline of less than 3 per cent for courses beginning in 2012 hardly dented the level of competition. The opening of new medical schools a decade ago was expected to ease this pressure on places, but there were still nearly 11 applications to every place in 2011.

The top four remain the same for the third year in succession, with Oxford ahead of Cambridge thanks largely to satisfaction levels that are 8 percentage points ahead of any other medical school. Cambridge has the highest entry standards and recorded the best results in the 2008 Research Assessment Exercise. At least 80 per cent of its research was considered world-leading or internationally excellent in all but one of the eight specialisms in which it submitted work. Universities were able to submit research in up to 12 areas (called units of assessment, UoA). Full details can be seen for UoA 1–9, 12, 14 and 15 at **www.rae.ac.uk/results**.

Employment scores are no longer used as a measure (although they are still shown for guidance) to avoid small differences distorting positions in a subject where virtually all graduates become junior doctors or researchers. Only four schools registered less than full employment in 2010 and none dropped below 98 per cent.

Undergraduates have to be prepared to work long hours, particularly towards the end of the course. But student satisfaction is generally high, even if it does not reach the levels seen in some subjects. Just Oxford managed to satisfy more than 85 per cent of undergraduates, but only five dropped below 70 per cent on this measure. Medicine is also second in the earnings league, with average starting salaries of more than £29,000 in 2010.

Nearly all schools demand chemistry and most biology. Physics or maths is required by some, either as an alternative or addition to biology Universities will want to see evidence of commitment to the subject through work experience or voluntary work. Almost all schools interview candidates, and several use one of the two specialist aptitude tests (*see* chapter 1). The figures for Exeter and Plymouth, in joint 14th place, relate to the Peninsula Medical School, which has been run jointly by the two universities. From 2013, the school will separate and applications should be made to the University of Exeter Medical School or Plymouth University Peninsula Medical School.

» British Medical Association: **www.bma.org.uk**
» NHS Careers: **www.nhscareers.nhs.uk**
» Student BMJ: **http://student.bmj.com**

Medicine

	Research quality	Entry standards	Student satisfaction %	Graduate prospects %	Overall rating
1 Oxford	1.4	620	95	100	100.0
2 Cambridge	1.6	631	85	100	98.0
3 Edinburgh	1.3	582	82	100	90.8
4 University College London	1.3	554	81	100	88.0
5 Aberdeen	1.1	540	87	100	87.5
6 Imperial College	1.2	560	80	100	87.0
7 Newcastle	0.8	531	87	100	84.3
8 St Andrews	0.7	538	85	98	82.4
9 Dundee	0.7	529	85	100	81.9
10 Hull-York	1.0	518	79	100	81.2
11 Queen Mary, London	1.1	499	79	100	81.1
12 Sheffield	0.7	511	83	100	79.6
13 Leeds	0.8	496	82	100	79.5
=14 Exeter	0.7	501	84	100	79.1
=14 Plymouth	0.7	501	84	100	79.1
16 Birmingham	0.9	534	73	100	79.0
17 Leicester	0.6	507	84	100	78.5
=18 King's College London	0.9	508	72	100	76.6
=18 Southampton	0.9	475	78	100	76.6
20 Nottingham	0.5	517	80	100	76.2
21 Glasgow	0.8	520	69	99	75.7
22 Manchester	1.0	498	68	100	75.5
23 Queen's, Belfast	0.6	505	75	99	75.3
24 Warwick	0.7		76	100	75.1
25 Bristol	0.9	508	68	100	75.0
26 Brighton & Sussex Medical School	0.5	471	83	99	74.2
27 Liverpool	0.8	484	68	100	72.2
28 Cardiff	0.7	521	64	100	71.9
29 St George's	0.6	463	76	100	71.8
30 East Anglia	0.6	465	76	100	71.7
31 Keele	0.4	464	71	100	68.6

Employed in graduate job:	91%	Employed in non-graduate job and studying:		0%
Employed in graduate job and studying:	3%	Employed in non-graduate job:		0%
Studying:	5%	Unemployed:		0%
Average starting graduate salary:	£29,141	Average starting non-graduate salary:		–

Middle Eastern and African Studies

Cambridge has overtaken Oxford in the ranking for Middle Eastern and African Studies by a fraction of a point, a year after rejoining the table. Cambridge has the highest entry standards and the most satisfied students, while the two ancient universities tie on research under the new method of calculating scores from the 2008 Research Assessment Exercise (RAE). The change mirrors the more selective allocation of research funds to universities in England. Leeds has the best employment record, but is only three places off the bottom of the table because it did not enter the RAE in these subjects. Durham, in third place, is the only other university where 80 per cent of graduates went straight into graduate-level jobs or onto more advanced courses. It is perhaps surprising, therefore, that the subjects have moved into the top half of the table for employment prospects, despite an above-average unemployment rate of 13 per cent.

St Andrews remains in fourth place in the ranking, just ahead of Edinburgh as the leading university north of the border. There are no representatives of Wales or Northern Ireland. Westminster is the only post-1992 university in the table.

The small numbers make for big swings even in the national statistics. The £20,500 average for starting salaries in graduate jobs, for example, is £4,500 down on the figure in last year's *Guide*. Middle Eastern Studies is the larger of the two subjects in terms of student numbers. There were fewer than 70 applications for African studies by March 2012, but almost 500 for Middle Eastern subjects. Entry standards are high: most students come with A levels or their equivalent and only one university averages less than 360 points on the UCAS tariff. A high proportion of students graduate with a first or 2:1.

Employed in graduate job:	45%	Employed in non-graduate job and studying:	3%
Employed in graduate job and studying:	5%	Employed in non-graduate job:	18%
Studying:	16%	Unemployed:	13%
Average starting graduate salary:	£20,537	Average starting non-graduate salary:	£15,872

Middle Eastern and African Studies	Research quality	Entry standards	Student satisfaction %	Graduate prospects %	Overall rating
1 Cambridge	1.5	548	89	69	100.0
2 Oxford	1.5	530	87	70	99.4
3 Durham	1.1	516	86	80	94.8
4 St Andrews	1.0	-	82	76	88.7
5 Edinburgh	1.2		65	71	82.0
6 School of Oriental and African Studies	1.1	392	70	70	81.2
7 Birmingham	1.0	375	84	60	81.1
8 Exeter	0.7	421	83	55	76.8
9 Leeds		423	86	84	76.0
10 Manchester	0.9	367	66	47	68.3
11 Westminster		263	64	47	49.7

» African Studies Association of the UK: **www.asauk.net**
» British Society for Middle Eastern Studies: **www.brismes.ac.uk**

Music

Music has been growing in popularity both for Honours and Foundation degrees, attracting almost 30,000 applications in 2011 – 5,000 more than in 2006. But the move to higher fees brought this expansion to an abrupt end, as applications dropped by almost 9 per cent in 2012. The number of places has kept pace with rising demand and there were little more than five applications to the place in 2011. Nine out of ten degree applicants come with A levels and most university departments expect music to be among them, although they may accept a distinction or merit in Grade 8 music exams. There is considerable variation in the character of courses, from the practical and vocational programmes in conservatoires to the more theoretical degrees in some of the older universities.

Music	Research quality	Entry standards	Student satisfaction %	Graduate prospects %	Overall rating
1 Oxford	1.8	490	87	80	100.0
2 Cambridge	1.8	521	78	81	97.1
3 Birmingham	1.9	451	85	71	95.3
4 Bristol	1.1	440	89	85	94.8
5 Newcastle	1.5	443	88	71	94.3
6 Manchester	1.9	467	82	70	94.2
7 King's College London	1.8	485	78	75	93.7
8 Southampton	1.8	418	84	71	92.8
9 Durham	1.2	459	84	77	92.5
10 York	1.8	417	81	73	91.6
11 Royal Holloway	2.1	395	80	67	90.9
12 Sheffield	1.7	378	77	86	90.6
13 Glasgow	1.4	480	83	61	90.1
14 Nottingham	1.4	446	82	67	89.1
15 Royal Academy of Music	1.2	324	78	96	87.7
16 Surrey	1.1	450	79	70	86.7
17 Cardiff	1.0	392	85	66	86.0
18 Edinburgh	1.1	448	79	64	85.1
19 Royal Conservatoire of Scotland	0.7	341		91	84.6
20 Bangor	1.2	325	81	73	83.6
21 Royal College of Music	0.8	303	77	94	83.0
22 Leeds	1.1	373	80	68	82.7
23 Aberdeen	0.6	395	83	67	82.5
24 Sussex	1.1	353	79	71	82.2
25 School of Oriental and African Studies	1.5	289		71	81.8
26 Queen's, Belfast	1.4	405	75	56	81.6
27 Keele	1.1	289	81	75	81.2
28 Goldsmiths College	1.3	364	74	67	80.9
29 Strathclyde		461		66	80.8
30 Huddersfield	1.2	324	79	66	80.5
31 Liverpool	0.8	362	81	59	79.5

32	Lancaster	1.3	339	71	70	78.7
33	Hull	0.5	335	84	61	77.9
34	East Anglia	0.4	375	81	61	77.5
35	Royal Northern College of Music	0.5	345	71	85	77.0
36	Birmingham City	0.7	252	75	87	76.7
37	City	1.3	361	66	65	75.7
38	Oxford Brookes	0.7	310	86	46	75.3
39	Bath Spa	0.5	346	75	66	74.9
40	Edinburgh Napier	0.1	397	68	79	74.0
41	Derby		333	86	53	73.6
42	Brunel	0.8	342	72	58	72.8
43	Chester	0.4	287	73	74	72.1
44	De Montfort	0.9	320	79	41	72.0
45	Kent		314	78	66	71.8
46	Gloucestershire		268	82	67	71.7
=47	Hertfordshire	0.3	328	79	46	69.4
=47	Canterbury Christ Church	0.5	240	79	55	69.4
=47	West of Scotland		318	87	37	69.4
50	Coventry	0.7	318	68	57	69.1
51	Plymouth	0.8	247	69	62	67.8
52	Glamorgan		324	67	71	67.7
53	Manchester Metropolitan		280	73	64	67.2
54	Cardiff Metropolitan		258	78	57	66.8
55	Southampton Solent		318	79	41	66.4
56	Westminster	0.5	288	67	57	65.9
57	Ulster	0.3	276	67	62	65.4
58	Chichester		288	76	49	65.0
59	Falmouth		227	74	62	64.5
60	Anglia Ruskin	0.3	267	66	62	64.0
61	Salford	0.3	275	70	52	63.8
62	Essex		240	76	51	63.7
63	Brighton	1.4	277	70	21	63.6
64	Kingston	0.1	296	66	55	62.5
65	West London	0.1	257	65	65	62.4
66	Cumbria		269	64	65	61.9
67	Middlesex		230	64	64	59.7
68	Buckinghamshire New		257	69	46	59.3
69	East London		243	63	61	59.0
70	Central Lancashire		301	64	44	58.6
71	Sunderland	0.3	284	69	30	58.4
72	Northampton	0.3		71	33	57.7
73	Liverpool John Moores		176	78	27	55.6

Employed in graduate job:	36%	Employed in non-graduate job and studying:	3%
Employed in graduate job and studying:	5%	Employed in non-graduate job:	26%
Studying:	21%	Unemployed:	9%
Average starting graduate salary:	£18,493	Average starting non-graduate salary:	£13,809

Music cont

Oxford remains at the head of the music ranking, despite not leading on any individual measure, but once again there has been considerable movement below it. Cambridge has replaced Bristol in second place and is the only university to average more than 500 points at entry. Birmingham has moved up six places to third, while further down the table, Aberdeen has jumped 15 places to 23rd.

The Royal Academy of Music again has the best employment score, and it is noticeable that the specialist institutions do far better than even the leading university departments on this measure. While the four specialists registered positive destinations for between 85 per cent and 96 per cent of their leavers, 12 universities in the bottom half of the table fell below 50 per cent.

Royal Holloway, just outside the top ten overall, had the best grades in a high-scoring set of research assessments, with no less than 90 per cent of its research considered world-leading or internationally excellent. Bristol, although down to fourth place, still has the most satisfied students. Huddersfield remains the top post-1992 university and the only one in the top 30. As in most subjects, the new universities suffer for their lower entry grades, although selection is more a matter of musical ability than academic achievement.

The 9 per cent unemployment rate in the latest survey remains no worse than the average for all subjects, despite the fact that career prospects for musicians are notoriously uncertain. Music finishes in the bottom half of the employment table because nearly 30 per cent of leavers were in non-graduate occupations six months after graduation. Salaries in those jobs were the lowest for any subject at the time of the latest survey, while the average in graduate-level employment was just outside the bottom ten, at less than £18,500.

» Incorporated Society of Musicians: **www.ism.org**
» Royal Musical Association: **www.rma.ac.uk**

Nursing

Nursing has seen the strongest growth at degree level of any area of higher education since moving towards becoming a graduate profession. There were more than 100,000 degree applications for the first time in 2010, and by March 2012 the subject was well on the way to 200,000, becoming by far the most popular choice of all. The withdrawal of the diploma route into the profession from September 2013 encouraged another 27 per cent rise in applications for degrees starting in 2012, following growth of 49 per cent in the previous year. It is all a far cry from 2008, when well-publicised stories of nurses finishing their training to face the dole led to a decline in the demand for places.

The number of places has not kept pace with such massive growth in demand. Indeed, the number of new enrolments dropped by 1,500 in 2011, making nursing one of the most competitive subjects, with almost nine applications for every place. The selection process may well tighten further in 2013, but entry requirements are certain to remain low. Despite the squeeze on places in 2010, only nine universities averaged more than 350 points for A levels and Highers. Entry scores are more closely bunched than in many tables: just two universities averaged less than 200 points.

Edinburgh remains top of the table, with the highest entry standards and good scores on the other measures. Glasgow has moved up to second, as the only other university to average 400 points at entry and sharing the top score in the 2011 National Student Survey with Liverpool, in fifth place. Fourth-placed Manchester produced the best grades in the 2008 Research Assessment Exercise, with 85 per cent of its submission considered world-leading or internationally excellent.

Chester, which is in the bottom ten overall, is one of 11 universities with 100 per cent employment records. The others are Liverpool, Ulster, York, Leeds, Cardiff, Sheffield Hallam, Bradford, Coventry, the joint school at Kingston and St George's, in south London, and Queen Margaret, Edinburgh. Only four universities saw fewer than nine out of ten nurses go straight into the profession or on to further study, leaving the subject in the top three for employment prospects. However, it is a different story in the earnings league, where nursing is 16th, with average starting salaries below £22,500.

Northumbria, which shares tenth place with East Anglia, is the only post-1992 university in the top ten of a ranking where less than a third of the institutions are older foundations. Queen Margaret, Kingston and St George's, Teesside and De Montfort join it in the top 20. Cardiff is the top university in Wales, while Ulster, which secured one of the best grades in the 2008 Research Assessment Exercise, outperforms Queen's, Belfast in Northern Ireland, sharing fifth place with Liverpool overall.

Almost two thirds of the students arrive without A levels, many of them upgrading other health-related qualifications. A quarter of those who join pre-registration programmes drop out, but the rate is nearer 10 per cent thereafter.

Employed in graduate job:	90%	Employed in non-graduate job and studying:	0%
Employed in graduate job and studying:	5%	Employed in non-graduate job:	2%
Studying:	1%	Unemployed:	2%
Average starting graduate salary:	£22,484	Average starting non-graduate salary:	£17,203

Nursing	Research quality	Entry standards	Student satisfaction %	Graduate prospects %	Overall rating
1 Edinburgh	1.3	442	91	95	100.0
2 Glasgow	0.9	436	93	93	98.1
3 Southampton	1.8	342	81	99	96.8
4 Manchester	1.9	352	76	98	95.7
=5 Liverpool	0.6	326	93	100	95.3
=5 Ulster	1.6	302	81	100	95.3
7 York	1.4	357	75	100	93.9
8 Nottingham	1.0	366	78	97	92.0
9 Leeds	1.1	305	77	100	91.3
=10 East Anglia	0.6	341	80	99	90.7
=10 Northumbria	0.8	291	83	99	90.7
12 Surrey	0.1	370	84	98	90.0
13 Cardiff	0.8	332	75	100	89.8
=14 City	1.3	297	74	97	89.6
=14 Queen Margaret Edinburgh		372	80	100	89.6

Nursing cont	Research quality	Entry standards	Student satisfaction %	Graduate prospects %	Overall rating
16 Queen's, Belfast	0.6	285	83	98	89.3
17 Teesside		349	83	99	89.2
18 King's College London	0.7	353	75	96	88.9
19 Kingston/St George's	0.8	295	76	100	88.8
20 De Montfort	0.5	302	81	98	88.4
21 Hertfordshire	1.1	280	75	98	88.2
22 Swansea	0.6	334	75	98	88.0
23 Sheffield Hallam	0.6	301	75	100	87.9
24 Edge Hill	0.4	246	86	96	87.3
25 Salford	0.6	299	79	95	87.1
26 Birmingham City		292	85	97	87.0
27 Birmingham		363	76	98	86.8
28 Staffordshire		273	85	98	86.6
29 Hull		320	80	98	86.4
30 Coventry		319	77	100	86.3
31 Keele		260	87	96	86.0
32 Bangor		280	82	97	85.5
=33 Greenwich	0.4	274	79	95	85.3
=33 London South Bank	0.5		77	96	85.3
=35 Oxford Brookes		297	80	97	85.2
=35 Glyndŵr	0.3	246	84	95	85.2
=37 Glamorgan	0.6	290	82	90	85.1
=37 West of England	0.5	282	72	98	85.1
=39 Edinburgh Napier	0.5	228	80	96	84.9
=39 Bradford	0.6	232	75	100	84.9
41 Bournemouth	0.6	332	71	93	84.5
42 Dundee	0.7	216	80	94	84.4
43 Brighton	0.2	301	72	98	84.2
44 Northampton		272	76	99	84.0
=45 West London	0.6	256	71	98	83.7
=45 Portsmouth		296	76	97	83.7
47 Cumbria		264	80	96	83.5
=48 Canterbury Christ Church		271	75	99	83.3
=48 Plymouth	0.5	286	71	96	83.3
=50 Leeds Metropolitan		232	85	94	83.2
=50 Bedfordshire		261	76	98	83.2
52 Manchester Metropolitan	0.3	241	76	97	83.1
53 Lincoln		326	69	98	82.8
54 Stirling	0.9	179	76	94	82.4
55 Glasgow Caledonian	0.9	259	82	81	81.6
=56 Chester	0.2	249	69	100	81.5
=56 Liverpool John Moores	0.5	252	72	94	81.5
58 Middlesex	0.5	195	77	94	80.8

59 West of Scotland		230	84	89	80.6
60 Anglia Ruskin		246	73	96	80.0
61 Robert Gordon		203	77	95	79.7
62 Worcester		279	64	97	78.6
63 Central Lancashire	0.7	279	77	77	77.7
64 Abertay		218		82	69.6

» NHS Careers: **www.nhscareers.nhs.uk**
» The Royal British Nurses' Association: **www.rbna.org.uk**
» Royal College of Nursing: **www.rcn.org.uk**

Other Subjects Allied to Medicine

The "allied to medicine" category covers audiology, complementary therapies, counselling, health services management, health sciences, nutrition, occupational therapy, optometry, ophthalmology, orthoptics, osteopathy, physiotherapy, podiatry, radiography and speech therapy. Taken together, the subjects are among the 20 most popular at degree level and suffered only a marginal decline at the introduction of higher fees. Applications were down by less than 3 per cent in March 2012, following increases of more than 15 per cent in both the preceding years.

Traditional universities monopolise the top ten, but big names such as Durham, Bristol and King's College London find themselves outside the top 30. Glasgow enters the ranking in first place, despite not leading on any of the four indicators, while Aston slips to second place. Cambridge moves up to third, with entry standards that are 160 points (the equivalent of more than one A*) ahead of its nearest challenger. Strathclyde, at equal fourth, has the most satisfied students, and eighth-placed Leeds and University College London, two places lower, share the best of a mediocre set of research grades.

Bangor, in 35th place, has the best employment score. It was the only university to see all its leavers go straight into graduate-level work or further study in 2010, although Exeter, in 15th place, came close. The choice of specialism naturally affects graduate employment rates, which range from better than 90 per cent positive destinations at ten universities to less than 50 per cent at a handful of universities in the bottom half of the table. Stiff competition for places in subjects such as optometry and physiotherapy has been pushing up entry grades, with 16 universities averaging at least 400 points on the UCAS tariff, while only five dropped below 250 in the latest survey.

The table is more mixed than most in terms of the performance of new and old universities. Portsmouth is the highest-placed post-1992 institution, while Oxford Brookes, Glasgow Caledonian, Robert Gordon and the West of England all join it in the top 20. Across the whole range of subjects, almost half of the students arrive without A levels.

The subjects are just outside the top ten for early employment prospects, having shot up the table in the last three years. Three quarters of all those completing a degree go straight into graduate jobs or continue their studies and only 8 per cent were unemployed at the time of the latest survey. Starting salaries have declined slightly since the last edition of the *Guide*, however, and are still not in the top 20.

Other Subjects Allied to Medicine cont

Employed in graduate job:	60%	Employed in non-graduate job and studying:	2%
Employed in graduate job and studying:	6%	Employed in non-graduate job:	17%
Studying:	8%	Unemployed:	8%
Average starting graduate salary:	£20,741	Average starting non-graduate salary:	£14,771

Other Subjects Allied to Medicine	Research quality	Entry standards	Student satisfaction %	Graduate prospects %	Overall rating
1 Glasgow	0.9	470	85		100.0
2 Aston	0.8	417	90	94	99.7
3 Cambridge		630	87	83	97.2
=4 Cardiff	1.0	425	82	93	96.5
=4 Strathclyde	0.9	434	91	72	96.5
6 Newcastle	0.9	447	87	75	95.5
7 Lancaster	1.0	371	89	75	93.8
8 Leeds	1.1	359	78	96	93.7
9 Manchester	0.9	435	79	86	93.2
10 University College London	1.1	415	81	78	93.0
11 Sheffield	0.9	411	84	76	92.5
12 Portsmouth	0.9	334	80	96	91.5
13 Nottingham	0.6	373	82	92	90.6
14 Keele	0.7	369	88	74	90.2
15 Exeter	0.9	416	69	98	89.7
16 Oxford Brookes	0.5	375	86	80	89.4
17 Glasgow Caledonian	0.9	407	79	75	89.0
18 Robert Gordon	0.3	406	81	88	88.0
19 Southampton	0.3	425	78	90	87.2
20 West of England	1.0	311	78	83	86.8
21 Bradford	0.5	374	78	89	86.7
22 Birmingham		430	85	79	86.6
23 Hull	1.0		79	69	86.3
24 Liverpool	0.6	344	75	93	86.2
=25 East Anglia	0.2	374	84	84	85.9
=25 Glamorgan	0.0	354	83	96	85.9
=25 Anglia Ruskin	0.3	371	84	81	85.9
28 Northumbria	0.4	358	82	80	85.3
29 Teesside	0.2	366	84	80	85.0
30 Swansea	1.0	374	69	84	84.8
31 Durham		405	86	74	84.7
32 Ulster	0.9	349	81	62	84.3
33 Hertfordshire	0.8	315	78	77	83.9
34 City	0.5	354	72	90	83.6
35 Bangor		296	80	100	83.0
36 Sheffield Hallam	0.3	343	79	84	82.7
37 King's College London	0.5	380	74	80	82.4

38	Brunel	0.5	359	77	76	82.1
39	Bournemouth		351	80	85	81.3
=40	Coventry	0.2	314	80	80	80.3
=40	Brighton	0.2	317	80	82	80.3
42	Kent	0.5	321	80	64	79.6
43	Central Lancashire	0.4	316	83	59	78.8
44	Manchester Metropolitan	0.4	343	74	76	78.7
45	Reading		400	75	76	78.5
46	Essex		321	79	79	78.3
47	Liverpool John Moores	0.4	316	76	73	78.0
=48	De Montfort	0.4	277	78	74	77.6
=48	Plymouth	0.1	319	76	80	77.6
=48	Westminster	0.6	300	71	79	77.6
51	Edinburgh Napier	0.2		76	78	77.4
=52	Salford	0.5	293	74	74	77.1
=52	Lincoln	0.1	264	84	70	77.1
=52	Cardiff Metropolitan	0.3	324	78	68	77.1
=52	St Mary's College		306	84	67	77.1
56	Nottingham Trent	0.9	307	72	59	77.0
57	East London	0.5	227	78	76	76.9
58	Queen Margaret Edinburgh	0.1	367	77	69	76.7
59	Middlesex	0.4	229	72	89	76.2
=60	Bristol		382	67	86	76.1
=60	Huddersfield		277	81	74	76.1
62	Cumbria	0.0	291	73	88	75.6
63	Chester	0.2	275	83	64	75.5
64	Birmingham City		296	76	79	75.4
65	London Metropolitan	0.4	271	76	68	74.8
66	St George's		354	70	77	74.1
67	West of Scotland	0.7	276	78	46	73.6
68	York St John	0.1	302	79	63	73.5
69	Greenwich		262	78	73	73.4
70	Leeds Metropolitan	0.1	306	78	61	73.1
71	Derby		276	75	75	72.8
72	Northampton	0.2	255	71	79	72.5
73	Marjon, Plymouth		382	68	67	71.8
74	Canterbury Christ Church	0.1	252	66	91	71.5
75	Bedfordshire		224	71	86	71.3
76	Sunderland	0.2	287	79	44	69.2
77	University College Birmingham		222	77	47	64.6
78	Abertay	0.1	247		50	63.2

» Association of Health Professions in Ophthalmology: **www.ahpo.org**
» British Association and College of Occupational Therapists: **www.cot.org.uk**
» British Society of Audiology: **www.thebsa.org.uk**
» Chartered Society of Physiotherapy: **www.csp.org.uk**
» General Chiropractic Council: **www.gcc-uk.org**

Other Subjects Allied to Medicine cont

» General Osteopathic Council: **www.osteopathy.org.uk**
» General Optical Council: **www.optical.org**
» Health Professions Council: **www.hpc-uk.org**
» NHS Careers: **www.nhscareers.nhs.uk**
» Royal College of Radiologists: **www.rcr.ac.uk**
» Royal College of Speech and Language Therapists: **www.rcslt.org**
» Society of Chiropodists and Podiatrists: **www.feetforlife.org**
» Society of Radiographers: **www.sor.org**

Pharmacology and Pharmacy

Pharmacology and pharmacy have been among the big successes of higher education, with big increases in applications and places in recent years. Applications continued to grow in spite of the switch to higher fees in 2012 and the subjects are in the top five for employment prospects. Only 3 per cent of new graduates were unemployed at the end of 2010, when 93 per cent were already in graduate-level jobs or continuing their studies. There were more than seven applications for every place in 2011, despite another increase in places for first-year students. Six more universities qualify for the latest table this year, making 13 additions in five years.

Departments in England are evenly split between those specialising in pharmacy and pharmacology. Only four cover both. Since 1997, pharmacy degrees have been converted to the four-year MPharm, whereas pharmacology is available either as a three-year BSc or as an extended course. Most degrees require chemistry and another science or maths at A level or the equivalent. Surprisingly, given graduates' success in the labour market, the subjects are not high in the earnings league: average starting salaries of just over £20,230 for graduate-level jobs place them 32nd out of the 62 subject groups.

Pharmacology and Pharmacy	Research quality	Entry standards	Student satisfaction %	Graduate prospects %	Overall rating
1 Cambridge	1.0	630	87	83	100.0
2 Nottingham	1.5	463	78	98	96.6
3 Cardiff	0.9	452	89	100	95.0
4 East Anglia	0.9	418	91	99	94.5
=5 Edinburgh	1.6		91	60	93.8
=5 Queen's, Belfast	0.9	440	87	100	93.8
7 Manchester	1.3	442	79	94	92.8
8 Newcastle	1.0	461	86	83	91.8
9 Bath	1.0	466	79	95	91.6
10 Dundee	1.2	425	91	69	90.5
=11 Aston	0.8	421	83	100	90.4
=11 King's College London	0.9	420	86	93	90.4
13 Strathclyde	0.9	481	78	93	89.6
=14 Leeds	0.9	386	89	75	86.8
=14 University College London	1.1	474	80	69	86.8

16 Bradford	0.9	353	82	96	86.5
17 School of Pharmacy	1.2	406	69	100	86.3
18 Robert Gordon		444	87	100	85.1
19 Liverpool	0.9	364	89	71	85.0
20 Huddersfield	0.3	382	94		84.6
=21 Glasgow	0.9	424	82	74	84.3
=21 Bristol	0.9	421	81	76	84.3
23 Brighton	0.6	373	82	94	83.7
24 Sunderland	0.2	427	82	96	83.2
25 Reading	0.7	364	76	100	82.6
26 Keele	0.2	391	83	100	82.5
27 Greenwich	0.4	284	95	86	81.8
28 Hertfordshire	0.5	346	85	87	81.5
29 Kent	0.5	330	80	98	81.0
30 Portsmouth	0.9	320	76	91	80.5
31 Liverpool John Moores	0.4	380	76	93	79.2
32 Nottingham Trent	0.9	313	77		77.9
33 De Montfort	0.6	311	77	87	77.0
34 Aberdeen		375	86	65	73.4
35 Glasgow Caledonian	0.4		84	55	71.3
36 Kingston	0.4	301	75	72	69.6
37 Hull		320	79	71	68.8
38 Ulster		367	69	71	66.6
39 East London		229	57	74	54.9
40 London Metropolitan		221	74	37	54.0

Employed in graduate job:	62%	Employed in non-graduate job and studying:	1%
Employed in graduate job and studying:	20%	Employed in non-graduate job:	6%
Studying:	9%	Unemployed:	3%
Average starting graduate salary:	£20,236	Average starting non-graduate salary:	£15,222

Cambridge remains top of the table, having taken the lead for the first time in five years in the 2012 *Guide*. The university's normal high entry standards make the difference: they are 150 points ahead of the rest. Nottingham, the leader two years ago, is back up to second place, followed by Cardiff, which was one of seven universities to register full employment for the class of 2010. The others were Aston, Keele, Queen's, Belfast, Reading, Robert Gordon and the University of London's School of Pharmacy.

Edinburgh, which shares fifth place with Queen's, has the best research score and remains the leading university in Scotland. Cardiff is again the only representative of Wales. Robert Gordon is the highest-placed post-1992 university and is joined in the top 20 by Huddersfield. Entry standards are high: nearly half of the universities in the table average more than 400 points and only three less than 300.

» Association of Pharmacy Technicians, UK: **www.aptuk.org**
» British Pharmacological Society: **www.bps.ac.uk**
» General Pharmaceutical Council: **www.pharmacyregulation.org**
» Royal Pharmaceutical Society: **www.rpharms.com**

Philosophy

Philosophy confounded the sceptics who predicted a decline for subjects without a clear pathway to employment in the era of £3,000 fees. With almost six applications to the place in 2011, it was one of the most competitive subjects in the arts and social sciences. Eight universities have average entry scores of more than 500 points and almost half more than 400 in the latest table. But there were ominous signs in March 2012, as fees rose again, with applications dropping by 16 per cent.

Cambridge has retaken the top place in philosophy that it lost to Oxford two years ago. Oxford still has the highest entry standards in the table, but Cambridge has the most satisfied students. The London School of Economics, in third place, has much the best employment record. Other employment scores are extremely variable, with over a quarter of all universities failing to secure "positive destinations" in employment or further study for at least 50 per cent of their graduates. Philosophy remains just in the bottom 20 subjects in the employment table, and nearly a third of leavers start their working life in non-graduate jobs.

As in previous years, scores in the National Student Survey were high throughout the table: none of the 46 universities failed to satisfy at least 70 per cent of its students. University College London, in fifth place, produced the best results in the 2008 Research Assessment Exercise, when three quarters of its submission was rated world-leading or internationally excellent. Fourth-placed St Andrews was close behind on research and remains the top university in Scotland. Cardiff remains top in Wales, while Brighton records the highest finish outside the old universities.

Relatively few philosophy undergraduates studied the subject at A level – indeed, Bristol warns that even an A in the subject is "not necessarily evidence of aptitude for philosophy at university". Degrees can require more mathematical skills than many candidates expect, especially when there is an emphasis on logic in the syllabus. The subject has usually resided in the bottom half of the earnings table, but a £1,000 increase in average starting salaries for graduate-level jobs has taken it close to the top 20 in the latest table.

Employed in graduate job:	31%	Employed in non-graduate job and studying:	4%
Employed in graduate job and studying:	5%	Employed in non-graduate job:	27%
Studying:	24%	Unemployed:	10%
Average starting graduate salary:	£21,096	Average starting non-graduate salary:	£14,512

Philosophy	Research quality	Entry standards	Student satisfaction %	Graduate prospects %	Overall rating
1 Cambridge	1.3	548	90	81	100.0
2 Oxford	1.4	590	85	81	99.1
3 London School of Economics	1.4	506	82	88	95.8
4 St Andrews	1.6	563	81	65	93.8
5 University College London	1.7	504	81	69	92.9
6 King's College London	1.5	476	82	72	92.1
7 Durham	0.9	539	83	78	91.8

8 Sheffield	1.4	466	86	61	91.4
9 Bristol	1.3	508	76	76	88.9
10 Sussex	0.8	404	89	67	88.7
11 Essex	1.2	369	86	69	88.3
12 York	0.9	465	81	70	86.5
13 Newcastle	0.8	406	88	56	85.3
14 Nottingham	1.1	411	81	65	85.0
15 Warwick	0.9	501	77	67	84.6
16 Reading	1.4	386	80	51	82.8
17 Glasgow	0.7	437	85	48	81.9
18 Exeter	1.0	464	75	62	81.5
19 Stirling	1.2	372	87	32	81.2
20 Leeds	1.1	410	76	59	80.5
21 Lancaster	0.6	389	78	69	80.4
22 Edinburgh	1.1	462	70	67	80.0
23 Southampton	0.5	432	82	51	79.5
24 Dundee	0.7	344	87	45	79.3
25 Cardiff	0.4	435	84	47	79.2
26 Birmingham	0.6	408	76	66	78.8
27 East Anglia	0.5	387	84	48	78.4
28 Brighton	1.4	286	81	39	77.3
29 Liverpool	0.3	395	81	55	77.0
30 Hull	0.5	323	82	57	76.7
31 Keele	0.5	332	79	61	76.6
32 West of England	0.2	298	82	67	75.9
33 Manchester	0.7	450	70	61	75.7
34 Aberdeen	0.3	356	79	62	75.5
35 Queen's, Belfast	0.8	396	75	48	75.3
36 Hertfordshire	0.4	320	81	54	74.9
37 Staffordshire	0.2	302	84	51	74.4
38 Oxford Brookes	0.0	323	84	48	73.2
39 Kent	0.6	363	74	50	72.7
40 Manchester Metropolitan	0.5	289	83	31	71.1
41 Roehampton		299	84	38	70.2
42 Heythrop College	0.1	345	73	54	68.5
43 Greenwich		262	80	41	67.3
44 Central Lancashire		275	83	27	66.5
45 Anglia Ruskin		226	82	31	65.1
46 Trinity St David	0.2	253	70	50	63.6

» British Philosophical Association: **www.bpa.ac.uk**
» Philosophical Society of England:
   http://atschool.eduweb.co.uk/cite/staff/philosopher/philsocindex.htm
» Royal Institute of Philosophy: **www.royalinstitutephilosophy.org**

Physics and Astronomy

There has been constant concern about the state of physics in recent years, with sixth-form numbers dropping and university departments closing. But applications were up by an astonishing 18 per cent in 2011 and even the prospect of £9,000 fees could not prevent another big rise in 2012. The 8 per cent growth in the demand for places even gave physics more applications than chemistry for the first time. The "Brian Cox effect" has been credited with the recent boom in popularity, in recognition of the engaging Manchester University professor's many television appearances.

There were almost six applications to the place in 2011 and physics is now one of the most competitive tables, with high scores among the leading universities. No fewer than nine universities, led by top-placed Cambridge, average more than 500 points at entry. Like last year, Cambridge has a slim lead over St Andrews, while Oxford has regained third place.

Aberdeen, in 20th place, was the only university to see over 90 per cent of its physicists find graduate-level employment or a postgraduate course within six months of completing a degree in 2010. But physics is among the top ten subjects nationally for employment prospects. Although unemployment is above average, at 11 per cent, almost half of all graduates continue their studies, either full or part-time.

Physics has also produced consistently high scores in the National Student Survey, with almost every university satisfying at least three quarters of their undergraduates in the 2011 results. Sussex, in fifth place, has the most satisfied students, with Lancaster close behind. By contrast, physics was one of the lowest-scoring subjects in the 2008 Research Assessment Exercise. Under the new scoring system used in the table this year, Lancaster shares the top score with Cambridge, St Andrews and Nottingham. Swansea has overtaken Cardiff to become the leading university in Wales for physics. Hertfordshire is the highest-placed of the five post-1992 universities in the table.

Most universities demand physics and maths at A level for both physics and astronomy, as well as good grades overall. Only one undergraduate in five is female and a similarly small proportion arrives without A levels or their equivalent. About 5 per cent transfer to other courses or drop out, usually at the end of the first year, but well over half of those who remain get firsts or 2:1s. The subjects are in the top 12 for starting salaries, averaging more than £23,650 in graduate-level jobs.

Employed in graduate job:	29%	Employed in non-graduate job and studying:	1%
Employed in graduate job and studying:	6%	Employed in non-graduate job:	12%
Studying:	40%	Unemployed:	11%
Average starting graduate salary:	£23,675	Average starting non-graduate salary:	£14,966

Physics and Astronomy	Research quality	Entry standards	Student satisfaction %	Graduate prospects %	Overall rating
1 Cambridge	1.2	630	87	83	100.0
2 St Andrews	1.2	563	88	84	99.2
3 Oxford	1.0	622	84	85	96.7

4 Durham	1.0	574	83	82	94.6
5 Sussex	0.9	420	92	80	94.3
6 Birmingham	1.0	506	87	79	94.2
7 Lancaster	1.2	443	91	66	93.5
8 Bath	1.1	469	84	78	92.5
9 Glasgow	1.0	477	87	76	92.4
10 Manchester	1.0	495	88	72	92.1
=11 Nottingham	1.2	453	84	76	91.8
=11 Imperial College	1.1	589	77	81	91.8
13 Sheffield	1.0	467	85	74	90.9
14 Leeds	0.8	435	85	84	90.7
15 Edinburgh	1.1	515	83	70	90.2
16 Bristol	1.0	498	81	79	90.1
17 Liverpool	1.0	404	87	73	89.4
18 Warwick	0.8	529	81	79	89.3
19 University College London	1.0	512	79	75	88.9
=20 Southampton	0.9	465	82	77	88.6
=20 Aberdeen	1.0	394	77	91	88.6
22 Surrey	0.8	421	86	78	88.5
23 Exeter	0.9	475	84	70	88.1
24 Loughborough	0.8	391	85	77	87.3
25 York	0.9	427	83	72	86.4
26 Heriot-Watt	0.9	388	85	71	86.3
=27 Strathclyde	0.5	399	89	71	85.3
=27 Royal Holloway	0.8	358	84	76	85.3
29 Leicester	0.9	383	82	72	84.8
30 Queen Mary, London	0.8	355	83	72	84.1
31 Kent	0.8	348	85	67	83.9
32 Swansea	0.7	344	84	74	83.5
33 King's College London	0.7	439	81	67	82.8
34 Keele	0.5	312	88	73	82.7
35 Salford	0.7	332	86	63	81.5
=36 Cardiff	0.6	431	83	62	81.4
=36 Hull	0.6	336	86	65	81.4
38 Hertfordshire	0.9	345		63	80.8
39 Queen's, Belfast	0.7	424	74	69	78.7
40 Nottingham Trent	0.9	298	74	73	78.2
41 Central Lancashire	0.5	309	81		76.2
42 West of Scotland	0.2	286	83		72.8
43 Aberystwyth	0.3	310	82	53	71.9
44 Glamorgan		286	75	46	62.3

» British Astronomical Association: **http://britastro.org**
» Institute of Physics: **www.iop.org**

Politics

Politics has been enjoying a boom as a degree subject, applications growing by almost a quarter in the first two years of the decade. The trend was reversed in 2012, with the prospect of higher fees, although even after a decline of almost 9 per cent, there were still more than 30,000 applications. With six applications for every place, entry scores have been rising. Almost 30 universities, six more than last year and twice as many as in the 2009 *Guide*, average over 400 points and only three less than 250 points.

Oxford holds onto top place with the highest entry grades, but Cambridge has overtaken Sheffield to secure second place. Cambridge ties with Leicester, in 25th place, for the most satisfied students. Sheffield shares the best score from the 2008 Research Assessment Exercise with Essex, in equal seventh place. Both had three quarters of their research rated world-leading or internationally excellent. Aberystwyth is the top university in Wales, while St Andrews is the leader in Scotland. Brighton is the highest-placed post-1992 university and is joined by Huddersfield in the top 40.

Satisfaction scores in politics were generally high in the 2011 National Student Survey: only two of the 71 universities failed to satisfy at least 70 per cent of their final-year undergraduates. The best employment prospects are at Bath, in sixth place. Scores elsewhere are variable, with ten universities failing to see half of their politics graduates go straight into graduate-level jobs or continue their studies. The subject is now in the top 20 in the earnings league, with average starting salaries of more than £21,500, but has yet to make the same progress in the employment of graduates. Unemployment is on the average for all subjects, at 9 per cent, but 30 per cent of graduates start off in lower-level jobs.

Employed in graduate job:	34%	Employed in non-graduate job and studying:	4%
Employed in graduate job and studying:	4%	Employed in non-graduate job:	26%
Studying:	23%	Unemployed:	9%
Average starting graduate salary:	£21,582	Average starting non-graduate salary:	£15,127

Politics	Research quality	Entry standards	Student satisfaction %	Graduate prospects %	Overall rating
1 Oxford	1.3	600	84	82	100.0
2 Cambridge	0.9	565	89	78	98.3
3 Sheffield	1.7	469	86	73	97.7
4 London School of Economics	1.2	535	76	82	92.5
5 Warwick	1.0	500	81	77	92.2
6 Bath	0.7	468	82	89	91.6
=7 St Andrews	0.7	522	83	75	90.7
=7 Essex	1.7	378	86	55	90.7
9 Durham	0.8	505	80	80	90.6
10 Exeter	1.0	458	81	71	89.0
11 University College London	1.1	514	71	86	88.6
12 Nottingham	0.8	447	79	78	87.8
13 Bristol	0.6	467	81	78	87.7
14 Aberystwyth	1.5	332	83	56	86.3

15	York	0.8	470	77	75	86.1
16	King's College London	0.8	474	78	68	85.5
17	Newcastle	0.7	410	81	69	84.9
18	Glasgow	0.8	457	81	60	84.3
19	Sussex	0.9	397	77	70	83.3
20	Loughborough	0.6	380	81	70	83.1
=21	Edinburgh	0.8	474	73	71	82.6
=21	Hull	0.6	372	84	61	82.6
=23	Birmingham	0.6	417	78	67	81.9
=23	Surrey	0.4	378	80	73	81.9
=25	Leicester	0.3	389	89	53	81.8
=25	Cardiff	0.8	442	77	61	81.8
=27	Leeds	0.3	423	78	75	81.4
=27	East Anglia	0.5	387	84	57	81.4
29	Strathclyde	0.3	429	83	57	81.1
30	Brighton	1.4	283	75		80.9
31	School of Oriental and African Studies	0.9	474	71	63	80.4
32	Reading	0.6	370	82	55	79.9
33	Brunel	0.4	320	83	65	79.8
34	Huddersfield	0.0	314	80	85	79.6
=35	Queen Mary, London	0.6	412	78	58	79.4
=35	Dundee	0.5	368	85	48	79.4
=37	Manchester	0.9	435	69	66	79.2
=37	City		342	83	70	79.2
39	Royal Holloway	0.4	410	74	72	79.1
40	Keele	0.5	312	81	65	79.0
41	Queen's, Belfast	0.7	386	76	59	78.8
42	Aston	0.3	367	78	68	78.6
43	Lancaster	0.3	408	77	65	78.3
=44	Kent	0.4	355	82	56	78.1
=44	Portsmouth	0.8	290	83	50	78.1
46	Southampton	0.4	432	73	64	77.3
47	Aberdeen	0.4	395	79	54	77.2
48	Plymouth	0.6	294	78	64	77.0
49	Bradford	0.8	276	79	53	76.5
50	Liverpool	0.2	407	78	55	75.4
51	Stirling	0.3	363	80	50	75.0
52	Ulster	0.6	260	79	55	74.6
53	Swansea	0.3	349	74	63	74.1
54	Goldsmiths College	0.5	328	74	57	73.8
55	Northumbria	0.5	306	73	61	72.7
=56	Salford	0.4	312	79	48	72.4
=56	West of England	0.2	314	79	53	72.4
58	Oxford Brookes	0.2	322	76	56	72.3
59	Lincoln	0.3	253	77	58	72.1
60	Coventry	0.2	283	76	55	70.9
61	Nottingham Trent		295	76	60	70.6

Politics cont

	Research quality	Entry standards	Student satisfaction %	Graduate prospects %	Overall rating
62 Cardiff Metropolitan		278	77	59	70.5
63 De Montfort	0.3	274	80	43	70.4
64 Central Lancashire	0.1	314	77	47	68.9
65 Manchester Metropolitan	0.2	269	76	47	68.4
66 Kingston	0.3	262	73	47	67.1
67 Westminster	0.3	292	65	58	65.7
68 London Metropolitan	0.3	217	73	46	65.3
69 Greenwich	0.0	205	78	43	65.0
70 Leeds Metropolitan		239	74	47	64.5
71 Birmingham City	0.3		70	38	61.7

» Political Studies Association: **www.psa.ac.uk**
» Study Politics: **www.studypolitics.org**

Psychology

Psychology is the biggest table in the *Guide*, with yet another university having joined the ranking this year. Applications fell by 6 per cent at the start of 2012, but only nursing and design attracted bigger totals. The subject remains among the most popular in spite of a relatively poor record in the graduate employment market: it is in the bottom six for the proportion of graduates with "positive destinations" and the bottom ten for average starting salaries in graduate-level jobs. Although unemployment is below average at 8 per cent, 44 per cent of graduates begin their careers in low-level jobs.

Most undergraduate programmes are accredited by the British Psychological Society, which ensures that key topics are covered, but the clinical and biological content of courses still varies considerably. Some universities require maths and/or biology A levels among an average of at least three Bs, but others are much less demanding. The contrast is obvious in the ranking, with 26 universities averaging more than 400 points at entry but eight below 250 points.

Cambridge has retained its lead over Oxford at the top of the table, recording the best scores on all four measures. Cambridge's entry grades were 80 points ahead of its ancient rival's and the proportion of psychologists going straight into graduate-level jobs or further study was 5 percentage points better. The student satisfaction measure was closer: Heriot-Watt, in 50th place, was only a point behind. But the 80 per cent of research considered world-leading or internationally excellent gave Cambridge comfortably the best grades in the 2008 Research Assessment Exercise.

The top four in the table are unchanged since last year, but there has been considerable movement further down. Cardiff and Royal Holloway have both moved up five places to enter the top ten, while Sheffield has slipped six places and out of it. Glasgow remains the top university in Scotland and Cardiff the same in Wales. Central Lancashire and Lincoln are the only post-1992 universities the top 40, while Northumbria and the West of England are the closest to joining them.

				Employed in non-graduate job and studying:	6%
Employed in graduate job:			27%		
Employed in graduate job and studying:			4%	Employed in non-graduate job:	38%
Studying:			16%	Unemployed:	8%
Average starting graduate salary:			£18,119	Average starting non-graduate salary:	£14,094

Psychology	Research quality	Entry standards	Student satisfaction %	Graduate prospects %	Overall rating
1 Cambridge	1.6	630	89	83	100.0
2 Oxford	1.5	550	87	78	94.7
3 University College London	1.4	526	84	72	89.8
4 Bath	1.5	498	80	68	86.8
5 Glasgow	1.0	475	85	71	85.8
6 Sussex	0.9	400	85	72	83.0
7 York	1.1	494	82	58	82.3
8 Durham	0.9	494	78	71	82.1
=9 Cardiff	1.2	462	80	62	82.0
=9 Royal Holloway	1.0	442	84	61	82.0
11 Sheffield	0.9	461	79	71	81.3
12 Exeter	0.9	464	82	63	81.0
13 Southampton	0.9	436	86	55	80.5
14 Bangor	1.1	318	87	57	79.2
15 Kent	0.6	398	82	68	78.2
16 Lancaster	0.6	434	79	67	78.0
17 Bristol	0.8	487	74	66	77.9
18 St Andrews	1.1	508	74	56	77.8
19 Loughborough	1.1	437	78	53	77.5
=20 Warwick	0.8	450	77	65	77.4
=20 Nottingham	0.8	446	75	68	77.4
=20 Birmingham	1.3	440	74	55	77.4
23 Aston	0.8	397	81	60	77.1
24 Surrey	0.6	425	77	68	76.4
25 Dundee	0.5	383	83	61	75.8
26 Edinburgh	0.9	464	78	48	75.4
27 Newcastle	0.6	431	76	64	75.1
28 Leeds	0.7	440	73	64	74.7
29 Aberdeen	0.6	377	81	55	74.0
30 Essex	0.8	345	82	52	73.6
=31 East Anglia	0.2	389	87	52	73.5
=31 Reading	0.8	394	78	52	73.5
33 Strathclyde	0.3	410	84	48	72.9
34 Central Lancashire	0.3	314	82	65	72.8
35 Lincoln	0.4	343	83	57	72.6
36 Stirling	0.3	363	83	53	71.8
37 Manchester	0.7	421	74	48	70.8
38 Leicester	0.3	399	76	60	70.7

Psychology cont

	Research quality	Entry standards	Student satisfaction %	Graduate prospects %	Overall rating
=39 Keele	0.3	323	79	62	70.6
=39 Bradford	0.7	253	83	50	70.6
=39 Goldsmiths College	0.7	338	79	49	70.6
42 Hull	0.5	359	81	48	70.3
43 Northumbria	0.3	352	79	58	70.1
44 West of England	0.5	342	79	50	69.9
45 Portsmouth	0.3	342	82	50	69.8
46 Brunel	0.5	349	77	53	69.5
47 Liverpool	0.4	396	79	44	69.4
48 Plymouth	0.4	320	78	55	69.1
49 Queen's, Belfast	0.4	372	79	45	68.7
50 Heriot-Watt	0.1	342	88	38	68.6
=51 Huddersfield		287	82	60	68.4
=51 Swansea	0.5	366	73	55	68.4
=53 Salford	0.5	326	78	48	67.9
=53 Chester	0.2	296	81	53	67.9
55 Staffordshire	0.3	267	81	52	67.4
56 Hertfordshire	0.4	330	76	51	67.3
57 Leeds Trinity	0.0	274	83	54	67.1
58 Cumbria		234	80	64	67.0
59 City	0.6	375	71	49	66.9
=60 Teesside		292	82	50	66.7
=60 Edinburgh Napier	0.1	309	82	47	66.7
62 Oxford Brookes	0.3	359	77	45	66.4
=63 York St John	0.0	334	86	34	65.9
=63 Edge Hill		298	83	45	65.9
65 Coventry	0.2	305	76	53	65.8
66 Ulster	0.4	295	83	35	65.6
=67 Sunderland	0.1	271	86	37	65.2
=67 Bournemouth	0.5	322	73	48	65.2
69 De Montfort		289	84	40	64.9
70 Westminster	0.2	304	70	62	64.3
71 Nottingham Trent	0.2	319	77	45	64.2
72 Sheffield Hallam	0.1	325	75	49	64.0
=73 Anglia Ruskin	0.6	258	75	45	63.7
=73 Newman		235	77	57	63.7
75 West London	0.0	195	82	52	63.6
=76 Roehampton	0.2	247	72	59	63.1
=76 St Mary's College		267	77	52	63.1
78 Manchester Metropolitan	0.5	318	70	44	62.9
79 Worcester		306	75	48	62.3
80 Middlesex	0.1	244	70	63	62.1
81 Buckinghamshire New		250	80	41	61.8

82 Derby	0.1	271	73	51	61.7
83 Winchester		311	73	46	61.2
84 Bath Spa	0.1	317	76	35	60.9
85 Greenwich	0.2	260	72	49	60.8
86 East London	0.2	217	75	46	60.6
87 Glamorgan	0.1	288	77	34	60.4
88 Queen Margaret Edinburgh		370	68	47	60.3
89 Gloucestershire	0.1	315	72	40	60.2
90 Brighton	0.4	306	72	34	60.0
=91 London South Bank	0.2	250	72	44	59.7
=91 Southampton Solent		282	77	35	59.7
93 Canterbury Christ Church		296	74	39	59.6
94 Bedfordshire		221	77	42	59.3
=95 Leeds Metropolitan		318	70	43	59.2
=95 Northampton		273	78	32	59.2
=97 Liverpool John Moores	0.4	288	75	26	59.0
=97 Newport		247	72	48	59.0
99 Abertay	0.2	267		39	58.9
100 Cardiff Metropolitan	0.3	265	70	43	58.8
101 Bolton	0.1	265	73	39	58.6
102 Glasgow Caledonian	0.1	364	66	41	58.3
103 West of Scotland		258	76	33	57.8
104 Kingston	0.2	282	69	37	57.3
105 London Metropolitan	0.1	256	68	36	55.1

» British Psychological Society: **www.bps.org.uk**

Russian and Eastern European Languages

Fewer than 100 students began degrees in Russian and/or Eastern European studies in 2011, following a 20 per cent drop in applications. Higher fees in 2012 brought an even more serious decline in the demand for places, and the small numbers make for exaggerated swings in statistics. Average starting salaries in graduate-level jobs have shot up by £4,600 in the latest table, for example, propelling the subjects almost into the top ten. The already healthy picture for general employment prospects has been maintained, with almost three quarters of graduates going on to further study or into jobs classified as "graduate level".

Cambridge has taken over from Oxford at the head of the ranking for Russian and Eastern European languages, establishing a clear lead for the first time in four years. Cambridge has the highest entry standards, the most satisfied students and the best employment score. The two ancient universities are well clear of Durham, in third place, and Bristol, in fourth, both of which have improved their positions in the latest *Guide*.

Oxford and Manchester tied for the best performance in the 2008 Research Assessment Exercise. Portsmouth is the sole representative of the post-1992 universities and there are no institutions from Wales or Northern Ireland. St Andrews remains the leader in Scotland, despite slipping six places since last year.

Russian has been growing in popularity in schools, although most undergraduates learn the language from scratch. Nationally, there were little more than five applications for each place in 2011. But entry standards are high throughout the table: no university averages less than 300 points on the UCAS tariff. Satisfaction levels are also high. Nearly every university in the table satisfied at least three quarters of its final-year undergraduates.

Employed in graduate job:	40%	Employed in non-graduate job and studying:	4%
Employed in graduate job and studying:	6%	Employed in non-graduate job:	19%
Studying:	24%	Unemployed:	8%
Average starting graduate salary:	£23,967	Average starting non-graduate salary:	–

Russian and East European Languages	Research quality	Entry standards	Student satisfaction %	Graduate prospects %	Overall rating
1 Cambridge	1.1	559	91	81	100.0
2 Oxford	1.4	527	87	74	96.9
3 Durham	0.5	516	85	80	91.0
4 Bristol	0.9	462	84	79	90.7
5 Exeter	0.7	473	82		86.9
6 Birmingham	0.9		80	71	86.0
7 University College London	0.7	451	77	80	85.7
8 Sheffield	1.2		80	60	84.5
9 St Andrews	0.2	482	83		83.6
10 Manchester	1.4	364	75		82.5
11 Nottingham	1.0	381	76	70	82.0
12 Bath	0.7	409	84	55	80.2
13 Glasgow	0.1		84	63	77.9
14 Leeds	0.3	404	69	73	74.8
15 Portsmouth		300	83	57	71.8

» British Association for Slavonic and East European Studies: **www.basees.org.uk**
» National Centre for Languages (CILT): **www.cilt.org.uk**

Social Policy

Social policy is the best bet for a degree place in the arts and social sciences, with barely three applications to the place and generally low entry grades. Even at such highly selective institutions as Bristol, Edinburgh and the London School of Economics (LSE), average entry points do not reach 450 in the new table. Three more universities have joined the table this year, reflecting a 14 per cent increase in applications in 2011. But this success was not repeated with the advent of higher fees: applications were down by 17 per cent in March 2012. Although two thirds of entrants come with A levels or their equivalent, some courses cater very largely for mature students – the group most reluctant to pay fees of up to £9,000 a year.

Social Policy

	Research quality	Entry standards	Student satisfaction %	Graduate prospects %	Overall rating
1 London School of Economics	1.8	425	74	78	100.0
2 City	1.1		73	100	95.7
3 Bristol	1.0	420	81	71	94.8
4 Bath	1.5	402	79	59	94.6
5 Edinburgh	1.3	428	75	56	90.4
6 Aston	0.3	383	86	72	89.7
7 Kent	1.3	294	79	64	89.1
8 Leeds	1.4	338	78	55	89.0
9 Cardiff	1.1	375	78	58	88.3
10 York	1.2	352	76	61	87.8
11 Nottingham Trent	0.9		74	74	87.2
12 Glasgow	0.8	371	74	68	86.2
13 Leicester	0.4	385	84	54	85.9
=14 Lincoln	0.5		82	67	85.8
=14 Stirling	0.8		82	53	85.8
16 Sheffield	1.1	367	74	58	85.5
=17 Loughborough	1.0	339	79	49	85.0
=17 Keele	1.0	320	79	56	85.0
19 Birmingham	0.9	332	77	59	84.7
20 London South Bank	0.9		81	43	83.4
21 Nottingham	0.7	355	75	54	81.7
22 Queen's, Belfast	1.0		72	56	80.6
23 Manchester	0.8		75	55	79.9
=24 Sheffield Hallam	0.9	307	77	37	78.8
=24 Bolton	0.6	192	83	60	78.8
26 Birmingham City	0.3	284	74	67	76.5
27 Salford	0.6	239	81	42	76.0
28 Bradford	0.7	215	78		75.7
29 West of Scotland	0.6		73	50	74.9
30 Swansea	0.8	339	66	41	73.6
31 Canterbury Christ Church		229	81	57	73.3
32 Ulster	0.8	254	77	25	72.8
33 Glyndŵr	0.2		66	73	71.3
34 Brighton	0.4	300	73	29	69.1
35 London Metropolitan	0.7		67	35	67.5
36 Plymouth	0.7	214	66	41	66.3
37 Leeds Metropolitan		244	68	55	65.6
38 Manchester Metropolitan	0.3		73	19	62.8
39 Anglia Ruskin	0.4	197	61	39	59.5

» National Institute of Economic and Social Research: **www.niesr.ac.uk**
» UK Social Policy Association: **www.social-policy.org.uk**

The London School of Economics (LSE) has retained its accustomed position at the head of the social policy ranking, with the best performance in the 2008 Research Assessment Exercise, when 80 per cent of its submission in the wider category of social work and policy and administration was rated world-leading or internationally excellent. City has come straight into the table in second place, with a 100 per cent employment record that is extremely rare in social policy. Elsewhere, only the LSE saw over three quarters of leavers go straight into graduate-level jobs or further study, and the success rate was below 40 per cent at six universities. Social policy is among the bottom five subjects for employment, although it does a little better in the earnings table.

Satisfaction levels are better, although six universities failed to satisfy at least 70 per cent of their final-year undergraduates in the 2011 National Student Survey. Aston produced the best score.

Edinburgh, with the highest entry standards, remains the leader in Scotland, despite dropping three places to fifth, while Cardiff is still well ahead of Swansea in Wales. A third of the 39 universities in the table are post-1992, but only three of them, compared with four last year, make the top 20. Nottingham Trent is by far the highest-placed, after a nine-place rise, while Lincoln and London South Bank are the other two.

Employed in graduate job:	31%	Employed in non-graduate job and studying:	4%
Employed in graduate job and studying:	4%	Employed in non-graduate job:	39%
Studying:	13%	Unemployed:	9%
Average starting graduate salary:	£19,540	Average starting non-graduate salary:	£14,410

Social Work

Despite the frequent pillorying of social workers in Parliament and the press, social work is among the most popular choices for higher education candidates. That may be partly because it is also in the top 20 for employment prospects and – more surprisingly – also in the top ten for starting salaries, which averaged almost £24,300 in 2010. Unemployment had crept up to 10 per cent in the latest survey, but more than 70 per cent of those completing social work degrees still went straight into graduate-level work or further study. There were signs of a change in 2012, however, when an 18 per cent drop in applications took the subject out of the top ten.

The social work table has grown by 48 universities in five years, a consequence of the move to a graduate profession. Thousands of places have been added at undergraduate level, but there were still more than seven applications for each one in 2011. Even so, entry grades are still the lowest in the *Guide*. Only Strathclyde, following the upgrading of the points awarded for Scottish sixth-form qualifications, averages more than 400 points, while six institutions have averages below 200 points.

Bath remains top of the table, although research is the only category in which it leads. Sheffield has jumped four places to second, just ahead of Strathclyde, which remains the leader in Scotland. For the second year in a row, Glamorgan has a 100 per cent employment record and is the top post-1992 institution and the leader in Wales, although it has slipped out of the top ten. Several others topped 90 per cent, but scores further down the table are surprisingly variable.

The most satisfied students are also at post 1992 universities: Robert Gordon and Chester, both of which are in the top 20. The majority of the institutions in the table are modern universities, but most are in the bottom half. Entry grades are largely responsible.

Employed in graduate job:	59%	Employed in non-graduate job and studying:	2%
Employed in graduate job and studying:	6%	Employed in non-graduate job:	18%
Studying:	5%	Unemployed:	10%
Average starting graduate salary:	£24,290	Average starting non-graduate salary:	£14,346

Social Work	Research quality	Entry standards	Student satisfaction %	Graduate prospects %	Overall rating
1 Bath	1.5	381	78	79	100.0
2 Sheffield	1.1	388	76	90	98.0
3 Strathclyde	0.5	437	85	85	97.6
4 Sussex	0.9	328	84	90	96.3
5 Leeds	1.4	354	82	68	96.0
6 Bristol	1.0	372	80	76	94.4
7 Keele	1.0	286	80	96	94.3
8 Queen's, Belfast	1.0	363	79	80	94.1
9 Kent	1.3	278	76	88	93.4
10 Lancaster	1.0	354	67	96	92.9
11 Stirling	0.8		82	87	92.2
12 Glamorgan	0.6	293	82	100	91.9
13 Hull	0.6	316	82	88	90.8
14 Robert Gordon		348	88	89	88.7
15 York	1.2	349	60	88	88.4
16 Huddersfield	0.7	299	79	82	87.0
17 Chester	0.2	276	88	92	86.9
18 Birmingham	0.9	338	74	70	86.8
19 Northumbria	0.5	277	86	81	86.3
20 East Anglia	0.8	294	82	69	85.9
21 Swansea	0.8		65	96	85.8
22 Glasgow	0.5		81	80	85.0
23 Glasgow Caledonian		327	84	86	84.9
24 Lincoln	0.5	271	79	87	84.6
25 Bedfordshire	0.6		77	79	83.8
26 Dundee	0.5	320	68	93	83.6
27 Ulster	0.8	283	78	68	83.2
28 Edinburgh	1.3	378	46	82	83.0
29 West of Scotland	0.6	334	78	63	82.9
30 Reading	0.6		69	89	82.7
31 Oxford Brookes		330	84	77	82.4
32 Sheffield Hallam	0.6	276	74	83	82.1

Social Work cont

		Research quality	Entry Standards	Student satisfaction %	Graduate prospects %	Overall rating
33	De Montfort	0.4	234	76	93	81.7
34	Bradford	0.7	256	73	78	81.0
35	Manchester	0.8		67	82	80.8
36	Coventry	0.4	268	78	81	80.6
37	Teesside		311	72	95	80.5
38	Middlesex	0.6	201	74	89	80.1
39	Nottingham Trent	0.9	222	75	69	79.7
40	West of England	0.3		72	90	79.3
41	Hertfordshire	0.2	288	68	97	79.2
=42	Bolton	0.6	211	83	70	79.0
=42	Newport	0.6		73	75	79.0
=44	Central Lancashire	0.6	251	73	74	78.5
=44	Southampton Solent		294	81	76	78.5
46	London South Bank	0.9		66	69	78.0
47	Goldsmiths College	0.6		77	64	77.2
48	Brunel	0.5	342	57	82	76.5
49	Brighton	0.4	215	75	79	75.8
50	Cardiff Metropolitan		226	77	86	75.1
51	Salford	0.6	289	68	61	74.8
52	Essex		240	84	69	74.5
53	Portsmouth		312	66	83	74.2
54	Derby		223	75	84	73.5
55	Northampton		241	76	77	72.8
56	Manchester Metropolitan	0.3	252	73	65	72.6
57	Gloucestershire	0.1	249	75	70	72.4
58	Bangor	0.4	269	75	53	72.2
59	Queen Margaret Edinburgh		341		56	71.8
60	Chichester		270	76	64	71.3
61	London Metropolitan	0.7	223	72	53	71.2
62	Plymouth	0.7	248	58	72	71.0
63	Marjon, Plymouth		196	82	68	70.2
64	East London	0.4	169	77	66	70.1
65	Anglia Ruskin	0.4	232	62	73	69.2
66	Worcester		225	79	59	68.8
67	Leeds Metropolitan		197	80	64	68.4
68	Sunderland		266	74	57	68.0
69	Edge Hill	0.2	254	79	45	67.9
70	Glyndŵr	0.2	179	66	79	67.4
71	Greenwich		229	68	71	66.7
72	Birmingham City	0.3	253	61	64	66.4
73	Liverpool John Moores		239	73	57	65.8
74	Staffordshire		158	68	82	65.5
75	Canterbury Christ Church		243	70	58	64.9

76 Winchester	283	69	45	63.4
77 Cumbria	185	68	59	60.6
78 Roehampton	210	72	45	60.4

» British Association of Social Workers: **www.basw.co.uk**
» General Social Care Council: **www.gscc.org.uk**
» Social Care Association: **http://socialcareassociation.co.uk**

Sociology

Sociology has slipped to second-bottom in the employment table this year, with more than half of those graduating in 2010 in low-level jobs or unemployed at the end of the year. The subject had been growing in popularity, with substantial increases in the demand for places in 2010 and 2011, but the prospect of higher fees brought an above-average decline of 11 per cent in 2012. Competition for places was already moderate for the social sciences, with fewer than five applications to the place and manageable entry grades.

Cambridge remains well clear in first place, despite uncharacteristically low grades for research. The sociology panel for the 2008 assessments was no respecter of reputations: neither Cambridge nor the London School of Economics is among the top 15 universities on this measure. But Cambridge has the most satisfied students and the best employment scores, while its entry grades are 100 points ahead of the nearest challenger.

Bath, which is up three places to third this year, has the best research score, with three quarters of the university's work judged to be world-leading or internationally excellent. Research grades in sociology were not as high as in many subjects, but Southampton, in 12th place, also did well, with 70 per cent of research in the top two categories. Glasgow, Aberdeen and Strathclyde (in that order) have all overtaken Edinburgh for sociology in Scotland, while Cardiff is best-placed in Wales. Portsmouth is the top post-1992 university and the only one in the top 30.

Sociology's low standing in the employment table is naturally reflected in the performance of individual universities. It is one of the few subjects in which not a single university saw 80 per cent of leavers go straight into graduate-level jobs or continue their studies. At 11 universities, over twice as many as last year, there were "positive destinations" for fewer than one new graduate in three.

Other subjects such as criminology, urban studies, women's studies and some communication studies are included in the category of sociology, and a large number of institutions teach the subject as part of a combined studies or modular programme. The subject's low standing in the employment ranking is not repeated in the comparison of graduate earnings, although it has slipped into the bottom half of the table this year after a drop of more than £1,000 in average starting salary in graduate-level jobs.

Employed in graduate job:	30%	Employed in non-graduate job and studying:	4%
Employed in graduate job and studying:	3%	Employed in non-graduate job:	42%
Studying:	13%	Unemployed:	9%
Average starting graduate salary:	£19,639	Average starting non-graduate salary:	£14,210

Sociology

Sociology	Research quality	Entry standards	Student satisfaction %	Graduate prospects %	Overall rating
1 Cambridge	1.0	565	89	78	100.0
2 Surrey	1.2	380	84	72	89.7
3 Bath	1.5	392	81	67	89.3
4 Warwick	1.2	422	81	62	87.3
5 London School of Economics	0.9	415	78	77	86.9
6 Durham	0.9	415	80	71	86.7
7 Glasgow	0.6	454	83	61	85.3
8 Sussex	1.1	374	82	57	84.1
9 Exeter	1.0	407	83	52	84.0
10 Lancaster	1.3	359	80	55	83.7
11 Leicester	0.5		88	57	82.3
12 Southampton	1.4	393	79	41	81.9
=13 Essex	1.3	336	81	49	81.8
=13 Aberdeen	0.9	372	84	50	81.8
15 Sheffield	1.1	367	79	57	81.6
16 York	1.2	374	79	47	81.2
17 Strathclyde	0.2	411	86	54	80.5
18 Keele	1.0	325	80	58	80.4
19 Kent	1.3	301	79	54	80.3
20 Leeds	1.4	359	75	51	80.1
21 Edinburgh	1.2	416	75	47	80.0
22 Bristol	0.7	410	77	57	79.9
23 Cardiff	1.1	384	77	49	79.8
24 Portsmouth	0.8	294	79	69	79.3
25 Newcastle	0.8	349	80	50	78.0
26 Loughborough	1.0	356	78	47	77.8
27 Goldsmiths College	1.3	320	75	50	77.7
=28 Stirling	0.8	336	82	43	76.4
=28 Manchester	1.4	384	67	49	76.4
30 Aston	0.3	371	79	56	76.2
31 Nottingham	0.7	356	74	57	76.0
32 Huddersfield	0.3	240	81	73	75.8
33 Robert Gordon	0.2	286	87	53	75.5
34 Hull	0.6	315	78	52	74.8
35 Northumbria	0.5	305	81	46	73.5
36 Birmingham	0.4	350	74	54	72.9
37 Coventry		278	86	50	72.6
=38 Birmingham City	0.3	273	84	45	72.4
=38 City	0.8	327	73	47	72.4
40 Lincoln		300	82	53	72.3
41 Brunel	0.7	314	77	38	71.7
=42 Bedfordshire	0.6	198	83	44	70.9
=42 Bangor		275	82	53	70.9

=44 Glasgow Caledonian	0.3	338	78	38	70.5
=44 Edinburgh Napier	0.1	316	82	40	70.5
46 Worcester		273	83	48	70.4
=47 Staffordshire	0.4	222	79	54	70.1
=47 Liverpool	0.4	375	72	44	70.1
49 Queen's, Belfast	1.0	355	69	34	69.3
50 Salford	0.7	296	75	37	69.1
51 Ulster		261	86	35	68.6
52 Chester	0.2	289	73	57	68.4
53 Central Lancashire		279	81	41	67.7
54 Southampton Solent		296	83	32	67.4
55 Bradford	0.7	205	78	37	67.2
56 Teesside	0.4	249	75	46	67.1
57 Brighton	0.4	282	78	31	66.8
58 Bath Spa		320	75	42	66.6
59 West of England	0.2	295	75	42	66.2
60 Sheffield Hallam		279	74	50	66.1
61 Canterbury Christ Church		261	78	44	66.0
62 West of Scotland		258	73	56	65.7
=63 Manchester Metropolitan	0.5	282	73	36	65.5
=63 Plymouth	0.5	295	66	50	65.5
65 Edge Hill		244	79	42	65.4
66 Leeds Metropolitan		259	76	45	65.1
67 Westminster		275	70	55	64.9
68 East London	0.6	192	77	33	64.6
69 Abertay		247		45	64.0
70 Liverpool John Moores		282	79	29	63.9
71 Nottingham Trent		271	74	40	63.5
72 Greenwich		236	78	37	63.1
73 Northampton		251	80	29	63.0
=74 Derby		274	77	31	62.8
=74 Roehampton	0.4	231	71	40	62.8
76 Sunderland		269	78	29	62.6
77 Kingston	0.3	264	71	36	62.5
78 Oxford Brookes		333	72	30	62.3
79 Middlesex		205	74	46	62.2
80 Anglia Ruskin		221	79	29	61.4
81 London South Bank		191	75	42	60.8
82 Buckinghamshire New		225	71	42	59.9
83 Glamorgan		259	71	33	59.2
84 Gloucestershire		271	66	39	58.7
85 London Metropolitan		208	68	43	57.8
86 St Mary's College		255		15	53.6

» The British Sociological Association: **www.britsoc.co.uk**

Sports Science

Sports science has been one of the big growth areas of UK higher education over the past decade – so much so that it has had its own table for the last four years. Even after an 8.5 per cent decline in applications in 2012, sports science remained on the verge of the top ten subjects at degree level. The subject covers more than 40 specialisms, from sports therapy to equestrian sport studies and marine sport technology. Many contain more science and less physical activity than candidates may expect. Brunel, for example, requires at least an AS level in one of the sciences. Many universities now offer sports scholarships for elite performers, but most are not tied to a particular course and, officially at least, do not mean that the normal entry requirements are waived.

Loughborough, the most famous name in university sport, tops the table, as it did in all three previous years of the ranking and when the broader classification was used. Surprisingly, it does not have the outright lead on any measure, although it ties with equal second-placed Birmingham for the best record in the 2008 Research Assessment Exercise. Both had 60 per cent of their research rated world-leading or internationally excellent. Glasgow, which shares second place with Birmingham, has the highest entry standards in a table where eight universities average less than 200 points.

Like last year, the most satisfied students are in Wales. Aberystwyth, the leader in Wales and 21st overall, had the top rating in the 2011 National Student Survey, followed by Glyndŵr, in Wrexham, reversing last year's leading scores on this measure. In both surveys, they were the only universities to satisfy more than 90 per cent of final-year undergraduates, although there were plenty of other good scores.

Sheffield Hallam is the only post-1992 university in the top ten, but Middlesex has the best employment score, despite only just making the top 40. At 20 universities and colleges, fewer than half of those completing a degree went straight into graduate jobs or onto a more advanced course. Sports science is just outside the bottom ten subjects for employment prospects and starting salaries this year. The unemployment rate is low, at only 6 per cent, but four out of ten graduates begin their working life in low-level jobs.

Employed in graduate job:	35%	Employed in non-graduate job and studying:	4%
Employed in graduate job and studying:	4%	Employed in non-graduate job:	36%
Studying:	15%	Unemployed:	6%
Average starting graduate salary:	£18,527	Average starting non-graduate salary:	£14,304

Sports Science	Research quality	Entry standards	Student satisfaction %	Graduate prospects %	Overall rating
1 Loughborough	1.1	412	84	72	100.0
=2 Glasgow	1.0	442	87	58	96.3
=2 Birmingham	1.1	399	83	65	96.3
4 Exeter	0.6	399	89	73	96.1
5 Durham	0.9	392	80	70	93.9
6 Edinburgh	0.8	405	69	79	90.2
7 Bath	0.7	368	84	61	89.3
8 Stirling	0.7	373	83	58	88.5

9	Sheffield Hallam	0.6	330	82	68	87.9
10	Aberdeen	0.4	419	84	53	86.6
11	Leeds	0.5	395	86	49	86.1
=12	Portsmouth	0.9	296	87	48	85.1
=12	East Anglia		352	87	67	85.1
=14	Strathclyde	0.9		81	53	84.2
=14	Leeds Metropolitan	0.7	284	80	63	84.2
16	Hertfordshire	0.5	321	80	66	84.1
17	Brunel	0.7	345	75	60	83.1
18	Liverpool John Moores	1.0	269	78	55	82.9
=19	Essex	0.5	341	83	52	82.6
=19	Ulster	0.4	300	89	51	82.6
21	Aberystwyth	0.2	251	94	58	82.4
22	Brighton	0.6	255	82	62	81.8
23	Chester	0.4	270	75	74	80.6
24	Huddersfield		258	83	73	80.1
25	Cumbria		268	81	72	79.4
=26	Bangor	0.6	265	82	52	79.1
=26	Chichester	0.3	301	83	53	79.1
=26	Heriot-Watt	0.5	347	76	53	79.1
29	Kent	0.8	263	75	57	79.0
=30	Central Lancashire		305	84	59	78.5
=30	Cardiff Metropolitan	0.4	268	83	55	78.5
32	Swansea	0.0	333	83	55	78.2
33	Hull	0.1	262	82	64	77.9
=34	Northumbria	0.3	303	73	64	77.4
=34	Gloucestershire	0.1	312	81	57	77.4
=34	Bournemouth		323	82	56	77.4
37	Manchester Metropolitan	0.4	252	73	67	77.0
38	Salford	0.5	292	87	36	76.9
=39	Lincoln		296	83	56	76.4
=39	Middlesex		206	76	81	76.4
41	Staffordshire	0.2	169	85	62	75.6
42	Dundee		405	82	35	74.8
43	Coventry	0.2	287	71	67	74.6
44	Newman	0.0	229	80	64	74.5
45	Teesside		273	84	51	74.3
46	Leeds Trinity		237	76	68	74.2
47	Oxford Brookes		320	82	46	74.0
48	Edinburgh Napier		309	80	50	73.9
=49	Southampton Solent		263	88	44	73.6
=49	Sunderland	0.4	259	80	44	73.6
51	Greenwich		264	75	64	73.5
52	St Mary's College	0.1	256	78	57	73.3
53	Winchester		245	83	53	73.1
54	Nottingham Trent	0.0	271	78	55	72.4
55	Worcester		287	76	54	71.9

Sports Science cont	Research quality	Entry standards	Student satisfaction %	Graduate prospects %	Overall rating
56 West of England		238	79	55	71.6
57 Glyndŵr		167	92	45	71.2
58 Abertay		248		55	70.9
59 Roehampton	0.0	220	70	69	70.3
60 London Metropolitan		221	75	58	69.5
61 Anglia Ruskin		167	73	68	68.9
62 Edge Hill		273	79	41	68.7
63 West of Scotland		283	75	46	68.4
64 London South Bank	0.4	210	73	46	67.9
65 Kingston		253	71	55	67.6
66 Glamorgan	0.3	246	77	35	67.1
67 East London		172	76	55	66.5
=68 Bedfordshire	0.3	215	66	53	66.1
=68 Marjon, Plymouth	0.0	205	79	44	66.1
=70 Derby		242	70	51	65.7
=70 York St John	0.0	235	75	45	65.7
72 Plymouth		272	68	50	65.5
73 Canterbury Christ Church	0.2	175	77	42	64.9
=74 Robert Gordon		316	64	47	64.8
=74 Northampton		205	75	47	64.8
76 Newport		192	79	41	64.6
77 Buckinghamshire New	0.1	199	65	43	58.6
78 Bolton		187	64	44	57.5

» British Association of Sport and Exercise Sciences: **www.bases.org.uk**
» English Institute of Sport: **www.eis2win.co.uk**
» Scottish Institute of Sport: **www.sisport.com**
» Sport Wales: **www.sportwales.org.uk**

Theology and Religious Studies

The table for theology and religious studies shows its third change of leadership in three years. Durham's lead over Cambridge could not be slimmer and Oxford is also less than a point behind in third place. Durham produced the best results in the 2008 Research Assessment Exercise, when two thirds of its work was considered world-leading or internationally excellent. Cambridge is a mere two points ahead of Oxford on entry standards, but the best scores on other measures come from outside the top three.

More than 1,300 students began degrees in theology or religious studies in 2011, but applications were down by 15 per cent in March 2012, as higher fees came in. It was already one of the least competitive subjects in the arts and social sciences: there were little more than four applications to the place in 2010. This is not fully reflected in the entry grades, however. Although only a dozen institutions average more than 400 points, none has an average of less than 250.

There is particularly keen competition north of the border, where Edinburgh and St Andrews have overtaken Aberdeen, but cannot be separated in the new table. Scottish universities occupied three of the top six places last year and still have four of the top 12. Exeter ties with St Andrews for the most satisfied students. Cardiff is the leader in Wales, while Leeds Trinity University College has the best employment record, but had been overtaken by Chichester and Chester as the highest-placed institution outside the old universities.

Surprisingly, theology and religious studies are close to the top 20 in the graduate destinations table, with an unemployment rate of only 6 per cent. By no means all graduates go into the church, but the vocation helps to maintain this record, as does the fact that four out of ten graduates continue studying.

Employed in graduate job:	30%	Employed in non-graduate job and studying:	4%
Employed in graduate job and studying:	4%	Employed in non-graduate job:	24%
Studying:	32%	Unemployed:	6%
Average starting graduate salary:	£20,068	Average starting non-graduate salary:	£14,099

Theology and Religious Studies	Research quality	Entry standards	Student satisfaction %	Graduate prospects %	Overall rating
1 Durham	1.5	456	88	84	100.0
2 Cambridge	1.3	517	84	87	99.9
3 Oxford	1.3	515	86	82	99.4
4 Exeter	0.7	452	92	76	93.1
=5 Edinburgh	1.2	440	83	74	91.6
=5 St Andrews	0.9	452	92	63	91.6
7 Nottingham	1.0	413	83	68	87.6
8 Bristol	0.8	432	80	77	87.0
=9 Glasgow	0.7	446	85	67	86.7
=9 Sheffield	1.1	398	85	64	86.7
11 Birmingham	0.9	373	83	74	86.1
12 Aberdeen	1.1	350	79	78	85.6
13 Manchester	1.2	404	82	59	85.0
14 Lancaster	0.9	373	81	74	84.9
15 Cardiff	0.5	422	81	71	83.2
16 Stirling	0.4	357	87	72	82.7
17 Kent	0.6	316	87	69	82.1
18 King's College London	0.9	410	70	72	80.4
19 Leeds	0.8	400	78	52	77.8
20 Bangor	0.4	312	85	63	77.5
21 Chichester	0.2	279	91	62	76.8
22 Queen's, Belfast		361	82	68	76.4
23 Chester	0.3	255	82	74	75.6
24 School of Oriental and African Studies	1.0	326	69	66	75.4

Theology and Religious Studies cont	Research quality	Entry standards	Student satisfaction %	Graduate prospects %	Overall rating
25 Leeds Trinity	0.4	250	72	88	75.2
26 Cumbria	0.3	295		71	74.1
27 St Mary's College	0.6	261	88	44	73.0
28 Newman		264	82	72	72.8
29 Heythrop College	0.1	331	79	62	72.7
=30 Winchester	0.1	323	83	56	72.4
=30 Roehampton	0.3	293	78	63	72.4
32 Oxford Brookes		318	82	57	71.5
33 Hull		346	79	56	70.4
34 York St John	0.1	282	85	50	69.6
35 Wales Trinity St David	0.5	268	68	60	66.6
36 Canterbury Christ Church	0.2	263	72	61	66.3
37 Bath Spa	0.1	316	67	59	64.9
38 Gloucestershire	0.4	304	74	27	61.3

» British Association for the Study of Religions: **http://basr.open.ac.uk**
» Society for the Study of Theology: **www.theologysociety.org.uk**

Town and Country Planning and Landscape

The demand for places on planning courses fell alarmingly during and after the last recession and, following a marginal rise in applications in 2011, there was another big drop in 2012. Even landscape and garden design, which had escaped the decline until then, saw applications drop by almost 20 per cent. Other courses were down by 16 per cent and seemed likely to increase their traditional reliance on Clearing. There were fewer than four applications for each of the 760 places filled in 2011.

Cambridge remains at the head of the planning table, with the best research grades and entry standards that are 70 points higher than the nearest challenger. Only three other universities average more than 400 points at entry, but only three drop below 250. Competition was tight in the 2008 Research Assessment Exercise: Cambridge had the most work placed in the top two categories, but Sheffield – which is back in second place this year – had a higher proportion judged to be world-leading.

Employment scores have recovered from a dip last year and are back in the top 20 for all subjects, having been in the top ten only three years ago. Reading again produces by far the best score on this measure. For the fifth year in a row, every graduate found high-level work or a place on a postgraduate course within six months of completing a degree.

Birmingham, in fifth place, again has the most satisfied students, closely followed by Leeds Metropolitan. Cardiff, in fourth place, is the top university outside England, while Glasgow Caledonian has overtaken Dundee to become the leader in Scotland for the first time. Northumbria is the only other post-1992 university in the top ten.

Unemployment is slightly above average, at 10 per cent, but 70 per cent of planners were in graduate-level jobs or still studying six months after graduating. Starting salaries in graduate-level jobs remain in the bottom half of the table, averaging just less than £20,000.

Employed in graduate job:	45%	Employed in non-graduate job and studying:	2%
Employed in graduate job and studying:	6%	Employed in non-graduate job:	18%
Studying:	19%	Unemployed:	10%
Average starting graduate salary:	£19,976	Average starting non-graduate salary:	£16,176

Town and Country Planning and Landscape

	Research quality	Entry standards	Student satisfaction %	Graduate prospects %	Overall rating
1 Cambridge	1.4	532	81	95	100.0
2 Sheffield	1.3	393	84	79	90.7
3 Cardiff	1.3	391	83	78	89.4
4 Reading	1.1	417	72	100	88.8
5 Birmingham	0.7	410	89	76	87.5
6 University College London	1.0	460	70	85	85.8
7 Newcastle	1.2	344	76	81	83.5
8 Loughborough	1.3	318	84	63	82.8
9 Glasgow Caledonian	0.9	347	74	82	80.5
10 Northumbria	0.6	301	84	79	79.4
11 Aberdeen	1.0	362		59	78.0
12 West of England	0.6	290	83	67	75.4
13 Gloucestershire	0.5	340		75	75.0
14 Sheffield Hallam	0.9	295	76	62	74.2
15 Oxford Brookes	0.5	334	75	73	73.9
16 Queen's, Belfast	0.5	340	68	84	73.7
17 Heriot-Watt	0.9	363	72	53	73.6
18 Manchester	1.0	352	71	53	73.5
19 Liverpool	0.7	370	75	52	72.9
20 Manchester Metropolitan	0.5		79	62	72.3
21 Nottingham Trent	0.3	306	76	69	70.5
=22 Liverpool John Moores	0.4		72	73	69.8
=22 Dundee	0.5		80	51	69.8
24 Leeds Metropolitan		308	87	50	68.7
25 Birmingham City	0.5	253	61	80	64.5
26 Greenwich		342	69	61	64.2
27 Westminster	0.4	243	73		63.1
28 Kingston	0.1	227	63	72	59.3
29 London South Bank		230	71	43	55.4
30 Ulster		250	67	41	53.9

» Royal Town Planning Institute: **www.rtpi.org.uk**
» Planning Officers Society: **www.planningofficers.org.uk**
» Landscape Institute: **www.landscapeinstitute.org**

Veterinary Medicine

Veterinary medicine was one of the select band of subjects to attract more applicants in spite of the move to higher fees. An increase of almost 8 per cent in the demand for places on courses beginning in 2012 was the third in succession. There were already almost nine applications per place and entry standards bettered only by medicine itself.

Veterinary medicine is another of the rankings in which employment scores have been removed from the calculations that determine universities' positions. The scores are still shown in the table, but the review group of academic planners consulted on the *Guide* agreed that employment rates in the subject were so tightly bunched that small differences could distort the overall ranking.

Nottingham is the newest of the seven schools, opening only in 2006, so the first students did not graduate in time for their statistics to be included in this edition of the *Guide*. But a clear lead on student satisfaction was enough to take it to the top, despite Cambridge's much higher entry standards. Edinburgh, in third place, produced the best performance in the 2008 Research Assessment Exercise. There are no degrees in veterinary medicine in Wales or Northern Ireland. Veterinary medicine remains in fourth place for employment this year but, surprisingly, the subject has dropped out of the top five for starting salaries in graduate-level jobs. Although the small numbers taking lower-level employment earned more than the graduates of any other subject in non-graduate work, vets have fallen behind economists and engineers in graduate-level jobs.

Most courses demand high grades in chemistry and biology, with some accepting physics or maths as one alternative subject. Cambridge and the Royal Veterinary College also set applicants a specialist aptitude test that is used by a number of medical schools. Few candidates win places without evidence of practical commitment to the subject, through work experience, either in veterinary practices or laboratories. The norm for veterinary science degrees is five years, but the Cambridge course takes six years and both Bristol and Nottingham provide a "pre-veterinary" year. Both Edinburgh and the Royal Veterinary College run four-year courses for graduates.

Employed in graduate job:	86%	Employed in non-graduate job and studying:	0%
Employed in graduate job and studying:	3%	Employed in non-graduate job:	5%
Studying:	4%	Unemployed:	3%
Average starting graduate salary:	£25,387	Average starting non-graduate salary:	£18,273

Veterinary Medicine	Research quality	Entry standards	Student satisfaction %	Graduate prospects %	Overall rating
1 Nottingham	0.9	494	90		100.0
2 Cambridge	0.6	601	84	87	98.5
3 Edinburgh	1.0	512	72	94	92.9
4 Glasgow	0.7	510	80	96	91.3
5 Royal Veterinary College	0.8	509	71	93	88.3
6 Liverpool	0.6	467	81	95	87.3
7 Bristol	0.4	456	77	90	81.6

» Royal College of Veterinary Surgeons: **www.rcvs.org.uk**

6 Making Your Application

In an era when there are relatively few interviews and more candidates each year achieve high A-level grades, what goes on your UCAS form is becoming more and more important – too important, many would say. The art of conveying knowledge of, and enthusiasm for, your chosen subject – preferably with supporting evidence from your school or college – can make all the difference.

Too many people take their eye off the ball when actually applying for a higher education place. Surprising numbers of applicants each year spell their own name wrongly, or enter an inaccurate date of birth, or the wrong course code. And that is to say nothing of the damage that can be done in the personal statement and teachers' references. While UCAS will decode misspelt names, other errors in grammar or spelling present admissions officers with an easy starting point in cutting applications down to a more manageable number.

There is talk of a new application system, with only two choices and later deadlines. But, for the moment, applicants will continue to have five choices of course, and to make decisions well before they have their results. You do not have to take advantage of all five – some people make only a single application, perhaps because they do not want to leave home or they have very particular requirements – but you will give yourself the best chance of success if you go for the maximum.

The application process

Most applications for full-time higher education courses go through UCAS, although specialist admissions bodies still handle applications to the music conservatoires (Conservatoires UK Admissions Service: **www.cukas.ac.uk**) and some postgraduate courses, including teacher training (Graduate Teacher Training Registry: **www.gttr.ac.uk**). The trend is towards the UCAS model even among specialist providers, however: recruitment to nursing and midwifery diploma and degree courses in Scotland switched to the UCAS system in 2010 and the art and design courses that used to recruit using the separate "Route B" scheme have also moved to the main system.

Universities that have not filled all their places, even during Clearing, will accept direct applications up to and after the start of the academic year, but UCAS is both the official route and the only way into the most popular courses.

Since 2006, all UCAS applications have been made online. The Apply electronic system is accessed via the UCAS website and is straightforward to use. For those who do not have the internet at home and prefer not to use school or college computers, the UCAS website lists 900 libraries, all over the UK, where you can make your application. Apply is available 24 hours a day, and, when the time comes, information on the progress of your application may arrive at any time.

Registering with Apply

The first step in the process is to register. If you are at a school or college, you will need to obtain a "buzzword" from your tutor or careers adviser – it is used when you log on to register. It links your application to the school or college so that the application can be sent electronically to your referee (usually one of your teachers) for your reference to be attached. If you are no longer at a school or college, you do not need a "buzzword" but you will need details of your referee. More information is given on the UCAS website.

To register, go to the UCAS website and click on "Apply". The system will guide you through the business of providing your personal details and generating a username and password, as well as reminding you of basic points, such as amending your details in case of a change of address. You can register separate term-time and holiday addresses – a useful option for boarders, who could find offers and, particularly, the confirmation of a place, going to their school when they are miles away at home. Remember to keep a note of your username and password in a safe place.

Throughout the process, you will be in sole control of communications with UCAS and your chosen universities. Only if you nominate a representative and give them your unique nine-digit application number (sent automatically by UCAS when your application is submitted), can a parent or anyone else give or receive information on your behalf, perhaps because you are ill or out of the country.

Once you are registered, you can start to complete the Apply screens. The sections that follow cover the main screens.

Personal details

This information is taken from your initial registration, and you will be asked for additional information, for example, on ethnic origin and national identity, used to monitor equal opportunities in the application process.

Choices

In most subjects, you will be able to apply to a maximum of five universities and/or colleges.

The main screens to be completed in UCAS Apply

» Personal details and some additional non-educational details for UK applicants.
» Student finance, a new section for UK-resident applicants.
» Your course choices.
» Details of your education so far, including examination results and examinations still to be taken.
» Details of any jobs you have done.
» Your personal statement.
» A reference from one of your teachers.
» Payment details (in 2012 applications cost £22, or £11 to apply to just one course).
» A declaration that you confirm that the information is correct and that you will be bound by the UCAS rules.

The exceptions are medicine, dentistry and veterinary science, where the maximum is four, but you can use your fifth choice as a back-up to apply for a different subject.

The other important restriction concerns Oxford or Cambridge, because you can only apply to one or the other; you cannot apply to both Oxford and Cambridge in the same year. For both Oxford and Cambridge you may need to take a written test (see pages 20–21) and submit examples of your work (depending on the course selected) and, in addition, for Cambridge, you will be asked to complete a Supplementary Application Questionnaire once Cambridge has received your application from UCAS. The deadline for Oxbridge applications – and for all medicine, dentistry and veterinary science courses – is 15 October. For all other applications the deadline is 15 January (or 24 March for some specified art and design courses).

Most applicants use all five choices. But if you do choose fewer than five courses, you can still add another to your form up to 30 June, as long as you have not accepted or declined any offers. Nor do you have to choose five different universities if more than one course at the same institution attracts you – perhaps because the institution itself is the real draw and one course has lower entrance requirements than the other. Universities are not allowed to see where else you have applied, or whether you have chosen the same subject elsewhere. But they will be aware of multiple applications within their own institution. It is, in any case, more difficult to write a convincing personal statement if it has to cover more than one subject.

For each course you select, you will need to put the UCAS code on the form – and you should check carefully that you have the correct code and understand any special requirements that may be detailed on the UCAS description of the course. You will also need to indicate whether you are applying for a deferred entry (for example, if you are taking a gap year – see page 203).

Education

In this section you will need to give details of the schools and colleges you have attended, and the qualifications you have obtained or are preparing for. The UCAS website gives plenty of advice on the ways in which you should enter this information, to ensure that all your relevant qualifications are included with their grades. While UCAS does not need to see qualification certificates, it can double-check results with the examination boards to ensure that no-one is tempted to modify their results.

Personal statements

As the competition for places on popular courses has become more intense, so the value attached to the personal statement has increased. Admissions officers look for a sign of potential beyond the high grades that growing numbers of applicants offer. Many (but not all) value success in extracurricular activities such as drama, sport or the Duke of Edinburgh's Award scheme. But your first priority should be to demonstrate an interest in and understanding of your chosen subject beyond the confines of the exam syllabus.

This is not easy in a relatively short statement that can readily sound trite or pretentious. You should resist any temptation to lie, particularly if there is any chance of an interview. A claim to have been inspired by a book that you have not read will backfire instantly under questioning and, even without an interview, experienced academics are likely to see through grandiose statements that appear at odds with a teacher's reference. Genuine experiences of after-hours clubs, lectures or visits – better still, work experience or actual reading around the syllabus – are much more likely to strike the right note. If you are applying for medicine, for example, any practical work experience or volunteering in medical or caring settings should be included. Take advice from teachers and, if there is still time before you make your application, look for some subject-related activities that will help fill out your statement.

Admissions officers are also looking for evidence of character that will make you a productive member of their university and, eventually, a successful graduate. Taking responsibility in any area of school or college life suggests this – leading activities outside your place of learning even more so. Evidence of initiative and self-discipline is also valuable, since higher education involves much more independent study than sixth-formers are used to.

UCAS top ten personal statement tips

1 Express interest in the subject and show real passion.
2 Go for a strong opening line to grab the reader's attention.
3 Relate outside interests to the course.
4 Think beyond university.
5 Get the basics right.
6 Don't try to sound too clever.
7 Take time and make it your best work.
8 Don't leave it until the last minute – remember the 15 January deadline!
9 Get a second opinion.
10 Honesty is the best policy.

Your overall aim in writing your personal statement is to persuade the admissions officer to pick you out of the piles of applications on his or her desk. That means trying to stand out from an often rather dull and uniform set of statements based around the curriculum and the more predictable sixth-form activities. Everyone is going to say they love reading, for example; narrow your interest down to an area of (real) interest. Don't be afraid to include the unusual, but bear in mind that an academic's sense of humour may not be the same as yours.

Give particular thought to why you want to study your chosen subject – especially if it is not one you have taken at school or college. You need to show that your interests and skills are well-suited to the course and, if it is a vocational degree, that you know how you envisage using the qualification. Admissions officers want to feel that you will be committed to their subject for the length of the course, which could be three, four or even five years, and capable of achieving good results.

Your school or college should be the best source of advice, since they see personal statements every year, but there are others. The UCAS website has a useful checklist of themes that you may wish to address, while sites such as **www.studential.com** also provide tips. But do not fall into the trap of cutting and pasting from the model statements included on such sites – both UCAS and individual universities have software that will spot plagiarism immediately. In one year, no fewer than one in twenty applicants came to grief in this way. Plagiarists of this type are unlikely to be disqualified, but they destroy the credibility of their application.

Try not to cram in more than the limited space will allow – admissions officers will have many statements to go through, and judicious editing may be rewarded. As long as you write clearly – preferably in paragraphs and possibly with sub-headings – it will be up to you what to include. It is a personal statement. But consider these points listed opposite and make sure that you can answer all the questions raised. Once you have completed your statement show it to others you trust. It is really important to have others read your statement before submitting it – sometimes things which are clear to you may not be to fresh eyes.

The Apply system allows 4,000 characters (including spaces), or 47 lines for your statement. While there is no requirement to fill all the space, it should not look embarrassingly short. UCAS recommends using a word-processing package to compile the statement before pasting it into the application system. This is because Apply will time-out after 35 minutes of inactivity, so there is a danger of losing valuable material. Working offline also has the advantage of leaving you with a copy and making it easier to show it to others.

References

Hand in hand with your personal statement goes the reference from your school, college or, in the case of mature students, someone who knows you well but is not a friend or family member. The reference has to be independent – you are specifically forbidden to change any part of it if you send off your own application – but that does not mean you should not try to influence what it contains. Most schools and colleges conduct informal interviews before compiling a reference, but it does no harm to draw up a list of the achievements that you would like to see included, and ensure your referee knows what subject you are applying for. Referees cannot know every detail of a candidate's interests and most welcome an aide-memoire.

The UCAS guidelines skirt around the candidate's right to see his or her reference, but it does exist. Schools' practices vary, but most now show the applicant the completed reference. Where this is not the case, the candidate can pay UCAS £10 for a copy, although at this stage it is obviously too late to influence the contents. Better, if you can, to see it before it goes off, in case there are factual inaccuracies that can be corrected.

Timing

The general deadline for applications through UCAS is 15 January but even those received up to 30 June will be considered if the relevant courses still have vacancies. After that, you will be limited to Clearing, or an application for the following year. In theory – and usually in practice – all applications submitted by the January deadline are given equal consideration. But the best advice is to get your application in early: before Christmas, or earlier if possible. Applications are accepted from mid-September onwards, so the autumn half-term is a sensible target date for completing the process. While no offers are usually made before the deadline, many admissions officers look through applications as they come in and may make a mental note of promising candidates. If your form arrives with the deadline looming, you may appear less organised than those who submitted in good time; and your application may be one of a large batch that receives a more cursory first reading than the early arrivals. Under UCAS rules, last-minute applicants should not be at a disadvantage, but why take the risk?

Key points to consider in writing your personal statement

» What attracts you to this subject (or subjects, in the case of dual or combined honours)?

» Have you undertaken relevant work experience or voluntary activities, either through school or elsewhere?

» Have you taken part in other extra-curricular activities that demonstrate character – perhaps as a prefect, on the sports field or in the arts?

» Have you been involved in other academic pursuits, such as Gifted and Talented programmes, widening participation schemes, or courses in other subjects?

» Which aspects of your current courses have you found particularly stimulating?

» Are you planning a gap year? If so, explain what you intend to do and how it will affect your studies. Some subjects – notably maths – actively discourage a break in studies.

» What other outside interests might you include that show that you are well-rounded?

Timetable for applications (based on 2011–12 dates)

May onwards	Find out about courses and universities. Attend open days.
September	Registration starts for UCAS Apply.
mid September	UCAS starts receiving applications.
15 October	Final day for applications to Oxford and Cambridge, and for all courses in medicine, dentistry and veterinary science.
15 January	Final day for all other applications from UK and EU students to ensure that your application is given equal consideration with all other applicants. Now also the deadline for all art and design courses except those which have a 24 March deadline (specified in UCAS Course Search).
16 January–30 June	New applications continue to be accepted by UCAS, but only considered by universities if the relevant courses have vacancies.
24 February	Start of applications through UCAS Extra.
24 March	Final day for applications for those art and design courses that specify this date.
31 March	Universities should have sent decisions on all applications received by 15 January, but decisions may be later than this.
9 May	Final day by which applicants have to decide on their choices if application submitted by 15 January and all decisions received by 31 March (exact date for each applicant will be confirmed by UCAS). **If you do not reply to UCAS, they will decline your offers.**
10 May	UCAS must receive all decisions from universities if you applied by 15 January.
7 June	Final day by which applicants have to decide on their choices if all decisions received by 10 May (exact date for each applicant will be confirmed by UCAS).
28 June	Final day by which applicants have to decide on their choices if all decisions received by 7 June (exact date for each applicant will be confirmed by UCAS).
1 July	Any new application received from this date held until Clearing starts.
4 July	Final day for applications through UCAS Extra.
19 July	Universities must give decisions on all applications submitted by 30 June. You must make a decision on these offers by 26 July.
7 August	SQA results published. Scottish Clearing starts.
16 August	GCE results published. Full Clearing and Adjustment starts.
31 August	Adjustment closes.
20 September	Last day UCAS will accept applications for courses about to start.
30 September	Clearing vacancy service closes. Contact universities directly about vacancies.
22 October	Last date by which a university can accept you through Clearing. Last day to add a Clearing choice.

Next steps

Once your application has been processed by UCAS, you will receive a welcome letter confirming your choices and summarising what will happen next. The letter will contain a reminder of your identification number and the username and password that you used to apply. These will also give you access to "Track", the online system that allows you to follow the progress of your application. Check all the details carefully: you have 14 days to contact UCAS to correct any errors. Since 2010 universities have been able to make direct contact with you through Track, including arranging interviews.

After that, it is just a matter of waiting for universities to make their decisions, which can take days, weeks or even months, depending on the university and the course. Some obviously see an advantage in being the first to make an offer – it is a memorable moment to be reassured that at least one of your chosen institutions wants you – and may send their response almost immediately. Others take much longer, perhaps because they have so many good applications to consider, or maybe because they are waiting to see which of their applicants withdraw when Oxford and Cambridge make their offers. Universities are asked to make all their decisions by the end of March, and most have done so long before that.

Interviews

Unless you are applying for a course in health or education that brings you into direct contact with the public, the chances are you will not have a selection interview. For prospective medics, vets, dentists or teachers, a face-to-face assessment of your suitability will be crucial to your chances of success. Likewise in the performing arts, the interview may be as important as your exam grades. Oxford and Cambridge still interview applicants in all subjects, and a few of the top universities see a significant proportion. But the expansion of higher education has made it impractical to interview everyone, and many admissions experts are sceptical about interviews.

What has become more common, however, is the "sales" interview, where the university is really selling itself to the candidate. There may still be testing questions, but the admissions staff have already made their minds up and are actually trying to persuade you to accept an offer. Indeed, you will probably be given a clear indication at the end of the interview that one is on its way. The technique seems to work, perhaps because you have invested time and nervous energy in a sometimes lengthy trip, as well as acquiring a more detailed impression of both the department and the university.

The difficulty can come in spotting which type of interview is which. The "real" ones require lengthy preparation, revisiting your personal statement and reading beyond the exam syllabus. Impressions count for a lot, so dress smartly and make sure that you are on time. Have a question of your own ready, as well as being prepared to give answers.

While you would not want to appear ignorant at a "sales" interview, lengthy preparation might be a waste of valuable time during a period of revision. Naturally, you should err on the side of caution, but if your predicted grades are well above the standard offer and the subject is not one that normally requires an interview, it is likely that the invitation is a sales pitch. It is still worth going, unless you have changed your mind about the application.

Offers

When your chosen universities respond to your application, there will be one of three answers:

» Unconditional Offer (U): This is a possibility only if you applied after satisfying the entrance requirements – usually if you are applying as a mature student, while on a gap year, after resitting exams or, in Scotland, after completing Highers.

» Conditional Offer (C): The university offers a place subject to you achieving set grades or points on the UCAS tariff.

» Rejection (R): You do not have the right qualifications, or have lost out to stronger competition.

If you have chosen wisely, you should have more than one offer to choose from, so you will be required to pick your favourite as your firm acceptance – known as UF if it was an unconditional offer and CF if it was conditional. Candidates with conditional offers can also accept a second offer, with lower grades, as an Insurance choice (CI). You must then decline any other offers that you have.

You do not have to make an Insurance choice – indeed, you may decline all your offers if you have changed your mind about your career path or regret your course decisions. But most people prefer the security of a back-up route into higher education if their grades fall short. You must be sure that your firm acceptance is definitely your first choice because you will be allocated a place automatically if you meet the university's conditions. It is no good at this stage deciding that you prefer your Insurance choice because UCAS rules will not allow a switch.

The only way round those rules, unless your results are better than your highest offer (see below), is through direct contact with the universities concerned. Your firm acceptance institution has to be prepared to release you so that your new choice can award you a place in Clearing. Neither is under any obligation to do so but, in practice, it is rare for a university to insist that a student joins against his or her wishes. Admissions staff will do all they can to persuade you that your original choice was the right one – as it may well have been, if your research was thorough – but it will almost certainly be your decision in the end.

UCAS Extra

If things do go wrong and you receive five rejections, that need not be the end of your higher education ambitions. From the end of February until the end of June, you have another chance through UCAS Extra, a listing of courses that still have vacancies after the initial round of offers. Extra is sometimes dismissed (wrongly) as a repository of second-rate courses. In fact, even in the boom year for applications of 2010, most Russell Group universities still had hundreds of courses listed in a wide variety of subjects.

You will be notified if you are eligible for Extra and can then select courses marked as available on the UCAS website. Applications are made, one at a time, through UCAS Track. If you do not receive an offer, or you choose to decline one, you can continue applying for other courses until you are successful. About half of those applying through Extra normally find a place.

Results Day

Rule Number One on results day is to be at home, or at least in easy communication – you cannot afford to be on some remote beach if there are complications. The day is bound to be stressful, unless you are absolutely confident that you achieved the required grades – more of a possibility in an era of modular courses with marks along the way. But for thousands of students Track has removed the agony of opening the envelope or scanning a results noticeboard. From midnight on the eve of A-level results day, the system informs those who have already won a place on their chosen course. You will not learn your grades until later, but at least your immediate future is clear.

If you get the grades stipulated in your conditional offer, the process should work smoothly and you can begin celebrating. Track will let you know as soon as your place is confirmed and the paperwork will arrive in a day or two. You can phone the university to make quite sure, but it should not be necessary and you will be joining a long queue of people doing the same thing.

If the results are not what you hoped – and particularly if you just miss your grades – you need to be on the phone and taking advice from your school or college. In a year when results are better than expected, some universities will stick to the letter of their offers, perhaps refusing to accept your AAC grades when they had demanded ABB. Others will forgive a dropped grade to take a candidate who is regarded as promising, rather than go into Clearing to recruit an unknown quantity. Admissions staff may be persuadable – particularly if there are extenuating personal circumstances, or the dropped grade is in a subject that is not relevant to your chosen course. Try to get a teacher to support your case, and be persistent if there is any prospect of flexibility.

One option, if your results are lower than predicted, is to ask for papers to be re-marked, as growing numbers do each year. The school may ask for a whole batch to be re-marked, and you should ensure that your chosen universities know this if it may make the difference to whether or not you satisfy your offer. If your grades improve, the university will review its decision, but if by then it has filled all its places, you may have to wait until next year to start the course.

If you took Scottish Highers, you will have had your results for more than a week by the time the A-level grades are published. If you missed your grades, there is no need to wait for A levels before you begin approaching universities. Admissions staff at English universities may not wish to commit themselves before they see results from south of the border, but Scottish universities will be filling places immediately and all should be prepared to give you an idea of your prospects.

Adjustment

If your grades are better than those demanded by your first-choice university, there is now an opportunity to "trade up". Introduced in 2009, the Adjustment Period runs for only five days after you have received your results, so there is no time to waste. First, go into the Track system and click on "Register for Adjustment" and then contact your preferred institutions to find another place. If none is available, or you decide not to move, your initial offer will remain open. More than 550 students switched places this way in 2011 – a small number, but worth considering if you are eligible. UCAS is yet to publish a breakdown of which universities were involved, but it is known that many students successfully went back to institutions that had rejected them at the initial application stage. The numbers using the system have risen gradually and it may well become more popular as it becomes better known, particularly if students become more cautious with their applications in response to the increased demand for places.

Clearing

If you do not have a place on Results Day, there will still be plenty of options through the UCAS Clearing scheme. Some 51,000 people – more than 10 per cent of all applicants –

found a place through this route in 2011. There is no reason to think there will be fewer places filled through Clearing in 2013. Although the most popular courses fill up quickly, many remain open up to and beyond the start of the academic year. And, at least at the start of the process, the range of courses with vacancies is much wider than in Extra. Most universities will list some courses, and most subjects will be available somewhere.

Clearing runs from A-level Results Day until the end of September, matching students without places to full-time courses with vacancies. As long as you are not holding any offers and you have not withdrawn your application, you are eligible automatically. You will be sent a Clearing number via Track to quote to universities.

Now it is just a matter of trawling through the lists on the UCAS website, and elsewhere, before making a direct approach to the university offering the course that appeals most, and where you have a realistic chance of a place – do not waste time on courses where the standard offer is far above your grades. Universities run Clearing hotlines and have become adept at dealing with a large number of calls in a short period, but you can still spend a long time on the phone at a time when the most desirable places are beginning to disappear. If you can't get through send an email setting out your grades and the course that interests you.

The best advice is to plan ahead and not to wait for Results Day to draw up a list of possible Clearing targets. Many universities publish lists of courses that are likely to be in Clearing on their websites from the start of August. Think again about some of the courses that you considered when making your original application, or others at your chosen universities that had lower entrance requirements. But beware of switching to another subject simply because you have the right grades – you still have to sustain your interest and be capable of succeeding over three or more years. Many of the students who drop out of degrees are those who chose the wrong course in a rush during Clearing.

In short, you should start your search straight away if you do find yourself in Clearing, and act decisively, but do not panic. You can make as many approaches as you like, until you are accepted on the course of your choice.

Most of the available vacancies will appear in Clearing lists, but some of the universities towards the top of the league tables may have a limited number of openings that they choose not to advertise – either for reasons of status or because they do not want the administrative burden of fielding large numbers of calls to fill a handful of places. If there is a course that you find particularly attractive – especially if you have good grades and are applying late – it may be worth making a speculative call. Sometimes a number of candidates holding offers drop grades and you may be on the spot at the right moment.

What are the alternatives?

If your results are lower than expected and there is nothing you want in Clearing, there are several things you can do. The first is to resit one or more subjects. The modular nature of most courses means that you will have a clear idea of what you need to do to get better grades. You can go back to school or college, try a "crammer". Although some colleges have a good success rate with re-takes, you have to be highly focused and realistic about the likely improvements. Some of the most competitive courses, such as medicine, may demand higher grades for a second application, so be sure you know the details before you commit yourself.

Other options are to get a job and study part-time, or to take a break from studying and return later in your career. The part-time route can be arduous – many young people find a job enough to handle without the extra burden of academic work. But others find it just the combination they need for a fulfilling life. It all depends on your job, your social life and your commitment to the subject you will study. It may be that a relatively short break is all that you need to rekindle your enthusiasm for studying. Many universities now have a majority of mature students, so you need not be out of place if this is your chosen route.

Taking a gap year

The other popular option is to take a gap year. About 7 per cent of applicants now defer their entry until the following year while they travel, or do voluntary or paid work. A whole industry has grown up around tailor-made activities, many of them in Asia, Africa or Latin America. Some have been criticised for doing more for the organisers than the underprivileged communities that they purport to assist, but there are programmes that are useful and character-building, as well as safe. Most of the overseas programmes are not cheap, but raising the money can be part of the experience. The alternative is to stay closer to home and make your contribution through organisations like Community Service Volunteers or to take a job that will make higher education more affordable when the time comes. Many admissions staff are happy to facilitate gap years because they think it makes for more mature, rounded students than those who come straight from school, and graduate employers also value the initiative and skills gained. The right programme may even increase your chances of winning a place, if it is relevant to your course. But there are subjects – maths in particular – that discourage a break because it takes too long to pick up study skills where you left off. From the student's point of view, you should also bear in mind that a gap year postpones the moment at which you embark on a career. This may be important if your course is a long one, such as medicine or architecture.

If you are considering a gap year, it makes sense to apply for a deferred place, rather than waiting for your results before applying. The application form has a section for deferments. That allows you to sort out your immediate future before you start travelling or working, and leaves you the option of changing your mind if circumstances change.

Useful websites

The essential website for making an application is, of course, that of UCAS:
www.ucas.com/students/applying
For applications to music conservatoires: **www.cukas.ac.uk**
For applications for graduate teacher training: **www.gttr.ac.uk**
For advice on your personal statement:
www.ucas.com/students/applying/howtoapply/personalstatement
www.studential.com

Gap years

To help you consider options and start planning: **www.gapadvice.org**
For links to volunteering opportunities in the UK: **www.do-it.org.uk**
For links to many gap year organisations: **www.yearoutgroup.org**
For work placements relevant to university courses (the Year in Industry Scheme):
www.etrust.org.uk

Also consult:
Community Service Volunteers: **www.csv.org.uk**
vInspired (the national young volunteers service): **www.vinspired.com**

7 University Tuition Fees

Undergraduate fees of up to £9,000 a year are finally on the way, and the sky has not fallen in on UK universities, but choosing a degree course will never be the same again for most applicants. Price may enter the equation both when deciding whether any degree is worth the money it will cost later, and in choosing between universities and sometimes even subjects.

One set of applications – not even enrolments – is no basis on which to judge how the new system will turn out. From the vantage point of March 2012, it is clear that increased fees will have a measurable, but not catastrophic, effect on the overall demand for higher education. Inevitably, some subjects and some universities will suffer more than others. But predictions that old universities and/or vocational subjects would prosper at the expense of the rest have already been shown to be too simplistic.

For many applicants, nothing has really changed. If you want to be a doctor, or a teacher or a social worker, there is no alternative to higher education. There will still be no requirement to pay upfront, even if £9,000 fees do mean a greatly extended repayment period once your salary tops £21,000. If you happen to live in Scotland, you will still have the option of paying nothing if you study in your home country, and there will be similar, if rather less generous, concessions in Wales and Northern Ireland.

Others will find it impossible to calculate exactly what a degree might cost, regardless of fee levels, because that will depend on their subsequent earnings, perhaps over 30 years, as that is the period after which any remaining loan is written off. And that is without taking account of the bewildering array of fee waivers, bursaries and scholarships that are now available, particularly to those from low-income families. Anyone with expectations of outstanding exam results and/or those from homes where the collective income is below £42,000 should scour the access agreements published by the Office for Fair Access to see if they qualify for extra support at universities they are interested in.

The Government estimates that only a third of graduates will pay off all their loans, so marginal differences in fee levels may make no difference at all to the amount that is repaid in the end. The catch is that there is no way of knowing whether you will be one of those who earns enough to pay off all your fees (with interest) or not. Judging from the first set of applications, many candidates have decided that the possibility of repaying £27,000, rather than perhaps £24,000, over 30 years is not going to sway their choice of university or course. If costs come down, it is more likely to be because of Government intervention in the allocation of places than any genuine fees market at work.

Some further education colleges are offering substantial savings on the cost of a degree, or Foundation degree, but it remains to be seen how successful they will be at attracting custom away from universities, as ministers would like. Similarly, the private sector may be expected to compete more vigorously in future, following the success of reasonably priced two-year degrees at Buckingham University and BPP University College. The exception will be at the New College of the Humanities, in London, which is charging £18,000 a year for University of London external degrees.

Elsewhere, even if it is closer to business as usual than many universities dared hope in the run-up to such a dramatic hike in fees, that does not mean that financial considerations will be irrelevant to the decision-making process. Students will want to keep their debts to a minimum and are bound to take the cost of living into account. They will also want the best possible career prospects and may choose their subject accordingly.

Impact on subject and university choice

While there has been no stampede out of purely academic subjects, higher fees do appear to have accelerated the drift towards more vocational degrees and those that are perceived to be winners in the labour market. Every group of subjects, with the sole exception of those allied to medicine, had seen a fall in applications at the start of 2012. The continued boom in nursing, where the number of applications rose by 28 per cent, was largely responsible for this bright spot. A more detailed look shows surprising variations – who would have guessed that anthropology would have enjoyed the biggest increase after nursing, with a rise of nearly 24 per cent, for example?

In general, the new fees have been bearable for the sciences and very bad news for languages and the creative arts. But sixth-formers studying English, history and French cannot suddenly switch to a chemistry degree. It will take time to detect whether the new fees regime brings about more fundamental changes in subject choice. In the first round of applications, vocational subjects such as mechanical engineering, medical technology and finance degrees are all up substantially, but others including architecture and degrees in hospitality, leisure, tourism and sport are down a lot. Even teacher training, journalism, media studies and social work – all subjects that have grown consistently in recent years – are down significantly.

In short, applicants are already looking more carefully at future career prospects when choosing a degree, but they have decided (rightly or wrongly) that some careers are more secure, or more lucrative, than others. Applications for law remain buoyant, while medicine is down only marginally, despite a long and now much more expensive training. Economics is another subject where applications have dropped only slightly, while the decline in mathematics is less than half the average for all subjects. Anthropology is not the only non-vocational subject to have held its own, however. The decline in history is lower than in mathematics, and the same is true of geography. There have been big drops in design and drama, but both remain among the 20 most popular subjects at degree level.

Nor is there a clear pattern in the applications to individual universities. Some of those charging maximum fees have been unaffected, or have even benefited. Durham, for example, had seen a 6 per cent rise in applications in January 2012, but Newcastle, 15 miles away, was 6 per cent down. Among those charging lower fees, Roehampton saw applications drop by 27 per cent, but Anglia Ruskin enjoyed an 11 per cent increase. There may have been regional factors at play, or distortions following particularly strong or weak recruitment in 2011, but there was no universal reaction to fee levels.

That is one reason why applicants for places in 2013 would be unwise to jump to conclusions about levels of competition in different subjects, or whole universities, based on the 2012 figures. The reaction to £3,000 fees, introduced in 2006, showed that the first year's applications were not representative of those that followed, either for particular subjects or institutions. An increased tendency to study at or near to home has continued and a trend towards more vocational subjects has also been sustained, but there were numerous examples of subjects and universities that recovered from an initial decline or fell away after an encouraging start. The only reliable forecast is that competition for places on the most popular courses will remain intense, just as it has been since before students paid any fees.

Getting the best deal

There is likely to be more variation in fees and student support packages in 2013, so it will be possible to shop around, particularly if your family income is low. But remember that the best deal, even in purely financial terms, is one that leads to a rewarding career. By all means compare the full packages offered by individual universities, but consider whether marginal differences in headline fees really matter as much as the quality of the course and the likely advantages it will confer in the employment market. Higher career earnings will soon account for more than £3,000 or even £6,000 in extra fees to be repaid over 30 years. It is all a matter of judgement – Scottish students can save themselves £27,000 by opting to study north of the border. That is a very different matter to the much smaller saving that is available to students in England, particularly if the Scottish university is of comparable quality to the alternatives elsewhere.

Nor can those who may be eligible for means-tested bursaries afford to ignore the financial assistance they offer, even if the attractions of a course at another university prove too strong to resist in the end. No one has to pay tuition fees while they are a student, but you still have to find thousands of pounds in living costs to take a full-time degree. In some cases, bursaries may make the difference between being able to afford higher education and having to pass up a potentially life-changing opportunity. Some are worth up to £3,000 a year, although most are less generous than this, often because large numbers of students qualify for an award.

Some scholarships are even more valuable – at the University of Bedfordshire, for example, the Vice-Chancellor's Scholarship is worth the full £27,000 fees to one student in each faculty. Most scholarships, including the Bedfordshire example, are not means-tested, but a few are open only to students who are both high performers academically and from low-income families.

For those who are swayed by fee levels, it is important to compare charges within universities as well as between them. While the big names will continue to charge £9,000 a year for every subject, many universities have a range of fees for different subjects. Some, like Bournemouth and Derby are charging more for their most popular and prestigious courses. Others are adding a premium for courses that cost most to run – generally engineering or science courses. Overall, the cheapest fees at any university in England in 2012–13 will be at London Metropolitan, where the expected average will be £6,850. Fees will range from £4,500 for some Foundation degrees to £9,000 for certain specialist degree subjects.

How the new fees work

Tuition fees for new British and EU undergraduates on full-time courses were fixed at a maximum of £9,000 a year for 2012 at universities and colleges in England, and at a maximum of £6,750 for part-time students. At the time of writing, fees for 2013 entry had not been set, but the Government had announced that the maximum would remain £9,000.

The maximum you can borrow for fees will also remain at £9,000, with lower sums set for private colleges and part-time study. The different levels of fees and support for UK students who are not from England is given below. Students from other EU countries will pay the same rate as home students in the UK nation in which they study. Those from outside the EU are not affected by the changes, and may well have to pay quite a lot more than home and European students.

With changes, large or small, becoming almost an annual occurrence, it is essential to consult the latest information provided on the websites of the relevant Government agencies What follows is a summary of the position for British students in spring 2012. While there are substantial differences between the four countries of the UK, there is one important piece of common ground. Up-front payment of fees is not compulsory, as students can take out a fee loan (see below) to cover them. This is repayable in instalments after graduation, when your earnings reach the £21,000 threshold set by the Government.

Fees in England

In England, the maximum tuition fee for full-time undergraduates from the UK or anywhere in the European Union will be £9,000 a year in 2013–14. The ceiling is unchanged from 2012–13, the first year of fees above £3,375. Some private colleges and further education colleges are charging considerably less than this for 2012–13, particularly for Foundation degrees, but very few university degrees will be available for the £6,000 fee that ministers once hoped would be the norm. Indeed, in 2012–13, every university set some or all of its fees above the basic level of £6,000.

The latest information on individual universities' fees at the time of going to press is listed at the end of this chapter and alongside their profiles in chapter 14. Most universities opted for fees of £9,000, or close to it, for 2012–13 in order to recoup the money removed from Government grants and leave room for further investment and student support. But this is only the headline figure: almost all universities offer bursaries and scholarships that bring the "real" average down. Some have lowered this average in order to be allowed to recruit additional students, and more may do the same in 2013, when the financial implications of the new arrangements are more obvious.

In many public universities, the lowest fees will be for Foundation degrees and Higher National Diplomas. Although some universities have chosen to charge the same for all courses, in many universities and further education colleges, these two-year courses will remain a cost-effective stepping stone to a full degree or a qualification in their own right. At Aston University, for example, fees for Foundation degrees were set at £6,000 for 2012–13, whereas Honours degrees cost £9,000.

Those universities that offer extended work placements as part of a degree course will charge much less than the normal fee for the "year out" – £1,000 in Aston's case. Fees are also reduced where universities offer a Foundation year to bring candidates up to the standard required on Honours courses. At Manchester Metropolitan University, for example, the Foundation year will cost £3,465 and the "sandwich year" £695 in 2012–13.

Fees in Scotland

At Scottish universities and colleges, students from Scotland and those from other EU countries outside the UK pay no fees directly. The universities' vice-chancellors and principals have appealed for charges to be introduced at some level to save their institutions from falling behind their English rivals in financial terms, but Alex Salmond, Scotland's First Minister, famously declared that the "rocks will melt with the sun" before this happens. Students whose home is in Scotland and are who studying at a Scottish university apply to the Student Awards Agency for Scotland (SAAS) to have their fees paid for them. Note, too, that three-year degrees are rare in Scotland, so most students can expect to pay four years of living costs.

Students from England, Wales and Northern Ireland studying in Scotland will pay fees at something like the level that applies in England and will have access to finance at similar levels to those available for study in England. Several Scottish universities are offering a "free" fourth year to bring their total fees into line with English universities, but Edinburgh and St Andrews are charging £9,000 in all four years of their degree courses.

Fees in Wales

Welsh universities have applied a range of fees up to £9,000, but a sizeable group have opted for fees below this level. Undergraduates who live in Wales will be able to apply for a Tuition Fee Loan as well as a Tuition Fee Grant, wherever they study. The grant was intended to pay fees beyond £3,465 a year in 2012.

Fees in Northern Ireland

The two universities of Northern Ireland are charging local students £3,465 a year for 2012–13. You can get a fee loan to postpone paying this until you are earning £15,975 a year. If you are from elsewhere in the UK, the fee is currently £6,000 a year at Ulster, still good value compared to much English provision, and £9,000 at Queen's, Belfast.

Useful websites

With changes, large or small, becoming almost an annual occurrence, it is essential to consult the latest information provided by Government agencies. It is worth checking the following websites for the latest information:

England: **www.direct.gov.uk/yourfuture**
Wales: **www.studentfinancewales.co.uk**
Scotland: **www.saas.gov.uk**
Northern Ireland: **www.studentfinanceni.co.uk**

For more information on Scottish fees and financial support for Scottish students and for any student studying in Scotland, visit:
www.scotland.gov.uk/Topics/Education/UniversitiesColleges/16640/financial-help

University tuition fees for UK/EU and international students

England

The fees given for UK/EU undergraduates are those for **2012–13**. At the time of going to press in spring 2012, fees for **2013–14** had not been announced. Approval from the Office for Fair Access is due at the end of July 2012. Please consult either the OFFA website (**www.offa.org.uk**) or university websites for the fees to be charged in **2013–14**. In the figures given below, the fees shown are for full degrees and do not include the sometimes lower fees charged for Foundation degrees or for science Foundation years (Year 0). The International student fees are for **2012–13** except where otherwise indicated (a few are for 2011–12 and for 2013–14). Please check university websites for the most recent information.

	Undergraduate fees UK / EU students 2012–13	Undergraduate fees International students 2012–13
Anglia Ruskin	£8,300	£9,500–£10,500
Aston	£9,000	£12,400–£15,600
Bath	£9,000	£12,300–£15,700
Bath Spa	£9,000	£10,030–£10,730
Bedfordshire	£9,000	£9,600
Birkbeck	£4,500–6,750[1]	£11,334–£11,925 (full-time courses)
Birmingham	£9,000	£11,730–£15,150; £15,150–£27,510 (medicine)
Birmingham City	£7,500–£9,000	£9,900–£11,200; £14,000–£17,000 (Conservatoire and acting)
Bolton	£6,300–£8,400	£9,400
Bournemouth	£8,200–£9,000	£9,500–£11,500
Bradford	£9,000	£11,000–£13,100
Brighton	£9,000	£10,500–£12,500; £23,678 (medicine)
Bristol	£9,000	£13,750–£16,750; £31,000 (dentistry, medicine, vet. medicine)
Brunel	£9,000	£11,330–£13,860
Buckingham	£11,250[2]	£16,000[2]
Buckinghamshire New	£6,000–£8,000	£8,900–£9,300
Cambridge	£9,000	£13,0119–£19,800[3] £31,494 (medicine)[3]
Canterbury Christ Church	£8,500	£9,425
Central Lancashire	£9,000	£9,450–£10,450
Chester	£8,000	£9,060
Chichester	£8,500	9,200–£10,500
City	£9,000	£10,000–£11,500
Coventry	£7,500–£9,000	9,375–£11,250 (Coventry); £10,375–£13,500 (London)
Cumbria	£7,850–£9,000	£9,600–£10,200
De Montfort	£9,000	£10,250–£10,750
Derby	£6,995–£7,995	£9,700–£10,250
Durham	£9,000	£12,600–£16,100
East Anglia	£9,000	£11,700–£14,400; £24,500 (medicine)
East London	£9,000	£9,900; £12,420 (architecture); £14,040 (physiotherapy)
Edge Hill	£9,000	£10,500
Essex	£9,000	£10,950–£12,950
Exeter	£9,000	£12,600–£14,500; £14,500–£22,000 (medicine)[4]
Gloucestershire	£8,250	£9,200
Goldsmiths	£9,000	£11,100–£15,400
Greenwich	£8,300; £9,000 (pharmacy)	£9,850

	Undergraduate fees UK / EU students 2012–13	Undergraduate fees International students 2012–13
Hertfordshire	£7,400–£8,500	£9,000–£10,000
Huddersfield	£7,950	£11,000–£12,000
Hull	£9,000	£11,200–£13,400; £24,080 (medicine)
Imperial	£9,000	£22,500–£25,000 £27,500–£39,150 (medicine)
Keele	£9,000	£10,200–£12,250; £20,000–£23,500 (medicine)
Kent	£9,000	£11,625–£13,875
King's College London	£9,000	£14,000–£17,800; £33,000 (medicine & dentistry)
Kingston	£8,500–£9,000	£9,950–£11,000[5]
Lancaster	£9,000	£12,070–£15,350
Leeds	£9,000	£12,500–£16,200; £18,000–£29,750 (medicine)
Leeds Metropolitan	£8,500	£11,000
Leicester	£9,000	£11,450–£14,645; £26,515 (medicine)
Lincoln	£9,000	£11,130–£12,755[6]
Liverpool	£9,000	£11,550–£14,850; £22,550 (dentistry & medicine)
Liverpool Hope	£8,250	£8,500
Liverpool John Moores	£9,000	£11,055–£12,040
London Metropolitan	£6,100–£8,100	£10,000–£10,700
London School of Economics	£8,500	£15,168
London South Bank	£8,450	From £10,000
Loughborough	£9,000	£12,250–£15,800
Manchester	£9,000	£12,300–£15,400; £15,400–£28,200 (medicine)
Manchester Metropolitan	£8,000–£9,000	£10,000–£15,500
Middlesex	£9,000	£10,400
Newcastle	£9,000	£11,500–£14,750 £14,750–£27,305 (medicine & dentistry)
Northampton	£8,500	£9,100
Northumbria	£8,500	£9,900–£10,600; £11,800 (physiotherapy)
Nottingham	£9,000	£11,990–£15,720; £16,570–£28,800 (medicine) £15,720–£23,300 (veterinary medicine)
Nottingham Trent	£8,500	£10,600–£11,300
Oxford	£9,000	£13,200–£18,550[7]; £15,150–£27,550 (medicine)[7]
Oxford Brookes	£9,000	£11,400–£12,640[6]
Plymouth	£9,000	£10,500; £14,500–£22,000 (medicine)[8]
Portsmouth	£8,500	£10,000–£11,300
Queen Mary	£9,000	£12,250–£13,925; £18,500–£28,200 (medicine)
Reading	£9,000	£11,440–£13,645
Roehampton University	£7,900–£8,250	£10,400
Royal Holloway	£9,000	£12,220–£13,860
Salford	£8,000–£9,000	£9,790–£12,170
School of Oriental and African Studies	£9,000	£13,890
Sheffield	£9,000	£12,160–£15,850; £28,650 (medicine)
Sheffield Hallam	£8,500	£10,320–£13,520
Southampton	£9,000	£12,420–£15,250; £29,450 medicine[6]
Southampton Solent	£7,800	£9,500–£10,500
Staffordshire	£7,490–£8,890	£9,875
Sunderland	£7,800–£8,500	£9,000[4]

	Undergraduate fees UK / EU students 2012–13	Undergraduate fees International students 2012–13
Surrey	£9,000	£11,550–£14,440
Sussex	£9,000	£12,300–£15,400; £23,678 (medicine)
Teesside	£7,450–£8,450	£10,450
University of the Arts, London	£9,000	£13,300
University College London	£9,000	£14,000–£18,500; £27,500 (medicine)
University for the Creative Arts	£8,500	£10,870
Warwick	£9,000	£13,800–£17,600
West London	£7,500–£8,200	£8,150–£9,540[5]
West of England	£9,000	£10,750
Westminster	£9,000	£10,975
Winchester	£8,500	£9,775
Wolverhampton	£8,000–£8,500	£9,925
Worcester	£8,100	£9,600
York	£9,000	£12,720–£16,540; £24,080 (medicine)
York St John	£8,500	£9,000–£11,500

1 On the basis of students studying for four years at 75 per cent intensity, equivalent to £6,000 to £9,000 full-time fees.
2 Courses starting in January 2013. Note that courses only lasts two years (eight terms).
3 Plus Cambridge College fees (£4,500–£5,500). UK & EU students who are eligible for tuition fee support not liable for College fees.
4 Figures for the Peninsula Medical School 2011–12. In 2013 Exeter will be providing its own medical course.
5 Figures for 2011/12.
6 Figures for 2013/14.
7 Plus Oxford College fees £6,157. UK & EU students who are eligible for tuition fee support not liable for College fees.
8 Figures for the Peninsula Medical School 2011–12. In 2013 Plymouth will be providing its own medical and dental courses.

Wales

For **2012–13**, universities can to charge up to £9,000 (with the Welsh Assembly paying fees above £3,465 for Welsh students). Indicative maximum fee levels for **2013–14** have been announced, which show some reductions in proposed fee levels for some institutions. The fees for International students are for **2012–13**. Please consult university websites for the details of fees to be charged in **2013–14**.

	Undergraduate fees UK / EU students 2012–13	Undergraduate fees International students 2012–13	Proposed maximum undergraduate fees UK / EU students 2013–14
Aberystwyth	£9,000	£9,500–£10,500	£9,000
Bangor	£9,000	£9,800–£11,900	£9,000
Cardiff	£9,000	£11,900–£15,000	£9,000
		£26,500 (medicine & dentistry)	
Cardiff Metropolitan	£9,000	£8,400–£9,600; £11,400 (podiatry)	£7,500
Glamorgan	£7,500	£10,750	£7,500
Glyndŵr	£5,850–£7,750	£7,950	£7,500
Newport	£8,250–£9,000	£8,700–£9,700	£7,500
Swansea	£9,000	£9,000	£9,000
Swansea Metropolitan	£8,500–£8,750	£9,000	£7,500
Trinity St David	£8,500–£9,000	£9,348	£7,500

Northern Ireland

For **2012–13** there will be different fees for students resident in Northern Ireland and students coming from other parts of the UK. There is some financial support from the universities specifically for students from the rest of the UK. The policy for **2013–14** had not been announced when this book went to print in May 2012. Please consult university websites for the fees to be charged in **2013–14**. The fees for International students are for **2012–13**.

	Fees for Northern Irish students and eligible non-UK EU students 2012–13	Fees for students from elsewhere in the UK 2012–13	Undergraduate fees International students 2012–13
Queen's Belfast	£3,465	£9,000	£11,266–£14,460
			£14,768–£27,860 (medicine)
			£22,624 (dentistry)
Ulster	£3,465	£6,000	£9,500

Scotland

In **2012–13** there are no fees for Scottish and EU students, but there are fees for students from elsewhere in the UK. As Scottish Honours degrees are 4 years in length, the cost of some degrees in Scotland for students from the rest of the UK will be higher than in England, although some universities have put a maximum cap on charges to maintain equality with English fees. There is some financial support from the universities specifically for students from the rest of the UK. The policy for **2013–14** had not been announced when this book went to print in May 2012. Please consult university websites for the fees to be charged in **2013–14**. The fees for International students are for **2012–13**.

	Fees for Scottish students and eligible non-UK EU students 2012–13	Fees for students from elsewhere in the UK 2012–13	Undergraduate fees International students 2012–13
Aberdeen	No fee	£9,000[1]	£11,000–£14,000; £24,500 (medicine)
Abertay	No fee	£7,000[2]	£9,975
Dundee	No fee	£9,000[1]	£9,700–£13,335
			£17,500–£26,750 (medicine & dentistry)
Edinburgh	No fee	£9,000	£12,650 or £16,650;
			£20,600–£34,850 (medicine)
			£19,950–£26,400 (veterinary studies)
Edinburgh Napier	No fee	£6,500	£9,690–£11,250
Glasgow	No fee	£6,725	£12,250–£15,750
		£9,000[3]	£28,500[3]
Glasgow Caledonian	No fee	£7,000[2]	£9,700–£10,500
Heriot Watt	No fee	£9,000[1]	£10,730–£13,530
Highlands and Islands	No fee	£7,500[4]	£8,000–£9,500
Queen Margaret	No fee	£6,750	£10,170–£11,790
Robert Gordon	No fee	£5,000–£8,500	£9,500–£11,800
St Andrews	No fee	£9,000	£15,500
			£23,550 (medical science)
Stirling	No fee	£6,750	£10,200–£12,250
Strathclyde	No fee	£9,000[1]	£10,200–£16,000
West of Scotland	No fee	£7,250	£10,000–£10,500

1 Capped at £27,000 for 4-year courses
2 Capped at £21,000 for 4-year courses
3 Medicine , dentistry, veterinary science
4 Capped at £22,500 for 4-year courses

8 The Cost of Studying

Anyone reading this *Guide* already knows that they need to think hard about how they will pay for their higher education. Fees at English universities are now equal to the top of the range worldwide, and of course you have to stay alive whilst studying. But funding is available, especially for those from less affluent backgrounds, to help make university affordable. Despite the costs, most independent research continues to show that it is worth investing in a degree – as long as you pick the right course and work hard enough to pass. The extra amount you earn, over and above what you would have made without a degree, should far outstrip the cost of your higher education in most subjects at most universities. In addition, there are many satisfying careers that are only open to graduates. However, graduates are no longer a tiny social elite, so a degree has ceased to have rarity value as an entry point to working life. An increasing number of careers now expect a higher-level qualification such as a Master's degree, not just a three- or four-year BA or BSc.

Funding help

Even under the new fees regime, there are sources of funding to enable most students to meet the costs of higher education and live reasonably. The drawback is that you will build up debts in the process. The Government points out that long-term finance is available to ease the pain of servicing this debt. But it will take perseverance to put together the best possible package. Depending on your family income and where you live in the UK, you may be entitled to a range of grants, bursaries or scholarships. Unlike loans, these have the great virtue that you don't have to pay them back. Altogether this means complex calculations on sources of financial support, fee levels, the length of courses and the cost of living at different universities. With many families feeling the pinch, it has never been more important to get it right.

Getting into debt is now a fact of life for almost all students. In mid-2011, graduates and current students still on courses owed £35.2 billion between them in England alone. Virtually all of this debt was in the form of income-contingent loans. The money was owed by 3.5 million borrowers, a figure which is itself up 9 per cent on a year earlier. So the average debt is almost exactly £10,000 per person. However, most of this debt was run up by students in an era of much lower fees than we see today. Most research now puts average graduate debt at around £20,000. In England, interest rates on these sums are less than for most commercial finance, currently at 5.3 per cent, and repayments begin when you are earning £21,000 a year. By the time you graduate, the interest rate will probably have changed and the repayment threshold will have risen, if only by inflation.

Careful financial planning and research into help that is available can go a long way to letting you emerge from your university education with a level of debt that is not going to become a millstone for life. As well as student loans, which will still be provided at relatively generous interest rates and under very favourable terms, you can shop around for university bursaries, scholarships and other sponsorship packages, and seek out supplementary support to which you may be eligible. You may be entitled to a maintenance grant: despite recent changes in eligibility, these are available to a much larger slice of the population than was the case in the early years of tuition fees. At the time of writing the University of Bristol, normally a £9,000-a-year institution, was offering a waiver for 2012 entrant students from households with incomes below £25,000, ranging from £5,500 as a fee waiver for those from homes with an income of less than £15,000 to a £3,000 fee waiver for children of families with incomes between £20,000 and £25,000. This is only an example, and such waivers are widespread under the so-called National Scholarship Programme (NSP).

However much you pay your university for your tuition, you will still need to survive the three or more years of your course. A range of grants and loans are available to help.

You can apply for a grant if you are from a household with an income of less than £42,600 in England. It can range from £3,250 a year for students from homes with less than £25,000 income all the way to a lavish £50 for those from homes whose incomes approach £42,600. (In common with many of the numbers in this chapter, this is the figure for 2012 entrants, and the 2013 figure had not been published at the time of writing. However, these figures can be used as a guideline and will change year-on-year only in line with inflation.)

You apply for such a grant via the Student Loans Company alongside your application for a loan, and if you get one, your loan will be correspondingly reduced.

The amount you can borrow as a so-called maintenance loan depends on your need. For 2012 entry it varies from £4,375 for those living at home, to £5,500 for people living away from home outside London, and £7,675 for those living away from home in London. (You can even get £6,535 for a year studying abroad as part of a UK course. This might be fine in Egypt, but will not get you far in Japan or Switzerland.)

How well you can live on these sums will vary from person to person. But most people will need to gather together all the resources they can just to survive. Analysis by the National Union of Students suggests that it is not possible to get by on student loans and grants alone. Savings, earnings, and help from family and friends have to be added to the pot. The information provided here and in the separate chapter on fees will help you understand how big your pot needs to be, and what you can expect to be added and taken away from it.

Student loans

Around 80 per cent of students take out a student loan, and it is not difficult to see why. First of all, as we saw earlier, it is very difficult to get by financially without one. If you don't take out a loan to cover your fees, then you will have to pay for them up front. And with living costs estimated to average more than £10,500 a year (over £11,700 in London), most students find it impossible to cover everything on savings and earnings alone. The only reasons to consider paying your fees up front might be if your parents are offering to meet the costs, or if a university is offering a discount if you do so. There are two types of student loan – one to cover the cost of tuition fees and another to help you cover the cost of living.

Tuition fees loan

In the case of fees loans, everyone can borrow up to the full amount needed to cover the cost of their tuition fees. Scots studying in Scotland are even better off, as there are no tuition fees for them to pay, so no need for a loan or for repayments later.

Maintenance loan

The second type of student loan, a maintenance loan, is means-tested. The amount you can borrow depends on a number of factors, including your family income, where you intend to study, and whether you expect to be living at home. Final-year students receive less than those in earlier years. As we saw above, the maximum maintenance loan for students starting in 2012 will be £5,500 outside London for those who leave home to study; £7,675 if you live away from home and study in London; and £4,375 for those living at home.

Sixty-five per cent of the maintenance loan is available to you regardless of your family circumstances, while the remaining 35 per cent is means-tested. If your parents are separated, divorced or widowed, then only the parent with whom you normally live will be assessed. However, if that parent has married again, entered into a civil partnership, or has a partner of the opposite sex, both their incomes will be taken into account.

Maintenance loans in Scotland

In Scotland, the rules and regulations for maintenance loans are different. The loans available are lower than the rest of the UK, particularly in the case of students going to study in London, and the proportion that is means-tested is higher. In 2011–12 the maximum loan available was £5,570 for a standard 30-week course. The least you can get (with a family income of over £61,000) is £940 a year. All the latest details can be found at **www.saas.gov.uk**. There are a wide range of non-repayable bursaries for students from households with lower total incomes.

Loans for mature students

Mature students (those who are over the age of 25, married, or have supported themselves for at least three years before entering university) are assessed for loan and grant entitlements on their own income plus that of their spouse or partner. Grants are also available for those with children, for single parents, and for students with adult dependents. Further support is available for students with children through the Childcare Grant, the Parents' Learning Allowance, the Adult Dependants' Grant and Child Tax Credit system. You have to be under 60 to get a living cost loan if you are studying full-time. But remember that the student finance system is mainly open only to people taking a degree for the first time.

Payment of loans

Maintenance loans are usually paid in three instalments a year into your bank or building society account. English students should apply for grants and loans through Student Finance England, Welsh students through Student Finance Wales, Scottish students through the Student Awards Agency for Scotland, and those in Northern Ireland through Student Finance NI or their Education and Library Board. You should make your application as soon as you have received an offer of a place at university. EU students from outside the UK will usually be sent an application form by the university that has offered them a place.

Repaying loans

Full-time students will begin accumulating interest during their course and will start repaying in the April after graduation, if they earn over £21,000. They will then pay 9 per cent of income above £21,000, but repayments will stop during any period in which annual income falls below the threshold. Repayments are normally taken automatically through the PAYE income tax system. If the loan has not been paid off after 30 years, no further repayments will be required.

During repayment periods, the amount of interest will vary according to how much you earn. If you earn less than £21,000, interest will be at the rate of inflation; between £21,000 and £41,000 you will be charged inflation plus up to 3 per cent; and if you earn over £41,000, interest will be at inflation plus the full 3 per cent. The Government website set up to guide prospective students through the changes includes a repayments calculator based on starting salaries for a range of careers, **http://yourfuture.direct.gov.uk/calculate**.

Grants

In the good old days, most students didn't have to pay fees and many received relatively generous maintenance grants to help them cover day-to-day costs. After a brief disappearance, these non-repayable grants have made a comeback, and are particularly significant if you come from a low-income family. The size and type of grants available, and the rules and regulations governing their distribution, are different for each country of the UK. To receive a grant, students whose homes are in England must apply through Student Finance England, in Wales to Student Finance Wales, those from Scotland must apply to the Student Awards Agency for Scotland, and those from Northern Ireland to Student Finance NI or their Education and Library Board. In addition, there are various types of bursaries and scholarships you can apply for, and other types of grants or support in each country to help students in particular circumstances, such as those that have a disability. What follows is a description of the maintenance grant arrangements country by country.

Maintenance grant and loan example for a first-year English student 2012

The mixture of grant and loan for a first-year English student in 2012–13 who is studying full-time and living away from home (but not in London). The maximum loan is £5,500, payable when the household income is £42,600. The loan thereafter declines to a minimum of £3,575 by £62,500.

Household income	Non-repayable grant	Maintenance loan	Total
£25,000 or less	£3,250	£3,875	£7,125
£30,000	£2,341	£4,330	£6,671
£35,000	£1,432	£4,784	£6,216
£40,000	£523	£5,239	£5,762
£45,000	£0	£5,288	£5,288
£50,000	£0	£4,788	£4,788
Over £62,500	£0	£3,575	£3,575

Department for Business, Innovation and Skills

England

Students from England can apply for a maintenance grant from the Government and a bursary from their university. Those on full-time courses are entitled to a full grant of £3,250 in 2012–13 if their household income is £25,000 or less, or a partial grant if household income is between £25,000 and £42,600. Grants are paid into the student's bank account at the beginning of each term. One important rule to bear in mind is that for every £1 you receive in maintenance grant, the amount you can borrow in student loans falls by £1. Thus, it is not possible to have both a full grant and a maximum student loan.

From 2012, there is also a new £150-million National Scholarship Programme to help English students from lower income families. Assistance may include reduced tuition fees (fee waivers) or accommodation discounts. Each university will determine its own pattern of support. Some examples are given alongside the university profiles in chapter 14 and details are available on university and college websites.

Bursaries and scholarships on offer from universities are discussed in a separate section below.

Northern Ireland

Students from Northern Ireland can get grants and loans on a similar basis to English students. The grants range from £3,475 for students with household incomes of less than £19,203, to zero if the figure is more than £41,065. Maintenance loans vary from £3,750 for students living at home, all the way to £6,780 for those studying in London. There are also extra sums for people doing courses longer than 30 weeks a year. As in England, there are also special funds for people with disabilities and other special needs, and for those with children or adult dependants.

Wales

In addition to the normal loans, students from low-income backgrounds in Wales will also be able to apply for Assembly Learning Grants of up to £5,600. They will be scaled according to household income, which in 2011–12 ranged from £18,370 for a full grant to £50,020 for the smallest payment.

Scotland

In Scotland, the maintenance grant is known as a Young Students' Bursary (YSB), and is also means-tested and does not have to be repaid. For 2012–13, the maximum bursary is £2,640 if you come from a family with an annual income of £19,310 or less. If your family income is between this amount and £34,195 you will be entitled to a partial bursary, but if it is higher than £34,195 you will receive nothing. You can get an additional student loan if your family income is £21,760 or less. If you qualify for the YSB, then you may also qualify for an additional loan of up to £605.

Part-time students

The most that universities or colleges can charge for part-time courses is between £4,500 and £6,750 a year for 2012, and they cannot charge more than 75 per cent of the full-time fee. New part-time students will be able to apply for a tuition fee loan that is not dependent on household income. Eligibility depends on the "intensity" of the course being at least 25 per cent of a full-time course, so that if a course takes six years to complete and the full-time equivalent takes three, the intensity will be 50 per cent.

Extra financial help will be available to disabled students studying on a part-time basis through Disabled Students' Allowances, which are paid in addition to the standard student finance package. They do not depend on income and do not have to be repaid.

Bursaries and scholarships

Bursaries and scholarships offered by universities and colleges are an important part of the student financial support system ushered in by the Labour Government and developed by the Coalition to try to ensure that no one is excluded from university because they cannot afford it. Virtually all institutions have expanded their activities in this area as fees have risen.

Most bursaries are targeted at students from poor backgrounds, but many scholarships are available purely on merit (for academic achievement or sporting prowess). Some combine eligibility by family circumstances with academic excellence. Most schemes focus on entrants to degree courses, but some also reward performance at university.

Confusingly, the biggest bursary scheme, established by the Government and with places available at most English universities, is called the National Scholarship Programme. Like many institutional schemes, it is open only to students resident in England whose family income is £25,000 or less. Other bursaries tend to have a sliding scale of payments up to family income of around £42,000.

Finding out about bursaries

There is now a bewildering variety of bursaries and scholarships on offer at UK universities.

Funding timetable

It is vital that you sort out your funding arrangements before you start university. Each funding agency has its own arrangements, and it is very important that you find out the exact details from them. The dates below give general indications of key dates.

March/April

» Online and paper application forms become available from funding agencies.
» You must contact the appropriate funding agency to make an application. For funding in England contact **www.studentfinanceengland.co.uk** rather than your LEA.
» Complete application form as soon as possible. At this stage select the university offer that will be your first choice.
» Check details of bursaries and scholarships available from your selected universities.

May/June

» Funding agencies will give you details of the financial support they can offer.
» Last date for making an application to ensure funding is ready for you at the start of term (exact date varies significantly between agencies).

August

» Tell your funding agency if the university or course you have been accepted for is different from that originally given them.

September

» Take letter confirming funding to your university for registration.
» After registration, the first part of funds will be released to you.

It is worth shopping around to see what you can get. The websites of individual institutions carry details of scholarships, bursaries and other financial support which they have available.

The system of bursaries and scholarships is overseen for England by the Office for Fair Access. It requires all universities to submit what are called "Access Agreements" that contain details of what fees they intend to charge and what scholarships and bursaries they are offering. Access Agreements also describe other kinds of financial support, such as "hardship funds". Some awards are guaranteed depending on your personal circumstances, while others are available through open competition. Copies of access agreements can be found at **www.offa.org.uk/students/introducing-bursaries** .

Applying for bursaries and scholarships

Do take note of the application procedures for scholarships and bursaries, as these vary from institution to institution, and even from course to course within individual institutions. There may be deadlines you have to meet to apply for an award. In some cases the university will work out for you whether you are entitled to an award by referring to your funding agency's financial assessment. If your personal circumstances change part-way through a course, your entitlement to a scholarship or bursary may be reviewed.

If you feel you still need more help or advice on scholarships or bursaries, you can usually find it on a university's website or in its prospectus. Some institutions also maintain a helpline. Some questions you will need answered include whether the bursary or scholarship is automatic or conditional and, if the latter, when you will find out whether your application has been successful. For some awards, you won't know whether you have qualified until you get your exam results.

Another obvious question is how the scholarship or bursary on offer compares with awards made by another university you might consider applying to. Watch out for institutions that list entitlements that others don't mention, but which you would get anyway.

Some institutions offer "fee remission" or "waivers" (a lower tuition fee) rather than scholarships or bursaries, which means you will have no more cash in hand during your course, but will owe less after you have graduated. Since two thirds of graduates are not expected to repay their loans in full, a cash bursary may be preferable to a smaller loan.

Living in one country, studying in another

As each of the countries of the UK develops its own distinctive system of student finance, the effects on students leaving home in one UK nation to go and study in another have become knottier. UK students who cross borders to study pay the tuition fees of their chosen university and are eligible for a fee loan, and maybe a partial grant, to cover them. They are also entitled to apply for the scholarships or bursaries on offer from that institution (excluding awards made under the English National Scholarship Programme). Any maintenance loan or grant will still come from the awarding body of their home country. You must check with the authorities in your home country. The funds available there may differ from those for home students.

European Union laws stipulate that EU students from outside the UK must be charged the same tuition fees as those paid by nationals of the country where they are studying, rather than the higher fees paid by students from outside the EU. They can also apply for a fee loan and may be considered for some of the scholarships and bursaries offered by individual institutions. Only students who have been living and studying in the UK for at least three years can apply for a maintenance loan or grant. If you haven't, then you will need to apply for such assistance from the authorities in your own country. Tuition fee rules for non-UK European Union students are the same in Scotland as for Scottish students – that is, you do not have to pay a tuition fee. There are also no fees to pay for exchange students coming to the UK, including those on the Socrates Programme.

Further sources of income

If you are feeling daunted by the potential costs, you can take some comfort from this section, which outlines just some of the ways you can raise additional funds.

Taking a gap year

Gap years have become increasingly popular both for travelling and, increasingly now, to earn some money to boost the bank balance in preparation for life as a student. Of course, there is more to taking a gap year than short-term financial gain. Both university admissions officers and employers look for evidence that candidates have more about them than academic ability. Work placements can be structured, as in the Year in Industry Scheme, or casual. Sponsorship is also available, mainly to those wishing to study engineering or business.

Additional Government support

There are various types of support available from Government sources for students in particular circumstances, other than the main loans, grants and bursaries.

» Undergraduates in financial difficulties can apply for help from the Access to Learning Fund (Financial Contingency Fund in Wales, Hardship Fund in Scotland, Support Funds in Northern Ireland). These are allocated by universities to provide support for anything from day-to-day study and living costs to unexpected or exceptional expense. The university decides which students need help and how much money to award them. These funds are often targeted at older or disadvantaged students and finalists.

» Students with children can apply for a Childcare Grant, worth £148.75 a week if you have one child and £255 a week if you have two or more children; and a Parents' Learning Allowance, for help with course-related costs, of between £50 and £1,508 a year.

» Students with disabilities can apply for a Disabled Students' Allowance, worth up to £20,520 a year for full-time students. This money can be used for equipment, extra travel costs, or costs such as a note-taker for lectures.

» Any students with a partner, or another adult such as a family member who is financially dependent on them, can apply for an Adult Dependants' Grant of up to £2,642 a year.

If you do not qualify for any of this kind of financial support you may still be able to apply for a Professional and Career Development Loan available from certain banks, in partnership with the Young People's Learning Agency. Students on a wide range of vocational courses can borrow from £300 to £10,000 at a fixed rate of interest to fund up to two years of learning.

Part-time work

The need to hold down a part-time job during term time is now a fact of life for more than half of students. Students from a working-class background are more likely to need to earn while they learn. A report by UNITE showed that 51 per cent of students from low-income families worked during term time, compared with just over a third of those from higher-income families. If you need or want to earn during term time, it is important to try to ensure that you do not work so many hours that it starts to affect your studies. A survey by the NUS found that 59 per cent of students who worked felt it had an impact on their studies, with 38 per cent missing lectures and over a fifth failing to submit coursework because of their part-time jobs.

Student employment agencies, which can now be found on many university campuses, can help you get the balance right. These introduce employers with work to students seeking work, sometimes even offering jobs within the university itself. But they also abide by codes of practice that regulate both minimum wages and the maximum number of hours worked in term time (typically 15 hours a week).

According to the Halifax bank, the average working student puts in about 18 hours a week, and makes around £6,000 a year out of this. Some firms, such as the big supermarkets, offer continuing part-time employment to their school part-time employees when they go to university. Some students make use of their expertise in areas like web design to earn some extra money, but most take on casual work in retail stores, restaurants, bars and call centres.

Most students, including those who don't work during term time, get a job during vacations. A Government survey found that 86 per cent of students in their second year of study or above worked during their summer vacation. Most of this kind of work is casual, but some is formalised in a scheme like STEP (**www.step.org.uk**) or may be part of a sponsorship programme. Many vacation jobs are fairly mundane, but it is possible to find more interesting work. Some students broaden their experience by working abroad, others work as film extras, or do a variety of jobs at big events such as festivals. It is also a good idea to try to use the summer holidays to get some work experience in a field that has some relevance to your career aspirations. Even if you don't get paid, this can significantly enhance your chances of finding employment after graduation.

What you will need to spend money on
Living costs

The NUS estimated that in 2010–11 the average student living outside London would spend £10,600 a year on regular living costs, including rent, food, personal items, travel and leisure. For those living in the capital, the estimated average expenditure was £11,700, not including tuition fees, books or equipment. Little surprise, then, that a growing number of students are choosing to live at home and study at a local university. However, even this option is not necessarily cheap, once travel to and from the university is taken into account.

Certain costs are unavoidable. You have to have a roof over your head, eat enough, clothe yourself, and probably do a certain amount of travelling. But the cost of even these essential items can be cut down significantly through a mixture of shopping around and careful budgeting. Some catering outlets at your university or in the students' union may well offer good value meals, but probably the most economical way to eat is to cook and share meals with fellow students with whom you may be living in a shared house. Make sure you make full use of student travel cards and other offers and facilities available locally to help you cut the cost of travel. In certain locations, a bicycle is a very worthwhile investment (as is buying a lock for it).

If you can keep your essential costs down, you will have more money for what you would probably prefer to spend your money on – going out and personal items. Most students spend a good proportion of their budget on socialising, and this is certainly an important part of the university experience. You can have plenty of fun and keep your leisure costs down by making the most of your student union's facilities and events.

The 2012 survey of student life by the company Sodexo suggests that students tend to spend £300–£500 a month on rent, much their biggest cost and far more than the cost of travel (under £100 a month) or food (less than £200). The same survey has spotted trends for lower levels of socialising among students and for more students to stay at home while studying. The same survey suggested that while 30 per cent of students graduating in 2012 expected to have debts of over £20,000, up from virtually zero in 2002, a growing percentage of students (75 per cent in 2012) regard university as a worthwhile investment.

Studying costs

The most recent NUS survey estimated that the average student spent £978 a year on costs associated with course work and studying, mainly books and equipment. That figure may have increased since the survey was conducted, but the amount you spend will be determined largely by the nature of your course and what you study. Additional financial support may be available for certain expenditure, but this is unlikely to cover you fully for spending on books, stationery, equipment, fieldwork or electives. A long reading list could prove very expensive if you tried to buy all of the required books brand new. Find out as soon as possible which books are available either in your university library or local libraries. Another approach is to buy books second hand from students who no longer need them. Your students' union or your university may run second-hand book sales or offer a service helping students to buy and sell books.

Other costs

Keep any other costs you may incur as low as possible. This may sound trite, but it is easy to let "other costs" get out of hand to the extent that they start to eat into your budget for day-to-day living. Mobile phone bills are a case in point. Look at your previous bills, or think carefully about your usage, and then shop around for the best deal to cover what you need. Extras like downloading games or music, or sending pictures, can add significantly to your bill. Most of all, try to avoid getting tied up with an expensive and inflexible contract.

Overdrafts and credit cards

Other costs it is best to avoid are the more expensive forms of debt. Many banks offer free overdraft facilities for students, but if you go over that limit without prior arrangement, you can end up paying way over the odds for your borrowing. Credits cards can be useful if managed properly. The best way to manage a credit card is to set up a direct debit to pay off your balance in full every month, which means you will avoid paying any interest. One of the worst ways is just paying the minimum charge each month, which can cost you a small fortune over a long period. If you are the kind of person who spends impulsively and doesn't keep track of their spending, you are probably better off without a credit card. That way, you can't spend money you don't have.

Insurance

One kind of additional spending that can actually end up saving you money is getting insurance cover for your possessions. Most students arrive at university with laptops, mobile phones and iPods, that are tempting to petty thieves. It is estimated that around a third of students fall victim to crime at some point during their time at university and yet around two thirds of students have no insurance. Your students' union will probably be able to advise you on the best deals. It may be possible to add cover cheaply to your parents' contents policy.

Planning your budget

University websites and many other sites offer guidance on preparing a budget, usually with the basic headings provided for you to complete. First, list all your likely income (grants, bursaries, loans, part-time work, savings, parental support) and then see how this compares with what you will spend. Try to be realistic, and not too optimistic, about both sides of the equation. With care, you will end up either only slightly in the red, or preferably far enough in the black for you to be able to afford things you would really like to spend your money on.

Above all, keep track of your finances so that your university experience isn't ruined by money worries, or finding you can't go to the ball because the cash machine has eaten your card. Spreadsheets make doing this simpler, and it is one skill you can learn that you are definitely going to need for the rest of your life.

Useful websites

This government website covers the basics of fees, loans, grants and other allowances:
www.direct.gov.uk/studentfinance

UCAS provides helpful advice: **www.ucas.com/students/studentfinance**
For England, visit Student Finance England through : **www.direct.gov.uk/studentfinance**
Office for Fair Access: **www.offa.org.uk**
For Wales, visit Student Finance Wales: **www.studentfinancewales.co.uk**
For Scotland, visit the Student Awards Agency for Scotland: **www.saas.gov.uk**
For Northern Ireland, visit Student Finance Northern Ireland: **www.studentfinanceni.co.uk**
All UK student loans are administered by the Student Loan Company: **www.slc.co.uk**
Educational Grants Advisory Service (EGAS):
www.family-action.org.uk/section.aspx?id=1924
HM Revenue and Customs: **www.hmrc.gov.uk/students**
NHS Student Bursaries for students on pre-registration health professional and social work training courses: **www.nhsbsa.nhs.uk/students**
For finding out about availability of scholarships: **www.scholarship-search.org.uk**

9 Finding Somewhere to Live

The first decision of your university life – even before choosing which course options to take – is where to live. As the number of students has risen in all parts of the UK, the search for affordable and acceptable housing has become tougher. The property bubble may have burst, but rents are continuing to rise, particularly in the student market. The National Union of Students (NUS) reported a 22 per cent rise in rents in the final years of the last decade, with the average student now paying more than £100 a week, although a recent survey by Standard Life put the average at closer to £80. The average rents for university accommodation quoted in chapter 14 show another significant increase this year.

Living at home

For a growing number of undergraduates, the solution to this problem is to live at home – particularly now that fees are rising so steeply. With repayments starting only after graduation, the new fee regime will leave students no worse off during their time at university. But many undergraduates will be more careful about the debts they run up, and housing is the biggest single item in the student budget.

The pattern of recent applications shows that the trend towards studying from home is accelerating, and there is no reason to think that will change while the downturn continues. Indeed, it may be a permanent shift, given the rising costs and the willingness of many young people to live with their parents well into their twenties.

The proportion of students living at home grew from 13 per cent to 18 per cent in three years before undergraduate fees went up, according to the *Sodexo University Lifestyle Survey*. This figure includes mature students, many of whom are restricted by family circumstances, but it would be surprising if it did not rise further in the immediate future. Women are more likely than men to stay at home: 20 per cent of them do, compared to 15 per cent of men. Asian women are particularly likely to take this option. Home study is four times more common at post-1992 universities than older institutions, again reflecting the larger numbers of mature students and a generally more affluent student population.

Living away from home

Most of those who can afford it still see moving away to study as integral to the rite of passage that student life represents. Some have little option because, in spite of the expansion of higher education, the course they want is not available locally. Others are happy to travel to secure their ideal place and widen their experience.

For the lucky majority, the search for accommodation will be over quickly because the university can offer a place in one of its halls of residence or self-catering flats. The choice may come down to the type of accommodation and whether or not to do your own cooking. For others, however, the offer of a degree place will be the start of an anxious search for a room in a strange city.

Going to university will oblige those who take the "away" route to think for the first time about practicalities of living independently. This can make the decision about where to live – both in terms of location and the type of accommodation – doubly difficult, but vital to get right. It may even influence your choice of university, since there are big differences across the sector in the cost and standard of accommodation – and your choice will have a significant impact on the quality of your life as a student.

How much will it cost?

Students in the UK are estimated to spend almost twice as much on rent as their combined spending on food, going out, books and music. The NUS survey found that even in 2009–10 students were paying a weekly rent of nearly £100, with those living in London paying more than £150 a week and those at the cheaper end of the spectrum in Belfast and Lancaster paying around £70 a week. But in this case, averages are becoming meaningless because the range of rents is so wide, particularly in London. Research by Drivers Jonas Deloitte suggested that the average in London was actually £145 a week, although this included students taking full board in halls, and that some were paying £300.

There is undoubtedly a growing luxury end to the student market, even while others live in much cheaper, often sub-standard accommodation. Most universities with a range of accommodation find that their most expensive rooms fill up first and students appear to have higher expectations – almost half of all the rooms in the NUS survey had en-suite facilities. The downside of this trend is that there can be fewer university-owned places available at the lowest price band. The privately run blocks, which the union blames for pushing up prices, certainly tend to be well-appointed as well as popular. The Deloitte survey found that 2,660 purpose-built residential places had been added in London in 2010–11, with another 7,700 under construction – almost twice as many as in the previous year.

Generally speaking, the cost of student accommodation is highest in London and the southeast of England and lowest in the Midlands and North of England, Wales, Scotland and Northern Ireland. But NUS surveys show considerable variations within those regions. Renting in new blocks of flats – and especially those that are en suite – is often more expensive than sharing a house with friends, but the latter is a lot more common after the first year.

It is important to remember that both your living costs and your potential earnings should be factored into your calculations when deciding where to live. While living costs in London

Term-time type of accommodation of full-time and sandwich students

	2010/11	2009/10
University maintained property	18.5%	19%
Private-sector halls	5%	4.5%
Parental/guardian home	19%	19%
Own residence	16%	17%
Other rented accommodation	29%	27.5%
Other	4%	5%
Not known	8.5%	8%

HESA 2012 (adapted)

are, unsurprisingly, by far the highest, potential earnings are nearly double those in other parts of the country. Students in London were earning more than £5,000 a year on average in 2009–10, according to the NatWest Student Living Index, making it the most cost-effective place to study in the bank's estimation. Of course, those earnings figures may be lower this year, whereas student rents undoubtedly have risen.

The choices you have

No longer are you faced with a straightforward choice between a university hall of residence and a poor quality rented house. A report from the NUS puts accommodation into 16 categories, ranging from luxurious university halls to a bedsit in a shared house. The choices include:

» University hall of residence, with individual study bedrooms and a full catering service; many will have en-suite accommodation.
» University halls, flats or houses where you have to provide your own food.
» Private, purpose-built student accommodation.
» Rented houses or flats, shared with fellow students.
» Living at home.
» Living as a lodger in a private house.

This chapter will provide you with more information to help you decide where you would like to live and whether you can afford it.

Making your choice

Financial considerations are not the only factor you should consider when deciding where to live. Feeling comfortable and happy in your student home is of crucial importance to your success at university and to the quality of your experience. It is therefore worth investing some time to find the right place, and to avoid the false economy of choosing somewhere cheap where you may end up feeling depressed and isolated. Most students who drop out of university do so in the first few months, when homesickness and loneliness can be felt most acutely.

Being warm and well fed is likely to have a positive effect on your studies. Perhaps for these reasons, most undergraduates in their first year plump for living in university halls, which offer a convenient, safe and reliable standard of accommodation, along with a supportive community environment. If meals are included, then this adds further peace of mind both for students and their parents. But nowadays most are self-catering, with groups of students sharing a kitchen. The sheer number of students – especially first years – in halls also makes this form of accommodation an easy way of meeting people from a wide range of courses and making friends.

Wherever you chose to live, there are some general points you will need to consider, such as how safe the neighbourhood seems to be, and how long it might take you to travel to and from the university – especially during rush hour. A recent survey of travel time between term-time accommodation and the university found that most students in London can expect a commute of at least 30 minutes and often over an hour, while students living in Wales are usually much less than 30 minutes away from their university. Be sure to make use of any local or national Student Travel Card and any university or students' union transport system that may be provided to help you get back to your accommodation cheaply and safely.

In the university profiles (chapter 14), we provide details of what accommodation each university offers, covering the number of places, costs and policy towards first-year students.

Continuing to live at home

The first decision must be whether to move at all. The potential financial benefits of remaining at home are obvious, and there may also be advantages in terms of academic work if the alternative involves shopping, cooking and cleaning, as well as the other distractions of a student flat. The downside is that you may miss out on a lot of the student experience, especially the social scene and the opportunity to make new friends.

There is no evidence that students living at home do any worse academically. The quality of your home environment should influence your decision when weighing up whether or not to take this option. If it is stressful or not conducive to studying, then you are probably better off moving out, even if it means having to take a job to make ends meet. On the other hand, there is a lot to be said for making use of supportive and flexible home conditions where these exist. If you are studying at a post-1992 university, you are more likely to have fellow students who also live at home.

What universities offer

You might think that opting to live in university accommodation is the most straightforward choice, especially since first-year students are invariably given priority in the allocation of places in halls of residence. Certainly if you go for university residences you benefit from being able to make arrangements in advance and at a distance, rather than having to be in the right place at the right time, as is often the way when searching for private housing. However, you may still need to select from a range of options because some universities will have a variety of accommodation on offer. You will need to consider which best suits your pocket and your preferred lifestyle.

New university accommodation

At the top end of the market, partnerships between universities and private firms have begun to lead the way in recent years. Private organisations such as UNITE plc and Liberty Living have been paid by universities to build and manage some of the most luxurious student accommodation the UK sector has ever seen. Rooms in these complexes are nearly always

---

Money paid monthly for accommodation

Average monthly spend

	Overall	Catered halls	Self-catered halls/flats houses	Rented flats/ houses off campus	Own flats/ houses off campus	Home parents/family off campus
	£342.70	£542.80	£428.20	£375.30	£334.20	£96.10

Monthly level of payments made by students as a percentage of all students surveyed*

£0	£1–£200	£201–£300	£301–£400	£401–£500	£501–£1,00	Over £1,001
15%	6%	19%	26%	14%	9%	2%

* In addition to the figures shown, 8 per cent of respondents did not know their monthly accommodation costs.

Adapted from Sodexo University Lifestyle Survey 2012

en suite and include facilities such as your own phone line, satellite TV and internet access. Shared kitchens are also top quality and fitted out with all the latest equipment. This kind of accommodation naturally comes at a higher price, but offers the advantages of flexibility both in living arrangements and through a range of payment options. Private companies have invested more than £5 billion into new student flats in recent years, continuing to do so even while the recession brought the rest of the construction business to a halt

Halls of residence

Many new or recently refurbished university-owned halls offer a standard of accommodation that is not far short of the privately built residences. One of the reasons for this is that rooms in these halls can be offered to conference delegates during vacations. Even though these halls are also at the pricier end of the spectrum, you will probably find that they are in great demand, and you may have to get your name down for one quickly to secure one of the fancier rooms. That said, you can often get a guarantee of some kind of university accommodation if you give a firm acceptance of an offered place by a certain date in the summer. This may not be the case if you have gained your place through Clearing – although rooms in private halls might still be on offer at this stage.

While a few halls are single-sex, most are mixed, and often house over 500 students. They are therefore great places for making friends and becoming part of the social scene. One possible downside is that they can also be noisy places where it can be difficult at times to get down to some work. The more successful students learn, before too many essay deadlines and exams start to loom, to get the balance right between all-night partying and escaping to the library for some undisturbed study time. Some libraries, especially new ones, are also now open 24 hours a day. If you feel in need of either personal or study support, this is often at hand either through a counselling service or from fellow students.

University self-catering accommodation

An alternative to halls, offered particularly by many older universities, are smaller, self-catering properties fitted out with a shared kitchen and other living areas. Students looking for a more independent and flexible lifestyle may prefer this option. Remember that if you choose this kind of university housing, you will be responsible for feeding yourself, and you may also have heating and lighting bills to pay. University properties are often on campus or nearby, and so travel costs should not pose a problem.

Catering in university accommodation

Many universities have responded to a general increase in demand from students for a more independent lifestyle, by providing more flexible catering facilities. A range of eateries, from fast food outlets to more traditional refectories, can usually be found on campus or in student villages. Students in university accommodation may now be offered pay-as-you-eat deals as an alternative to full-board packages.

What after the first year?

After your first year of living in university residences you may well wish, and will probably be expected, to move out to other accommodation. The main exceptions are the collegiate universities – particularly Oxford and Cambridge – which may allow you to stay on in college halls for another year or two, and particularly for your final year. Students from outside the EU are also sometimes guaranteed accommodation. There are also some universities, such as

Loughborough, where it is not uncommon for students to move back in to halls for their final year.

Practical details

If you have decided to start out in university accommodation, then you will probably be expected to sign an agreement to cover rent. Contract lengths vary. They can be for around 40 weeks, which includes the Christmas and Easter holiday periods or for just the length of the three university terms. These term-time contracts are common when a university uses its rooms for conferences during vacations, and you will be required to leave your room empty during these weeks. It is therefore advisable to check whether the university has secure storage space for you to leave your belongings – otherwise you will have to make arrangements to take all your belongings home or to store them privately between terms. International students may be offered special arrangements, in which they can stay in halls during the short vacation periods. Organisations like **www.hostuk.org** can also arrange for international students to stay in a UK family home at holiday times such as the Christmas break.

Parental purchases

One option for affluent families is to buy a house or flat and take in student lodgers. Naturally, this might not be the safe bet it once appeared, but it is still tempting for many parents. *The Sodexo University Lifestyle Survey* found a surprisingly large number of students living in houses owned by their own or fellow students' parents. Those who are considering this route tend to do so from the first year of study to maximise the return on the investment.

Being a lodger or staying in a hostel

A small number of students live as a lodger in a family home, an option most frequently taken up by international students. The usual arrangement is for a study bedroom and some meals to be provided, while other facilities such as a washing machine are shared. Students with particular religious affiliations or those from certain countries may wish to consider living in one of a number of hostels run by charities catering for certain groups. Most of these can be found in London.

Renting from the private sector

More than a third of students live in privately rented flats or houses, according to the *Sodexo University Lifestyle Survey*. Every university city or town is awash with such accommodation, available via agencies or direct from landlords. Indeed, there has been so much of it that so-called "student ghettoes", where local residents feel outnumbered, have become hot political issues. Into this traditional market in rented flats and houses have come the new private-sector complexes and residences, often created in partnership with universities, adding considerably to the private-sector options. Some are on university campuses. Others are in city centres and usually open to students of more than one university. Examples can be seen online; some sites are listed at the end of this chapter.

While there are always exceptions, a much more professional attitude and approach to managing rented accommodation has emerged among smaller providers, thanks to a combination of greater regulation and increasing competition. Nevertheless, it is wise to take certain precautions when seeking out private residences.

How to start looking for rented property

Contact your university's accommodation service and ask for their list of approved rented properties. Some have a Student Accommodation Accreditation Scheme, run in collaboration with the local council. To get onto an approved list under such schemes, landlords must show they are adhering to basic standards of safety and security, such as having an up-to-date gas and electric safety certificate. University accommodation officers should also be able to advise you on any hidden charges. For instance, you may be asked to pay a booking or reservation fee to secure a place in a particular property, and fees for references or drawing up a tenancy agreement are also sometimes charged. The practice of charging a "joining fee", however, has been outlawed. It would also be wise to speak to older students with first-hand experience of renting in the area. Certain companies in the area will often be notorious among second and third years and therefore you can seek to avoid them.

Making a choice

Once you have made an initial choice on the area you would like to live in and the size of property you are looking for, the next stage is to look at possible places. If you plan to share, it is important that you all have a look at the property. If you will be living by yourself, take a friend with you when you go to view a property, since he or she can help you assess what you see objectively, and avoid any irrational or rushed on-the-spot decisions. Don't let yourself be pushed into signing on the dotted line there and then. Take time to visit and consider a number of options. It is often helpful to spend some time in the area in which you may be living, to check out the local facilities, transport and the general environment at various times of the day and different days of the week.

If you are living in private rented accommodation, it is likely that at least some of your neighbours will not be students. Local people often welcome students, but resentment can build up, particularly in areas of towns and cities that are dominated by student housing. It is important to respect your neighbours' rights, and not to behave in an anti-social manner.

Preparing for sharing

The people you are planning to share a house with may have some habits that you find at least mildly irritating. How well you cope with some of the downsides of sharing will be partly down to the kind of person you are – where you are on the spectrum between laid back and highly strung – but it will help a lot if you are co-habiting with people whose outlook on day-to-day living is not too far out of line with your own. Some students sign for their second year houses as early as November and while it is good to be ahead of the rush, in such a short time at the university you may not have met your best friends yet. If you have not selected your own group of friends, universities and landlords can help by taking personal preferences and lifestyle into account when grouping tenants together. You can make this task easier if you give full details about yourself when filling in accommodation application forms.

Potential issues to consider when deciding whether to move into a shared house include whether any of the housemates smoke, own a loud musical instrument that they may decide to play at any time of the day or night, or have a habit of spending hours on the telephone. With most students owning a mobile phone, the latter should not be a problem unless someone decides to save on their mobile bills by using a landline in your shared house instead. If this is the case, then you should arrange for individual billing, provided by a number of phone companies. It will also be important to sort out broadband arrangements

that will work for everyone in the house, and that you will be able to arrange access to the
university system. It is also a good idea to agree from the outset a rota for everyone to share
in the household cleaning chores. Otherwise it is almost certain that you will live in a state of
unhygienic squalor or that one or two individuals will be left to clear up everyone else's mess.

The practical details about renting

It is a good idea to ask whether your house is covered by an accreditation scheme or code of
standards. Such codes provide a clear outline of what constitutes good practice as well as the
responsibilities of both landlords and tenants. Adhering to schemes like the National Codes
of Standards for Larger Student Developments compiled by Accreditation Network UK
(**www.anuk.org.uk**) may well become a requirement for larger properties, including those
managed by universities, now that the Housing Act is in force.

At the very least, make sure that if you are renting from a private landlord, you have his
or her telephone number and home address. Some can be remarkably difficult to contact
when repairs are needed or deposits returned.

Multiple occupation

If you are renting a private house it may be subject to the 2004 Housing Act in England
and Wales (similar legislation applies in Scotland and Northern Ireland). Licenses are
compulsory for all private Houses in Multiple Occupation (HMOs) with three or more
stories that house five or more unrelated residents. The provisions of the Act also allow local
authorities to designate whole areas in which HMOs of all sizes must be licensed. The good
news is that these regulations can be applied in sections of university towns and cities where
most students live. This means that a house must be licensed, well-managed and must meet
various health and safety standards, and its owner subject to various financial regulations.
The bad news is that this could lead to a reduction in the number and range of privately
rented properties on the market, or an increase in rental prices. Oxford City Council was the
first authority to require HMOs of all sizes within the city to be licensed by January 2012.

Tenancy agreements

Whatever kind of accommodation you go for, you must be sure to have all the paperwork in
order and be clear about what you are signing up to before you move in. If you are taking up
residence in a shared house, flat or bedsit, the first document you will have to grapple with
is a tenancy agreement or lease offering you an "assured shorthold tenancy". Since this is a
binding legal document you should be prepared to go through every clause with a fine-tooth
comb. Remember that it is much more difficult to make changes or overcome problems
arising from unfair agreements once you are a tenant than before you become one.

You would be well advised to seek help, in the likely event of your not fully understanding
some of the clauses. Your university accommodation office or students' union are a good
place to start – they should know all the ins and outs, and have model tenancy agreements
to refer to. A Citizens Advice Bureau or Law Advice Centre should also be able to offer
you free advice. In particular, watch out for clauses that may make you jointly responsible
for the actions of others with whom you are sharing the property. If you name a parent as
a guarantor to cover any costs not covered by you, then they may also be liable for charges
levied on all tenants for any damage that might not be your fault. A rent review clause
could allow your landlord to increase the rent at will, whereas without such a clause, they
are restricted to one rent rise a year. Make sure you keep a copy of all documents, and get

a receipt (and keep it somewhere safe) for anything you have had to pay for that is the landlord's responsibility.

Contracts tend to be longer than for university accommodation – they will frequently commit you to paying rent for 52 weeks of the year. There are probably more advantages than disadvantages to this kind of arrangement. It means you don't have to move out during vacation periods, which you might have to in university halls. You can store your belongings in your room when you go away (but don't leave anything really valuable behind if you can help it). You may be able to negotiate a rent discount for those periods when you are not staying in the property. The other advantage, particularly important for cash-strapped students, is that you have a base from which to find work and hold down a job during the vacations. Term dates are also not as dictatorial as they might be in halls; if you rent your own house then you can come back when you wish.

Deposits

On top of the agreed rent, you will need to provide a deposit or bond to cover any possible breakages or damage. This will probably set you back the equivalent of another month's rent. The deposit should be returned, less any deductions, at the end of the contract. However, be warned that disputes over the return of deposits are quite common, with the question of what constitutes reasonable wear and tear often the subject of disagreements between landlords and tenants. To protect students from unscrupulous landlords who withhold deposits without good reason, the 2004 Housing Act has introduced a National Tenancy Deposit Scheme under which deposits are held by an independent body rather than by the landlord. This is designed to ensure that deposits are fairly returned, and that any disputes are resolved swiftly and cheaply.

Inventories and other paperwork

You should get an inventory and schedule of condition of everything in the property. This is another document that you should check very carefully – and make sure that everything listed is as described. Write on the document anything that is different. The NUS even suggests taking photographs of rooms and equipment when you first move in (putting the date on the pictures if you are using a digital camera), to provide you with additional proof should any dispute arise when your contract ends and you want to get your deposit back. If

---

Security in rented accommodation

Students in private housing are twice as likely to be burgled as those in university halls. When looking at accommodation, use this NUS security checklist:

» Check that the front and back doors are fitted with five-lever mortise locks in addition to standard catch locks.
» Make sure the door to your room has a lock, and always lock up when you leave it, especially for long periods such as during vacations.
» Check the locks and catches on accessible windows, especially those at ground-floor level.
» Before you move in, try to talk to neighbours about how safe the area is and whether there have been many instances of burglary or car crime.
» Ask your landlord to ensure that all previous tenants and holders of keys no longer have copies.
» If you find a property that you like but have some security concerns, discuss these with the letting agency or landlord. They may be able to make the necessary changes to make the property more secure before you move in.

you are not offered an inventory, then make one of your own. You should have someone else witness and sign this, send it to your landlord, and keep your own copy. Keeping in contact with your landlord throughout the year and developing a good relationship with him or her will also do you no harm, and may be to your advantage in the long run.

You should ask your landlord for a recent gas safety certificate issued by a qualified CORGI engineer, a fire safety certificate covering the furnishings, and a record of current gas and electricity meter readings. Take your own readings of meters when you move in to make sure these match up with what you have been given, or make your own records if the landlord doesn't supply this information. This also applies to water meters if you are expected to pay water rates (although this isn't usually the case).

If you are sharing a house only with other full-time students, then you will not have to pay Council Tax. However, you may be liable to pay a proportion of the Council Tax bill if you are sharing with anyone who is not a full-time student. You may need to get a Council Tax exemption certificate from your university as evidence that you do not need to pay Council Tax or should pay only a proportion, depending on the circumstances.

Safety and security

Once you have arrived and settled in, remember to take care of your own safety and the security of your possessions. You are particularly vulnerable as a fresher, when you are still getting used to your new-found independence. This may help explain why a fifth of students are burgled or robbed in the first six weeks of the academic year. Take care with valuable portable items such as mobile phones, iPods and laptops, all of which are tempting for criminals. Ensure you don't have them obviously on display when you are out and about and that you have insurance cover. If your mobile phone is stolen, call your network or 08701 123123 to immobilise it. Students' unions, universities and the police will provide plenty of practical guidance when you arrive. Following their advice will reduce the chance of you becoming a victim of crime, and so able to enjoy living in the new surroundings of your chosen university town.

Useful websites

In the university profiles later in this book, we give an indication of costs for university-provided accommodation and details of university accommodation websites.

For advice on a range of housing issues, visit: **www.nus.org.uk/en/student-life/housing-advice**
The Shelter website has separate sections covering different housing regulations in England, Wales, Scotland and Northern Ireland: **www.shelter.org.uk**

As examples of providers of private hall accommodation, visit:
www.unite-students.com or **www.libertyliving.co.uk**

There are a number of sites that will help you find accommodation and/or potential housemates. Among the best-known are:

www.accommodationforstudents.com   **www.let4students.com**
www.homesforstudents.co.uk   **www.studentbunk.com**
www.studentaccommodation.org   **http://student.spareroom.co.uk**
www.studentpad.co.uk

10 Sporting Opportunities

Until recently, sport was a side issue at best for most students choosing universities. It still does not rate with the quality of course or the location of the university in the list of most applicants' priorities, but you only have to look at the investment in campus facilities to know that universities themselves think it is important. University sports facilities have improved out of all recognition over the past decade – and continue to do so. Recent developments at Leeds and Birmingham are just the most striking examples of a trend that has spread across the university system. Such has been the scale of investment that some of the biggest multi-sports developments in recent years have been on university campuses, where facilities nationally are said to be worth an astonishing £20 billion. As a result, half of all universities were chosen as pre-Olympics training bases for Great Britain squads and 30 will host other nations' teams in the run-up to the Games themselves.

University sport may not be big business, as it is in the USA, but it has become increasingly important in the student experience. Gone are the days when physical exercise was a minority pursuit on campus and regarded as not cool. Today it is said that at least 1.7 million students take part in regular physical activity, from gym sessions to competitive individual or team sports. Some specialist facilities may be reserved at times for elite (often international) performers. As at the Beijing Olympics, a significant proportion of Team GB at London 2012 are either students or relatively recent graduates.

Sporting opportunities

Being a full-time student offers unrivalled opportunities to discover and play a vast range of sports. Many universities still encourage departments not to schedule lectures and seminars on Wednesday afternoons, to give students free time for sport. Even those who spend long hours in the laboratory have more time for leisure activities as a student than they will be able to spare later in life. There are student-run clubs for all the major sports and – particularly at the larger universities – a host of minor ones. Or you can content yourself with high-quality gyms, with staff on hand to devise personalised training regimes and run popular activities such as zumba and pilates. The cost varies widely between universities, and membership fees can represent a large amount to lay out at the start of the year, but most provide good value if you are going to be a regular user.

More and more students want to keep fit, even if they do not play competitive sport, and universities have joined a race of their own to provide the best facilities. Sport may still be a secondary consideration for most applicants, but particularly good (or particularly poor) facilities can sometimes tip the balance.

Sport for all

For most universities, it is in the area of "sport for all" that most attention has been focused. Beginners are welcomed and coaching provided in a range of sports, from ultimate Frisbee to tai-chi, that would be difficult to match outside the higher education system. Check on university websites to see whether your usual sport is available, but do not be surprised if you come across a new favourite when you have the opportunity to try out some new sports as a student. Many universities have programmes designed to encourage students to take up a new sport, with expert coaching provided.

All universities are conscious of the need to provide for a spread of ability. Sports scholarships for elite performers are now commonplace, but there will be plenty of opportunities, too, for beginners. University teams demand a hefty commitment in terms of training and practice sessions – often several times a week – and in many sports standards are high. University teams often compete in local and national leagues.

For those who do not aspire to such heights, or whose interests are primarily social, there are thriving internal, or intramural, leagues. These provide opportunities for groups from halls of residence or faculties, or even a group of friends, to form a team and participate on a regular basis. A recent survey conducted by British Universities and Colleges Sport (BUCS) found 41,000 participants in the intramural programmes of 41 institutions. The largest programme was at the University of Brighton, where more than 6,000 students were playing sports ranging from football, rugby and badminton to softball, orienteering and fencing. Nor is university sport a male preserve – student teams were among the pioneers in mixed sport and are still strong in areas such as women's cricket, football and rugby. More than a third of the teams entered in national leagues in 2010–11 – nearly 4,300 teams – were female.

First-year sport

Halls of residence and university-owned flats will often provide an array of sports teams. At some universities, these are part of the intramural network of leagues, while others have separate arrangements for first years. In such cases, a Sports Captain, elected the year previously as part of the Junior Common Room, takes responsibility for organising trials and picking the teams, as well as arranging fixtures for the year. Hall sport is a great way of meeting like-minded people from your accommodation and over the course of the years, friendly rivalries often develop with other halls or flats. Generally there will be teams for football (both five- and 11-a-side), hockey, netball, cricket, tennis, squash, badminton and even golf. If your lodgings are smaller then don't worry, they are often twinned with similar flats to enable as many first-year students as possible to get involved in freshers' sport.

Other opportunities

You may even end up wanting to coach, umpire or referee – and this is another area in which higher education has much to offer. Many university clubs and sports unions provide subsidised courses for students to gain qualifications that may be of use to the individual in later life, as well as benefiting university teams in the short term. Or you might want to try your hand at some sports administration, with an eye to your career. In most universities there is a sports (or athletic) union, with autonomy from the main students' union, which organises matches and looks after the wider interests of those who play. There are plenty of opportunities for those seeking an apprenticeship in the art of running a club, or larger organisation. Southampton Solent University, for example, deploy students on volunteer coaching placements in more than 70 local schools. These placements increase a university's community engagement as well as enhancing student employability with minimal investment.

Universities that excel

A few universities are known particularly for sport – Exeter and Loughborough men's teams play national Premier League hockey, for example, while Bath and Northumbria both have teams in the Netball Super League. The University of London women's volleyball team has won the English Volleyball Championships, and "Team Bath" have tasted success in the FA Cup as a university team. Several of this elite group had a head start as former physical education colleges. Loughborough is probably the best-known of them, but Leeds Metropolitan and Brunel are others with a similar pedigree. Other universities with different traditions, such as Bath and the University of East Anglia, also have a variety of outstanding facilities, while the likes of Stirling and Cardiff Metropolitan have the same in a narrower range of sports. As in so much else, Oxford and Cambridge are in a category of their own. The Boat Race and the Varsity Match (in rugby union) are the only UK university sporting events with a big popular following – although there are varsity matches in several university cities that have become big occasions for students – and there is a good standard of competition in other sports. But you should not assume that success in school sport will be a passport to an Oxbridge place, for the days of special consideration for sporty undergraduates appear to be over.

Representative sport

Competitive standards have been rising in university sport. British Universities and Colleges Sport (BUCS; **www.bucs.org.uk**) runs competitions in almost 50 sports, and ranks participating institutions based on the points earned in the competitive programme. There is also international competition in a number of sports, and many students have been selected for Olympic and professional teams. The World Student Games have become one of the biggest occasions in the international sporting calendar.

BUCS is the national organisation for higher education sport in the UK, providing a comprehensive, multi-sport competition structure and managing the development of services and facilities for participative, grass-roots sport and healthy campuses, through to high-performance elite athletes. Its mission is to raise the profile of student sport and drive the university sport agenda by influencing government and key stakeholders in the sector.

University sports facilities

Even the smallest university should provide reasonable indoor and outdoor sports facilities – a sports hall, modern gym equipment and outdoor pitches (usually including an all-weather surface and floodlights). Many will also have a swimming pool and extras such as climbing walls, but some smaller universities make arrangements for students to use local sports centres and clubs when it is not feasible to provide for minority sports. The same goes for the really expensive sports, like golf, which is usually the subject of an arrangement with one or more local clubs that give students a discount. Specialist facilities, like boat houses and climbing huts, obviously depend on location, but the most landlocked university is likely to have a sailing club that organises regular activities away from campus, and a skiing club that runs at least annual trips to the mountains.

Many of the larger universities have spent millions of pounds improving their sports facilities, sometimes in partnership with local authorities or national sporting bodies. University campuses are ideal locations for national coaching centres, and many have been established in recent years. Although elite coaching generally takes place in closed sessions, students can occasionally find themselves rubbing shoulders with star players.

It is estimated that close to £500 million has been spent on new or upgraded sports facilities at UK universities over the past decade, and planned investment for the next three years will add at least £170 million to this figure. Universities now boast a significant proportion of the UK's 50-metre pools, for example, and more are planned to follow the recent opening at the University of Surrey. Other innovative schemes include Leeds Metropolitan's development of the Headingley cricket and rugby league grounds, providing teaching space for students during the week and improved facilities for players and spectators on match days.

Both the scale of investment and the emphasis on sport has increased as the 2012 Olympics approached. The BUCS Visa Outdoor Athletics Championships was chosen as the test event for the Olympic Stadium and the Olympic Torch relay visits many university campuses between May and July 2012. The legacy for students – not just in London – should be considerable, as it was following the Commonwealth Games in Manchester and the World Student Games in Sheffield.

Beyond scrutinising the prospectus for the extent of university facilities, there are two important questions to ask: how much do they cost and where are they? Neither is easy to track down on the average university website.

How much?

University prospectuses tend to major on the quality of the sports facilities without being as forthcoming about the prices. Students who are used to free (if inferior) facilities at school often get a nasty surprise when they find that they are expected to pay to join the Athletic Union and then pay again to use the gym or play football. Because most university sport is subsidised, the charges are reasonable compared to commercial facilities, but the best deal may require a considerable outlay at the start. Some campus gyms and swimming pools now charge more than £300 a year, for example, which is still considerably cheaper than paying per visit if you intend to use the facilities regularly (and provides an incentive to carry on doing so). Some universities are offering sports facility membership as part of the £9,000 fee, but most offer a variety of peak and off-peak membership packages – some for the entire length of your course.

Outdoor sports are usually charged by the hour, although clubs will also charge a membership fee. You may be required to pay up to £25 for membership of the Athletic Union (although not all universities require this). Fees for intramural sport are seldom substantial; teams will usually pay a fee for the season, while courts for racket sports tend to be marginally cheaper per session than in other clubs.

How far away?

The other common complaint by students is that the playing fields are too far from the campus – understandable in the case of city-centre universities, but still aggravating if you have to arrange your own transport. This is where campus universities have a clear advantage. For the rest, there has to be some trade-off between the quality of outdoor facilities and the distance you have to travel to use them. But universities are beginning to realise that long journeys depress usage of important (and expensive) facilities, and some have tried to find suitable land closer to lectures and halls of residence. Indoor sports centres should all be within easy reach.

Sport as a degree subject

Sports science and other courses associated with sport had seen consistent increases in applications until the imposition of higher fees. Even after an 8 per cent fall in 2012, the subject was in the top dozen in terms of popularity, with more than 47,000 applications at degree level. A separate ranking for the subject is published on page 186. If you are hoping to be rewarded with an academic qualification for three years on the sports field, you will be disappointed because there is serious science involved. However, sport is a growing employment field and one that demands qualifications like any other.

Other degrees in the sports area are more closely focused on management, with careers in the leisure industry in mind – golf course management, for example, has proved popular with students despite being a target of those who see anything beyond the traditional academic portfolio as "dumbing down". The question is not whether the courses are up to standard, but whether a less specialised one will offer more career flexibility if a decline in popularity for the particular sport limits future opportunities.

Sports scholarships

The number and range of sports scholarships have expanded just as rapidly as courses in the subject, but the two are usually not connected. Sports scholarships are for elite performers, regardless of what they are studying – indeed, they exist at universities with barely any degrees in the field. Imported from the USA, scholarships now exist in an array of sports. At Birmingham University, for example, there are specialist golf awards (as there are at ten other universities) and a scholarship for triathletes, as well as others open to any sport.

The value of scholarships varies considerably – sometimes according to individual prowess. The Royal and Ancient scholarships for golfers, for example, range from £500 for promising handicap golfers to £10,000 for full internationals. All of them demand that you meet the normal entrance requirements for your course and maintain the necessary academic standards, as well as progressing in your sport. In practice, most departments will be flexible about attendance and deadlines, as long as you make your requests well in advance.

Many sports scholarships offer benefits in kind, in the form of coaching, equipment or access to facilities. The Government-funded Talented Athlete Scholarship Scheme (TASS), which is restricted to students at English universities who have achieved national recognition at under-18 level and are eligible to represent England, is one such example. Winning Students is a similar scheme in Scotland. No fewer than 21 of the medallists in the Beijing Olympics were current or former TASS athletes. The scholarships are worth £3,500 a year and can be put towards costs such as competition and training costs, equipment or mentoring. Further details are available at **www.tass.gov.uk.**

Part-time work

University sports centres are an excellent source of term-time (and out-of-term) employment. You may also be trained in first aid, fire safety, customer care and risk assessment – all useful skills for future employment. The experience will help you secure employment in commercial or local authority facilities – and even for jobs such as stewarding at football grounds and music venues. Most universities also have a sabbatical post in the Athletic Union or similar body, a paid position with responsibility for organising university sport and representing the sporting community within the university.

University sporting facilities

Different students look for different things from their sport while at university and the table overleaf gives an initial guide to what's on offer at different institutions and, where appropriate, their various campuses.

The table is based on a detailed survey of university sport undertaken by British University and Colleges Sport (BUCS) in early 2012. The information in the table relates only to the facilities and services that universities provide centrally for all their students and does not include any facilities there may be in halls of residence or colleges.

The table contains a mix of factual information and "1–5" rankings, with five dots the best and one dot the worst. If there is no dot there is no facility. All the ratings take account of the number of students at each university, or on each campus, so they provide comparative information. The information in the table includes:

» The university's overall BUCS ranking and number of teams in BUCS competitions. Teams get points each year for their success in inter-university competitions and BUCS uses them to compile an annual league table. Some multi-site universities (eg, Manchester Metropolitan) have a BUCS ranking for each of their campuses, others (eg, Cumbria) have only one.

» The type of pool, if any (25m, 50m or other) at each university and the extent of its availability to students. The availability rating takes account of the extent to which the pool may be reserved for outside users, for example by a local swimming club or squad.

» Ratings for the range and availability of indoor dry sports facilities, such as sports halls, dance studios, squash courts and fitness gyms, derived from the total at-one-time capacity of the facilities and number of students. The more dots in the "Range" column, the more extensive the facilities in relation to the student population. A significant difference in the rating for range and availability indicates that while facilities exist, students may have restricted access to them.

» The total number of fitness training machines, plus an asterisk if the university's fitness facilities are accredited under the Inclusive Fitness Initiative (IFI) by the English Federation of Disability Sport. However, note that the IFI scheme does not operate in Northern Ireland, Scotland or Wales.

» Ratings for the range and availability of outdoor grass and artificial pitches and tennis or netball courts.

» The number of sports with intramural competitions.

» The availability of taught or instructor-led classes.

» The number of sports scholarships or bursaries available; they may be any mix of funding and free access to facilities or elite athlete support services.

» The number of different forms of support for achieving sporting excellence, such as coaching, sports psychology, nutritional advice, access to sports medicine or specialist strength and conditioning training.

University sports websites are given in the university profiles (chapter 14).

University sporting facilities

Name	BUCS Ranking 2010–11	Teams in BUCS Premier Leagues	Swimming pool	Availability of pools	Range of indoor dry sports facilities	Availability of indoor dry sports facilities
Aberdeen	27	3	Other	•	•••••	••••
Abertay	96	0			••	•••
Aberystwyth	55	1	Other	••	••••	•••••
Anglia Ruskin	85	0			•••	•••
Aston	89	0	Other	•	••••	••••
Bangor	68	5			•••	••••
Bath	5	18	50m	•••••	•••	••••
Bath Spa	132	No information available				
Bedfordshire	72	0			•••••	•••••
Birmingham	2	14	25m	•••	••	••
Birmingham City	112	No information available				
Bolton	141	No information available				
Bournemouth	30	4			•	••
Bradford	90	0	25m	•	••••	••••
Brighton (Brighton)	35	4			•••	••
Brighton (Eastbourne)	35	4	25m	••	•••••	•••••
Bristol	11	6			••	•
Brunel West London	24	No information available				
Buckingham	92	0			•••••	•••••
Cambridge	14	6			•••••	••••
Canterbury Christ Church	78	No information available				
Cardiff	12	5			•••••	•••••
Cardiff Metropolitan	13	12			•	•
Central Lancashire	43	10			••	•••
Chester (Chester)	86	No information available				
Chester (Warrington)	135	No information available				
Chichester	56	2			•••••	•••••
City	130	0			•	•
Coventry	50	0			••	•••
Cumbria (Ambleside)	114	0			••••	•••••
Cumbria (Carlisle)	114	0			•	•
Cumbria (Lancaster)	114	0			•	••
Cumbria (Penrith)	114	0			•••••	•••••
Cumbria (Preston)	114	0			•	•••
De Montfort	95	0			•	•
Derby	104	0			••	••
Derby (Buxton)	136	No information available				
Dundee	39	0	25m	•••	•••	••••
Durham	4	18			••••	•••
East Anglia	60	No information available				
East London	81	0			•	•
Edge Hill	76	1			•••	•••
Edinburgh	6	10	25m	•••	•••••	••••
Essex	38	5			••••	••••
Exeter	8	12	25m	•••	•••••	•••••

Fitness machines	Number of winter pitches	Availability of winter pitches	Outdoor courts	Availability of outdoor courts	Sports with intramural competitions	Availability of taught classes	Sports scholarships/ bursaries	Forms of elite athlete support
200	•••••	•••••	•	•	1	•••••	29	6
35					1	•	0	10
76	••••	••••	•••••	•••••	1	•••••	30	5
20					3	••••	25	0
103	••••	•••	•	••	0	••	6	2
93	•••	•••	••	••	6	•••	10	0
101*	••••	•••	••••	•••	2	•••	400	10
19	•••	•••	•••	•••	6	•	67	2
90*	••••	••••	•	•	6	•••••	67	10
55					10	•••	55	9
100*	••	•	•••	•••	17	•••	8	0
88	•••	•••	••••	••••	8	•	30	10
47	••••	••••	•••••	•••••	7	••••	30	10
100	••••	•••	••••	•	9	••	26	10
16	••	••			1	•••••	0	0
470					19	••	15	5
90	••	•••	•	••	3	••	60	9
55	•	•	•	•	2	•	28	6
108	••	•	••••	••••	1	••••	12	8
28	•••••	•••••	•••	•••	2	•	16	3
0					5	••	0	0
86	••	••			10	••	65	10
0	•	•			0	••	0	3
0					0	••	0	3
0	•••	•••			0	•	0	5
0	•••••	•••••			0		0	8
0	••	••	••••	•	0	•	0	8
90					6	•	0	0
37	•	•	••	••	0		6	10
125	••	••	•••	•••	8	•••••	12	10
242	•••••	•••••	••••	••••	20	•••	45	10
10					6	•	22	10
56	••••	•••			0	••••	18	10
266	••	••	•	••	11	••••	278	10
88	•••	••••	•••	•••	20	•••	7	10
125	•••••	•••••	•••••	•••••	16	•••••	60	10

Name	BUCS Ranking 2010–11	Teams in BUCS Premier Leagues	Swimming pool	Availability of pools	Range of indoor dry sports facilities	Availability of indoor dry sports facilities
Exeter (Falmouth)	8	0			•••	••••
Glamorgan	51	3			••••	•••••
Glasgow	34	0	25m	•••••	••	•
Glasgow Caledonian	87	0			•	•
Gloucestershire	40	4			•••••	•••••
Glyndŵr	134	No information available				
Goldsmiths	131	0			••••	•
Greenwich	118	0			•	••
Harper Adams	100	3			•••••	•••••
Heriot-Watt	46	0			•••	•••
Hertfordshire	61	1	25m	••••	•••	•••
Highlands and Islands	124	No information available				
Huddersfield	107	0			•	•
Hull	70	1			•	••
Imperial College	17	6	25m	•••••	•••••	•••••
Keele	77	0			••••	•••••
Kent	36	0			•	•
King's College London	42	1			••	••
Kingston	80	0			•	•
Lancaster	47	0	25m	••••	••••	••••
Leeds	16	7	25m	••••	•••	••
Leeds Metropolitan	3	11	Other	••	•••	•••
Leicester	66	0			••••	••
Lincoln	67	1			••	••
Liverpool	32	1	25m	••••	••	•••
Liverpool Hope	103	No information available				
Liverpool John Moores	52	No information available				
London Metropolitan	59	No information available				
LSE	64	No information available				
London South Bank	87	No information available				
Loughborough	1	22	50m	•••••	•••••	••••
Manchester	9	12	50 m	•••	••	••
Manchester Metropolitan (MMU)	71	0			••••	•••
MMU (Cheshire)	73	0			••••	••••
Middlesex	65	1			••	••
Napier	63	2			••	•••
Newcastle	15	4			••	••••
Northampton	93	No information available				
Northumbria	20	6	25m	•	•••••	•••
Nottingham	7	9	25m	•••••	•••	••••
Nottingham Trent	19	4			•••	••
Oxford	10	No information available				
Oxford Brookes	54	1	25m	••	••••	••
Plymouth	41	1			•	•
Portsmouth	28	1			••	•••

Fitness machines	Number of winter pitches	Availability of winter pitches	Outdoor courts	Availability of outdoor courts	Sports with intramural competitions	Availability of taught classes	Sports scholarships/ bursaries	Forms of elite athlete support
40			•••	•••	2	••••	6	3
134	••••	••••			7	•••	24	9
145	•••	•••	••••	••••	4	•••••	38	4
110					0	•••••	18	5
40*	•••••	•••••	•••••	•••••	4	•••••	18	10
113	•	•	••	••	3	••••	0	0
38*	•	•	•••	•••	0		0	3
22	•••••	•••••	•••••	•••••	0	••••	1	1
51	••••	••••	•••	••••	5	•••••	41	6
102*	•••••	•••••	•••	•••	2	•••	20	10
26					3	••	0	0
53*	•••	••	•••	•••	2	•	0	10
242	•••••	•••••	••	•••	7	••••	44	10
57	•••	•••	•	•	1	••••	0	2
110					9		51	9
32	••	•••	••	••	0	•	0	1
40	•	•	••	•	3	•	8	10
90	•••	••••	••	•••	16	•••••	0	0
221*	•	••	••	••	17	•••	35	10
169	•••	••••	•••	••••	4	•	52	10
96	••	••	••••	••••	13	•••	5	4
44*	••••	••••	••	••	5	••	15	7
92	•••	••••	••	••	7	••••	40	10
233	•••••	•••••	•••••	•••••	45	••••	135	10
105	•	•	•	••	12	•••	40	8
178*			•	•	0		0	10
50	•••••	•••••	•••••	•••••	3		0	10
78			•	•	8	••	43	10
57					0	•	4	1
108	••	•••	••	••	7	••	32	9
240	•••	•••			0		100	10
184	•••	••••	•••••	•••••	8	•••	35	10
140	••••	••••	••	••	4	•••	50	10
107	•••	•••	•••••	•••••	5	••••	25	8
43					10	••	20	6
96	•	•	••	••	13	•••••	15	6

University sporting facilities cont

Name	BUCS Ranking 2010–11	Teams in BUCS Premier Leagues	Swimming pool	Availability of pools	Range of indoor dry sports facilities	Availability of indoor dry sports facilities
Queen Margaret	113	3			•••••	•••••
Queen Mary	84	1			•••	••
Queen's, Belfast	102	No information available				
Reading	31	1			••••	••••
Robert Gordon	74	0	25m		••••	•••
Roehampton	91	0			•••	••••
Royal Holloway	57	0			•••	•••
St Andrews	25	1			•••	•••
Salford	110	0	25m	••	•	•
SOAS	115	No information available				
Sheffield	23	2	25m	••••	••	•
Sheffield Hallam	33	5			•	•
Southampton	18	No information available				
Southampton Solent	58	1			•••••	•••••
Staffordshire	83	0			•••••	•••
Stirling	22	3	50m	•••••	••••	•••••
Strathclyde	49	0	Other	•	••	•
Sunderland	98	0			••	••
Surrey	53	0	50m	•••••	•••••	•••••
Sussex	43	0			•••	••
Swansea	26	No information available				
Swansea Metropolitan	129	No information available				
Teesside	82	0			••	••
Trinity St David	143	No information available				
Ulster	127	0			•	•
University College London	37	1			•	•
University for the Creative Arts	141	No information available				
University of the Arts London	125	No information available				
UWE, Bristol	29	1			••	•
UWE, Hartpury	69	No information available				
Wales, Newport	105	0			•••	••••
Warwick	27	3	25 m	••••	••••	•••
West London	145	No information available				
West of Scotland	116	No information available				
Westminster	117	No information available				
Winchester	97	No information available				
Wolverhampton	99	0			•	•
Wolverhampton (Walsall)	99	0	25 m	•	•••••	•••••
Worcester	62	1			••••	••••
York	48	1	25 m	•••	•••	•••
York St John	94	0			•	••

Fitness machines	Number of winter pitches	Availability of winter pitches	Outdoor courts	Availability of outdoor courts	Sports with intramural competitions	Availability of taught classes	Sports scholarships/ bursaries	Forms of elite athlete support
50					0	•••••	0	0
70	•	•			4	•••	0	2
103	•••	•••	••••	••••	3	•••••	40	7
98*					0	••••	20	9
37*	•	•	••••	••••	0		23	10
48	••	••	•••••	•••••	0		28	4
45	•••••	•••••	•••••	•••••	14	••••	15	8
46	•	•			0	•	0	6
140	••	••			0		27	5
98	•	•	•	•	5	•••	36	10
175	••••	••	•	•	20	•••	28	10
68	•••••	•••••	•••••	•••••	2	••	0	10
86	••••	••••	••••	••••	3	•••••	91	8
97	•	••			3	•••	44	5
60					0		10	10
110	•••••	•••••	••••	••••	0		14	10
103	•••	••	•••	•••	5	•••	27	4
50*	••	••			3	••••	12	10
45	••	••			2	•	0	9
75*	•	•	•	•	3	••	26	7
100*	•	•			5	••	19	10
35*	•	•	•••	••••	3	•••••	15	10
98*	••••	••••	••	•	7	••••	No	9
17					7	••	0	10
38	••••	••••	••••	••••	7	••••	30	10
60	•••••	••••			1	••	27	10
71*	•••	••	•••••	•••••	14	•	13	4
18	••	•••			0		1	9

11 What Parents Should Do

When upfront fees were abolished in 2006 and responsibility for repayment shifted to graduates, some thought that parents would become less involved in their children's higher education. Far from it: spiralling student debt left parents feeling just as obliged as before to help their children through university. The shift to much higher fees appears to have sparked even more parental interest, with record numbers accompanying their children to open days and playing an active part in questioning academics and administrators. That involvement often continues in pursuing value for money from the student experience. This chapter looks at where to draw the line between constructive involvement and unwelcome interference.

Nearly all students are adults, and university offers an environment where they can begin to make their own decisions and develop as individuals. A good starting point is to offer advice only when it is sought, and to leave direct contact with university administrators and academics to the student. Of course, throughout the *Guide*, all references to parents apply equally to guardians and step-parents.

Student finance and parental involvement

No matter how independent students are meant to be, most parents will still want to help out when they can. The new student finance system is designed to enable undergraduates to pay their own way through a degree course – albeit building up considerable debts. Student loans are repayable after graduation only when the graduate's salary reaches £21,000 – a £6,000 increase on the previous threshold. Parents will not even know when repayments begin, let alone be required to make a contribution. However, remember that part of the maintenance loan is income-assessed and you may need to contribute to living expenses, especially in Scotland, where loans are less generous.

In any case, students still have to live, and the combination of loans and bursaries that comprises the new system will seldom be enough to make ends meet. Hundreds of thousands of students – particularly mature students – do pay their own way through university. But every survey shows that families play an important financial (and, until now, growing) role where students move straight from school to higher education.

"Helicopter parents"

Universities have found that anxious mothers and fathers are more inclined than ever to question what their children are getting for their increasingly substantial fees. There have been stories of parents challenging not just the amount and quality of tuition, but even the marking of essays and exams. The phenomenon, first reported in the USA, has given rise to the phrase "helicopter parents" – so called because they hover over their children's education when they should be letting go. No one wants to think of themselves in that category, but it is not surprising – or reprehensible – that parents are taking more of an interest. Many more of today's parents have been to university themselves, so have the knowledge and confidence to offer advice, both in choosing where and what to study, and in the decisions facing students at university. One of the reasons that some then overstep the mark is that they are shocked that the amount of teaching and size of seminar groups are not what they recall from their own "free" higher education. The new fees are meant to herald improvements in the student experience, including more contact hours, but it remains to be seen if these materialise. Few universities now have more money to spend on teaching, and it may be that fewer and larger seminars are here to stay in the arts and social sciences, where almost all state support has been withdrawn.

An associated reason for greater parental involvement is that family relationships have changed. Many teenage applicants are happy to accept a lift to an open day to get a second opinion on a university and their prospective course. They are also more likely than previous generations of students to come home at the weekend – or to live there in the first place – and to air any grievances.

Laying the ground

The first thing any parent can do to smooth the path to university is to be encouraging about the value of higher education. Ideally, this should have started long before the application process, but it is especially important at this point. Now that student debt has become a frequent media topic and the economic downturn has hit graduate employment prospects, it is only natural for sixth-formers and others to have second thoughts about higher education.

The lure of a regular wage packet will be tempting, should one be available, and there are plenty of young people who are not suited to full-time higher education. More big companies are choosing to employ promising 18-year-olds, rather than rely entirely on graduate recruitment. And even after the years of rapid university expansion, most people still do not go to university. Nevertheless, those who are capable of going generally do not regret the decision. Many people look back on their student days as the best period of their life, as well as the one that shaped their personality and their career. Time as a student should still pay off for the individual in terms of lifetime earnings, as well as personal development. A little reassurance at this stage may make all the difference.

Making the choice

Any parent wants to help a son or daughter through the difficult business of choosing where and what to study. How big a role you play will depend on a number of factors, not the least of which is the extent to which your advice is wanted. In the end, it is the student's decision, and you can do no more than offer relevant information.

One important factor is the quality of advice available at school or college. If this is good, parental involvement should be marginal. But often that is not the case, and you may have to call on other resources, including your own research.

A second factor is your own level of expertise: you may have opinions about particular universities or subjects, but are they up-to-date and based on evidence? Try not to give advice that is coloured by memories of your own student days. That was probably a quarter of a century ago, and higher education has changed out of all recognition in the intervening years. Avoid second-hand opinions gleaned through the media or dinner party gossip. You may think that some subjects are a sure-fire route to lucrative employment, while others are shunned by employers, but are you right? And do you really know the strengths and weaknesses of more than 100 universities? The tables in chapters 2 and 4 offer a reality check, but even they cannot take account of the differences within institutions. The subject tables in chapter 5 show that the best graduate employment rates are often not at the obvious universities.

Above all, do not try to rewind your own career decisions through your children. The fact that you enjoyed – or hated – a subject or a university does not mean that they will. You may have always regretted missing out on the chance to go to Oxbridge or to become a brain surgeon, but they have their own lives to lead. Students who switch courses or drop out frequently complain that they were pressured into their original choice by their parents.

Check that choices are being made for sensible reasons, not on the basis of questionable gossip or trivial criteria. But beyond that, you should stay in the background unless there is a very good reason to play a more substantive role. Make a point of looking for important aspects of university life that the applicant might miss. Security, for example, usually does not feature near the top of a teenager's list of priorities; likewise other practical issues, such as the proximity of student accommodation to lectures, the library and the students' union.

Many universities now publish guides specifically for parents and put on programmes for them at Open Days. The latter may be a way of separating prospective applicants from their more demanding "minders", but the programmes themselves can be interesting and informative. Do not worry that you will be an embarrassment by attending Open Days – thousands of parents do so, and you may add a critical edge to the proceedings. Like prospectuses, Open Days are part of the sales process, and it is easy for a sixth former to be carried away by the excitement surrounding a lively university. You are much more likely to spot the defects – even if they are ignored in the final decision.

Finding a place

Once the choices have been made, get to know the UCAS system and quietly ensure that deadlines are being met. The school should be doing this, but there is no harm in providing a little back-up, especially on parts of the process that take time and thought, such as writing the personal statement. There is little a parent can do as the offers and/or rejections come rolling in, other than to be supportive. If the worst happens and there are five rejections, you may have to start the advice process all over again for a new round of applications through UCAS Extra. If so, a cool head is even more necessary, but the same principles apply.

Results day

Then, before you know it, results day is upon you. Make sure you are at home, rather than in some isolated holiday retreat. Your son or daughter needs to have access to instant advice at school or college, and to be able to contact universities straight away if Clearing or Adjustment is required. And your moral support will be much more effective face to face, rather than down a telephone line. Whatever happens, try not to transmit the anxiety that you will inevitably be feeling to your son or daughter, especially if the results are not what was wanted. It is easy to make rash decisions about re-sitting exams or rejecting an insurance offer in the heat of the moment. Try to slow the process down and encourage clear and realistic thinking. Make sure you know in advance what might be required, such as where to access Clearing lists, and if it is Clearing or Adjustment, you will need to be on hand to offer advice and help with for visits to possible universities. Clearing or Adjustment is all but over in a week, so the agony should be short-lived.

Before they go

Little more than a month after the tension of results day, everything should be ready for the start of term. Unless your son or daughter is one of the growing band choosing to stay at home to study, there will be forms to fill in to secure university accommodation, as well as student loans to sort out and registration to complete. You can perform useful services, like supplying recipe books if the first year is to be spent in self-catering accommodation, but now is the time for independence to become reality. Make sure that important details like insurance are not forgotten, but otherwise stand clear.

Then it is just a matter of agreeing a budget, assuming you are in a position to make a financial contribution. How large that contribution is will depend on family circumstances and your attitude to independent living. Some parents want to ensure that their children leave university debt-free; others could never afford to do that, while yet others believe that paying your own way is part of the learning experience. The important thing is that students and parents know where they stand.

After they've left

Any new student is going to be nervous if he or she is leaving home for the first time and having to settle into a strange environment. But in most cases it is not going to last long because everyone is in the same boat and freshers' weeks hardly leave time for homesickness. In any case, they will not want to let their apprehension show. The people who are most likely to be emotional are the parents – especially if they are left with an empty nest for the first time. It can take a while to get used to an orderly, quiet house after all those years of mayhem.

Resist any temptation to decorate their bedroom and turn it into an office – it is more common than you might think, and psychologists say it can do lasting damage to family relationships. Keep in touch by phone, text or email, but try not to pry. You're not going to be told everything anyway – which is probably just as well. They will be back soon enough and, just as you were getting used to having the place to yourself, a weekend visit or the Christmas vacation will remind you of how things used to be. If things are not going smoothly at university, this may be the time for more reassurance – more students drop out at Christmas of their first year than at any other time.

Lastly, do not become a helicopter parent. Your son or daughter may well seek your advice if they are dissatisfied with the course, their accommodation or some other aspect of university life. By all means, give advice, but leave them to sort the problem out. Universities will cite the Data Protection Act, in any case, to say they can only deal with students, not parents. What they really mean is that students are adults and should look after themselves.

Useful websites

Many universities have sections on their websites for parents of prospective students.
UCAS has a Parents section and a regular newsletter on its website: **www.ucas.com/parents**
To find out more about open days, visit: **www.opendays.com**
There is helpful information: **www.direct.gov.uk/parentsguidetohe**

12 Coming to the UK to Study

All around the world, more and more young people are choosing to study outside their own country – 3.7 million did so in 2009. Sometimes this is because their home universities are poorly regarded, or just full. In other cases it is to master a different language, experience another culture or take the first step on an international career ladder.

The UK is one of the prime destinations of choice for those seeking to broaden their horizons. Only the USA, with its vast higher education system, attracts more international students. Global surveys have shown that UK universities are seen as offering high quality in a relatively safe environment. And, while their Achilles heel in such research is the perceived cost, there are compensations in the recent state of the pound and in the reduced living expenses offered by courses that are relatively short by international standards.

UK universities have been growing in popularity among international students for many years, although their "market share" has dropped as countries such as Australia and Germany have competed aggressively. Numbers have risen further as the value of the pound has made courses more affordable, while higher visa charges and changes in immigration regulations seem not to have dimmed global enthusiasm for UK higher education. The country's international student population rose by more than 5 per cent in 2010–11, and overseas applications for undergraduate places were up again at the start of 2012.

Both EU students (who pay the same fees as their British counterparts) and those from the rest of the world (who pay considerably more) have shared in the boom, but applications for 2012 courses saw a predictable parting of the ways. Those from EU countries for first degree courses were down by 12 per cent, as fees rose at English universities. Beyond the EU, where the new fees do not apply, applications were up by another 13 per cent. When postgraduates are included, the largest numbers continue to come from China and India.

There have been suggestions, even from the Prime Minister, that fees for non-EU students may fall (or at least rise more slowly) when British students are paying more. The logic behind the argument is that if the new rates for UK and other EU undergraduates reflect the full cost of teaching, international applicants and their sponsors will not expect to pay more. There is little sign as yet, however, of universities moving towards a single fee.

Why study in the UK?
Aside from the strong reputation of UK degree courses and the opportunity to be taught

and immerse yourself in English, new research shows that most graduates are handsomely rewarded when they return home. A report from the Department for Business, Innovation and Skills (BIS) shows that UK graduates earn much higher salaries than those who studied in their own country. The starting salaries of UK graduates in China and India were more than twice as high as those for graduates educated at home, while even those returning to the USA enjoyed a salary premium of more than 10 per cent.

Some premium is to be expected – you are likely to be bright and highly motivated if you are prepared to uproot yourself to take a degree. And most students have to be from a relatively wealthy background to afford the fees and other expenses of international study. A higher salary will probably be a necessity to compensate for the cost of the course. But the scale of increase demonstrated in the report suggests that a UK degree remains a good investment. Three years after graduation, 95 per cent of the international graduates surveyed were in work or further study. More than 90 per cent had been satisfied with their learning experience and almost as many would recommend their university to others.

A popular choice

Nearly all UK universities are cosmopolitan places that welcome international students in large numbers. Recent surveys by i-graduate, the student polling organisation which also

The top countries for sending international students to the UK

EU Countries (top 20)		%	Non-EU Countries (top 20)		%
France	7,325	10.5	China	28,694	25.3
Germany	7,294	10.4	Malaysia	9,865	8.7
Ireland	6,437	9.2	Hong Kong	7,951	7.0
Cyprus (EU)	5,735	8.2	India	6,485	5.7
Poland	4,708	6.7	Nigeria	5,216	4.6
Greece	4,628	6.6	United States	3,872	3.4
Bulgaria	3,597	5.1	Saudi Arabia	3,818	3.4
Lithuania	3,372	4.8	Singapore	3,140	2.8
Romania	3,349	4.8	Pakistan	3,041	2.7
Spain	2,843	4.1	Norway	2,722	2.4
Italy	2,689	3.8	Canada	2,411	2.1
Sweden	2,381	3.4	Sri Lanka	2,236	2.0
Belgium	1,828	2.6	Korea (South)	2,030	1.8
Cyprus (Other*)	1,814	2.6	Vietnam	1,481	1.3
Latvia	1,671	2.4	Russia	1,476	1.3
Netherlands	1,441	2.1	Bangladesh	1,456	1.3
Finland	1,263	1.8	Brunei	1,431	1.3
Portugal	1,239	1.8	United Arab Emirates	1,398	1.2
Slovakia	967	1.4	Switzerland	1,335	1.2
Austria	854	1.2	Kenya	1,316	1.2
All EU Students	**70,045**		**All non-EU students**	**113,318**	

Note: First degree non-UK students

*Domicile coding changed in 2007/8 for Cyprus students. 'Other' includes students from Northern Cyprus and all students from Cyprus entering prior to the change.

produced the BIS report, put the country close behind the USA among the world's most attractive study destinations. More than 420,000 international students were taking higher education courses in the UK in 2010–11, around half of them at undergraduate level. They now make up over 17 per cent of all students at UK universities and colleges. More full-time postgraduates – the fastest-growing group – come from outside the UK than within it. In many UK universities you can expect to have fellow students from over 100 countries.

More than 90 per cent of international students declare themselves satisfied with their experience of UK universities in i-graduate surveys, although they are less sanguine in the National Student Survey and more likely than UK students to make official complaints. Nevertheless, satisfaction increased by 8 percentage points in four years, according to i-graduate, reflecting greater efforts to keep ahead of the global competition. International students are particularly complimentary about students' unions, multiculturalism, teaching standards and places of worship. Their main concerns tend to be financial, with the UK considered the second-most expensive study location in the world (after the USA), partly because of a lack of employment opportunities (in one survey, only 56 per cent were satisfied with the ability to earn money while studying).

One way round this in a growing number of countries is to take a UK degree through a local institution or a full branch campus of a UK university. Indeed, there are now almost as many international students taking UK degrees in their own country as there are in Britain, 320,000 of them outside the EU. The numbers grew by 70 per cent in a decade and are likely to rise further if the UK Government prevents universities increasing the number of students coming to Britain.

Where to study in the UK

The vast majority of the UK's universities and other higher education institutions are in England. Of the 120 universities covered in *The Times Good University Guide*, 93 are in England, 15 in Scotland, 10 in Wales and 2 in Northern Ireland. Fee limits in higher education for UK and EU students are determined separately in each administrative area, which in some cases has brought benefits for EU students. All undergraduates from other EU countries are charged the same fees as those from the part of the UK where their chosen university is located, so EU students currently pay no tuition fees in Scotland, for example.

Within the UK, the cost of living varies by geographical area. Although London is the most expensive, accommodation costs in particular can also be high in many other major cities. You should certainly find out as much as you can about what living in Britain will be like. Further advice and information is available through the British Council at its offices worldwide, at more than 60 university exhibitions that it holds around the world every year, or at its Education UK website (**www.educationuk.org**). Another useful website for international students is provided by the UK Council for International Student Affairs (UKCISA) at **www.ukcisa.org.uk**.

Universities in all parts of the UK have a worldwide reputation for high quality teaching and research, as evidenced in global rankings such as those shown on pages 49–51. They maintain this standing by investing heavily in the best academic staff, buildings and equipment, and by taking part in rigorous quality assurance monitoring. The main regulatory bodies include the Quality Assurance Agency for Higher Education (QAA), higher education funding councils for each country of the UK, and the Office for Standards in Education, all of which publish reports on their websites. Professional bodies also play an important role, and there is an Independent Adjudicator for Higher Education who handles student complaints that have not been resolved by universities' own internal procedures.

Although many people from outside the UK associate British universities with Oxford and Cambridge, in reality most higher education institutions are nothing like this. Some universities do still maintain a traditional culture, but most are modern institutions that place at least as much emphasis on teaching as research and offer many vocational programmes, often with close links with business, industry and the professions. The table below shows the universities that are most popular with international students at undergraduate level. Although some of those at the top of the lists are among the most famous names in higher education, others achieved university status only in the last 20 years.

What subjects to study?

One of the reasons for such diversity is that strongly vocational courses are favoured by international students. Many of these in professional areas such as architecture, dentistry or medicine take one or two years longer to complete than most other degree courses. Traditional first degrees are mostly awarded at Bachelor level (BA, BEng, BSc, etc.) and last three to four years. There are also some "enhanced" first degrees (MEng, MChem, etc.) that take four years to complete. The relatively new Foundation degree programmes are almost all vocational and take two years to complete as a full-time course, with an option to study for a further year to gain a full degree. The tables at the end of this chapter select the 20 most popular subjects and show which universities for each subject have the greatest numbers of students. Remember, though, that you need also to consider the details of any course that

The universities most favoured by EU and non-EU students

Institution (top 20)	EU Students	Institution (top 20)	Non-EU Students
Aberdeen	1,638	Manchester	3,942
Coventry	1,616	Nottingham	2,901
Edinburgh	1,496	University of the Arts, London	2,895
London Metropolitan	1,483	University College London	2,753
Middlesex	1,402	Warwick	2,313
Manchester	1,394	Edinburgh	2,293
University of the Arts, London	1,388	Imperial College	2,288
Edinburgh Napier	1,368	Hertfordshire	1,935
Westminster	1,318	Sheffield	1,915
Glasgow	1,286	Coventry	1,889
University College London	1,156	Northumbria	1,866
Essex	1,119	Greenwich	1,837
Portsmouth	1,100	Liverpool	1,764
Kingston	1,073	Sheffield Hallam	1,646
King's College London	1,061	Middlesex	1,638
Brighton	1,027	Portsmouth	1,637
Kent	1,018	St Andrews	1,598
Salford	1,005	East London	1,574
Anglia Ruskin	985	Leeds	1,542
Ulster	958	Southampton	1,477

you wish to study and to look at the ranking of that university in our main league table in chapter 4 and in the subject tables in chapter 5.

English language proficiency

The universities maintain high standards partly by setting high entry requirements, including proficiency in English. For international students, this usually includes a score of 6 or 7 in the International English Language Testing System (IELTS), which assesses English language ability through listening, speaking, reading and writing tests. Under new visa regulations introduced in 2011, universities for a student's ability in English. This proficiency will need to be equivalent to an "upper intermediate" level (level B2) of the CEFR (Common European Framework of Reference) for studying at an undergraduate level.

There are many private and publicly funded colleges throughout the UK that run courses designed to bring the English language skills of prospective higher education students up to the required standard. However, not all of these are Government approved. Some private organisations such as INTO (**www.into.uk.com**) have joined with universities to create centres running programmes preparing international students for degree-level study. The British Council also runs English language courses at its centres around the world.

Tougher student visa regulations were introduced in April 2012. Although universities' international students will not be denied entry to the UK, some lower-level preparatory

The most popular subjects for international students

Subject Group	EU Students	Non-EU Students	Total	%
Business and administrative studies	16,302	35,716	52,018	28%
Engineering and technology	6,915	17,757	24,672	13%
Social studies	7,084	9,828	16,912	9%
Creative arts and design	6,238	6,189	12,427	7%
Subjects allied to medicine*	4,516	6,600	11,116	6%
Law	3,574	6,574	10,148	6%
Computer science	3,590	5,857	9,447	5%
Biological sciences	5,291	4,092	9,383	5%
Languages	4,339	2,721	7,060	4%
Architecture, building and planning	2,431	2,828	5,259	3%
Physical sciences	2,253	2,590	4,843	3%
Mathematical sciences	1,152	3,592	4,744	3%
Mass communication and documentation	2,396	2,120	4,516	2%
Medicine and Dentistry	1,089	3,422	4,511	2%
Historical and philosophical studies	1,755	1,555	3,309	2%
Education	500	630	1,131	1%
Veterinary science	109	645	754	0%
Agriculture and related subjects	301	341	642	0%
Combined	209	261	470	0%
Total	**70,045**	**113,318**	**183,363**	**100%**

Note: First degree non-UK students
* Subjects allied to medicine include pharmacy and nursing

courses taken by international students will be affected. It is, therefore, doubly important to consult the official UK government list of approved institutions (web address given at the end of this chapter) before lodging an application.

How to apply

You should read the information below in conjunction with that provided in chapter 6, which deals with the application process in some detail.

Some international students apply directly to a UK university for a place on a course, and others make their applications via an agent in their home country. But most applying for a full-time first degree course do so through the Universities and Colleges Admissions Service (UCAS). If you take this route, you will need to fill in an online UCAS application form at home, at school or perhaps at your nearest British Council office. There is lots of advice on the UCAS website about the process of finding a course and the details of the application system (**www.ucas.com/students/wheretostart/nonukstudents**).

Whichever way you apply, the deadlines for getting your application in are the same. For those applying from within an EU country, application forms for most courses starting in 2013 must be received at UCAS by 15 January 2013. Note that applications for Oxford and Cambridge and for all courses in medicine, dentistry and veterinary science have to be received at UCAS by 15 October 2012, while some art and design courses have a later deadline of 24 March 2013.

If you are applying from a non-EU country to study in 2013, you can submit your application to UCAS at any time between 1 September 2012 and 30 June 2013. Most people will apply well before the 30 June 2013 deadline to make sure that places are still available and to allow plenty of time for immigration regulations, and to make arrangements for travel and accommodation.

Entry and employment regulations

Visa regulations have been the subject of frequent controversy in the UK and many new rules and regulations have recently been introduced, often hotly contested by universities. The Government was criticised for increasing visa fees, doubling the cost of visa extensions, and ending the right to appeal against a refusal of a visa.

It also introduced a points system for entry – known as Tier 4 – which came into effect in March 2009. Under this scheme, prospective students can check whether they are eligible for entry against published criteria, and so assess their points score. Universities are also required to provide a Certificate of Acceptance for Study to their international student entrants and they must have "Highly Trusted" status on the Register of Sponsors. Prospective students have to demonstrate that, as well as the necessary qualifications, they have English language proficiency and enough money for the first year of their specified course. This has now increased to £1,000 a month in inner London and £800 a month elsewhere. Under the new visa requirements, details of financial support will be checked in more detail.

Since September 2007, all students wishing to enter the UK to study have been required to obtain entry clearance before arrival. The only exceptions are British nationals living overseas, British overseas territories citizens, British Protected persons, British subjects, and non-visa national short-term students who may enter under a new Student Visitor route. Visa fees have been increased again and the details of the regulations have been reviewed by the UK Border Agency. You can find more about all the latest rules and regulations for entry and visa requirements at **www.ukba.homeoffice.gov.uk/visas-immigration/studying**.

The rules and regulations governing permission to work vary according to your country of origin and the level of course you undertake. If you are from a European Economic Area (EEA) country (the EU plus Iceland, Liechtenstein and Norway), you do not need permission to work in the UK, although you will need to be ready to show an employer your passport or identity card to prove you are a national of an EEA country. Students from outside the EEA who are here as Tier 4 students are allowed to work part-time for up to 20 hours a week during term time and to work full-time during vacations. These arrangements apply to students on degree courses; stricter limits were introduced in 2010 for lower-level courses. If you wish to stay on after you have graduated, you can apply for permission under Tier 2 under the new points-based immigration system, but you will need a sponsor and the work must be considered "graduate level", commanding a salary of at least £20,000. The latest reforms abolished the Tier 1 two-year post-study period for graduates who do not have such a sponsor. They will be required to apply for a new visa from scratch. Full details are on the UK Border Agency website.

A new Graduate Entrepreneur Scheme will enable up to 1,000 graduates to remain in the UK longer than others if they have developed "world class innovative ideas or entrepreneurial skills". Successful applicants, who will be selected by their university, will be allowed to stay in the UK for 12 months, with the possibility of a further 12-month extension.

Bringing your family

Since 2010, international students on courses of six months or less have been forbidden to bring a partner or children into the UK, and the latest reforms extend this prohibition to all undergraduates except those who are government sponsored. Postgraduates will still be able to bring dependants to the UK and most universities can help to arrange facilities and accommodation for families as well as for single students. The family members you are allowed to bring with you are your husband or wife, civil partner (a same-sex relationship that has been formally registered in the UK or your home country) and dependent children.

If you are a national of any country from outside the EEA, your family will be subject to immigration policy. Those who are eligible to bring dependants will need to show that they can support them financially, arrange appropriate accommodation, and that they will leave the UK when the student has finished his or her studies. Such family members will usually be able to study (children under 16 are required to attend full-time education), and any over the age of 16 should be able to work as long as you have permission to stay for over 12 months and are following a degree or Foundation degree course. You can find out more about getting entry clearance for your family at **www.ukcisa.org.uk/student/info_sheets/your_family.php**.

Support from British universities

Support for international students is more comprehensive than in many countries, and begins long before you arrive in the UK. Many universities have advisers in other countries. Some will arrange to put you in touch with current students or graduates who can give you a first-hand account of what life is like at a particular university. Pre-departure receptions for students and their families, as well as meet-and-greet arrangements for newly arrived students, are common. You can also expect an orientation and induction programme in your first week, and many universities now have "buddying" systems where current students are assigned to new arrivals to help them find their way around, adjust to their new surroundings and make new friends. Each university also has a students' union that organises social, cultural and sporting events and clubs, including many specifically for international students. Both the university and the students' union are likely to have full-time staff whose job it is to look after the welfare of students from overseas.

International students also benefit from free medical and subsidised dental and optical care and treatment under the UK National Health Service, plus access to a professional counselling service and a university careers service.

At university, you will naturally encounter people from a wide range of cultures and walks of life. Getting involved in student societies, sport, voluntary work, and any of the wide range of social activities on offer will help you gain first-hand experience of British culture, and, if you need it, will help improve your command of the English language.

The 20 most popular subjects and universities for international students

1 Business Studies

	EU	Non-EU
Middlesex	288	771
Coventry	343	626
Aston	281	667
Westminster	507	339
Northumbria	149	662
Manchester	212	579
Anglia Ruskin	441	333
London Metropolitan	411	342
Cardiff Metropolitan	109	573
Sunderland	90	590
All overseas students	**11,829**	**21,799**

2 Accounting & Finance

	EU	Non-EU
Manchester	93	532
City	106	426
Exeter	16	486
Essex	103	383
Sheffield Hallam	15	466
Lancaster	111	364
Bangor	4	407
Warwick	74	310
Hull	63	274
Kent	29	264
All overseas students	**2,095**	**11,457**

3 Law

	EU	Non-EU
King's College London	260	269
Leicester	195	285
Kent	114	285
Manchester	88	251
Warwick	52	258
Essex	229	77
Northumbria	15	281
Buckingham	27	238
London School of Economics	32	224
Queen Mary, London	109	133
All overseas students	**3,574**	**6,574**

4 Computer Science

	EU	Non-EU
East London	28	631
Greenwich	38	380
Middlesex	66	294
Coventry	165	160
Teesside	64	238
Imperial College	150	97
Manchester	118	109
Portsmouth	104	120
Bedfordshire	47	167
Edinburgh	166	43
All overseas students	**3,590**	**5,857**

The 20 most popular subjects and universities for international students cont

5 Economics

	EU	Non-EU
University College London	101	521
Warwick	105	429
London School of Economics	59	415
Manchester	63	324
Essex	127	174
Royal Holloway	76	208
Exeter	60	218
York	77	184
Leicester	28	231
St Andrews	56	169
All overseas students	**2,248**	**5,977**

6 Art & Design

	EU	Non-EU
University of the Arts, London	820	2,053
Middlesex	165	69
Kingston	57	149
Northumbria	31	167
Nottingham Trent	51	147
University for Creative Arts	150	46
Birmingham City	92	92
Coventry	83	93
London Metropolitan	100	59
Goldsmiths College	48	106
All overseas students	**3,172**	**4,228**

7 Electrical and Electronic Engineering

	EU	Non-EU
Imperial College	87	321
Manchester	36	243
Birmingham	16	235
Northumbria	18	223
Liverpool	9	232
Sheffield	29	211
Birmingham City	42	186
Strathclyde	25	188
Coventry	22	172
Southampton	36	121
All overseas students	**1,194**	**5,679**

8 Mechanical Engineering

	EU	Non-EU
Imperial College	103	215
Coventry	48	205
Nottingham	32	193
Sheffield	17	176
Birmingham	6	163
Bath	73	95
Manchester	20	133
Hertfordshire	26	120
Southampton	48	98
University College London	31	112
All overseas students	**1,338**	**3,987**

9 Politics

	EU	Non-EU
St Andrews	76	334
Kent	240	50
Aberdeen	175	37
Edinburgh	38	165
London School of Economics	56	141
Warwick	67	119
Essex	105	61
University College London	90	59
Aberystwyth	107	35
Royal Holloway	90	50
All overseas students	**2,971**	**2,273**

10 Biological Sciences

	EU	Non-EU
Edinburgh	200	134
Imperial College	83	181
University College London	63	146
Manchester	83	99
Aberdeen	139	22
Cambridge	60	68
St Andrews	44	75
Oxford	48	63
Nottingham	31	76
Liverpool	13	88
All overseas students	**2,343**	**2,404**

The 20 most popular subjects and universities for international students cont

11 Mathematics

	EU	Non-EU
Imperial College	68	322
University College London	68	305
Warwick	74	263
Manchester	67	221
Liverpool	9	239
London School of Economics	23	223
Cambridge	104	135
Oxford	47	162
Leicester	27	111
Southampton	16	119
All overseas students	**1,152**	**3,592**

12 Hospitality, Leisure, Recreation & Tourism

	EU	Non-EU
West London	135	304
University College Birmingham	197	229
University of the Arts, London	51	196
Surrey	72	175
Brighton	173	34
Bournemouth	85	119
London Metropolitan	116	54
Edinburgh Napier	60	85
Oxford Brookes	88	50
Sheffield Hallam	16	114
All overseas students	**2,272**	**2,249**

13 Civil Engineering

	EU	Non-EU
Edinburgh Napier	217	31
Nottingham	44	159
Coventry	69	113
Imperial College	67	113
Cardiff	53	117
East London	46	119
Brighton	81	79
Bradford	114	44
University College London	44	113
Birmingham	17	114
All overseas students	**1,866**	**2,467**

14 Communication and Media Studies

	EU	Non-EU
University of the Arts, London	147	184
Liverpool John Moores	12	198
Goldsmiths College	60	141
Middlesex	129	55
Westminster	115	61
London Metropolitan	115	57
Bedfordshire	45	83
Southampton Solent	108	10
Coventry	74	38
Central Lancashire	34	74
All overseas students	**2,293**	**1,899**

15 Medicine

	EU	Non-EU
Manchester	45	247
King's College London	83	167
Imperial College	64	174
Nottingham	38	199
Glasgow	55	125
University College London	57	119
Leicester	28	147
Edinburgh	25	149
Cambridge	50	121
Birmingham	19	137
All overseas students	**1,019**	**3,159**

16 Psychology

	EU	Non-EU
Aberdeen	160	34
Glasgow	149	14
University College London	52	100
York	28	112
St Andrews	53	69
Middlesex	65	42
Essex	48	45
Nottingham	32	62
East London	56	30
Edinburgh	34	46
All overseas students	**2,429**	**1,539**

The 20 most popular subjects and universities for international students cont

17 Other Subjects Allied to Medicine

	EU	Non-EU
Bournemouth	181	170
Queen Margaret Edinburgh	131	118
Imperial College	54	137
Greenwich	93	60
Cambridge	62	70
Cardiff	25	91
Bedfordshire	68	46
Hertfordshire	60	45
Sheffield	20	84
Robert Gordon	102	0
All overseas students	**2,044**	**1,794**

19 Nursing

	EU	Non-EU
Glyndŵr	0	314
West London	64	226
Hertfordshire	30	255
Northampton	3	218
Liverpool John Moores	20	165
Glasgow Caledonian	25	158
Edinburgh Napier	104	78
Anglia Ruskin	29	135
Winchester	0	135
Glamorgan	13	100
All overseas students	**848**	**2,242**

18 Architecture

	EU	Non-EU
Nottingham	66	266
Manchester Metropolitan	87	85
Portsmouth	99	43
Westminster	92	49
Edinburgh	56	79
London Metropolitan	84	48
East London	86	41
Plymouth	98	14
Dundee	76	31
University of the Arts, London	45	61
All overseas students	**1,835**	**1,675**

20 Pharmacology & Pharmacy

	EU	Non-EU
Sunderland	115	252
Nottingham	15	262
Brighton	151	91
Robert Gordon	187	6
Liverpool John Moores	20	172
Manchester	23	140
Bath	23	139
Strathclyde	11	130
Kingston	46	67
School of Pharmacy	17	96
All overseas students	**949**	**2,077**

Useful websites

The British Council, with its dedicated Education UK site designed for those wishing to find out more about studying in the UK:

www.educationuk.org

The UK Council for International Student Affairs (UKCISA) produces a wide range of factsheets on all aspects of studying in the UK:

www.ukcisa.org.uk

UCAS, for full details of courses available and an explanation of the application process:

www.ucas.com/students/wheretostart/nonukstudents

For the latest information on entry and visa requirements, visit the UK Border Agency:

www.ukba.homeoffice.gov.uk/visas-immigration/studying

Register of Sponsors for Tier 4 educational establishments:

**www.ukba.homeoffice.gov.uk/sitecontent/documents/employersandsponsors/
pointsbasedsystem/registerofsponsorseducation**

For a general guide to Britain, available in many languages:

www.visitbritain.com

13 Applying to Oxbridge

Oxbridge (as Oxford and Cambridge are called collectively) not only dominates UK higher education; the two universities are recognised as among the best in the world, regularly featuring among the top five in global rankings. But that is not why they merit a separate chapter in this *Guide*.

The two ancient universities have different admissions arrangements to the rest of the higher education system. Although part of the UCAS network, they have different deadlines from other universities, you can only apply to one or the other, and selection is in the hands of the colleges rather than the university centrally. Most candidates apply to a specific college, although you can make an open application if you are happy to go anywhere.

There have been reforms to the admissions system at both universities in recent years, in order to make the process more user-friendly to those who do not have school or family experience to draw upon. In particular, the business of choosing a college has been intimidating for many prospective applicants. Candidates are now distributed around colleges more efficiently, regardless of the choices they make initially.

There is little to choose between the two universities in terms of entrance requirements, and a formidable number of successful applicants have the maximum possible grades. However, that does not mean that the talented student should be shy about applying: both have fewer applicants per place than many less prestigious universities, and admissions tutors are always looking to extend the range of schools and colleges from which they recruit. For those with a realistic chance of success, there is little to lose except the possibility of one wasted space out of five on the UCAS application.

Overall, there are about five applicants to every place at Oxford and Cambridge, but there are big differences between subjects and colleges. As the tables in this chapter show, competition is particularly fierce in subjects such as medicine and English, but those qualified to read geology or classics have a much better chance of success. The pattern is similar to that in other universities, although the high degree of selection (and self-selection) that precedes an Oxbridge application means that even in the less popular subjects the field of candidates is certain to be strong.

The two universities' power to intimidate prospective applicants is based partly on myth. Both have done their best to live down the *Brideshead Revisited* image, but many sixth-formers still fear that they would be out of their depth there, academically and socially. In fact, the state sector produces nearly 55 per cent of entrants to Oxford and over 59 per cent to Cambridge, and the dropout rate is lower than at almost any other university. The "champagne set" is still present and its activities are well publicised, but most students are hard-working high achievers with the same concerns as their counterparts on other campuses. A joint poll by the two universities' student newspapers showed that undergraduates were spending much of their time in the library or worrying about their employment prospects, and relatively little time on the river or even in the college bar.

State school applicants

Both universities and their student organisations have put a great deal of effort into trying to encourage applications from state schools, and many colleges have launched their own campaigns. Such has been the determination to convince state school pupils that they will get a fair crack of the whip that a new concern has grown up of possible bias against independent school pupils. In reality, however, the dispersed nature of Oxbridge admissions rules out any conspiracy. Some colleges set relatively low standard offers to encourage applicants from the state sector, who may reveal their potential at interview. Some admissions tutors may give the edge to well-qualified candidates from comprehensive schools over those from highly academic independent schools because they consider theirs the greater achievement in the circumstances. Others stick with tried and trusted sources of good students. The independent sector still enjoys a degree of success out of proportion to its share of the school population.

Choosing the right college

Simply in terms of winning a place at Oxford or Cambridge, choosing the right college is not quite as important as it used to be. Both universities have got better at assessing candidates' strengths and finding a suitable college for those who either make an open application or are not taken by their first-choice college.

Cambridge: The Tompkins Table 2011

College	2011	2010	College	2011	2010
Trinity	1	2	Sidney Sussex	16	18
Emmanuel	2	1	Downing	17	15
Trinity Hall	3	4	Peterhouse	18	7
Clare	4	8	Robinson	19	19
Pembroke	5	10	King's	20	14
Christ's	6	12	Fitzwilliam	21	22
Selwyn	7	6	Murray Edwards	22	23
Jesus	8	16	Girton	23	21
Magdalene	9	5	Newnham	24	25
Churchill	10	3	Wolfson	25	24
St. Catharine's	11	9	Homerton	26	26
Corpus Christi	12	13	Hughes Hall	27	27
Gonville and Caius	13	11	St Edmund's	28	28
Queens'	14	17	Lucy Cavendish	29	29
St. John's	15	20			

At Oxford, subject tutors from around the university put candidates into bands at the start of the selection process, using the results of admissions tests as well as exam results and references. Applicants are spread around the colleges for interview and may not be seen by their preferred college if the tutors think their chances of a place are better elsewhere. Almost a quarter of last year's successful candidates were offered places by a college other than the one they applied to.

Cambridge relies on the "pool", which gives the most promising candidates a second chance if they were not offered a place at the college to which they applied. Those placed in the pool are invited back for a second round of interviews early in the new year. The system lowers the stakes for those who apply to the most selective colleges – in 2010 over 18 per cent of offers came via the pool. Cambridge still interviews about 90 per cent of applicants, whereas the new system at Oxford has resulted in more immediate rejections in some subjects. In medicine, fewer than a third of Oxford's applicants were interviewed in 2010, while in biochemistry almost all were.

However, most Oxbridge applicants still apply direct to a particular college, not only to maximise their chances of getting in, but because that is where they will be living and socialising, as well as learning. Most colleges may look the same to the uninitiated, but there are important differences. Famously sporty colleges, for example, can be trying for those in search of peace and quiet.

Thorough research is needed to find the right place. Even within colleges, different admissions tutors may have different approaches, so personal contact is essential. The tables in this chapter give an idea of the relative academic strengths of the colleges, as well as the varying levels of competition for a place in different subjects. But only individual research will suggest where you will feel most at home. For example, women may favour one of the few remaining single-sex colleges (Murray Edwards, Newnham and Lucy Cavendish at Cambridge). Men have no such option.

Oxford: The Norrington Table 2011

College	2011	2010	College	2011	2010
Merton	1	3	Corpus Christi	16	2
Christ Church	2	7	Trinity	17	25
New	3	5	St Anne's	=18	18
Magdalen	4	1	St Hilda's	=18	21
Hertford	5	12	Keble	20	28
Worcester	6	8	Balliol	21	9
Wadham	7	13	Lady Margaret Hall	22	20
Jesus	8	10	St Hugh's	23	19
Exeter	9	27	Queen's	24	16
Brasenose	10	22	St Catherine's	25	14
St John's	11	4	Somerville	26	24
Mansfield	12	29	St Edmund Hall	27	23
Pembroke	13	17	St Peter's	28	26
University	14	6	Oriel	29	11
Lincoln	15	15	Harris Manchester	30	30

Oxford applications and acceptances by course

Arts	Applications		Acceptances		Acceptances to Applications %	
	2011	2010	2011	2010	2011	2010
Ancient and Modern History	74	84	16	23	21.6	27.4
Archaeology and Anthropology	87	83	25	26	28.7	31.3
Classical Archaeology and Ancient History	107	82	22	22	20.6	26.8
Classics	292	294	117	122	40.1	41.5
Classics and English	36	34	7	6	19.4	17.6
Classics and Modern Languages	38	31	12	9	31.6	29
Economics and Management	1,086	1,169	89	89	8.2	7.6
English	1,152	1,307	220	224	19.1	17.1
English and Modern Languages	166	158	20	24	12	15.2
European and Middle Eastern Languages	54	56	15	26	27.8	28.6
Fine Art	193	156	23	25	11.9	16
Geography	344	389	81	86	23.5	22.1
Modern History	960	1,035	225	224	23.4	21.6
Modern History and Economics	85	73	14	14	16.5	19.2
Modern History and English	86	85	13	9	15.1	10.6
Modern History and Modern Languages	94	119	16	18	17	15.1
Modern History and Politics	316	344	48	45	15.2	13.1
History of Art	105	88	14	14	13.3	15.9
Law	1,223	1,153	202	192	16.5	16.7
Law with Law Studies in Europe	341	345	28	31	8.2	9
Mathematics and Philosophy	95	104	16	16	16.8	15.4
Modern Languages	582	584	185	170	31.8	29.1
Modern Languages and Linguistics	68	73	15	24	22.1	32.9
Music	232	210	65	67	28	31.9
Oriental Studies	150	151	41	40	27.3	26.5
Philosophy and Modern Languages	79	88	16	18	20.3	20.5
Philosophy and Theology	96	86	25	21	26	24.4
Physics and Philosophy	116	126	25	17	21.6	13.5
Philosophy, Politics and Economics (PPE)	1,676	1,668	248	238	14.8	14.3
Theology	107	112	31	45	29	40.2
Theology and Oriental Studies	6	7	2	2	33.3	28.6
Total Arts	**10,046**	**10,294**	**1,876**	**1,877**	**18.7**	**18.2**

The findings in the Tompkins Table (see page 262) are not officially endorsed by Cambridge University itself. However, since 2007 we have been able to publish the "official" Norrington Table from Oxford. Sanctioned or not, both tables give an indication of where the academic powerhouses lie – information which can be as useful to those trying to avoid them as to those seeking the ultimate challenge. Although there can be a great deal of movement year by year, both tables tend to be dominated by the rich, old foundations. Both tables are compiled from the degree results of final-year undergraduates. A first is worth five points;

Oxford applications and acceptances by course cont

Sciences	Applications		Acceptances		Acceptances to Applications %	
	2011	2010	2011	2010	2011	2010
Biochemistry	391	329	90	91	23	27.7
Biological Sciences	399	382	102	107	25.6	28
Biomedical Sciences	204	–	31	–	15.2	–
Chemistry	560	573	188	181	33.6	31.6
Computer Science	151	148	25	19	16.6	12.8
Earth Sciences (Geology)	146	123	35	35	24	28.5
Engineering Science	820	757	156	150	19	19.8
Engineering, Economics and Management	131	125	11	10	8.4	8
Experimental Psychology	262	270	47	50	17.9	18.5
Human Sciences	167	106	28	25	16.8	23.6
Materials Science (including MEM)	106	125	28	31	26.4	24.8
Mathematics	1133	1046	173	173	15.3	16.5
Mathematics and Computer Science	99	91	26	20	26.3	22
Mathematics and Statistics	209	194	26	22	12.4	11.3
Medicine	1487	1469	151	154	10.2	10.5
Physics	893	841	166	162	18.6	19.3
Physiological Sciences	–	95	–	24	–	25.3
Psychology, Philosophy and Physiology (PPP)	–	176	–	23	–	13.1
Psychology and Philosophy	139	–	27	–	19.4	–
Total Sciences	**7,297**	**6,850**	**1,310**	**1,277**	**18**	**18.6**
Total Arts and Sciences	**17,343**	**17,144**	**3,186**	**3,154**	**18.4**	**18.4**

Note: the dates refer to the year in which the acceptances were made

a 2:1, four; a 2:2, three; a third, one point. The total is divided by the number of candidates to produce each college's average.

In both universities, teaching for most students is based in the colleges. In practice, however, in the sciences this arrangement holds good only for the first year. One-to-one tutorials, which are Oxbridge's traditional strength for undergraduates, are by no means universal. Teaching groups remain much smaller than in most universities, and the tutor remains an inspiration for many students.

The applications procedure
Both universities have set a UCAS deadline of 15 October 2012 for entry in 2013. You may also need to take a written test and submit examples of your work – the exact requirements vary depending on the course you select, so check this carefully. See pages 20–21 for details of application tests. In addition, once Cambridge receives your UCAS form, you will be asked to complete an online Supplementary Application Questionnaire (SAQ). The deadline for this will be 22 October 2012 in most cases. For international applications to Cambridge you must also submit a Cambridge Online Preliminary Application (COPA), in some cases

Cambridge applications and acceptances by course

Arts	Applications		Acceptances		Acceptances to Applications %	
	2010	2009	2010	2009	2010	2009
Anglo-Saxon, Norse and Celtic	47	52	21	25	44.7	48.1
Archaeology and Anthropology	181	163	66	69	36.5	42.3
Architecture	464	499	37	43	8	8.6
Asian and Middle Eastern Studies	149	188	48	61	32.2	32.4
Classics	148	173	71	88	48	50.9
Classics (4 years)	33	34	13	11	39.4	32.4
English	875	1,035	204	221	23.1	21.4
Geography	337	332	101	99	30	29.8
History	731	772	199	210	27.2	27.2
History of Art	139	126	31	34	22.3	27
Linguistics	86	–	23	–	26.7	–
Modern and Medieval Languages	580	605	164	191	28.3	31.6
Music	157	182	56	71	35.7	39
Philosophy	254	312	45	52	17.7	16.7
Theology and Religious Studies	111	124	46	58	41.4	46.8
Total Arts	**4,292**	**4,597**	**1,125**	**1,233**	**26.2**	**26.8**
Social Science	2010	2009	2010	2009	2010	2009
Economics	1,342	1,396	169	178	12.6	12.8
Land Economy	230	261	56	56	24.3	21.5
Law	1,143	1,062	213	219	18.6	20.6
Social and Political Sciences	798	689	124	110	15.5	16
Total Social Sciences	**3,513**	**3,408**	**562**	**563**	**16**	**16.5**
Science and Technology	2010	2009	2010	2009	2010	2009
Computer Science	272	329	76	69	27.9	21
Engineering	1,798	1,546	336	307	18.7	19.9
Mathematics	1,196	1,177	232	244	19.4	20.7
Medical Sciences	1,968	1,857	304	299	15.4	16.1
Natural Sciences	2,378	2,278	637	647	26.8	28.4
Veterinary Medicine	446	414	78	75	17.5	18.1
Total Science and Technology	**8,058**	**7,601**	**1,663**	**1,641**	**20.6**	**21.6**
Education	103	98	44	42	42.7	42.9
Total	**15,966**	**15,704**	**3,394**	**3,479**	**21.3**	**22.2**

Note: the dates refer to the year in which the acceptances were made. Information for 2011 had not been published when this guide went to press.
Mathematics includes mathematics and mathematics with physics. Medical sciences includes medicine and the graduate course in medicine.
The Tripos courses in chemical engineering, management studies and manufacturing engineering can be taken only after Part 1 in another subject. Applications and acceptances for these courses are recorded under the first year subjects taken by the applicants involved.
Linguistics could only be taken after Part 1 of another Tripos for 2009 entry. From 2010 entry onwards, however, this subject became available as a full three-year degree programme

by 9 September 2012. Check both university websites for full details.

You may apply to either Oxford or Cambridge (but not both) in the same admissions year, unless you are seeking an Organ award at both universities. Interviews take place in December for those short-listed (for international applicants, Cambridge hold some interviews overseas while Oxford holds some interviews over the internet, though medicine interviewees must come to Oxford). Applicants to Oxford will receive either a conditional offer or a rejection by Christmas, while in Cambridge the news arrives early in the new year. For more information about the application process and preparation for interviews, visit **www.cam.ac.uk/admissions** and **www.ox.ac.uk/admissions**.

Oxford College Profiles

Balliol

Oxford OX1 3BJ	01865 277777	www.balliol.ox.ac.uk
Undergraduates: 383	Postgraduates: 316	undergrad.admissions@balliol.ox.ac.uk

Famous as the *alma mater* of many prominent post-war politicians, Balliol has maintained a strong presence in university life and is usually well represented in the Union and most other societies. Academic standards are formidably high, as might be expected in the college of Wyclif and Adam Smith, notably in the classics and social sciences, though, surprisingly, it fell to 21st in the 2011 Norrington Table. PPE is notoriously oversubscribed. Library facilities are good and include the Taylor law library. Balliol began admitting overseas students in the 19th century and has cultivated an attractively cosmopolitan atmosphere. It is now the only college to have an entirely student-run bar, the focal point for evening socialising. Most undergraduates are offered guaranteed accommodation in college for their first and final years, with second year accommodation off-site and a few rooms in college for those who would rather stay on campus. Graduate students are usually lodged in the Graduate Centre at Holywell Manor.

Brasenose

Oxford OX1 4AJ	01865 277510 (admissions)	www.bnc.ox.ac.uk
Undergraduates: 365	Postgraduates: 209	admissions@bnc.ox.ac.uk

Brasenose may not be the most famous Oxford college, but it makes up for its discreet image with an advantageous city-centre position, nestled beside the stunning Radcliffe Camera. The alma mater of David Cameron, Brasenose was one of the first colleges to admit women in the 1970s, and now usually has a near-even split within each year. BNC, as the college is often known, has a strong rugby reputation, having won the rugby cuppers 14 times over the years, and also has among the lowest proportions of students from state schools in the university. Named after the door knocker on the 13th-century Brasenose Hall, the college has a pleasant, intimate ambience which most find conducive to study. Law, PPE, medicine and modern history are traditional strengths, and competition for places in these subjects is intense. The library is open 24 hours a day and there is a separate law library. Sporting standards are as high as at many much larger colleges and the college's rowing club is one of the oldest in the university. The annexe at Frewin Court means nearly all undergraduates can live in, and many postgraduates can also live in the St Cross Building.

Christch Church

Oxford OX1 1DP   01865 276181 (admissions)   www.chch.ox.ac.uk

Undergraduates: 438   Postgraduates: 223   admissions@chch.ox.ac.uk

The college founded by Cardinal Wolsey in 1525 and affectionately known as "The House" has come a long way since Evelyn Waugh mythologised its aristocratic excesses in *Brideshead Revisited*. A little under half of offers tend to be made to state school pupils, which still leaves Christ Church with among the highest proportion of private school students. Academic pressure is reasonably relaxed, although natural high achievers prosper, and the college's history and law teaching is highly regarded. The college was second in the Norrington Table in 2011, rising from seventh year before. The magnificent 18th-century library is one of the best in Oxford and is supplemented by a separate law library. Christ Church has its own art gallery, which holds over 2,000 works of mainly Italian Renaissance art. Sport, especially rugby and football, is an important part of college life. The college has good squash courts and the river is close by for the aspiring oarsman, with the men's crew retaining its position at Head of the River this year. Accommodation for all three years is rated by college undergraduates as excellent and includes flats off Iffley Road as well as a number of beautifully panelled shared sets (double rooms) in college. Its chapel is also the cathedral of the Diocese of Oxford – England's smallest medieval cathedral.

Corpus Christi

Oxford OX1 4JF   01865 276693 (admissions)   www.ccc.ox.ac.uk

Undergraduates: 248   Postgraduates: 105   admissions.office@ccc.ox.ac.uk

Corpus, one of Oxford's smallest colleges, is naturally overshadowed by its Goliath-like neighbour, Christ Church, but makes the most of its intimate, friendly atmosphere and exquisite beauty. Although the college has only around 350 students including postgraduates, it has an admirable library open 24 hours a day. Academic expectations are high and English, Classics, PPE and medicine are especially well-established. The college came 16th in the Norrington Table in 2011, a significant fall from 2nd the year before. Perhaps unsurprisingly, Corpus has stormed to victory in University Challenge twice in recent years, although after their 2008 win the team were subsequently disqualified and stripped of their title. Corpus is able to offer accommodation to all its undergraduates, one of its many attractions to those seeking a smaller community in Oxford. The college is also one of the most generous with bursaries, giving travel, book and vacation grants at an almost unparalleled level across the university. Scholars are particularly well rewarded.

Exeter

Oxford OX1 3DP   01865 279648 (academic secretary)   www.exeter.ox.ac.uk

Undergraduates: 343   Postgraduates: 201   admissions@exeter.ox.ac.uk

Exeter is the fourth oldest college in the university and was founded in 1314 by Walter de Stapeldon, Bishop of Exeter. Nestling between the High Street and Broad Street, site of most of the city's bookshops, it could hardly be more central. The college boasts handsome buildings, the exceptional Fellows' garden and attractive accommodation for most undergraduates for all three years of their university careers, although many second year students currently live out. The college has recently refurbished its graduate accommodation in the east of the city to a high standard. Exeter does have academic pedigree and has climbed up the Norrington Table lately, rising from 27th to 9th in 2011. It is, however, often accused of being rather dull. Given its glittering roll-call of alumni, which includes Martin

Amis, J.R.R. Tolkien, Alan Bennett, Richard Burton, Imogen Stubbs and Tariq Ali, this seems an accusation that, on the face of it at least, is hard to sustain. The arrival of Frances Cairncross, the former managing editor of *The Economist*, in 2004 has created a new dynamic at the college, with regular, high-profile speaker events, and the incorporation of a college careers service. The college has taken over the buildings of Ruskin College in Walton Street, which will provide further accommodation.

Harris Manchester

Oxford OX1 3TD	01865 271009 (admissions tutor)	www.hmc.ox.ac.uk
Undergraduates: 85	Postgraduates: 108	enquiries@hmc.ox.ac.uk

Founded in Manchester in 1786 to provide education for non-Anglican students, Harris Manchester finally settled in Oxford in 1889 after spells in both York and London. A full university college since 1996, its central location with fine buildings and grounds in Holywell Street is very convenient for the Bodleian, although the college itself does have an excellent library. Harris Manchester admits only mature students to read for both undergraduate and graduate degrees, predominantly in the arts. All students must be 21 or older, though the average age has come down slightly in recent years. There are also groups of visiting students from American universities and students training for the ministry. Most members live in and all meals are provided – indeed the college encourages its members to dine regularly in hall. The college has few sporting facilities (a croquet lawn and a college punt), but members can use two central Oxford gyms without charge and can play football, cricket, swimming and chess as well as playing on other college or university teams. Other outlets include the college Drama Society and the chapel, a focal point for many there.

Hertford

Oxford OX1 3BW	01865 279404 (admissions)	www.hertford.ox.ac.uk
Undergraduates: 396	Postgraduates: 172	admissions@hertford.ox.ac.uk

Though tracing its roots to the 13th century, Hertford is determinedly modern. It was one of the first colleges to admit women (in 1975). Hertford also helped set the trend towards offers of places conditional on A-levels, which paved the way for the abolition of the entrance examination. It is still popular with state school applicants, and is one of the least stuffy colleges, with a reputation for attracting students from a broad range of backgrounds. The college lacks the grandeur of Magdalen, of which it was once an annex, but has its own architectural trademark in the Bridge of Sighs. It is also close to the History Faculty library (Hertford's neighbour), the Bodleian and the King's Arms, perhaps Oxford's most popular pub. Academic pressure at Hertford is relaxed, but the quality of teaching, especially in English, is generally thought admirable. Accommodation has improved, thanks in part to the Abingdon House and Warnock House complex close to the Thames near Folly Bridge, and the college can now lodge all of its undergraduates at any one time, often at subsidised rates, albeit in disparate parts of the city. The bar, offering some notorious cocktails, serves as a central social hub, and is popular with students across the university.

Jesus

Oxford OX1 3DW	01865 279721 (admissions)	www.jesus.ox.ac.uk
Undergraduates: 347	Postgraduates: 168	admissions.officer@jesus.ox.ac.uk

Jesus, the only Oxford college to be founded in the reign of Elizabeth I, suffers from something of an unfair reputation for insularity. Its students, whose predecessors include T.E.

Lawrence and Harold Wilson, describe it as "friendly but gossipy" and shrug off the legend that all its undergraduates are Welsh. Close to most of Oxford's main facilities, Jesus has three compact quads, the second of which is especially enticing in the summer. The college's JCR is well-equipped, with a pool table, large projector screen television, and a hatch serving tea and toast throughout the day. Academic standards are high and most subjects are taught in college. Physics, chemistry and engineering are especially strong. Rugby and rowing also tend to be taken seriously. Accommodation is almost universally regarded as excellent and relatively inexpensive, and the new Ship Street Centre was opened last year with 33 en-suite rooms for first-year students and a lecture theatre. Self-catering flats in north and east Oxford have enabled every graduate to live in throughout his or her Oxford career. The range of accommodation available to undergraduates is similarly good and is available for the full length of any course. The college's Cowley Road development, also the site of the college's sports ground, has been described by the students' union as "some of the plushest student housing in Oxford".

Keble

Oxford OX1 3PG   01865 272711 (admissions)   www.keble.ox.ac.uk
Undergraduates: 423   Postgraduates: 200   college.office@keble.ox.ac.uk

Keble is one of Oxford's most distinct colleges, with its unmistakable Victorian Gothic architecture and newly cleaned brickwork walls gleaming around the grand quads. Named after John Keble, the leader of the Oxford Movement, Keble was founded in 1870 with the intention of making Oxford education more accessible, and the college remains proud of "the legacy of a social conscience". With around 400 undergraduates, Keble is one of the biggest colleges in Oxford and its academic performance varies from year to year. It is strong in the sciences, where it benefits from easy access to the Science Area, the Radcliffe Science Library and the Mathematical Institute. The college's sporting record remains exemplary, with the rugby team regularly dominating university competitions. Though the overflow of the sporting ethos into the college's social life can be a little overbearing, it by no means dominates the life of a college, which has numerous music and drama societies as well as a highly successful annual Arts Week. Undergraduates are guaranteed accommodation in their first two years and the college can also accommodate most undergraduates in their final year. The cosy, wood-panelled library is open 24 hours a day. The college hall, where students wishing to dine must wear gowns six nights a week, has recently been intensively cleaned to restore it to its former glory and is one of the most impressive in the university. The college also has a well-equipped gym and the modern O'Reilly theatre, the acoustics of which are rated the best in the university.

Lady Margaret Hall

Oxford OX2 6QA   01865 274310 (admissions)   www.lmh.ox.ac.uk
Undergraduates: 400   Postgraduates: 185   admissions@lmh.ox.ac.uk

Lady Margaret Hall, Oxford's first college for women, has been co-educational since 1978 and now enjoys an equal gender balance. For many students, LMH's comparative isolation – the college is three-quarters of a mile north of the city centre – is a real advantage, ensuring a clear distinction between college life and university activities, and a refuge from tourists. For others it means a long journey to central library facilities. Although the neo-Georgian architecture is not to everyone's taste, the college's beautiful gardens back onto the Cherwell river, allowing LMH to have its own punt house and 12 acres of land. The students' union describes life at the college as "relaxed". It generally hovers around the lower reaches of the Norrington Table (22nd in 2011), although English is strong, producing a high proportion of firsts each year, as do maths, physics and history. Accommodation is guaranteed for first, second and third years since the opening of the Pipe Partridge building, which has considerably enlarged undergraduate accommodation and houses a new JCR, dining hall and lecture theatre. Ongoing building works aim to provide further graduates rooms as well as a new gym, due for completion by autumn 2014. LMH shares most of its sports facilities with Trinity College, though it has tennis courts on site and has become a leading rowing college. The library is open 24 hours and is well-stocked for English and Classics, with a separate law library. It has long been one of Oxford's dramatic centres, with at least five student productions a year, put on at the Simpkins Lee lecture theatre.

Lincoln

Oxford OX1 3DR   01865 279836 (admissions)   www.lincoln.ox.ac.uk

Undergraduates: 318   Postgraduates: 291   admissions@lincoln.ox.ac.uk

Small, central Lincoln cultivates a lower profile than many other colleges with comparable assets. The college's 15th-century buildings and beautiful library – a converted Queen Anne church – combine to produce a delightful environment in which to spend three years. Academic standards are high, particularly in arts and social science subjects, although the college's relaxed atmosphere is justly celebrated. City-centre accommodation is provided by the college for all undergraduates throughout their careers and includes rooms above the Mitre, a medieval inn. The college has a healthy rivalry with neighbouring Brasenose. Historically, Lincoln students must invite their Brasenose counterparts into the bar for free drinks every Ascension Day, in recognition of a time when a Lincoln and Brasenose student were both being chased by a town mob and the Brasenose student was denied access to Lincoln, leaving him to be killed by the mob. Graduate students have their own centre a few minutes' walk away in Bear Lane and at the EPA Science Centre close to the university science area. Finalists live in a recently refurbished complex on Museum Road, by Keble and the University Parks. Lincoln's small size and self-sufficiency have led to the college being accused of insularity. Lincoln's food is outstanding, among the best in the university. Sporting achievement is impressive for a college of this size, in part a reflection of its good facilities, with a successful cup-winning football team.

Magdalen

Oxford OX1 4AU   01865 276063 (admissions)   www.magd.ox.ac.uk

Undergraduates: 415   Postgraduates: 189   admissions@magd.ox.ac.uk

Perhaps the most beautiful college in Oxford or Cambridge, Magdalen is known around the world for its tower, its deer park and its May morning celebrations – when students threw themselves off Magdalen Bridge into the River Cherwell. This practice has now been banned after shallow water resulted in a large number of injuries. The college has shaken off its public school image to become a truly cosmopolitan place, with a large intake from overseas and an increasing proportion of state school pupils. Magdalen's record in English, history and law is second to none, while its science park at Sandford is bound to bolster its reputation in these subjects. The college is academically very strong and topped the Norrington Table for the first time in 2010, coming fourth in 2011, with over half of the finalists last year achieving firsts. Library facilities are excellent, especially in history and law. First-year students are accommodated in the Waynflete Building and are allocated rooms in subsequent years by ballot. Undergraduates can be housed in college for the full length of their course. Rents are not cheap compared to other colleges, but there is always financial help on offer. Magdalen is also conveniently placed between the city centre and east Oxford, where there is a plethora of pubs and restaurants and a lively music scene. The college bar is one of the best in Oxford and the college is a pluralistic place, proud of its drama society and choir. In recent years the college has become particularly strong at rowing. Elsewhere, enthusiasm on the sports field makes up for a traditional lack of athletic prowess.

Mansfield

Oxford OX1 3TF   01865 270920 (admissions)   www.mansfield.ox.ac.uk

Undergraduates: 226   Postgraduates: 81   admissions@mansfield.ox.ac.uk

Mansfield's graduation to full Oxford college status in 1995 marked the culmination of a long history of development since 1886. Its spacious, attractive site is fairly central, close to the libraries, the shops, the University Parks and the river Cherwell. With just over 200 undergraduates, the community is close-knit, although this can verge on the claustrophobic. Recent moves to increase intake numbers may change that. The less intimidating atmosphere of Mansfield is, perhaps, helped by its strong representation of state-school students; among the highest ratio in the university. First and third years live in college accommodation while second-years live in private houses nearby. The library is open 24 hours and the JCR is among the largest of any college, while Mansfield students share Merton's excellent sports ground and have numerous college teams. In recent years the college has produced many student journalists and contributes many performers to theatre and music productions. Despite its former theological background, students are not admitted on the basis of religion and can read a wide variety of subjects. Mansfield is home to the Oxford Centre for the Environment, Ethics and Society (OCEES) and the American Studies Institute backs onto its gardens, evidence of the strong links between Mansfield and the USA, which is reflected by some 35 visiting students annually. It also spearheads the Oxford FE Initiative, which encourages applications to the university from further education colleges.

Merton

Oxford OX1 4JD   01865 276299 (admissions)   www.merton.ox.ac.uk

Undergraduates: 314   Postgraduates: 289   admissions@admin.merton.ox.ac.uk

Founded in 1264 by Walter de Merton, Bishop of Rochester and Chancellor of England, Merton is one of Oxford's oldest and most prestigious colleges. Quiet and beautiful, with the oldest quad in the university, Merton has high academic expectations of its undergraduates, consistently reflected in its position at or near the top of the Norrington Table. History, English, physics, PPE and chemistry all enjoy a formidable track record. The medieval library is the envy of many other colleges. Accommodation is some of the cheapest in the university, of a good standard and offered to students for all three years. Merton's food is well-priced and among the best in the university; formal Hall is served six times a week. Kitchens are provided for second years who live in off-site accommodation while Merton's many diversions include the Merton Floats, its dramatic society, the Neave Society (politics), an excellent Christmas Ball and the peculiar Time Ceremony, which celebrates the return of GMT. Sports facilities are excellent, although participation tends to be more important than the final score.

New College

Oxford OX1 3BN   01865 279512 (admissions)   www.new.ox.ac.uk
Undergraduates: 418   Postgraduates: 217   admissions@new.ox.ac.uk

New College is actually rather old (founded in 1379 by William of Wykeham), large and much more relaxed than most expect when first confronting its daunting facade. It is a bustling place, as proud of its excellent music and its bar as of its strength in classics, chemistry, music and maths. The college came third in the Norrington Table in 2011, climbing from fifth the year before. Traditionally in the bottom third of colleges for attracting state-school students, the college has been making particular efforts to increase this proportion, inviting applications from schools that have never sent candidates to Oxford. The Target Schools Scheme, designed to increase applications from state schools, is well established. All first, second and fourth-year students can live in college and almost all of the third-years who want to live in usually can. The college's library facilities are impressive, especially in law, classics and PPE. The sports ground is nearby and includes good tennis courts. Women's sport is particularly strong, especially on the river. A sports complex, named after Brian Johnston, opened in 1997, at St Cross Road. The sheer beauty of New College remains one of its principal assets and the college gardens are a memorable sight in the summer, especially the other-worldly Mound in the heart of the college. Music is a feature of college life, and the college has some of the best practice facilities in the university. The Commemoration Ball, held every three years, is a highlight of Oxford's social calendar.

Oriel

Oxford OX1 4EW   01865 276522 (admissions)   www.oriel.ox.ac.uk
Undergraduates: 302   Postgraduates: 158   admissions@oriel.ox.ac.uk

In spite of its reputation as a rower's paradise, Oriel is a friendly, centrally located college with a strong sense of identity. The college is traditionally described as having "a strong crew spirit" reflecting its traditions on the river, though the last few years have not been quite so glorious for the actual Oriel crew. Academic pressure is relaxed by Oxford standards and it tends to inhabit the middle reaches of the Norrington Table, though fell to 29th in 2011 from 11th the year before. The well-stocked library is open 24 hours a day. Oriel's sporting reputation is certainly deserved and its rowing eight is rarely far from the head of the river. Other sports are well catered for, even if their facilities are considerably farther away than the boathouse, which is only a short jog away. Accommodation is of variable quality, but Oriel can provide rooms for the duration of the course – be it three years or four – for those students who require them. Extensive new accommodation has been completed one mile away off the Cowley Road and at the Island Site on Oriel Street. Oriel also offers a lively drama society, a Shakespearian production taking place each summer in the front quad. College meals are cheap, with students charged little more than £6 for three meals a day in hall.

Pembroke

Oxford OX1 1DW   01865 276412 (admissions)   www.pmb.ox.ac.uk
Undergraduates: 367   Postgraduates: 141   admissions@pmb.ox.ac.uk

Although its alumni include such extrovert characters as Dr Johnson and Michael Heseltine, Pembroke is stereotypically one of Oxford's least dynamic colleges. The college is historically poor financially, though its modern art collection draws in visitors and revenue. Mid-table in terms of exam results, the college has Fellows and lecturers in almost all the major university subjects. Pembroke will be able to accommodate all undergraduates when a new extension is opened in October 2012, and the Sir Geoffrey Arthur building on the river, ten minutes' walk from the college, offers excellent facilities; in addition to 100 student rooms there is a concert room, computer room and a multi-gym. College food is reasonable, with formal hall three times a week. Rugby and rowing are strong, with Pembroke usually behind only Oriel and Magdalen on the river, and squash and tennis courts are available at the nearby sports ground. The college's netball, football and hockey teams have all reached the finals of college cup competitions in recent years. Over the past few years Pembroke's intake has had among the lowest proportion of state-school students in the university, though it is running access schemes to improve this ratio.

Queen's

| Oxford OX1 4AW | 01865 279161 | www.queens.ox.ac.uk |
| Undergraduates: 343 | Postgraduates: 124 | admissions@queens.ox.ac.uk |

One of the most striking sights of the High Street, Queen's is one of Oxford's liveliest and most attractive colleges. The college's academic record is average, although results had improved recently, before dropping to 24th in the Norrington Table in 2011. Modern languages, chemistry and mathematics are reckoned among the strongest subjects. Queen's does not normally admit undergraduates for the single honour schools of theology, computer science or geography, but is seen as strong in history and politics. The library is as beautiful as it is well stocked. All students are offered accommodation, first years being housed in modernist annexes in east Oxford, and the college has converted a large number of rooms into en-suite facilities. Queen's can be insular and is largely apolitical, but has a strong college enthusiasm for sport, particularly rugby and netball. The college's beer cellar is one of the most popular in the university and the JCR facilities are also better than average. An annual dinner commemorates a student who is said to have fended off a bear by thrusting a volume of Aristotle into its mouth. Postgraduates are accommodated in St Aldate's House, a modern building close to the centre of town.

St Anne's

| Oxford OX2 6HS | 01865 274840 (admissions) | www.st-annes.ox.ac.uk |
| Undergraduates: 444 | Postgraduates: 233 | enquiries@st-annes.ox.ac.uk |

Architecturally uninspiring (a Victorian row with concrete "stack-a-studies" dropped into their back gardens), St Anne's makes up in community spirit what it lacks in awesome grandeur. One of the largest colleges, it has a relatively high proportion of state-school students. A women's college until 1979, its academic standing has fluctuated, having been in last place in the Norrington Table in the middle of the last decade, but now scoring around mid-table – equal 18th place in 2011. PPE is particularly strong. The library, which is now open 24 hours, is very well-stocked and is rich in law, Chinese and medieval history texts. The college has a strong presence in the university journalism scene and its football teams usually do very well. Accommodation is guaranteed to all undergraduates, and the college also operates an equalisation scheme which gives up to £800 to students wishing to live out. The college is situated to the north of the city centre, although not as far out as St Hugh's. Three new accommodation blocks contain 150 student rooms, including four for disabled students, while the older rooms have been refurbished. Half of all rooms are en suite.

St Catherine's

Oxford OX1 3UJ   01865 271703 (admissions)   www.stcatz.ox.ac.uk

Undergraduates: 499   Postgraduates: 216   admissions@stcatz.ox.ac.uk

Arne Jacobsen's modernist design for "Catz", one of Oxford's youngest and largest under-graduate colleges, has attracted much attention as the most striking contrast in the university to the lofty spires of Magdalen and New College. Close to the law, English and social science faculties, the university science area and the pleasantly rural Holywell Great Meadow, St Catherine's is nevertheless only a few minutes' walk from the city centre. Academic standards are especially high in mathematics and physics. The well-liked Wolfson library is open till midnight on most days. Rooms are small but tend to be warmer than in other, more venerable colleges, and are now available on site for first, second and third years. There is an excellent theatre, as well as an on-site punt house, gym and squash courts. The college is host to the Cameron Mackintosh Chair of Contemporary Theatre, currently held by Meera Syal. Previous incumbents include Kevin Spacey, Arthur Miller and Sir Ian McKellen. St Catherine's has one of the best JCR facilities in Oxford.

St Edmund Hall

Oxford OX1 4AR   01865 279011 (admissions)   www.seh.ox.ac.uk

Undergraduates: 404   Postgraduates: 166   admissions@seh.ox.ac.uk

St Edmund Hall – "Teddy Hall" – has one of Oxford's smallest college sites but also one of its most populous. The college offers students the chance to live in its medieval quads right in the heart of the city. With the male/female ratio nearly equal, the college is shedding its image as a home for "hearties", and the authorities have gone out of their way to tone down younger members' rowdier excesses. Nonetheless, the sporting culture is still vigorous and the college usually does well in rugby, football and hockey. Academically, Teddy Hall tends to yo-yo between the middle and the bottom of the Norrington Table; in 2011 it was 27th. But the college has some impressive names among its fellowship as well as a marvellous library, originally a Norman church. It hosts three annual prizes for journalism, including a £500 award for a student from St Edmund Hall. College accommodation is reasonable and can be offered for three years, either on the main site or in three annexes, one near the University Parks, and two on Iffley Road, where many of the rooms have private bathrooms.

St Hilda's

Oxford OX4 1DY   01865 286620 (admissions)   www.st-hildas.ox.ac.uk

Undergraduates: 398   Postgraduates: 139   college.office@st-hildas.ox.ac.uk

October 2008 marked a milestone for St Hilda's and the university as a whole, as the college welcomed its first mixed sex intake. Although the college, founded in 1893, lasted more than 100 years as an all-female institution, the governing body voted in 2006 to admit men. Male students now make up nearly half of the first year in incoming years. The college has long languished at the bottom end of the Norrington Table, though is slowly rising towards mid-table. However, it is a distinctive part of the Oxford landscape and is usually well represented in university life. The library is growing fast and accommodation for readers was extended in 2005. St Hilda's also boasts one of the largest ratios of state-school to independent undergraduates in Oxford. Accommodation is guaranteed to first years and finalists and the bar and common room are being renovated and enlarged and disabled access improved for the summer of 2012. The JCR has its own punts, which are available free for college members and their guests. Many of the rooms offer some of the best river views in Oxford. The standard of food is high, and the college has recently stopped fining students for serious misbehaviour, but rather asking them to do community service.

St Hugh's

Oxford OX2 6LE   01865 274910 (admissions)   www.st-hughs.ox.ac.uk
Undergraduates: 397   Postgraduates: 219   admissions@st-hughs.ox.ac.uk

One of the lesser-known colleges, St Hugh's was criticised by students in 1986 when it began admitting men. There is now an equal male/female ratio, a better balance than at most Oxford colleges. Like Lady Margaret Hall, St Hugh's picturesque setting is a bicycle ride from the city centre. It is an ideal college for those seeking a place to live and study away from the madding crowd, and is well liked for its pleasantly bohemian atmosphere and beautiful gardens. Academic pressure remains comparatively low. After a brief jump up the Norrington Table the college is now back in the lower regions at 23rd in 2011. St Hugh's guarantees accommodation to undergraduates for all three years, although the standard of rooms is variable. Sport, particularly football, is taken quite seriously. As the college enjoys extensive grounds compared to most colleges, there is space for a croquet lawn and tennis courts. A new building for the study of China will start construction in 2012 after a £10-million donation from a Hong Kong businessman.

St John's

Oxford OX1 3JP   01865 277317 (admissions)   www.sjc.ox.ac.uk
Undergraduates: 399   Postgraduates: 213   admissions@sjc.ox.ac.uk

St John's is one of Oxford's powerhouses, excelling in almost every field and boasting arguably the most beautiful gardens in the university. Founded in 1555 by a London merchant, it is richly endowed and makes the most of its resources to provide under-graduates with an agreeable and challenging three years. The work ethic is very much part of the St John's ethos, and academic standards are high, with English, chemistry and history among the traditional strengths, though all students benefit from the impressive library. The college is usually challenging for the top spot in the Norrington Table though it fell to 11th in 2011. It also has one of the highest proportions of state-school students in Oxford. As might be expected of a wealthy college, the accommodation is excellent and guaranteed for three or four years, boosted by the completion of a brand new quad with en-suite rooms and a new gym, café and law library. The college's riches allow it to subsidise accommodation costs to a large degree, as well as providing generous book grants and prizes. St John's has a strong sporting tradition and offers good facilities, but the social scene is relatively limited. As befits such an all-round strong college, entry is fiercely competitive. The college is very close to two of Oxford's landmark pubs: the Eagle and Child and the Lamb and Flag.

St Peter's

Oxford OX1 2DL   01865 278863 (admissions)   www.spc.ox.ac.uk
Undergraduates: 348   Postgraduates: 92   admissions@spc.ox.ac.uk

Opened as St Peter's Hall in 1929, St Peter's has been an Oxford college since 1961. Its medieval, Georgian and 19th-century buildings are in the city centre and close to most of Oxford's main facilities. Though still young, St Peter's is well represented in university life and has pockets of academic excellence, rising to tenth in the Norrington Table in 2004, although it has since fallen far back into the bottom half, languishing in 28th in 2011. History tutoring is particularly good and accommodation is offered to students in their first and third years. Student rooms vary from traditional rooms in college to new purpose-built rooms a few minutes' walk away. The college's facilities are impressive, including one of the university's best JCRs. The college has a proud sporting heritage, being particularly strong at rugby and rowing. St Peter's is known as one of Oxford's most vibrant colleges socially. It is strong in acting and journalism, and has a recently refurbished bar, although the college has recently suffered from a severe shortage in funding.

Somerville

Oxford OX2 6HD   01865 270619 (admissions)   www.some.ox.ac.uk
Undergraduates: 401   Postgraduates: 80   secretariat@some.ox.ac.uk

The announcement, early in 1992, that Somerville was to go co-educational sparked an unusually acrimonious and persistent dispute within this most tranquil of colleges. Protests were doomed to failure, however; the first male undergraduates arrived in 1994 and men now account for half the students as peace has returned. The college's atmosphere appears to have survived the momentous change. The college has relatively strong state-school representation. Accommodation, including 30 small flats, is of a reasonable standard, and was supplemented by a new 68-room building last year, so that all first, third and fourth-year students can live in, as well as around three-quarters of second-years. There are kitchens in all college buildings, but hall food is towards the cheaper end of the university. Sport is strong at Somerville and the women's rowing eight usually finishes near the head of the river. The college's hockey pitches and tennis courts are nearby. The library is open 24 hours a day and is the second largest college library as well as one of the most beautiful in Oxford. The college also has an active music society and strong drama presence.

Trinity

Oxford OX1 3BH   01865 279860 (admissions)   www.trinity.ox.ac.uk
Undergraduates: 300   Postgraduates: 98   admissions@trinity.ox.ac.uk

Architecturally impressive and boasting beautiful lawns (which you can actually walk on), Trinity is one of Oxford's least populous colleges, admitting some 80 undergraduates each year. It is ideally located, beside the Bodleian, Blackwell's bookshop and the White Horse pub, a short stroll from the University Parks and the town centre. Cardinal Newman, an alumnus of Trinity, is said to have regarded Trinity's motto as "Drink, drink, drink". Academic pressure varies, but the college had recently made impressive steps up the ranks of the Norrington Table of academic performance and climbed from 25th to 17th in 2011, with a fair share of firsts, especially in arts subjects. Trinity has shaken off its reputation for apathy, and whilst members are active in all walks of university life, the college has its own debating and drama societies, as well as sharing a fierce rivalry with neighbouring Balliol. Usually, all undergraduates are given a room on the main site in their first and second years, with the majority of third and fourth years living in a purpose-built block a mile and a half north of the main site. Students rate the food highly and the atmosphere is close-knit.

University

Oxford OX1 4BH   01865 276959 (admissions)   www.univ.ox.ac.uk
Undergraduates: 364   Postgraduates: 205   admissions@univ.ox.ac.uk

University is the first Oxford college to be able to boast a former student in the Oval Office as the former President Clinton was a Rhodes Scholar at University in the late 1960s. The college is probably Oxford's oldest – a claim fought over with Merton – though highly unlikely to have been founded by King Alfred, as legend claims. Academic expectations are high and the college prospers in most subjects. It was 14th in 2011 in the Norrington Table, having come 6th the year before. Physics, PPE and maths are particularly strong. Students who are accepted to read courses with a mathematical element are invited to a free week-long maths course just before the beginning of their first term, providing a head start in their studies. Accommodation is guaranteed to undergraduates for all three years, with third years lodged in an annexe in north Oxford about a mile and a half from the college site on the High Street, although the vast majority of third years choose to live out in rented accommodation. Sport is strong and University has been well represented and successful on the rugby field in the last few years, but the college has a reputation for being quiet socially. Students from the state sector are poorly represented, despite a generous bursary scheme, but the college's proactive access schemes in recent years have resulted in a shift in state-sector applications.

Wadham

Oxford OX1 3PN   01865 277545 (admissions)   www.wadh.ox.ac.uk

Undergraduates: 458   Postgraduates: 125   admissions@wadh.ox.ac.uk

Founded by Dorothy Wadham in 1609, Wadham is known in about equal measure for its academic track record – the college generally ranks just above mid-table, rising to seventh in 2011 – and its leftist politics. The JCR – or student union as it has rebranded itself – is famously dynamic and politically active, although the breadth of political opinion is greater than its left-wing stereotype suggests. Wadham students are notoriously trendy, although some in the university find the atmosphere at the college slightly forced. That said, the college is very strong on admitting students from state schools. And for somewhere supposedly unconcerned with such fripperies, its gardens are surprisingly beautiful. The somewhat rough-hewn chapel is similarly memorable. The college has a good 24-hour library. Accommodation is guaranteed for at least two years and there are many large, shared rooms on offer. Journalism, music and drama play an important part. Highlights in the social calendar are Queer Festival, a riotous celebration of all things gay, and Wadstock, the college's open-air summer music festival. Tickets to both are always sold out.

Worcester

Oxford OX1 2HB   01865 278391 (admissions)   www.worc.ox.ac.uk

Undergraduates: 416   Postgraduates: 186   admissions@worc.ox.ac.uk

Worcester is to the west of Oxford what Magdalen is to the east: an open, rural contrast to the urban rush of the city centre. The college's rather mediocre exterior conceals a delightful environment, including some characteristically muscular Baroque Hawskmoor architecture, a garden and a lake. The college has been rising up the Norrington Table and was ranked sixth in 2011. The 24-hour library is strongest in the arts. Accommodation, guaranteed for two years and provided for the majority of third years, varies in quality from ordinary to conference standard in the Canal Building. More en-suite accommodation, next to the new gym, is also available. Sport plays an important part in college life, as befits the only college with playing fields on site. Worcester's hockey team is not quite what it once was, but the college has had five successful rowing teams since the first term of 2010/11 and is a noted powerhouse in men's football. Reasonably priced formal halls are available four nights a week. Like Magdalen and New, it is home to the Commemoration Ball once every three years, a highlight of the Oxford social calendar. Of the 2011 intake, 55 per cent was from the state system (fairly representative for the college), and 61 per cent was female.

Cambridge College Profiles

Christ's

Cambridge CB2 3BU   01223 334983 (admissions)   www.christs.cam.ac.uk
Undergraduates: 440   Postgraduates: 111   admissions@christs.cam.ac.uk

Christ's is much bigger than it first appears and, with an entrance leading out directly onto the city centre, it is one of the most conveniently located colleges. Rooms on offer vary from the gothic splendour of some of the old buildings to the more modern New Court, dubbed "the Typewriter", which was refurbished in 2008, offering students en-suite accommodation and private balconies. The college has a visual arts centre, where the college's artist in residence works, and a recently refurbished gallery and performance space, the Yusuf Hamied Centre. Christ's Films – widely considered to be one of the best film societies in the university – and the Christ's Amateur Dramatics Society are active student groups. Sport flourishes and the football team has historically won Cuppers more times than any other college. The playing fields, shared with St Catharine's, are situated on Barton Road, about two miles away. Christ's prides itself on its academic strength, and although it has not been at the top of the Tompkins Table for over a decade, it climbed back up to 6th place in 2011 from 12th the year before. In 2010 some 63 per cent of students accepted came from the state sector. Christ's is one of the last Cambridge colleges to give "easy offers", confident in its ability to identify potential high-flyers at interview. However, such offers are rare and applicants need "an outstanding record of GCSE grades and strong support from your school". Christ's has a reputation for being dominated by hard-working medics, natural scientists and mathematicians, although it is also strong in history and English. It counts amongst its notable alumni Charles Darwin and the poet John Milton.

Churchill

Cambridge CB3 0DS   01223 336202 (admissions)   www.chu.cam.ac.uk
Undergraduates: 500   Postgraduates: 255   admissions@chu.cam.ac.uk

The first of the male colleges to take female students, the progressive atmosphere even stretches to being allowed to walk on the grass. This informality stems from the youth of the college – it celebrated its 50th anniversary in 2008 – as well as its relatively high state-school intake. Lack of ceremony does not undermine academic performance however, and it has remained in the top ten of the Tompkins Table for the past four years. Founded to help meet "the national need for scientists and engineers and to forge links with industry", the college has a noticeably high proportion of scientists. The student body has also been largely male dominated, although now women make up just over a third of the most recent intake. Compared to the soaring architecture of other Cambridge colleges, Churchill's modern and functional architecture strikes many as ugly. Another perceived flaw is its distance from the city centre – about a 15-minute walk away– while others rate the college's spacious and leafy grounds. One undeniable advantage is Churchill's ability to provide every undergraduate with a room in college for all three years. There are extensive on-site playing fields, and the college does well in rugby, hockey and rowing. The university's only student radio is based here, and it frequently wins national awards for best student radio station. The College Archive Centre houses the papers of both the college's namesake, Winston Churchill, and former prime minister, Margaret Thatcher.

Clare

Cambridge CB2 1TL   01223 333246 (admissions)   www.clare.cam.ac.uk
Undergraduates: 490   Postgraduates: 258   admissions@clare.cam.ac.uk

Though the second oldest college in Cambridge, founded in 1326, Clare is far from austere. It occupies a quiet yet central position behind Caius, in the shadow of King's College Chapel and looking onto "the Backs". Clare is known among students as one of the friendliest and most welcoming places to study, with an active bar, frequent live music and comedy in Clare Cellars, a magnet for students all across town. Accommodation is guaranteed for all three years, either in college – where life centres around the 17th-century Old Court – or nearby hostels. In 2009, the college opened Lerner Court which provides en-suite undergraduate accommodation and conference facilities. The college has made systematic attempts to raise the proportion of state-educated students and places are amongst the most sought after usually averaging five applicants per place. Although it is academically strong, Clare's extracurricular life is a big attraction. Music thrives, and the choir records and tours regularly. The student acting group, the Clare Actors, are well-known in college, whilst Clare Comedy provides a night of stand-up every month. One of the few complaints is that its playing fields, which are shared with Peterhouse and the graduate college, Clare Hall, are a 15-minute bicycle ride away. Clare isn't known for its sporting prowess.

Corpus Christi

Cambridge CB2 1RH   01223 338056 (admissions)   www.corpus.cam.ac.uk
Undergraduates: 273   Postgraduates: 185   admissions@corpus.cam.ac.uk

Corpus is one of the oldest colleges, founded by the townsfolk of two guilds in the fourteenth century; the Old Court has changed little since then– students still have to venture outdoors for a bathroom. The small size makes it one of the most intimate colleges. As well as a fine hall and excellent formal food, Corpus boasts a state-of-the-art college library, which holds many world-famous manuscripts. Students are offered a range of accommodation and, whilst some students dislike the college's policy of allocating rooms partly on the basis of academic results, all undergraduates are allocated a room in college or neighbouring hostels for at least three years. The latest statistics showing 60 per cent of undergraduates at the college came from the state sector. The sporting facilities, at Leckhampton (just over a mile away), are among the best in the university and include a popular outdoor swimming pool. However, the size of the college means that its sporting reputation owes more to enthusiasm than success. Drama is also well catered for, with The Fletcher Players put on a number of productions each term, and the college has just funded the refurbishment of the Corpus Playroom, the university's best small theatre, to the tune of £100,000. Music is likewise strong at Corpus— it has one of the best student-run choirs and a beautiful chapel in which to practise.

Downing

Cambridge CB2 1DQ   01223 334826 (admissions)   www.dow.cam.ac.uk
Undergraduates: 445   Postgraduates: 222   admissions@dow.cam.ac.uk

With spacious grounds, set within a neo-Classical quadrangle, Downing feels like a haven of calm off the bustling thoroughfare of Regent Street. Although it was founded in 1800 for the study of law, now medicine, natural sciences and engineering are considered to be the college's strong subjects. It is not all work and no play at Downing though. The college is well known for coming "head of the river" in the "Bumps" rowing competition and with its own on-site tennis, netball and squash courts, a gym and plenty of open space, it has many successful sports teams. First and third years generally live on site, with second years offered houses on Lensfield Road, which backs on to the college. In addition to this, a new accommodation block will be unveiled in June 2012. The library, opened in 1993, has won an award for its architecture. There is a good mix between students with state and independent school backgrounds among new undergraduates. The student-run bar/party room has improved college social life, and meals are of a high standard, as is formal hall, which is often held in candlelight. For those of a less sporting persuasion, meetings of the student debating society and the Blake Society, named after alumnus Quentin Blake, are important events in the student calendar. Music at the college is strong, and a new student theatre, providing a venue for drama, music and exhibitions, opened in 2010.

Emmanuel

Cambridge CB2 3AP   01223 334290 (admissions)   www.emma.cam.ac.uk
Undergraduates: 513   Postgraduates: 160   admissions@emma.cam.ac.uk

On average the most successful college academically, Emmanuel, more commonly known as "Emma", was only just pipped to its regular spot at the top of last year's Tompkins Table by Trinity. The college is proud of students' achievements in sport and music and has one of the most popular of the smaller May Balls. Despite being one of the wealthiest of the colleges, Emma has an unpretentious atmosphere: its wealth does make for additional benefits to students though, such as funding for books, travel grants and plentiful provision of welfare activities including popular film nights. It is also the only college to offer students a laundry service inclusive in their rent. The library has been newly renovated and opened in 2010. For the last few years Emma has fairly consistently kept the state to independent student ratio at about 60:40, and around half of all undergraduates are women. All students are guaranteed accommodation for the duration of their course. Second years can choose to stay on site or nearby in college-owned houses. With self-catering facilities limited, most students eat in hall and the college chefs were recently voted best in the university. Although formal hall is good, most popular is the Sunday brunch: a late-morning affair with fry-ups or pastries and the Sunday papers. In the summer, the college gardens, with tennis courts, croquet and an outdoor swimming pool, offer a welcome haven from exam pressures. The sports grounds are excellent, if some distance away, and the women's rowing team have excelled in recent years.

Fitzwilliam

Cambridge CB3 0DG   01223 332030 (admissions)   www.fitz.cam.ac.uk
Undergraduates: 487   Postgraduates: 229   admissions@fitz.cam.ac.uk

It may not be the most beautiful of colleges but "Fitz", a ten-minute cycle from the city centre, makes up for what it lacks in architectural splendour through a lively atmosphere and laid-back appeal. The college was established in 1869, with the aim of widening access to the university – a continuing tradition which attracts a larger than average proportion of applicants from the state sector. The college is notably "unstuffy", with a good college bar serving drinks at night and homemade cakes during the day, excellent ENTS events and a strong sporting reputation. The football and rugby teams have enjoyed great success, and there are extensive and well-kept sports facilities close by, including a gym, football, rugby, cricket, hockey and tennis grounds – as well as squash courts on site. Music also thrives at the college: Fitz is the only Cambridge college to have access to a professional string quartet. The college has a 250-seater auditorium for performances, and a new state-of-the-art library and IT centre, designed by the award-winning architect Edward Cullinan and recently the beneficiary of a £1.4 million endowment. Undergraduates are guaranteed college accommodation for three or four years, either on site or in nearby housing, and like its flower-filled gardens, its newly built accommodation is spacious and bright.

Girton

Cambridge CB3 0JG 01223 338972 (admissions) www.girton.cam.ac.uk
Undergraduates: 551 Postgraduates: 168 admissions@girton.cam.ac.uk

Amongst students at the university, Girton is best known for being "a trek" away from the city centre – in reality, only a 15-minute bicycle ride but in Cambridge terms this seems a lengthy commute. However, its comparative isolation inevitably encourages a strong community spirit, and its beautiful grounds are a well-kept secret. Girton stands in 50 acres and all facilities, including an indoor swimming pool, gym, squash and tennis courts are on site, as well as an orchard through which to meander if academic pressure proves too much. There is no question of overcrowding: rooms are available for the entire course. The majority of second-year students live in the self-contained Wolfson Court (near the University Library, closer to town). Some find that the long corridors remind them of a boarding school, but the accommodation, which includes a number of self-contained houses, is noticeably cheaper than some other colleges. Since becoming coeducational in 1977, the college has maintained a balanced admissions policy. At least 60 per cent of the undergraduates admitted are from state schools, and just under half are women. Girton also has one of the highest proportion of female Fellows in any mixed college. The college is active in most sports and particularly strong in football. Given its comparative isolation, many people eat and socialise in college. The food is reported to be excellent.

Gonville and Caius

Cambridge CB2 1TA 01223 332440 (admissions) www.cai.cam.ac.uk
Undergraduates: 559 Postgraduates: 234 admissions@cai.cam.ac.uk

Gonville and Caius College – to confuse the outsider, the college is usually known as Caius (pronounced "keys") – is among the most beautiful of Cambridge's colleges, as well as one of the most central. It has an excellent academic reputation, especially in medicine and history, although maths and law are also highly rated. Caius also has one of the largest and most architecturally impressive student libraries in Cambridge. It was formerly the library for the whole university and is housed next door to the college in the impressive Cockerell Building. Accommodation, though guaranteed for three years, varies in quality. Most first years are housed in Harvey Court, a five-minute walk away across the river, which boasts recently renovated en-suite accommodation. Many second years are in houses near the train station, a 10–15 minute bicycle to main faculties. Adjacent to Harvey Court is the £13-million Stephen Hawking Building, named after the college's most famous fellow, which opened in October

2006. This provides en-suite accommodation for 75 students and eight fellows, and boasts some of the highest standard student accommodation in Cambridge. Third years live in the idyllic surroundings of the old courts. An on-going gripe is that undergraduates are obliged to eat in hall most nights of the week, having to purchase 34 meal tickets a term. There is also formal hall every night of the week, for which the food is no different from informal hall, but students wear gowns, and dine with fellows by candlelight. The college is working to diminish its public school reputation – more than 60 per cent of new students now come from state schools. Caius has one of the best and most competitive boat clubs in the university, and has won the "Bumps" numerous times over the last few years.

Homerton

Cambridge CB2 8PH   01223 747252 (admissions)   www.homerton.cam.ac.uk

Undergraduates: 607   Postgraduates: 452   admissions@homerton.cam.ac.uk

Originating in 18th-century London, Homerton moved to Cambridge in 1894. The college has been part of the university for about 40 years, and in 2010 was awarded a Royal Charter as a college of the university. Established as a teaching training college, Homerton remains home to those taking a PGCE course, in addition to offering a wide range of university courses. Its position, a mile from the city centre in its own large grounds, however, is sometimes a point of contention. It does not appear to stop Homertonians from being among the most active in university life though. The college has great facilities on site, with "lots of green space", sports grounds, and some popular societies. On the music front, it is home to an orchestra, two choirs and, more unusually, a steel band which holds regular concerts. Homerton Amateur Theatrical Society (HATS) not only showcases student acting talent, but also puts on highly popular cabarets twice a year. College accommodation, in modern en-suite rooms, is offered for all three years of a student's course. The students that make up the Homerton community come from all over the world, making Homerton one of the most internationally diverse colleges in the town. To add to this diversity, most of the students from the UK come from state schools.

Hughes Hall

Cambridge CB1 2EW   01223 334897 (admissions)k   www.hughes.cam.ac.uk

Undergraduates: 113   Postgraduates: 427   admissions@hughes.cam.ac.u

Despite its air of mystery (hidden away overlooking Fenner's cricket ground and tucked in behind the city's main gym and swimming pool), Hughes Hall is home to a lively and cosmopolitan population of postgraduate students and mature undergraduates over the age of 21. The oldest graduate college in the university, it was founded in 1885 for the training of graduate women teachers. It is now home to some 550 students of both sexes, with provision for study in nearly all the degrees Cambridge offers. It has a large international community and supports the applications of overseas students. Hughes is well known for its friendly and egalitarian ethos and its excellent food. Plus, being just off the much-loved Mill Road, some of Cambridge's best international eateries can be found just around the corner. Accommodation within the college is available for all single undergraduates and affiliated students throughout their course, though family accommodation can be difficult to secure. The site comprises a good mixture of modern and refurbished accommodation with a new library and IT suite. Hughes Hall forms a close-knit community, with a well-frequented bar, and the MCR (student council) lay on social and academic events regularly.

Jesus

Cambridge CB5 8BL   01223 339455 (admissions)   www.jesus.cam.ac.uk
Undergraduates: 515   Postgraduates: 251   undergraduate-admissions@jesus.cam.ac.uk

Jesus is perhaps best known for its extra-curricular prowess, although it performs well academically, too. Its rugby team is reputedly fearsome and with football, rugby and cricket pitches as well as three squash and ten tennis courts, it's not surprising that Jesus is popular amongst the more sports inclined students. Culture features high on the agenda as well, with regular sculpture exhibitions in the grounds and the consistently well-attended "Chapel Sessions", which puts on an eclectic variety of music in the college chapel every Tuesday. Although Jesus lacks a theatre of its own, the college is active in university drama and the ADC theatre is a three-minute walk. The college also hosts one of the most popular of the May Balls. On the teaching front, the fellows-to-undergraduates ratio is generous. There is an excellent and stylish new library which is open 24 hours. Rooms in college are guaranteed for all first and half of third-year students, whilst all other students live in college houses, just over the road. The college recently spent £10 million renovating some quarters and in September will open the newly refurbished Chapel Court. Around 60 per cent of new undergraduates are state educated and the college is keen to encourage more applications from the state sector. The college grounds are attractive and contain some of the oldest buildings in the university, dating to the 12th century. Jesus' location of the edge of town makes it convenient for the centre, but keeps it away from the flurry of the main streets.

King's

Cambridge CB2 1ST   01223 331255 (admissions)   www.kings.cam.ac.uk
Undergraduates: 430   Postgraduates: 225   undergraduate.admissions@kings.cam.ac.uk

It may have been founded to provide a home for Eton boys at Cambridge, but King's is now one of the most accessible colleges for state school pupils and ethnic minorities. It has a reputation for its radical leftist values which, despite ongoing debate as to whether the communist flag should be removed from above the bar, still thrive. Yoga, debates and green activities feature high on the agenda and despite having amongst the most famous and beautiful buildings in Cambridge, the college has done away with many of the typical university traditions – gowns, the Fellows' "High Table" at dinner (though they still sit separately), and superior rooms to reward good results. Formal halls are rare, and the May Ball has been replaced by a more rowdy "King's Affair". The college was among the first of the all-male colleges to admit women, and is actively involved in an initiative to increase the number of candidates from socially and educationally disadvantaged backgrounds. The college has a reputation for accepting a high proportion of state-school applications, usually over 70 per cent. The college has fewer undergraduates than the grandeur of its buildings might suggest, one result being that accommodation is guaranteed, either in college or in hostels. With the highest ratio of fellows to undergraduates in Cambridge, it is not surprising that King's has a strong academic reputation. The world-famous chapel and choir form the heart of an outstanding music scene.

Lucy Cavendish

Cambridge CB3 0BU   01223 330280 (admissions)   www.lucy-cav.cam.ac.uk
Undergraduates: 142 (women only) Postgraduates: 132 lcc-admissions@lists.cam.ac.uk

Lucy Cavendish pitches itself as the college for "smart, inspirational women". Since its creation in 1965, Lucy Cavendish has given hundreds of women over the age of 21 the opportunity to read for Tripos subjects. Around 20 per cent of students are over 40 years of age, and some are in their 60s. The college has a number of bursaries available, including some that give preference to single parents and applicants from the northwest of England. The college has particularly strong provision for the teaching of medicine and veterinary medicine, and has a good reputation for social sciences and English literature. Accommodation is provided for all who request it, either in the college's three Victorian houses or in its three modern residential blocks. The college's small size enables all students to get to know one another within an informal atmosphere, although some find it a little too quiet. However, others appreciate a more relaxed, egalitarian atmosphere, with the lack high table in the dining hall being a prime example. The college has its own annual women's politics and literature festival, Women's Word. All the fellows are women, and there is a well-established network of university teachers for subjects not taught in college.

Magdalene

Cambridge CB3 0AG   01223 332135 (admissions)   www.magd.cam.ac.uk
Undergraduates: 379   Postgraduates: 146   admissions@magd.cam.ac.uk

It is taking time for Magdalene to shake off its image as the college of public school "lads", particularly since it was the last college to admit women (1988). However, times are changing: the gender balance is around 50:50, and more than half of new undergraduates come from the state sector. With the most expensive May Ball ticket in Cambridge and a daily formal hall by candlelight, it certainly knows how to play *Brideshead*. The sporty emphasis, on rugby and rowing in particular, is also undeniable. The nearby playing fields are shared with St John's and the college has its own Eton fives court. Magdalene's academic standing has improved of late – previously languishing towards the bottom of the Tompkins Table, it has steadily improved and finished ninth last year. Undergraduates may also be eligible for travel grants from the college, ranging from £50 to £2,000. Rowan Williams, the Archbishop of Canterbury, will become college Master next January. Students are heavily involved in university-wide activities from drama to journalism, as well as sport. Accommodation is provided for all undergraduates, either in college or in one of 21 houses and hostels, all within two minutes' walk. Magdalene is proud of its river frontage, the longest in the university, which is especially memorable in the summer. Students enthuse about supportive academic staff and friendly porters, but complain about the poor canteen food.

Murray Edwards

Cambridge CB3 0DF   01223 762229 (admissions)   www.murrayedwards.cam.ac.uk
Undergraduates: 373 (women) Postgraduates: 113 admissions@murrayedwards.cam.ac.uk

One of three all women's colleges in Cambridge, Murray Edwards has only recently come to be known by its current name. The college was established in 1954 to allow more young women to study in Cambridge, becoming known as "New Hall", and remaining officially unnamed for more than 50 years. In 2008 however, Ros Smith, a New Hall graduate, and her Oxford-educated husband, Steve Edwards, gave the college a £30-million endowment, and, at last, a new name. Murray Edwards enjoys a largely erroneous reputation for feminism and academic underachievement, although it has yet to emerge from the bottom half of the Tompkins Table. The college is particularly proud of its collection of contemporary women's art, the second largest in the world, and students are politically active. Unlike many colleges, Murray Edwards has no religious leanings and thus no chapel. Despite modern buildings, the grounds are lovely and the "dome" makes a light and airy dining hall with very good food. There are also practice rooms for musicians and an art room with dark room facilities for the artistically inclined. The college is known for its unusual split-level bar, but many students choose to socialise elsewhere. Accommodation has improved in recent years, with new rooms, 40 per cent of which are en suite, now on offer. Sport is a good mixture of high-fliers and enthusiasts, with grounds, shared with Fitzwilliam, half a mile away. It is another "hill" college, meaning a bicycle and a strong disposition is a must.

Newnham

Cambridge CB3 9DF   01223 335783 (admissions)   www.newn.cam.ac.uk
Undergraduates: 385 (women)   Postgraduates: 185   admissions@newn.cam.ac.uk

First established as a residence for women who were admitted to attend lectures in an all-male university, Newnham has long had to battle with a bluestocking image. Its entry in the university prospectus used to insist that it was "not a nunnery" and that the atmosphere in this all-women college was no stricter than elsewhere. It is, however, proud of its history as the first women's college in the university and counts amongst its alumnae A.S. Byatt, Germaine Greer and Sylvia Plath. The college still has all-women fellows, and Newnham is in the perfect location for humanities students, with the lecture halls and libraries of the Sidgwick Site just a step across the road. Nearly all students live in for all three years, and room rents are the same for all types of accommodation. Newnham students are anything but insular and are some of the most active in the social, sporting and artistic life of the university. As well as being blessed with the largest and most beautiful lawns in Cambridge (upon which students can both walk and sunbathe), Newnham has its playing fields and tennis courts on site. The boat club has been notably successful, while the college competes to a high standard in tennis, cricket and a number of minority sports.

Pembroke

Cambridge CB2 1RF   01223 338154 (admissions)   www.pem.cam.ac.uk
Undergraduates: 465   Postgraduates: 203   adm@pem.cam.ac.uk

Pembroke is a hidden gem. The gardens and buildings are amongst the most beautiful in Cambridge. Rowing and rugby are a prominent feature of Pembroke life, thanks in part to a public school tradition that it is doing much to shake off. Women undergraduates have recently outnumbered men for the first time, and its traditional reputation is giving way to a more relaxed atmosphere. Around two-thirds of all undergraduates live in college, including all first years. The rest are housed in fairly central college hostels, though the standards of these are variable. That said, the college has recently completed a student accommodation block that contains a gym, music rooms, and a new art room. Academically, Pembroke is towards the top of the Tompkins Table, steadily featuring in the top ten over the last decade, with traditional strengths in engineering and natural sciences. The New Cellars venue lends itself to plays, parties and gigs. The famed Pembroke Players generally stage one play a term in the Old Reader, which also doubles as the college cinema, and many Pembroke students are involved in university dramatics. The Old Library is a popular venue for classical concerts. Indeed music is a Pembroke strength. Nestled in one of the quads is the college chapel, designed by Sir Christopher Wren. Pembroke formal hall has become synonymous with good eating and is a sought-after ticket from students across the university.

Peterhouse

Cambridge CB2 1RD   01223 338223 (admissions)   www.pet.cam.ac.uk

Undergraduates: 273   Postgraduates: 124   admissions@pet.cam.ac.uk

Thanks to its position as the oldest and smallest of the undergraduate colleges, Peterhouse has been lumbered with an unenviable image as male-dominated, Conservative, and public school. The male–female ratio is now about 60:40, and over 55 per cent of undergraduates come from state schools. Most first years are accommodated in a row of houses just beside college or in the more modern William Stone Building. During the remaining years students live on site or in college hostels, most within ten minutes' walk. The college's diminutive size makes for a familiar college populus, but this does not mean that its undergraduates never venture beyond the cosy Peterhouse bar. It is known above all as "the history college", and while history is indeed seen as a traditional strength, it is home to a number of important and very active university societies: the Peterhouse Politics Society, the Heywood Society (resident dramatic society), the intellectual Perne Club, the scientific Kelvin Club, and the Music Society. Academically, the college is generally a mid-table performer. The 13th-century candle-lit dining hall provides one of the most beautiful, but perhaps not the most delicious, of formal halls in the university. The sports grounds are shared with Clare and are about a mile away.

Queens'

Cambridge CB3 9ET   01223 335540 (admissions)   www.queens.cam.ac.uk

Undergraduates: 536   Postgraduates: 380   admissions@queens.cam.ac.uk

Queens' has one of the largest undergraduate bodies but this does not prevent it from being renowned for being tightly knit. Although some accommodation is less architecturally beautiful than others – indeed Queens' showcases the most eclectic mix of architecture of any college from medieval cloisters to 1970s concrete – it is all comfortable, and undergraduates can be housed in college for the full three years. The bar is large and popular and Queens' "Bops" which happen regularly in the large Fitzpatrick Hall are well known to be good parties. The bar in Cripps Court is linked over the River Cam by the Mathematical Bridge, designed by Sir Isaac Newton, under which the college-owned punts are moored. More than half of new undergraduates come from the state sector, and about 45 per cent of undergraduates are women. Facilities are excellent and, in addition to three excellent squash courts on site, Queens' is also home to Cambridge's first college nursery. Academically, the college generally hangs around the middle of the Tompkins Table, and is known better for its contribution to the Footlights and university journalism. The amateur dramatics society, BATS, produces some of the best in-college theatre productions. There is a gym and a dance studio on site. The playing fields (one mile away) are shared with Robinson.

Robinson

Cambridge CB3 9AN   01223 339143 (admissions)   www.robinson.cam.ac.uk

Undergraduates: 421   Postgraduates: 130   apply@robinson.cam.ac.uk

Robinson is one of the youngest colleges in Cambridge and admitted its first students in 1979. Its unspectacular architecture has earned it the unfortunate nickname "the car park". On the other hand, having been built with one eye on the conference trade, what Robinson lacks in grand architecture, it makes up for with excellent facilities and vast, idyllic gardens. Rooms are more comfortable than most, and the majority are en suite with a balcony. Almost all students live in college or in nearby houses, and the college is one of the few with rooms adapted for disabled students. Robinson tends to be found in the middle of the Tompkins Table, but it by no means flounders. One in four fellows are women, one of the highest proportions in any mixed college. Its youth and admissions policy (the college typically accepts around 60 per cent from state schools) ensure that Robinson has one of the more unpretentious atmospheres. The auditorium is the largest of any college and is a popular venue for films, plays and concerts. The sports fields (shared with Queens') provide training grounds for excellent rugby and hockey sides, and the boat club is also successful. The atmosphere at the optional twice-weekly formal halls are described by students as "very down to earth". The college has two newly built graduate buildings providing state-of-the-art facilities as well as 48 new graduate rooms.

St Catharine's

Cambridge CB2 1RL   01223 338319 (admissions)   www.caths.cam.ac.uk
Undergraduates: 482   Postgraduates: 174   undergraduate.admissions@caths.cam.ac.uk
Known to everyone as "Catz", this medium-sized, 15th-century college stands opposite Corpus Christi on King's Parade. The principal college site, with its distinctive three-sided main court, though small, provides accommodation for all its first and third years. Rooms are small, but amongst the cheapest in Cambridge. The majority of second years live in four- or five-room flats at St Chad's Court, a ten-minute walk away. Once not considered one of the leading colleges academically, its status is much changed. Having been top of the Tompkins Table in 2005, the college has hovered around the top ten ever since. It has a reputation as a friendly place. About half of the students are women, and the split between independent and state-school undergraduates accepted to the college is around 40:60. A new library and JCR have improved the facilities considerably, and there is a strong musical tradition. In 2006 St Catharine's proudly announced that it was the first college to be awarded Fair Trade status. With a reputation for being sporting rather than sporty, Catz is one of the few colleges that regularly puts out three rugby XVs, last year provided two blues for the Boat Race, has a history of success at hockey and is the only Cambridge college with its own world-class Astroturf pitch. The playing fields are a ten-minute walk away.

St Edmund's

Cambridge CB3 0BN   01223 336086 (admissions)   www.st-edmunds.cam.ac.uk
Undergraduates: 154   Postgraduates: 269   admissions@st-edmunds.cam.ac.uk
St Edmund's is primarily a graduate college, with over half its students coming from overseas. Students say this diversity gives the college a unique atmosphere. The college is set in quiet grounds and is conveniently placed to the northwest of the city centre. The college buildings currently house more than 200 single students, and some of the accommodation has been constructed specifically for students with physical disabilities. There is brand new accommodation block for couples and, in addition, there are a small number of maisonettes suitable for students with children or married couples. A new building with an additional 70 student rooms opened in 2006, and the college has recently invested in a new library, teaching rooms, a gym and music practice rooms. In recent times, St Edmund's students have become regulars in the university sports team, particularly rugby and rowing, earning an impressive number of "blues" (awarded for competing in a varsity match against Oxford), whilst a number of the college's international students also represent their own countries as well. The college bar may be sparsely populated, but it is an ideal place for mature students seeking a quiet life.

St John's

Cambridge CB2 1TP   01223 338703 (admissions)   www.joh.cam.ac.uk
Undergraduates: 615   Postgraduates: 334   admissions@joh.cam.ac.uk

Second only to Trinity in size and wealth, St John's has an enviable reputation in most fields. Johns' wealth translates into excellent facilities and accommodation in college, as well as book and travel grants available to all as well as a new 24-hour library. St John's straddles the River Cam, linked by the magnificent Bridge of Sighs, and its chapel spire is the highest point between the town and Ely Cathedral. Its May Ball was famously voted the "seventh-best party in the world". St John's has had a formidable academic record, although it has dropped into the lower half of the Tompkins Table in recent years. This might be thanks to its persistent reputation for sportiness and to the female intake being below average at just below 40 per cent. St John's receives relatively few applications from state-school students, who make up around 52 per cent of St John's students, among the lowest among the colleges. Some students find the atmosphere "posh" and the college's events "terribly formal". The boat club has a powerful reputation, but hockey, cricket and the rugby "Red Boys" are all traditionally strong teams. Extensive playing fields shared with Magdalene are a few hundred yards away, and the boathouse is extremely good. The college film society organises popular screenings in the Fisher Building, which also contains an art studio and drawing office for architecture and engineering students. Music is dominated by the world-famous choir. Excellent as the facilities are, some students find that the sheer size of St John's can be daunting. Others argue that it provides an excitingly diverse atmosphere.

Selwyn

Cambridge CB3 9DQ   01223 335896 (admissions)   www.sel.cam.ac.uk
Undergraduates: 403   Postgraduates: 159   admissions@sel.cam.ac.uk

Selwyn is one of the less assuming colleges, with a relatively unpressured atmosphere behind "the Backs", and adjacent to the Sidgwick site where most humanities are taught, making it an ideal position for arts and humanities students, though engineering is also a perceived strength. Its position also means it is far from town, which is less of a problem since new accommodation blocks mean everyone is housed within 400 yards of the centre quad. It also hides one of the most beautiful college gardens. In recent years it has consistently appeared in the top ten of the Tompkins Table, coming seventh in 2011. One of the first colleges to admit women (in 1976), now almost half of Selwyn's undergraduates are female. Around 70 per cent of new undergraduates are from state schools. Food has improved enormously in recent years and it has a popular college bar. As well as the usual college groups, the music society is especially well supported. Selwyn bucks the trend for a summer ball or June event, and hosts the popular Snow Ball each December. In sport, the novice boat crews have done well in recent years, as have the hockey and badminton sides, but the emphasis is as much on enjoyment as achievement. The sports grounds are shared with King's and are just under a mile away.

Sidney Sussex

Cambridge CB2 3HU   01223 338872 (admissions)   www.sid.cam.ac.uk
Undergraduates: 380   Postgraduate: 170   admissions@sid.cam.ac.uk

Despite its central location, the college's large private gardens award the student with a tranquil environment behind the redbrick walls. All students are housed either in college or one of 11 nearby hostels. The college's unpretentious atmosphere is cultivated by the students, half of whom are women. Despite its size, Sidney has an active social life, boasting one of just two student-run bars in the university and maintaining fortnightly "bops". The college choir has produced critically acclaimed recordings, and tours regularly in the UK and overseas, and being very close to the ADC theatre means that a thespian community thrives. Sports are taken less seriously, with enthusiasm and enjoyment the focus of the students' sporting endeavours. Exam results at the college are not amongst the highest in Cambridge but have improved steadily for a number of years with Sidney achieving 16th place in the 2011 Tompkins ratings. Sports grounds are shared with Christ's and are a ten-minute bicycle ride away. Sidney's size means that the college is a tight-knit community, although some students find such insularity suffocating rather than supportive. Certainly, the students enjoy coming together for Sidney formal hall, which has a solid reputation.

Trinity

Cambridge CB2 1TQ   01223 338422 (admissions)   www.trin.cam.ac.uk
Undergraduates: 734   Postgraduates: 328   admissions@trin.cam.ac.uk

The legend that you can walk from Oxford to Cambridge without ever leaving Trinity land typifies Cambridge undergraduates' views about the college, even if it is not true. Indeed, the college is almost synonymous with size and wealth – it is the largest and wealthiest of all Cambridge colleges. Founded by Henry VIII, its endowment is almost as big as the other colleges' put together. There was a view that every Trinity student was an arrogant public schoolboy. Though less true than it was, the number of students from the state sector has been historically low – the figure has only risen from 38 per cent in 2007 to 43 per cent in 2010, and only 36 per cent of undergraduates are women. Being rich, Trinity offers book grants to every student as well as generous travel grants. The rooms are amongst the cheapest at the university as they are subsidised by the college, and are also known for being spacious. The huge number of rooms at Trinity means students can stay in residence for the duration of their course. Consistently strong academically, it topped the Tompkins Table last year and is known for its large population of "mathmos" (mathematics students). Keen to dispel a reputation for being overly serious, students have set up a new Cocktail Society and promote the annual May Ball that has reputedly never run out of champagne. Christopher Wren designed the college's iconic library, which backs onto the river and keeps the original Winnie-the-Pooh manuscripts amongst other treasures. With playing fields only half a mile away, Trinity excels in most sports, most notably cricket.

Trinity Hall

Cambridge CB2 1TJ   01223 332535 (admissions)   www.trinhall.cam.ac.uk
Undergraduates: 400   Postgraduates: 240   admissions@trinhall.cam.ac.uk

Trinity Hall or "Tit Hall" is one of the oldest and smallest colleges in Cambridge, resulting in a remarkably close community of students. The outstanding performance of its oarsmen has ensured the prevailing view of Trinity Hall as a "boaty" college, but it is also known for its drama, music and bar. The Preston Society is one of the better college drama groups, and stages regular productions. Weekly recitals keep the music society busy. The size of the bar (tiny) is inversely proportional to the number of people who frequent it (large). The college is strong academically, and at third in the Tompkins Table in 2011, it stepped up a place from the previous year. It has equal numbers of students studying arts and sciences. Just over half of the undergraduates are women, and in recent years the college has increased the number of state-school students, with over 55 per cent of new undergraduates coming from the state sector. All first years and approximately half the third years live in college, which is situated on "the Backs" behind Caius. The remainder take rooms either in two large hostels close to the sports ground, or in college accommodation about five minutes' walk away. The college offers a number of travel bursaries and hardship funds for current students.

Wolfson

Cambridge CB3 9BB   01223 335918   www.wolfson.cam.ac.uk

Undergraduates: 124   Postgraduates: 510   ugadministrator@wolfson.cam.ac.uk

Wolfson, although primarily a graduate college, has around 120 mature or affiliated undergraduates. Wolfson is one of three colleges that admit students for the graduate course in medicine. The average age is 27 and life is enriched by the high proportion (about 50 per cent) of overseas students, reflected in popular societies and events, such as the salsa night. It likes to style itself "the most cosmopolitan college in Cambridge". The relationship between senior and junior members is informal; common rooms, facilities and social activities are equally open to both. The college has a relaxed atmosphere and like King's, does not subscribe to many of the more traditional college customs such as fellows eating at a high table. It is also headed by a President (currently the historian, Richard Evans), rather than a Master. The college regularly hosts senior academic visitors, journalists and specialists, many of whom give open talks at the college. Wolfson is situated in west Cambridge, close to the University Library and the arts faculties – or as the students say, nearer to the M11 than the Cam. The location, however, means the green fields and popular pathway to nearby Grantchester are a short hop away. The main buildings of Wolfson College were built in the 1970s around attractive garden courts. The college has accommodation for most students who want to live in, and there is also some accommodation for couples.

14 University Profiles

The following profiles contain valuable information about each university. Each profile contains contact details, including the postal address, the telephone number for admission enquiries, email or web addresses for admissions and prospectus enquiries, web address for the university, the students' union and for sports facilities, and any university grouping that the institution is affiliated to (Russell Group, etc.). In addition, each profile provides:

The Times **rankings** These figures are taken from the main league table. See chapter 4, *The Top Universities*, for this table and the sources of the data. The headings follow those in the main league table.

Undergraduates The first figure is for full-time undergraduates. The second figure (in brackets) gives the number of part-time undergraduates. The figures are for 2010–11, and are the most recent provided by HESA.

Postgraduates The first figure is for full-time postgraduates. The second figure (in brackets) gives the number of part-time postgraduates. The figures are for 2010–11, and are the most recent provided by HESA.

Mature students The percentage of first degree entrants who were 21 or over at the start of their studies. The figures are from 2010–11, and are from HESA.

Overseas students The number of undergraduate overseas students (both EU and non-EU) as a percentage of full-time undergraduates. The figures relate to 2010–11, and are based on HESA data.

Applications per place The number of applicants per place for 2011 as calculated by UCAS.

From state-school sector The number of young full-time undergraduate entrants from state schools or colleges in 2010–11 as a percentage of total young entrants. The figures are published by HESA.

From working-class homes The number of young full-time undergraduate entrants in 2010–11 whose parental occupations are skilled, manual, semi-skilled or unskilled (NS-SEC classes 4–7) as a percentage of total young entrants. The figures are published by HESA.

Accommodation The information was obtained through a survey made of all university accommodation services, and their help in compiling this information is gratefully acknowledged.

Undergraduate fees and support

Details of tuition fees and financial support for students starting in 2012–13 are given. Figures for 2013–14 were not available at the time this book went to press in spring 2012, and some changes can be expected. It is of the utmost importance that you check university websites for the latest information. In England the Office for Fair Access (**www.offa.org.uk**) will announce approved university fees and financial support at the end of July 2012, and all English university "Access Agreements" for 2013–14 will then be available on the OFFA website. In the summary given, RUK describes students from the Rest of the UK at Scottish universities and NSP stands for National Scholarship Programme, a scheme of awards part-funded by the Government which are only available to English students from households with a family income of below £25,000. English universities offer a limited number of NSP awards according to additional criteria that they select. Universities also offer a variety of scholarships and bursaries, for example, in particular subjects or to help people from particular places. There is not space in this book to give full details of such awards, and, again, you are advised to check university websites for details. For the principles behind the fees and funding systems, see chapters 7 and 8.

Comments on campus facilities apply to the universities' own sites only. Newer universities, in particular, operate "franchised" courses at further education colleges, which are likely to have lower levels of provision. Prospective applicants should check out the library and social facilities before accepting a place away from the parent institution.

We include profiles on the two major suppliers of part-time degrees, the Open University and Birkbeck College. However, we do not give profiles to separate business and medical schools, specialist colleges or institutions that only offer postgraduate degrees, such as Cranfield University (**www.cranfield.ac.uk**) and London Business School (**www.lbs.ac.uk**). Specialist institutions such as the Royal College of Music (**www.rcm.ac.uk**) and St George's, University of London medical school (**sgul.ac.uk**) could not fairly be compared with generalist universities. Their omission is no reflection on their quality, simply a function of their particular roles. A number of colleges with degree-awarding powers also do not appear because they have yet to be granted university status. However, at the end of the book, we list higher education colleges with their addresses and websites.

University of Aberdeen

Aberdeen has launched an academic recruitment drive to make the most of a new range of courses, as well as strengthening its research. While other universities are retrenching, it has created 100 new posts to deliver the new range of "Sixth Century Courses", which include cross-disciplinary degrees such as risk in society, sustainability, and the digital society. They provide the option of "sustained study programmes" in a language, computing or a business-related subject. The aim is to give graduates broader knowledge and more intellectual flexibility.

The early years of the university's sixth century have also seen a series of big capital projects. Aided by one the most successful fundraising schemes at any UK university, Aberdeen has spent £28 million on a sports centre that opened in 2009 and £57 million on a futuristic new library that followed in 2011. Student services had already been transformed and the redeveloped Butchart Centre has given the Students' Association a new social centre on campus. In all, the university expects to spend another £148 million by 2019.

Aberdeen registered some good results in the 2008 Research Assessment Exercise, when more than half of the work submitted was judged to be world-leading or internationally excellent. Health services research and theology, divinity and religious studies produced the best results in the UK, while computer science and informatics, anthropology, English and history also did particularly well. Research income grew by more than a third over five years, cementing Aberdeen's ambitions to be recognised among the top 100 universities in the world.

The demand for places showed only slight growth in 2012, following the trend elsewhere in Scotland, but this followed big increases in the two preceding years. Female students now outnumber the men, but Aberdeen still considers itself a "balanced" university because roughly half of its students study medicine, science or engineering, half the arts or social sciences. Even on traditional degree programmes, students can try out three or four subjects before committing themselves at the end of their first or even second year. The modular system is so flexible that the majority of students change their intended degree before graduation. The mixture secured Aberdeen a place in the top 30 in the National Student Survey in 2011. English, history, archaeology, medicine, dentistry, sociology and sports science produced the best results.

Aberdeen established the English-speaking world's first chair in medicine and has produced its share of advances since. The Institute of Medical Sciences, which has brought together all Aberdeen's work in this

---

King's College
Aberdeen AB24 3FX

01224 272090/91 (admissions)
sras@abdn.ac.uk
www.abdn.ac.uk
www.ausa.org.uk
Affiliation: none

The Times **Rankings**
Overall Ranking: **39**

Student satisfaction:	=17	(81%)
Research quality:	34	(0.62)
Entry standards:	29	(401)
Student–staff ratio:	=37	(16.2)
Services & facilities/student:	52	(£1,428)
Expected completion rate:	=69	(81.6%)
Good honours:	=41	(68.7%)
Graduate prospects:	=32	(71.5%)

area, boasts high quality laboratory facilities. Another £20 million was invested in the Suttie Centre, which opened in 2009 as a new teaching and learning centre for medical education and clinical skills. Education is now also considered among Aberdeen's strengths, while biological sciences have developed considerably in recent years, becoming second only to the social sciences in terms of size. Biomedicine is particularly strong, and the university's links with the oil industry show in geology's high reputation.

Today's university is a fusion of two ancient institutions which came together in 1860. With King's College dating back to 1495 and Marischal College following almost a century later, Aberdeen likes to boast that for 250 years it had as many universities as the whole of England. The original King's College buildings are the focal point of an appealing campus, complete with cobbled main street and some sturdily handsome Georgian buildings, about a mile from the city centre.

Medicine is at Foresterhill, a 20-minute walk away, adjoining the Aberdeen Royal Infirmary. Buses link the two sites with the Hillhead residential complex. Almost a third of all students come from the north of Scotland, but taking one in six from outside Britain ensures a cosmopolitan atmosphere. Students from England and the 120 nationalities from further afield are

generally prepared for Aberdeen's remote location and, although the winters are long, the climate is warmer than the uninitiated might expect. As the energy capital of Europe, transport links are good. Students find the city lively and welcoming but expensive: the JobLink service provides a good selection of part-time jobs.

Student facilities are good and the students' centre – The Hub – brings together dining and retail outlets with support services, including the Students' Association and the careers service. There is also a city centre bar and first-class sports facilities, which have improved still further with the opening of the Aberdeen Sports Village, part-funded by the City Council and Sports Scotland. The ICT network has over 1,500 computers for student use. The university's residential stock has been growing and all new undergraduates are guaranteed a place.

Undergraduate Fees and Bursaries

» Fees for Scottish and EU students 2012–13   No fee
» Fees for Non-Scottish UK (RUK) students for 2012–13: £9,000 capped at a maximum of £27,000 regardless of course length, with the exception of enhanced degrees and medicine.
» Fees for international students 2012–13   £11,000–£14,000
  Medicine   £24,500
» For RUK students, access scholarships: household income below £20K, £3,000 for three years; household income £20K–£30K, £2,000 for three years. Merit scholarships (AAB at A level or equivalent), £3,000 for four years.
» Check the university's website for the latest information.

Students

Undergraduates:	**10,850**	**(1,345)**
Postgraduates:	**2,510**	**1,475)**
Mature students:	**13.6%**	
Overseas students:	**19.4%**	
Applications per place:	**8**	
From state-sector schools:	**79.8%**	
From working-class homes:	**24.7%**	

For detailed information about sports facilities:
www.abdn.ac.uk/sportandexercise

Accommodation

Number of places and costs refer to 2011–12
University-provided places: about 2,717
Percentage catered: 14%
Catered costs: £137–£157 a week (39 weeks).
Self-catered costs: £70–£133 (studio) a week (39–50 weeks).
First-year students are guaranteed accommodation.
International students: as above.
Contact: studentaccomm@abdn.ac.uk

University of Abertay Dundee

Abertay fended off the suggestion that it might merge with neighbouring Dundee University as the forerunner of a Scottish Government plan to create regional institutions. Instead, the two universities have agreed to work more closely together. The initial speculation was fuelled by a long-running dispute over the leadership of the university, which saw the departure of the long-serving Principal and eventual replacement by his deputy. However, Abertay's popularity appears undiminished: two huge increases in applications were followed by a more modest rise in 2012. The university doubled in size during the 1990s and has grown further since tuition fees were abolished for Scottish students, although there are still only 5,500 students in total. They are based mainly in Dundee, but with several hundred in locations as far afield as Malaysia, Canada and China. There have been dramatic improvements to a dropout rate that once stood at more than one in three of all those starting degrees: the latest rate was one in ten – well below the benchmark for the university's courses and entry qualifications. More than a third come from working-class homes and practically all attended state schools.

The former Dundee Institute of Technology had already established its academic credentials when university status arrived in 1994, with teaching in economics rated more highly than in some of Scotland's elite universities. Subsequent assessments were solid, without living up to that early promise in most subjects. More recently, Abertay has established a leading reputation in computer arts and games design. Its courses hold 5 of only 12 degree accreditations in these areas awarded by Skillset, the Government-sponsored training council for the creative industries. The university has been accredited as the first Interactive Media Academy in the UK and also the first national Centre for Excellence in Computer Games Education. Staff and students in the Institute for Art, Media and Computer Games work with industrial partners from across the broadcast, interactive and wider digital media sectors. The university has a partnership with Peking University (one of China's top two) on computer games.

Research is not being ignored. Abertay is proud of its record in establishing a series of specialist centres, in areas as diverse as wood technology, urban water systems, bioinformatics, earth systems and environmental sciences. The university opened Europe's first research centre dedicated to computer games and digital entertainment, and a major environmental science centre. Earth systems and environmental sciences

Bell Street
Dundee DD1 1HG

01382 308080
sro@abertay.ac.uk
www.abertay.ac.uk
www.abertayunion.com
Affiliation: million+

The Times **Rankings**
Overall Ranking: **112**

Student satisfaction:	n/a	
Research quality:	=86	(0.09)
Entry standards:	87	(280)
Student–staff ratio:	116	(25.2)
Services & facilities/student:	86	(£1,208)
Expected completion rate:	114	(67.7%)
Good honours:	104	(51.3%)
Graduate prospects:	111	(48.8%)

and general engineering, mineral and mining engineering produced the best scores in the latest research assessments. Those for law and psychology were the best at any post-1992 Scottish university.

Abertay plays to its strengths with a limited range of courses, and is not shy about its achievements. Among them is a high-tech approach that permeates all four of the university's schools, while spending on libraries and computers is among the highest per student in Britain, providing one computer for every four students.

All the university's buildings are within 15 minutes' walk of each other, mainly in the centre of Dundee. They are modern and functional, with new facilities being added gradually, such as the innovative White Space facility, the university's flagship creative learning and working environment, where students study alongside industry professionals who are working on real commercial or broadcast projects. A 500-bed student village opened in 2010 and new premises for a £5-million Business Prototyping Project to support the UK's creative industries followed in 2011.

Entrance requirements have been rising, although for most courses other than high-demand areas such as computer games, they are still modest. Well-qualified A-level students are eligible for direct entry into second year. Degrees are predominantly vocational, with more subjects being added every year. Food and consumer sciences, creative sound production, and ethical hacking and countermeasures are recent examples. All courses can be taken on a part-time basis, and new programmes aim to offer students the chance to spend at least 30 per cent of their time in industry.

The university's revamped modular degree scheme means that undergraduates take a maximum of eight modules a year. Students can complete a Certificate of Higher Education after one year, a diploma after two, an ordinary degree after three, or honours in four years. Abertay is piloting problem-based and work-based approaches to learning across a wide range of courses, focusing on real-world issues and teamwork rather than sitting in conventional lectures.

Dundee has a large student population and the cost of living is modest. Around 30 per cent of the undergraduates are over 21 on entry, many living locally. This lifts the pressure on university-owned beds sufficiently to allow all first years to be given priority for accommodation.

Undergraduate Fees and Bursaries

» Fees for Scottish and EU students 2012–13   No fee
» Fees for Non-Scottish UK (RUK) students for 2012–13   £7,000 capped at £21,000 for all courses.
» Fees for international students 2012–13   £9,975
» For RUK students: household income below £25K, annual bursary £1,500. Academic merit or personal achievement in music or sport scholarships, £1,500 a year.

Students

Undergraduates:	**4,200**	**(320)**
Postgraduates:	**320**	**(135)**
Mature students:	**29.1%**	
Overseas students:	**17.1%**	
Applications per place:	**4.9**	
From state-sector schools:	**96.4%**	
From working-class homes:	**35.8%**	

For detailed information about sports facilities:
www.sport.abertay.ac.uk/

Accommodation

Number of places and costs refer to 2011–12
University-provided places: 668
Percentage catered: 0%
Self-catered costs: £54.11–£104.00 a week (38, 42 or 51 weeks).
New first years are given priority provided conditions are met.
Some residential restrictions.
International students: prioritised by distance from Dundee.
Contact: accommo@abertay.ac.uk

Aberystwyth University

Aberystwyth slipped out of the leading position for student satisfaction in the 2011 National Student Survey, but still boasted the most satisfied undergraduates in Wales. Physical geography and environmental science, sports science, zoology, economics, Celtic studies, animal science and accounting all produced outstanding results. Overseas students were even more satisfied, giving Aberystwyth the third-best results out of 239 universities worldwide in the International Student Barometer. The university is investing over £48 million in its residences and teaching facilities to ensure it maintains its popularity. The new prospectus includes QR (quick response) codes giving people with smart phones direct links to a website or video presentation.

Although the oldest of the Welsh universities, Aberystwyth has long prided itself on a modern outlook: it was among the pioneers of the modular degree system and allowed students flexibility between subjects even before that. Uniquely in the UK, every student is offered the opportunity of a year's work experience in commerce, industry or the public sector, either at home or abroad. Those who have taken advantage of the scheme have achieved better than average degrees and enhanced their employment prospects.

An attractive seaside location does the university no harm when the applications season comes around. Aber had seen strong growth in the demand for places over several years until experiencing a decline in line with the average in Wales in 2012. Less than a third of the students are from the Principality and more than half from other parts of the UK. Over 90 per cent of the undergraduates come from state schools or colleges – a higher proportion than the mix of subjects would imply – and almost a third of the entrants come from working-class homes. The projected dropout rate, which remained slightly above 10 per cent in the latest survey, is one of the lowest in Wales.

Recent developments include a new building on the main Penglais campus for the Institute of Biological, Environmental and Rural Sciences, which serves more than 1,000 undergraduate and research students and has a remit to look for creative solutions to the major challenges facing the world in sustainable land use, climate change, renewable energy and the security of food and water supplies. The institute, which has a link with Bangor University, has over 300 staff and an annual budget in excess of £25 million, making it one of the largest groups of scientists and support staff working in this field in Europe. The institute won a Queen's Anniversary Prize for its work in 2010 and gives Aber the widest range of land-related courses in the UK.

Old College
King Street
Aberystwyth
Ceredigion SY23 2AX

01970 622021 (admissions)
ug-admissions@aber.ac.uk
www.aber.ac.uk
www.aberguild.co.uk
Affiliation: University
Alliance

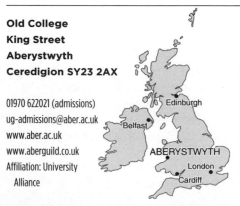

The Times **Rankings**
Overall Ranking: **47**

Student satisfaction:	=7	(83%)
Research quality:	=35	(0.61)
Entry standards:	=57	(307)
Student–staff ratio:	=74	(19.1)
Services & facilities/student:	=69	(£1,307)
Expected completion rate:	46	(85.9%)
Good honours:	=73	(59.2%)
Graduate prospects:	102	(52.1%)

Other additions to the university estate include a new student health centre and crèche, new psychology and education buildings, as well as a new phenomics research facility on the Gogerddan campus. A £1.5-million Student Welcome Centre, opened in 2009, bringing together services such as the fees office and student support services that were previously distributed around the campus or in town.

Entrance scholarships and bursaries are available in a range of subjects, even though Welsh students have been spared the full impact of top-up fees. Aber boasts one of higher education's most informative websites and also publishes a 12-page guide for parents. There is 24-hour access to the computer network, and the four university libraries are complemented by the National Library of Wales.

International politics produced the best results in the 2008 research assessments, with 40 per cent of work rated world-leading. Computer science, geography and earth sciences, Welsh, and theatre, film and television also did well.

The town of Aberystwyth is compact and travel to other parts of the UK slow, so applicants should be sure that they will be happy to spend three years or more in a tight-knit community. The students' guild is the largest entertainment venue in the region and the prize-winning arts centre has been extended at a cost of £3.5 million.

The seaside town of 25,000 people was voted the best university location in Wales and eighth in the UK in one survey. There is plenty of out-of-season accommodation to supplement the university's 3,700 places, all of which are now online. Another 1,000 residential places should become available in 2014 on land immediately adjacent to the award-winning Pentre Jane Morgan Student Village, and within easy walking distance of its all facilities on the Penglais campus. Sports facilities are good for the size of institution and well used – participation in exercise classes increased by 90 per cent last year. A 400-metre running track has just been added to 50 acres of playing fields, a new 3G pitch, refurbished swimming pool, a climbing wall and specialist outdoor facilities for water sports.

Undergraduate Fees and Bursaries

» Fees for UK/EU students for 2012–13: £9,000, with Welsh Assembly non-means-tested grant to pay fees above £3,465 for Welsh students.
» International student fees 2012–13   £ 9,500–£10,500
» For all UK students: household income less than £18,371, a bursary of £1,100 a year; £18,371– £23,610, £950; £23,611–£28,850, £800; £28,851–£34,090, £700.
» Scholarships based on circumstances or by competition.
» Check the university's website for the latest information.

Students		
Undergraduates:	**7,390**	**(1,950)**
Postgraduates:	**990**	**(810)**
Mature students:	**8.4%**	
Overseas students:	**12.2%**	
Applications per place:	**3.8**	
From state-sector schools:	**93.1%**	
From working-class homes:	**30.9%**	

For detailed information about sports facilities: www.aber.ac.uk/sportscentre/

Accommodation

Number of places and costs refer to 2012–13
University-provided places: 4,000
Percentage catered: 12%
Catered costs: £71.40–£110.60 a week (31 or 37 weeks).
Self-catered costs: £56.00–£104.30 a week (37 weeks).
First years are guaranteed accommodation if conditions are met.
International students: accommodation guaranteed for students classed as overseas for fees.
Contact: www.aber.ac.uk/residential
accommodation@aber.ac.uk

Anglia Ruskin University

Applications to Anglia Ruskin were up by more than 18 per cent at the start of 2012, bucking the national trend and building on an even bigger increase in 2011 despite the introduction of fees for degree courses of more than £8,000 a year. The university offered extra fee waivers for students from less wealthy backgrounds in order to qualify for additional places and will have 550 more available as a result – the biggest allocation to any university. Anglia Ruskin has invested over £81 million in the last five years in the latest learning environments, including the £35-million redevelopment of the Cambridge campus and two buildings dedicated to Health and Social Care on the Chelmsford campus. It has committed to invest a further £58 million over the next three years. Among the specialist study facilities are four university libraries and a mock courtroom.

The two very different locations are far enough apart to limit contact, although electronic networking and a central administration mean that key academic facilities are available throughout the university. The university has around 30,000 full and part-time students, who are taught primarily on the two main campuses, but also through a growing network of regional and international partners. Already one of the largest universities in the east of England, Anglia Ruskin has signed up to deliver higher education courses in Peterborough, Harlow and King's Lynn in partnership with local further education colleges. Three quarters of the full-time undergraduate leavers who find jobs in the UK are working in East Anglia.

Anglia was the last university to retain a polytechnic title, but discarded it in 2005 to avoid confusion among employers and overseas applicants. The former APU took the name of John Ruskin, who founded the Cambridge School of Art, which evolved into the university. It has since acquired the former Homerton College School of Health Studies in Cambridge, after a long period of partnership, and added a new health and social care building in Chelmsford, with bespoke counselling rooms, simulated hospital wards, operating theatres, and a complementary medicine suite. The 22-acre Rivermead campus also boasts an impressive business school and a sports hall, as well as the £15-million Marconi Building, completed in 2008, for law students. At the same time, the university has made considerable strides in becoming more "green", performing consistently well in the Green League, compiled by People and Planet and becoming the Walking Works Employer of the Year 2010.

Nearly all the students attended state schools or colleges and more than a third

---

Chelmsford Campus:
Bishop Hall Lane,
Chelmsford CM1 1SQ
Cambridge Campus:
East Road,
Cambridge CB1 1PT
0845 271 3333 (enquiries)
contact via website
www.anglia.ac.uk
www.angliastudent.com
Affiliation: million+

The Times **Rankings**
Overall Ranking: **107**

Student satisfaction:	=98	(74%)
Research quality:	=101	(0.05)
Entry standards:	107	(241)
Student–staff ratio:	=74	(19.1)
Services & facilities/student:	104	(£1,064)
Expected completion rate:	82	(79.2%)
Good honours:	87	(55.6%)
Graduate prospects:	90	(54.8%)

are from working-class homes. The projected dropout rate had worsened slightly in the latest survey, but is still significantly better than the national average for the university's subjects and entry grades. The best results in the 2011 National Student Survey were history, ophthalmics and sociology. Only 71 academics were entered for the Research Assessment Exercise in 2008, but almost a third of their work was considered world-leading or internationally excellent. All but one of the nine subject areas had some top-rated research, with history, English and psychology producing the best grades. Psychology produced the best results among the new universities.

Each undergraduate has an adviser to help compile a degree package which looks at the chosen subject from different points of view to maximise future job prospects. There is also an employer mentoring scheme for second-year undergraduates planning for the transition from study to work. Each student is carefully matched with a mentor from their chosen career field who volunteers time to provide skills-building, support and encouragement.

Employers play a part in planning courses which are integrated into a modular system extending from degree level to professional programmes, including a modest selection of vocational two-year Foundation degrees. The business school, for example, has developed a work-based course with Barclays Bank, where the students are sponsored and salaried for all three years of their course. The programme is now being offered to other businesses in order to aid retention and staff development.

Famous alumni include Pink Floyd members Dave Gilmour and the late Syd Barrett. The social scene varies between the two campuses, but the university has two art galleries and a theatre. There is limited collaboration with Cambridge University on the Cambridge Centre for Cricketing Excellence, and a base for Anglia Ruskin's Rowing Club. In the past, some students have found Chelmsford dull, but the social scene is said to be improving. In the summer, the town is also home to the V Festival at Hylands Park and neither base is far from London by train.

Undergraduate Fees and Bursaries

» Fees for UK/EU students 2012–13 £8,300
  Foundation degree £7,500
» International student fees 2012–13 £9,500–£10,500
» Household income below £25K, fee waiver of £1,500 a year; household income £25K–£35K, fee waiver of £500 a year.
» For English students Anglia Ruskin NSP awards (177 available): household income below £25K), fee waiver of £6,800 over three years.
» Check the university's website for the latest information.

Students		
Undergraduates:	11,710	(6,870)
Postgraduates:	1,720	(1,465)
Mature students:	34.2%	
Overseas students:	12.6%	
Applications per place:	4.1	
From state-sector schools:	96.3%	
From working-class homes:	34.2%	

For detailed information about sports facilities:
www.anglia.ac.uk/sport

Accommodation
Number of places and costs refer to 2012–13
University-provided places: Cambridge, 719 plus 212 referral rooms; Chelmsford, 511
Percentage catered: 0%
Self-catered costs: Cambridge: £75–£155 a week; Chelmsford: £94.00–£101.50 a week.
Most first years are accommodated. Distance restrictions apply.
International students: conditions and deadline apply
Contact: cambaccom@anglia.ac.uk
essexaccom@anglia.ac.uk

Aston University

Aston was the first university outside the elite Russell and 1994 groups to announce £9,000 fees. Professor Julia King, the vice-chancellor, was a member of the Browne Review, which recommended higher fees, and she believes that Aston's strong record for graduate employment justified the charges. There are still more than 9,000 applications for 2,000 places, but demand has declined substantially in both years of higher charges. Small and lively, set in the heart of Birmingham, the university has remained resolutely specialist in science and technology, business, languages and social science, concentrating on the sandwich degrees which have served its graduates so well in the employment market. But it is now aiming for "sustainable growth in key areas" to provide an improving student experience and the size necessary to boost research performance and become a top ten university.

Aston did break into the top 20 in *The Times* table, although it has slipped back recently, mainly due to less favourable staffing levels and lower spending on student facilities. Despite some modest growth, the university still has fewer than 8,000 undergraduates. But, with healthy funding from industry and commerce, Aston has been investing in its future, boosting staffing in business, engineering and languages, and developing the campus with a £215-million programme of improvements. An impressive new library, with glazed façade, opened in 2010. The Woodcock Sport Centre, including a Grade II listed swimming pool, followed in 2011.

Business and management led the way in the 2008 Research Assessment Exercise, with health subjects also producing good grades from a smaller submission. The university submitted far more staff for assessment than in 2001 but, while 45 per cent of the work in the four subject areas was judged to be world-leading or internationally excellent, the high entry helped to place Aston near the bottom of the tables of pre-1992 universities. New research centres have since been established in entrepreneurship, healthy ageing, Europe and neuroscience and child development. The £6-million Aston Brain Centre opened last year, combining research and teaching in a single unique facility.

As befits a one-time college of advanced technology, Aston is strong in engineering and the sciences, although the highly rated business school accounts for almost half of the students. A £20-million extension to the business school has seen an increase in staff from 80 to over 120. New undergraduates are offered 12 online study skills modules before the formal start of their course, covering areas such as essay writing. Aston

---

Aston Triangle
Birmingham B4 7ET

0121 204 4444 (course enquiries)
ugenquiries@aston.ac.uk
www.aston.ac.uk
www.astonguild.org.uk
Affiliation: none

BIRMINGHAM
Edinburgh
Belfast
Cardiff
London

The Times Rankings

Overall Ranking: =36

Student satisfaction:	=34	(80%)
Research quality:	50	(0.40)
Entry standards:	38	(383)
Student–staff ratio:	48	(17.0)
Services & facilities/student:	40	(£1,564)
Expected completion rate:	=31	(89.7%)
Good honours:	=43	(67.8%)
Graduate prospects:	17	(75.7%)

is also introducing a free programme of language tuition for all students, to ensure that no one need graduate without having some proficiency in a second language and to help boost employability further.

There is a wide range of joint honours programmes for those who prefer not to specialise. More than 87 per cent of Aston graduates – far more than the national average – go straight into jobs, often returning to the scene of work placements, which have become the norm for seven out of ten undergraduates. The tuition fee for the placement year is set at £1,000, and most students are paid by their host company. At the forefront of employer-led degrees, the university was awarded £1.6 million to set up a Foundation Degree Centre to establish new courses and explore other ways of delivering qualifications. Aston consistently features among the top 20 in the "High Fliers" survey of employers' favoured universities for graduate recruitment.

Student satisfaction increased considerably in 2011, with social policy, sociology and ophthalmics leading the way. The dropout rate has been improving and was still ahead of the national average for Aston's subjects in the latest statistics, despite slipping back to almost 9 per cent. The intake is diverse, with close to 40 per cent of the undergraduates coming from working-class homes. Six out of ten undergraduates come from outside the West Midlands, about a third of them from outside the UK.

The 40-acre campus is a ten-minute walk from the centre of Birmingham. Recent building programmes have brought all Aston's residential and academic accommodation onto one carefully landscaped site. Almost half of the undergraduates live on campus, with places guaranteed for first years and overseas students. A new phase of construction for residential accommodation began in 2008 and will have added 2,400 en-suite rooms by 2014. More than half of them became available in 2010. Recent developments have helped Aston to a place in the top ten of the People and Planet Green League of sustainability for the past two year. The Aston Students' Guild remains very active, both socially and in student welfare matters.

Undergraduate Fees and Bursaries

- » Fees for UK/EU students 2012–13 £9,000
- » International student fees 2012–13 £12,400–£15,600
- » Excellence scholarships (AAB at A level or equivalent), fee waiver of £1,000 per year (inc. placement year).
- » Household income up to £14.5K, fee waiver of £3,000 year 1, other years £500, plus placement year £1,000; household income £14.5K–£18K, fee waiver of £1,000 year 1, other years £500, plus placement year £1,000; household income £18K–£42K, fee waiver £500 a year with no fee waiver for placement year.

Students

Undergraduates:	**7,435**	**(695)**
Postgraduates:	**2,270**	**(920)**
Mature students:	**9.6%**	
Overseas students:	**23.3%**	
Applications per place:	**6.5**	
From state-sector schools:	**91.4%**	
From working-class homes:	**38.7%**	

For detailed information about sports facilities:
www.aston.ac.uk/sport

Accommodation

Number of places and costs refer to 2012–13
University-provided places: 2,309
Percentage catered: 0%
Self-catered accommodation: range £78 (standard) – £129 (en-suite deluxe) a week.
First years are guaranteed accommodation if they fulfil requirements and apply by the deadline.
International fee-paying students: as above.
Contact: accom@aston.ac.uk;
www.aston.ac.uk/accommodation

Bangor University

Bangor has the "fairest" workload of any UK university, according to polls of students published in 2009 and 2010, and it moved into the top 50 for overall satisfaction levels in the latest National Student Survey. Final-year undergraduates in psychology, initial teacher training and business studies gave particularly high marks in the 2011 satisfaction survey. The "small and friendly" nature of the university and the city no doubt helped – students have given it high marks for security in other surveys.

Bangor's community focus dates back to a 19th-century campaign which saw local quarrymen putting part of their weekly wages towards the establishment of a college. The School of Education and Lifelong Learning continues the tradition with courses across North Wales, but the university has also built a worldwide reputation in areas such as environmental studies and ocean sciences. Like Swansea and Aberystwyth, it is another part of the University of Wales to have asserted its independence by taking the title of Bangor University and awarding its own degrees.

The 2008 research assessments identified some world-leading work in all Bangor's 19 subject areas. The university claimed the grades for accounting and finance to be the best in the UK, with electronic engineering second and both sports science and Welsh in the top ten in their respective subjects. Teaching assessments were impressive, with half of the subjects rated as excellent. There is a high proportion of small-group teaching and tutorials, as well as one of Britain's largest peer guiding schemes, which sees senior students mentoring new arrivals.

Bangor merged with a nearby teacher training college, Coleg Normal, in 1996, and that site is now part of the university. The 23 academic schools are grouped into six colleges: arts and humanities; business, social sciences and law; natural sciences; health and behavioural sciences; physical and applied sciences and education and lifelong learning. All schools are within walking distance of each other, apart from ocean sciences, which is two miles away in Menai Bridge.

The university estate has been re-developed, with the addition of a £5-million environmental sciences building, while a £3.5-million Cancer Research Institute is attracting specialists of international repute. A combination of private funds and a £5-million European grant was used to establish a new Business Management Centre on a waterfront site. A £35-million Arts and Innovation Centre is due to open in 2013, forming a bridge between the university's upper campus and the nearby science site. Part-funded by the Welsh Assembly, it will include an "innovation

---

Bangor

Gwynedd LL57 2DG

01248 382017 (admissions)
admissions@bangor.ac.uk
www.bangor.ac.uk
www.undeb.bangor.ac.uk
Affiliation: none

The Times Rankings

Overall Ranking: **56**

Student satisfaction:	=17	(81%)
Research quality:	=45	(0.48)
Entry standards:	=68	(295)
Student–staff ratio:	=74	(19.1)
Services & facilities/student:	98	(£1,106)
Expected completion rate:	79	(79.7%)
Good honours:	70	(60.2%)
Graduate prospects:	=62	(61.9%)

hub", as well as teaching and performance spaces that will include a 500-seat theatre and an outdoor amphitheatre.

Based little more than a stone's throw from Snowdonia with its attractions for sports enthusiasts, Bangor is an expanding centre for Welsh-medium teaching. Although a majority of students come from outside Wales – there is a strong link with Ireland, for example – around a quarter of the students speak the language and one of the halls of residence is Welsh-speaking.

The university also has a flourishing international exchange programme. Summer courses in South Korea, a year in Australia or a semester in Finland are some of the opportunities available to undergraduates.

Bangor does better than most traditional universities when judged against access benchmarks. Almost 95 per cent of the students come from state schools or colleges, and four in ten come from working-class homes. The university is spending £3 million a year on bursaries and scholarships. There are approximately 40 merit scholarships of up to £3,000 for students who excel in the university's annual entrance scholarships examinations, sports scholarships worth up to £2,000 a year and £5,000 excellence scholarships in several subject areas. The university's Talent Opportunities Programme, which operates in schools across North Wales, targets potential applicants from lower socio-

economic families, who have little or no history of going on to university. Applications had increased steadily in recent years but demand for places was down by more than 10 per cent at the start of 2012, following the trend in most of Wales.

There is a strong focus on student support – the Peer Guide Scheme supports new students in the transition to university life, while the pioneering dyslexia unit offers individual and group support throughout students' courses. Eleven new halls of residence have opened in recent years. The work was part of a £35-million upgrade at the main university accommodation site, which helped Bangor to a place in the top 10 at the WhatUni? Student Choice Awards in 2011. Bangor is one of the most cost-effective places in which to study – one survey made it the second-cheapest university in the UK.

Undergraduate Fees and Bursaries

» Fees for UK/EU students for 2012–13: £9,000, with Welsh Assembly non-means-tested grant to pay fees above £3,465 for Welsh students.

» International student fees 2012–13   £9,800–£11,900

» Bangor Bursary: household income below £25K, £1,500 a year; household income £25K–£40K, £750 a year. Care leaver bursary (£1,000), Welsh-medium study bursaries.

» Scholarships include Excellence Scholarships (up to £5,000) in some subjects and Merit Scholarships (up to £3,000), awarded on Entrance Scholarship examinations.

» Check the university's website for the latest information.

Students		
Undergraduates:	**7,395**	**(1,015)**
Postgraduates:	**1,800**	**(965)**
Mature students:	**20.3%**	
Overseas students:	**10%**	
Applications per place:	**5.1**	
From state-sector schools:	**94.1%**	
From working-class homes:	**39.5%**	

For detailed information about sports facilities: www.maesglas.co.uk

Accommodation

Number of places and costs refer to 2012–13

University-provided places: approx 2,300

Percentage catered: 0%

Self-catered costs: £71–£88 (standard); £99–£117 (en-suite or larger rooms) a week (40-week contract).

All first-year students are guaranteed places.

International students: as above.

Contact: halls@bangor.ac.uk; www.bangor.ac.uk/accommodation

University of Bath

Bath saw a surge in student satisfaction in 2011, placing it among the most popular universities and helping it to move up *The Times* league table. Aerospace engineering, and molecular biology, biophysics and biochemistry both achieved 100 per cent ratings from final-year undergraduates, while accounting, finance, architecture, chemistry, civil engineering, sociology and Italian all showed very high levels of satisfaction. Students like the community feel of campus life, and one of the lowest dropout rates in Britain suggests that they are well supported.

Bath is a relatively small university with a high proportion of postgraduates. The university enjoys both an attractive location and a high academic reputation – it has never been out of the top 20 in *The Times* League Table. Despite this, Bath has not seen the sharp growth in demand for places experienced by many of its peers in recent years. Applications were flat at the start of 2011 and grew by only 2 per cent in the boom year of 2010. However, there are signs that this may be changing. At the start of 2012, when most universities were experiencing a fall in applications, Bath bucked this trend with 4 per cent growth.

Few can fail to be impressed by the magnificence of the city's architecture. The modern campus on the edge of Bath, with some undistinguished buildings dating from its origins as a technological university in the 1960s, is hardly in the same league. But the 200-acre site has pleasant grounds and is functional, with academic, recreational and residential facilities in close proximity. The university is nearing the end of a four-year expansion and refurbishment of its campus that has cost more than £100 million. It has added further facilities for teaching and research, as well as extra student accommodation and social space, including a new student centre and a dedicated centre for postgraduates, both of which opened in 2010. More lecture theatres and computer laboratories have eased the pressure on teaching space and 468 new study bedrooms have also been added recently. The latest addition was a new building for computer science and there are plans for a £10-million Arts Centre. The central Parade now features a lively and contemporary café, while the library is open 24 hours a day, seven days a week.

Research is Bath's greatest strength: 60 per cent of the work submitted for the 2008 Research Assessment Exercise was judged to be world-leading or internationally excellent. Social work and social policy, business and management, physics, pharmacy and maths did particularly well, but there were good results in a number of areas. The university's

---

Claverton Down
Bath BA2 7AY

01225 383019 (admissions)
admissions@bath.ac.uk
www.bath.ac.uk
www.bathstudent.com
Affiliation: 1994 Group

The Times Rankings
Overall Ranking: **9**

Student satisfaction:	=4	(84%)
Research quality:	=23	(0.70)
Entry standards:	12	(461)
Student–staff ratio:	49	(17.1)
Services & facilities/student:	29	(£1,742)
Expected completion rate:	=6	(96.4%)
Good honours:	9	(81.1%)
Graduate prospects:	8	(79.1%)

research grants and contracts portfolio is worth around £100 million. Most degree courses have a practical element, and assessors have praised the university for the work placements it offers. The majority of undergraduates take courses with placements or a period of study abroad, which helps to produce consistently outstanding graduate employment figures. Student entrepreneurship is actively encouraged through a number of initiatives and projects.

The university's other great claim to fame lies in its sports facilities, which were already among the best in Britain before the addition of a £35-million training village, funded with Lottery money. The campus acquired a 50-metre swimming pool by this route, to which it added an indoor running track, a multipurpose sports hall, eight indoor tennis courts, an indoor jumps and throws hall, air pistol and fencing sale, a judo dojo and even a simulated bobsleigh. There is even a skeleton start area, as used by Amy Williams, 2010 Olympic gold medallist. There is a strong tradition in competitive sports: the university pioneered sports scholarships more than 20 years ago and there are also courses to do the facilities justice. The university has begun to charge students for more of its facilities, but they still represent an exceptional resource. The campus is hosting the British Paralympic team and the Malaysian Olympic team in the run up to London 2012.

Students – nearly a quarter of whom were educated at independent schools – may find the campus quiet at weekends and struggle to afford some of Bath's attractions, but they value its location. When they tire of the beauty of Bath, the nightlife of Bristol is only a few minutes away by public transport. The two cities have a combined student population of more than 50,000. The popular students' union – one of only four in the country to hold a SUEI Gold Award – is very active, and the university has been upgrading its student support services. Improvements include the introduction of a new virtual learning environment and establishment of a central base for the full range of student services. More than nine out of ten students surveyed say they would recommend the university to family and friends.

Undergraduate Fees and Bursaries

» Fees for UK/EU students 2012–13   £9,000
   Foundation degree   £7,500
» International student fees 2012–13   £12,300–£15,700
» Household income £16K or below and other criteria, fee waiver of £4,500 years 1 and 2, full fee waiver in placement year, and £1,000 fee waiver in further years of study.
» Household income £16K or below and student has AAB at A level or equivalent, a bursary of £2,000 year 1, £1,000 year 2 and £1,500 for unpaid placement or study abroad year.
» Check the university's website for the latest information.

Students

Undergraduates:	**9,625**	**(450)**
Postgraduates:	**1,950**	**(3,295)**
Mature students:	**8.9%**	
Overseas students:	**21.4%**	
Applications per place:	**7**	
From state-sector schools:	**72.4%**	
From working-class homes:	**17.6%**	

For detailed information about sports facilities:
www.bathstudent.com/sport

Accommodation

Number of places and costs refer to 2012–13
University-provided places: 3,394
Percentage catered: 7%
Catered cost: £158–£195 a week.
Self-catered cost: £60 (shared) – £145 (single) a week.
First years guaranteed accommodation if conditions are met, and applications received by 31 July.
International students: as above. Exchange students are housed on a reciprocal basis.
Contact: www.bath.ac.uk/study/ug/accommodation/index.html

Bath Spa University

Bath Spa is one of a number of universities with a specific focus on teaching created since the millennium under Government reforms. But it is far from new in other respects and has some notable research strengths. The history of the predecessor colleges goes back 160 years, and it boasts some famous alumni, including Body Shop founder Anita Roddick and Turner Prize winner Sir Howard Hodgkin. The university's Newton Park headquarters, four miles outside the World Heritage city of Bath, is in grounds landscaped by Capability Brown in the 18th century, with a handsome Georgian manor house owned by the Duchy of Cornwall as its centrepiece.

In recent years, the new university has undertaken significant improvements to its campuses to cater for growing student numbers. Applications rose by over 40 per cent in five years, although at the start of 2012 they were down nearly 17 per cent, with the introduction of £9,000 fees for all but Foundation degrees. With around 8,800 students, Bath Spa is still comparatively small, but has begun to punch above its weight in *The Times* league table, rising 14 places this year.

Newton Park is the base for all students except those taking art and design subjects, and provides a study environment where historic buildings blend sympathetically with modern facilities such as the new 200-seat University Theatre. The Creative Writing Centre is housed in the 14th-century gatehouse, a scheduled ancient monument. Significant further development is taking place at Newton Park and should be complete in early 2014. The £70-million development will provide new teaching, social and residential facilities that will enable another 600 students to be housed on campus. The university is in a strong financial position and is one of the few higher education institutions currently with no borrowing on its balance sheet.

A second campus at Sion Hill, in Bath itself, houses the Bath School of Art and Design. It has recently undergone a £6-million redevelopment and boasts facilities that are among the most modern in the country. Meanwhile, the university has established a postgraduate centre at Corsham Court, a 16th-century manor house near Chippenham, and there is a teacher training centre on the site of Culverhay School, in Bath. About a third of the students are postgraduates, including a large cohort training to be teachers.

Bath Spa has been awarding its own taught degrees since 1992 – much longer than some of the other new arrivals on the university scene – and research degrees since 2007. Results in all the National Student Surveys have been good, especially

---

Newton Park
Newton St Loe
Bath BA2 9BN

01225 875609 (admissions)
admissions@bathspa.ac.uk
www.bathspa.ac.uk
www.bathspasu.co.uk
Affiliation: million+

The Times **Rankings**
Overall Ranking: **70**

Student satisfaction:	=55	(78%)
Research quality:	=86	(0.09)
Entry standards:	61	(304)
Student–staff ratio:	=106	(21.6)
Services & facilities/student:	114	(£821)
Expected completion rate:	=40	(87.7%)
Good honours:	47	(67.0%)
Graduate prospects:	=92	(53.7%)

for teaching quality. Business studies, education, and philosophy and religions produced the best results in 2011. Students like the "small and friendly" atmosphere. The university was designated a national centre for excellence in teaching and learning in the creative industries, bringing significant investment in the Schools of Music and Performing Arts, Humanities and Cultural Industries and Bath School of Art and Design. Half of the subjects in which the university entered the 2008 Research Assessment Exercise (art and design, communication, cultural and media studies, English, history and music) were judged to have some world-leading work.

Despite a setting that would seem to be a magnet for applicants from independent schools, almost 95 per cent of the home intake is state-educated and more than 40 per cent are from working-class homes. Two thirds of the students are female, reflecting the arts and social science bias in the curriculum and a quarter are over 25. The latest projected dropout rate, at 7.6 per cent, is an improvement on last year and better than the national benchmark for the university's courses and entry grades. There are about 250 overseas students from a variety of countries, and the university is actively seeking additional partnerships with institutions abroad.

Bath Spa has a number of partner colleges in the region, both in the further education and private sectors, where a range of vocational two-year Foundation degrees are delivered. Many students then progress to the university campuses to complete an honours degree. Employment opportunities and skills are emphasised throughout all degree courses, and links with employers help ensure that job prospects are good.

About 90 per cent of first years attending Bath Spa itself are offered university managed residential accommodation. Once the planned new halls of residence are completed on campus in 2014, all eligible first-year students will be guaranteed housing. The university is proud of its environmental success and is ranked seventh in the People and Planet Green League 2011.

Sports facilities are not extensive, but a new gym in the students' union has improved them, and some of the university's sports teams fare well in local competitions.

Undergraduate Fees and Bursaries

» Fees for UK/EU students 2012–13 £9,000
  Foundation degree £7,500
» International student fees 2012–13 £10,030–£10,730
» Bursary scheme: household income up to £17K, £500 a year; £17K–£22K, £400 a year, £22K–£25K, £300 a year.
» For English students 172 NSP awards: household income below £25K and other conditions, year 1 £2,000 fee waiver and £1,000 bursary, years 2 and 3, £500 bursary plus bursary scheme awards as above.
» Check the university's website for the latest information.

Students		
Undergraduates:	**5,285**	**(410)**
Postgraduates:	**680**	**(2,595)**
Mature students:	**20.6%**	
Overseas students:	**2.7%**	
Applications per place:	**7.4**	
From state-sector schools:	**94.5%**	
From working-class homes:	**40.8%**	

For detailed information about sports facilities:
www.bathspasu.co.uk

Accommodation
Number of places and costs refer to 2011–12
University provided places: 1,083 in halls; 132 in Accredited Independent Housing
Percentage catered: 0%
Self catered: £83–£123 a week; £141 (studio flat) for 36 or 45 weeks.
First years are housed provided requirements are met. Residential restrictions apply. Students with a disability or medical condition have priority.
International students: as above; Homestay option available
Contact: http://housing.bathspa.ac.uk

University of Bedfordshire

Bedfordshire has ploughed £180 million into its estate since taking over De Montfort University's Bedford campus and establishing a new identity in 2006. The move made the former Luton University the main provider of higher education in a relatively prosperous county and allowed it to shed a name that – however unfairly – had become a liability. The new university has seesawed in *The Times* League Table, but the demand for places has increased dramatically. The number of applications nearly doubled between 2008 and 2011, while the small decline at the start of 2012 was much less serious than at most universities.

The new university is expanding and developing its five campuses, having spent £60 million on the two main sites, adding a well-equipped media arts centre and an impressive learning resources centre in Luton. The Bedford redevelopment is now complete, with a new campus centre comprising a 280-seat auditorium and a students' union, as well as an accommodation block for 500 students.

Work is now underway on developments costing another £74 million on the Luton campus. A new campus centre opened in 2010, with teaching and exhibition space as well as the students' union, information desks and the careers and employment centre. New £40 million student halls are nearing completion, with en-suite facilities, phone and high-speed internet access. With 500 rooms already in use, the rest should follow during 2012. The third phase of the redevelopment programme, due to open in 2013, is a £15-million postgraduate and continuing professional development centre.

Although there are partner colleges in Bedford, Dunstable and Milton Keynes, the bulk of the students remain in Luton. The centrepiece of the campus, in the midst of the shopping area, is the striking atrium which leads into the learning resources centre.

The Bedford campus is a 20-minute walk from the town centre in a "self-contained leafy setting". It houses the Faculty of Education, Sport and Tourism, with 3,000 students, making it the UK's largest provider of physical education teacher training, as well as a national centre for other subjects at primary and secondary level.

There is also an attractive management centre and conference venue at Putteridge Bury, a neo-Elizabethan mansion outside Luton. Nursing and midwifery students in the growing Faculty of Health and Social Sciences are based at the Butterfield Park campus, near Luton, or at the Oxford House development, in Aylesbury, Buckinghamshire. There are additional teaching facilities at Stoke Mandeville and Wycombe General hospitals. A postgraduate

---

Park Square
Luton
Bedfordshire LU1 3JU

0844 848 2234
admissions@beds.ac.uk
www.beds.ac.uk
www.ubsu.co.uk
Affiliation: million+

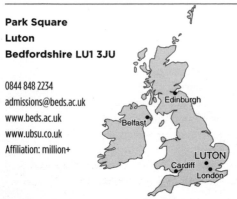

The Times Rankings
Overall Ranking: **88**

Student satisfaction:	=74	(77%)
Research quality:	=101	(0.05)
Entry standards:	116	(206)
Student–staff ratio:	80	(19.4)
Services & facilities/student:	17	(£2,004)
Expected completion rate:	106	(74.6%)
Good honours:	97	(53.6%)
Graduate prospects:	79	(57.4%)

medical school is run in partnership with Hertfordshire and Cranfield universities.

Courses in the new university are largely vocational. The portfolio of two-year Foundation degrees, for example, is among the largest in the country, stretching from animal management and graphic design to animation for industry and sustainable construction. The university pioneered electronic assessment, with more than 10,000 students in disciplines from accountancy to biology tested by computer. Bedfordshire was also awarded a national centre of excellence in personal development planning and employability, aiming to link student learning with life after university.

Almost all of Bedfordshire's entrants are from state schools and nearly 43 per cent come from working-class backgrounds. Four in ten of the undergraduates are over 20 on entry, many taking access courses to bring them up to degree or diploma standard, and about a third take part-time courses. Clearing numbers have dropped from nearly one in three to only one in ten, but the projected dropout rate of more than 20 per cent remains high, taking into account the university's courses and entry qualifications. Surprisingly high numbers – nearly a third – are from outside the EU, many of them taking postgraduate courses.

The university celebrated much-improved results in the 2008 Research Assessment Exercise, registering at least some world-leading work in earth systems and environmental science, social work, social policy and administration, sport, tourism and leisure, English language and literature, and communications, cultural and media studies. Satisfaction scores rose considerably in the 2011 National Student Survey, but Bedfordshire remained in the lower reaches of the table. The only subjects to satisfy at least 90 per cent of final-year undergraduates were English studies and initial teacher training.

Both Luton and Bedford have their share of pubs, clubs and restaurants, and London is only half an hour away by train. Bedford's impressive sports facilities are set to host athletes for the 2012 Olympics.

Undergraduate Fees and Bursaries

» Fees for UK/EU students 2012–13   £9,000
    Foundation degree   £6,000
» International student fees 2012–13   £9,600
» For English students with household income below £25K: grant of £1,000 in year 1. For those leaving care, £1,000 grant a year. Students from partner colleges, grant of £338: NSP award: £1,000 grant year 1, and further support in vouchers to value of £2,000.
» Students with AAB at A level or equivalent: Centenary Scholarship, £3,000 a year provided students maintain a 2:1 average. Students with 280 UCAS points eligible for Academic Scholarships, £1,000 on entry; other scholarships available.
» Check the university's website for the latest information.

Students

Undergraduates:	**10,585**	**(4,570)**
Postgraduates:	**3,600**	**(1,780)**
Mature students:	**23.6%**	
Overseas students:	**18.2%**	
Applications per place:	**4.6**	
From state-sector schools:	**98.6%**	
From working-class homes:	**42.6%**	

For detailed information about sports facilities:
www.beds.ac.uk/sportbeds

Accommodation

Number of places and costs refer to 2012–13
University-provided places: about 2,440
Percentage catered: 0%
Self-catered costs: £96–£140 a week.
First years cannot be guaranteed a place but help is available to find alternative housing in the private sector.
International students: as above.
Contact: www.beds.ac.uk/studentlife/accommodation
Bedford campus: accommodationqueries@beds.ac.uk
Luton campus: info@studentvillagebeds.com

Birkbeck, University of London

Birkbeck saw by far the biggest increase in applications of any university at the start of 2012, as the demand for its three-year degrees taught through evening classes more than doubled. The unprecedented rise was due partly to expansion in the number of subjects offered, but it also reflects more general interest in combining study and work. Birkbeck's much larger programme of part-time degrees, taken over four years, has also grown in popularity in spite of a considerable fees increase. The introduction of the first Government loans for part-time undergraduates has enabled Birkbeck students to afford fees of £6,000 a year for standard part-time degree courses, which is pro-rata the £8,000 a year cost for the three-year evening programme. Further cash bursaries and fee waivers are on offer for students with household incomes below £25,000.

Birkbeck does not appear in the overall ranking of universities published in this *Guide* because, as a specialist provider of part-time, evening higher education, it cannot be compared fairly with other institutions on some of the measures. But the college has become an increasingly popular and prestigious choice for Londoners of all ages. There will be over 70 part-time undergraduate degree courses to choose from in 2013. The college encourages applications from people without traditional qualifications and there is a flexible policy for entry at undergraduate level. Students aged over 21 are not asked for formal qualifications, but the college makes its own assessment of skills and knowledge, on the basis of interviews and/or short tests.

The Labour Government's removal of funding in 2007 for students returning to take a different qualification cost Birkbeck 40 per cent of its income and student numbers. The college reorganised into a smaller number of "super-schools", increased its recruitment activity and set about improving the student experience. The strategy appears to be succeeding and brought the college a leadership award. Among the innovations has been the introduction of full-time undergraduate degrees, still taught in the evenings.

Founded in 1823, Birkbeck offers a surprisingly wide range of subjects, from law, business and management to criminology, history of art, psychology and planetary science. Most are in the arts and social science, but the 20 full-time evening degrees include law, English and accounting. Students apply for full-time courses through UCAS, rather than direct to the college, as is the case for the part-time portfolio. Birkbeck took only 210 students onto the narrower programme of full-time courses in

Malet Street
Bloomsbury
London WC1E 7HX

020 7631 6000 (general enquiries)
contact via website
www.bbk.ac.uk
http://bbk.ukmsl.net
Affiliation: 1994 Group

The Times Rankings
The available data do not match the data used to rank the other full-time universities, so Birkbeck could not be included in the League Table this year.

2011 but, with only 883 applications, it represented a better-than-average chance of entry to a high-quality degree course. The 156 per cent growth in applications for 2012 suggests that this may not be the case for long.

There are now almost 18,000 students at the college, and the My Birkbeck Student Centre acts as a front door to all the college's student support services, from help in choosing courses and submitting applications to information about financial support and study skills. Nine out of ten academics at the college are researchers as well as teachers. More than half of the work submitted to the 2008 Research Assessment Exercise was considered world-leading or internationally excellent. Earth Sciences, psychology, history, classics and archaeology and history of art, film and visual media were rated in the top five nationally. Its research strength has helped Birkbeck to a place among the top 150 universities in the world, according to the 2011 *Times Higher Education* rankings.

Birkbeck is located in the heart of the University of London, in Bloomsbury, close to the university's Senate House head-quarters and main facilities. Almost £20 million has been spent consolidating the college's buildings and bringing them under one roof. Teaching also takes place in Stratford, where there is a unique partner-ship with the University of East London. A new shared £33-million university building in Stratford will welcome its first cohort of students in 2013. University Square Stratford is the first shared project of this kind in the capital, allowing a broad mix of 3,400 adults to take a wide variety of courses throughout the day and evening. Degree courses will include business and community development and public policy, while Foundation degrees include environmental management and web technologies.

Bloomsbury is easily accessible by public transport and cycle routes. The campus is next door to the University of London Union, where facilities include the Energy Base, which offers a 60-station gymnasium with cardio theatre, a 33-metre swimming pool and two studios. as well as a wide range of sports clubs. Most Birkbeck students already live in the capital, but those looking for housing can apply to the University of London Accommodation Office.

Undergraduate Fees and Bursaries

» Fees for UK/EU students 2012–13   £4,500–£6,750 (on the basis of students studying for four years at 75 per cent intensity, equivalent to £6,000–£9,000 full-time fees).

» International student fees 2012–13   £11,334–£11,925 (full-time courses)

» Household income under £25K, cash bursary up to £1,000 a year, depending on intensity of study. For English students, NSP awards: household income below £20K, fee waiver of up to £3,000 a year depending on intensity of study.

» Check the university's website for the latest information.

Students		
Undergraduates:	210	(12,535)
Postgraduates:	1,235	(3,840)
Mature students:	67.0%	
Overseas students:	6.2%	
Applications per place:	2.5	
From state-sector schools:	84.4%	
From working-class homes:	35.7%	

For detailed information about sports facilities:
www.ulu.co.uk/content/621793/energybase/

Accommodation

As the courses provided are part-time, the university has a limited number of places in the intercollegiate halls of residence, and these are normally reserved for full-time international students. For further accommodation information see: www.bbk.ac.uk/mybirkbeck/services/facilities/accommodation

International students should also contact www.bbk.ac.uk/prospective/international/accommodation

University of Birmingham

The original "redbrick" university, Birmingham has been rediscovering the energy of its pioneering early days. Professor David Eastwood said on his appointment as Vice-Chancellor that he wanted the university to be the "best of the rest" outside Oxbridge and the top London colleges, and a series of initiatives in teaching and research are taking the university in the right direction.

Birmingham is part way through a long-term programme of investment in its facilities, services and staff. Recent developments costing £700 million include a student facilities building at the medical school, a new home for sport and exercise sciences and a well-equipped learning centre, as well as refurbished student accommodation. The programme has also included a new music building with 450-seat auditorium, improved library and IT services, and enhanced student support. The university has also invested £3.5 million on an employability initiative which will include internships and mentoring by some of the university's most successful alumni.

Birmingham's 28,000 students include 4,000 from 150 different countries. The university slipped out of the top 30 for student satisfaction in the 2011 National Student Survey, but still finished well up the table. Planning produced a second successive 100 per cent satisfaction score, while archaeology, biology, chemistry, electronic engineering, European languages, geology, music and physics all produced good results. Birmingham encourages interdisciplinary study, for example allowing undergraduates to combine technology with subjects ranging from Latin or modern Greek to the management of floods and other natural disasters. Entry standards are high, averaging the equivalent of more than ABB at A level. With over seven applicants for each place, they are likely to remain so, but aspiring students still flock to the largest open days in Britain each June.

The university has stepped up its efforts to widen participation to coincide with the introduction of £9,000 fees. Over 4,000 students are expected to benefit from its package of enhanced financial support for those from lower income backgrounds. The Access to Birmingham (A2B) scheme, which encourages students from the West Midlands whose families have little or no experience of higher education to apply to university, will be extended to students outside the Midlands.

The university's enduring reputation is based on its research, with 16 per cent of the work submitted for the Research Assessment Exercise regarded as world-leading. Birmingham took satisfaction from the broad range of subjects in which

---

Edgbaston
Birmingham B15 2TT

0121 415 8900 (admissions)
admissions@bham.ac.uk
www.bham.ac.uk
www.guildofstudents.com
Affiliation: Russell Group

The Times **Rankings**
Overall Ranking: **=24**

Student satisfaction:	=55	(78%)
Research quality:	=21	(0.72)
Entry standards:	21	(435)
Student–staff ratio:	31	(15.5)
Services & facilities/student:	14	(£2,036)
Expected completion rate:	13	(94.4%)
Good honours:	18	(76.1%)
Graduate prospects:	20	(74.0%)

it produced good results, with music, physics, computer science, mechanical engineering, European studies, primary care, cancer sciences, psychology and law all doing well. The university is now going to partner Nottingham University on a range of research projects. Birmingham is the national hub for a new STEM programme, a national initiative to promote interest in science, technology, engineering and maths among young people and enhance higher level skills in the workplace. It has also become the first link in a chain of Cancer Research UK Centres, while a £60-million fundraising campaign launched in 2009 will support projects ranging from research into brain injury, ageing and clean energy to scholarships and a centre for heritage and cultural learning.

The 230-acre campus in leafy Edgbaston is dominated by a 300-foot clocktower, which is one of the city's best-known landmarks, and boasts its own station. Dentistry is located in the city centre, while part of the School of Education is in Selly Oak, a mile from the Edgbaston campus. Drama is also located there, along with the BBC Drama Village, which is part of a strategic alliance between the university and the corporation.

Most of the halls and university flats are conveniently located in an attractive parkland setting near the main campus. There are more than 4,200 university-owned beds, and accommodation in the private sector is also plentiful. The campus is less than three miles from the city centre, but the area has plenty of shops, pubs and restaurants. With its own nightclub among the facilities on campus, some students do not even stray that far, but the city is acquiring a growing reputation among the young. Some 40 per cent of Birmingham graduates make the city their home.

Student facilities on campus are on a par with the best in the country, and include a medical practice. An outdoor pursuits centre is by Coniston Water, in the Lake District. Birmingham has traditionally been concerned with the body as well as the mind, and the voluntary Active Lifestyles Programme attracts 4,000 students to 150 different courses. Birmingham has ranked in the top four in British Universities sports competitions for the past 15 years.

Undergraduate Fees and Bursaries

» Fees for UK/EU students 2012–13   £9,000
» International student fees 2012–13   £11,730–£15,150
   Clinical medicine   £27,510
» Household income up to £42.6K, tapered fee or accommodation waiver or cash bursary, £2,000–£250. For English students, NSP awards, for a care leaver or applicant eligible for free school meals and living in university accommodation, £4,750 accommodation waiver; not in university accommodation £3,000 fee waiver; household income below £16,190, accommodation or fee waiver, £3,000.
» Check the university's website for the latest information.

Students		
Undergraduates:	**17,565**	**(1,445)**
Postgraduates:	**6,740**	**(4,910)**
Mature students:	**7.3%**	
Overseas students:	**10.5%**	
Applications per place:	**7.8**	
From state-sector schools:	**76.1%**	
From working-class homes:	**21.1%**	

For detailed information about sports facilities:
www.sport.bham.ac.uk

Accommodation
Number of places and costs refer to 2011–12
University-provided places: 4,267
Percentage catered: 42%
Catered costs: £109.50–£165.50 a week.
Self-catered costs: £77.50–£133.50 a week.
All first years are guaranteed housing (subject to conditions).
International students: as above.
Contact: ugradaccomm@bham.ac.uk
www.birmingham.ac.uk/students/accommodation

Birmingham City University

Birmingham City University (BCU) is constructing a new campus in the heart of Birmingham, the first phase of which is due to open in September 2013. Diggers and cranes have moved into the Eastside district to create the first phase of the university's £61-million City Centre Campus, next to Millennium Point. The project is intended to create a Learning Quarter and is part of BCU's overall £180-million investment in new facilities. The five-storey building will provide a home for the Birmingham Institute of Art and Design (BIAD), one of the six faculties that make up the university. The building will also feature a "media hub" with industry-standard TV, radio and photographic studios that will underpin the university's media production courses.

The university has thrived since adopting its new name in 2007. Applications shot up, although the move to higher fees saw a drop of 6 per cent at the start of 2012. The switch from the previous identity as UCE Birmingham (originally the University of Central England) was designed to emphasise the university's location, reinforce its close links with the city and give the university a stronger identity. The Vice-Chancellor's strategy has been to build on the university's traditionally close links with business and the professions.

As a pioneer in green technology, BCU is attracting support from national and regional partners to help support a green economy with the potential to create thousands of jobs. There is a strong emphasis on making graduates "job-ready", with training and education resources to help develop skills and knowledge for the workplace. High-powered visiting lecturers and an innovative iLearning strategy contribute to this agenda, with students having access to learning tools and facilities, such as Shareville – a virtual town where students can engage with real-life scenarios.

The university registered a big improvement on previously disappointing satisfaction levels in the 2011 National Student Survey, with accounting, media studies, initial teacher training and sociology producing the best results. The prize-winning Student Academic Partners scheme has spawned a formal agreement between the university and the students' union to improve the student experience. Internal student surveys have led to the introduction of internet tutorials in engineering and new help with research for undergraduates in law and social science.

More than 40 per cent of the students come from working-class homes and 97 per cent were state educated. About half come from the West Midlands, many from ethnic minorities. The drop-out rate has been improving and is now close to the national

---

Perry Barr

Birmingham B42 2SU

0121 331 5595 (enquiries)
access via website
www.bcu.ac.uk
www.bcusu.com
Affiliation: million+

The Times **Rankings**

Overall Ranking: =75

Student satisfaction:	=55	(78%)
Research quality:	=93	(0.07)
Entry standards:	=82	(283)
Student–staff ratio:	101	(21.1)
Services & facilities/student:	44	(£1,516)
Expected completion rate:	91	(77.8%)
Good honours:	=73	(59.2%)
Graduate prospects:	=62	(61.9%)

average for the university's courses and entry grades. The university also has one of the largest programmes of part-time courses in Britain, making it the biggest provider of higher education in the region. Many students enter through the network of associated further education colleges, which run foundation and access programmes.

Eight campuses straggle across the city, but about half of students are concentrated on the modern City North Campus at Perry Barr. The university's estate has already been significantly remodelled, engineering and computing relocating to Millennium Point in 2001, for example. Facilities in the £114-million Lottery-funded centre are open to the public. The Birmingham School of Acting also moved into purpose-built facilities at Millennium Point in 2007.

The Edgbaston campus has been refurbished for the Faculty of Health, with a prize-winning library, IT suites, teaching facilities and recreational space. The Birmingham Institute of Art and Design spreads over four campuses from the city centre to Bourneville, where the refurbished facility occupies part of the Cadbury village. The largest institute of its kind outside London, it also includes the world-famous School of Jewellery in the city's Jewellery Quarter.

One of BCU's best-known features is its Conservatoire, housed in part of the city's smart convention centre. Courses from opera to world music have given it a reputation for innovation. Teacher education courses consistently produce among the best scores in Ofsted inspections. The university was also awarded a national teaching centre in health and social care.

The university has been increasing its portfolio of high-tech degree courses such as electronic commerce, communications and network engineering, and electronic systems. The 2008 Research Assessment Exercise recorded some world-leading work in all seven areas covered by the university's submission. In art and design, 30 per cent were given the top grade, placing Birmingham City in the top ten for the subject.

University-owned accommodation is guaranteed for first years, and there is plentiful private housing sector. The city's student scene is highly rated and has been charted in a Lonely Planet guide.

Undergraduate Fees and Bursaries

» Fees for UK/EU students 2012–13 £7,500–£8,200
   Specialist courses (including Conservatoire) £9,000
   Foundation degree £6,000
» International student fees 2012–13 £9,900–£11,200
   Conservatoire and Acting £14,000–£17,000
» For English students, 370 NSP awards: fee waiver of £3,000 if household income typically below £16,190 with conditions.
» Scholarships and bursaries based on circumstances or by competition.
» Check the university's website for the latest information.

Students		
Undergraduates:	**15,530**	**(4,315)**
Postgraduates:	**1,975**	**(2,140)**
Mature students:	**28.9%**	
Overseas students:	**7.9%**	
Applications per place:	**6.2**	
From state-sector schools:	**97.5%**	
From working-class homes:	**41.6%**	

For detailed information about sports facilities:
www.bcusu.com/sports

Accommodation
Number of places and costs refer to 2011–12
University-provided places: 2,485
Percentage catered: 0%
Self-catered costs: £83.00–£109.50 a week (40–43 weeks).
Accommodation guaranteed for first years if conditions are met.
International students are guaranteed accommodation.
Contact: www.bcu.ac.uk/accommodation
accommodation@uce.ac.uk

University of Bolton

Bolton will have among the lowest fees at any university in 2013, averaging less than £6,500 after all forms of financial support are taken into consideration. Applications were still down by more than 11 per cent at the start of 2012, however, reversing two years of healthy increases in demand. The university now has a single campus in the centre of the town, as well as a branch campus in the United Arab Emirates that is part of a longer-term inter-nationalisation strategy. The rationalisation of sites in Bolton has provided additional and enhanced teaching space, facilities to inter-act with industry and a new students' union.

The university traces its roots back as far as 1824 to one of the country's first three mechanics institutes. There are now over 9,000 students but there are no plans for further dramatic growth. The university sees itself as a regional institution, with three quarters of the students coming from the North West, many through partner colleges. But the international dimension includes long-established links in Malaysia, China, Zambia, Malawi and Vietnam, as well as a regular contingent coming to Bolton from 60 different countries. The Ras as Khaimah campus opened in 2008, offering a range of undergraduate and postgraduate courses identical to those taught at Bolton. The £1-million development near Dubai has 270 students and is intended to take 700 within five years. Students at Bolton will also have the opportunity to study in the UAE for part of their degree course.

Student satisfaction improved slightly in 2011 without matching the early days of the National Student Survey, when Bolton almost made the top ten. It has since dropped into the bottom half of the table on this measure, although there were good scores in 2011 for design studies and social studies. At the other end of the scale, law students were among the least satisfied. In 2012, law students will benefit from a £100,000 mock court room and there will be a major investment in the university's IT infrastructure The university has done better in the International Student Barometer, which tracks the views of overseas students at UK institutions.

The university is not research-driven, but has been accredited for research degrees for more than a decade. About 1,800 of the students are postgraduates, taking qualifications up to and including PhDs. Engineering, architecture and the built environment, social work and social policy all contained some world-leading research in the 2008 assessments. An institute for research and innovation in materials was the first of a series of "knowledge exchange zones". Institutes for educational cybernetics and renewable energy and

---

Deane Road
Bolton BL3 5AB

01204 903903 (course enquiries)
enquiries@bolton.ac.uk
www.bolton.ac.uk
www.ubsu.org.uk
Affiliation: million+

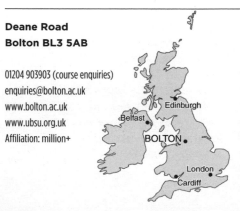

The Times Rankings

Overall Ranking: **115**

Student satisfaction:	=89	(75%)
Research quality:	=95	(0.06)
Entry standards:	110	(234)
Student–staff ratio:	=83	(19.6)
Services & facilities/student:	116	(£679)
Expected completion rate:	115	(62.4%)
Good honours:	110	(48.6%)
Graduate prospects:	116	(41.4%)

environmental technologies have followed, as well as a research centre for health and wellbeing.

The £11.3-million building programme at the Deane campus has included a design studio and three floors of teaching and learning space where students work on actual briefs for companies seeking design solutions, an Innovation Factory housing, among others, special effects laboratories and a product design studio. Also included within this development is a new social learning zone which includes a students' union bar and social facilities, a computer access room and new students' union offices and advice centre. The combined student services centre covers floor space equivalent to the size of a football pitch. Bespoke facilities for arts students have been developed across the top floor of Eagle Tower and a multi-faith chaplaincy opened in 2010.

A swimming pool and sports complex built in partnership with the local authority and NHS Bolton opened in 2012, offering students access to the 25-metre pool, gym and dance studio, sports courts and climbing wall, as well as health service facilities. The university will also have its own teaching and research space within this building, named Bolton One. The 700 reasonably priced residential places go a long way in an institution with a high proportion of home-based students. Almost half of the undergraduates are over 21 at entry.

The university exceeds all the access measures designed to widen participation in higher education: nearly 41 per cent are from working-class homes and the proportion from areas without a tradition of higher education is among the highest in the UK. The downside – and an important one – is that the dropout rate is the highest of any university in England: more than 31 per cent of the first years who entered in 2009 are projected to leave without a qualification – ten percentage points worse than the national average for Bolton's degree subjects and entry grades.

Undergraduate Fees and Bursaries

» Fees for UK/EU students 2012–13

Classroom-based courses	£6,300
Studio-based and resource-intensive courses	£7,200
Laboratory and specialist courses using dedicated facilities	£8,400

» International student fees 2012–13   £9,400

» Students with household income below £42K on science, engineering and mathematics courses with fees of £8,400, excluding sport and psychology, fee waiver of £1,200 a year. For English students, 180 NSP awards: household income below £25K on courses as above, year 1 fee waiver of £1,200, benefits to value of £800, and scholarship of £1,000 on successful completion of year. Grant of £500 in year 1 for students from partner colleges.

» Vice Chancellor's Award, up to £15,000, for most outstanding and academically gifted, students (maximum three awards a year).

» Check the university's website for the latest information.

Students

Undergraduates:	**4,070**	**(3,375)**
Postgraduates:	**760**	**(1,030)**
Mature students:	**43.8%**	
Overseas students:	**8.5%**	
Applications per place:	**3.8**	
From state-sector schools:	**99.2%**	
From working-class homes:	**40.5%**	

For detailed information about sports facilities:
http://bolton.ac.uk/Sport/Home.aspx

Accommodation

Number of places and costs refer to 2011–12
University-provided places: 700
Percentage catered: 0%
Self-catered costs: £2,790 (40 weeks); £69.75 a week.
All first years are generally accommodated.
International students: accommodation is secured for these students.
Contact: accomm@bolton.ac.uk

Bournemouth University

Once a university that gloried in the absence of traditional academic disciplines, Bournemouth has been subtly changing its image. It appointed 150 academics in three years to "facilitate the transformation of its staff profile and foster the development of an academically-led culture". Research moved up the agenda with a £1-million investment in 80 PhD studentships – only three universities showed more improvement in the last set of research assessments – and the aim is to increase undergraduates' entry qualifications. The university rose 27 places up *The Times* League Table in four years but has lost much of that ground in the latest edition after a big fall in student satisfaction.

The university suffered a 15 per cent drop in applications at the start of 2012, following the announcement of £8,200 fees for most of its degrees. A few "flagship" courses – carefully not listed on the university's website, but including multimedia journalism and computer visualisation and animation – will cost £9,000. Bournemouth has particular strengths in media subjects and boasts the National Centre of Computer Animation. State-of-the-art equipment includes a motion capture facility for real-time animation, which is used in teaching and available for use by outside companies. The university was designated as England's only centre for excellence in media practice.

Bournemouth claims a number of firsts in its growing portfolio of courses, notably in the area of tourism, media-related programmes and conservation. Degrees in public relations, retail management, script-writing and tax law were all ahead of their time. Foundation degrees, which will cost £6,000 a year, are delivered in five further education colleges in Dorset and Somerset, as well as on the main campus. They support the needs of business in the creative arts, media and tourism. One even serves soldiers based in Afghanistan, who are studying business and management via the internet. Top-up courses are available for those who wish to turn their qualification into an honours degree.

A majority of undergraduates take sandwich courses, and 70 per cent do work placements. The result is that nearly four out of five graduates went straight into jobs at the time of the latest survey. The retail management degree notched up eight successive years of full employment. Virtually all students take up the offer of personal development planning, both online and with trained staff, while 1,400 first years also take advantage of peer-assisted learning, receiving advice and mentoring from more experienced undergraduates.

In the 2008 Research Assessment Exercise, eight of the ten subject areas contained at least some world-leading

Fern Barrow
Talbot Campus
Poole
Dorset BH12 5BB

08456 501501 (enquiries)
askBUenquiries@
  bournemouth.ac.uk
www.bournemouth.ac.uk
www.subu.org.uk
Affiliation: University Alliance

The Times Rankings
Overall Ranking: =81

Student satisfaction:	=114	(69%)
Research quality:	=71	(0.13)
Entry standards:	54	(328)
Student–staff ratio:	90	(20.4)
Services & facilities/student:	63	(£1,335)
Expected completion rate:	=51	(85.0%)
Good honours:	51	(64.8%)
Graduate prospects:	=52	(65.1%)

research, with art and design and communication, cultural and media studies producing the best grades. The results have tripled Bournemouth's research grant and the university won a £6-million research grant, its largest ever, to establish an Industrial Doctorate Centre in Computer Animation with the University of Bath. However, the university suffered a disastrous set of results in the 2011 National Student Survey. Overall satisfaction declined by 7 percentage points – more than at any other university – leaving it in the bottom three. Only complementary medicine, publicity studies and sports science satisfied nine out of ten final-year undergraduates.

New teaching and residential accommodation has been added in recent years, with more to come. There is a wide range of accommodation, from around 2,900 places in university halls to bed-and-breakfast lets and shared houses. Students based in halls of residence in Poole enjoy a millionaire's view of Poole Harbour. Recent developments include a new Executive Business Centre, which is a focus for services to local companies and £1.5 million has been spent on improvements to information technology. There are now two campuses – the original Talbot site in Poole and a dedicated campus in Bournemouth – with partner colleges in Bridgwater, Yeovil, Bournemouth and Poole, Dorchester and Weymouth.

The southern seaside location and the subject mix attract more middle-class students than most new universities, although almost 94 per cent attended state schools. The campuses are served by a subsidised bus service and students are discouraged from bringing cars. The area has plenty to offer during the summer season, and Bournemouth no longer shuts up when the tourists go home. The students' union's Old Fire Station bar is the favourite among many nightlife options. The new surf reef, recently completed off Boscombe seafront, is helping to transform the area into the UK's latest surfing hotspot and other water sports are catered for in Poole Harbour. The university is also benefiting from the Lottery-funded Free your Fitness campaign, which gives students a chance to take up a new sport or return to a former favourite.

Undergraduate Fees and Bursaries

» Fees for UK/EU students 2012–13 £8,200
  Flagship degrees, for example in computer animation, journalism, television production, tourism £9.,000
  Foundation degrees £6,000–£8,200
» International student fees 2012–13 £9,5u⊃–£11,500
» For English students, BU Maintenance Bursary for household income below £25K (limited number): year 1, cash £400, fee or accommodation waiver £2,000, living expenses vouchers £600; years 2 and 3: cash £300, fee or accommodation waiver £1,000, living expenses vouchers £200. BU Care Leaver Bursary as above but with fee or accommodation waiver £4,500 each year, £900 cash each year.
» Check the university's website for the latest information.

Students

Students		
Undergraduates:	**12,560**	**(3,355)**
Postgraduates:	**1,635**	**(1,240)**
Mature students:	**21.6%**	
Overseas students:	**6.7%**	
Applications per place:	**5.8**	
From state-sector schools:	**94.0%**	
From working-class homes:	**28.0%**	

For detailed information about sports facilities: www.bournemouth.ac/things/sportbu

Accommodation

Number of places and costs refer to 2012–13
University-provided places: about 2,910 (2,310 in halls; 600 head tenancy)
Percentage catered: 0%
Self-catered costs: £100–£110 (single); £125–£140 (studio) a week.
The university expects to offer all first years a place to live. Residential restrictions apply.
International students: guaranteed if conditions are met.
Contact: accommodation@bournemouth.ac.uk

University of Bradford

Bradford has been a leading light in the green movement in higher education, with its "ecoversity" programme addressing issues of sustainable development in all the university's practices, including the curriculum. The most visible sign was the opening in 2011 of The Green, a sustainable student village catering mainly for first-year and international students. The development is part of a £70-million modernisation plan that includes a £7-million investment in new and upgraded teaching facilities. Another project produced the distinctive four-storey Atrium, which has brought together all student support services in a single, open-plan social space.

The university is at the heart of a new "Learning Quarter", an area of education institutions and creative and knowledge-based industries, which is levering in over £40-million worth of investment to the area. Still a relatively small university, Bradford has carved out a niche for itself with mature students, who now make up around a quarter of all undergraduates. They relish the vocational slant and the accent on work experience and placement courses, which regularly place Bradford towards the top of the graduate employment tables.

Nearly half of the undergraduates are from working-class homes – the biggest proportion of any pre-1992 university. The demand for places has recovered in recent years after a difficult period, despite rising admission requirements. Applications were slightly up at the start of 2012, when most other universities were experiencing a decline. Nearly 18 per cent of the university's students are from overseas, many of them taught in partner institutions in locations as diverse as Poland, India, Iceland and Hong Kong. Nearer home, there are alliances with a number of further education colleges to help boost participation in a region where it is well below the national average. The colleges offer Foundation degrees in areas such as public sector administration, community justice, engineering technology and enterprise in IT. Perhaps the best known is in health and social care, where the university was already expanding opportunities locally, bringing about a fourfold increase in enrolments by young women from South Asian families.

The relatively small, lively campus is close to the city centre. Health students have moved into a new state-of-the-art facility on campus; the highly rated management school is two miles away in a 14-acre parkland setting. Improvements in recent years have included upgraded laboratories for chemical and forensic science, and new sports facilities including a gym and climbing wall and an improved sports hall. New students will be amongst the first to

Richmond Road
Bradford
West Yorkshire BD7 1DP

0800 073 1225 (freephone)
course-enquiries@bradford.ac.uk
www.bradford.ac.uk
www.ubuonline.co.uk
Affiliation: University
  Alliance

The Times Rankings
Overall Ranking: **67**

Student satisfaction:	=55	(78%)
Research quality:	54	(0.30)
Entry standards:	88	(279)
Student–staff ratio:	=53	(17.6)
Services & facilities/student:	53	(£1,411)
Expected completion rate:	75	(80.4%)
Good honours:	105	(50.8%)
Graduate prospects:	42	(69.0%)

use the brand new accommodation and "Student Central", the new students' union which will hold social and study spaces, bars and nightclub venues.

The university maintained its recent improvements in the National Student Survey in 2011, remaining in the top 60 with good results in anatomy, history, sociology and forensic and archaeological science. Bradford is harnessing the power of technology: a so-called "e-induction" offers online preparation for university life, while those who do win a place are offered a "self-audit" that gauges new students' levels of confidence in different academic areas and allows them to develop an action plan with their personal tutor.

Some 80 per cent of the work submitted for the 2008 Research Assessment Exercise was placed in the top two categories, although more than a third of the academics were not entered. Social work and social policy, politics, civil engineering and pharmacy produced the best results. Politics includes the university's best-known offering of peace studies, which has acquired an international reputation, while the human studies programme, which combines psychology, literature and sociology with philosophy, is another imaginative construct.

The university has launched suites of ICT and media studies courses to add to those in e-commerce and internet computing, computer animation and special effects, interactive systems and video games design. Computer-assisted learning is increasing in many subjects, making use of unusually extensive IT provision and a new wireless network. Some courses feature online assessment and the use of laptops in lectures.

More southerners are being attracted to Bradford's status as Britain's cheapest student city. Places in halls are reasonably priced and all have internet connections. Another 1,000 places were added when The Green opened, a highly energy-efficient development with a central hub building containing a laundrette and small retail/coffee shop, within five minutes of the city centre. The university has particularly good provision for disabled students, who account for 6 per cent of the university population. Bradford's senior management group includes a Dean of Students to ensure that the student voice is heard in future developments.

Undergraduate Fees and Bursaries

» Fees for UK/EU students 2012–13   £9,000
    Foundation degree   £7,500
» International student fees 2012–13   £11,000–£13,100
» UK students with AAB at A level or equivalent, £1,500 cash in year 1, £1,000 cash in years 2 and 3.
» For English students, 228 NSP awards: household income below £25K meeting certain criteria, £3,000 fee waiver in year 1 and placement year fees waived.
» Check the university's website for the latest information.

Students

Undergraduates:	**8,920**	**(1,605)**
Postgraduates:	**1,375**	**(1,670)**
Mature students:	**22.5%**	
Overseas students:	**17.3%**	
Applications per place:	**4.8**	
From state-sector schools:	**93.3%**	
From working-class homes:	**49.6%**	

For detailed information about sports facilities:
www.bradford.ac.uk/unique/

Accommodation

Number of places and costs refer to 2012–13
University-provided places: 1,051
Percentage catered: 0%
Self-catered costs: £88.98 (town house) – £96.72 (en suite) a week (42-week contracts).
All first-year undergraduate students are guaranteed accommodation (terms and conditions apply).
Contact: halls-of-residence@bradford.ac.uk
www.brad.ac.uk/accommodation

University of Brighton

Brighton has been increasing its focus on the careers of its graduates to coincide with the introduction of £9,000 fees. Career planning and development, as well as employability skills, are built into every course, while leadership skills, management training and enterprise are available as modules or in workshops. More than nine out of ten courses include a work placement or a sandwich year. Degrees are designed in collaboration with employers in the public and private sectors, three quarters of them endorsed by professional associations. The job-focused approach is popular: only five post-1992 universities attract more applicants, although the demand for places was 14 per cent down at the start of 2012.

A series of new developments have been completed recently. The School of Education, as well as languages and literature students, moved into the new Checkland Building on the Falmer campus, which now also boasts a £7.3-million sports centre. Meanwhile, at the Moulsecoomb site, the £23-million Huxley Building has provided a new home for pharmacy and biosciences.

Brighton came of age as one of the first new universities to be awarded a medical school, but is equally well known for imaginative initiatives in its region. It has set up a centre in Hastings and runs a number of schemes to draw people from the region into higher education and to help them with practical problems. The £28.5-million medical school, run jointly with Sussex University, is training 128 doctors a year. Brighton was already heavily engaged in other health subjects, such as nursing and midwifery. The medical school's head-quarters, on Brighton's Falmer campus, has also provided a new base for applied social sciences, such as criminology and applied psychology, which are among the university's most sought-after degrees.

The two universities have been collab-orating since Brighton was a polytechnic. There is a joint research building for science policy and management studies, and a joint accord guarantees the offer of a place to all suitably qualified applicants from the Channel Island of Jersey. Brighton does the same for applicants from Sussex and leads a Learning Network for the county. Almost a third of undergraduates now come through these accords.

Brighton was again one of the top new universities in the last Research Assessment Exercise. Art and design produced the best results, with two thirds of the work submitted considered world-leading or internationally excellent. Business management, sports studies and mechanical and aeronautical engineering also did well. Biology, communications and information studies, history and archaeology, philosophy

Mithras House
Lewes Road
Brighton BN2 4AT

01273 600900 (switchboard)
enquiries@brighton.ac.uk
www.brighton.ac.uk
www.bsms.ac.uk
www.ubsu.net
Affiliation: none

The Times Rankings
Overall Ranking: **69**

Student satisfaction:	=55	(78%)
Research quality:	55	(0.29)
Entry standards:	=74	(292)
Student–staff ratio:	68	(18.6)
Services & facilities/student:	110	(£948)
Expected completion rate:	=53	(84.8%)
Good honours:	60	(62.0%)
Graduate prospects:	98	(52.7%)

and medicine achieved the best scores in the 2011 National Student Survey.

Brighton's strengths in art and design – recognised in the award of national teaching centres in design and creativity – have been at the forefront of the university's popularity. But the university also has a growing reputation in areas such as sport and hospitality, as well as scoring well in teacher education rankings.

The Design Council's national archive is lodged on campus, and the four-year fashion textiles degree offers work placements in the USA, France and Italy, as well as Britain. Teaching facilities include a flight simulator, a fully functional newsroom for the university's sports journalists, modern clinical skills laboratories for pharmacy, and a custom-designed culinary arts studio. At Eastbourne there is a new library and extensive leisure and sports facilities, including three gymnasia and a dance studio, a refurbished swimming pool and fitness facilities, which attracted the Swedish tennis team for its pre-Olympic preparations. Sport science laboratories and 354 en-suite residential places have been added, and improvements made to the learning resources centre, lecture theatres and refectory.

Four sites house the five faculties. Art and design has the prime location opposite the Royal Pavilion, with sports science, service management and the health professions at Eastbourne and the other subjects on the outskirts of Brighton, at Falmer and Moulsecoomb. The university has a cosmopolitan air, with more overseas students and a more middle-class UK intake than most of the former polytechnics. Around a third of the full-time undergraduates are over 21 on entry, often attracted by strongly vocational courses. Students have a personal tutor to advise on combinations within the modular degree scheme and there is an award-winning student services department for other problems.

Students have taken to Studentcentral, an interactive service providing online access to teaching materials and other information. Most like Brighton's lively social scene, despite the high cost of living for those not in hall. Eastbourne is also surprisingly popular, and both towns offer plentiful accommodation to supplement the university's stock.

Undergraduate Fees and Bursaries

» Fees for UK/EU students 2012–13 — £9,000
Foundation degrees at partner colleges — £7,000–£8,300
» International student fees 2012–13 — £10,500–£12,500
Medicine — £23,678
» For English students, NSP awards: household income below £25K, plus other criteria, year 1, cash £1,000, fee waiver £1,000, fee waiver or discounted university service £1,000. No cash payments in years 2 and 3.
» Aimhigher bursary for local students, cash £1,000, fee waiver, £1,000 a year; also care leaver's bursary and bursaries for those studying architecture, pharmacy and teaching.

Students

Undergraduates:	**14,020**	**(3,335)**
Postgraduates:	**1,510**	**(2,260)**
Mature students:	**27.0%**	
Overseas students:	**10.7%**	
Applications per place:	**7**	
From state-sector schools:	**93.3%**	
From working-class homes:	**28.7%**	

For detailed information about sports facilities:
www.brighton.ac.uk/sportbrighton

Accommodation

Number of places and costs refer to 2012–13

University-provided places: 2,015; 300 in private sector university-managed houses or flats.

Percentage catered: 44%

Catered costs: £128–£150 a week.

Self-catered costs: £97–£150 a week.

First years have priority for housing if conditions are met.

International students: guaranteed accommodation if conditions are met.

Contact: accommodation@brighton.ac.uk

University of Bristol

Bristol is the most popular multi-faculty university in Britain, judged in terms of applications per place – more than ten hopefuls vie for every degree slot. It has long been a natural alternative to Oxbridge, favoured particularly by independent schools, whose pupils take more than a third of the places. In order to broaden the intake, departments may make slightly lower offers to the most promising applicants from the bottom 40 per cent of schools and colleges at A level. Applications were down by 6 per cent at the start of 2012, but this was better than the national average and competition for places remained intense.

The university's academic credentials are not in doubt –the QS rankings for 2011 placed it in the top 30 in the world. Entry standards are among the highest at any UK university and Bristol continued to live up to expectations in the last Research Assessment Exercise, when almost two thirds of the work submitted was rated in the top two categories. Epidemiology and public health, health services research, chemistry, mathematics, drama, mechanical engineering and economics produced the best results. There are 33 Fellows of the Royal Society and similar numbers in other learned societies.

Scores in the National Student Survey have improved markedly, placing Bristol among the top 30 universities in 2011. Biology, human and social geography, chemistry and computer science scored particularly well. There has been gradual expansion to 12,625 full-time under-graduates, the university offering a limited number of additional places in arts and science subjects in 2012 for applicants with at least AAB at A level. But Bristol remains a relatively small city university.

Bristol has found it difficult to attract working-class teenagers, despite spending more than £15 million since 2006 on recruiting and supporting students from disadvantaged backgrounds. Some fear that they would be out of place socially, and few come from Scotland or the north of England. In 2010–11 only 14 per cent came from a working-class home – one of the lowest proportions outside Oxbridge. Generous bursaries and fee waivers represent the latest attempt to broaden the intake. Local students who take the Access to Bristol course while at school or college will receive free education if their family income is less than £25,000.

The university celebrated its centenary in 2009 and launched a new fundraising campaign with a target of £100 million by 2014. The previous campaign helped the university to create new chairs and embark on a number of building projects, including a well-appointed centre for the highly rated

---

Senate House
Tyndall Avenue
Bristol BS8 1TH

0117 928 9000 (switchboard)
ug-admissions@bristol.ac.uk
www.bristol.ac.uk
www.ubu.org.uk
Affiliation: Russell Group

The Times **Rankings**
Overall Ranking: **11**

Student satisfaction:	=17	(81%)
Research quality:	=7	(0.89)
Entry standards:	9	(478)
Student–staff ratio:	18	(14.3)
Services & facilities/student:	18	(£1,992)
Expected completion rate:	=6	(96.4%)
Good honours:	3	(83.2%)
Graduate prospects:	7	(79.2%)

chemistry department. Both chemistry and medical sciences were chosen to house national teaching and learning centres, and the university was also awarded four centres to train doctoral scientists and engineers.

An extensive programme of investment in academic facilities and student services is continuing. The Arts and Social Sciences Library has been refurbished and a £55-million life sciences building is due to open early in 2014. A new hall of residence at the Stoke Bishop site should be ready in the same year, ensuring that the university continues to fulfil its accommodation guarantee to new first years. A rolling programme of refurbishment is underway to modernise the existing halls.

An impressive sports complex with a well-equipped gym has been developed at the heart of the university precinct, where the careers centre has also been refurbished. The students' union houses one of the city's biggest live music venues as well as a café, bars, theatre and swimming pool. A £25-million refurbishment and redesign commenced in 2011, which will transform the building over the next four years, providing space for community activities and the 180 student societies and 50 sports clubs.

The city is one of the most attractive in Britain, as well as possessing a vibrant youth culture. It is also relatively prosperous, offering job opportunities to students and graduates alike. The university merges into the centre, its famous gothic tower dominating the skyline from the junction of two of the main shopping streets. Despite its hills, Bristol is England's first Cycling City and was the only UK city to be shortlisted for the European Green Capital Award 2010.

The current students' union is less of a social centre than in some universities, partly because of the intense competition from nightclubs. Most students enjoy life in Bristol, although the high cost of living can be a drawback. The dropout rate is among the lowest in Britain and one student in five stays in the city after graduation. Parts of the city suffer from the same security concerns as any big conurbation, but the university won a police-approved Secured Environments award for its crime protection work.

Undergraduate Fees and Bursaries

» Fees for UK/EU students 2012–13 £9,000
    For students with household income £15K or below £3,500
    For students with household income £20K or below £4,500
    For students with household income £25K or below £6,000
» International student fees 2012–13 £13,750–£16,750
    Dentistry, medicine, veterinary medicine £31,000
» For students in the Access to Bristol scheme with household income of £25K or below a full fee waiver and maintenance bursary of £3,750.
» Increased funding for university hardship funds.
» Scholarships and bursaries based on circumstances or by competition.
» Check the university's website for the latest information.

Students

Undergraduates:	**12,625**	**(1,450)**
Postgraduates:	**4,140**	**(1,775)**
Mature students:	**4.4%**	
Overseas students:	**12.2%**	
Applications per place:	**10.7**	
From state-sector schools:	**60.2%**	
From working-class homes:	**14.0%**	

For detailed information about sports facilities:
www.bris.ac.uk/sport

Accommodation

Number of places and costs refer to 2011–12
University-provided places: about 3,950
Percentage catered: 46%
Catered costs: £111.00 (shared room) – £184.50 a week.
Self-catered costs: £64 (shared room) – £130 a week.
First years are guaranteed one offer of accommodation provided conditions are met.
International students: accommodation is guaranteed provided conditions are met.
Contact: www.bristol.ac.uk/accommodation/

Brunel University

Still less than 50 years old, Brunel has invested more than £300 million in teaching, research and sporting facilities in recent years. The building programme has included a £6.5-million outdoor sports complex and a £7-million indoor athletics and netball centre, making a fitting home for the former Borough Road College and its illustrious sporting traditions, as well as serving the modern-day university. There is also a hugely extended university library, increased residential accommodation, more catering and social amenities and enhanced teaching and research facilities. A new accommodation complex comprising 1,188 en-suite rooms, 40 specially adapted rooms for disabled students and 112 studio flats opened in 2008. Other developments include a new engineering and design annex and a student facilities complex, featuring an atrium that opens onto a dining area, bars, the students' union and retail outlets.

In recent years, Brunel has introduced more variety into a portfolio of degrees that was once given over almost entirely to sandwich courses. Many undergraduates still take four-year degrees with extended work placements, but new developments have tended to be conventional three-year arts, humanities or sports programmes. There has also been significant growth in courses specialising in new technologies, such as multimedia design and broadcast media, as well as health and social care. Other innovations include creative writing, journalism, sonic arts, aviation engineering and pilot studies, motorsport engineering and games design.

Work placements and the inclusion in degree courses of skills modules, such as oral and written communication, business and computer literacy, have helped maintain a consistently good record in the graduate employment market. Many courses are validated by professional institutions. A recent survey placed Brunel graduates 13th in the UK for average starting salaries. At more than £22,000, the figure was almost £3,000 above the national average.

Substantial investment in research centres and academic recruitment produced significant improvements in the last Research Assessment Exercise, when Brunel registered one of the biggest increases in the numbers of staff entered. Almost nine out of ten academics were assessed, compared with barely more than six out of ten in 2001. With 43 percent of the work submitted judged to be world-leading or internationally excellent, the outcome was a 54 per cent increase in Brunel's research allocation from the Higher Education Funding Council for England. The extra money is being invested in 40 senior academic posts. Benjamin Zephaniah has recently taken

---

Uxbridge
Middlesex UB8 3PH

01895 265265 (admissions)
admissions@brunel.ac.uk
www.brunel.ac.uk
www.brunelstudents.com
Affiliation: none

The Times **Rankings**
Overall Ranking: **43**

Student satisfaction:	=17	(81%)
Research quality:	=42	(0.51)
Entry standards:	=44	(343)
Student–staff ratio:	59	(18.0)
Services & facilities/student:	32	(£1,680)
Expected completion rate:	44	(86.1%)
Good honours:	56	(63.1%)
Graduate prospects:	65	(61.3%)

up his first academic position as Chair of creative writing. Brunel's Institute for the Environment won a Queen's Anniversary Prize for its pioneering research revealing the link between chemicals in rivers and reproductive health.

Recent reviews of NHS-funded health programmes, including physiotherapy and occupational therapy, have been satisfactory and Brunel also scored well in its last institutional audit. Sporting excellence is also being maintained, with four graduates winning Olympic medals in 2008 and several students competing in the Games – notably Montell Douglas, who broke the British 100 metres record the day before she graduated. Brunel has also been selected as a pre-training site for the 2012 Olympics and is the training base for the South Korean Olympic team.

More than a third of the undergraduates are from working-class homes – significantly more than the national average for the subjects on offer – and more than half come from ethnic minorities. There is a large contingent of international students, some of whom benefited from a £100,000 scholarship programme in 2011. Applications have fluctuated in recent years, dropping in 2010 and increasing above the national average in 2011. At the start of 2012 there had been another decline, but only by 2.3 per cent, much less than most universities. The projected total of less than 10 per cent

leaving without a qualification is much better than the UK average for Brunel's subjects and entry grades, and an improvement on previous years.

Student union facilities are good and students like Brunel's intimacy, although this had not been reflected in National Student Surveys until 2011, when the university recorded the biggest improvement in the UK. Students in design, mathematics and statistics, history and anatomy were among the most satisfied in the country, as Brunel moved from the bottom ten universities into the top half of the table.

Residential stock has been greatly increased and all new first years are now guaranteed accommodation on campus. Brunel has won awards for its provision for disabled students, and its placement service.

Undergraduate Fees and Bursaries

» Fees for UK/EU students 2012–13   £9,000
» International student fees 2012–13   £11,330–£13,860
» For English students with household income below £25K, over 300 NSP awards: £2,000 fee waiver and £1,000 cash, voucher or fee waiver (1 year only); 380 Access scholarships for students from under-represented groups or who are mature: £1,000 (year 1), £1,500 (year 2), £2,000 (year 3) cash, voucher or fee waiver. Foundation Year scholarships, £1,000.
» Academic Excellence scholarship (AAA at A level and above), £3,000 fee waiver each year; six Local Borough scholarships, £5,000 fee waiver each year; other scholarships based on circumstances or by competition.

Students

Undergraduates:	**10,180**	**(455)**
Postgraduates:	**4,065**	**(1,515)**
Mature students:	**16.0%**	
Overseas students:	**14.1%**	
Applications per place:	**6.8**	
From state-sector schools:	**94.3%**	
From working-class homes:	**37.1%**	

For detailed information about sports facilities:
www.brunel.ac.uk/services/sport

Accommodation

Number of places and costs refer to 2012–13
University-provided places: 4,549
Percentage catered: 0%
Self-catered costs: £94.01 (standard) – £119.77; £180.04 (studio flat) a week (36 weeks).
All new full-time first-year students are eligible for on-campus accommodation.
International students: as above.
Contact: www.brunel.ac.uk/life/accommodation
accom-uxb@brunel.ac.uk

University of Buckingham

Britain's only private, not-for-profit university re-entered *The Times* League Table last year after an absence of more than a decade and almost made the top 20. Buckingham had too few students to be classified in some measures in the intervening period, but has seen dramatic growth in the last few years – the number of new entrants increased by 70 per cent in 2011. But the university has been a victim of its own success this year, falling 20 places because staffing levels and spending on student facilities have not kept pace with the expansion. Buckingham also suffered a big drop in graduate employment in 2010. Nevertheless, in the last six National Student Surveys, Buckingham students have emerged as among the most satisfied in England. The best results were in economics and politics, but almost every subject satisfied at least 90 per cent of final-year undergraduates in 2011.

Even before the latest rise in fees elsewhere, Buckingham claimed to be no more expensive than other universities because its intensive two-year degrees cut maintenance costs and accelerate entry into employment. Total fees for UK undergraduates taking the two-year degree from January 2013 are now £22,500, and there are further discounts for payment in advance. Overseas students pay £32,000 and there is a range of scholarships for both home and overseas candidates.

The university, which celebrated its 35th anniversary in 2011, still has only around 1,500 students and staffing levels that are bettered by only one university in the UK. One-to-one tutorials, which have all but disappeared outside Oxbridge and are by no means universal there, are common at Buckingham. The average teaching group contains about six students. Only its absence from the Research Assessment Exercise (which is open only to state-funded institutions) prevented the university from finishing even higher in the table. However, the university has a number of research groups and nearly 100 research students. Research income in 2011 was around £2 million.

A Conservative-backed experiment of the 1970s, Buckingham is now an accepted part of the university system. Although in 1992 it installed Baroness Thatcher as Chancellor, the university has no party political ties. Professor Terence Kealey, a biochemist from Cambridge University, has been Vice-Chancellor since April 2001, declaring an ambition for Buckingham to "one day" challenge the cream of American higher education. He has recruited a number of high-profile libertarians, including Sir Chris Woodhead, former Chief Inspector of Schools. The university's degrees carry full currency in the academic world and

---

Hunter Street
Buckingham MK18 1EG

01280 814080
info@buckingham.ac.uk
www.buckingham.ac.uk
www.buckingham.ac.uk/
   life/social/su
Affiliation: none

The Times **Rankings**
Overall Ranking: **41**

Student satisfaction:	=1	(87%)
Research quality:		(n/a)
Entry standards:	92	(276)
Student–staff ratio:	2	(10.7)
Services & facilities/student:	57	(£1,396)
Expected completion rate:	81	(79.3%)
Good honours:	117	(42.2%)
Graduate prospects:	14	(76.4%)

teaching standards are high. Education courses now have accreditation from the Training and Development Agency for Schools. Student numbers have doubled over the past three years, and were set to rise again at the start of 2012, when Buckingham enjoyed an unprecedented 200 per cent increase in UCAS applications.

The university runs on calendar years, rather than the traditional academic variety, although some courses give the option of entering in July or September. Most degree courses run for two 40-week years, minimising disruptive career breaks for the many mature students. Around 60 per cent of the students are from overseas, but the proportion from Britain has been growing. Students have the option of a three-year degree in the humanities and other schools are now following suit. Recent additions to the subjects on offer in Buckingham include a BSc in business enterprise and Masters programmes in finance and investment, security and intelligence studies and diplomacy. Masters programmes in biography, military history, modern war studies and decorative arts are now taught in London. A new BA in art history and heritage management offers the opportunity of a term at the British Institute in Florence. The most striking development, however, has been the postgraduate medical school launched in 2008 with a two-year MD in clinical medicine. The course attracts overseas medical graduates who find it difficult to secure junior doctor posts as a result of Government restrictions.

Buckingham operates on two sites within easy walking distance of each other. An academic centre containing computer suites, lecture theatres and student facilities provides a focal point that was missing previously. Two historic buildings have recently been refurbished at the cost of almost £2 million and a new six-acre site has been acquired to make room for future expansion. The social scene is predictably quiet, given the size of the university and the workload, especially at weekends. There is a university cinema and the town of Buckingham is pretty, with a good selection of pubs and restaurants. Milton Keynes or Oxford are nearby. Although Buckingham has no rail station, good bus services operate throughout the week with extra buses at weekends.

Undergraduate Fees and Bursaries

» Fees for UK/EU students for degree course starting in January 2013, £11,250 a year. Note that the course only lasts two years (eight terms).

» Fees for International students for degree course starting in January 2013, £16,000 a year. Note that the course only lasts two years (eight terms).

» For UK students with household income below £42K, a bursary of £1,000 a year.

» Check the university's website for the latest information.

Students

Undergraduates:	**935**	**(40)**
Postgraduates:	**520**	**(35)**
Mature students:	**35.9%**	
Overseas students:	**59%**	
Applications per place:	**4.2**	
From state-sector schools:	**75.6%**	
From working-class homes:	**22.9%**	

Accommodation

Number of places and costs refer to 2011–12
University-provided places: 567
Percentage catered: 0%
Self-catered accommodation: £92.31–£166.15 a week (47–50 weeks).
All new first-year students are guaranteed accommodation if they apply by the deadline.
International students: same as above.
Contact: accommodation@buckingham.ac.uk

Buckinghamshire New University

The start of 2012 saw the first decline in applications since Buckinghamshire New University took on its current status in 2007. But the intervening period had brought such growth in the demand for places that its popularity still far outstrips its days as a college of higher education. The first phase of a £200-million campus redevelopment was completed in 2009 and students have been responding enthusiastically to a portfolio of innovative courses and an attractive package of financial support and extra-curricular benefits for students.

The redevelopment allows most students to be based at the main campus in High Wycombe – the exception being those taking nursing, who have moved into a new building in nearby Uxbridge. The prize-winning Gateway Building at High Wycombe has transformed the town-centre campus with improved teaching, social and administrative space. The complex includes a new sports hall, gym, treatment rooms and sports laboratory, which are available to the public as well as to students. At the same time, collaboration with two of the world's biggest IT companies is resulting in one of the most advanced student networks in UK higher education.

Sport is an important part of life at the new university, which partners the London Wasps rugby union team in a relationship which trades coaching for Bucks students for courses for Wasps players. But the university's main aim is to contribute to the social and economic life of the region, embracing workplace learning and close ties with local businesses. Employees of the bed company Dreams, which is based in High Wycombe, take a new Foundation degree in retail management while at work, for example. A further innovation in 2010 was the establishment of the National School of Furniture with local employers and further education colleges, offering qualifications from certificate level to PhD.

Bucks has also won awards for its training of commercial pilots and its courses for music industry management. Other Foundation degrees include animation and visual effects, protective security management and sports coaching and performance, all run at partner colleges.

There are more than 9,000 full and part-time students, three quarters of whom are taking first degrees and 25 per cent of whom are over 25. Nearly 60 per cent of the students are female. Academic departments are divided into two faculties: Design, Media and Management, and Society and Health. The nursing provision is the largest in the London area and has growing links with the Imperial College London Healthcare Trust,

Queen Alexandra Road
High Wycombe
Buckinghamshire
HP11 2JZ

0800 0565 660 (enquiries)
advice@bucks.ac.uk
www.bucks.ac.uk
www.bucksstudent.com
Affiliations: Guild HE,
   million +

Edinburgh
Belfast
Cardiff
HIGH WYCOMBE
London

The Times Rankings

Overall Ranking: **106**

Student satisfaction:	=98	(74%)
Research quality:	=112	(0.02)
Entry standards:	111	(231)
Student–staff ratio:	112	(23.3)
Services & facilities/student:	23	(£1,923)
Expected completion rate:	64	(83.2%)
Good honours:	115	(47.2%)
Graduate prospects:	112	(48.7%)

including a joint appointment designed to promote innovation. The child nursing courses attract particularly good ratings. Only 26 staff were entered for the 2008 Research Assessment Exercise – half of them in art and design, which registered the only world-leading research. However, an institutional audit expressed "broad confidence" in academic standards.

The projected dropout rate for first years entering in 2009 improved again and, at less than 11 per cent, was considerably lower than at most comparable institutions and a full 8 percentage points better than the national average for its subjects and entry qualifications. Nor was this achieved by neglecting the Government's widening participation agenda: almost all the entrants are from state schools or colleges, and 37 per cent are from working-class homes. The university has a particular focus on student support: a third of its fee income was devoted to bursaries under the previous fee regime – one of the biggest proportions in England. The university's Big Deal, which was in place before the fees went up, provides free entertainment, recreational activities, events, and sports. A new mission statement stresses the university's determination to "put students first".

However, one disappointment has been the consistently low scores in the National Student Survey. Despite a big increase in the overall satisfaction rate in 2011, Bucks remained among the bottom ten universities. Only law and social work satisfied more than 80 per cent of final-year under-graduates in 2010, when language students registered a particularly low score. The university's own annual survey, carried out by independent academics, has been more complimentary. And the courses and lecturers attracted some of the most positive verdicts of any university on a national student reviews website.

Beyond the campus, High Wycombe has the usual range of pubs and clubs for a medium-sized town and central London is only 40 minutes away by train. More residential accommodation will be provided in the town centre in September 2012.

Undergraduate Fees and Bursaries

» Fees for UK/EU students 2012–13

New business degree	£6,000
Majority of degrees	£7,500
Art, design and production-based courses using workshops or studios	£8,000
» International student fees 2012–13	£8,900–£9,300

» For English students with household income below £25K and meeting criteria , NSP awards will provide £3,000 (year 1) or £1,500 (years 2 and 3) as fee waiver, accommodation voucher or a similar institutional service, or to include a cash bursary of up to £1,000 a year.

» "Big Deal" package which encourages participation in a range of sporting, recreational and social activities.

» Check the university's website for the latest information.

Students

Undergraduates:	**5,205**	**(3,280)**
Postgraduates:	**255**	**(510)**
Mature students:	**24.5%**	
Overseas students:	**9.1%**	
Applications per place:	**4.8**	
From state-sector schools:	**98.1%**	
From working-class homes:	**37.9%**	

For detailed information about sports facilities: www.bucksstudent.com

Accommodation

Number of places and costs refer to 2011–12
University-provided places: 780
Percentage catered: 0%
Self-catered costs: £87.64 (standard)–£136;.64 (studio) a week (42 weeks).
First-year students cannot be guaranteed accommodation.
Residential restrictions apply.
International students: priority allocation for first years.
Contact: accom@bucks.ac.uk

University of Cambridge

Cambridge had the most satisfied students in the UK in the 2011 National Student Survey (NSS), adding to a string of other accolades. It maintained its position as the top university in the world in the QS rankings, which place more emphasis on research than is the case in the undergraduate-focused *Times* table. Until 2001, Cambridge had also enjoyed an unbroken run at the top of our table, and even now it is practically inseparable from first-placed Oxford. The university produced the best results in the 2008 Research Assessment Exercise and still tops far more of our subject tables than any of its rivals. Nearly a third of its research was considered world-leading and over 70 per cent was rated in the top two categories. The university is particularly strong in the sciences, but has also increased its reputation in other areas.

Cambridge already had the highest entry standards of any UK university when it became the first to announce plans to use the new A* grade for admissions. As a result, the standard offer for entry in 2013 will be AAA* at A level. The only good news for applicants is that, for most degrees, the top grade can come in any subject. The bad news is that there will still be additional tests, such as Cambridge's own STEP papers, in a number of subjects.

At first, Cambridge students did not respond in sufficient numbers for the university to be included in the NSS. But in 2011, undergraduates in classics and philosophy were 100 per cent satisfied, while politics, sociology, religious studies, psychology, history, European languages, anthropology and archaeology all came close. The tripos system was a forerunner of the currently fashionable modular degree, allowing students to change subjects (within limits) midway through their courses. Students receive a classification for each of the two parts of their degree.

Almost 60 per cent of undergraduates now come from the state system, but the proportion of working-class undergraduates remains low, at little more than 10 per cent. Summer schools, student visits and, in some colleges, sympathetic selection procedures are helping to attract more applications from comprehensive schools and further education colleges. Although Cambridge is charging the full £9,000 undergraduate fee, there are £6,000 fee waivers for the poorest students and additional bursaries according to parental income. The application system has been simplified slightly, with candidates no longer required to complete an initial Cambridge form, as well as their UCAS form. However, they are still sent the Supplementary Application Questionnaire, after they have submitted their UCAS

The Old Schools
Trinity Lane
Cambridge CB2 1TN

01223 333308 (admissions)
admissions@cam.ac.uk
www.cam.ac.uk
www.cusu.cam.ac.uk
Affiliation: Russell Group

The Times Rankings
Overall Ranking: **2**

Student satisfaction:	=1	(87%)
Research quality:	1	(1.35)
Entry standards:	1	(596)
Student–staff ratio:	=7	(11.8)
Services & facilities/student:	3	(£2,994)
Expected completion rate:	1	(98.8%)
Good honours:	2	(87.4%)
Graduate prospects:	3	(84.4%)

form, covering the applicant's academic experience in more detail.

A lively alternative prospectus, available from the students' union, used to say there was no such thing as Cambridge University, just a collection of colleges. Where applications are concerned, this is still true. Making the right choice of college is crucial, both to maximise the chances of winning a place and to ensure an enjoyable three years if you are successful. Applicants can take pot luck with an open application if they prefer not to opt for a particular college. But, though the statistics show that this route is equally successful, only a minority takes it. Most teaching is now university-based, especially in the sciences, and a shift of emphasis towards the centre has been taking place more generally.

Cambridge boasts numerous successful partnerships with the private sector, several of which benefit undergraduates as well as researchers. The university was also chosen for a Government-sponsored partnership with the Massachusetts Institute of Technology to promote entrepreneurship and, more recently, was selected to host one of five Academic Health Science Centres to lead biomedical innovation.

A £1-billion funding appeal to mark the university's 800th anniversary, in 2009, reached its target two years early, making Cambridge the first university outside the USA to raise such a sum. The money has gone into bursaries and scholarships, professorships and teaching posts, and new buildings for research, teaching and student accommodation. Such is the scale of development that almost £500-million worth of building is either planned or under construction, with longer-term plans for expansion to the west of the city. Work is under way on new premises for materials science and metallurgy, and a £16-million sports centre is due to open in 2013.

With fewer than five applicants for each place – fewer still if you choose your subject carefully – the competition for places appears less intense than at the popular civic universities, but the real difference is that nine out of ten entrants have at least three A grades at A level. The amount of high-quality work to be crammed into eight-week terms can prove a strain, although the projected dropout rate of 1.1 per cent is the lowest at any university.

Undergraduate Fees and Bursaries

» Fees for UK/EU students 2012–13 — £9,000
» International student fees 2012–13 — £13,011–£19,800
   Medicine — £31,494
   College fees — £4,500–£5,500
» A bursary of £3,500 for students with household income less than £25K, tapered down to £50 for income of £42.6K, payable either as a grant or fee waiver.
» In addition for English students around 136 NSP awards of £6,000 fee waiver a year to students with low-income backgrounds.

Students

Undergraduates:	**12,015**	**(285)**
Postgraduates:	**6,460**	**(1,635)**
Mature students:	**4.7%**	
Overseas students:	**17.1%**	
Applications per place:	**4.8**	
From state-sector schools:	**59.0%**	
From working-class homes:	**10.6%**	

Accommodation

See chapter 13 for information about individual colleges.

For detailed information about sports facilities:
www.sport.cam.ac.uk

Canterbury Christ Church University

Canterbury Christ Church is celebrating the 50th anniversary of its establishment as a Church of England college, but the most rapid development has come in the seven years since it became a university. There are now 20,000 students on five campuses and the university has become the largest provider of higher education to the public services in Kent, particularly for teaching, health and social care, nursing and policing. The teacher training courses are rated "outstanding" by Ofsted. Primary Education has a unique record of successive outstanding ratings since 1996.

The network of campuses spreads across Kent, the most populous county in England but, until recently, one of the most sparsely provided with higher education. The purpose-built campus at Broadstairs, for example, focuses on arts and media courses such as commercial music, digital media, photography, and child and youth studies. There is an imposing country house outside Tunbridge Wells, mainly for postgraduates, as well as a newly expanded Medway site at Chatham that is shared with Greenwich and Kent universities and offers education and health programmes at a variety of levels, from Foundation degree to postgraduate.

The University Centre at Folkestone, also developed in partnership with Greenwich, offers performing and visual arts.

The majority of the students, however, are at the university's headquarters at Canterbury, a world heritage site and one of the safest university cities in Britain. The main campus, which dates from 1962, is a few minutes' walk from the city centre, but the university has several buildings in other parts of Canterbury. Augustine House and a £35-million library and student services centre, with specialist teaching and IT facilities, opened in 2009. It includes a café, two garden terraces, an atrium and multipurpose floor space for public events, conferences, exams, teaching and exhibitions. The Sidney Cooper Gallery, in the heart of the city, hosts exhibitions and workshops from visiting artists as well as work by students before the best goes on to be exhibited in London galleries.

The Church of England link was underlined with the installation of the Archbishop of Canterbury as the university's first Chancellor. A residential course for church music has recently been developed. The subject mix, with an emphasis on health subjects and education, means that seven out of ten students are female. Just over 97 per cent of the undergraduates are state-educated and more than a third come from working-class homes. The dropout rate improved significantly in the latest

---

North Holmes Road
Canterbury CT1 1QU

01227 782900 (enquiries)
admissions@canterbury.ac.uk
www.canterbury.ac.uk
www.ccsu.co.uk
Affiliation: Cathedral Group

The Times **Rankings**
Overall Ranking: **85**

Student satisfaction:	=89	(75%)
Research quality:	=101	(0.05)
Entry standards:	103	(258)
Student–staff ratio:	=53	(17.6)
Services & facilities/student:	99	(£1,098)
Expected completion rate:	=51	(85.0%)
Good honours:	=75	(59.0%)
Graduate prospects:	58	(62.9%)

projections and, at 11 per cent, is significantly better than average for the university's courses and entry qualifications. Graduates' job prospects are relatively good, with three-quarters going straight into employment and only 4 per cent unemployed six months after graduation.

Scores in the National Student Survey rose in 2011, and met the average for all institutions. Art registered a rare 100 per cent satisfaction rate, while education subjects also produced particularly good scores. Canterbury Christ Church was one of the new "teaching-led" universities, but was given the power to award research degrees in 2009. The university entered staff in seven areas in the 2008 Research Assessment Exercise. The best grades came in education and music, both of which had 10 per cent of their work assessed as world-leading.

All campuses are interconnected by a high speed regional data network, providing access to online teaching and learning materials, the student web portal and email. A new student and staff support service – i-zone – was introduced in 2009, which can be accessed online or via staff at the i-zone desks. The new Drill Hall Library at Medway provides 110,000 items, 400 computers and 280 study spaces. The bookshop on the Canterbury campus has been refurbished and extended, with a new "grab and go" café opposite.

Social and sports facilities naturally vary between the campuses, although the students' union is present on all of them. A new sports centre in Canterbury includes a fitness suite and a hall big enough for eight badminton courts. There is also a tennis court and netball court on campus and the university also has facilities at Polo Farm Sports Club close to the city. There are 12 acres of playing fields about a mile from the main campus.

Residential accommodation is available to all first years. The pressure is eased to some extent because more than 60 per cent of the students come from Kent, many of them among the 7,400 taking part-time courses. Another 204 single, en-suite student bedrooms and 10 three-bedroom family houses will be available in 2012 close to the main campus, where a student centre with a café bar, internet café and office space for the students' union will also open.

Undergraduate Fees and Bursaries

» Fees for UK/EU students 2012–13 £8,500
   Foundation degree at partner colleges £4,500
» International student fees 2012–13 £9,425
» Household income below £25K, fee waiver of £1,000 a year and bursary of £500 a year; for English students, household income below £25K and other criteria, NSP awards of £2,000 fee waiver and £1,000 cash bursary in year 1 only.
» Sports, music and other scholarships based on circumstances or by competition.

Students		
Undergraduates:	**9,240**	**(4,740)**
Postgraduates:	**1,520**	**(2,685)**
Mature students:	**27.8%**	
Overseas students:	**9.2%**	
Applications per place:	**4.4**	
From state-sector schools:	**97.4%**	
From working-class homes:	**33.8%**	

For detailed information about sports facilities:
www.canterbury.ac.uk/sport

Accommodation
Number of places and costs refer to 2012–13
University-provided places: 1,783
Percentage catered: 0%
Self-catered costs: £83–£175.00 a week.
Accommodation guaranteed for first years if conditions are met.
International students: as above.
Contact: accommodation@canterbury.ac.uk
www.canterbury.ac.uk/support/accommodation

Cardiff University

Cardiff offered the biggest inducement to high-fliers of any university in 2012, with the winner of its "Ultimate Scholarship" entitled to free tuition for life, even if he or she went on to take an MBA or a PhD. The eye-catching initiative was not born out of any threat to the university's position as the front-runner in Welsh higher education. Cardiff is the Principality's only member of the Russell Group of research-led universities and has two Nobel Laureates on its staff. Entry requirements have been rising and more than half of all applicants achieve at least AAB grades at A Level.

The university now has more than 28,000 students and nearly 6,000 staff. The student population is diverse with international students accounting for around 12 per cent, while a third of the intake comes from Wales. Applications dropped slightly in 2004, but by much less than the average for Wales or the UK as a whole. The 2008 Research Assessment Exercise rated almost 60 per cent of the submitted work in the top two categories, with 33 of the 34 subject areas containing some world-leading research. Journalism, media and cultural studies, English, city and regional planning, and business produced the best results.

Courses are accredited by more than 50 different professional bodies. An audit by the Quality Assurance Agency complimented the university on its "powerful academic vision and well-developed and effectively articulated mission to achieve excellence in teaching and research". Student support services, including counselling facilities and the help offered to dyslexics, were among the features singled out for praise. Cardiff was the first Welsh university to be awarded the Frank Buttle Trust Quality Mark which recognises support for students who were in care.

Cardiff has been a consistent performer in the National Student Survey. In 2011 some 86 per cent of final-year students were satisfied with the quality of their course. Planning, ophthalmics, physical geography and English were among the best performers. Many full-time degrees share a common first year, and the modular system makes undergraduate study flexible thereafter. Recent additions at degree level include marine geoscience, an MMath degree and a new portfolio of computing courses. Cardiff has been bucking the national trend with increases in applications in the physical sciences. One undergraduate in six comes from an independent school, but nearly one in five have a working-class background. The projected dropout rate is comfortably the lowest in Wales, at a little over 6 per cent.

The university occupies a significant part of the civic complex around Cathays Park

---

Cardiff
Wales CF10 3XQ

029 2087 4455 (enquiries)
enquiry@cardiff.ac.uk
www.cardiff.ac.uk
www.cardiffstudents.com
Affiliation: Russell Group

Edinburgh
Belfast
London
CARDIFF

The Times **Rankings**
Overall Ranking: **32**

Student satisfaction:	=42	(79%)
Research quality:	=32	(0.63)
Entry standards:	19	(437)
Student–staff ratio:	19	(14.4)
Services & facilities/student:	=69	(£1,307)
Expected completion rate:	20	(92.9%)
Good honours:	=32	(71.7%)
Graduate prospects:	15	(76.1%)

in the Welsh capital. The five healthcare schools at the Heath Park campus share a 53-acre site with the University Hospital of Wales. The university's new health education centre opened in 2011, offering students the latest teaching, library and simulation facilities. The Cochrane Building provides teaching and learning facilities for all healthcare schools based on the Heath Park Campus.

In recent years, there has been major investment in new buildings and equipment, and extensive refurbishment including a £4-million extension to the School of Biosciences and a £21-million building to house the School of Optometry and Vision Sciences. Current projects include a £30-million building which will house highly advanced facilities for some of the university's world-leading scientific teams.

Library services continue to be transformed in order to improve access to resources, increase the range of electronic resources, extend self-service provision and improve the environment for the study of rare collections. A new IT working environment gives students online access to information about their studies and social life, from reading lists and timetables to social events and networking groups. The campus is also wireless enabled, with over 1,300 access points.

Other recent developments include the Cardiff Award providing students with an opportunity to gain official recognition for learning acquired via extracurricular activities to support their employment prospects, and the students union's state-of-the-art "Lounge" aimed at international students. The School of Dentistry recently launched a new Dental Education Clinic offering students some of the UK's most modern training facilities, enabling them to treat patients in real-life situations.

Providing more than 5,100 study bedrooms, Cardiff's students can apply for residences which best suit their situations. The main residential site at Talybont boasts a "sports training village", and there is also a newly refurbished city-centre fitness suite and a sports ground available to students. It is to be an official training centre for Olympic football at the 2012 Games.

Undergraduate Fees and Bursaries

» Fees for UK/EU students for 2012–13: £9,000, with Welsh Assembly non-means-tested grant to pay fees above £3,465 for Welsh students.

» International student fees 2012–13   £11,900–£15,000
Medicine, dentistry   £26,500

» Cardiff University Bursaries for students with household income below £30K, top up to £7,500 the value of maintenance grants and loans; £30–£42.6K, top up to £6,750 the value of maintenance grants and loans. Care leaver and Community First bursaries also available.

» Around 100 scholarships of £1,500 (year 1) and £750 (years 2 and 3) to students achieving grades AAA at A-level in certain subject areas; other scholarships available.

Students

Undergraduates:	**16,765**	**(3,930)**
Postgraduates:	**4,405**	**(3,740)**
Mature students:	**13.1%**	
Overseas students:	**11.1%**	
Applications per place:	**6.2**	
From state-sector schools:	**82.9%**	
From working-class homes:	**19.8%**	

For detailed information about sports facilities:
www.cardiff.ac.uk/sport

Accommodation

Number of places and costs refer to 2012–13
University-provided places: 5,171
Percentage catered: 5.4%
Catered costs: £86–£103 a week.
Self-catered costs: £71–£101 a week.
All first years (except Clearing students) are guaranteed accommodation if conditions are met.
Policy for international students: as above
Contact: residences@cardiff.ac.uk

Cardiff Metropolitan University

Cardiff Metropolitan adopted a new name on its departure from the University of Wales, stressing its location in the Welsh capital, and almost immediately came under pressure to change it again by merging with two of its rivals. The former University of Wales Institute Cardiff has resisted ministerial demands for amalgamation with Glamorgan and Newport universities, and threatened legal action to maintain its independence. Students seeking places for 2013 will apply to Cardiff Met and will pay fees of £7,500, rather than the £9,000 charged in 2012, after the funding council agreed to reimburse universities that lowered their fees. Those from Wales will probably continue to pay only £3,465.

The university's three campuses have been benefiting from a £50-million programme of improvements. The £20-million Cardiff School of Management opened on the Llandaff campus in 2010, offering improved facilities for business, hospitality and tourism. A new campus centre, with a shop and catering facilities, was also added in 2010, along with an Information Zone for student services such as accommodation. The Cyncoed campus already had a new student centre with a nightclub and all the normal catering and leisure facilities. Next, a £10-million building on the Llandaff campus will bring Cardiff School of Art and Design together on one site.

The university had the best scores among the post-1992 universities in Wales in the 2011 National Student Survey. English studies, medical subjects, dance, history and food science led the way. Ratings by overseas students in the International Student Barometer were even more positive, placing the university top in Wales. Applications had been rising, but there was a 17 per cent decline at the start of 2012.

Two thirds of the 13,500 students are Welsh, half of them from Cardiff or the Vale of Glamorgan. Some 94 per cent attended state schools and nearly a third come from working-class homes. The dropout rate slipped back above 15 per cent in the latest survey and is marginally worse than the UK average for the university's subjects and entry grades.

Cardiff Met is one of Britain's leading centres for university sport, with team performances to match some excellent facilities. In recent years, the university has had British university champions in sports ranging from archery and gymnastics to squash, weightlifting and judo. More than 300 past or present students are internationals in 30 sports. Fourteen of them appeared at the New Delhi Commonwealth Games, bringing home three medals. The

---

Llandaff Campus
Western Avenue
Cardiff CF5 2YB

029 2041 6070 (enquiries)
courses@cardiffmet.ac.uk
www.cardiffmet.ac.uk
www.cardiffmetsu.co.uk
Affiliation: University
 Alliance

The Times **Rankings**
Overall Ranking: **=78**

Student satisfaction:	**=55**	(78%)
Research quality:	**=80**	(0.10)
Entry standards:	**93**	(272)
Student–staff ratio:	**=88**	(19.9)
Services & facilities/student:	**79**	(£1,263)
Expected completion rate:	**65**	(82.9%)
Good honours:	**92**	(54.6%)
Graduate prospects:	**=99**	(52.2%)

£7-million National Indoor Athletics Centre is Cardiff Met's pride and joy, but other facilities are also of high quality.

Academically, the large Cardiff School of Art and Design is the star performer, with 70 per cent of the work submitted to the 2008 Research Assessment Exercise rated either world-leading or internationally excellent. Sport also registered some world-leading research and all six teacher training courses are rated as excellent by Estyn, the school inspectorate.

Entrance requirements are generally modest, but the menu of largely vocational courses means that many students come with qualifications other than A levels. Just over a fifth are mature students and more than 1,000 are international students from 143 different countries. Many are postgraduates, who make up nearly a quarter of the student population – the largest proportion in Wales. Cardiff Met courses are also taught at partner colleges in Kuala Lumpur, Singapore and Dhaka.

The three Cardiff sites are all within three miles of the city centre. The Cyncoed campus, housing education and sport, is the main centre of activity, particularly for first years. As well as the new student centre, the athletics centre is there, together with a multitude of outdoor facilities and also the Welsh Sports Centre for the Disabled. Student facilities have been upgraded recently. The IT suite has 250 computers available 24 hours a day. For the moment, Howard Gardens is the home of fine art, while the Llandaff campus hosts design, engineering, food science and health courses. The student centre at Llandaff includes a dyslexia support unit among a number of advice and representation services, and a learning centre with more than 300 computers.

The enterprising students' union owns a nightclub and bar in the city centre to add to the campus choices. During term-time, the Rider bus service links all the campuses with other parts of Cardiff. There are enough hall places to accommodate most first years, but recent expansion means that some have to rely on the private sector. Cardiff Met has been awarded the Government's Charter Mark four times, the judges commenting particularly on the level of satisfaction among students.

Undergraduate Fees and Bursaries

» Fees for UK/EU students for 2012–13 £9,000, with Welsh Assembly non-means-tested grant to pay fees above £3,465 for Welsh students. For 2013–14, fees £7,500.

.» International student fees 2012–13 £8,400–£9,600
Podiatry £11,400

» Bursaries for care leavers, £1,000 a year; bursaries for Welsh students from Community First areas, £1,000 a year.

» Scholarships for highest academic achievers on entry, based on UCAS score (£3,000), Welsh study scholarships (up to £3,000).

Students

Undergraduates:	**7,540**	**(840)**
Postgraduates:	**1,800**	**(3,300)**
Mature students:	**21.1%**	
Overseas students:	**11.9%**	
Applications per place:	**4**	
From state-sector schools:	**94.1%**	
From working-class homes:	**31.7%**	

For detailed information about sports facilities: www3.uwic.ac.uk/English/sport

Accommodation

Number of places and costs refer to 2012–13
University-provided places: 934
Percentage catered: 34%
Catered cost: £125.50–£135.50 a week (£81.50–£91.50 outwith term)
Self-catered costs: £82.50–£100.50 a week.
First-year students have no guarantee; terms and conditions apply.
International students: accommodation is reserved, subject to availability and if conditions are met.
Contact: accomm@cardiffmet.ac.u

University of Central Lancashire (UCLan)

At the heart of the city of Preston, the University of Central Lancashire (UCLan) has developed into one of the largest universities in the country, with 38,000 students. UCLan has invested over £100 million in new buildings and facilities, including the £13-million Sir Tom Finney Sports Centre and a £12.5-million building to house the university's forensic science, chemistry and fire courses – both of which opened in 2011. New facilities for business, computing, dentistry, health, media, nuclear science, pharmacy, psychology and sport have been added in recent years, as well as an award-winning students' union building. The campus also boasts Europe's largest 3-D lecture theatre and a 24-hour-access library. The dental school was one of the first to open in over a century, while the architecture degree launched in 2009 was the first new such course for ten years.

To coincide with the new fees and funding system, the university has launched the UCLan Advantage: a new package of benefits that aims to help its students once they graduate. The scheme includes the provision of guaranteed structured work experience for every student who requests it. Many undergraduates also have the opportunity to study abroad for a period. UCLan has a strong international dimension, including research collaborations such as the work undertaken by a nanotechnology research team based in China. Travel bursaries enable students to undertake periods of overseas work experience and they have the opportunity to study a range of world languages, including Arabic, Chinese, Japanese and Russian. UCLan was the only UK university to break into the QS World University Rankings in 2010.

The university also has a strong focus on entrepreneurship and has established a range of business incubation facilities for its students and graduates. The Futures Centre brings together advice on careers and work placements, employability and enterprise course electives, business start-up and self-employment services. UCLan ranks in the top five nationally for the number of student business start-ups.

A former polytechnic, UCLan has a high reputation in some apparently unlikely fields. Astrophysics benefits from two observatories in Britain and a share in the Southern African Large Telescope, its academics working closely with NASA. Linguistics and journalism were classed as world-leading in the last Research Assessment Exercise and in total, 17 areas contained work considered world-leading or internationally excellent. The Confucius Institute promotes and supports

---

Preston
Lancashire PR1 2HE

01772 892400 (enquiries)
cenquiries@uclan.ac.uk
www.uclan.ac.uk
www.yourunion.co.uk
Affiliation: million+

Edinburgh
Belfast
PRESTON
London
Cardiff

The Times Rankings
Overall Ranking: **71**

Student satisfaction:	=55	(78%)
Research quality:	=78	(0.11)
Entry standards:	67	(297)
Student–staff ratio:	=64	(18.5)
Services & facilities/student:	36	(£1,639)
Expected completion rate:	104	(74.3%)
Good honours:	100	(52.3%)
Graduate prospects:	77	(57.7%)

the development of Chinese language and culture throughout the North West region.

UCLan's Burnley campus gives local students the opportunity to take degree or Foundation degree courses without leaving home. In collaboration with Cisco Systems, the campus is the location for an advanced manufacturing "factory of the future" facility incorporating robotics, computer vision, non-destructive testing and component assembly. There is a Centre for Outdoor Education at Llangollen, North Wales, while the university's West Cumbrian Campus, in Westlakes, focuses primarily on nuclear skills training. Ranked as the fourth greenest university in the UK, UCLan has become one of only five higher education institutions to hold both ISO 14001 certification and the Carbon Trust Standard. The university runs modules in sustainability and was the first in the UK to install solar trackers.

Electives are used to broaden the curriculum, so that up to 11 per cent of students' time is spent on subjects outside their normal range. Scores in the National Student Survey have been steady, with fine art, tourism, transport and travel, media studies, sports science, drama and law ranked in their respective top 20s for 2011. The university reluctantly opted for £9,000 fees, promising a "comprehensive student package" to ensure that UCLan remains accessible to all. Nearly four out of ten

Central Lancashire students come from working-class homes, and a high proportion of students are local people in their 20s or 30s. Almost 20 per cent of the university's students are taught in colleges and UCLan has won official praise for the quality of its external programmes. Applications increased in 2010 and 2011. Although they dropped at the start of 2012, the decline was well below the national average.

UCLan's impressive sports facilities will be used as official training venues for the Olympic Games and the 2013 Rugby League World Cup. Preston's social scene may not compare with Manchester or Liverpool, but neither do the security risks, and the cost of living is low. The students' union, which boasts one of the biggest student venues in the country, won the "Best Campus Venue 2011" award from Live UK Music.

Undergraduate Fees and Bursaries

» Fees for UK/EU students 2012–13 £9,000
  Burnley campus £7,000
» International student fees 2012–13 £9,450–£10,450
» UCLan Advantage will provide portable financial credits to contribute, for example, towards the cost of UCLan accommodation, buying food on campus or an overseas placement: a student with household income below £25K will receive a bursary of £3,000 in year 1 with opportunities for bursaries in years 2 and 3.
» Scholarships, including "Excellence in Sport" scholarships based on circumstances or by competition.

Students

Undergraduates:	**18,640**	**(9,205)**
Postgraduates:	**1,425**	**(2,775)**
Mature students:	**24.4%**	
Overseas students:	**9.2%**	
Applications per place:	**4.6**	
From state-sector schools:	**98.2%**	
From working-class homes:	**39.2%**	

For detailed information about sports facilities:
www.uclan.ac.uk/sport.

Accommodation

Number of places and costs refer to 2012–13
University-provided places: around 2,000
Percentage catered: 0%
Self-catered costs: £83.00 (standard) – £99.47 (en suite) a week (42 weeks).
The Student Accommodation Service will assist all first years find suitable accommodation either in University owned/leased halls of residence, private sector registered halls, or shared houses.
International students: as above.
Contact: www.uclan.ac.uk/study/accommodation/index.php

University of Chester

Chester cut its intended fee for degree courses by £1,000 to gain access to the pool of places reserved for universities with low charges, but it was not enough to prevent a 13 per cent fall in applications. However, the university did secure nearly 300 extra places as a result, and healthy increases in demand over the previous two years left it with plenty of competition for entry. There were almost nine applications to the place in 2011.

The picturesque Roman city of Chester is one of those places that outsiders probably always expected to have its own university. Indeed, William Gladstone was among the founders of the first Church of England teacher training college there in 1839. Although it took until 2005 for that college to achieve university status, it had been building up a solid reputation in a number of subjects beyond education.

The main campus is only a short walk from the centre of Chester, a 32-acre site boasting manicured gardens and a number of new developments. A new students' union is just one of a stream of improvements, including the opening of a second campus in the city in 2007. A third base was added in 2010, following the purchase of historic County Hall in Chester, which now houses the faculties of Health and Social Care and Education and Children's Services.

The Warrington campus, which has eight halls of residence, focuses on the creative industries and public services. It has seen the addition of high-quality production facilities in collaboration with Granada Television. The university has also signed a partnership agreement with the BBC, which is intended to open up new employment opportunities and develop new talent following the transfer of parts of the corporation to Salford in 2011. The library has been tripled in size, and a business centre opened for students and local firms. Warrington is expected to be the focus of future developments. Around £1 million has been spent on sports provision, including two new tennis courts, a 100-metre sprint track, and a floodlit, 3G multi-use sports pitch.

Chester was among the top ten universities in the first National Student Survey, but then slipped down the table. The 2011 survey showed a big increase in satisfaction, with archaeology, English, geography, nursing and theology leading the way to the university's best-ever results and helping the university to move 12 place up *The Times* League Table. Chester was the first of the universities created in 2005 to be granted the power to award research degrees. Four of the ten subject areas entered for the last Research Assessment Exercise contained at least some world-leading work. History was the most

---

Parkgate Road
Chester CH1 4BJ

01244 512528 (admissions)
enquiries@chester.ac.uk
www.chester.ac.uk
www.chestersu.com
Affiliation: Cathedral Group

The Times **Rankings**
Overall Ranking: **59**

Student satisfaction:	=42	(79%)
Research quality:	=108	(0.03)
Entry standards:	=82	(283)
Student–staff ratio:	=42	(16.6)
Services & facilities/student:	60	(£1,364)
Expected completion rate:	84	(78.6%)
Good honours:	71	(60.0%)
Graduate prospects:	45	(67.1%)

successful, with nearly half of its submission placed in the top two categories.

With more than 15,400 students, including part-timers, Chester is among the biggest of the new universities. More than a fifth of the undergraduates are over 20 on entry and two-thirds are female. Nearly all are state-educated, and 36 per cent have working-class roots. The projected dropout rate has been improving and, at 14 per cent, now matches the national average for the university's courses and entry standards. About a third of the undergraduates take combined honours degrees. There is also a limited range of Foundation degrees, mainly in health subjects. The Foundation degree in mortuary science was the first of its kind, as was one for guide dog trainers. Even the more traditional degrees have been designed to support the practical and vocational demands of the professions. Many include an extended period of work experience. Initial teacher training courses have been rated "outstanding" by Ofsted.

A student contract of the type that is set to become universal in higher education sets out clear conditions on the offer of a place, as well as detailing the university's responsibilities. Students promise to "study diligently, and to attend promptly and participate appropriately at lectures, courses, classes, seminars, tutorials, work placements and other activities which form part of the programme." The university undertakes to deliver the student's programme, but leaves itself considerable leeway beyond that. However, Chester offers considerable academic support for its students. It was the first UK university to receive the maximum five-star rating from the British Quality Foundation for its student support and guidance and for its careers and employability departments.

There are extensive sports facilities at Warrington and especially on the main campus at Chester, catering partly for the large sports science and physical education programmes. Most first years are offered one of the growing number of hall places, although there is not yet enough university accommodation to make this a guarantee. Student union facilities form the basis of the social scene on both campuses, but the city of Chester also has a great deal to offer.

Undergraduate Fees and Bursaries

» Fees for UK/EU students 2012–13   £8,000
    Foundation degrees   £7,000
» International student fees 2012–13   £9,060
» Household income below £25K, £500 a year fee waiver; for English students, 200 NSP awards for students with lowest household income below £25K, fee waiver year 1 £3,000, years 2 and 3 £500; students from targeted partner schools and colleges with household income below £42K eligible for £500 a year fee waiver.
» Scholarships and bursaries based on circumstances or by competition.
» Check the university's website for the latest information.

Students

Undergraduates:	**7,565**	**(4,235)**
Postgraduates:	**880**	**(2,720)**
Mature students:	**22.2%**	
Overseas students:	**1.7%**	
Applications per place:	**8.5**	
From state-sector schools:	**97.1%**	
From working-class homes:	**36.0%**	

For detailed information about sports facilities:
www.chester.ac.uk/campus-life

Accommodation

Number of places and costs refer to 2011–12
University-provided places: approx 1,040
Percentage catered: 45% (including semi-catered)
Catered costs: £70.70–£129.50 a week.
Self-catered costs: £63.35–£102.90 a week.
First years cannot be guaranteed accommodation.
International students: guaranteed accommodation if they apply by the advertised date.
Contact: www.chester.ac.uk/campus-life/accommodation

University of Chichester

The smallest of the nine universities created in 2005, Chichester features consistently among the leading modern universities in league tables. It resumed its position as the top post-1992 university in the 2011 National Student Survey after a big increase in overall satisfaction to 87 per cent throughout the university. History and philosophy registered 100 per cent satisfaction and drama and education were not far behind. However, none of this prevented a drop of more than 20 per cent in the number of applications when fees rose to £8,500 for degree courses in 2012. Chichester added extra fee waivers to qualify for places from the pool of 20,000 reserved for institutions charging the lowest fees and was awarded more than 150.

The university traces its history back to 1839, when the college that subsequently bore his name was founded in memory of William Otter, the education-minded Bishop of Chichester. It became a teacher training college for women, who still account for two thirds of the places. Two further stages preceded university status – 20 years as the West Sussex Institute of Higher Education, following an amalgamation with the nearby Bognor Regis College of Education, and then seven as University College Chichester. The Chichester campus – now the larger of two – continues to carry the Bishop Otter name, signifying a continuing link with the Church of England.

The two faculties each operate on both sites, one covering business, teacher training and IT; the other the arts, history, media, sport and social sciences. The portfolio of some 300 courses ranges from adventure education to humanistic counselling, fine art and the psychology of sport and exercise. The PE teacher training course is one of the largest in the country – recently training one in five PE teachers in England – and is highly rated by Ofsted. Sport was the only area in which the university registered any world-leading work in the 2008 Research Assessment Exercise, but history and drama, dance and performing arts also produced good results.

The university is financially stable, having reported a surplus of more than £2 million last year. It holds nearly £10 million in reserves and considers itself one of the best placed institutions to deal with the challenges of the future. It is near to completing developments in Bognor Regis that cost £13 million, the majority of which has be spent transforming the Dome into a business and research centre and creating a new learning and resource centre.

The Alexandra Theatre, in Bognor, is used as a base for the musical theatre programme and there are links, too, with the Chichester Festival Theatre. The

---

Bishop Otter Campus
College Lane
Chichester
W. Sussex PO19 6PE

01243 816002 (admissions)
admissions@chi.ac.uk
www.chi.ac.uk
www.chisu.org
Affiliation: Cathedral
Group

The Times **Rankings**
Overall Ranking: **61**

Student satisfaction:	=17	(81%)
Research quality:	=101	(0.05)
Entry standards:	=68	(295)
Student–staff ratio:	=62	(18.4)
Services & facilities/student:	96	(£1,147)
Expected completion rate:	=34	(89.0%)
Good honours:	=75	(59.0%)
Graduate prospects:	95	(53.5%)

Mathematics Centre, at Bognor, has an international reputation, working with over 30 countries as well as teaching the university's own students. It has become a focal point for curriculum development in Britain and elsewhere. Chichester runs short courses for education ministries in countries as diverse as Bhutan, Russia and the Seychelles.

Graduate employment rates have been good for a number of years. In the last survey published, only 4 per cent were thought to be jobless, but the relatively high proportion starting off in non-graduate work pushes Chichester down our table on this measure. About 20 per cent of the 5,000 students are over 20 on entry and almost a third come from working-class homes, although this is less than the average for the university's courses and entry grades. The projected dropout rate remained below 8 per cent in the latest survey, approaching half the benchmark figure. The university runs summer taster sessions and has a series of partnerships with schools in the Channel Islands and Sussex to encourage a broader intake. Courses are also run in collaboration with Isle of Wight College.

Both of the university's campuses are within ten minutes' walk of the sea and the 647 residential places are roughly equally divided between them. There is a university bus service linking the two and students' union bars at each. Sports facilities are good and competitive teams surprisingly successful for such a small university. The university was chosen to provide training facilities for competitors in athletics, boxing, road cycling and table tennis before the 2012 Olympic Games. The Barbados team will be taking advantage of Chichester's expertise in sports science and medicine in the run-up to the Games.

The small cathedral city of Chichester is best known as a yachting venue and, while Bognor's days as a leading holiday resort are well in the past, it is said to have the longest stretch of coastline in the south where all types of water sports are available. Both locations offer a good supply of private housing and some student-oriented bars. Much of the surrounding countryside has been designated an area of outstanding natural beauty.

Undergraduate Fees and Bursaries

» Fees for UK/EU students 2012–13   £8,500
» International student fees 2012–13   £9,200–£10,500
» Students with household income below £25K, £1,500 as fee waiver, £1,000 as bursary or fee waiver; with a household income of £25K–£42K, £1,000 as bursary or fee waiver; for English students, NSP award for year 1 £3,000 fee waiver, year 2 £2,000 as fee waiver, £1,000 as bursary or fee waiver, year 3 £1,500 as fee waiver, £1,000 as bursary or fee waiver; care leaver bursaries available.
» Scholarships and bursaries based on circumstances or by competition.
» Check the university's website for the latest information.

Students		
Undergraduates:	**3,680**	**(715)**
Postgraduates:	**335**	**(980)**
Mature students:	**20.6%**	
Overseas students:	**2.6%**	
Applications per place:	**5.8**	
From state-sector schools:	**96.5%**	
From working-class homes:	**31.7%**	

For detailed information about sports facilities:
www.chi.ac.uk/student-life/life-campus/sport

Accommodation

Number of places and costs refer to 2011–12
University-provided places: 647
Percentage catered: 66.5%
Catered costs: £116.41 (twin) – £155.05 (single, en suite) a week (37 or 40 weeks).
Self-catered costs: £91.00 (shared) – £128.10 (en suite) a week (37 or 40 weeks).
First years are accommodated on a first come, first served basis.
International students: as above.
Contact: www.chi.ac.uk/student-life/accommodation

City University London

City set the highest undergraduate fee in England for 2012–13 after fee waivers and other financial support were taken into account, according to the Office for Fair Access. The university has a better record than most of its peers for widening participation in higher education, with over 40 per cent of its undergraduates coming from working-class homes. But, despite offering over 70 National Student Scholarships and investing more than £1 million a year in outreach and retention activities such as summer schools, City was expected to spend only £270 of each £9,000 fee promoting wider access. However, the university has promised to invest heavily in new academic staff and student related facilities, focusing particularly on the recruitment of more research-oriented academics. City is aiming to be ranked among the top 2 per cent in the world and to be London's only university to be committed to business and the professions, as well as academic excellence. It set out to be "significantly more selective" in 2012, when degree applications dropped by 15 per cent.

Marketing itself as the "international university in the heart of London", City added the name of the capital to its title to make the most of its greatest asset. Students come from more than 160 different countries to study on the borders of the financial district. Once a college of advanced technology, City now has roughly a quarter of its students taking business courses, another quarter health and community subjects, and the remaining half law, computing, mathematics, engineering, journalism and the arts.

The university reaps the benefits of its strong links with business and the professions with consistently good graduate employment figures. City's graduates play their part, with nearly 2,000 of them offering practical help to current students through an online careers network. Courses have a practical edge, and many of the staff hold professional, as well as academic, qualifications. A number of interdisciplinary centres have been launched to increase collaborative teaching and research, as well as to build stronger links between industry and academia. There are now more than 17,000 students, and because around a fifth of them are from outside the EU and around 40 per cent are postgraduates, City is less dependent on Government funding than many other universities. It is also among the most popular, with over eight applications for each undergraduate place.

Development is continuing at the university's Islington campus. Some £20 million went into an impressive new building for the School of Social Sciences, interactive classrooms and a modern

---

Northampton Square
London EC1V 0HB

020 7040 5060
contact via website
www.city.ac.uk
www.culsu.co.uk
Affiliation: none

The Times Rankings

Overall Ranking: **46**

Student satisfaction:	=89	(75%)
Research quality:	48	(0.43)
Entry standards:	41	(372)
Student–staff ratio:	=42	(16.6)
Services & facilities/student:	25	(£1,865)
Expected completion rate:	=47	(85.7%)
Good honours:	39	(69.0%)
Graduate prospects:	31	(71.7%)

electronics laboratory in 2009 for the School of Engineering and Mathematical Sciences. The library has been renovated at a cost of £2.3 million, giving students more space, upgraded technology and better support. More recently, the Student Centre and Careers Centre, have been refurbished and a new common room for students was put in over the summer of 2011. Future projects include moving the School of Health Sciences to the main campus with new facilities including a new biomedical and clinical skills centre. The School of Law will also be having their accommodation upgraded over the summer of 2012.

The £42-million Cass Business School is one of City's great strengths. It has 3,000 students and is ranked among the top 50 business schools in the world. Based in the heart of the financial district, it has built up an impressive cadre of visiting practitioner lecturers who find it easy and convenient to visit. City has links with 50 European universities and many more farther afield, and many students spend a year of their course abroad. The City Law School, which incorporated the Inns of Court School of Law in 2001 was the first in London to offer a "one-stop shop" for legal training, from undergraduate to professional courses. The School of Journalism, within the School of Arts is highly regarded and the university has launched the UK's first graduate school of journalism in new £12-million facilities. There is a flourishing short course programme for adults, which ranges from sitcom writing to e-business.

City has a particularly high reputation in music, where it is associated with the Guildhall School of Music and Drama. Together with nursing and midwifery, music achieved the university's best results in the 2008 Research Assessment Exercise. Social work and social policy also produced good results. Like other universities in London, City has struggled to make an impression in the National Student Survey, finishing low down the table in 2011. Aerospace engineering and music received high marks for teaching, while finance, management and business studies produced high overall satisfaction levels.

The students' union is popular, but sports facilities are poor by current standards. However, the Sports Centre is due to undergo a planned £7.2-million investment and redevelopment.

Undergraduate Fees and Bursaries

» Fees for UK/EU students 2012–13 £9,000
» International student fees 2012–13 £10,000–£11,500
» For English students with household income below £16K and other criteria, 150 NSP awards of £2,000 fee waiver and £1,000 cash bursary or fee waiver.
» For students with at least AAB or equivalent, Lord Mayor of London Scholarship of up to £3,000 a year and other scholarships based on circumstances or by competition.
» Check the university's website for the latest information.

Students

Undergraduates:	**7,780**	**(1,850)**
Postgraduates:	**4,945**	**(2,930)**
Mature students:	**26.3%**	
Overseas students:	**24.5%**	
Applications per place:	**8.8**	
From state-sector schools:	**91.0%**	
From working-class homes:	**41.2%**	

For detailed information about sports facilities: www.city.ac.uk/sport-and-leisure..

Accommodation

Number of places and costs refer to 2012–13
University-provided places: 1,141
Percentage catered: 0%
Self-catered costs: £144–£284 a week.
Accommodation is guaranteed for first years if conditions are met.
Residential restrictions apply.
International students: preference is given to new overseas students.
Contact: accomm@city.ac.uk
www.city.ac.uk/study/why-study-at-city/accommodation

Coventry University

Coventry took its rivals by surprise by opening its own university college for 2012 as a cut-price option for people who do not want the full student experience. Its courses will lead to Coventry degrees or diplomas, but fees are only £4,800 a year because most campus facilities will not be available. The initiative appears not to have affected the demand for places on the main university courses, where fees range from £7,500 for classroom-based degrees to £9,000 for specialist subjects such as automotive engineering. Overall applications had risen by 2 per cent at the start of 2012.

Coventry is in the throes of a £160-million investment to rejuvenate its 33-acre campus close to the city centre. Much of the ten-year programme involves student facilities such as the showpiece turreted library, which cost £20 million. The latest development is a brand new Students' building, containing the new students' union offices, a live music venue for up to 800 people, three floors of informal study space, convenience stores and restaurants. A new home for the Faculty of Engineering and Computing will open in September 2012, and there are plans to pedestrianise much of the university. Other facilities have already been added, including more residential accommodation, a £7-million arts centre and a sports centre.

Coventry traces its origins back to 1843 and its links with the motor industry of the Midlands were reflected in its earlier title of Lanchester Polytechnic, named after a leading engineering figure. It has adopted an innovative approach to computer-assisted learning, supported by an expanded computer network. The university was chosen to house national centres of excellence in teaching for e-learning in health and social care, as well as in maths, and transport and product design.

The university has a focus on employment, which is reflected in a predominantly vocational curriculum. The Start-Up Café encourages business networking and local employers are engaging with the programme of work-based learning. The Add+vantage scheme is designed to help full-time under-graduate students improve their employability whilst studying. Its modules cover a wide range of skills and help students gain work-related knowledge and prepare for a career.

The majority of students exercise their right to take "free-choice modules" that cover the full range of university provision, with IT skills and languages particularly popular. Coventry has been building up its portfolio of courses, introducing eye-catching degrees in subjects such as ethical hacking and network security, disaster management, forensic chemistry, criminology and boat design.

Priory Street
Coventry CV1 5FB

024 7615 2222 (admissions)
studentenquiries@coventry.ac.uk
www.coventry.ac.uk
www.cusu.org
Affiliation: million+

The Times **Rankings**
Overall Ranking: **55**

Student satisfaction:	=17	(81%)
Research quality:	=93	(0.07)
Entry standards:	80	(287)
Student–staff ratio:	=29	(15.4)
Services & facilities/student:	=87	(£1,205)
Expected completion rate:	=89	(78.0%)
Good honours:	64	(61.2%)
Graduate prospects:	48	(66.8%)

The 2011 National Student Survey saw a big increase in satisfaction levels, helping to move Coventry 20 places up the main table this year. There were wide subject variations, with politics students 100 per cent satisfied and those in sociology and social policy only a fraction behind. But transport registered an unusually low score. Research grades improved in the 2008 assessments, when small amounts of world-leading work were recognised in seven of the 16 areas the university submitted. Art and design and electrical and electronic engineering produced the best results. Design benefits from a revolutionary £1.6-million digital modelling workshop, sponsored by the Bugatti Trust, which provides full-scale vehicle modelling facilities.

Among the initiatives to improve the student experience has been the introduction of tangible rewards for excellent teaching and further development of electronic learning. The Centre for Academic Writing offers advice on essays and theses, with group sessions and one-to-one appointments, while the Maths Support Centre includes a statistics advisory service and specialist support service for students with dyslexia.

More than most universities, Coventry is a creature of its city, and the civic-minded approach of the university has created many town–gown links. The university's main buildings open out from the ruins of the bombed cathedral, as university and public facilities mingle in the city. Student residences are within easy walking distance of the campus and city centre. However, the university has also opened a business-oriented campus in London, which enrolled its first undergraduates in 2011. A degree in global business management will include a workplace project and a period of study abroad. The campus, close to Liverpool Street station, also offers one-year top-up programmes giving international students entry into the final year of a BA degree.

Students in Coventry welcome the relatively low cost of living there. Almost 40 per cent of the undergraduates have working-class backgrounds. The projected dropout rate had improved significantly in the latest survey, and, at 14 per cent, is better than the national average for the university's courses and entry qualifications.

Undergraduate Fees and Bursaries

» Fees for UK/EU students 2012–13   £7,500–£9,000
    Foundation degree   up to £6,000
» International student fees 2012–13: £9,375–£11,250 (Coventry)
    £10,375–£13,500 (London)
» Household income below £25K, around 200 NSP awards for students from local institutions plus other criteria, fee waiver, £2,000, £500 cash and £500 credit for university services for year 1, continued into years 2 and 3, based on performance
» Students with AAB at A Level or equivalent eligible for Academic Excellence scholarship of £1,000 cash or £1,500 discount on university accommodation each year.
» Sports scholarships up £3,000 a year.

Students

Undergraduates:	**14,620**	**(8,050)**
Postgraduates:	**3,015**	**(2,125)**
Mature students:	**19.4%**	
Overseas students:	**15%**	
Applications per place:	**5.5**	
From state-sector schools:	**96.1%**	
From working-class homes:	**37.5%**	

For detailed information about sports facilities:
www.coventry.ac.uk/sportandrecreation

Accommodation

Number of places and costs refer to 2012–13
University-provided places: 2,439 (includes 235 beds on Nomination Agreements)
Percentage catered: 24%
Catered costs: £117 a week (10 meals).
Self-catered costs: £97.50–£145.00 a week.
First-year students are guaranteed housing provided conditions are met.
International students: as above.
Contact: www.coventry.ac.uk/cu/accommodation

University of Cumbria

Cumbria is reshaping its network of campuses after mothballing one of them and cutting a number of courses to cope with serious financial problems. Plans for a £70-million development in Carlisle had already been put on hold and the Ambleside campus closed pending a review. Now Ambleside is to be reopened – although not accommodating students until 2014 – for the university's forestry, outdoor studies and science programmes. The Newton Rigg campus, outside Penrith, which presently houses some of these courses, will become a field centre for research and development. It has been a turbulent period for the university, which is only five years old, but the finances are now said to be on an even keel and the demand for places has held up. Degree applications were up by 5 per cent at the start of 2012, although other courses saw a more serious decline. This followed three years of strong growth in the demand for places at all levels.

The new university, which has more than 12,000 students, was finally established in 2007, after a series of false starts. It was formed by the amalgamation of a former teacher training college and an arts institute, with the addition of the two Cumbrian campuses of the University of Central Lancashire.

The university is by far the largest provider of higher education in the historically underprovided county of Cumbria. It is divided between Carlisle, Penrith, Ambleside and Lancaster, as well as running a specialist teacher education centre in east London. There are partnerships with the four further education colleges in the county to provide higher education locally. The university is opening a base of its own at Furness College, in Barrow in Furness, and has already established Learning Gateway West, another teaching centre, at the Energus Building in Workington.

Although the headquarters remain in Carlisle, the biggest of the component parts is the former St Martin's College, which was founded in Lancaster by the Church of England in 1964 to train teachers and expanded during the 1990s with the addition of a nursing college. It forms the new university's main base, a ten-minute walk from Lancaster town centre. The Gateway, a £9.2-million development, opened in 2009 providing a range of student services and there is a modern library and excellent sports facilities, including a £2.5-million sports complex, gymnastics centre and fitness centre.

There are two main sites in Carlisle, the larger of which is in a parkland setting close to the River Eden. The second campus, closer to the city centre, boasts a new Learning Gateway, an innovative

---

Fusehill Street
Carlisle, Cumbria CA1 2HH

0845 606 1144 (enquiries)
enquirycentre@cumbria.ac.uk
www.cumbria.ac.uk
www.thestudentsunion.
    org.uk
Affiliations: Cathedral Group,
    Guild HE

The Times **Rankings**

Overall Ranking: **=97**

Student satisfaction:	**=108**	(72%)
Research quality:	**=115**	(0.01)
Entry standards:	**=96**	(268)
Student–staff ratio:	**50**	(17.2)
Services & facilities/student:	**91**	(£1,174)
Expected completion rate:	**72**	(81.1%)
Good honours:	**=65**	(61.1%)
Graduate prospects:	**69**	(60.4%)

multimedia learning resource centre, and a sports centre with a four-court sports hall and well-equipped fitness room. The former Cumbria Institute of the Arts can trace its history in Carlisle back to 1822, eventually becoming the only specialist institute of the arts in the North West, and one of only a small number of such institutions in the country. The creative arts are one of the main areas for development in the university's initial planning. Policing will also move to Carlisle as part of the reorganisation.

Further education courses taught at Newton Rigg, a former agricultural college with two farms, are being taken over by Askham Bryan College. All other courses will be fully transferred by 2015 and some of the land sold off to help finance the reorganisation of the university's estate. The Ambleside campus will be refurbished and new amenities provided in conjunction with the Lake District National Park Authority. Research has already restarted there and the campus is intended to host more business and enterprise activity, as well as some new courses.

Cumbria made its debut in the lower reaches of *The Times* League Table, but is now only just in the bottom 20 despite a 15-place drop this year. However, the university was bottom of the initial rankings from the 2008 Research Assessment Exercise, recording only a small amount of world-leading research in theology, divinity and religious studies. There was a big improvement in National Student Survey scores in 2011, but Cumbria remained among the bottom ten universities. Forensic science and some of the health courses produced excellent results, but no other subjects satisfied 90 per cent of final-year undergraduates.

The focus of the university has been on attracting more students from a region of low participation in higher education, as well as on serving the social and economic needs of the county. Almost all the students are from state schools and colleges and more than a third are from working-class homes. The proportion from areas without a tradition of higher education is also well above the national average for the university's subjects and entry grades.

Undergraduate Fees and Bursaries

- » Fees for UK/EU students 2012–13 £7,850
  Foundation degree £6,000
  Teacher training £9,000
- » International student fees 2012–13 £9,600-£10,200
- » Household income less than £25K, 296 Cumbria bursaries of £1,500 cash a year. For English students with household income below £25K and other criteria, 128 NSP awards, year 1, £2,000 fee waiver, £1,000 cash, years 2 and 3, £1,500 cash.
- » Scholarships and bursaries based on circumstances or by competition.
- » Check the university's website for the latest information.

Students

Undergraduates:	**5,700**	**(2,595)**
Postgraduates:	**1,065**	**(1,820)**
Mature students:	**29.9%**	
Overseas students:	**1.4%**	
Applications per place:	**3.5**	
From state-sector schools:	**97.8%**	
From working-class homes:	**35.7%**	

For detailed information about sports facilities: www.cumbria.ac.uk/StudentLife/Sport

Accommodation

Number of places and costs refer to 2012–13

University-provided places: 1,000

Percentage catered: 65%

Catered costs: £72.00–£78.00 a week (plus catering plan).

Self-catered costs: £51.50–£95.00 a week.

First years are guaranteed halls accommodation if Cumbria is first choice.

International students: guaranteed halls accommodation if conditions are met.

Contact: www.cumbria.ac.uk/FutureStudents/Accommodation

De Montfort University

De Montfort has recovered some of the ground it lost last year in *The Times* League Table, thanks particularly to improved student satisfaction and completion rates. It already had one of the best scores for research at any post-1992 university, having seen 43 per cent of its work rated world-leading or internationally excellent in the last Research Assessment Exercise. Almost all the subject areas contained some world-leading research and in the case of English language and literature the proportion reached an outstanding 40 per cent. Drama, dance and performing arts and communication and media studies also produced excellent results.

Successes in the previous assessments laid the foundation, helping to bring in an income of about £10 million a year in external research grants and contracts. The university has 500 staff engaged in research and 600 research degree students. Much of the successful work took place in the Institute of Creative Technologies, which acts as a catalyst for research that defies the traditional boundaries of computer science, the digital arts and humanities, and which excites the interest of the business world. Some £3.7 million was spent on creative technology studios, which feature video, audio and radio production suites, recording studios and laboratories with the latest broadcast and audio analysis technology. A Performance Arts Centre for Excellence allows the university to deliver innovative teaching for students of dance, drama and music technology.

Once a network of campuses spreading far beyond Leicester, De Montfort has invested £143 million on returning to a more manageable estate. The entire institution is now once again on one campus. The last piece in the jigsaw saw nursing and midwifery move into new premises for the health and life sciences. Four further education colleges across the East Midlands are associates, linked into the university's network and offering its courses.

Other campus developments included the diversion of part of the ring road to allow the university to open up the 15th-century Magazine Gateway building, which has become the focal point of a university quarter with public open spaces and new links to the city centre. A prize-winning building for business and law, which opened in 2010, is at its heart. The Hugh Aston Building, which cost £35 million and caters for around 6,000 students, includes a court room, law library, dedicated law clinic and bookshop, as well as more conventional teaching facilities. Elsewhere, the 24-hour library has been remodelled with wireless networks and rooms equipped with audio visual and IT facilities, and new game

---

The Gateway
Leicester LE1 9BH

08459 454647 (enquiries)
contact via website
www.dmu.ac.uk
www.demontfortstudents.
 com
Affiliation: University
 Alliance

The Times Rankings
Overall Ranking: **72**

Student satisfaction:	=42	(79%)
Research quality:	60	(0.18)
Entry standards:	=78	(288)
Student–staff ratio:	=60	(18.1)
Services & facilities/student:	100	(£1,084)
Expected completion rate:	68	(81.7%)
Good honours:	=98	(52.8%)
Graduate prospects:	84	(56.0%)

development studios have been installed to enable students to see their work in 3-D. An £8-million leisure centre, with a 25-metre swimming pool, eight courts for indoor sports, a gym, multipurpose studios, a climbing wall and a café, opens in July 2012 and will also be available to the public.

The professional accounting courses achieved "premier" status in a global accreditation scheme, and the university was awarded a national teaching centre for drama, dance and theatre studies. Recent results in the National Student Survey have been good, with history, human resource management, marketing and English producing the best results in 2011. However, applications had still dropped by 11 per cent – a little more than the national average – at the start of 2012.

Among the recent additions to the portfolio of courses is a degree in digital marketing and social media. Others include a BSc in green energy technology and another in public and community health, tackling issues such as increases in sexually transmitted infections and obesity. Strong links with local business and industry manifest themselves in courses such as the BSc in media production, run in conjunction with the BBC. There is also a new agreement to work with Hewlett-Packard on innovative educational programmes to better connect academia and business, as well as to collaborate on research.

The dropout rate has improved considerably: at 13 per cent, it is now lower than the national average for the university's courses and entry grades. De Montfort has gone back to a three-term year, partly because it believed the prospect of imminent assessment encouraged some students to give up at Christmas in their first year. The university has a proud record for widening access to higher education with almost 40 per cent of students coming from working-class homes. It was one of the first to set up an employment agency to help students find part-time work as well as find careers upon graduation.

Accommodation difficulties have been addressed, with the addition of new halls within walking distance of lectures, although all first years cannot be guaranteed a place in halls. Rents in the private sector are low.

Undergraduate Fees and Bursaries

» Fees for UK/EU students 2012–13 £9,000
   Foundation degree £6,000
» International student fees 2012–13 £10,250–£10,750
» Household income below £25K, DMU Bursary of £1,000 cash a year. For English students, 480 NSP awards for those with lowest household income, year 1, £2,000 fee waiver and £1,000 cash, years 2 and 3, £1,500 fee waiver.
» Care leaver and estranged student bursaries.
» Academic scholarships of £1,000 a year; bursaries of £1,000 a year for students on access courses.
» Check the university's website for the latest information.

Students

Undergraduates:	**14,545**	**(3,215)**
Postgraduates:	**1,360**	**(3,295)**
Mature students:	**14.1%**	
Overseas students:	**6.7%**	
Applications per place:	**5.1**	
From state-sector schools:	**96.8%**	
From working-class homes:	**38.8%**	

For detailed information about sports facilities: www.dmu.ac.uk/study-information/ student_services/..

Accommodation

Number of places and costs refer to 2012–13
University-provided places: around 2,680
Percentage catered: 0%
Self-catered costs: £95–£164 a week.
First years cannot be guaranteed accommodation.
International students: new students are guaranteed accommodation.
Contact: accommodation@dmu.ac.uk

University of Derby

Derby was one of the universities that suffered most in terms of applications in the switch to higher fees. Although the university restricted most fees to £6,995, with some specialist subjects costing £7,995, the demand for places dropped by almost a quarter at the start of 2012. The good news was that the decline followed two of the biggest increases in applications at any university, so the total was little different to that in 2010. Derby's adjustment was aided by its success in the allocation of more than 300 extra places from the national pool reserved for universities with low fees.

The university has enjoyed a rise of 18 places in this year's *Times* league table, but its own target is to become the pre-eminent university of its type by 2020. Its yardsticks are student satisfaction, employability, service to business and flexibility, delivered cost effectively.

Higher entry grades have coincided with the recruitment of more students from affluent families, but still almost four in ten undergraduates are from working-class homes and two in ten are from areas of low participation in higher education – well above the national average for the courses and entry qualifications. The latest projected dropout rate had improved considerably, but was still above 20 per cent, a little above the benchmark figure for the university.

Campus developments are continuing, all part of a £75-million estates strategy that has created a University Quarter for the city of Derby. The second campus in Buxton is based in the former Devonshire Royal Hospital and offers courses in spa, outdoor recreation and hospitality management, as well as further education programmes. The landmark building, which has a bigger dome than St Paul's Cathedral, houses a training restaurant, a beauty salon and a health spa, as well as more conventional teaching facilities. A new Sports Centre opened in Buxton in 2011.

There are two main sites in Derby: an extended academic campus at Kedleston Road, two miles from the city centre, and a residential campus close to the city's entertainment district. Kedleston Road caters for most of the main subjects including all business, computing, science, humanities and law courses. The Markeaton cluster hosts arts, technology and some social science and health. The students' union, multi-faith centre and main sports facilities are here. The £1.5-million clinical skills suite features hospital wards, counselling rooms and diagnostic radiography facilities. The site's three tower blocks have been refurbished in a £13.5-million project, which will make them more energy efficient with the installation of photovoltaic panels and wind turbines.

Kedleston Road
Derby DE22 1GB

01332 590500 (admissions)
askadmissions@derby.ac.uk
www.derby.ac.uk
www.udsu.co.uk
Affiliation: million+

The Times **Rankings**
Overall Ranking: **89**

Student satisfaction:	=55	(78%)
Research quality:	=108	(0.03)
Entry standards:	=89	(278)
Student–staff ratio:	=60	(18.1)
Services & facilities/student:	66	(£1,326)
Expected completion rate:	=96	(76.1%)
Good honours:	101	(52.0%)
Graduate prospects:	=99	(52.2%)

A new all-weather sports pitch was added in 2009. The university has acquired the 550-seat Derby Theatre to house theatre arts programmes as well as continuing as a producing theatre. Students have access to the main auditorium as well as their own 112-seat studio theatre.

The sites are within 10 minutes walk of each other as well as being linked by free shuttle buses and the UniBus service, which also connects with the train station and city centre. Derby also has a centre in Chesterfield to teach nursing.

A Foundation programme allows students to begin work at a partner college before transferring to the university. Derby has also awarded more work-based qualifications than any other UK university. Business and management is by far the university's biggest academic area, but work placements are encouraged in all relevant subjects. The accent on employability continues through the "Skillbuilder" career development programme, which covers a range of transferable skills to give graduates an edge in the employment market. Derby is at the forefront of development of a Higher Education Achievement Record that students can make available electronically to prospective employers.

Derby was quick to adopt new teaching methods, pioneering the use of interactive video for a national scheme. Distance learning is a growth area, either online or through Derby's nine regional centres. Prospective students can even sample a virtual open evening. A variety of courses, from Foundation degrees to postgraduate qualifications, are available online. The university won an award for the imaginative use of distance learning.

The university spent £30 million in five years to maintain its guarantee of accommodation for all first years and has improved student facilities. Students seem to appreciate these efforts because Derby comes out well in its own satisfaction surveys, although this has not been reflected in the national equivalent. Scores in the National Student Survey continue to improve, but the university remained in the bottom half of the table in 2011. History and music both achieved 100 per cent satisfaction, with initial teacher training not far off this mark.

Undergraduate Fees and Bursaries

» Fees for UK/EU students 2012–13

Classroom-based courses (40 per cent)	£6,995
Resource -intensive courses (40 per cent)	£7,495
Specialist "signature courses" (20 per cent)	£7,995

» International student fees 2012–13   £9,700–£10,250
» For English students with household income below £25K and other criteria, 300 NSP awards, £2,000 fee waiver and £1,000 cash grant in year 1 only. Retention bursaries available.
» Scholarships based on circumstances or by competition.
» Check the university's website for the latest information.

Students

Undergraduates:	**10,490**	**(4,150)**
Postgraduates:	**815**	**(2,145)**
Mature students:	**29.6%**	
Overseas students:	**9.4%**	
Applications per place:	**6.1**	
From state-sector schools:	**97.6%**	
From working-class homes:	**38.5%**	

For detailed information about sports facilities:
www.teamderby.com

Accommodation

Number of places and costs refer to 2012–13
University-provided places: 2,500
Percentage catered: 0%
Self-catered costs: £89.32–£112.49.
First-year students are guaranteed accommodation if they apply before 31 July.
Policy for international students: as above.
Contact: studentliving-housingteam@derby.ac.uk;
www.derby.ac.uk/halls
Student Living – tel: 01332 594111 (126 Nuns St, Derby, DE1 3LQ))

University of Dundee

Dundee has doubled in size over the past 20 years and has been enjoying a surge in popularity recently. Applications rose again in 2012, following a 15 per cent increase in the previous year, when some of the university's competitors saw a decline in demand for places. There are now has nearly 17,000 students, including a healthy number from overseas. Dundee has been looking outwards to achieve the "critical mass" which experts regard as essential to break into the higher education elite, with the acquisition of education, nursing and art colleges, which greatly increased its scope. But it resisted ministerial encouragement to amalgamate with Abertay University in 2012 but agreed instead to collaborate more closely with its neighbour.

Dundee describes itself as "Scotland's most enterprising university" and, while there would be other claimants to that title, it has certainly been among the liveliest in recent years. A long series of good quality ratings have been complemented by high-profile research successes, especially in the life sciences and medicine. A £200-million campus redevelopment designed by the leading architect, Sir Terry Farrell, is now complete. Almost £40 million of this was spent on wireless-networked student residences. The IT facilities include a "superfast" broadband network and are among the best in the UK, allowing the latest technologies to be used to enhance teaching. Education and social work moved into a new teaching block on the main campus in 2008, and there have been extensions to the library and the sports centre. Best-known for the life sciences, where research into cancer and diabetes is recognised as world-class, the university has already opened new buildings for clinical research, interdisciplinary research and applied computing.

Set in 20 acres of parkland, the medical school is the one of the few components of the university outside the compact city-centre campus – some of the nursing and midwifery students are 35 miles away in Kirkcaldy. Biochemistry is the flagship department, housed in a complex that includes the £13-million Wellcome Trust Building and the Sir James Black Centre, which cost £21 million. Its academics were the first in Britain to be invited to take part in Japan's Human Frontier science programme and are now the most-quoted researchers in their field. The university is also to lead one of four "knowledge exchange hubs for the creative economy", tasked with bringing academics together with business and charities, and raising public awareness of the creative industries.

More than half the work submitted for the 2008 Research Assessment Exercise was

---

Nethergate
Dundee DD1 4HN

01382 383838 (enquiries)
contactus@dundee.ac.uk
www.dundee.ac.uk
www.dusa.co.uk
Affiliation: none

The Times **Rankings**
Overall Ranking: **44**

Student satisfaction:	=34	(80%)
Research quality:	47	(0.47)
Entry standards:	39	(382)
Student–staff ratio:	17	(14.2)
Services & facilities/student:	73	(£1,299)
Expected completion rate:	=69	(81.6%)
Good honours:	34	(71.2%)
Graduate prospects:	43	(68.2%)

rated world-leading or internationally excellent. Dundee recorded the best results in Scotland for art and design, civil engineering, biological and laboratory-based clinical sciences. The university has also produced consistently good scores in the National Student Survey. In 2011, there was 100 per cent satisfaction in history and politics, with high scores in physical geography and environmental science, medicine and pharmacology, law, European languages, English, economics, computer science and anatomy.

Vocational degrees predominate, helping to produce the university's consistently good graduate employment record. The university sends more graduates into the professions than any other institution in Scotland, and only Oxbridge graduates came out ahead of Dundee's in a national survey of starting salaries. Most degrees include a career planning module and an internship option, and students are now provided with their own personal development website. Among the new courses introduced recently are dual qualifying law (Scots and English), digital interaction design and business computing. The highly rated design courses are taught at the former Duncan of Jordanstone College of Art.

There has been an emphasis on opportunities for women ever since Dundee's separation from St Andrews University, in 1967, and the addition of teacher training has increased the female majority. Two thirds of Dundee's students are from Scotland and nearly one in ten from Northern Ireland. One in five come from areas with little tradition of higher education and more than a quarter are from working-class homes. Private accommodation is plentiful for those who are not housed by the university. Applicants have access to MyDundee, an online portal giving further information about the university during the application process and to prepare them for the academic year.

The city is profiting from recent regeneration programmes. The university has been at the heart of a successful campaign to bring the Victoria and Albert Museum to Dundee by 2014. Spectacular mountain and coastal scenery are close at hand, but social life tends to be concentrated on one of the largest and most active students' union in Scotland.

Undergraduate Fees and Bursaries

» Fees for Scottish and EU students for 2012–13   No fee
» Fees for Non-Scottish UK (RUK) students for 2012–13: £9,000 a year, capped at a maximum of £27,000 regardless of course length.
» Fees for international students for 2012–13   £9,700–£13,335
   Medicine   £17,500–£26,750
» For RUK students, bursary or fee waiver of £3,000 a year if household income below £20K, and £1,000 a year if household income £20K–£42K.
» Check the university's website for the latest information.

Students

Undergraduates:	**9,280**	**(1,350)**
Postgraduates:	**1,865**	**(3,665)**
Mature students:	**25.8%**	
Overseas students:	**9.5%**	
Applications per place:	**7.4**	
From state-sector schools:	**88.5%**	
From working-class homes:	**27.9%**	

For detailed information about sports facilities:
www.dundee.ac.uk/ise

Accommodation

Number of places and costs refer to 2012–13
University-provided places: 1,587
Percentage catered: 0%
Self-catered costs: £107.66–£125.44 a week.
First-year students are guaranteed accommodation if conditions are met. No residential restrictions.
International students are guaranteed accommodation if conditions are met.
Contact: residences@dundee.ac.uk
www.dundee.ac.uk/studentservices/residences

Durham University

Durham was one of four universities to join the Russell Group of leading research universities in 2012. Many people already assumed that it was a member. Long established as a leading alternative to Oxford and Cambridge, Durham has a collegiate structure and picturesque setting that attracts a largely middle-class student body. The university has been attracting more applicants from non-traditional backgrounds, but more than 40 per cent of undergraduates still come from independent schools. All those who receive an offer are invited to a special open day to see if Durham is the university for them. Since around 80 per cent come from outside the northeast of England, most are seeing the small cathedral city for the first time.

Undergraduates apply to one of 14 colleges, all of which have been mixed since 2004. Colleges range in size from 300 to 1,100 students and are the focal point of social life, although all teaching is done in central departments. There are significant differences in atmosphere and student profile, ranging from the historic University College, in Durham Castle, to modern buildings on the city's outskirts and on Queen's Campus, 23 miles away at Stockton-on-Tees.

Durham has been among the top 20 universities in the National Student Survey for the last four years, with 90 per cent of final-year undergraduates satisfied in 2011. Theology recorded 100 per cent satisfaction, while history, classics and ancient history, business and modern languages all scored highly. Entrance requirements are among the highest in Britain – and with a dropout rate just over 2 per cent, Durham is among the top for degree completion. Durham has moved into the top five in *The Times* League Table this year and has also been moving up the world rankings, finishing in the top 100 in both the *Times Higher Education* and QS world rankings in 2011.

More than 60 per cent of the work submitted for the 2008 Research Assessment Exercise was rated world-leading or internationally excellent. Applied maths, archaeology and theology were among the best results in the UK. Music, English and geography and environmental science also did well. Investment continues on the Science Site, which will see the completion of a major development project in 2012. This will improve the student facilities and includes a library extension, a brand new law school and a student services building, the Palatine Centre.

As the third-oldest university in England, Durham is generally quite traditional. Wherever possible, teaching takes place in small groups and most assessment is by written examination. However, the

---

University Office
Old Elvet
Durham DH1 3HP

0191 334 6128 (admissions office)
admissions@dur.ac.uk
www.dur.ac.uk
www.dsu.org.uk
Affiliation: Russell Group

Edinburgh
Belfast
DURHAM
London
Cardiff

The Times Rankings
Overall Ranking: **5**

Student satisfaction:	=7	(83%)
Research quality:	=7	(0.89)
Entry standards:	6	(503)
Student–staff ratio:	=25	(15.3)
Services & facilities/student:	7	(£2,281)
Expected completion rate:	8	(96.2%)
Good honours:	7	(81.8%)
Graduate prospects:	9	(78.5%)

establishment of Queen's Campus in Stockton-on-Tees broke the mould. Initially a joint venture with Teesside University, Stockton is now home to a wide range of courses including applied psychology, business and business finance, anthropology and primary education. The campus has also seen the fulfilment of Durham's long-held ambition to restore the medical education it lost when Newcastle University went its own way in 1963. An innovative joint project allows students to do the first two years of their training at Stockton, concentrating on community medicine, before transferring to Newcastle to complete their degree.

Significant investment has been made to improve social facilities for the 2,000 students on the Queen's Campus, including the opening of a £5.5 million sports centre and facilities, relocating some of the university's elite sports activities from Durham as part of a strategy to increase integration between the two sites. The university's aim is for the campus to be equal in academic status to Durham City, focusing on interdisciplinary research and covering the full range of research, taught postgraduate and undergraduate study. The strategy would see both student and staff numbers at the campus double.

The university dominates the city of Durham to an extent which sometimes causes resentment, but adds considerably to the local economy. The 2009 National Student Housing Survey rated Durham top for private sector accommodation and second for halls of residence. For those looking for nightlife, or just a change of scene, Newcastle is a short train journey away. Sports facilities are excellent – with strong investment in facilities at both Durham and Stockton – and Durham is among the premier universities in national competitions: it came fourth in national student championships in 2010/11. Among the alumni are the current and former England cricket captains, Andrew Strauss and Nasser Hussain, and rugby World Cup winner, Will Greenwood. The university hosts centres of excellence in cricket, rowing and fencing, and offers a range of sports scholarships. Nine out of ten students take part in sport on a regular basis and Durham's College Sport programme is the largest intramural competition in the UK. Some 380 teams compete in 15 sports every week.

Undergraduate Fees and Bursaries

» Fees for UK/EU students 2012–13 £9,000
» International student fees 2012–13 £12,600–£16,100
» "Promise of Support" packages: household income below £25K, £3,000 a year support package as money off college living expenses or cash if living out, household income £25K–£42K, £1,000 a year support package.
» Academic, music, art and sports scholarships based on circumstances or by competition, up to £2,000.
» Check the university's website for the latest information.

Students

Undergraduates:	**11,300**	**(155)**
Postgraduates:	**3,155**	**(1,750)**
Mature students:	**7.3%**	
Overseas students:	**10.7%**	
Applications per place:	**6.5**	
From state-sector schools:	**59.5%**	
From working-class homes:	**14.0%**	

For detailed information about sports facilities:
www.teamdurham.com

Accommodation

Number of places and costs refer to 2012–13
University-provided places: 4,751
Percentage catered: 67%
Catered costs: £149.29 (38 weeks) – £165.94 (33 weeks).
Self-catered costs: £118.97 (38 weeks, Durham); £118.97 (38 weeks, Queen's campus).
All full-time students become members of one of the university's colleges or societies and are allocated housing if they want it.
International students: first years are guaranteed housing.
Contact: admissions@durham.ac.uk

University of East Anglia

UEA has been one of the big winners in the National Student Survey. Eight out of ten final-year undergraduates were satisfied overall in 2011, despite slipping to just outside of the top ten for the first time since results were published. Molecular biology, biophysics and biochemistry achieved 100 per cent satisfaction levels and so did aural and oral studies, while occupational therapy, physiotherapy and speech and language therapy were top in their field. Biological sciences, human and social geography for international development, and psychology, also registered extremely high scores. Students appear to like the scale of this relatively small campus university, as well as the quality of its courses. There had been strong growth in the demand for places until the 2012 fees rise, when they fell by 14 per cent – rather more than the national average.

The university has been engaged in an ambitious building and refurbishment programme on the 129-acre site on the outskirts of Norwich. It has included the provision of 700 more en-suite student bedrooms, a new health centre and the extension and refurbishment of the central library, catering facilities and students' union. The Square, the university's social centre, has been regenerated and new buildings added for the schools of nursing and midwifery and medicine, as well as for an INTO English language centre for overseas students. In keeping with the university's strong "green" credentials, a biomass generator facility is reducing the university's carbon emissions. An Enterprise Centre to develop students' entrepreneurial skills is planned for 2013.

Some of the broad subject combinations that the university pioneered from its origins in the 1960s are still highly regarded in the academic world. With successive 5* ratings for research followed by a good result in the 2008 Research Assessment Exercise, environmental sciences is the flagship school. UEA contributed more than any other university in the world to the 2007 Nobel Prize-winning Intergovernmental Panel on Climate Change. The Climatic Research Unit and the Government-funded Tyndall Centre for Climate Change Research, which has a hub in Shanghai, are among the leaders in the investigation of climate change. The university was at the centre of international controversy regarding climate data manipulation, but enquiries on two continents concluded that the allegations were groundless, although a lack of openness was criticised.

History of art and culture and media did even better in the latest RAE, with half of their research considered world-leading. Art history has the benefit of the Sainsbury Centre for the Visual Arts, perhaps the greatest resource of its type on any British campus. The refurbished and extended centre

---

Norwich NR4 7TJ

01603 591515 (admissions office)
admissions@uea.ac.uk
www.uea.ac.uk
www.ueastudent.com
Affiliation: 1994 Group

Edinburgh
Belfast
NORWICH•
London
Cardiff

The Times Rankings
Overall Ranking: **28**

Student satisfaction:	=12	(82%)
Research quality:	=32	(0.63)
Entry standards:	=32	(396)
Student–staff ratio:	=14	(13.9)
Services & facilities/student:	31	(£1,689)
Expected completion rate:	36	(88.4%)
Good honours:	38	(69.6%)
Graduate prospects:	59	(62.8%)

houses a priceless collection of modern and tribal art in a building designed by Norman Foster. Creative writing is another star-studded area, with authors Andrew Cowan, Giles Foden and Lavinia Greenlaw taking up where Andrew Motion and the late Malcolm Bradbury left off.

Health studies have been among UEA's fastest-developing areas. The university was awarded one of the first new medical schools for 20 years, and has since added pharmacy and speech and language therapy degree courses. Its first doctors graduated in 2007.

Almost nine out of ten undergraduates come from state schools or colleges, and over a fifth have a working-class background. Most have the opportunity of work experience as part of their course. An academic adviser guides all students on their options under the modular course system and monitors their progress through to graduation. The university is proposing to focus even more on employability with the introduction of £9,000 fees. Almost a third of undergraduates are expected to benefit from fee waivers or bursaries of up to £3,000 and there will be scholarships of £1,500 for students who achieve three A grades at A level or the equivalent. Dropout rates have fluctuated, but the latest projected figure of less than 9 per cent was below the national average for the university's subjects and entry standards.

Most students come from outside the region, although there is an unusually large contingent of mature students for a traditional university, who tend to be more regional. UEA opened University Campus Suffolk in 2007, in partnership with Essex University, with a main site in Ipswich and smaller bases in Bury St Edmunds, Great Yarmouth, Lowestoft and Otley.

The university is situated in parkland, with easy access to Norwich, which has been voted one of the best small cities in the world. The Sportspark, which was extended recently, boasts an Olympic-sized swimming pool, fitness and aerobics centres, athletics track, gymnastics facilities, climbing wall, courts and pitches. The university was chosen as the base for the English Institute of Sport in the East.

Undergraduate Fees and Bursaries

» Fees for UK/EU students 2012–13 £9,000
» International student fees 2012–13 £11,700–£14,400
  Medicine £24,500
» For each year of study, UK students with household income below £16K, £3,000; household income £16K–£20K, £2,000; household income £20K–£30K, £1,000; care leaver £3,000; all can be taken as full fee waiver, full accommodation discount, £1,000 cash plus remainder as fee waiver, or, from year 2, as cash.
» Entry Scholarships £1,500 cash for students with AAA or equivalent. Subject scholarships and annual Excellence Awards (£1,000) also available.
» Check the university's website for the latest information.

Students		
Undergraduates:	**10,730**	**(2,050)**
Postgraduates:	**2,610**	**(1,905)**
Mature students:	**18.1%**	
Overseas students:	**14.1%**	
Applications per place:	**7.1**	
From state-sector schools:	**89.2%**	
From working-class homes:	**22.6%**	

For detailed information about sports facilities:
http://sportspark.co.uk

Accommodation
Number of places and costs refer to 2012–13
University-provided places: 3,457
Percentage catered: 0%
Self-catered costs: £2,261.00–£4,184.18 (38 weeks)
First years are guaranteed accommodation if conditions are met. Distance restrictions.
International students (non EU) are guaranteed accommodation if conditions are met.
Contact: accom@uea.ac.uk
www.uea.ac.uk/accommodation

University of East London

The nearest university to the 2012 Olympic Park is making full use of the Games to cement its local links and project the high quality of its sports and academic facilities. The United States Olympic team is to be based at East London (UEL), using a new £21-million sports and academic centre at the Docklands campus, called the Sports Dock, which opened in March. Professor Patrick McGhee, the new Vice-Chancellor, has said that that the university's Olympic and Paralympic involvement, together with its location and the diversity of its students, give it a unique role in the area's regeneration.

The capital's first new campus for 50 years gave the university a new focal point, with its modern version of traditional university features like cloisters and squares. The university has spent more than £190 million on its Docklands campus, and is now unrecognisable from its early days as a pioneering polytechnic. Student residences and recreational facilities sit side by side with academic buildings in a prize-winning waterside development. The final pieces in the jigsaw were the business school and Knowledge Dock, a support centre for local companies, and a £40-million student village by the Royal Albert Dock, which added 800 more beds. The campus has helped to attract a 31 per cent increase in applications in 2010 and another 13 per cent rise in the following year. Student numbers have almost doubled since 2001, with students coming from 120 countries. However at the start of 2012, UEL could not escape the nationwide fall, and applications dropped by more than 15 per cent. UEL charged the full £9,000 undergraduate tuition fee in every subject. It also offered a "generous package" of scholarships and bursaries to ensure that potential students were not deterred from accessing higher education.

The university's original Stratford campus is being redeveloped, with a new library and learning centre, student residences and facilities for part-time and evening courses. The Great Hall in University House boasts a high-tech, 230-seat fully retractable lecture theatre, while the health and bioscience laboratories have been refurbished. The new Cass School of Education has now opened and law is next on the development agenda. A unique partnership project between UEL and Birkbeck, University of London, will see a new campus open in Stratford in 2013. The Stratford Island University Centre will house a selection of departments from each university and incorporate a range of flexible teaching and administrative spaces, alongside dedicated spaces for subjects including law, performing arts, dance, music and information technology.

Stratford Campus
Water Lane
London E15 4LZ

020 8223 3333 (admissions)
study@uel.ac.uk
www.uel.ac.uk
www.uelunion.org
Affiliation: million+

The Times **Rankings**
Overall Ranking: **=116**

Student satisfaction:	=77	(76%)
Research quality:	=75	(0.12)
Entry standards:	117	(205)
Student–staff ratio:	114	(23.7)
Services & facilities/student:	113	(£852)
Expected completion rate:	116	(61.1%)
Good honours:	116	(43.9%)
Graduate prospects:	113	(48.6%)

All but one of the nine subject areas in which UEL entered the 2008 Research Assessment Exercise contained at least some world-leading research. Communication, culture and media studies, produced particularly good results, while art and design and sociology also did well. Teacher training courses have been given good marks by Ofsted. Engineering and technology, psychology, social work and sports science achieved the highest satisfaction rates in what was a much improved set of results in the 2011 National Student Survey, which saw UEL move up 5 percentage points overall.

UEL is more concerned with extending access to higher education than competing with the elite universities. Barely more than half of first years arrive with A levels and very nearly half are over 21 on entry – many choosing to start courses in February. Many degrees are vocational and employers are closely involved in course planning. Almost 1,000 businesses are involved in mentoring programmes and/or a work-based learning initiative which offers accredited placements.

More than 40 per cent of UEL's students come from working-class homes and almost all are state-educated, many from the area's large ethnic minority populations. A successful mentoring scheme for black and Asian students has become a model for other institutions, while a guidance unit advises local people considering returning to education. UEL is also strong on provision for disabled students and houses the Rix Centre for Innovation and Learning Disability. The projected dropout rate has been improving – the latest figure of 14.5 per cent is better than average for UEL's courses and entry qualifications.

University housing is not plentiful, although there are now 1,200 bedspaces and the rents are good value for London. Priority is given to disabled students and those living farthest away. The social mix means that UEL has not been the place to look for the archetypal partying student lifestyle, although the Docklands campus is beginning to change this. Sports facilities and new students' union premises have been added at both Stratford and Docklands.

Undergraduate Fees and Bursaries

» Fees for UK/EU students 2012–13	£9,000
» International student fees 2012–13	£9,900
Architecture	£12,420
Physiotherapy	£14,040

» For students from local schools or colleges with household income below £25K, NSP awards in year 1 as £1,000 cash, £2,000 credit against accommodation and other study-related costs using UEL Progress Card.

» UEL Progress Bursary available for all who complete first semester: year 1, £500, years 2 and 3, £300 as credits to UEL Progress Card; care leaver bursary £1,000 per year; free textbook offer and enhanced study skills support.

» Other scholarships and bursaries are available.

Students

Undergraduates:	**13,880**	**(3,625)**
Postgraduates:	**3,750**	**(3,665)**
Mature students:	**49.5%**	
Overseas students:	**14.5%**	
Applications per place:	**4.1**	
From state-sector schools:	**97.8%**	
From working-class homes:	**42.6%**	

For detailed information about sports facilities: uel.ac.uk/sport.

Accommodation

Number of places and costs refer to 2012–13

University-provided places: 1,200

Percentage catered: 0%

Self-catered costs: £110.70 (en-suite single) – £146.50 (studio flat) a week (39 weeks).

First years are guaranteed accommodation if conditions are met; priority given to disabled students. Residential restrictions apply. International students: same as above.

Docklands Campus 020 8223 5409

dlres@uel.ac.uk

Edge Hill University

Edge Hill surprised many observers with its decision to charge £9,000 undergraduate fees in all subjects. But the decision paid off handsomely, with a 13 per cent increase in applications across all programmes at the start of 2012 defying the national trend. The university will use most of the income to continue enhancing its students' learning experience after losing 95 per cent of its teaching grant. Based at Ormskirk, Edge Hill has been one of the fastest growing universities in the UK, as well as one of the newest. It has more than doubled its complement of students since the millennium to reach 25,000, although only 8,000 of them are on full-time undergraduate courses. Edge Hill moved 22 places up *The Times* League Table in the last two years and remains in the top 80 in the new edition.

There are plans for significant expansion with the recent purchase of land adjoining the existing site, which include a new sports complex and further on-campus student accommodation, some of which will be available for the 2013 intake. Some £135 million has been spent on the existing campus. A £8-million Business School opened in 2009, when additional student residences also came on stream. A new £13.5-million Student Hub opened in 2011, providing dining outlets, extensive ICT facilities and a new central location for the Students' Union.

Although university status arrived only in 2005, Edge Hill moved to its 75-acre landscaped campus in the 1930s and has been training teachers since the 19th century. It has long since expanded into other subjects, but remains the largest provider of secondary teacher training and courses for classroom assistants. It has also won the lion's share of funding to deliver further training for qualified secondary school teachers. In 2011, the Faculty of Education achieved an unprecedented "outstanding" grade in all 33 possible graded areas of its Ofsted inspection across all three phases of its teacher-training provision.

A £5-million expansion of resources for the performing arts opened in 2005 and are set to expand further, with the refurbishment of the current theatre facilities and an extension which will house a new café and performance space. There are industry-standard facilities for animation, TV and other media areas. The SOLSTICE (Supported Online Learning for Students using Technology for Information and Communication in their Education) e-learning centre is recognised officially as a national centre of excellence in teaching and learning. It has a particular focus on learning in the workplace, but is involved with

---

St Helens Road
Ormskirk
Lancashire L39 4QP

01695 575171
study@edgehill.ac.uk
www.edgehill.ac.uk
www.edgehillsu.com
Affiliation: none

The Times **Rankings**
Overall Ranking: =73

Student satisfaction:	=17	(81%)
Research quality:	=112	(0.02)
Entry standards:	98	(266)
Student–staff ratio:	=64	(18.5)
Services & facilities/student:	108	(£1,005)
Expected completion rate:	83	(79.1%)
Good honours:	84	(56.4%)
Graduate prospects:	61	(62.0%)

curriculum development and delivery in all three of the university's faculties. Nursing, midwifery and other health care programmes have been commended by inspectors. Three quarters of all graduates leave with professional accreditation. Recent additions to the portfolio of degrees are digital marketing and music, sound and enterprise.

All students have a personal tutor, as well as access to counsellors and financial advice. Satisfaction levels have been consistently above average in the National Student Survey, with particularly good scores for students' personal development, in which Edge Hill was second only to Oxford in 2011. Dance students were the most satisfied in the UK, while geography, imaginative writing, law and history all scored well.

Beyond Ormskirk, there are seven satellite campuses in Liverpool, Manchester and other parts of the North West to facilitate local learning. In addition, a range of further education colleges in the region teach the university's Foundation degrees. Edge Hill has one of the highest proportions of state-educated students in England – almost 99 per cent. Over 40 per cent of undergraduates have a working-class background and one in five come from areas without a tradition of higher education – far above the national average for the university's courses and entry qualifications.

The projected dropout rate of 13 per cent is also better than the university's benchmark.

Before the fees went up, Edge Hill won an award for a student finance support package that rewarded achievement, as well as encouraging students to complete their studies, rather than simply offering incentives for enrolling. Bursaries and scholarships have been expended since, and there are separate awards in sport, the performing arts, volunteering and the creative arts. The university was chosen as a pre-Olympic training centre for athletics, road cycling and archery and is hosting teams from the Marshall Islands, Palau and American Samoa in the run-up to the games. The £3.9-million Sporting Edge complex, which was part funded by a Lottery grant, is open to staff, students and the local community.

Undergraduate Fees and Bursaries

» Fees for UK/EU students 2012–13 £9,000
  Foundation degree £6,000
» International student fees 2012–13 £10,500
» For English students with household income below £25K plus academic conditions, over 110 NSP year 1 awards of £1,000 cash and £2,000 university accommodation discount or fee waiver.
» Scholarship of £1,000 for those with over 360 UCAS points with conditions. Competitive "Excellence" scholarships on entrance, of up to £2,000 over three years, not linked to subject choice, in sport, performing arts, creative arts and volunteering.

Students

Undergraduates:	**8,685**	**(5,405)**
Postgraduates:	**805**	**(13,060)**
Mature students:	**29.6%**	
Overseas students:	**1.6%**	
Applications per place:	**4.5**	
From state-sector schools:	**98.7%**	
From working-class homes:	**41.1%**	

For detailed information about sports facilities: www.edgehill.ac.uk/EdgeHillSport

Accommodation

Number of places and costs refer to 2012–13
University provided places: 1,045
Percentage catered: 29%
Catered costs: £87 a week (38–40 weeks)
Self-catered costs: £90 a week (40 weeks)
First years cannot be guaranteed housing. Residential restrictions apply.
Students designated overseas for fees are guaranteed accommodation if conditions are met.
Contact: www.edgehill.ac.uk/study/accommodation

University of Edinburgh

Edinburgh became one of the two most expensive universities in the UK for undergraduates from England, Wales and Northern Ireland in 2012, charging £9,000 for the full four years of a degree course. But it still recorded an increase in applications of almost 4 per cent at the January deadline. The university retains a special status in Scotland, where it is regarded as the nearest thing to Oxbridge north of the border. Despite having to play second fiddle to St Andrews in our League Table recently, it is seldom far from the top ten in the UK and was in the top 20 universities in the world in the latest QS global rankings. The presence of more than 6,000 international students testifies to its worldwide reputation.

Edinburgh is the largest university in Scotland, with around 27,000 students. The university's buildings are spread around the city, but most border the historic Old Town. These include the university's main library, which has been redeveloped at a cost of £60 million. The science and engineering campus is two miles to the south. Competition for places remains intense: nine applications for each place in 2011.

Like Oxbridge, Edinburgh has been trying to widen its intake, spending more than £1 million on 700 undergraduate bursaries of at least £1,000 a year in 2010/11. Other measures include an eight-week summer school for teenagers from local schools and support for students in the transition to higher education and later in their courses. The university has always attracted a high proportion of middle-class candidates – many from England – and is a favourite in independent schools, whose students take about a quarter of the places. Selection guidelines aim to look beyond grades to consider candidates' potential, giving particular weight to references and personal statements. The university gives extra credit in some oversubscribed programmes to applicants from Scotland and parts of the north of England.

Edinburgh, a member of the Russell Group of leading UK research universities, has stepped up its fundraising activities. The campaign has contributed to a new informatics building, as well as to the development of a "BioQuarter", a ground-breaking collaboration between the university and a number of public bodies that is intended to consolidate Scotland's reputation as a world leader in biomedical science. In 2010, the author J.K. Rowling gave £10 million to the university to set up a new research clinic for multiple sclerosis.

The Business School has relocated to the heart of the main campus and a new research centre has been established for the study of Islamic civilisation

---

Old College
South Bridge
Edinburgh EH8 9YL

0131 650 4360 (admissions)
sra.enquiries@ed.ac.uk
www.ed.ac.uk
www.eusa.ed.ac.uk
Affiliation: Russell Group

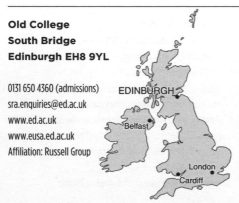

The Times Rankings
Overall Ranking: **14**

Student satisfaction:	=77	(76%)
Research quality:	6	(0.98)
Entry standards:	10	(476)
Student–staff ratio:	=14	(13.9)
Services & facilities/student:	19	(£1,989)
Expected completion rate:	=25	(92.3%)
Good honours:	=5	(82.8%)
Graduate prospects:	18	(74.5%)

and issues relating to Islam in Britain. Elsewhere a £90-million redevelopment of the university's Easter Bush site is nearing completion. A vet school building, a research building for the recently incorporated Roslin Institute and a cancer centre opened in 2011, followed by a new building to house the MRC Centre for Regenerative Medicine at Little France.

Almost two thirds of the work submitted for the last Research Assessment Exercise was rated as world-leading or internationally excellent, the highest proportion in Scotland. The university's entry was among the largest in the UK and produced strong results across the board. The College of Medicine and Veterinary Medicine was the star performer, with all of the work in hospital-based clinical subjects rated at the international level and 40 per cent at the highest grade. Informatics, linguistics and English literature also produced outstanding results.

Scores in the National Student Survey slipped slightly in 2011, although Edinburgh was still well up the table. There was 100 per cent satisfaction in archaeology for the second year in a row. Nursing and other health subjects were close behind, while chemistry, medicine and physics also scored well. Departments organise visiting days in October for those thinking of applying and in the spring for those holding offers, as well as the annual open day in June.

New undergraduates generally take three subjects in both their first and second years. Every student has a Director of Studies to help them narrow down the selection of a final degree and give personal advice when necessary.

A new £4.5-million extension to the university's Centre for Sport and Exercise was unveiled in 2010, adding to the already impressive sports facilities. Considerable sums have also been spent making the university more accessible to disabled students. The students' union operates on several sites and there is a regular bus link between the science areas and the main university around George Square. The city is a treasure-trove of cultural and recreational opportunities, and most students thrive on Edinburgh life, despite a relatively high cost of living. The plentiful stock of residential accommodation has been increased recently.

Undergraduate Fees and Bursaries

- » Fees for Scottish and EU students for 2012–13   No fee
- » Fees for Non-Scottish UK (RUK) students for 2012–13: £9,000 a year, for up to 4 years (total £36,000)
- » Fees for international students 2012–13   £12,650 or £16,650
  Medicine   £20,600–£34,850
  Veterinary studies   £19,950–£26,400
- » For RUK students, the Edinburgh RUK Bursary taken as fee waiver or cash: household income below £16K, £7,000 a year, £16K–£20K, £5,700, £20K–£25K, £4,000, £25K–£30K, £2,000, £30K–£35K, £1,500, £35K–£42.6K, £500.
- » Check the university's website for the latest information.

Students		
Undergraduates:	**16,985**	**(585)**
Postgraduates:	**5,870**	**(2,260)**
Mature students:	**12.2%**	
Overseas students:	**20.2**	
Applications per place:	**9**	
From state-sector schools:	**74.4%**	
From working-class homes:	**17.1%**	

For detailed information about sports facilities:
www.sport.ed.ac.uk

Accommodation

Number of places and costs refer to 2011–12
University-provided places: about 6,300
Percentage catered: about 30%
Catered costs: £113–£226 a week
Self-catered costs: £58–£127 a week.
First years are guaranteed an offer of accommodation providing they fulfil requirements. Residential restrictions apply.
International students: accommodation guaranteed if conditions are met.
Contact: www.accom.ed.ac.uk

Edinburgh Napier University

Edinburgh Napier is one of the largest universities in Scotland with over 18,000 students, including nearly 5,000 international students, from more than 100 different countries. Professor Dame Joan Stringer, who was the first woman to lead a university north of the border, has set Napier a target of becoming "one of the leading modern universities in the United Kingdom". For two years in a row, the university enjoyed among the biggest increases in applications in the UK and it defied the national trend in 2012 by registering another significant rise. Although partly fuelled by UK-wide changes in art and design and nursing qualifications, the unprecedented demand for places has been a reflection of the university's growing popularity.

As part of the university's £100-million investment, the newly opened Sighthill campus has brought the Faculty of Health, Life and Social Sciences together on one site for the first time. The student-focused campus includes a five-storey learning resource centre, 25 specialised teaching rooms including clinical skills laboratories, an environmental chamber and biomechanics laboratory, a crime scene scenario room, three IT-enabled lecture theatres and seminar rooms as well as integrated sports facilities. The Merchiston

campus will also be refurbished in 2012. A new reception complex will include gallery space to display student work and new sound-proofed, state-of-the-art music studios to the rear of the campus.

Once Scotland's first and largest polytechnic, the university is named after John Napier, the inventor of logarithms. The tower where he was born still sits among the concrete blocks of the Merchiston campus, in the city's main student district. The 500-seat computing centre is open all hours, and students have access to online lecture notes and study aids via WebCT. There are fully networked libraries at each campus, and a multimedia language lab and adaptive technology centre for students with special needs.

The Craiglockhart campus houses the business school. It features a glass atrium housing a cyber café and two spherical lecture theatres with a total of 600 seats, as well as a new fitness suite. The Screen Academy Scotland, run in partnership with Edinburgh College of Art, reflects the university's strong reputation in film education. The university is also planning a new 725-bed student residence in the city centre, which should be ready for the start of the 2013 academic year. There are several smaller sites, mainly in the leafy south of Edinburgh, ranging from a converted church to a former school, as well as outposts in Melrose and Livingston.

Craiglockhart Campus
Edinburgh EH14 1DJ

08455 203050 (admissions)
ugadmissions@napier.ac.uk
www.napier.ac.uk
www.napierstudents.com
Affiliation: million+

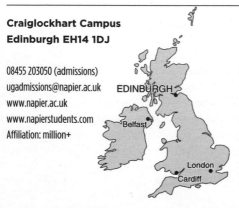

EDINBURGH
Belfast
London
Cardiff

Edinburgh Napier has over 3,000 students taking its degrees in Hong Kong, Singapore and India. It also has agreements with a number of partner universities and colleges that enable students to complete their qualifications, either as undergraduates or postgraduates. A new dual degree with the State University of New York (SUNY) allows students to complete a degree from Napier and SUNY in four years.

Closer to home, some 2,000 college "articulation routes" enable students to use their college qualifications to gain direct entry into year two or three of a university degree. Widening participation is high on the university's list of priorities, although the 30 per cent share of undergraduate places going to students from working-class homes is less than that UK average for the university's subjects and entry grades.

Most of Edinburgh Napier's avowedly vocational courses include a work placement, and the close relationship with industry and commerce helps to produce consistently good graduate employment figures. The modular course system allows movement between courses at all levels and has allowed students the option of starting courses in February, rather than September.

Edinburgh Napier has been held up as a model to other universities trying to reduce non-completion rates. The university uses its own students to mentor newcomers, runs bridging programmes and offers pre-term introductions to staff and information on facilities, as well as running summer top-up courses in a variety of subjects and teaching employability skills and personal development. The latest projected dropout rate of more than 15 per cent, is only marginally better than average for the subjects on offer, but represents a significant improvement on previous years.

Nine Institutes of Research Excellence have been established at Edinburgh Napier, offering expertise in different areas. Library and information management achieved by far the best results in the 2008 Research Assessment Exercise, when just over a fifth of the university's submission was considered world-leading or internationally excellent. The university's Building Performance Centre was awarded the Queen's Anniversary Prize in 2009 for "innovative housing construction for environmental benefit and quality of life".

Undergraduate Fees and Bursaries

» Fees for Scottish and EU students for 2012–13   No fee
» Fees for Non-Scottish UK (RUK) students for 2012–13: £6,500 a year, for up to 4 years (total £26,000).
» Fees for international students 2012–13   £9,690–£11,250
» For RUK students, household income below £25K, bursary of £2,000 a year; household income £25K–£42.6K, bursary of £1,000 a year.
» Scholarships and bursaries based on circumstances or by competition.
» Check the university's website for the latest information.

Students		
Undergraduates:	**9,390**	**(1,865)**
Postgraduates:	**1,380**	**(1,335)**
Mature students:	**41.1%**	
Overseas students:	**19.3**	
Applications per place:	**5.5**	
From state-sector schools:	**94.5%**	
From working-class homes:	**29.7%**	

For detailed information about sports facilities: www.napier.ac.uk/engage/Pages/Home.aspx

Accommodation

Number of places and costs refer to 2012–13
University-provided places: 957
Percentage catered: 0%
Self-catered costs: £101–£103 average cost a week.
First years and direct entrant undergraduates are guaranteed a place provided requirements are met. Residential restrictions apply.
International students: as above.
Contact: accommodation@napier.ac.uk

University of Essex

Essex has announced new developments costing more than £200 million in the run-up to its 50th anniversary in 2014. A new Student Centre and library extension on the main Colchester campus, and a new library and learning centre at Southend are planned for coming years. The Colchester library has already been extended once and its Large Reading Room is open all hours during the week and every day in the summer term. Sustainable energy and technology are being used whenever possible, with recent projects featuring ground source heat pumps and a wind turbine. Work is currently underway on the £10-million transformation of the historic Wivenhoe House, in the Colchester grounds, into the UK's first country house hotel to be run and staffed by students, supervised by industry professionals.

The introduction of £9,000 fees for all degree courses did not dampen demand. Two years of strong growth in applications were followed by another increase in 2012. Another good performance in the 2011 National Student Survey saw Essex placed among the top 20 mainstream universities. American studies, philosophy, politics and sociology produced the best results. The social sciences also led a strong set of results in the last Research Assessment Exercise (RAE), which saw 22 per cent of the university's submission rated as world-leading and over 90 per cent as internationally excellent. Both politics and sociology produced the best results in the country, while economics was ranked third in the UK and linguistics fourth. In addition, Essex Business School was ranked second for accounting and finance, and the humanities achieved good results with history ranked second and philosophy tenth.

Essex has been building up its science departments, and biological sciences is now one of its largest. Computer science and electronic engineering is also strong and a BSc in computer games shows Essex keeping pace with changing demands in graduate employment. But improvements in the university's academic performance could not disguise the fact that its original glass and concrete campus, set in 200 acres of parkland on the outskirts of Colchester, was showing distinct signs of wear and tear. The university has been carrying out major refurbishments at the same time as expanding student facilities. These have included the conversion of an old boiler house into a colourful teaching centre, a £1.4-million investment in new gym, refurbishment of the students' union bar, a café with adjoining learning space and an innovative shared IT workspace. Future developments include the Knowledge Gateway development, which will provide

---

Wivenhoe Park
Colchester
Essex CO4 3SQ

01206 873666 (enquiries)
admit@essex.ac.uk
www.essex.ac.uk
www.essexstudent.com
Affiliation: 1994 Group

The Times **Rankings**

Overall Ranking: **40**

Student satisfaction:	=17	(81%)
Research quality:	=27	(0.68)
Entry standards:	52	(331)
Student–staff ratio:	35	(15.9)
Services & facilities/student:	43	(£1,536)
Expected completion rate:	42	(87.6%)
Good honours:	58	(62.5%)
Graduate prospects:	=92	(53.7%)

space for social sciences, research and development, and business, as well as a home for the Institute for Democracy and Conflict Resolution.

The incorporation of the East 15 Acting School, in Loughton, was the university's first venture beyond Colchester. It became a department of the university. There has since been heavy investment in a third campus, the Gateway Building in Southend, which opened in 2007, offering courses in business, health and the arts. Situated in the town centre, the Southend campus includes the Clifftown Studios and a church that has been restored as a theatre, to provide a beautiful and atmospheric venue for performances. The university has recently added new student accommodation in the town. Another regional project has seen Essex collaborate with the University of East Anglia on University Campus Suffolk, which offers courses in Ipswich and at smaller centres across the county. Essex degrees are also taught at Writtle College, near Chelmsford, the Colchester Institute and South East Essex College, in Southend.

The university now has more than 11,000 undergraduates. The student population is unusually diverse for a traditional university, with high proportions of mature and overseas students. More than a third of undergraduates are from working-class homes and 95 per cent went to state schools or colleges – both higher figures than the subject mix would suggest.

Essex champions academic breadth, and students follow a common first year before specialising. They may take four or five different subjects before committing themselves to a particular degree. Most courses include an opportunity to study abroad, for a term or for the third year of a four-year course, and Essex has abolished the fee for undertaking a full year as this experience enhances learning and widens career prospects upon graduation. Social and sporting facilities are good, with an active students' union and some 40 acres of land at the Colchester Campus devoted to sports facilities.

All first years are guaranteed university accommodation which is now networked to the IT system. Some ground-floor flats have been adapted for disabled students.

Undergraduate Fees and Bursaries

» Fees for UK/EU students for 2012–13 £9,000
» International student fees 2012–13 £10,950–£12,950
» Household income below £25K, bursary of £1,500 a year; care leaver's bursary of up to £1,000; refugee bursary of up to £1,000. For English students with household income up to £10K, 200 NSP awards of £3,000 accommodation subsidy for university accommodation in year 1.
» Academic Excellence scholarships for UK students with AAB at A Level or equivalent, £2,000 a year. Other scholarships are available.
» Check the university's website for the latest information.

Students

Undergraduates:	**9,455**	**(2,185)**
Postgraduates:	**2,160**	**(965)**
Mature students:	**21.2%**	
Overseas students:	**22.9**	
Applications per place:	**5.5**	
From state-sector schools:	**95.0%**	
From working-class homes:	**34.1%**	

For detailed information about sports facilities:
www.essex.ac.uk/sport

Accommodation

Number of places and costs refer to 2012–13
University-provided places: 4,266
Percentage catered: 0%
Self-catered costs: Colchester: £67.97 (South Towers) – £115.99 (South Court en suite) a week; Southend: £119.98 (en suite) – £147.98 (studio flat)
New first years are guaranteed accommodation if conditions met.
International students: new students are guaranteed accommodation if conditions are met.
Contact: admit@essex.ac.uk

University of Exeter

Exeter was one of the first universities to announce its intention to charge the maximum fee, arguing that £9,000 was needed to direct resources at widening participation, fair access and improving the student experience. Applications had held steady at the start of 2012, when Exeter was one of four institutions to join the Russell Group of leading research universities. Exeter has recorded a string of high finishes in *The Times* League Table, thanks particularly to outstanding results in the National Student Survey and a good performance in the Research Assessment Exercise (RAE). Selection remains highly competitive – especially in English literature, drama, law, history and psychology. The university is launching new programmes in liberal arts, art history and visual culture, natural sciences and environmental science in 2013.

Exeter has featured among the top ten universities in every year of the National Student Survey and maintained this record in 2011. There was 100 per cent satisfaction among final-year theology undergraduates, while sports science, archaeology and geology all produced high scores. The 2008 RAE saw Exeter move up the pecking order of research universities, with most of its work judged to be world-leading or internationally excellent despite a much larger submission (involving 95 per cent of academics) than most of its peers. English, classics, archaeology, and accounting and finance did particularly well. The successes produced one of the biggest increases in research funding at any university.

Exeter boasts one of the most attractive settings of any university, and will complete a £270-million investment programme on its main campus ahead of the new academic year. This ambitious programme includes £130 million for student residences, substantial investment in the business school, a new Moods Disorders Centre and new facilities for biosciences. The jewel in the crown of the new developments is the Forum, a new £48-million development which creates a central hub and features an extended library, new student services centre, technology-rich learning spaces, a new auditorium and additional social and retail facilities. Another big development was the opening of Peninsular College of Medicine and Dentistry, in association with Plymouth University in 2006. The two partners will go their separate ways in 2013, leaving Exeter with its own (smaller) medical and dental school.

Exeter has targeted schools and colleges in the rural South West in order to broaden its social mix. Although almost a third of the undergraduates come from independent schools – a much higher proportion than the

---

Northcote House
The Queen's Drive
Exeter, Devon EX4 4QJ

0844 620 0012 (admissions)
ug-ad@exeter.ac.uk
www.exeter.ac.uk
www.pcmd.ac.uk
www.exeterguild.org
www.fxu.org.uk
Affiliation: Russell Group

The Times Rankings
Overall Ranking: **10**

Student satisfaction:	=12	(82%)
Research quality:	=13	(0.84)
Entry standards:	13	(459)
Student–staff ratio:	=64	(18.5)
Services & facilities/student:	16	(£2,017)
Expected completion rate:	9	(96.1%)
Good honours:	=5	(82.8%)
Graduate prospects:	=22	(73.0%)

national average for Exeter's subjects – this figure has been dropping. Location is partly responsible: despite sophisticated shopping and a lively entertainment scene, South West cathedral cities are not necessarily what every teenager is looking for. Nevertheless, the city has been attracting new businesses like the Met Office and benefiting from major investment such as the £235-million Princesshay shopping centre.

A £100-million campus near Falmouth has helped boost applications. Shared with University College Falmouth, the Cornwall campus offers Exeter degrees in bioscience, geography, English, history and politics plus a range of degrees, such as mining engineering, that are not available in Exeter. The latest development is a £30-million Environment and Sustainability Institute that will help put the university at the forefront of environmental and climate change research. The university has announced a further £100-million investment in sports, IT and science facilities there.

Exeter's longstanding international focus is exemplified by the growing range of four-year programmes "with international study" and by its 180 partner universities worldwide. All students are offered tuition in foreign languages and even some three-year degrees include the option of a year abroad. Career management skills are built in and students can gain work experience through employability and business project programmes. The Employability and Graduate Development Service has been expanded to increase students' work experience and placement opportunities, and employability has been improving despite the recession. The university's Exeter Award provides official recognition of all the extracurricular activities that students undertake. There is a particularly strong record of voluntary activities.

The centrally located Streatham campus has a lively social scene. The highly rated department of sport and health sciences and the graduate school of education are a mile away at the St Luke's campus. Some £11 million has been invested in sports facilities, and Exeter is one of only nine UK universities to have indoor tennis facilities to national competition standards. A new £2-million cricket centre opened in 2009.

Undergraduate Fees and Bursaries

» Fees for UK/EU students for 2012–13 £9,000
» International student fees 2012–13 12,600–£14,500
  Medicine (2011–12) £14,500–£22,000
» Household income below £25K, bursary of £1,500 a year; household income £25K–£35K, £1,000; household income £35K–£42.6K, £500. In addition, around 300 NSP awards: household income below £16K, £3,000 fee waiver (or £2,000 fee waiver, £1,000 accommodation bursary) a year; household income £16K–£20K, £2,000 fee waiver; household income £20K–£25K, £1,000 fee waiver.
» Care leaver support includes full fee waiver for all years plus financial support for accommodation outside term dates.

Students

Undergraduates:	**13,325**	**(80)**
Postgraduates:	**3,465**	**(1,160)**
Mature students:	**7.5%**	
Overseas students:	**20.3**	
Applications per place:	**6.2**	
From state-sector schools:	**66.8%**	
From working-class homes:	**15.2%**	

For detailed information about sports facilities:
www.sport.ex.ac.uk

Accommodation

Number of places and costs refer to 2012–13
University-provided places: 5,495
Percentage catered: 26%
Catered costs: £124.95–£206.64 a week (32 weeks).
Self-catered costs: £79.80–£142.94 a week (40, 42, 44 or 51 weeks).
Unaccompanied first years are guaranteed accommodation provided conditions are met.
International students: as above.
Contact: sid@exeter.ac.uk

University of Glamorgan

Glamorgan, which added Cardiff and Pontypridd to its title to stress its location, has been under pressure to merge with two of its rivals to form the Principality's largest university, serving the whole of southeast Wales. Its new partners would be Newport and Cardiff Metropolitan, which was the subject of a similar merger proposal almost a decade ago. Whatever the outcome, applications in 2013 will be to Glamorgan, which is going ahead with £28 million of investment in its campuses in Cardiff and Treforest. More than half will be spent on an expansion of the university's ATRiuM campus in the heart of Cardiff, while the rest will go on improvements to Glamorgan's original campus.

The university has already invested £130 million in new facilities. Recent developments included a £15-million expansion for health, science and sport students, new halls of residence and specialised teaching facilities. There has also been a new students' union building on the Treforest campus, a new home for the Law School in a listed building and the £35-million ATRiuM building, which houses the Cardiff School of Creative and Cultural Industries. The opening of the ATRiuM in 2007, which followed a merger with the Royal Welsh College of Music and Drama, with its conservatoire courses, boosted the demand for courses based in the capital by more than 60 per cent. The extension will make room for another 2,500 students. Although Glamorgan's applications were down in 2012, this followed growth of 43 per cent over four years.

Most of Glamorgan's 24,000 students remain on the Treforest campus, 20 minutes by train from Cardiff, overlooking the market town of Pontypridd. The Law School's upgraded facilities include a moot courtroom, while accommodation for mathematics and computing has had a £5-million refurbishment. The business school – the largest in Wales – is also based there. Health, sport and science are on the Glyntaff site, a short walk from the main campus. They are housed in new buildings and restored tramsheds. The popular Institute of Chiropractic is one of only two university-based centres for training chiropractors in the UK. Other students take Glamorgan courses in five overseas centres or in a growing number of further education colleges across Wales. Four have become accredited colleges, guaranteeing places on degree courses if students meet set conditions, while Merthyr Tydfil College has merged with the university.

Glamorgan produced good results in the last Research Assessment Exercise, albeit from a low entry in most subjects. Almost a third of the work submitted was judged

---

Pontypridd
Mid Glamorgan CF37 1DL

08456 434 030 (enquiries)
contact via website
www.glam.ac.uk
www.glamsu.com
Affiliation: University
Alliance

to be world-leading or internationally excellent, with English and nursing and midwifery doing especially well. The university also improved its scores in the 2011 National Student Survey, although it remained in the bottom half of the table. Electronics and imaginative writing had the most satisfied students in the UK, while social studies, finance and accounting also produced high scores.

The range of two-year courses has expanded rapidly, covering subjects as diverse as football and rugby coaching, surveying and costume construction. A vocational approach at all levels pays dividends for graduate employment, which is consistently good. The Faculty of Advanced Technology has been designated a centre of excellence for Wales, while three National Partnership awards testify to high standards in course design and delivery. Degrees in computer forensics, computer games development, lighting and design technology and aerospace courses are all designed with the involvement of employers.

Glamorgan exceeds all its access benchmarks: almost 40 per cent of undergraduates come from working-class homes and 14 per cent are from areas with no tradition of higher education. Three quarters of the 17,000 campus-based students are from Wales, but a healthy 3,700 are from outside the UK. However, the projected dropout rate, at more than 22 per cent, is above average for the university's courses and entry qualifications.

Many students live around Pontypridd, while others choose Cardiff, which is both livelier and a better source of accommodation. Students there also have access to 1,206 rooms in privately run halls of residence. However, amenities on the Pontypridd campus have been developing, with a modern a recreation centre as well as the new students' union. The sports facilities were good enough for Glamorgan to have been awarded the 2001 British University Games and have continued to improve: a £4-million sports park opened in 2011. The university also hosts one of six centres of excellence in cricket. Glamorgan is successful in student competitions, especially in rugby, and offers a number of sports bursaries for students with international potential.

Undergraduate Fees and Bursaries

» Fees for UK/EU students for 2012–13 £7,500, with Welsh Assembly non-means-tested grant to pay fees above £3,465 for Welsh students.

» International student fees 2012–13 £10,750

» Centenary Bursary of £1,500 in year 1 university accommodation discount and £1,000 cash in years 2 and 3 for those paying full fees. Not available to those receiving Welsh Government tuition fee grant.

» Bursaries or scholarships available for widening participation, care leaver's, Welsh-medium study, sports and some academic subjects.

Students

Undergraduates:	**12,020**	**(4,170)**
Postgraduates:	**2,175**	**(1,850)**
Mature students:	**27.3%**	
Overseas students:	**10.7%**	
Applications per place:	**3.7**	
From state-sector schools:	**97.4%**	
From working-class homes:	**38.1%**	

For detailed information about sports facilities: http://sport.glam.ac.uk/

Accommodation

Number of places and costs refer to 2012–13
University-provided places: 1,206
Percentage catered: 0%
Self-catered accommodation: £94 (standard) – £110 (premium) a week (39 weeks); £140 (studio flat, 42 weeks).
First-year students are offered accommodation. Local restrictions apply.
International students are guaranteed housing.
Contact: accom@glam.ac.uk

University of Glasgow

More distinctively Scottish than its rivals in Edinburgh or St Andrews, almost half of Glasgow's students come from within 30 miles of the city and two-thirds are from north of the border. There was always a high proportion of home-based undergraduates, but the university also attracts students from 120 countries, buoyed by Glasgow's position in the top 60 in the QS World University Rankings. They seem to enjoy the experience, for they voted Glasgow first in the UK in i–graduate's independent International Student Barometer. British students are also pretty satisfied – Glasgow was in the top ten in the National Student Survey published in 2011, with 90 per cent of all final-year undergraduates giving their seal of approval. The university achieved 100 per cent satisfaction ratings in dentistry, genetics, sports science, accounting and finance. In addition, students in nursing and geology were the most satisfied in the UK.

Glasgow enjoys the rare distinction of having been established by Papal Bull, and began its existence in the chapterhouse of Glasgow Cathedral in 1451. Since 1871 it has been based on the Gilmorehill campus in the city's fashionable West End, with its 104 listed buildings – more than any other British university. A new student centre opened in 2008.

Education occupies a separate campus nearby, while the Veterinary School and outdoor sports facilities are located at Garscube, four miles away. A £15-million small animal hospital for the Vet School opened in 2009, with state-of-the-art facilities. The centre won two architecture awards, while the environmental research building has also won awards as one of the "greenest" in Scotland.

Glasgow has adopted an increasingly outward-looking style in recent years, and opened its first overseas branch in its 560-year history in 2011, as part of an agreement with the Singapore Institute of Technology (SIT) to deliver joint engineering and mechatronics degree programmes. Students will complete three years at one of SIT's partner polytechnics before finishing their studies at the University of Glasgow Singapore. The university's Commonwealth Scholarship scheme celebrates the city's success as host of the 2014 Commonwealth Games by offering 53 awards for students from developing countries. The Centre for International Development, which was the first of its kind in Scotland and the largest in the UK, has helped to secure more than £20 million of research income. The university also has a campus at Dumfries, which is taking liberal arts and teacher education degrees to southwest Scotland.

Glasgow is no stranger to innovation: it was the first university in Britain to have

University Avenue
Glasgow G12 8QQ

0141 330 2000 (switchboard)
contact via website
www.gla.ac.uk
www.theguu.com
www.qmu.org.uk
Affiliation: Russell Group

GLASGOW
Edinburgh
Belfast
London
Cardiff

The Times Rankings

Overall Ranking: **15**

Student satisfaction:	=7	(83%)
Research quality:	20	(0.73)
Entry standards:	11	(465)
Student–staff ratio:	=25	(15.3)
Services & facilities/student:	9	(£2,186)
Expected completion rate:	=37	(88.3%)
Good honours:	24	(74.1%)
Graduate prospects:	12	(77.0%)

a school of engineering, for example, and the first in Scotland to have a computer. It has now appointed Scotland's first Gaelic language officer and the country's first chair of Gaelic to promote both learning opportunities and cultural events. Glasgow is a member of the Russell Group of leading research universities. More than half of the work submitted for the last Research Assessment Exercise was considered world-leading or internationally excellent. Art history was the most highly rated in the UK and the Vet School joint top in its field, while the university finished in the top ten in 18 subject areas. The Business School has been rated among the world's top 100:

Almost half of the university's applications are for arts or sciences degrees, rather than specific subjects, reflecting the popularity of a flexible system that allows students to delay choosing a specialism until the end of their second year. Applications have resumed their upward trend, following a blip in 2011, growing by more than 10 per cent at the start of 2012. The projected dropout rate had improved in the latest statistics but, at over 11 per cent, is above average for Glasgow's subjects and entry qualifications.

The Club 21 programme, which provides students with paid work experience placements, involves more than 100 employers from Santander to T-Mobile, some of whom sponsor undergraduates at £1,000 a year, as part of an arrangement to forge closer links with local business.

Nearly 20 per cent of the students are from working-class homes. The university operates a number of access initiatives, including the Top Up programme, which has been working with schools in the West of Scotland since 1999, and the Talent Awards, which are worth £1,000 a year to 50 academically able entrants who could face financial difficulties in taking up a place at Glasgow.

Most students like the combination of campus and city life, with the added bonus that Glasgow has been rated among the most cost-effective cities in which to study. Undergraduates have the choice of two students' unions, plus a sports union supporting more than 40 clubs and activities.

Undergraduate Fees and Bursaries

» Fees for Scottish and EU students for 2012–13   No fee
» Fees for Non-Scottish UK (RUK) students for 2012–13, £6,725 a year (total £27,000); medicine , dentistry, veterinary science £9,000 (total £36,000).
» Fees for international students 2012–13   £12,250–£15,750 Medicine, dentistry and veterinary medicine   £28,500
» For RUK students, £1,000 in year 1, as fee waiver or cash. Scholarship of £1,000 a year for students with AAB at A Level or equivalent and household income below £42.6K. Tuition fee waiver of £2,000 a year when household income below £42.6K.
» Scholarships and other bursaries based on circumstances or by competition.

Students

Undergraduates:	**15,855**	**(4,505)**
Postgraduates:	**4,050**	**(2,140)**
Mature students:	**14.9%**	
Overseas students:	**10.5%**	
Applications per place:	**6.6**	
From state-sector schools:	**85.1%**	
From working-class homes:	**19.1%**	

For detailed information about sports facilities:
www.gla.ac.uk/services/sport

Accommodation

Number of places and costs refer to 2012–13
University-provided places: 3,521
Percentage catered: 6.7%
Catered costs: £141.19–£156.17 a week.
Self-catered costs: £79.59–£129.15 a week.
First years are guaranteed accommodation if conditions are met. Deadline applies.
International students: first years are guaranteed accommodation if conditions are met. 20% of returners are also housed.
Contact: accom@gla.ac.uk

Glasgow Caledonian University

Glasgow Caledonian was the first Scottish university to open a campus in London and it also has bases in Oman, China and Bangladesh. But its top priority remains the modern city-centre campus that continues to draw home and international students to Glasgow. Degree applications were steady at the start of 2012. The university has spent more than £70 million transforming once mediocre facilities into a single campus that does justice to a thriving institution of more than 16,000 students, and more investment is planned. The health building brings together teaching and research facilities that include a virtual hospital. Other learning resources include multimedia studios, a Fashion Factory and an eye clinic equipped with latest technologies for teaching and research. Student facilities include the Arc sports centre, 24-hour computer labs, an employability centre and a dedicated Students' Association building.

Many GCU courses benefit from accreditation from professional bodies and more than half include work placement opportunities. The university is one of the largest providers of health-related graduates to the NHS in Scotland, covering a wide range of professions, including nursing, podiatry, radiography, social work and physiotherapy. As the only Scottish university delivering optometry degrees, for example, it trains 90 per cent of the country's eye care specialists. GCU recently launched its new Scottish Ambulance Academy, the only education establishment in the UK to be formally endorsed by the College of Paramedics and certified by the Health Professions Council. The School of Engineering and Built Environment teaches more than 75 per cent of Scotland's part-time construction students.

The Caledonian Business School boasts more undergraduates than any other such institution in Scotland, with almost 1,000 in each year group. The university pioneered subjects such as entrepreneurial studies and risk management – the only university in the country to do so – and offers highly specialist degrees, such as tourism management, fashion marketing, leisure management and consumer protection. A more recent innovation was the first full-time university MA course in fiction writing for television.

Widening participation in higher education has always been one of the university's main aims. More than a third of the undergraduates are from working-class homes and almost three-quarters are the first in their family to attend university. GCU's Caledonian Club for children and families from disadvantaged communities

---

Cowcaddens Road
Glasgow G4 0BA

0141 331 8681 (enquiries)
studentenquiries@gcu.ac.uk
www.gcu.ac.uk
www.caledonianstudent.com
Affiliation: University Alliance

GLASGOW
Edinburgh
Belfast
London
Cardiff

***The Times* Rankings**

Overall Ranking: **=81**

Student satisfaction:	=77	(76%)
Research quality:	=86	(0.09)
Entry standards:	48	(338)
Student–staff ratio:	97	(20.9)
Services & facilities/student:	55	(£1,405)
Expected completion rate:	98	(76.0%)
Good honours:	48	(66.8%)
Graduate prospects:	=85	(55.5%)

was recognised by *Times Higher Education* magazine as a national example of best practice in raising aspirations, building life skills and opening the university to the local community. However, the projected dropout rate shot up to 25 per cent in the most recent survey, the UK average for GCU's courses and entry qualifications. Caledonian has introduced a series of measures – such as monitoring non-attendance at lectures and better academic, social and financial support – for those at risk of dropping out.

The university's scores in the 2011 National Student Survey were close to the average for its subjects and entry grades. Optometry registered 100 per cent satisfaction among final-year students, while nutrition and social work also produced particularly high scores. The GCU Students' Association was named Scottish University Students' Association of the Year in 2011, when the university continued a run of good results in the International Barometer survey for overseas students. GCU has 1,500 international students and offers engineering in Oman, nursing in Bangladesh and joint degrees in a variety of subjects at the Caledonian College at the University of Jinan, in China. The London campus is for postgraduates only, but undergraduates are encouraged to participate in international exchanges and study abroad.

Half of the 14 subject areas in which the university entered the 2008 Research Assessment Exercise contained at least some world-leading work, with 30 per cent of all researchers judged to have produced world-leading or internationally excellent work. Health subjects registered the best results and entered the largest numbers for assessment. There were particularly good results in rehabilitative health sciences, which covers long-term health conditions such as arthritis and strokes.

Sports and social facilities have been among the priorities in the building programme. GCU is committed to environmental sustainability and has had success in the EcoCampus Environmental Management and Awards Scheme. Some students find that the high proportion of their peers living at home detracts from the social scene, but Glasgow is a very lively city with a large student population.

Undergraduate Fees and Bursaries

» Fees for Scottish and EU students for 2012–13　No fee
» Fees for Non-Scottish UK (RUK) students for 2012–13, £7,000 a year, capped at a maximum of £21,000 regardless of course length.
» Fees for international students 2012–13　£9,700–£10,500
» For RUK students, household income below £25K, £2,000 a year fee waiver to max. total of £6,000. Scholarship of £1,000 a year fee waiver to max. total of £3,000 for students with AAB at A Level or equivalent.
» Scholarships based on circumstances or by competition.

Students

Undergraduates:	**10,685**	**(3,125)**
Postgraduates:	**2,090**	**(1,435)**
Mature students:	**31.7%**	
Overseas students:	**6.6%**	
Applications per place:	**6.4**	
From state-sector schools:	**97.3%**	
From working-class homes:	**33.9%**	

For detailed information about sports facilities:
www.gcal.ac.uk/arc/

Accommodation

Number of places and costs refer to 2011–12
University-provided places: 660
Percentage catered: 0%
Self-catered costs: £86–£99 a week (39 weeks).
Students under 19 living outside the Glasgow area have priority for accommodation.
International students: new non-EU students guaranteed housing.
Contact: www.gcu.ac.uk/study/undergraduate/accommodation

University of Gloucestershire

Gloucestershire remains among the leading post-1992 universities in *The Times* League Table following a big rise in student satisfaction in 2011. The university's scores in the National Student Survey were close to the national average, with particularly good results in biological sciences, geography and environmental science. Applications were down by less than the national average at the start of 2012, after the university reduced its average fee to qualify for extra places. Its allocation was one of the highest awarded to any university. Although the fee remained £8,250, the average to be paid by students from less wealthy backgrounds was put at £7,500 after fee waivers.

Gloucestershire is investing £5 million in new teaching accommodation and social space after closing two campuses, one in London, and dividing its courses between the university's three remaining sites. The other campus casualty is the Pittville campus, in Cheltenham, where only student accommodation will remain. The reorganisation, in response to financial problems, has maintained the full range of subjects and added a media hub with new studio areas for fine art, photography and specialist design. Art and design students are transferring to the nearby Francis Close Hall, which they will share with a new Institute of Education and Public Services.

The Park Campus is the main base for the Faculty of Business, Education and Professional Studies, which includes accounting and law. Sport and exercise sciences, playwork, leisure, tourism, hospitality and event management will continue to be based at the Oxstalls campus in Gloucester, which will also house the Countryside and Community Research Institute, the largest rural research centre in the UK.

Gloucestershire has a longstanding focus on green issues, finishing in the top two for the last two years in the Green League of Universities for its all-round environmental performance. There are allotments for students, diplomas in environmentalism and an International Research Institute in Sustainability that brings together researchers from around the world, undertaking work for agencies such as UNESCO. Students are discouraged from bringing cars to university and bus fares between campuses are subsidised.

A recent additions to the list of universities, Gloucestershire was the first for more than a century to have formal links with the Church of England. Although its religious origins have been played down recently, and students of all faiths are welcomed, the university includes church

---

The Park Campus
The Park
Cheltenham GL50 2RH

0844 8011100 (enquiries)
enquiries@glos.ac.uk
www.glos.ac.uk
www.yourstudentsunion
.com
Affiliations: Cathedral
Group, million+

The Times Rankings
Overall Ranking: **=65**

Student satisfaction:	=55	(78%)
Research quality:	=95	(0.06)
Entry standards:	=71	(293)
Student–staff ratio:	=103	(21.4)
Services & facilities/student:	84	(£1,213)
Expected completion rate:	=61	(83.9%)
Good honours:	=41	(68.7%)
Graduate prospects:	96	(53.3%)

appointees on its governing body. Lord Carey, formerly archbishop of Canterbury, was its first Chancellor. This did not prevent the university dropping theology at degree level as part of a curriculum review, although the subject is now taught by distance learning. The university prides itself on a good range of work placements, which include Airbus and Renault. The Degreeplus initiative, launched in 2012, combines internships with additional training to improve students' chances of getting a good job after graduating.

The main campus is on the attractive site of the former College of St Paul and St Mary, a mile outside Cheltenham. There has also been considerable development of the Gloucester campus, on the site of a former domestic science college which became part of the university in 2002. The two centres are only seven miles apart and students are not as isolated as they are in some split-site institutions.

The university's intake is diverse, with over 95 per cent of undergraduates from state schools and almost a third from working-class homes. About a third are recruited from Gloucestershire, and another third from elsewhere in the South West of England. The projected dropout rate has improved dramatically, with the latest projection of less than 8 per cent well below the national average for the university's subjects and entry qualifications. The Gloucester campus, where participation in higher education has always been low, focuses particularly on access initiatives.

Gloucestershire did not quite reiterate the success it enjoyed in the previous research assessments when the exercise was repeated in 2008. Some world-leading research was found in five of the 12 areas in which the university submitted work, with the small education entry producing the best results. But less than 20 per cent of all work reached the top two categories.

The sports facilities include a sports hall, gym and tennis courts. First years are given preference for the 1,349 hall places, and the university has access to private sector places. At both sites facilities overall are improving.

Undergraduate Fees and Bursaries

» Fees for UK/EU students 2012–13 £8,250
Foundation degrees £6,000
» International student fees 2012–13 £9,200
» Household income up to £25K, £1,000 fee waiver in year 1. Academic scholarship of £2,000 in year 1 for students with AAB at A Level or equivalent and £1,000 fee waiver for students with household income below £42.6K who show academic potential.
» For English students with household income below £20K, 92 NSP awards, with fee waiver of £3,000 in year 1 and £1,500 in years 2 and 3; priority will be given to care leavers, disabled students and students from Compact schools or colleges. For other students from Compact schools and colleges, £1,000 fee waiver a year.

Students

Undergraduates:	**6,185**	**(1,000)**
Postgraduates:	**805**	**(1,565)**
Mature students:	**20.0%**	
Overseas students:	**5.7%**	
Applications per place:	**4**	
From state-sector schools:	**95.2%**	
From working-class homes:	**34.1%**	

For detailed information about sports facilities:
www.glos.ac.uk/living/sport

Accommodation

Number of places and costs refer to 2011–12
University-provided places: about 1,349
Percentage catered: 0%
Self-catered costs: £81–£109 a week.
First-year undergraduates have priority for halls.
International students: first-year undergraduates are guaranteed accommodation if conditions are met.
Contact: accommodation@glos.ac.uk

Glyndŵr University

Glyndŵr set average fees £2,000 lower than those at other universities in Wales in 2012, but paid an even bigger price than expected when the rest were encouraged to reduce their charges and compensated for loss of income. Glyndŵr could lose 20 per cent of its public funding as a result, despite experiencing only a small drop in applications. Only Cardiff has a better graduate employment rate among universities in Wales.

The former North East Wales Institute of Higher Education took the name of the 15th-century Welsh prince Owain Glyndŵr, who championed the establishment of universities throughout Wales, when it was awarded university status in 2008. The new university is based on two campuses in Wrexham and one at Northop, in Flintshire, on the site of the former Welsh College of Horticulture. The Flintshire campus is the first university presence in the county, and £1.7 million has been invested to make it a centre of excellence for land and animal-based studies.

In 2011, Glyndŵr became the only university to own an international football stadium – the oldest in the world – when it bought the Racecourse Ground to safeguard the future of Wrexham FC and provide more facilities for its students. The purchase included the club's well-equipped training ground. Glyndŵr already had a partnership with the club, whose land, next door to the university's Plas Coch site, hosts the new student accommodation complex. The campus also contains a modern sports centre with two floodlit artificial pitches, including an international standard hockey pitch, a human performance laboratory and indoor facilities that include a sports hall with a 1,000 square-metre sprung floor.

The two campuses in Wrexham are within five minutes' walk of each other. The university's art school is based at the Regent Street campus, nearer the town centre. The university has also opened a new campus in London offering mainly business courses. Based at Elephant and Castle, in South London, the new development is the result of a partnership with the London School of Management and Science.

Glyndŵr has fewer than 4,000 full-time students and another 3,700 part-timers, but has been growing fast. Nearly 55 per cent of the undergraduates are over 20 on entry and almost a third of all students are from overseas, many from other EU countries, India or China. As NEWI, there were only two applications per place – a lower ratio than at any UK university. But Glyndŵr enjoyed the customary boost that accompanies a change of status, and sustained it with another 13 per cent in applications at the start of 2011.

Mold Road
Wrexham
N. Wales LL11 2AW

01978 293439 (student enquiries)
sid@glyndwr.ac.uk
www.glyndwr.ac.uk
www.glyndwr.ac.uk/
  en/Ourstudentsupport/
  StudentsGuild/
Affiliation: none

The Times **Rankings**
Overall Ranking: **=97**

Student satisfaction:	=77	(76%)
Research quality:	=106	(0.04)
Entry standards:	113	(220)
Student–staff ratio:	=98	(21.0)
Services & facilities/student:	35	(£1,654)
Expected completion rate:	107	(73.7%)
Good honours:	94	(54.4%)
Graduate prospects:	47	(66.9%)

The new university has embarked on a series of academic developments, including the opening of a £2-million Centre for the Child, Family and Society, based on a Scandinavian concept, to allow those working in the field of child development to hone their skills in both an academic and practical manner. The Advanced Composite Training and Development Centre, a partnership with Airbus, who have a large plant nearby, followed in 2010. Research carried out at the centre will help to improve the efficiency of aircraft and will feed into the university's undergraduate engineering courses, which are also developed in association with Airbus. The Centre for the Creative Industries opened in 2011 with new TV, radio and online production studios for students from disciplines such as art and design, media and computing. It plays a key role in the university's television degree, and is also the new regional home of BBC Cymru Wales.

Glyndŵr registered a big increase in satisfaction levels in the 2011 National Student Survey, pulling away from the foot of the table. There was 100 per cent satisfaction on education courses and outstanding scores in English and nursing. Fewer than half of the undergraduates are school-leavers and nearly all are state-educated. More than 40 per cent are from working-class homes – far more than average for the university's subjects and entry grades. Glyndŵr also has the largest proportion of disabled students in Wales and was nominated for an award for its provision for them. There is a dedicated centre for students with disabilities that assesses students' needs before they embark on a course.

The university entered only 27 academics for the last Research Assessment Exercise, but almost a quarter of their work was judged to be world-leading or internationally excellent. Computer science and materials both reached the top grade for a small proportion of their work, and the university's research funding more than doubled as a result.

Two thirds of the students are local, many living at home, which inevitably affects the social scene. But Wrexham is not without nightlife, and both Manchester and Liverpool are within easy reach.

Undergraduate Fees and Bursaries

» Fees for UK/EU students for 2012–13   £5,850-£7,750, with Welsh Assembly non-means-tested grant to pay fees above £3,465 for Welsh students.
     Foundation degrees   £3,850
» International student fees 2012–13   £7,950
» Care Leaver's scholarship of £1,000 a year and other scholarships available..
» Check the university's website for the latest information.

Students

Undergraduates:	**3,850**	**(3,720)**
Postgraduates:	**780**	**(605)**
Mature students:	**53.0%**	
Overseas students:	**36.9%**	
Applications per place:	**2.7**	
From state-sector schools:	**98.8%**	
From working-class homes:	**42.3%**	

For detailed information about sports facilities: www.glyndwr.ac.uk/en/ourstudentsupport/ Sportandrecreation

Accommodation

Number of places and costs refer to 2011–12
University-provided places: 615
Percentage catered: 0%
Self-catered costs: £65–£95 (shared) – £98 (single en suite) a week (37–40 weeks).
First-year undergraduates are guaranteed accommodation.
International students: guaranteed housing.
Contact: www.glyndwr.ac.uk/en/Ourstudentsupport/ Accommodation/
accommodation@glyndwr.ac.uk

Goldsmiths, University of London

Goldsmiths has a stellar reputation in the arts, with alumni such as Damien Hirst, Antony Gormley, Julian Clary, Malcolm McLaren and Linton Kwesi Johnson. Graduates of the college have won the Turner Prize no fewer than six times. But it stresses that it brings the same creative approach to a wider range of subjects, spanning humanities, social sciences, computing and teacher training. More than half of the work submitted for the last Research Assessment Exercise was considered world-leading or internationally excellent. Indeed, it was among the top ten universities for the proportion of work (22 per cent) placed in the highest category. Sociology was rated joint top in the UK, while communication, cultural and media studies, music and art and design all did well. Recent world university rankings have placed Goldsmiths in the world's top 100, and the UK's top 20 for arts and humanities, but the portfolio of courses includes computing and psychology.

Goldsmiths also has a long tradition of community-based courses, which predates its membership of the University of London. Evening and other part-time classes are still as popular as conventional degree courses and many subjects can be studied from basic to postgraduate levels. A history of providing educational opportunities for women is reflected in one of the largest proportions of female students of any university in England.

Determinedly integrated into its southeast London locality, the campus has a cosmopolitan atmosphere. Around 30 per cent of new undergraduates are over 21 on entry (many of them at least 25), with a strong representation from the area's ethnic minorities, and there is a growing cohort of international students. The age profile helped Goldsmiths to a rise in applications in advance of the switch to £9,000 fees, but the start of 2012 saw a 23 per cent decline in the demand for places.

The campus is a mixture of old and new. The latest addition, a purpose-built, eco-friendly building for media and communications facilities and the Institute for Creative and Cultural Entrepreneurship, opened in September 2010. The Rutherford Building, containing library and IT services and a Grade II listed former baths building has been converted to provide more space for research and art studios. The Ben Pimlott Building, featuring a dramatic sculptural "scribble" by the acclaimed architect Will Alsop, contains state-of-the-art studio facilities and two multidisciplinary centres for interaction between the arts and social sciences.

There are nearly 6,700 full-time students and around 1,500 part-timers at Goldsmiths. Scores in the National Student Survey

---

Lewisham Way
New Cross
London SE14 6NW

020 7919 7766 (enquiries)
course-info@gold.ac.uk
www.gold.ac.uk
www.goldsmithssu.org
Affiliation: 1994 Group

The Times **Rankings**

Overall Ranking: **48**

Student satisfaction:	=77	(76%)
Research quality:	=18	(0.74)
Entry standards:	43	(347)
Student–staff ratio:	55	(17.7)
Services & facilities/student:	111	(£946)
Expected completion rate:	71	(81.3%)
Good honours:	=36	(70.1%)
Graduate prospects:	=99	(52.2%)

improved in 2011, taking satisfaction levels close to the national average. In common with other London universities, really high scores have been hard to come by, however. Only design studies, fine art and psychology satisfied 90 per cent of final-year undergraduates, although anthropology and sociology came close. Employment prospects are good, especially for an institution with such a high proportion of students taking performing arts subjects, where a period of unemployment after graduation is commonplace. Goldsmiths places great emphasis on equipping students with creative thinking skills and has introduced workshops to help students develop entrepreneurial skills. Personal development opportunities include the Gold Award, which encourages students to develop the skills and experience that employers are looking for. However, the projected dropout rate of more than 18 per cent is above average for the courses and entry qualifications.

Student politics has survived at Goldsmiths to an extent not seen at many universities, while a college in which Alex James and Graham Coxon, from Blur, are just two of a number of successful rock alumni cannot fail to have a thriving music scene. The union has a strong tradition in volunteering and an award-winning newspaper/magazine, and in recent years have been winners of several Sound Impact Awards, in recognition of work on ethical and environmental issues.

Sky-high prices for loft conversions may put top-end apartments beyond the reach of most students, but there are plenty of more reasonably priced options in the vicinity. There are over 1,000 halls of residence places within walking distance of the campus – not enough to guarantee all first years accommodation, but international students can be housed throughout their course. There is a well-equipped and affordable gym on campus plus a swimming pool and indoor complex in Deptford, but the main pitches are eight miles away. Goldsmiths expects to make more of a contribution to the cultural programme than the sporting one at the 2012 Games, although two students have been selected to take part in the Olympic torch relay.

Undergraduate Fees and Bursaries

» Fees for UK/EU students 2012–13   £9,000
» International student fees 2012–13   £11,100–£15,400
» Ten £9,000 a year fee waivers for best students from Lewisham. £1,000 bursary for UK students from area of low participation and household income below £50K; £750 bursary for any students from local boroughs with household income below £50K, £500 for any other English student with household income below £25K. For English students with household income below £25K, 65 NSP awards of £6,000, £1,000 of which can be cash, the remainder fee waiver.
» Range of scholarships and bursaries for mature students, care leavers, disabled students, computer and music students; £1,000 a year for students with AAB at A Level or equivalent.

Students

Undergraduates:	**4,745**	**(560)**
Postgraduates:	**1,945**	**(910)**
Mature students:	**27.3%**	
Overseas students:	**15.5%**	
Applications per place:	**6.7**	
From state-sector schools:	**89.2%**	
From working-class homes:	**35.8%**	

For detailed information about sports facilities: www.gold.ac.uk/sports/

Accommodation

Number of places and costs refer to 2011–12
University-provided places: 973 (college halls); 46 studio flats through McMillan Student Village (private hall provider)
Percentage catered: 0%
Self-catered costs: £94–£126 a week (studio flats in McMillan Student Village are £170–£212 a week)
Priority is given to new full-time students; distance restrictions apply.
International students will be given priority for accommodation.
Contact: www.goldsmiths.ac.uk/accommodation

University of Greenwich

Greenwich has the most satisfied students of any post-1992 university in London. After a series of improvements, the university finished in the top third of all universities in the 2011 National Student Survey. Maths and pharmacy both recorded 100 per cent satisfaction rates, while law and civil, chemical and other engineering courses were all in the top three in the country. But following two years of strong growth in the demand for places, applications were down by 11 per cent at the start of 2012 – more than the national average.

The university claims to have "one of the grandest university settings in the world", and it is hard to argue. Its move, completed in 2002, into the former Royal Naval College buildings designed by Sir Christopher Wren provided a campus worthy of one of the most desirable titles of any university. Its name has always conjured up images of history and science in equal measure, and the main campus is now part of a World Heritage Site. Wren's baroque masterpiece is being used, with the former Dreadnought Hospital, to teach over half the university's students in humanities, business, law, maths, computing and maritime studies. Four halls provide 2,300 rooms.

The prize-winning Medway campus, centred on the former naval base at Chatham, has been developed in partnership with Kent and Canterbury Christ Church universities. New student accommodation opened there in 2008, together with an improved café in the main Pembroke building. Greenwich put £20 million into the campus, which houses one of the first new schools of pharmacy for 20 years, as well as the schools of science and engineering, the Natural Resources Institute, nursing and some business courses. A joint learning resources centre serves the Chatham Maritime campus and the University of Kent's neighbouring premises. Another shared facility has improved teaching facilities and expanded student services, the campus having already exceeded the original target of 6,000 students. A BSc in paramedic science combines academic study, assessments and laboratory exercises with learning as part of an ambulance crew.

Other schools are situated at Avery Hill, a Victorian mansion on the outskirts of southeast London, where a £14-million sports and teaching centre opened in 2006, with a new gym and refurbished café following in 2008. As well as a sports hall and 220-seat lecture theatre, there are laboratories for health courses that replicate NHS wards. A neighbouring building is now the main base for the School of Health and Social Care. The campus also contains a student village of 1,300 rooms,

---

Old Royal Naval College
Park Row
Greenwich
London SE10 9LS

020 8331 9000 (course enquiries)
courseinfo@greenwich.ac.uk
www.gre.ac.uk
www.suug.co.uk
Affiliation: million+

The Times **Rankings**
Overall Ranking: **=91**

Student satisfaction:	=34	(80%)
Research quality:	=86	(0.09)
Entry standards:	104	(257)
Student–staff ratio:	109	(22.1)
Services & facilities/student:	51	(£1,444)
Expected completion rate:	105	(74.2%)
Good honours:	102	(51.5%)
Graduate prospects:	88	(55.1%)

as well as teaching accommodation for the social sciences, architecture, landscape and construction, and the large education faculty, which is one of the few to offer both primary and secondary teacher training courses. The Avery Hill TV studio has also been refurbished to meet current industrial standards.

The university has also bought a large site in Greenwich town centre, where it plans to invest £76 million in a new library and a new home for the School of Architecture and Construction. The development will increase student numbers in the town by about 20 per cent.

The university achieved good results from a large entry to the last Research Assessment Exercise, which showed a quarter of the work reaching world-leading or internationally excellent levels. The small mechanical, aeronautical and manufacturing engineering group produced by far the best results, but architecture and history also did well. A fifth of the university's income is from research and consultancy – the largest proportion at any former polytechnic, and externally sponsored research and consultancy income has leapt by a massive 60 per cent in two years, to £15.3 million annually. Taking into account government funding, the university's total research revenues have almost doubled since 2007–8.

Eleven associated colleges in Kent and London teach the university's courses, while strong links with institutions outside the UK provide a steady flow of overseas students, as well as exchange opportunities for those at Greenwich. The 5,000 overseas students put the university among the top international recruiters, attracting more students than any other UK institution from India, and large numbers from Bangladesh, Ghana, Sri Lanka, Mauritius and Nigeria.

A commitment to extending access is reflected in a high proportion of mature students. More than 97 per cent of undergraduates are state-educated, and 54 per cent come from working-class homes – the biggest proportion in England. Both figures are significantly higher than the national average for Greenwich's courses and entrance qualifications. The downside has been the dropout rate. The latest projection of 22 per cent is still higher than the university's benchmark.

Undergraduate Fees and Bursaries

» Fees for UK/EU students 2012–13   £8,300
       MPharm   £9,000
       Foundation degree   £6,000
       Partner college   £7,900
» International student fees 2012–13   £9,850
» For English students with household income below £25K and other criteria, NSP awards of £1,000 cash and £2,000 fee waiver in year 1 and £1,000 fee waiver in years 2 and 3.
» For students with AAB at A Level or equivalent, £2,500 fee waiver for each year of study.
» Check the university's website for the latest information.

Students		
Undergraduates:	**15,820**	**(6,100)**
Postgraduates:	**3,480**	**(2,345)**
Mature students:	**37.7%**	
Overseas students:	**12.7%**	
Applications per place:	**6.8**	
From state-sector schools:	**97.8%**	
From working-class homes:	**54.6%**	

For detailed information about sports facilities:
www.gre.ac.uk/about/sports

Accommodation
Number of places and costs refer to 2012–13
University-provided places: 2,300
Percentage catered: 0%
Self-catered costs: £99.40–£174.86 a week.
First years are guaranteed a place. Conditions apply.
International students: new students get priority.
Contact: www2.gre.ac.uk/study/accommodation
ah.accommodation@gre.ac.uk (Avery Hill Campus)
gr.accommodation@gre.ac.uk (Greenwich Campus)
me.accommodation@gre.ac.uk (Medway Campus)

Heriot-Watt University

Heriot-Watt enjoyed the biggest increase in applications of any Scottish university at the start of 2012, as the demand for places grew by 20 per cent. Its student satisfaction ratings have also been rising, leaving the university close to the UK top 30 in the 2011 National Student Survey. There was 100 per cent satisfaction among chemical engineers and particularly good scores in civil engineering and chemistry, as well as the top ratings in Scotland for psychology and biology.

The university is investing £5 million a year to boost its teaching and research in business and technology as part of a commitment to become a world-leading university within ten years. The university is already Scotland's most international institution, with a new, purpose-built campus in Dubai and another to follow in Malaysia. There are around 12,000 students in approved learning centres overseas or taking distance learning courses in 150 different countries. Overseas students also fill nearly a third of the places on the university's Edinburgh campus – one of the biggest proportions in the UK. Heriot-Watt won an award from the Scottish Council of Development and Industry, partly for its support for international students.

Heriot-Watt's strengths lie in the physical sciences, mathematics, engineering and in the built environment. Concentration on these areas is fitting for a university which commemorates James Watt, the pioneer of steam power, and George Heriot, financier to King James VI. The university has fostered inter-disciplinary teaching and research, with a battery of employment-related degrees.

The subject mix serves graduates well: Heriot-Watt is seldom far from the top of graduate employment league tables. The latest jobs figures showed further significant improvement at a time when many other universities experienced a decline. The projected dropout rate of almost 11 per cent is just below the UK average for the university's subjects and entrance qualifications. More than half of the undergraduates are from Scotland, and just under 20 per cent from other parts of Britain. Nearly 95 per cent of them are from state schools and colleges, while the proportion from working-class backgrounds has risen to well above average for the courses and entry grades.

Heriot-Watt is one of the most commercially diversified universities in Britain, deriving over 60 per cent of its income from non-government sources, particularly research income generated from business and industry. Its Research Park was the first of its kind in Europe, providing

---

Edinburgh Campus
Edinburgh EH14 4AS

0131 449 5111
enquiries@hw.ac.uk
www.hw.ac.uk
www.hwunion.com
Affiliation: none

EDINBURGH
Belfast
London
Cardiff

The Times **Rankings**
Overall Ranking: **42**

Student satisfaction:	=17	(81%)
Research quality:	41	(0.54)
Entry standards:	37	(384)
Student–staff ratio:	=69	(18.8)
Services & facilities/student:	=61	(£1,341)
Expected completion rate:	67	(81.8%)
Good honours:	40	(68.8%)
Graduate prospects:	=32	(71.5%)

direct access to university expertise for a range of companies. The university also has a £6.5-million project to transfer knowledge and expertise to Scottish businesses which will benefit the wider economy and foster partnerships. More than half of the work submitted for the last Research Assessment Exercise was rated world-leading or internationally excellent. Mathe-matics produced by far the best results, but there were good grades, too, in petroleum engineering, physics, general engineering, the built environment, and art and design.

The main campus, in an attractive park-land setting at Riccarton, close to Edinburgh Airport and 20 minutes drive from the city centre, still has a modern feel more than 40 years after it opened. The university remains small in terms of full-time students – there are about 7,500 on the Edinburgh campus. Students in Dubai take business, engineering, science, technology or textiles and design courses. Numbers in the Gulf state had risen to about 3,000 by the end of 2011 and are expected to grow quickly towards 5,000. The new Heriot-Watt campus in Malaysia is due to open in 2014.

Science, engineering, management and languages are located on the Edinburgh campus. The Scottish Borders Campus in Galashiels, 35 miles south of Edinburgh, specialises in textiles, fashion, design and management. Heriot-Watt and Borders College have signed a partnership

agreement for a long-term collaboration to deliver higher and further education in the historically under-provided region, both institutions now sharing new campus facilities. In addition, there is a postgraduate campus at Stromness in Orkney, specialising in renewable energy

The Edinburgh campus has the students' union at its heart and halls of residence conveniently placed. Edinburgh students have complained that the six-mile journey to the city centre leaves them isolated, but there are frequent bus services. Sports enthusiasts are well provided for, and representative teams do well. Music also thrives: there is a professional musician-in-residence and a number of music scholarships, as well as a varied programme of events.

Undergraduate Fees and Bursaries

» Fees for Scottish and EU students for 2012–13   No fee
» Fees for Non-Scottish UK (RUK) students for 2012–13, £9,000 a year, capped at a maximum of £27,000 for 3 or 4 year courses; enhanced 5-year undergraduate courses (MEng, MPhys, MChem, MMath) capped at £36,000.
» Fees for international students 2012–13   £10,730–£13,530
» For RUK students entering at year 1, fee waiver of £2,250 a year plus £1,500 cash bursary in year 1; for students entering at year 2 with household income below £25K, £3,000 cash bursary a year; household income £25K–£42.6K, £2,000 cash bursary a year. Academic scholarship of £1,000 a year for students who achieve AAA or AAB depending upon subject at A Level, or equivalent.

Students		
Undergraduates:	5,580	(695)
Postgraduates:	1,905	(2,995)
Mature students:	16.4%	
Overseas students:	28.4%	
Applications per place:	5.4	
From state-sector schools:	94.3%	
From working-class homes:	30.2%	

For detailed information about sports facilities:
www.hw.ac.uk/sports

Accommodation
Number of places and costs refer to 2011–12
University places provided: 1,624
Percentage catered: 19%
Catered costs: £119.84–£131.87 a week.
Self-catered costs: £86.29 (standard) – £103.93 (en suite) a week.
All new first years are guaranteed accommodation provided conditions are met and applications in place by 22 August.
International students: as above.
Contact : halls@hw.ac.uk; www.hw.ac.uk/student-life/campus-life.htm

University of Hertfordshire

Hertfordshire was among the minority of universities to see an increase in degree applications at the start of 2012, having added more fee waivers for students from low-income homes to qualify for extra places. The university was already charging less than £8,000 for most courses, and allocation of an additional 350 places will ease the transition to the new higher education economy. Hertfordshire has become a model for the "business-facing" university, serving the needs of local employers and improving the job prospects of its students in the process. The university lived up to this reputation by winning the *Times Higher Education* "Entrepreneurial University of the Year" in 2010. It even runs the local bus service and plays an important role in steering the local economy.

A purpose-built £120-million campus, close to the existing Hatfield headquarters, opened in 2003, bringing the university together for the first time and providing outstanding facilities. The de Havilland campus, named after the aircraft manufacturer which once occupied the site, houses business, education and the humanities. It has a 24-hour learning resources centre, £15-million sports complex and 1,600 networked, en-suite residential places. The two sites are linked by cycleways, footpaths and university-owned shuttle buses.

As Hatfield Polytechnic, the university's reputation was built on engineering and computer science, but health subjects now account for by far the largest share of places. An innovative degree in paramedic science was Britain's first, its students using the UK's largest medical simulation centre to train how to treat patients in emergency situations. The university is still hoping for a medical school, although its last bid was not successful. A new School of Pharmacy and a postgraduate medical school strengthened its position. The university is also working with the NHS Trusts in the East of England as a preferred provider for BSc healthcare science degree. Increased research activity resulted in the establishment of the Health and Human Sciences Institute.

The creative arts are also growing, particularly the multimedia courses. In 2005, the university launched what is now the School of the Creative Arts. In 2007, a £10-million media centre was completed, with the latest technology for the teaching of music, animation, film, television and multimedia, based on the College Lane campus. This includes one of the largest art galleries in the eastern region. An Automotive Centre has upgraded the teaching facilities for that branch of engineering, as well as boosting interaction with industry. On the De Havilland campus, a 460-seat auditorium enhances the cultural programme.

College Lane
Hatfield
Herts AL10 9AB

01707 284800 (admissions)
contact via website
www.herts.ac.uk
www.uhsu.co.uk
Affiliation: University
  Alliance

The Times **Rankings**
Overall Ranking: **68**

Student satisfaction:	=55	(78%)
Research quality:	=80	(0.10)
Entry standards:	=64	(300)
Student–staff ratio:	=85	(19.8)
Services & facilities/student:	37	(£1,636)
Expected completion rate:	88	(78.2%)
Good honours:	=61	(61.8%)
Graduate prospects:	67	(60.7%)

Hertfordshire saw 30 per cent growth in applications in two years before the fees went up. The student intake is more diverse than might be expected, given the location and subject mix: four in ten come from working-class homes and 97 per cent are state-educated. However, the projected dropout rate slipped close to 20 per cent in the latest survey, having previously outperformed the national average for the university's subject mix and entry grades.

Many Hertfordshire students include work placements in their degrees, and the close links with employers contribute to a consistently good graduate employment record. The university's Careers and Placements Service offers graduates lifelong support on employment and career development issues.

There has been steady and consistent improvement in scores in the National Student Survey. Hertfordshire was close to the national average in 2011, with the most satisfied students in anatomy, physiology and pathology, physics and astronomy, and human resource management.

Hertfordshire produced some of the best results of any post-1992 university in the 2008 Research Assessment Exercise, when nearly half of its submission was judged to be world-leading or internationally excellent. History, nursing and midwifery, engineering and computing collected the highest grades.

The award-winning library and resource centre on the main campus is Britain's biggest, offering 24-hour access to hundreds of computer workstations. A second centre on the de Havilland campus provides another 1,100 workstations. The StudyNet information system has been a leader in its field, giving all staff and students their own storage space. Students can use it for study, revision or communication, as well as to access university information.

In September 2009, the university opened the Forum, a new student venue on the College Lane campus. It includes an auditorium for live gigs and club nights, a nursery, a convenience store and a multistorey car park, as well as quiet areas. A £15-million sports complex, the Hertfordshire Sports Village, is principally for student use, but it is also open to local residents.

Undergraduate Fees and Bursaries

» Fees for UK/EU students 2012–13 £7,400–£8,500
» International student fees 2012–13 £9,000–£10,000
» For English students with household income below £25K, around 250 NSP awards, year 1 £1,000 fee waiver, £1,000 accommodation or computer voucher plus other vouchers to value of £1,000; years 2 and 3, £500 cash and £1,000 in support and book vouchers.
» 60 awards of £3,000 a year for academically talented students. Scholarships of £2,000 a year for students with 450 UCAS points. Scholarships of £1,500 for students with AAB at A Level or equivalent.

Students

Undergraduates:	**17,155**	**(4,310)**
Postgraduates:	**3,255**	**(2,980)**
Mature students:	**26.1%**	
Overseas students:	**14.9%**	
Applications per place:	**5.6**	
From state-sector schools:	**97.5%**	
From working-class homes:	**40.3%**	

Accommodation

Number of places and costs refer to 2012–13
University-provided places: 3,400
Percentage catered: 0%
Self-catered costs: £71–£118 a week.
First years are guaranteed accommodation if conditions are met.
International students: as above.
Contact: Accommodation@herts.ac.uk

For detailed information about sports facilities:
www.student.hertssportsvillage.co.uk

University of the Highlands and Islands

The University of the Highlands and Islands (UHI) is the only institution to be added to the complement of UK universities in the last two years. As a federation of 13 colleges and research institutions, spread across hundreds of miles in the Highlands and Islands of Scotland, it is also the most unusual. UHI waited almost 20 years for university status – indeed, its establishment was recommended in 1990 in a report to the Highland Regional Council which envisaged that the process might take four years. The region had to wait a lot longer than that for a university: Perth was first identified as a suitable location for a university in 1425.

The university's development has come in stages since its establishment was formally recommended in 1992. As the UHI Millennium Institute, it became a higher education institute in 2001 and received degree-awarding powers in 2008. University status finally came in February 2011, by which time it had 8,000 students spread around its many campuses. It made its debut in *The Times* League Table last year in the bottom ten, and remains there. But some data – notably on staffing levels – will be refined in future years.

The 13 colleges spread from Dunoon in the south to the village of Scalloway, the ancient capital of the Shetland Islands, in the north. But that does not begin to do justice to the university's network of campuses. Argyll College, for example, has 13 sites on the mainland and on islands such as Arran, Islay and Mull. UHI provides educational opportunities at more than 50 learning centres located throughout the Highlands and Islands, Moray and Perthshire. Some colleges are relatively large and located in the urban centres of the region such as Perth, Elgin and Inverness. Others are smaller institutions, including some whose primary focus is research. The university insists, however, that all have a student-centred culture and an individual approach.

Several of the colleges are in spectacular locations. Lews Castle College UHI, in Stornoway, in the Outer Hebrides, for example, is set in 600 acres of parkland. It claims "possibly the UK's most attractive location to study art" for its harbourside Lochmaddy campus in North Uist. Sabhal Mòr Ostaig UHI is the only Gaelic-medium college in the world, set in breathtaking scenery on the Isle of Skye, while the Highland Theological College UHI is in Dingwall. West Highland College UHI does not even have a central campus, although the single degree, in adventure tourism management, is taught in Fort William. close to Ben Nevis.

Executive Office
Ness Walk
Inverness IV3 5QS

01463 279 000 (general enquiries)
contact via website
www.uhi.ac.uk
www.uhisa.org.uk
Affiliation: none

The Times **Rankings**
Overall Ranking: **114**

Student satisfaction:		n/a
Research quality:	=95	(0.06)
Entry standards:	95	(269)
Student–staff ratio:		n/a
Services & facilities/student:	115	(£760)
Expected completion rate:	117	(57.5%)
Good honours:	16	(77.0%)
Graduate prospects:	117	(39.4%)

UHI's priority is to give students living in the region local access to learning and research relevant to their needs and to those of local employers. Students take a broad range of qualifications, from higher national certificates and diplomas and degrees to professional development awards. The university is widely acknowledged as a major asset to the regional economy, helping to create and sustain businesses, as well as championing local culture and the environment. But UHI also attracts students from further afield with a wide choice of locations, extensive use of information technology, including online materials and video conferencing, and small class sizes. Many courses are also available by online distance learning, including a new international degree in sustainable development.

The university offers more than 100 undergraduate courses. Degree courses intended to lead to careers in renewable engineering, tourism and hospitality, health care, and children's services are among the options for 2013. A degree in childhood practice was launched in 2011, catering for day care managers in children's services and nurseries. Those offered in 2012 include archaeology; fine art textiles; music business; tourism and hospitality practice; enterprise and e-marketing, and electrical and energy engineering. Courses such as audio engineering; health studies for rural health or health and welfare, and adventure tourism management have added an honours year of study.

UHI became the first higher education institution to publish a Gaelic language plan in 2010, setting out plans to provide students with unique opportunities to learn Gaelic, improve existing skills, or study for qualifications entirely through the language. There is now a growing community of students with Gaelic skills throughout the UHI network. The university's mission statement is published in five languages, of which Gaelic is the first and staff are offered a one-day Gaelic Awareness course.

Environmental science produced the best results and made by far the largest submission in the 2008 Research Assessment Exercise, but there was some world-leading research in Celtic studies and archaeology. There are a dozen research centres specialising in everything from agronomy to Nordic studies, diabetes and rural childhood.

Undergraduate Fees and Bursaries

» Fees for Scottish and EU students for 2012–13   No fee
» Fees for Non-Scottish UK (RUK) students for 2012–13, £7,500 a year, capped at a maximum of £22,500 for 3 or 4-year courses.
» Fees for international students 2012–13   £8,000–£9,500
» For RUK students, household income below £20K, fee waiver of £1,500; £20K–£22.5K, fee waiver of £1,000; £22.5–£25K, fee waiver of £500.

Students		
Undergraduates:	**3,445**	**(3,175)**
Postgraduates:	**85**	**(365)**
Mature students:	**61.7%**	
Overseas students:	**2.9%**	
Applications per place:	**n/a**	
From state-sector schools:	**97.2%**	
From working-class homes:	**39.0%**	

Sports provision for each campus is through local community facilities.

Accommodation

On-site halls of residence are available at four of the partner colleges. The other colleges provide lists of local lodgings or private rented accommodation. Some international students prefer to stay with host families.

Contact: Perth College UHI: pc.enquiries@perth.uhi.ac.uk
Sabhal Mòr Ostaig UHI: trusadh@smo.uhi.ac.uk
Lews Castle College UHI: enquiries@lews.uhi.ac.uk
NAFC Marine Centre UHI: www.nafc.ac.uk/Accommodation.aspx

University of Huddersfield

A big rise in student satisfaction has helped Huddersfield improve its position in *The Times* League Table, as well as coinciding with a healthy increase in applications for degree places. The university's improvement in the 2011 National Student Survey was among the largest at any university and took it into the top half of the table. Initial teacher training, medical science and pharmacy recorded 100 per cent satisfaction rates, while history and biology were close behind. The university's own satisfaction surveys suggest that students value the friendliness and helpfulness of staff. The dropout rate had been improving, but the latest projection of almost 20 per cent is higher than the national benchmark.

Huddersfield is living up to its mission to widen participation in higher education. Some 43 per cent of full-time undergraduates are from working-class homes – far more than the national average for the university's courses and entry qualifications – and the numbers coming from areas without a tradition of higher education are among the highest in the country. The university has opened satellite centres in Barnsley and Oldham to widen participation further.

Imaginative conversions and new buildings have brought the university together on one town-centre campus. The university capitalised on Huddersfield's industrial past to ease the strain on facilities that were struggling to cope with student numbers that have now passed 21,000. Canalside, a refurbished mill complex, provided extra space for mathematics and computing, and education occupies another mill site. The university has created "pocket parks" and a landscaped area along the reopened Narrow Canal to provide additional green space. Human and health sciences also have new premises, and £4 million was spent on a new students' union, allowing drama courses to take over the existing union complex. The union building includes alcohol-free social areas to encourage participation by those overseas students and ethnic minorities who would otherwise avoid the facilities. The latest additions include a striking creative arts building, which cost around £16 million. A similar sum was spent on a new business school, which opened in 2010.

The 19th-century Ramsden Building – the historical heart of the university – has been refurbished and there are ultra modern facilities behind its carefully preserved exterior. Over the next 18 months the university plans to invest some £58 million in facilities including a £20-million sport, learning and leisure complex and improvements to teaching and research space. A tradition of vocational education

---

Queensgate
Huddersfield
West Yorkshire HD1 3DH

0870 901 5555 (prospectus)
prospectus@hud.ac.uk
www.hud.ac.uk
www.huddersfield
  student.com
Affiliation: University
  Alliance

The Times Rankings

Overall Ranking: **57**

Student satisfaction:	=17	(81%)
Research quality:	=95	(0.06)
Entry standards:	=59	(305)
Student–staff ratio:	=56	(17.9)
Services & facilities/student:	56	(£1,398)
Expected completion rate:	92	(77.7%)
Good honours:	86	(55.7%)
Graduate prospects:	=40	(69.3%)

dates back to 1841, and the university has a long-established reputation in areas such as textile design and engineering. The university was awarded an £8-million Centre for Innovative Manufacturing in Advanced Metrology by the Engineering and Physical Sciences Research Council. Other strengths include music and social work, as well as teacher training, for which Huddersfield was awarded a national centre of excellence.

Most of the areas in which Huddersfield entered the 2008 Research Assessment Exercise contained at least some world-leading work. A third of the university's submission was placed in the top two categories, with music producing by far the best results and social work also doing well. The results brought a 45 per cent increase in research funding. A flourishing relationship with industry produces more private income than is achieved in many larger institutions, as well as influencing courses. The university has sealed partnerships recently with the National Physical Laboratory, the Food and Environment Research Agency and the Royal Armouries in developments that it expects to benefit undergraduates as well as researchers.

The most popular courses are in human and health sciences. Many arts and social science courses have a vocational slant – politics features a six-week placement, which often takes students to the House of Commons. The university's Chancellor, the actor Sir Patrick Stewart, coaches drama students in his capacity as professor of performing arts, as well as undertaking other duties. A third of the students in all subjects take sandwich courses, one of the highest proportions in Britain, and more than 4,000 have some element of work experience. The approach has been paying off in terms of graduate employment, which is the healthiest at any of England's post-1992 universities.

Most residential accommodation is now concentrated in the Storthes Hall Park student village, but additional housing is available at Ashenhurst, just over a mile from the campus. Recent developments mean that there are enough residential places to guarantee accommodation to first years, and private housing is cheap and plentiful in Huddersfield. Town–gown relations are good. although students tend to base their social life around the students' union. There is easy public transport access to Leeds and Manchester.

Undergraduate Fees and Bursaries

- » Fees for UK/EU students 2012–13   £7,950
  Placement year   £500
- » International student fees 2012–13   £11,000–£12,000
- » For English students, 1,000 NSP awards of a £3,000 fee waiver to students with a minimum of 280 UCAS points and with household income below £25K.
- » Additional support for care leavers.

Students

Undergraduates:	**12,340**	**(4,800)**
Postgraduates:	**1,400**	**(2,640)**
Mature students:	**30.7%**	
Overseas students:	**7.1%**	
Applications per place:	**5**	
From state-sector schools:	**98.3%**	
From working-class homes:	**43.3%**	

For detailed information about sports facilities: www.hud.ac.uk/sportandfitness/

Accommodation

Number of places and costs refer to 2012–13
University-provided places: 1,665 in privately-owned halls
Percentage catered: 0%
Self-catered costs: £73–£105 a week.
First years are housed on a first come, first served basis provided conditions are met.
International students: as above.
Contact: www.digstortheshall.co.uk/; www.digashenhurst.co.uk

University of Hull

Hull has moved up *The Times* League Table this year, thanks partly to striking improvement in graduate employment. The careers service approaches undergraduates early in their time at Hull and sets up meetings with potential employers on campus. Students are also offered a 20-credit module on career management skills. The approach helped the university to a top-20 finish in the 2011 National Student Survey, the latest in a string of excellent performances. There was 100 per cent satisfaction in American studies and physics, while chemistry, history, archaeology, physical geography and biomedical science all came close. The medical school, jointly run with the University of York, was even more popular with students.

The university and the city have always commanded loyalty among students, who appreciate the modest cost of living and ready availability of accommodation, as well as the quality of courses. Nevertheless, applications dropped sharply with the introduction of £9,000 fees in 2012, following a run of healthy increases. Even the medical school, which handles its own admissions, suffered a decline in the demand for places.

There are now around 20,000 students on the main campus and at the former site of University College Scarborough. The medical school, which opened in a landmark building on the former Humberside (now Lincoln) University campus after a long period as a postgraduate school, takes 150 students a year. The West Campus also contains a Business Quarter, incorporating the Business School and a new Enterprise Centre to support local firms.

The original 94-acre main campus has seen considerable development, with improvements to social facilities, new buildings for languages and chemistry, a Graduate Research Institute and a state-of-the-art sport, health and exercise science laboratory. The campus, with its art gallery and highly automated library, is less than three miles from the centre of Hull. In 2010, the university opened a history centre in partnership with the city council, telling the story of the city over the centuries. It attracted 10,000 visitors in its first six weeks. The university spent more than £13 million in the summer of 2010 upgrading the teaching facilities and student accommodation, as well as bringing together student welfare and other advice services.

The Scarborough campus has also seen investment, with new laboratories for music technology and digital arts, and a renovated café bar. A new enterprise lab opened in 2010, helping new start-up firms and existing businesses to harness their innovations. Students' union facilities and teaching rooms have also been refurbished. Hull has

Cottingham Road
Hull HU6 7RX

01482 466100 (admissions)
admissions@hull.ac.uk
www.hull.ac.uk
www.hyms.ac.uk
www.hullstudent.com
Affiliation: none

The Times Rankings
Overall Ranking: **49**

Student satisfaction:	=17	(81%)
Research quality:	=52	(0.33)
Entry standards:	53	(329)
Student–staff ratio:	=88	(19.9)
Services & facilities/student:	68	(£1,313)
Expected completion rate:	=55	(84.5%)
Good honours:	96	(53.9%)
Graduate prospects:	44	(67.8%)

always maintained a roughly equal balance between science and technology and the arts and social sciences, but the Scarborough campus tips the scales towards the arts.

A longstanding focus on Europe shows in the wide range of languages available at degree level, with the purpose-built Language Institute heavily used by all the students. Strength in politics – confirmed by one of three top research grades – is reflected in a steady flow of graduates into the House of Commons. The Westminster Hull Internship Programme (WHIP) offers a year-long placement and month-long internships for British politics and legislative studies students. A new Legal Advice Centre, staffed by law students, provides guidance and advice to the public. The university offers 400 adult education modules, as well as 2,000 courses for its full-time students.

Research plaudits have been relatively thin on the ground, however. Hull had the lowest proportion of world-leading research among England's older universities in the 2008 exercise. Health subjects, geography and environmental science, and drama, dance and performance achieved the best grades. An Institute for Learning encourages aca-demics to put research findings into practice, developing training courses and developing the university's interest in lifelong learning.

More than 90 per cent of Hull's undergraduates are state-educated, while almost a third are from working-class homes. The projected dropout rate of less than 11 per cent is better than the national average for the university's courses and entry qualifications.

Student leisure facilities have been upgraded as part of the campus building programme. The students' union has been refurbished and more than £2 million has been spent remodelling University House, which accommodates student services as well as the union. New football pitches have been added recently on campus and the Sports and Fitness Centre has been attracting praise. There is a rolling programme of refurbishment of the halls of residence in both Hull and Scarborough.

Undergraduate Fees and Bursaries

» Fees for UK/EU students 2012–13   £9,000
    Foundation degree   £7,000
» International student fees 2012–13   £11,200–£13,400
    Medicine   £24,080
» For students from England with household income below £25K, NSP awards (the Hull Bursary): £3,000, including at least £1,500 fee waiver, accommodation or resources discounts and up to £1,000 cash.
» £3,000 a year including at least £1,500 fee waiver, accommodation or resources discounts and up to £1,000 cash, for students with household income below £25K and who achieved AAB at A Level or equivalent.

Students

Undergraduates:	**12,715**	**(6,765)**
Postgraduates:	**2,440**	**(1,400)**
Mature students:	**16.3%**	
Overseas students:	**10.8%**	
Applications per place:	**4.1**	
From state-sector schools:	**92.8%**	
From working-class homes:	**32.6%**	

For detailed information about sports facilities:
www.hullstudent.com/au

Accommodation

Number of places and costs refer to 2012–13
University-provided places: 2,601 (owned stock); 150 (leased/associated stock)
Percentage catered: 49%
Catered costs: £121.31–£137.55 (31 weeks).
Self-catered costs: £59.22–£120.19 a week (34–50 weeks).
Unaccompanied first years are guaranteed accommodation if conditions are met.
International students: as above.
Contact: www2.hull.ac.uk/student/accommodation.aspx

Imperial College of Science, Technology and Medicine

Regularly in the top four in *The Times* League Table, London's specialist university of science, engineering and medicine is also in the top ten of both the QS and *Times Higher Education* world rankings. The 6,000 academic staff include 73 Fellows of the Royal Society, 71 Fellows of the Royal Academy of Engineering and 79 Fellows of the Academy of Medical Sciences. Imperial's submission for the 2008 Research Assessment Exercise contained a higher proportion of world-leading or internationally excellent work (73 per cent) than any other university's submission. The college achieved the best results in the UK for pure mathematics, chemical engineering, civil engineering, mechanical, aeronautical and manufacturing engineering, and history of science.

Imperial is not recommended for academic slouches, but tough entrance requirements ensure that they are a rare breed in any case. Even in subjects that struggle for candidates elsewhere, entrants average better than AAB at A level. There were almost 15,000 applications for 2,400 places in 2011, and demand held steady at the start of 2012, when most other universities were in decline. More than a third of the undergraduates are from independent schools – one of the highest proportions at any university and considerably more than the national average for Imperial's courses. Approaching 30 per cent of the 14,000 students are from outside the EU. The projected dropout rate has halved since last year and, at only 4 per cent, is among the lowest in the UK.

The Faculty of Medicine is one of Europe's largest in terms of its staff and student numbers, as well as its research income. The UK's first Academic Health Science Centre (AHSC), run in partnership with Imperial College Healthcare NHS Trust, aims to translate research advances into patient care. The centre is one of only five in the country, denoting international excellence in biomedical research, education and patient care. The medical school has teaching bases attached to a number of hospitals in central and west London, and Imperial is also collaborating with Nanyang Technological University, in Singapore, to jointly run a new medical school on the island from 2013.

Engineering degrees last four years and lead to an MEng. Imperial is unique in the UK for providing teaching and research in the full range of engineering disciplines. The growing business school is Imperial's main concession to the academic world beyond science, technology and medicine. There is also an environmental research campus at

---

Exhibition Road
South Kensington
London SW7 2AZ

020 7589 5111 (switchboard)
contact via website
www.imperial.ac.uk
www.imperialcollege
union.org
Affiliation: Russell Group

The Times **Rankings**
Overall Ranking: **4**

Student satisfaction:	=55	(78%)
Research quality:	=4	(0.99)
Entry standards:	3	(556)
Student–staff ratio:	5	(11.6)
Services & facilities/student:	1	(£3,588)
Expected completion rate:	10	(95.9%)
Good honours:	8	(81.7%)
Graduate prospects:	2	(87.1%)

Silwood Park, 25 miles west of London.

Scientists and engineers can develop and broaden their skills by taking humanities or business modules. Many of the courses offered involve placements and students are actively encouraged to seek summer internships. The Undergraduate Research Opportunities Programme offers "hands-on" research experience. It is especially popular in the summer vacation, when students can be paid bursaries and international undergraduates can participate without needing a work permit. The Careers Advisory Service's award-winning website has section dedicated to aiding international students, as well as supplementing the normal advice for home students. On average, Imperial's graduates have the highest starting salaries in the UK.

Imperial celebrated its centenary in 2007 and has left the University of London to trade on its global reputation. It has been redeveloping and expanding facilities on its main campus, in the heart of South Kensington's museum district. Construction of a new sports centre, a second complex of halls of residence and refurbishments to the central library were followed by improvements to the students' union bar and nightclub. Most recently, a new headquarters for the AHSC has opened on the Hammersmith medical campus.

Student satisfaction levels are above the national average and particularly good for London, where many universities have struggled in the National Student Survey. Geology, medicine, and civil engineering produced the best results in the survey published in 2011, when there were high levels of satisfaction on the quality of teaching, library and IT resources and personal development.

Imperial's specialisms have the effect of making it one of the most male-dominated university institutions in Britain, although the number of female students doubled during the 1990s and now stands at more than a third. The social scene has improved and the students' union claims to have the largest selection of clubs and societies in the country. Outdoor sports facilities are remote, but there is a new and well-equipped sports centre at the South Kensington campus offering students free gym and swimming facilities. Wednesday afternoons are left free to encourage participation in sporting activities.

Undergraduate Fees and Bursaries

» Fees for UK/EU students 2012–13   £9,000
» International student fees 2012–13   £22,500–£25,000
    Medicine   £27,500–£39,150
» Sliding scale of annual support: household income under £25K, bursary of £3,500 and fee waiver of £2,500 and then 7 bands until household income £55K–£60K, bursary of £900.
» Subject scholarships and 70 Rector's Scholarships of £1,000 for those with household income £25K–£45K.
» Check the university's website for the latest information.

Students

Undergraduates:	**8,865**	(–)
Postgraduates:	**4,945**	(**1,365**)
Mature students:	**9.3%**	
Overseas students:	**36.3%**	
Applications per place:	**6.2**	
From state-sector schools:	**62.2%**	
From working-class homes:	**16.4%**	

For detailed information about sports facilities:
www.imperial.ac.uk/sports

Accommodation

Number of places and costs refer to 2012–13
University-provided places: 2,494
Percentage catered: 0%
Self-catered costs: £59.64–£244.94 a week.
First-year undergraduates are guaranteed accommodation if application received by 27 July.
International students: as above.
Contact: accommodation@imperial.ac.uk

Keele University

Some £110 million has been spent on the Keele's 600-acre campus – the largest in the country – since the turn of the century. The latest phase aims to transform the heart of the campus, reconfiguring the Union Square plaza and providing a social hub for both informal and formal events. Two thirds of all undergraduates, as well as many postgraduates and even some staff, live on a campus which has won a clutch of environmental awards. The university shares top place with Manchester United football club in the Environment Agency's energy efficiency ranking and is opening a Sustainability Hub building to bring together universities, researchers, local communities, schools, national and international experts in the field. A degree in environment and sustainability was introduced in 2009, and all undergraduates can take a module in sustainability or environmental studies.

The broad Foundation course and four-year degree that made the university's name is a fading memory, but half of the undergraduates still take more than one subject. The new Distinctive Keele Curriculum builds on the existing degree structure, combining core academic activities with a purposeful range of co-curricular activities. There will be a new student charter from September 2012 and a focus on ten "graduate attributes" throughout the portfolio of degrees. These will include independent thinking, synthesizing information, creative problem solving, communicating clearly, and appreciating the social, environmental and global implications of all studies and activities.

All degree courses are modular, with the academic year divided into two 15-week semesters, with breaks at Christmas and Easter. Nearly all undergraduates have the option of spending a semester abroad at one of Keele's 50 partner universities. Keele remains small by modern standards, with fewer than 10,000 students at all levels. The proportion of postgraduates has been growing, and almost a third of the students now take higher degrees. Substantial increases in applications for undergraduate places in 2010 and 2011 were among the biggest at any pre-1992 university, however. Although there was a 6 per cent drop at the start of 2012, this was still better than the national average. The university has been trying to broaden its intake by targeting 12- and 13-year-olds with a special website, as well as running masterclasses in local schools and hosting a summer school. More than nine out of ten undergraduates are state educated and approaching 30 per cent come from working-class homes.

Keele has an excellent record in the

Keele
Staffordshire ST5 5BG

01782 734005 (admissions)
home-euadmissions@
 paa.keele.ac.uk
www.keele.ac.uk
www.kusu.net
Affiliation: none

The Times Rankings
Overall Ranking: **45**

Student satisfaction:	=7	(83%)
Research quality:	51	(0.38)
Entry standards:	47	(339)
Student–staff ratio:	36	(16.0)
Services & facilities/student:	=87	(£1,205)
Expected completion rate:	43	(86.9%)
Good honours:	49	(66.0%)
Graduate prospects:	30	(71.8%)

National Student Survey, with 90 per cent of final-year undergraduates satisfied in 2011, placing it among the top 10. There was 100 per cent satisfaction in human resource management and extremely good scores in education, anatomy, maths, physical geography and environmental science, physics and social work. The projected dropout rate of less than 9 per cent is well below the national average for the university's subjects and entry qualifications.

Health subjects have been the main focus of development in recent years. First degrees in physiotherapy and nursing and midwifery were added to the well-established postgraduate medical school. Keele also offers a five-year undergraduate medical course. Some 130 students each year are taught in new facilities on the Keele campus, at the University Hospital of North Staffordshire NHS Trust, three miles away, and at the Associate Teaching Hospital at the Shrewsbury and Telford Hospitals NHS Trust in Shropshire. Students take the new Keele undergraduate degree programme, which is in the process of validation by the GMC. New improved facilities for pharmacy and the natural sciences opened in 2010.

An increased emphasis on research brought limited success in the last Research Assessment Exercise. Almost half of the work submitted was judged to be world-leading or internationally excellent, but Keele was still towards the bottom of the traditional universities on this measure. The most successful subjects were history and music, with some world-class work in primary care, physics, applied mathematics, business and management, law, social policy and administration, politics, Russian and English language and literature.

Located on the outskirts of Stoke, the university is within an hour's drive of Manchester and Birmingham, and under two hours by train from London. The cost of living in the Potteries and the surrounding area is relatively low. The students' union offers entertainment on campus every night of the week and houses five bars and two purpose-built entertainment venues. The sports facilities have benefited from a new all-weather pitch, and the leisure centre has a refurbished fitness suite. A new £2.9-million nursery will accommodate more than 100 children from three months to school age.

Undergraduate Fees and Bursaries
» Fees for UK/EU students 2012–13   £9,000
» International student fees 2012–13   £10,200–£12,250
    Medicine   £20,000–£23,500
» For English students with household income below £25K with conditions, 160 NSP awards of £3,000 a year; £1,000 cash bursary for all others with household income below £25K.
» Scholarships for those with AAA at A Level or equivalent (£2,000) or AAB (£1,000).
» Check the university's website for the latest information.

Students		
Undergraduates:	**7,175**	**(800)**
Postgraduates:	**1,020**	**(1,880)**
Mature students:	**12.7%**	
Overseas students:	**10.6%**	
Applications per place:	**8.9**	
From state-sector schools:	**90.7%**	
From working-class homes:	**27.9%**	

For detailed information about sports facilities:
www.keele.ac.uk/sport

Accommodation
Number of places and costs refer to 2012–13
University-provided places: 3,200
Percentage catered: 0% (optional meal plan available)
Self-catered costs: £68–£124 a week.
First years are guaranteed accommodation on campus if Keele is first or firm choice university.
International students: guaranteed accommodation for the duration of their course. Deadlines apply.
Contact: accomenq@keele.ac.uk

University of Kent

Kent is up five places in this year's *Times* League Table, almost matching the university's best-ever position, thanks to an improvement in already impressive student satisfaction scores and a much better completion rate. The university was in the top 20 in the 2011 National Student Survey, with excellent scores in archaeology, finance, history, linguistics and politics. The university takes teaching standards seriously, encouraging all academics to take a Postgraduate Certificate in Higher Education. Kent academics have been awarded National Teaching Fellowships in each of the last four years.

The university has capitalised sensibly on its position near the Channel ports, specialising in international programmes, as well as in the flexible degree structures that have been the hallmark of most 1960s universities. Styling itself "the UK's European university", Kent now has postgraduate sites in Brussels and Paris, as well as giving many undergraduates the option of a year abroad. There are partnerships with over 100 European universities and Kent is one of the UK's most enthusiastic participants in the EU's Erasmus exchange programme, providing its undergraduates with study or work opportunities in countries from Spain to the Czech Republic.

The university has been broadening its horizons at home as well, assuming a regional role. Access courses throughout the county allow students to upgrade their qualifications to university standard, but the main focus is on the Medway towns, where Kent is involved in ambitious projects with Greenwich and Canterbury Christ Church universities and Mid-Kent College. The Medway campus, based in the old Chatham naval base, has already exceeded its target of 6,000 students, a third of whom are from Kent. The School of Pharmacy, which now has more than 550 undergraduates and nearly 300 postgraduates, is the main feature of a £50-million development.

The original low-rise campus, set in 300 acres of parkland overlooking Canterbury, is tidy rather than architecturally distinguished. The student centre has a nightclub large enough to attract big-name bands, as well as a theatre, cinema and bars, and a new concert hall and music building will be completed in August 2012. The university has another base in Tonbridge serving 3,000 part-time students across Kent, mainly taught in associate colleges. Entry grades for full-time degrees have been rising in most subjects. Offers are pitched according to the UCAS points tariff, although those taking A levels are expected to pass at least three subjects

---

Canterbury
Kent CT2 7NZ

01227 827272 (admissions)
information@kent.ac.uk
www.kent.ac.uk
www.kentunion.co.uk
Affiliation: none

The Times **Rankings**
Overall Ranking: **34**

Student satisfaction:	=34	(80%)
Research quality:	=42	(0.51)
Entry standards:	42	(352)
Student–staff ratio:	21	(14.6)
Services & facilities/student:	=61	(£1,341)
Expected completion rate:	=31	(89.7%)
Good honours:	=43	(67.8%)
Graduate prospects:	39	(69.6%)

(one of which may be general studies).

Applications had been increasing, partly thanks to the Medway development. While Kent was not immune to the general decrease in applications in 2012, the 6 per cent decline was better than the national average. The university has a more mixed intake than many in the south of England: over nine out of ten undergraduates are from state schools and over a quarter come from working-class homes. Graduates of all disciplines fare well in the employment market – the university regularly features among the top 20 for graduate starting salaries.

The university was also much more successful in the 2008 research assessments than in previous exercises, with more than half of its submission placed in the top two categories. Thirty per cent of research in social policy was considered world-leading. Kent has since been awarded 10 prestigious Erasmus Mundus doctoral fellowships in the humanities. The university has been building up its science departments, among which computing is particularly well regarded, but still a majority of the students take arts or social science subjects.

Kent opted for £9,000 undergraduate fees for 2012–13, but has committed £6 million to fee waivers, scholarships and bursaries to preserve access for such groups. Students come from 120 countries, and campus security is good, although some complain that Canterbury itself is expensive and limited socially.

Students on the main campus are attached to one of four colleges, although they do not select it themselves. The colleges act as the focus of social life, and include academic as well as residential facilities. The £25-million redevelopment of Keynes College in 2011 added 500 residential places. Further development of the Park Wood student village has brought the number of places available in Canterbury close to 5,000. Other recent developments on the main campus have included a new School of Arts building, the Canterbury Innovation Centre and a new sports pavilion. Future developments on the Medway campus, will bring the number of residential places to 1,100 by September 2013. An expanded presence in the dockyard part of the site will provide extra space for fine art and music.

Undergraduate Fees and Bursaries

» Fees for UK/EU students 2012–13 £9,000
» International student fees 2012–13 £11,625–£13,875
» For English students with household income below £42.6K and from areas of low participation, NSP awards of £4,000 (year 1); £2,000 (years 2 and 3).
» Scholarship of £2,000 a year for those with AAA at A Level or equivalent.
» Check the university's website for the latest information.

Students

Undergraduates:	**13,820**	**(2,060)**
Postgraduates:	**1,750**	**(1,320)**
Mature students:	**12.1%**	
Overseas students:	**15.2%**	
Applications per place:	**5.3**	
From state-sector schools:	**91.7%**	
From working-class homes:	**26.9%**	

For detailed information about sports facilities: www.kent.ac.uk/sports.

Accommodation

Number of places and costs refer to 2011–12
University-provided places: 4,981
Percentage catered: 16%
Catered costs: £115–£129 a week.
Self-catered costs: £95–£138 a week.
First years are guaranteed accommodation provided applications received before 31 July.
International students: as above
Contact: hospitality-enquiry@kent.ac.uk

King's College London

King's remains on the fringe of the top 20 in *The Times* League Table, but has an even higher reputation internationally. It is rated among the top 30 in the world by QS in the more research-oriented World University Rankings. Sixty per cent of the work submitted to the last Research Assessment Exercise was judged to be world-leading or internationally excellent, with cardiovascular medicine, dentistry, nutritional sciences, philosophy, languages and the digital humanities among the leaders in their fields. King's is one of the oldest and largest of London University's colleges. It is Europe's largest centre for the education of doctors, dentists and other healthcare professionals and home to six Medical Research Council centres.

King's is concentrated on four main campuses close to the Thames, within walking distance of each other. The original Strand site and the Waterloo campus, which includes the largest university building in London, house most of the non-medical departments. Nursing and midwifery and some biomedical subjects are also based at Waterloo, while medicine and dentistry are mainly at Guy's Hospital, near London Bridge, and in the St Thomas' Hospital campus, across the river from the Houses of Parliament. A fifth site, at Denmark Hill,

in south London, houses the Institute of Psychiatry, as well as more medicine and dentistry. Libraries are located on all the main campuses, specialising in the subjects taught locally. There is college-wide wireless network coverage, and broadband access in all halls of residence, providing fast, secure internet access.

The expansion of the Strand Campus into the East Wing of Somerset House early in 2012 is a historic moment in the history of King's. The renovated wing bridges the worlds of higher education, policy and the arts, and provides impressive new premises for the 175-year-old School of Law. The college has invested in new student centres on each campus and has recently completed a major upgrade of the library and student space at the Waterloo Campus, as well as teaching and social spaces at the Strand and Guy's. The conversion of the former Public Record Office in Chancery Lane created the largest new university library in Britain since World War II. A donation of £4 million by a graduate allowed the spectacular Maughan Library to be equipped with 1,600 networked reader places.

Following increased demand for places in the last two years, applications were down 14.5 per cent at the start of 2012, which was well above the average decline nationwide. About one student in five is

Strand
London WC2R 2LS

020 7836 5454 (enquiries)
contact via website
www.kcl.ac.uk
www.kclsu.org
Affiliation: Russell Group

The Times Rankings
Overall Ranking: **22**

Student satisfaction:	=55	(78%)
Research quality:	=23	(0.70)
Entry standards:	14	(458)
Student–staff ratio:	6	(11.7)
Services & facilities/student:	21	(£1,938)
Expected completion rate:	=25	(92.3%)
Good honours:	14	(78.7%)
Graduate prospects:	6	(79.6%)

from outside the European Union, many of them among the 8,800 postgraduates. King's slipped slightly this year in the 2011 National Student Survey, but still satisfied 84 per cent of final-year undergraduates. There were particularly strong scores in pharmacy, classics, and electronic and electrical engineering. An institutional audit by the Quality Assurance Agency gave King's the highest mark, stressing the excellence of the student support services.

Once known primarily for science, King's now excels in a wide range of subjects in nine schools of study, including such unusual features as War Studies. Four language departments were rated as internationally outstanding in the latest research assessments. Graduates enjoy one of the best employment rates in the UK and typically also earn among the highest starting salaries. The college's central location means King's students are in an enviable position for accessing opportunities for work experience. A new Internships Office is working with King's Careers Service to support development in this area.

More than a quarter of the undergraduates come from independent schools, despite the college's efforts to widen its intake. King's has recently launched a new Enhanced Support Dentistry Programme to attract talented school-leavers from lower performing schools, along the lines of its celebrated Access to Medicine course. An £18-million upgrade of student facilities on the Strand, Waterloo and Guy's campuses is underway, and the active students' union, which runs bars, cafes and a nightclub, puts on an extensive programme of events. The college is well provided with accommodation in a variety of residences, in busy central locations as well as quieter, residential areas. Students have access to privately run residences and others run by the University of London, as well as more than 2,500 places in university-owned provision. Some of the outdoor sports facilities are a long way from the college, but are accessible by train. There are facilities for all the main sports, as well as rifle ranges, two gyms and a swimming pool.

Undergraduate Fees and Bursaries

» Fees for UK/EU students 2012–13   £9,000
» International student fees 2012–13   £14,000–£17,800
   Medicine and dentistry   £33,000
» For English students with household income below £25K, 116 NSP awards of £6,000 fee waiver in year 1.
» Bursaries and merit scholarships, including 30 STEM awards of £9,000 fee waiver and £1,000 cash a year.
» Check the university's website for the latest information.

Students

Undergraduates:	**12,695**	**(3,105)**
Postgraduates:	**5,440**	**(4,120)**
Mature students:	**25.1%**	
Overseas students:	**17.7%**	
Applications per place:	**9.8**	
From state-sector schools:	**70.3%**	
From working-class homes:	**22.0%**	

For detailed information about sports facilities: www.kcl.ac.uk/campuslife/student/sport/index.aspx

Accommodation

Number of places and costs refer to 2011–12
University-provided places: 2,649; 752 intercollegiate.
Percentage catered: 17.9% King's Residences; 100% intercollegiate
Catered costs: £118.23 King's Residence; £126.00–£227.50 intercollegiate a week.
Self-catered costs: £78.82–£151.13 (40 weeks); £255.00 single studio.
New full-time undergraduate students are guaranteed the offer of one year in accommodation if specific conditions are met.
International students: priority for new students.
Contact: 020 7848 2759; www.kcl.ac.uk/accomm

Kingston University

Kingston is one of the largest universities in the country at undergraduate level, taking almost 7,000 new students in 2011 after a period of rapid growth. It was still among the most popular institutions in 2012, but applications dropped by more than 14 per cent as higher fees were introduced. Charges ranged from £6,000 a year for Foundation degrees to £8,500 for nearly all honours degrees, and the university expected to give financial support to at least 1,750 students. Kingston has one of the most ethnically mixed student populations of any UK university, and many undergraduates are also the first in their family to experience higher education.

The university is revitalising its four campuses, opening three impressive new buildings as part of a £123-million programme which will run to 2018. The new facilities, which include multiple projection systems, video conferencing, interactive displays and built-in voting systems, have won plaudits from staff and students alike. The centrepiece is the £20-million John Galsworthy Building at the heart of the Penrhyn Road campus, which incorporates lecture theatres, flexible teaching space and information technology suites as well as a "Knowledge Centre" giving students a

spacious setting, including at a laptop bar, in which to do course work.

There have been extensive upgrades of the library facilities on each campus. Learning resource centres bring together library, computing and multimedia facilities to encourage interactive and group learning. There are bookable study rooms with multimedia facilities and specially equipped spaces dedicated to meeting the needs of disabled users. The main centres are open 24 hours a day during term-time weekdays and a high-tech self-issue system makes borrowing much quicker and easier.

The university markets itself as in "lively, leafy London", making a virtue of its suburban location southwest of central London as well as its proximity to the bright lights. Two of its four campuses are close to Kingston town centre; another, two miles away, is at Kingston Hill; the fourth is in Roehampton Vale, where a site once used as an aerospace factory now contains a new technology block. A flight simulator and the university's own Learjet as well as a Foundation degree in aeronautical engineering continue the tradition. Kingston boasts the third-largest engineering faculty in London.

Approaching a third of the university's submission to the 2008 Research Assessment Exercise was rated world-leading or internationally excellent. The star performance was in history of art,

---

River House
53–57 High Street
Kingston upon Thames
Surrey KT1 1LQ

0844 855 2177 (application
 enquiries)
aps@kingston.ac.uk
www.kingston.ac.uk
www.kusu.co.uk
Affiliation: million+

KINGSTON
UPON THAMES

The Times **Rankings**
Overall Ranking: **101**

Student satisfaction:	=102	(73%)
Research quality:	=80	(0.10)
Entry standards:	86	(281)
Student–staff ratio:	=85	(19.8)
Services & facilities/student:	94	(£1,154)
Expected completion rate:	77	(80.2%)
Good honours:	67	(61.0%)
Graduate prospects:	81	(56.6%)

architecture and design, where half of the submission was at least internationally excellent. In nursing, 15 per cent of the work reached the top level, and in business and management studies, the proportion was 10 per cent, making Kingston the highest-rated new university in the field.

Nursing is part of the Faculty of Health and Social Care Sciences, a collaboration with St George's Hospital Medical School, which now has more than 4,000 students and also covers midwifery, radiography, physiotherapy, social work, paramedic science and biomedical sciences. Radiotherapy students are among the first in the country to hone their clinical skills in a simulated cancer treatment room, while the Centre for Paramedic Science serves as a hub for course delivery and a raft of revolutionary research projects. The Royal Marsden School of Cancer Nursing and Rehabilitation launched a new collaboration with the faculty in 2010.

More than a quarter of Kingston's places go to mature students and around 40 per cent to those from working-class families – both groups with low completion rates nationally. Students get extra support in their first year. The latest projected dropout rate is just over 15 per cent, lower than the national average for the subjects on offer. Results in the National Student Survey are slightly below the average for London universities, but accounting,

chemistry, English studies, imaginative writing and initial teacher training all scored well in 2011.

Students like the university's location, although they complain about the high cost of living. A "one-stop shop" deals with student issues ranging from careers and accommodation to complaints and financial advice. There is also a new unit, thought to be the first of its kind in the UK, offering free mediation of disputes involving local people. Each session is conducted by a student, but supervised by members of staff from the university law school who are accredited mediators. More than £20 million has been spent on halls of residence and Kingston's sports facilities have improved. A new £2.65-million sports pavilion, designed to suit both able-bodied and disabled users, and an upgraded sports ground opened in 2010.

Undergraduate Fees and Bursaries

» Fees for UK/EU students 2012–13 £8,500–£9,000
  Foundation degree £3,000–£6,000
» International student fees 2011–12 £9,950–£11,000
» For English students with household income below £25K with conditions, 528 NSP awards of £2,000 fee waiver and £1,000 as cash or voucher. First generation HE students on full maintenance grant, £1,000 bursary; care leaver's bursary available.
» Check the university's website for the latest information.

Students

Undergraduates:	**18,565**	**(2,140)**
Postgraduates:	**3,575**	**(3,320)**
Mature students:	**29.0%**	
Overseas students:	**12.3%**	
Applications per place:	**6.8**	
From state-sector schools:	**96.0%**	
From working-class homes:	**40.9%**	

For detailed information about sports facilities: www.kingston.ac.uk/sport.

Accommodation

Number of places and costs refer to 2012–13
University-provided places: 2,365; private hall: 214
Percentage catered: 0%
Self-catered costs: £96.00–£120.25 a week (university provided); £99.25 and £192.75 (private hall).
Offers accommodation to many first-years who make Kingston their firm choice.
International students: offered places if conditions met, subject to availability.
Contact: www.kingston.ac.uk/accommodation/

Lancaster University

Lancaster's two-year stay in the top ten of *The Times* League Table has ended for now, but the university is still 18 places better off than it was only seven years ago and is easily top in the north-west of England. Although a dip in staffing levels has cost the university its coveted top-ten place, students are more satisfied, entry grades have risen and employment prospects are brighter than last year. Lancaster has done well in all six National Student Surveys. Biology and linguistics recorded 100 per cent satisfaction ratings in 2011, when business studies, English and physics also did well. The university has also won nine National Teaching Fellowships since the scheme was launched in 2000.

Having celebrated its 45th birthday and almost completed a £300-million makeover for its campus, Lancaster has been expanding its overseas activities in line with its ambition to be truly international. The campus hosts students from more than 100 countries, but there will soon be more graduating with the university's degrees in India, Malaysia and Pakistan than in Lancaster itself. The university has opened a campus near Delhi in partnership with an Indian group and in the latest development, is offering dual degrees with COMSATS Institute of Information Technology, in Pakistan.

With the prospect of a new campus in the Guangdong province of China, the university is poised to become one of the first to have campuses in both India and China.

At home, recent campus developments will increase its capacity by up to 50 per cent. A £10-million building for the Lancaster Institute for the Contemporary Arts has brought together art, music and theatre studies with the university's public art gallery, concerts and theatre. A £20-millon sports centre opened in 2011. Still a relatively small institution, Lancaster has established itself among the leading research universities. More than 60 per cent of Lancaster's work was rated as world-leading or internationally excellent in the last Research Assessment Exercise. Physics was the star performer, with the best grades in the country, but there were good results in health studies, computer science, art and design, management and sociology. In an unusual move, the university has also acquired the London-based think tank, the Work Foundation.

A new 24-hour student learning space at the centre of the campus will provide flexible learning environments and social space with up-to-date technology. Infolab 21, the £15-million centre of excellence in information communication technology, acts as a technology transfer and incubation facility and houses a training facility for high-tech businesses. Other recent

---

Bailrigg
Lancaster LA1 4YW

01524 592028 (admissions)
ugadmissions@lancaster.ac.uk
www.lancaster.ac.uk
www.lusu.co.uk
Affiliation: 1994 Group

The Times **Rankings**
Overall Ranking: **12**

Student satisfaction:	=12	(82%)
Research quality:	12	(0.85)
Entry standards:	26	(410)
Student–staff ratio:	22	(14.8)
Services & facilities/student:	26	(£1,795)
Expected completion rate:	17	(93.4%)
Good honours:	=26	(73.4%)
Graduate prospects:	21	(73.6%)

developments include a leadership centre for the highly rated Management School and the establishment of the Lancaster University Confucius Institute as a hub for Chinese language teaching and culture.

Lancaster is another of the campus universities which has always championed a flexible degree structure. Most undergraduates can broaden their first-year studies by taking a second or third subject. The final choice of degree comes only at the end of that year. Combined degree programmes, with 200 courses to choose from, are especially popular. The degree portfolio now includes medicine, with students taking a five-year course following the Liverpool University curriculum. New developments include a research centre specialising in bipolar disorder and a new Centre for Organisational Health and Wellbeing.

The projected dropout rate of 6 per cent is lower than average for the subjects on offer. Lancaster also exceeds expectations for the recruitment of state-educated students, and the proportion from working-class homes is only marginally below the benchmark for the university's courses and entry grades.

Students join one of eight residential colleges on campus, which become the centre of most students' social life. Most house between 800 and 900 students in self-catering accommodation and each has its own bar and social facilities. The pioneering 800-room Eco Residence, which opened in 2008, has won an environmental award. Students can live in town houses with shared facilities and monitor their bills. As part of the developments, Cartmel and Lonsdale colleges have transferred to the New Alexandra Park area of the campus with enhanced social facilities.

The campus has been praised by students, especially for its refurbished lecture theatres and academic areas. Lancaster itself is a ten-minute bus ride away. Both the campus and city have been rated among the safest in the UK. Sports facilities are good and conveniently placed. The new sports centre includes a climbing wall built to Chancellor Sir Chris Bonington's specifications. For the outdoor life, the Lake District is within easy reach and there is a "trim trail" with a series of fixed exercise stations through the woodland surrounding the campus. Road and rail communications are good, but Lancaster is inevitably more limited than larger university centres for off-campus life.

Undergraduate Fees and Bursaries

» Fees for UK/EU students 2012–13 £9,000
» International student fees 2012–13 £12,070–£15,350
» For English students with household income below £25K, £5,000 package of fee waiver and support over 3 years.
» Scholarship of £1,000 a year for those with A*AA at A Level or equivalent.
» Check the university's website for the latest information.

Students

Undergraduates:	**8,550**	**(470)**
Postgraduates:	**2,085**	**(1,420)**
Mature students:	**6.2%**	
Overseas students:	**16.9%**	
Applications per place:	**6.2**	
From state-sector schools:	**88.9%**	
From working-class homes:	**21.3%**	

For detailed information about sports facilities:
www.sportcentrelancaster.co.uk

Accommodation

Number of places and costs refer to 2012–13
University-provided places: 6,600 (plus about 1,050 places in university-managed houses)
Percentage catered: 5%
Catered costs: £116.97 (standard) – £150.92 (en suite).
Self-catered costs: £78.75 (standard) – £134.40 (studio) a week.
All first years are normally accommodated; no formal guarantee for Insurance, Clearing and late applicants.
International students are guaranteed accommodation.
Contact: accommodation@lancaster.ac.uk

University of Leeds

Leeds is spending more than any other university on financial support for its students in the new era of £9,000 fees. It expects a third of English and EU undergraduates to benefit from subsidies, which they can choose to take as fee waivers, bursaries or accommodation discounts. This assistance may have helped to limit the decline in applications at the start of 2012, which, at less than 6 per cent, was considerably below the national average. Only Nottingham and Manchester had attracted more. An unusually wide range of degrees gives applicants more than 500 undergraduate programmes to choose from.

A curriculum enhancement programme is intended to deliver significant improvements to degree courses in 2013, without altering the integration of teaching and research that the university regards as its greatest strength. A new employability strategy encourages early career planning and offers regular engagement with employers and professional bodies. The Leeds for Life initiative helps students to identify opportunities such as work placements and volunteering to develop their skills. A partnership document introduced in 2011 sets out students' rights and responsibilities.

The university scaled back its campus development plan, but is still spending heavily on new facilities that are designed to propel it into the top 50 universities in the world. It is already comfortably in the top 100 in the QS World Rankings. A member of the Russell Group of research-led universities, it occupies a 98-acre site within walking distance of the city centre. The buildings are a mixture of Victorian and modern. The latest developments are a new £4.4-million home for the Institute of Communications Studies with 41 edit suites, TV and radio studios, newsroom and 60-seat cinema; a £12.5-million Energy Research building that contains a suite of advanced laboratories; and a £9.5-million refurbishment of the Leeds Dental Institute.

Leeds is part of the Worldwide Universities Network, which brings together 18 research-led universities to collaborate on research and postgraduate programmes. There is a thriving study abroad programme and the university has links with over 200 universities around the world. A free-standing language unit caters for casual learners as well as specialists. Around 15 per cent of undergraduates take joint honours or interdisciplinary combinations such as nanotechnology, women's studies or international studies.

Leeds has been awarded 16 National Teaching Fellowships – more than any other university in England. Scores in the National Student Survey improved significantly in 2011, taking the university well above the average for its subjects and

---

Leeds
West Yorkshire LS2 9JT

0113 343 2336 (enquiries)
contact via website
www.leeds.ac.uk
www.leedsuniversityunion.
  org.uk
Affiliation: Russell Group

Edinburgh
Belfast
LEEDS
London
Cardiff

The Times **Rankings**
Overall Ranking: **30**

Student satisfaction:	=17	(81%)
Research quality:	=27	(0.68)
Entry standards:	25	(413)
Student–staff ratio:	34	(15.7)
Services & facilities/student:	=81	(£1,216)
Expected completion rate:	30	(90.9%)
Good honours:	15	(77.3%)
Graduate prospects:	=22	(73.0%)

entry grades. Final-year undergraduates in civil engineering, aural and oral sciences, and human and social geography were 100 per cent satisfied, while medicine, French, fine art and landscape design all did well. The verdict on learning resources was especially positive, thanks to one of the largest libraries at any UK university and an extensive IT network.

More than 60 per cent of the university's submission was rated as world-leading or internationally excellent in the last Research Assessment Exercise. Electrical and electronic engineering produced the best results in the country, with social work and social policy, English, Italian, geography and nursing also highly rated. Income from research grants and contracts has grown consistently over recent years.

Sports and social facilities are first rate. Leeds teams regularly excel in competition and the university hosts one of six centres of cricketing excellence. Sustainability is a priority for the university, and Leeds has won a number of environmental awards, and was in the "highly commended" category at the 2011 Green Gown Awards for "promoting positive behaviour". The university is committed to a 35 per cent reduction in carbon emissions by 2020.

More than a quarter of the undergraduates attended independent schools and only a fifth come from working-class homes – both significantly below average for the university's subjects and entry grades. The already large students' union, famous for its long bar and big-name rock concerts, has been extended to provide better services and more space for students to socialise. It was named the NUS Students' Union of the Year for 2009–10 and is one of only three gold accredited students' unions recognised under a national evaluation scheme.

The rise of Leeds as a shopping and clubbing centre has added to the attractions of a university which has long been one of the giants of the higher education system. Town–gown relations are generally good, although residents in Headingley, the main student area for both of the city's universities, have complained about the impact on their neighbourhood. The wider local community benefits from 2,000 student volunteers.

Undergraduate Fees and Bursaries

» Fees for UK/EU students 2012–13 £9,000
» International student fees 2012–13 £12,500–£16,200
  Medicine £18,000–£29,750
» For English students with no income: £6,000 in year 1, £3,000 in years 2 and 3 as fee waiver and cash; household income below £25K: £3,000 fee waiver, cash or accommodation discount; £25K–£42.6K: sliding scale to £1;000 cash or fee waiver.
» A range of scholarships and bursaries are available.
» Check the university's website for the latest information.

Students		
Undergraduates:	22,595	(1,660)
Postgraduates:	5,295	(2,885)
Mature students:	9.1%	
Overseas students:	8.8%	
Applications per place:	7.7	
From state-sector schools:	72.6%	
From working-class homes:	20.0%	

For detailed information about sports facilities:
www.leeds.ac.uk/sport

Accommodation
Number of places and costs refer to 2011–12
University-provided places: 7,900
Percentage catered: 23%
Catered costs: £102–£161 a week.
Self-catered costs: £74–£139 a week.
Single first years are guaranteed a place provided conditions are met.
International students: guaranteed to full fee-paying undergraduates if conditions are met.
Contact: www.leeds.ac.uk/accommodation

Leeds Metropolitan University

Only six universities had attracted more applications than Leeds Met at the start of 2012, despite a drop of 11 per cent in the demand for degree places. Having seen big increases in applications in the two preceding years, the university resisted the temptation to reduce its planned charge of £8,500 a year to qualify for extra funded places. A low-pricing strategy backfired when other universities went for the £3,000 maximum at the introduction of top-up fees in 2006. This time, the university was determined to recoup lost Government funding, establish schemes to provide financial support for fee-payers and boost retention, and find new ways to improve the student experience.

Student satisfaction scores have been improving, but the university remains among the bottom 20 universities in the National Student Survey. Nevertheless, human and social geography registered an outstanding 100 per cent satisfaction in 2011 and there were extremely good results in landscape design and fine art. Only just over half all undergraduates are taking conventional full-time degrees, such is the popularity of sandwich and part-time courses. Some 2,500 international students come from 90 different countries, including 200 from Africa.

Leeds Met has a longstanding reputation for widening participation in higher education: well over 90 per cent of undergraduates are state-educated and almost a third come from working-class homes. A quarter of the students come from the Yorkshire and Humberside region, and around one in five is over 21 on entry. There is also a wide range of summer schools, including one for Asian women and one for Afro-Caribbean boys. An early application scheme allows sixth-formers and college students to secure a place eight months ahead of the UCAS process, and provides feedback to enable unsuccessful candidates to improve their applications. A Regional University Network of 24 further education colleges, which stretches from Belfast to Stamford via Glasgow, enables students to take Leeds Met courses locally. The university's projected dropout rate of 16 per cent has improved, but is still above average for its courses and entry qualifications.

There are two bases in Leeds: the Civic Quarter campus, close to the city centre, and the Headingley campus, three miles away in the 100 acres of park and woodland of Beckett Park. The latter boasts outstanding sports facilities, including the £2-million Carnegie Regional Tennis Centre, as well as teaching accommodation for education, informatics, law and business. Over 7,000 students take part in some form of sporting activity, and there is a range of £2,000 sports

---

City Campus
Leeds
West Yorkshire LS1 3HE

0113 812 3113 (enquiries)
contact via website
www.lmu.ac.uk
www.leedsmetsu.co.uk
Affiliation: million+

The Times Rankings
Overall Ranking: **104**

Student satisfaction:	=89	(75%)
Research quality:	=95	(0.06)
Entry standards:	99	(263)
Student–staff ratio:	=81	(19.5)
Services & facilities/student:	112	(£936)
Expected completion rate:	73	(80.9%)
Good honours:	93	(54.5%)
Graduate prospects:	94	(53.6%)

scholarships. The university has been named a UK centre for coaching excellence. Two synthetic turf pitches were added in 2011 and the university will receive further investment from England Basketball in 2012 to develop a multi-sport arena with seating for 700.

The Civic Quarter campus is the subject of a £100-million development programme, which began with the opening of a new film school. A futuristic lecture theatre complex next to Leeds Civic Hall now houses the business school. The former BBC building has reopened as Old Broadcasting House, while next door Broadcasting Place has become the new home of the Faculty of Arts and Society. In the first developments of their kind, a new stand was built at the Headingley rugby ground, with classrooms, coaching facilities and social space for use by the university and the two professional clubs, and a new pavilion at the adjacent Test and County Cricket ground has similar multi-use facilities. It hosts students on media, events management and hospitality courses.

Relatively few academics were entered for the 2008 Research Assessment Exercise, but nearly a third of their work was judged to be world-leading or internationally excellent. Communication, cultural and media studies, sport, and library and information management produced the best results. Students are included on the committees that design and manage courses.

A growing emphasis on educational technology is enhanced by a £20-million learning resources centre. More than 400 computers, audiovisual presentation studios and study areas are available all hours. Contacts with small and medium-sized businesses have been carefully fostered as part of the university's successful attempts to maintain a good record in graduate employment.

Like its older neighbour, Leeds Met is benefiting from the city's growing reputation for nightlife, but it is making its own contribution with a famously lively entertainments scene. With 4,500 bed spaces, those who accept places before Clearing are guaranteed university accommodation. Carnegie Village, a self-contained residential facility on the Headingley campus, has added to the places available. The Athletic Union hosts 32 clubs and university teams – especially for women – are among the most successful in national competition. A season pass for both the Headingley campus and Civic Quarter facilities costs around £100.

Undergraduate Fees and Bursaries

» Fees for UK/EU students 2012–13 £8,500
» International student fees 2012–13 £11,000
» For English students with household income below £25K with conditions, 520 NSP awards of £1,000 cash and £2,000 credit to use on university services.
» Scholarship of £1,000 for those with AAB at A Level or equivalent.
» Check the university's website for the latest information.

Students

Undergraduates:	**17,940**	**(4,980)**
Postgraduates:	**1,760**	**(2,340)**
Mature students:	**19.3%**	
Overseas students:	**5.1%**	
Applications per place:	**5.8**	
From state-sector schools:	**93.5%**	
From working-class homes:	**32.2%**	

For detailed information about sports facilities: www.leedsmet.ac.uk/sport

Accommodation

Number of places and costs refer to 2011–12
University-provided places: 4,500
Percentage catered: 0%
Self-catered costs: £82–£145 a week (41–51 weeks).
First years with Conditional Firm or Unconditional Firm offers guaranteed accommodation.
International students: guaranteed accommodation if conditions are met.
Contact: www.leedsmet.ac.uk/accommodation

University of Leicester

Leicester has become a fixture in the top 20 of *The Times* League Table, with consistently high levels of student satisfaction, generous staffing levels and high spending on student facilities. The university has shown the scale of its ambitions with a £1-billion development plan. The Queen opened the £32-million library in 2008 and another £16 million has been spent more recently on an award-winning students' union.

Applications have risen substantially over several years, although they were down 11 per cent at the start of 2012, which was rather more than the national average. Leicester was among the top 20 universities in the 2011 National Student Survey. American and Australasian studies, archaeology, biology, chemistry, French, geology, medicine, physical science, social policy and sociology produced the best results, outdone only by genetics, which registered 100 per cent satisfaction. The university has been trialling the use of social media to improve feedback in an attempt to increase satisfaction levels even more. A new web technologies facility keeps staff up to date with the latest developments in e-learning.

Although Leicester celebrated its 90th anniversary in 2011, fewer than 10,000 full-time undergraduates are based on its main campus, representing little more than half of the student population. But substantial postgraduate and distance learning programmes bring Leicester close to the size of other big city universities. Vice-Chancellor, Professor Sir Robert Burgess has focused on strengthening research, and Leicester entered a much larger proportion of its academics than many of its peers in the 2008 Research Assessment Exercise. As a result of the large entry, less than half of the university's submission was considered world-leading or internationally excellent, but there was a big increase in research funding. The star performers were the nine entrants in museum studies, who produced the highest proportion of world-leading research in any subject at any UK university, with almost two thirds of their work placed in that top category.

Leicester has the most socially diverse intake of any university in our top 20, aided by initiatives such as a summer school for local teenagers. An £8-million scholarship programme is designed to keep it that way, offsetting the impact of £9,000 undergraduate fees. Nearly nine out of ten undergraduates come from state schools and more than a quarter are from working-class homes. The 7 per cent projected dropout rate falls below the national average for the university's courses and entry grades.

Leicester was awarded national centres of excellence for teaching and learning

---

University Road
Leicester LE1 7RH

0116 252 2522 (switchboard)
admissions@le.ac.uk
www.le.ac.uk
http://leicesterunion.com
Affiliation: 1994 Group

The Times **Rankings**
Overall Ranking: **17**

Student satisfaction:	=4	(84%)
Research quality:	=38	(0.60)
Entry standards:	=27	(409)
Student–staff ratio:	13	(13.7)
Services & facilities/student:	10	(£2,175)
Expected completion rate:	23	(92.5%)
Good honours:	35	(70.4%)
Graduate prospects:	=52	(65.1%)

in geography, genetics and physics. The university also has a long-established reputation in space science, with Europe's largest university-based space research facility, including the £52-million National Space Centre. The medical school, which allows graduates in the health and life sciences to qualify in four years, has among the most modern facilities in Britain, including a new £12.6-million cardiovascular research centre. The siting of a medically based interdisciplinary research centre at the university was another indication of strength. The genetics department, where DNA genetic fingerprinting was discovered, has helped make Leicester's academics among the most cited in Britain, according to the Scopus database, which monitors research.

Clinical medicine is taught at the city's three hospitals, but all other teaching and much residential accommodation is concentrated in a leafy suburb a mile from the city centre. Its location, adjacent to one of Leicester's main parks, is popular with students. The new library has doubled the available space and brought the total number of workspaces to 1,500.

The refurbished students' union has won numerous design awards and achieved the Gold Standard at the 2011 NUS Environmental Awards for good ethical and environmental practice. The union is the only one in the country to contain an O2 Academy which has hosted gigs from the likes of Kasabian and Noah and the Whale.

Extensive residential accommodation includes a £21-million 600-bed en-suite development. The university has over 3,500 student bed spaces so first years are guaranteed a residential place. Many second and third-year students also live in hall, although the majority choose to live in the reasonably priced private accommodation available nearby. The main sports facilities are conveniently located: in 2011–12, students paid £75 a year to use them.

As a city, Leicester is not one of the most fashionable student destinations, but its ethnic diversity makes for a rich cultural experience. It is big enough to provide all the normal sports and entertainment opportunities, but also offers events such as the biggest Diwali celebrations outside India. The Demos Bohemian index rated Leicester the second most creative city in Britain behind London, and Birmingham is also easily accessible via public transport.

Undergraduate Fees and Bursaries

» Fees for UK/EU students 2012–13 £9,000
» International student fees 2012–13 £11,450–£14,645
Medicine £26,515
» For English students with household income below £25K and with academic potential, NSP awards of £1,000 cash and £2,000 fee waiver a year.
» Annual £2,000 fee waiver for those with AAA at A Level or equivalent (not medical students); £1,250 fee waiver for meeting course A Level standards.

Students

Undergraduates:	**9,465**	**(1,235)**
Postgraduates:	**3,065**	**(2,810)**
Mature students:	**11.2%**	
Overseas students:	**17.1%**	
Applications per place:	**7.2**	
From state-sector schools:	**88.5%**	
From working-class homes:	**24.6%**	

For detailed information about sports facilities:
www.le.ac.uk/sports

Accommodation

Number of places and costs refer to 2012–13
University-provided places: 4,697
Percentage catered: 32%
Catered costs: £119.70–£213.50 a week (30 weeks).
Self-catered costs: £79.80–£162.40 (42 weeks).
First-year students are guaranteed accommodation if conditions are met.
International students: as above, with priority to those returning.
Contact: www.le.ac.uk/accommodation

University of Lincoln

Lincoln achieved the most progress up *The Times* League Table of any institution over the last two years and now ties with Oxford Brookes as the top post-1992 university in England. Much-improved graduate employment, higher entry standards, better staffing levels and extra spending on student facilities produced the latest rise. The opening of an impressive purpose-built campus alongside a marina in the centre of Lincoln in 1996 brought about the most dramatic transformation of any university in recent times. Humberside University, as it had been, even gave its new location pride of place in its title. Five years later it went a step further, selling the previous headquarters campus in Hull and becoming the University of Lincoln. While not moving out of Hull entirely, the university has concentrated its activities there on a much smaller city-centre site.

The switch has paid undoubted dividends, helping to attract high-quality academics. The number of professors grew from eight to 87 in four years. Student applications have increased for most of the last decade, despite rising admission requirements. Even the introduction of £9,000 fees for every subject did not prevent applications from rising again (albeit only slightly) at the start of 2012. New entrants were offered support packages worth up to £3,000 to soften the blow.

The most recent addition to the campus is the £7-million Engineering Hub, opened in 2011. New science laboratories, sports facilities, an architecture school, a library in a converted warehouse and a students' union and entertainment venue in a former railway engine shed were previous developments in a £100-million capital programme. The various projects have won two regeneration awards. Another £30 million has been committed to complete the main campus.

A £6-million performing arts centre contains a 450-seat theatre and three large studio spaces, while the Human Performance Centre is a regional facility for excellence in sport, coaching and exercise science. In addition, the Lincoln Business School has been given its own dedicated building and a new business incubation unit is fully open. There is a one-stop-shop for students to get careers advice, enhance their CVs, gain work experience and find jobs, as well as supporting graduates who are setting up their own businesses. The university expanded its graduate internship scheme and launched a new summer placement programme in 2011.

Lincoln initially concentrated on social sciences, but the university now has a much wider range of courses. The School of Architecture, for example, has over 400 students. Art and design is based in the

---

Brayford Pool
Lincoln LN6 7TS

01522 886644 (enquiries)
contact via website
www.lincoln.ac.uk
www.lincolnsu.com
Affiliation: University
 Alliance

The Times Rankings

Overall Ranking: **=52**

Student satisfaction:	**=55**	(78%)
Research quality:	**=64**	(0.15)
Entry standards:	**56**	(316)
Student–staff ratio:	**=69**	(18.8)
Services & facilities/student:	**77**	(£1,272)
Expected completion rate:	**=47**	(85.7%)
Good honours:	**79**	(58.6%)
Graduate prospects:	**46**	(67.0%)

city centre, while animal, biological and equine studies are at Riseholme Park, a 1,000-acre site ten minutes outside Lincoln. Riseholme has been chosen as one of the training centres for equine events ahead of the 2012 Olympic Games, while the Egyptian Paralympic Team will use the sports facilities in Lincoln. Only the School of Health and Social Care remains in Hull, following the transfer of art and design degree provision in the city to Hull College.

The university was determined to achieve a high-profile return in the Research Assessment Exercise in 2008 to match a sharp rise in its research income. Lincoln entered more of its academics for assessment than many institutions in its peer group and improved on previous results, with 28 per cent of its submission judged to be world-leading or internationally excellent. The result was a £2-million boost in research grants. Communication, cultural and media studies and computer science and informatics produced the highest grades. The university has also had successes in applied research and knowledge transfer, notably with the National Centre for Food Manufacturing, based in Holbeach, which specialises in the production of chilled foods.

All students take the Effective Learning Programme, which uses computer packages backed up by weekly seminars to develop necessary study skills, and produce a detailed portfolio of all their work. Some degrees can be taken as work-based programmes, with credit awarded for relevant aspects of the jobs. Lincoln was the first university to win a Charter Mark for exceptional service. Results in the National Student Survey have improved and reached the average for all universities in 2010 and 2011. Drama, accounting, English, languages, law and nursing all recorded high levels of satisfaction.

Almost 37 per cent of the undergraduates come from working-class homes and the improved dropout rate of 11 per cent is below the average for the subjects on offer, given the entry standards. The city is adapting to its new student population with new bars and clubs, although the social scene there is not the prime draw for students. The campus now has around 1,000 beds, while private developments close to the university now provide well over 2,000 further residential places.

Undergraduate Fees and Bursaries

» Fees for UK/EU students 2012–13 £8,500
» International student fees 2013–14 £11,130–£12,755
» Students with household income below £25K, a support package of £3,000 in year 1 and £700 in years 2 and 3; £25K–£30K, £600 a year; £30K–£40K, £450 a year.
» Check the university's website for the latest information.

Students		
Undergraduates:	**8,515**	**(1,900)**
Postgraduates:	**575**	**(1,015)**
Mature students:	**15.5%**	
Overseas students:	**4.2%**	
Applications per place:	**3.7**	
From state-sector schools:	**97.7%**	
From working-class homes:	**36.9%**	

For detailed information about sports facilities:
www.lincoln.ac.uk/home/campuslife/
sportsandsocieties

Accommodation

Number of places and costs refer to 2011–12
University-provided places: Lincoln, 1,037; Riseholme Park, 180
Percentage catered: 13% (Riseholme Park only)
Catered costs: £91–£129 a week (half-board)
Self-catered costs: £96–£109 a week.
Student accommodation prioritised by distance within application date.
International students are given detailed information and assistance.
Contact: www.lincoln.ac.uk/accommodation

University of Liverpool

Liverpool has moved back into the top 30 in *The Times* League Table after improvements in student satisfaction, graduate employment and spending on student facilities. The university is investing £600 million in additional student accommodation, as well as new and upgraded teaching and research facilities. The teaching environment for the physical sciences is being transformed by new centralised teaching laboratories, while the first phase of a proposed £70-million interdisciplinary research facility has also opened recently. The finished article will bring together more than 600 scientists to focus on the major health challenges of the 21st century. The university is planning to invest £32 million in teaching facilities for the humanities and social sciences, as well as extending the Management School and refurbishing the Guild of Students building. Other new developments include major improvements in student social space and a £4-million investment in sports facilities.

A major beneficiary of recent investment has been the university's library, which underwent a £17-million redevelopment in 2008 and now offers 24-hour access to computers. The 2011 National Student Survey found that 88 per cent of students were satisfied with its resources, compared with 81 per cent nationally. Liverpool achieved an overall satisfaction rate of 86 per cent – well above the sector average. The most satisfied students were in archaeology, dentistry, English, French, history, nursing, physics, classics and veterinary science. More than half of the work submitted for the last Research Assessment Exercise was judged to be world-leading or internationally excellent. Computer science, materials, architecture, English and history produced particularly good results.

Applications had dropped by 11 per cent at the start of 2012, as £9,000 fees were introduced, all but wiping out an increase of similar proportions a year earlier. The university intends to commit more than 30 per cent of its additional fee income in 2012–13 to support for students from lower-income backgrounds and enhanced measures to prevent students from dropping out. More than a quarter of new undergraduates will qualify for a financial support package totalling £3,000 in their first year and £2,000 a year for the rest of their course. The 5 per cent projected dropout rate is significantly better than average for Liverpool's subjects and entry grades. Liverpool was among the first traditional universities to run access courses for adults without traditional qualifications. The proportion of undergraduates from working-class homes is the highest among the civic universities, at almost a third.

Liverpool L69 3BX

0151 794 5927 (enquiries)
contact via website
www.ljmu.ac.uk
www.lgos.org
Affiliation: Russell Group

The Times Rankings

Overall Ranking: **29**

Student satisfaction:	=42	(79%)
Research quality:	=38	(0.60)
Entry standards:	=27	(409)
Student–staff ratio:	10	(13.0)
Services & facilities/student:	13	(£2,041)
Expected completion rate:	=21	(92.7%)
Good honours:	29	(72.7%)
Graduate prospects:	36	(71.0%)

Liverpool is developing a growing international presence and opened a new university in Suzhou, China, in partnership with Xi'an Jiaotong University, in 2006. Chinese students can complete the latter part of their studies in Liverpool, while Liverpool-based students are offered work experience at Suzhou Industrial Park, which is home to 84 "Fortune 500" companies. Since September 2011, students in electrical engineering and electronics, computer science and maths have been given the opportunity to spend a year studying in China. All staff and students across the university can take a course in Mandarin for £10. Liverpool is planning further collaborations with universities in Chile, Mexico and Spain that will allow students to complete part of their degree at one or more of these institutions via a range of options such as projects or placements. Students will have access to a full range of support services while abroad.

Back in Liverpool, one of Europe's largest facilities for training dentists opened in 2007, marking the start of another big investment programme following the award of an additional 125 dental places from 2009. There has also been substantial investment in new educational technology. But by far the biggest spending programme, totalling some £250 million, is devoted to student accommodation. A 710-bedroom development, featuring shops and a 250-seat restaurant, will open on the city-centre campus in the summer of 2012. Existing accommodation is being refurbished and another 1,500 study bedrooms are planned on the main campus. New residences will also be built at the Greenbank site, at suburban Mossley Hill, to provide a self-contained student village.

The Guild of Students is the natural centre of social activity, but the city is also famous for its nightlife. The university's indoor and outdoor sports facilities are undergoing a £4.5-million refurbishment programme and a new gym has opened at the Greenbank halls site. The university has one of the largest careers resources centres in the UK and has recently introduced an innovative programme of "boot camps" giving new graduates opportunities for networking with employers while developing a range of employability skills. Over the next two years, more than £2 million will be invested in student and graduate internships, most of them paid and lasting for substantial periods of time.

Undergraduate Fees and Bursaries

» Fees for UK/EU students 2012–13 £9,000
» International student fees 2012–13 £11,550–£14,850
   Dentistry and medicine £22,550
» Household income below £25K, £3,000 fee waiver, year 1 for English students (£2,000 for other UK students) and £2,000 for years 2 and 3; £25K–£35K, £1,000 a year.
» Scholarships and bursaries are available.
» Check the university's website for the latest information.

Students		
Undergraduates:	**14,540**	**(2,280)**
Postgraduates:	**2,520**	**(1,525)**
Mature students:	**11.8%**	
Overseas students:	**13.4%**	
Applications per place:	**8.1**	
From state-sector schools:	**85.6%**	
From working-class homes:	**23.5%**	

For detailed information about sports facilities:
www.liv.ac.uk/sports

Accommodation
Number of places and costs refer to 2012–13
University-provided places: 4,369
Percentage catered: 59%
Catered costs: £119.90–£155.00 a week.
Self-catered costs: £86.45–£115.00 a week.
First-year students are guaranteed accommodation if requirements are met.
International students: as above.
Contact: accommodation@liverpool.ac.uk
www.liv.ac.uk/accommodation

Liverpool Hope University

Liverpool Hope continues to opt out of league tables after finishing at the bottom of our table on its only appearance in *The Times Good University Guide*. It has improved some scores since then, but the university believes that the criteria used in league tables are biased in favour of wealthier institutions with a longer history. It insists that its objections "can't be summed up in one sentence". Hope even hides its latest application rates from public view, although UCAS's annual datasets show that there were big increases in 2010 and 2011.

Hope is a unique ecumenical institution formed from the merger of two Catholic and one Church of England teacher training colleges in 1980. A university since 2005, it describes itself as "teaching led, research informed and mission focused" and includes "taking faith seriously" among its five key values. The university opened its own joint Church of England and Roman Catholic academy in September 2011, replacing two comprehensive schools. There are also partnerships with the Royal Liverpool Philharmonic Orchestra, Liverpool Tate and the National Museums Liverpool to develop cultural programmes and new curricular areas such as art history and curating.

Student satisfaction rates improved in 2011, but still left Hope among the bottom 20 universities. There was 100 per cent satisfaction in arts and design, history and physical geography, while theology came close to this mark, but music was the only other subject to satisfy 90 per cent of final-year undergraduates. Most students opt for combined subject degrees, choosing after the first year whether to give them equal weight or to go for a major/minor arrangement. Hope is moving away from modular degrees to an "integrated undergraduate curriculum" in order to give students a more rounded view of their subject. The university has significantly increased its national recruitment profile, with nearly 60 per cent of students now coming from beyond Merseyside. Entry standards have increased: the university average of 318 points in 2011 would have placed Hope in mid table on this measure.

Hope undergraduates can register for the Service and Leadership Award, which is credit-rated and runs alongside their degree work. The award recognises service work, learning and leadership development. Students can volunteer locally, within the region or internationally as part of Global Hope, the university's award winning overseas charity.

More than a quarter of the academics were entered for the 2008 Research Assessment Exercise – a higher proportion than at most comparable institutions.

Hope Park
Liverpool L16 9JD

0151 291 3111 (enquiries)
enquiries@hope.ac.uk
www.hope.ac.uk
www.hopesu.com
Affiliation: Cathedral Group

Edinburgh
Belfast
LIVERPOOL
London
Cardiff

The Times Rankings
Liverpool Hope blocked the release of data from the Higher Education Statistics Agency and so we cannot give any ranking information.

Theology was the top scorer, although a small amount of world-leading work was found in applied social sciences. Overall, only 12 per cent of the university's submission reached the top two grades – placing it among the bottom five on this measure.

Nearly 30 per cent of the undergraduates are over 20 on entry and female students outnumber their male counterparts by more than two to one. Hope comfortably exceeds all of the official benchmarks for widening participation in higher education. Almost all the undergraduates are state educated, approaching a half are from working-class families and almost one in five is from an area with little tradition of higher education – one of the highest proportions in England. This is partly the result of the Network of Hope, which brings university courses to sixth-form colleges across the North West of England, in areas where there is limited higher education. Single honours and Foundation degrees are taught in Bury and Blackburn. At 12 per cent, the projected dropout rate is well below average for the university's courses and entry qualifications.

Hope's own premises are now concentrated on two sites in Liverpool, and there is a residential outdoor education centre in Snowdonia, North Wales. The main campus – Hope Park – is three miles from the city centre in the suburb of Childwall, while the creative and performing arts are based at the more central Creative campus in Everton, where a new performance centre opened in 2010. It houses one of only three Steinway Schools in England, as well as practice rooms, recording spaces and a theatre. The £5-million main library, on the Hope campus, has 270,000 items and 700 study spaces, with electronic access from other sites.

Other recent campus developments have included a Centre for Education and Enterprise, which supports local business as well as hosting the Faculty of Education. More than £1 million has been spent on a new food court and a dedicated library and reading room has opened on the Creative campus, with a Renaissance-style garden which includes an outdoor performance area. Sports facilities have been improving. The university has a range of residential accommodation, some of it provided by a private firm, and guarantees places for international students and first years who apply before Clearing.

Undergraduate Fees and Bursaries
- » Fees for UK/EU students 2012–13 £8,250
- » International student fees 2012–13 £8,500
- » For English students with household income below £15K with conditions, 65 NSP awards of £6,000 (£3,000 accommodation discount, year 1; £1,000 credit against university services, years 2 and 3; £1,000 cash year 3).
- » £5,000 over length of course for those with AAB at A Level or equivalent.

Students

Undergraduates:	**4,740**	**(920)**
Postgraduates:	**885**	**(830)**
From state-sector schools:	**99.0%**	
From working-class homes:	**40.0%**	

For detailed information about sports facilities:
.www.hope.ac.uk/hopeparksports

Accommodation

Number of places and costs refer to 2012–13
University-provided places: 1,195
Percentage catered: 0%
Self-catered costs: £83 (shared); £102–£108 (en suite) a week.
First years are guaranteed accommodation if Liverpool Hope is their first choice and they apply before Clearing.
International students: housing is subject to availability.
Contact: accommodation@hope.ac.uk

Liverpool John Moores University (LJMU)

Liverpool John Moores (LJMU) is among a minority of post-1992 universities charging undergraduate fees of £9,000 in 2012. It said the maximum fee was necessary to promise students a "distinctive, life-changing experience worth the financial commitment". Degree applications dropped by 6 per cent, but the decline was steeper at many of the universities with lower fees. The university will use some of the fee income to improve student facilities and enhance its prizewinning World of Work (WoW) initiative. Work-related learning is included in every degree and all undergraduates are encouraged to become expert in up to eight transferable skills, applicable to a wide range of professions and careers.

The programme has been shaped and steered by leading companies and business organisations. More than 150 local employers have taken the time to be trained as WoW skills verifiers, working with LJMU to deliver graduate-entry-level interviews. In future, all students will have their skills verified through an employer-validated statement. The Centre for Entrepreneurship supports students and graduates who want to start up in business, become self-employed or work freelance, as well as working closely with programme teams to provide enterprise education through the curriculum.

Naming itself after a football pools millionaire set a pattern of innovation for LJMU. Early examples included Britain's first student charter, which became a template for others. The university also launched the first degrees in sports science and criminal justice, and the first distance learning degree in astronomy. It has been investing £180 million to transform its three campuses by 2013. Developments include the award-winning Art and Design Academy and the £25.5-million life sciences building, opened by Liverpool footballer and LJMU honorary fellow Steven Gerrard, where the world-class facilities include an indoor 70-metre running track and labs for testing cardiovascular ability, motor skills and biomechanics functions. A new professional centre, housing the Liverpool Screen School, Liverpool Business School and the School of Law, opens in June.

There is a learning resource centre in each of the three campuses and a state-of-the-art media centre that is open all hours. The university's Virtual Learning Environment enables students to access most teaching materials and a range of other support features online. Scores in the National Student Survey improved in 2011, although they were still below the sector average. Only accounting, finance, English

---

Roscoe Court
4 Rodney Street
Liverpool L1 2TZ

0151 231 5090 (course enquiries)
courses@ljmu.ac.uk (enquiries)
www.ljmu.ac.uk
www.l-s-u.com
Affiliation: University
  Alliance

Edinburgh
Belfast
LIVERPOOL
London
Cardiff

The Times **Rankings**
Overall Ranking: **=93**

Student satisfaction:	**=77**	(76%)
Research quality:	**=78**	(0.11)
Entry standards:	**91**	(277)
Student–staff ratio:	**=98**	(21.0)
Services & facilities/student:	**83**	(£1,214)
Expected completion rate:	**63**	(83.5%)
Good honours:	**=68**	(60.6%)
Graduate prospects:	**103**	(51.8%)

and imaginative writing satisfied 90 per cent of final-year undergraduates.

Mainly concentrated in an area between Liverpool's two cathedrals, the university is now one of Britain's biggest with 26,000 students in the city and another 4,500 taking LJMU courses overseas. Arts and science courses occupy separate sites within easy reach of the city centre, with the IM Marsh campus three miles away for education and community studies. Nearly half of the students are drawn from the Merseyside area.

A growing research reputation is a source of particular pride. A third of the research assessed in 2008 was rated as world-leading or internationally excellent, with 12 of the 17 subject areas having some work in the top category. LJMU was among the top four of post-92 universities for electrical and electronic engineering, general engineering, sports-related studies, architecture and built environment, anthropology, physics, biological sciences, and computer sciences and informatics. A £1.6-million maritime centre features the UK's most advanced 360-degree ship-handling simulator.

The university's efforts to extend access to higher education are successful: almost all the undergraduates are state-educated and approaching four in ten are from working-class homes. A new range of scholarships and bursaries will accompany the new fees in 2012. Among them are the John Lennon Imagine Awards, match-funded through a gift of £260,000 from Yoko Ono, which help students who have either been in local authority care or who are estranged from their parents. LJMU also has a wide range of disability support services and has been addressing concerns about its dropout rate, which is now better than the national average for the university's courses and entry grades. A new assessment room is available for students with disabilities and requiring additional support to test out a range of different furniture, equipment and technologies based on their own specific needs.

Student facilities have been improving. The university has partnerships with a range of private accommodation providers so that all new students are guaranteed accommodation if they require it. LJMU students also have free off-peak access to Lifestyles Fitness Centres around Liverpool.

Undergraduate Fees and Bursaries

» Fees for UK/EU students 2012–13 £9,000
» International student fees 2012–13 £11,055–£12,040
» For English students with household income below £25K with conditions, 442 NSP awards of £2,000 fee waiver and £1,000 cash.
» For any student with household income below £25K, £500 a year cash bursary.
» Further academic, sports and care leaver's awards including six Vice Chancellor's Scholarships of £10,000 a year.

Students

Undergraduates:	**16,715**	**(3,695)**
Postgraduates:	**1,710**	**(2,565)**
Mature students:	**20.9%**	
Overseas students:	**9.8%**	
Applications per place:	**5.3**	
From state-sector schools:	**97.0%**	
From working-class homes:	**37.7%**	

For detailed information about sports facilities:
www.ljmu.ac.uk/sport

Accommodation

Number of places and costs refer to 2012–13
University-provided places: 3,200 plus 15,000 through Liverpool Student Homes.
Percentage catered: 0%
Self-catered costs: £73–£118 a week.
All new students are guaranteed a place in university housing, even if applying through Clearing.
International students: as above
Contact: accommodation@ljmu.ac.uk
www.ljmu.ac.uk/accommodation

University of London

The federal university is by far Britain's biggest conventional higher education institution, with more than 120,000 students. The majority study at colleges in the capital, but such is the global prestige of the university's degrees that over 50,000 students in 180 different countries take University of London International Programmes.

The university, which celebrated its 175th anniversary in 2011, consists of 18 self-governing colleges, an institute in Paris and the School of Advanced Study, which comprises ten specialist institutes for research and postgraduate education. The members include some of the most famous names in UK higher education, although Imperial College left in 2007. The university's students have access to joint residential accommodation, sporting facilities and the University of London Union, but most identify with their college.

Other prestigious colleges have considered following Imperial in going their own way and applied for their own degree-awarding powers to hold in reserve, but they remain bound together by the London degree. Reforms to the university's governance have given the colleges more autonomy and look to have staved off further departures for now.

The following colleges – some of which have dropped the word from their title to underline their university status – have separate entries in this chapter. Each also appears in the main university league table, with the exception of Birkbeck, whose overwhelmingly part-time provision does not lend itself to a full comparison on the measures used in our *Guide*.

» Birkbeck College
» Goldsmiths, University of London
» King's College London
» London School of Economics and Political Science
» Queen Mary, University of London
» Royal Holloway
» School of Oriental and African Studies
» University College London

Many of London's teaching hospitals have now merged with colleges of the university:

» King's College London now incorporates Guys and St Thomas's (the United Medical and Dental Schools of Guys and St Thomas's).
» Queen Mary now incorporates St Bartholomew's and the Royal London School of Medicine and Dentistry.
» University College London now incorporates the Royal Free Hospital Medical School and the Eastman Dental Hospital.

The School of Slavonic and Eastern European Studies is now part of University College, and, from 2012, the School of Pharmacy also became part of University College London.

Senate House
Malet Street
London WC1E 7HU

020 7862 8000
enquiries@london.ac.uk
www.london.ac.uk
www.ulu.co.uk

Edinburgh
Belfast
Cardiff
LONDON

Enquiries: to individual colleges, institutes or schools.

Nine colleges do not have separate entries in the *Guide*. These are listed below, with postal, telephone and electronic contacts.

Central School of Speech and Drama

Eton Avenue , London NW3 3HY
020 7449 1648 (undergraduate admissions)
admissions@cssd.ac.uk
www.cssd.ac.uk
600 undergraduates. Acting and theatre practice.
Undergraduate fees £9,000.

Courtauld Institute of Art

Somerset House, Strand
London WC2R 0RN
020 7848 2645 (admissions)
ugadmissions@courtauld.ac.uk
www.courtauld.ac.uk
150 undergraduates. History of art degree.
Undergraduate fee £9,000.

Heythrop College

Kensington Square, London W8 5HN
020 7795 6600 (switchboard)
admissions@heythrop.ac.uk
www.heythrop.ac.uk
540 undergraduates. Degrees in theology and philosophy.
Undergraduate fees £8,250.

Institute of Education

20 Bedford Way, London WC1H 0AL
020 7612 6000 (switchboard)
enquiries@ioe.ac.uk
www. ioe.ac.uk
Mainly postgraduate education courses;
200 undergraduates.
Undergraduate fees £7,500.

London Business School

Regent's Park, London NW1 4SA
020 7000 7000 (switchboard)
webenquiries@london.edu
www.london.edu
Postgraduate MBA and other courses.

London School of Hygiene and Tropical Medicine

Keppel Street, London WC1E 7HT
020 7299 4646 (admission enquiries)
registry@lshtm.ac.uk
www.lshtm.ac.uk
Postgraduate medical courses.

Royal Academy of Music

Marylebone Road, London NW1 5HT
020 7873 7393 (registry)
registry@ram.ac.uk
www.ram.ac.uk
330 undergraduates. Degrees in music.
Undergraduate fees £9,000.

Royal Veterinary College

Royal College Street, London NW1 0TU
020 7468 5147 (undergraduate admissions)
enquiries@rvc.ac.uk
www. rvc.ac.uk
1,500 undergraduates. Degrees in veterinary medicine.
Undergraduate fees £9,000 (veterinary nursing £7,500)

St George's, University of London

Cranmer Terrace, London SW17 0RE
020 8672 9944 (switchboard)
contact via website
www.sgul.ac.uk
3,000 undergraduates. Degrees in medicine.
Undergraduate fees £9,000.

London Metropolitan University

London Met set the lowest average fees in England for 2012–13 and cut the number of courses from more than 550 to fewer than 200. The new Vice-Chancellor, Professor Malcolm Gillies, said drastic action was necessary to tackle well-publicised financial difficulties and prepare for the new fees regime. With far fewer courses, it was no surprise that applications dropped by almost 15 per cent. The university is still at the foot of *The Times* League Table, having rejoined it last year after a six-year absence, but a single point now covers the bottom three.

Undergraduates entering in 2012 will pay fees ranging from £4,500 to £9,000, according to the course, and averaging £6,850. The university was rewarded for its approach with the second-largest allocation of places (564) to be funded from the national pool reserved for universities and colleges with low fees. Subjects such as history and philosophy have gone, under protest from academics, but the university has vowed to maintain the diversity of its intake. London Met has always catered particularly for groups who are under-represented at traditional universities. It has been considering making some parts of the university alcohol-free in deference to the large number of Muslim students. More than a third of the students are Afro-Caribbean and the proportion of mature students is among the highest in England. Almost 45 per cent come from working-class homes, far above the average for the courses and entry qualifications.

The changes are part of a "radical overhaul of undergraduate education", which includes a move to year-long modules consisting of 30 weeks of timetabled teaching. Over a year, students will typically study four modules worth 30 credits each and receive a minimum of 60 teaching hours per module. The university expects first-year students to have 12 hours of teaching a week, giving more opportunity for development and guidance. Student support services, from admission to careers advice, have been remodelled and there is a particular emphasis on academic and pastoral counselling on entry and at other key points of courses. But the projected dropout rate had risen to more than 27 per cent at the time of the latest survey – the second-highest rate in England.

Student satisfaction rates rose by a full 7 percentage points in the midst of the furore over course cuts, but London Met was still among the bottom five universities in 2011. There was 100 per cent satisfaction in maths and statistics, but no other subjects satisfied 90 per cent of final-year undergraduates. The new administration

---

166–220 Holloway Road
London N7 8DB

020 7133 4200 (enquiries)
contact via website
www.londonmet.ac.uk
www.londonmetsu.org.uk
Affiliation: million+

Edinburgh
Belfast
Cardiff
LONDON

The Times Rankings

Overall Ranking: **=116**

Student satisfaction:	=114	(69%)
Research quality:	=80	(0.10)
Entry standards:	112	(228)
Student–staff ratio:	78	(19.2)
Services & facilities/student:	117	(£630)
Expected completion rate:	110	(71.3%)
Good honours:	108	(50.1%)
Graduate prospects:	114	(47.9%)

has promised a "renewed focus on student satisfaction and the quality of student learning". There has been increased investment in the campus, with more study zones and a £13.5-million refurbishment programme. A refurbished library on the Holloway Road site has more computers, informal learning spaces, technobooths and teaching rooms, as well as a café. There is also a new headquarters for the students' union on the site. At the same time, the university has been working hard to reduce its carbon footprint. A 12 per cent reduction led to the award of the Carbon Trust Standard in 2011.

Earlier developments saw four "business-related" departments join together to form the London Metropolitan Business School which, with 10,000 students, is one of Europe's largest. The biomedical sciences degree, launched in 2008, leads on to an MD course from the University of Health Studies, in Antigua. The six-year programme is based in London and graduates will complete the United States Medical Licensing Examination, enabling them to practise in America.

Since its establishment from the merger of London Guildhall and North London universities, the level of UK applications to London Met has been uneven, but overseas enrolment has remained healthy. Only three universities recruit more students from the EU, and 20 per cent of all London Met's undergraduates are from outside the UK. The university's sites are centred on the City of London and north London's Holloway Road. The graduate school was designed by Daniel Libeskind and there is an impressive £30-million science centre, which features a "superlab" of 280 workstations that is Europe's largest, as well as a multipurpose gym and sports therapy facilities.

London Met entered more academics than most former polytechnics in the 2008 Research Assessment Exercise, when almost a quarter of its work was placed in the top two categories. About half of the 21 subject areas contained some world-leading research, with architecture, media studies, education and social studies producing the best results.

Residential accommodation is limited, but many of London Met's students live at home. Sports facilities are still not extensive, although competitive teams are successful. However, the social scene is lively, particularly in north London.

Undergraduate Fees and Bursaries

» Fees for UK/EU students 2012–13   £6,100–£8,100
    Foundation year   £4,500
» International student fees 2012–13   £10,000–£10,700
» For English students with household income below £20K with conditions, 188 NSP awards of £3,000 fee waiver, year 1; £1,500 fee waiver, years 2 and 3.
» Check the university's website for the latest information.

Students

Undergraduates:	**12,695**	**(3,855)**
Postgraduates:	**3,180**	**(3,105)**
Mature students:	**51.1%**	
Overseas students:	**20.2%**	
Applications per place:	**3.5**	
From state-sector schools:	**96.5%**	
From working-class homes:	**44.8%**	

For detailed information about sports facilities:
www.londonmet.ac.uk/sports

Accommodation

Number of places and costs refer to 2011-12
University-provided places: Students have access to accommodation in a wide range of halls of residences provided by specialist student accommodation providers.
Percentage catered: 0%
Self-catered costs: approximately £103–£305 a week.
The university cannot guarantee a place in halls.
All students have access to halls spaces.
International students: as above.
Contact: accommodation@londonmet.ac.uk

London School of Economics and Political Science (LSE)

Even the gesture of setting undergraduate fees £500 below the new maximum allowable in England did not save LSE from the decline in applications that afflicted most universities in 2012. But the 8 per cent drop in demand hardly made a dent in the most intense competition for admission at any UK university. There were almost 14 applications for every place in 2011. Always one of the big names of British higher education, the LSE is in the top five social science institutions in the world, according to the QS Global Rankings. The LSE has closed the gap a little on Oxford and Cambridge in the latest *Times* League Table, and has the best record of any university for graduate employment.

The school endured a difficult year in 2011, when Sir Howard Davies, the Director, resigned over the LSE's links to the Gadaffi regime in Libya. Craig Calhoun, the American sociologist who has chaired the US Social Science Research Council for more than a decade, takes over in September 2012. The school has a long history of political involvement, from its foundation by Beatrice and Sidney Webb, pioneers of the Fabian movement. Sir Howard's predecessor, Professor Anthony

Giddens, was the academic face of Tony Blair's Third Way and before the 2010 General Election, 31 MPs and 42 members of the House of Lords were alumni. The tradition lives on, not only among the academics, but in a students' union which claims to be the only one in Britain to hold weekly general meetings at which every student may attend and vote.

The LSE has added 1,000 places in recent years, having seized the chance to tackle a longstanding shortage of teaching space by acquiring former Government buildings near the school's Aldwych headquarters. However, most of the extra capacity has gone on postgraduate courses. The campus has a cosmopolitan feel that derives from the highest proportion of overseas students at any publicly funded university. Only the much larger Manchester University has more applications from overseas. More than 30 past or present heads of state have either been students at, or taught at, the university, as have 16 Nobel prizewinners in economics, literature and peace – including George Bernard Shaw, Bertrand Russell, Friedrich von Hayek and Amartya Sen. The latest of them is Professor Christopher Pissarides, who shared the prize for economics in 2010.

Its international character not only gives the LSE global prestige but also an unusual degree of financial independence. Less than a fifth of its income is from the Higher Education Funding Council for

---

Houghton Street

London WC2A 2AE

020 7955 7125 (admissions)
ug.admissions@lse.ac.uk
    (admissions)
www.lse.ac.uk
www.lsesu.com
Affiliation: Russell Group

The Times **Rankings**

Overall Ranking: **3**

Student satisfaction:	=42	(79%)
Research quality:	3	(1.16)
Entry standards:	4	(527)
Student–staff ratio:	=7	(11.8)
Services & facilities/student:	4	(£2,625)
Expected completion rate:	=4	(96.5%)
Good honours:	11	(80.9%)
Graduate prospects:	1	(87.8%)

England, although the LSE has still been affected by cuts in Government funding. A third of British students are from independent schools – one of the highest ratios in the country and higher than the funding council's benchmark figure. Efforts are being made to attract a broader intake with Saturday classes and summer schools. The projected dropout rate of less than 4 per cent is among the lowest at any university. Scores in the National Student Survey have been the LSE's Achilles heel, but a second successive big improvement produced overall satisfaction above the sector average in 2011. Even so, only law satisfied more than 90 per cent of final-year undergraduates.

Areas of study range more broadly than the name suggests: law, management and history are all on the curriculum and there is even a small contingent of scientists. Only Cambridge recorded higher average scores than the LSE in the 2008 Research Assessment Exercise, which saw almost 70 per cent of the work submitted rated world-leading or internationally excellent. Ninety-five per cent of the economics submission, 80 per cent in social policy and 75 per cent in law reached the top two categories.

Improvements have been made to the campus over a number of years. A £30-million Norman Foster-designed redevelopment of the Lionel Robbins Building houses a much-improved library.

The move was a welcome one since the number of books borrowed by LSE students is more than four times the national average, according to one survey. Routes between most of the buildings have been pedestrianised and a new student services centre has opened. In 2008 the Queen opened the LSE's £71-million eco-friendly academic building, which helped it to second place in the "Green League" of universities in the following year. A new student centre is due to open in 2013.

Partying is not the prime attraction of the LSE for most applicants, who tend to be serious about their subject, but London's top nightspots are on the doorstep for those who can afford them. The 3,650 residential places for 9,000 full-time students offer a good chance of avoiding central London's notoriously high private sector rents.

Undergraduate Fees and Bursaries

» Fees for UK/EU students 2012–13   £8,500
» International student fees 2012–13   £15,168
» For English students, max. £3,500 for those with household income below £25K decreasing in 5 bands to £500 for household income £40–£42.6K. In addition NSP award for household income £3K or less, £3,000 support year 1; £1,500 fee waiver years 2 and 3.
» Scholarships and bursaries available.
» Check the university's website for the latest information.

Students

Undergraduates:	**3,885**	**(95)**
Postgraduates:	**5,040**	**(510)**
Mature students:	**2.0%**	
Overseas students:	**44.3%**	
Applications per place:	**13.9**	
From state-sector schools:	**66.5%**	
From working-class homes:	**19.0%**	

For detailed information about sports facilities
www.lsesu.com/facilities/sportoncampus:

Accommodation

Number of places and costs refer to 2012–13
University-provided places: 3,650
Percentage catered: about 38%
Catered costs: from £95–£197 a week.
Self-catered costs: £86–£336 a week.
First-year undergraduates are guaranteed an offer of accommodation.
Policy for international students: same as above.
Contact: accommodation@lse.ac.uk
to apply online: www.lse.ac.uk/accommodation

London South Bank University (LSBU)

London South Bank (LSBU) graduates were the best-paid of any post-1992 university at the time of the latest survey, thanks in large part to a carefully tailored programme of vocational courses. The university is charging fees of £8,450 for degrees, but was one of the few to enjoy increased applications at that level at the start of 2012. The growth in demand was doubly impressive since 55 per cent of LSBU's first-degree entrants are over 21, the group that has seen the biggest drop in applications nationally. The university added extra fee discounts in order to be allowed to accept more applicants in 2012–13 and received one of the biggest allocations from the pool of places reserved for universities with average fees below £7,500 across all courses after allowing for student support.

Three quarters of the students are from the capital and more than half are drawn from ethnic minorities. Of almost 19,000 undergraduates, 43 per cent study part-time and many are on sandwich courses. Fewer than half enter with traditional academic qualifications. The diversity of the intake is encouraged by initiatives such as the summer school for local people to upgrade their qualifications. The courses, some catering for mature students and others for younger students, start at the end of June and are limited to 15 hours a week so as not to affect students' benefit entitlement.

South Bank has always given a high priority to widening participation in higher education. It won a London education award for its work with non-traditional learners who have no family history or aspirations to apply to university. Diploma and degree courses run in parallel so that students can move up or down if they are better suited to another level of study. However, the official dropout rate has frequently been among the highest in the country and well above the average for LSBU's courses and entry qualifications. The university is targeting much of its fee income on measures to ensure that more students complete their courses in the expected time.

The university has invested over £50 million in modern teaching facilities in recent years, and developments costing another £38 million are planned. A new student centre will open in September, bringing the students' union and many support services together to make them more convenient and accessible. An Enterprise Centre will showcase the achievements of students and staff and provide start-up units for students who have created their own businesses. LBSU is one of the top universities for "knowledge transfer partnerships" with firms and other outside organisations, its projects spanning construction,

---

103 Borough Road
London SE1 0AA

0800 923 8888 (course enquiries)
course.enquiry@lsbu.ac.uk
www.lsbu.ac.uk
www.lsbsu.org
Affiliation: million+

The Times **Rankings**
Overall Ranking: **111**

Student satisfaction:	=102	(73%)
Research quality:	=91	(0.08)
Entry standards:	115	(212)
Student–staff ratio:	111	(22.4)
Services & facilities/student:	105	(£1,062)
Expected completion rate:	=96	(76.1%)
Good honours:	89	(55.1%)
Graduate prospects:	66	(61.0%)

manufacturing, energy and environment, food, information technology, health and the creative industries.

Specialist facilities such as the Centre for Explosion and Fire Research carry the vocational theme through into research. Although the university entered only 87 academics for the 2008 Research Assessment Exercise, their average grades were among the best of the new universities. More than 40 per cent of the submission was rated as world-leading or internationally excellent, with social policy, engineering and communication, culture and media studies leading the way. LSBU has struggled in the National Student Survey, however, and was among the bottom 20 universities in 2011. Accounting and business studies produced the best results. Psychology degrees have been revamped for 2012–13, making the university one of the first to adopt industry recommendations for an integrated curriculum that provides a deeper knowledge of the subject.

The main campus is in Southwark, near the Elephant and Castle, and not far from the South Bank arts complex. It includes the Centre for Efficient and Renewable Energy in Buildings, a unique teaching, research and demonstration resource for low carbon technologies, and the UK's first inner city green technology research centre. Some health students are based on the other side of London, in hospitals in Romford and Leytonstone, where there is a smaller satellite campus in Havering to supplement that in Southwark. The university now trains 40 per cent of London's nurses. It is ranked first for occupational therapy, second for mental health nursing, adult nursing, diagnostic radiography, and therapeutic radiography in NHS London's quality assessments.

A new hall of residence means that the university now has residential places within ten minutes' walk of the main campus, but first year students cannot yet be guaranteed housing. Some of the capital's biggest attractions are on the doorstep of the main campus for those who can afford them. Sports facilities include a 40-station fitness suite, a dedicated free weights room, exercise classes and a sports injury clinic. The university provides a large and comprehensive sports scholarship scheme, and has the number one men's and women's university basketball teams in London.

Undergraduate Fees and Bursaries

» Fees for UK/EU students 2012–13 £8,450
   Foundation degree £5,950
» International student fees 2012–13 from £10,000
» For English students with household income below £25K, 100 NSP awards of full fee waiver of £8,450 for year 1, 150 awards of £3,000 fee waiver for year 1, or award of £1,000 fee waiver year 1.
» Sports and other scholarships and care leaver's bursaries available.
» Check the university's website for the latest information.

Students

Undergraduates:	**11,590**	**(8,235)**
Postgraduates:	**1,735**	**(3,715)**
Mature students:	**53.3%**	
Overseas students:	**7.9%**	
Applications per place:	**6.3**	
From state-sector schools:	**97.3%**	
From working-class homes:	**45.7%**	

For detailed information about sports facilities:
www.lsbu.ac.uk/sports

Accommodation

Number of places and costs refer to 2012–13
University-provided places: 1,400
Percentage catered: 0%
Self-catered costs: £104–£107 (standard) – £128 (en suite) a week.
First-year UK students are not guaranteed accommodation, but high priority is given to those who live outside the Greater London area.
International students: first years are guaranteed accommodation if conditions are met.
Contact: accommodation@lsbu.ac.uk

Loughborough University

Loughborough has regained the four places in *The Times* League Table that it lost last year, despite slipping slightly in its traditional strength of student satisfaction. It has moved up the top 20 with much higher spending on student facilities and greatly improved graduate employment. Sixth-formers seem well aware of the university's qualities: a drop in applications of less than 4 per cent when £9,000 fees were introduced was far below the sector average.

The university remains best known for its successes on the sports field. As well as capturing a 31st consecutive British Universities and Colleges Championship in 2010, Loughborough was chosen as the official preparation camp headquarters for Team GB prior to the London 2012 Olympic Games. The campus is being used for pre-Games training in many sports. Past and present students and Loughborough-based athletes won a total of 44 medals at the 2010 Commonwealth Games in Delhi. If the university had been a country, it would have finished eighth in the medal table.

But Loughborough has also enhanced its academic reputation recently, consistently finishing well up *The Times* rankings and improving its performance in the 2008 Research Assessment Exercise. Although the results were patchy, more than half of the research in art and design was considered world-leading, and there were particularly good results in architecture and sport. The Office for Standards in Education also rates Loughborough in its top category for teacher training in physical education, design and science.

Loughborough has been one of the universities with the most satisfied students every year since the National Student Survey was launched. There was near total satisfaction in chemistry, accounting and civil engineering in 2011 and very high scores in human and social geography, management and physical science. Loughborough also won five successive *Times Higher Education* awards for the best student experience.

The university remains a major centre of engineering, with more than 2,800 students in a £20-million integrated engineering complex. Loughborough headquarters the £1-billion national Energy Technologies Institute, as part of a consortium with Birmingham and Nottingham universities, concentrating on low-carbon energy. Civil, aeronautical and automotive engineering are particularly strong.

The original 216-acre campus has benefited from a sustained construction programme which included a large student union extension and a new business school, as well as the gradual refurbishment of residential accommodation. The first phase of a £68-million on-campus accommodation development opened in 2008 and more than 5,000 rooms now all have telephone and

Ashby Road
Loughborough
Leicestershire LE11 3TU

01509 263171 (switchboard)
access via website
www.lboro.ac.uk
www.lufbra.net
Affiliation: 1994 Group

The Times Rankings
Overall Ranking: **16**

Student satisfaction:	=4	(84%)
Research quality:	=18	(0.74)
Entry standards:	34	(393)
Student–staff ratio:	=45	(16.7)
Services & facilities/student:	28	(£1,768)
Expected completion rate:	18	(93.2%)
Good honours:	=36	(70.1%)
Graduate prospects:	26	(72.1%)

internet connections. The development will eventually provide another 1,300 bedrooms in four new halls.

The purchase of the adjacent Holywell Park site increased the size of the campus by 75 per cent. This will become the focus for research and collaboration with industry, including a £59-million BAE-sponsored Systems Engineering Innovation Centre. The university prides itself on a close relationship with industry, which accounts for its record haul of six Queen's Anniversary Prizes. Arts facilities are improving with the upgrading of the Cope Auditorium to serve the campus and local community. An £8-million building for Health, Exercise and Biosciences opened in 2010 and a new Design Centre, the first project in a wider masterplan for the East Park area of the campus, opened its doors in October 2011.

Most subjects are available either as three-year full-time or four-to-five-year sandwich courses, which include a year in industry. This has helped to give graduates an outstanding employment record, as well a dropout rate of only 6 per cent, which is particularly low for the subjects Loughborough offers. The university is a leader in the use of computer-assisted assessment, offering students the chance to gauge their own progress online.

However, Loughborough misses all its access benchmarks: fewer than a quarter of the undergraduates are from working-class homes and little more than 5 per cent are from areas of low participation in higher education. The

university has promised up to £7 million in scholarships and bursaries worth £3,000 a year in accommodation discounts and other support to students from disadvantaged backgrounds.

The programme of sports scholarships is the largest in the university system. The campus boasts a 50-metre swimming pool, national academies for cricket and tennis, a gymnastics centre and a high-performance training centre for athletics. The university also boasts the UK's only centre for disability sport and has spent £15 million on its Sports Technology Institute. SportPark, a bespoke hub for some of the country's leading sports bodies, allows a variety of organisations to share best practice and innovation.

Social activity is concentrated on the students' union. The relatively small town of Loughborough, a mile away, is never going to be a clubber's paradise, but both Leicester and Nottingham are within easy reach.

Undergraduate Fees and Bursaries

» Fees for UK/EU students 2012–13 £9,000
» International student fees 2012–13 £12,250–£15,800
» For English students, household income below £18K, £3,000 package each year: £18K–£22K, £2,000 package; £22K–£25K, £1,000 bursary; £25K–£32K, £500 bursary. Enhanced support for mature students and care leavers.
» Year of Entry Merit Scholarships of £1,000 for certain courses.
» A range of sports scholarships are available.
» Check the university's website for the latest information.

Students

Undergraduates:	**11,285**	**(405)**
Postgraduates:	**2,470**	**(1,955)**
Mature students:	**4.6%**	
Overseas students:	**10.5%**	
Applications per place:	**6.3**	
From state-sector schools:	**81.5%**	
From working-class homes:	**22.6%**	

For detailed information about sports facilities:
http://sdc.lboro.ac.uk

Accommodation

Number of places and costs refer to 2011–12
University-provided places: 5,600
Percentage catered: 42.5%
Catered costs: £4,395.60 – £5,752.30.
Self-catered costs: £2,733.90 – £5,539.80.
Undergraduate first-year first-choice students are guaranteed accommodation.
International students: guaranteed housing in same residence for two years.
Contact: http://accommodation.lboro.ac.uk

University of Manchester

Manchester is spending £20 million to recruit top academics to further its stated aims of breaking into higher education's "golden triangle" of Oxford, Cambridge and London, and becoming one of the top 25 universities in the world by 2020. Although not in the top 30 in *The Times* League Table, it fares better in the more research-oriented world rankings. The new recruits will join three Nobel prize-winners on the staff. Professors Andre Geim and Professor Konstantin Novoselov brought the all-time complement of laureates to 25 when they took the physics prize in 2010. Sir John Sulston, who chairs the Institute of Science, Ethics and Innovation, won the prize for physiology and medicine in 2002. Manchester also has its first female vice-chancellor in Dame Nancy Rothwell.

The merger with the neighbouring University of Manchester Institute of Science and Technology (UMIST) in 2004 created the biggest conventional university in the UK outside the federal University of London. Some departments were already administered jointly with UMIST and the two institutions only separated fully in 1993, so the new institution was able to avoid some of the problems associated with other university mergers. A £400-million building and refurbishment programme,

the largest ever in UK higher education has been completed and another £250 million of investment is planned by 2015. Work has begun on the development of the University's £30-million "Learning Commons" building, which will open in the summer of 2012. The first phase will provide more than 1,000 flexible learning spaces, high quality IT facilities, and a campus hub for student-centred activities and learning support services.

Manchester was among the top ten universities in the 2008 Research Assessment Exercise, with almost two thirds of its submission considered world-leading or internationally excellent. There were particularly strong performances in cancer studies, nursing, biology, dentistry, engineering, sociology, development studies, Spanish, and music and drama. But scores in the 2011 National Student Survey left Manchester close to the bottom 20 universities for undergraduate satisfaction levels. There was, nevertheless, 100 per cent satisfaction in archaeology and good results in biology, chemistry, dentistry, Italian, physics and astronomy, zoology and philosophy.

The university has been trying to broaden its intake, with a particular focus on increasing recruitment from the city and its surrounding area. But it is yet to reach the national average for its courses and entry qualifications for the recruitment of state-

---

Oxford Road
Manchester M13 9PL

0161 275 2077 (admissions)
ug-admissions@manchester.ac.uk
www.manchester.ac.uk
www.umsu.manchester.ac.uk
Affiliation: Russell Group

Edinburgh
Belfast
MANCHESTER
London
Cardiff

The Times **Rankings**

Overall Ranking: **33**

Student satisfaction:	=77	(76%)
Research quality:	11	(0.86)
Entry standards:	23	(425)
Student–staff ratio:	24	(15.2)
Services & facilities/student:	30	(£1,732)
Expected completion rate:	19	(93.0%)
Good honours:	=30	(71.8%)
Graduate prospects:	38	(70.5%)

educated students or those from working-class homes. The governors agreed only "very reluctantly" to charge £9,000 fees, and Manchester intends to spend about 30 per cent of the additional income on bursaries and fee waivers of up to £3,000 a year for undergraduates from the least wealthy homes. Applications were 10 per cent down at the start of 2012.

UMIST's legacy was a strong reputation among academics and employers alike in its specialist areas of engineering, science and management. Surveys of employers frequently place Manchester among their favourite recruiting grounds, helping to produce an unrivalled network of industrial sponsorship. Employers have also rated Manchester's careers service the best at any university. The merger also produced the largest engineering school in the UK, with a £20-million budget and 1,200 students. The first phase of a new chemical engineering facility, with a sophisticated industrial pilot plant, as well as teaching laboratories, opened in 2011.

A £39-million research centre dedicated to biomedical science opened in 2009, housing one of the largest complexes of its kind in Europe. A £60 million development will create a new hotel, conference venue, and executive education centre for Manchester Business School in the strategically important Oxford Road Corridor. The business school is among the strengths of the merged institution, as is the medical school, which was rewarded for impressive teaching ratings with extra places. A new teaching block helps to cater for 2,000 undergraduates following a problem-based curriculum. Google is helping to fund new research that could help blind people to find their way around the worldwide web.

The city's famed youth culture and the university's position at the heart of a huge student precinct help to ensure keen competition for places – and hence high entry standards – in most subjects. First-rate sports facilities have improved further since the city hosted the Commonwealth Games. Students get discount rates at the on-campus aquatics centre opened for the Games, for example. The university sports teams are also high achievers, ranking 11th overall in the BUCS league. The city's reputation for violent crime has subsided, but the students' union runs late-night minibuses, self-defence classes, and regular safety campaigns.

Undergraduate Fees and Bursaries

» Fees for UK/EU students 2012–13 £9,000
» International student fees 2012–13 £12,300–£15,400
Medicine £15,400–£28,200
» Household income below £25K, £3,000 package, year 1, £2,500 other years; £25K–£35K, £1,000 cash each year.
» Scholarships and bursaries and available. Enhanced fee discounts for years out.

Students		
Undergraduates:	**27,415**	**(1,270)**
Postgraduates:	**7,955**	**(3,775)**
Mature students:	**9.6%**	
Overseas students:	**18.9%**	
Applications per place:	**7.1**	
From state-sector schools:	**77.5%**	
From working-class homes:	**21.2%**	

For detailed information about sports facilities:
www.manchester.ac.uk/sport

Accommodation

Number of places and costs refer to 2012–13
University-owned/managed places: 9,229
Percentage catered: approx 26%
Catered costs: £3,402–£6,520 (40 weeks).
Self-catered costs: £3,651–£5,103 (40 weeks).
First years are guaranteed housing provided conditions are met.
International students paying overseas fees are guaranteed accommodation if conditions met.
Contact: accommodation@manchester.ac.uk
www.manchester.ac.uk/accommodation

Manchester Metropolitan University

Manchester Metropolitan (MMU) saw the demand for places drop by 16 per cent at the start of 2012, despite setting lower fees than many of its rivals, but still only three universities in the UK attracted more applications. The average fee for 2012–13 was among the lowest in England, at little more than £6,500 after allowing for discounts and student support, although some degrees in specialist scientific, healthcare, and art and design subjects were priced at £9,000 a year because they require the use of expensive facilities.

With over 35,000 students, including nearly 7,500 part-timers, MMU is one of the largest universities in Britain. Almost 1,000 courses cover more than 70 subjects. But the giant institution boasts quality as well as quantity: more than a third of the work entered for the 2008 Research Assessment Exercise was rated as world-leading or internationally excellent. Education, English, and art and design produced the best results. The Poet Laureate, Professor Carol Ann Duffy, is Creative Director of the Writing School in the English department.

The university takes teaching seriously: small groups are used whenever possible and staff are encouraged to take a three-year MA in teaching. MMU has more professionally accredited courses than any other university and many courses involve work placements. Longstanding commitments to extending access are being continued: a fifth of the full-time undergraduates are over 25 and almost four in ten come from working-class homes. Yet scores in the 2011 National Student Survey left the university inside the bottom ten. Only aural and oral sciences, maths and statistics, imaginative writing and philosophy satisfied more than 90 per cent of final-year undergraduates. The projected dropout rate was more than 22 per cent in the latest survey, significantly worse than average for the subjects and entry qualifications.

Education courses have fared well in the Teaching Agency's performance indicators, however, especially for primary training. The university trains more teachers than any other and has launched a Centre for Urban Education to develop its expertise further. Some 800 trainees and other students taking contemporary arts and sports science are at the former Crewe and Alsager College campus in Crewe, 40 miles south of Manchester and now rebranded as MMU Cheshire. The remaining education students are based at Didsbury, five miles from the centre of Manchester, with those taking community studies. A single Institute of Education covers both centres.

The former campus at Alsager has been

All Saints Building
All Saints
Manchester M15 6BH

0161 247 2000 (general enquiries)
enquiries@mmu.ac.uk
www.mmu.ac.uk
www.mmunion.co.uk
Affiliation: University
    Alliance

The Times Rankings
Overall Ranking: **102**

Student satisfaction:	=108	(72%)
Research quality:	=71	(0.13)
Entry standards:	=71	(293)
Student–staff ratio:	72	(18.9)
Services & facilities/student:	97	(£1,116)
Expected completion rate:	94	(77.3%)
Good honours:	80	(58.5%)
Graduate prospects:	76	(58.1%)

merged with the Crewe campus in the area now known as the University Quadrant. There is a £30-million student village and arts subjects have switched to Crewe with the opening of a £6-million drama, music and dance centre. A new £10-million Sport Science Centre opened in 2010 and the Business School followed early in 2012. Exercise and sport science students were the final group to make the six-mile move to Crewe, and now only sports facilities remain at Alsager.

The five sites in Manchester will eventually be reduced to two linked campuses. The university will move from leafy Didsbury in the southern suburbs and create a £120-million "Campus for the Professions" in the city centre that will be one of the most environmentally sustainable in the UK, uniting provision for teachers, nurses, health and youth workers. The new site is close to the existing All Saints campus, on the university's border with Hulme and Moss Side.

New science and engineering buildings at All Saints cost £42 million – part of a £300-million building programme for the university as a whole. The large business school will benefit from a new £65-million building next to the Mancunian Way. Overseas links have expanded rapidly in recent years, with MMU offering exchange opportunities in Europe and further afield, as well as establishing teaching bases abroad. However, more than half of the students come from the Manchester area, easing the pressure on accommodation in a city of nearly 70,000 students. The university plays an important role in the region's economy, not least because 70 per cent of graduates stay and work in the North West. MMU is currently offering up to 100 of its own graduates paid internships for up to 12 months. The university's financial impact on the region has been put at £690 million a year and rising.

All first years who request accommodation can be housed, with priority for university-owned halls going to the disabled and those who live furthest from Manchester. The city's attractions do no harm to recruitment levels, but much depends on where the course is based; students at Crewe can feel isolated. Some potential applicants are daunted by the sheer size of the university, but individual courses and sites usually provide a social circle.

Undergraduate Fees and Bursaries
» Fees for UK/EU students 2012–13   £8,000–£9,000
» International student fees 2012–13   £10,000–£15,500
» Household income below £25K, £3,000 support package, year 1; £1,000, year 2.
» Bursary of £1,500, year 1; £500, years 2 and 3, for those with AAB at A Level or equivalent.

Students
Undergraduates:	**24,540**	**(3,195)**
Postgraduates:	**2,810**	**(4,220)**
Mature students:	**18.6%**	
Overseas students:	**6.5%**	
Applications per place:	**6.5**	
From state-sector schools:	**96.1%**	
From working-class homes:	**35.5%**	

For detailed information about sports facilities:
www.mmu.ac.uk/sport

Accommodation
Number of places and costs refer to 2012–13
University provided places: 3,530
Percentage catered: 3.9%
Catered costs: £102.50 a week
Self-catered costs: Manchester £83.50–£108.00; Cheshire £83.50–£94.00 a week.
All new full-time students will be housed if applications are received by 15 August and requirements are met.
International students: as above.
Contact: www.mmu.ac.uk/accommodation/

Middlesex University

Only one university in England will have higher average fees than Middlesex in 2012–13, after allowing for fee discounts, according to the Office for Fair Access. But the £9,000 fees and relative shortage of bursaries and fee waivers seems not to have deterred applicants. The overall demand for places was barely down at the start of 2012, when many other universities were suffering big declines. This followed two big increases in applications in successive years, buoyed by changes in nursing and art and design. The university's growing popularity has coincided with the culmination of a programme of reorganisation that introduced a new pattern of courses and more international recruitment. Middlesex also rationalised its schools to focus on its strengths in business, computing and the arts, registering particular successes with work-based courses, which drew praise from quality assessors. The university reports higher spending on student facilities than any institution outside the top four in the table and £1,000 per student higher than most of its peers.

While making its network of London campuses more manageable in recent years, the university has spread its wings to other parts of the world. Middlesex has an established campus in Dubai, and has become the first UK university to open a campus in Mauritius. The university's latest overseas venture is at Noida, east of the Indian capital of Delhi, where a new campus opened in 2011. Current Indian legislation requires students at international universities to complete their course at that university's home campus, but Indian students will be able to choose between London, Dubai or Mauritius. There are now 40,000 students taking Middlesex qualifications, 9,000 of them outside the UK. With more than 1,000 EU students coming to London each year as part of a longstanding commitment to Europe, the proportion of non-UK students at all levels is now 30 per cent.

The highly flexible course system allows students to start some courses in January if they prefer not to wait until autumn, and offers the option of an extra five-week session in the summer to try out new subjects or add to their credits. The introduction of year-long modules have the benefit of instilling a deeper level of learning, allowing students to get to grips with a subject before assessment. Nine out of ten students take vocational courses. Media students, for example, benefit from a Skillset Academy. The business school is the biggest subject area, but almost half of the undergraduates are on multidisciplinary programmes. About a third are over 21 on entry and half of the full-timers come from

The Burroughs
London NW4 4BT

020 8411 5555 (enquiries)
contact via website
www.mdx.ac.uk
www.musu.mdx.ac.uk
Affiliation: million+

The Times Rankings

Overall Ranking: **90**

Student satisfaction:	=89	(75%)
Research quality:	=64	(0.15)
Entry standards:	114	(218)
Student–staff ratio:	108	(21.9)
Services & facilities/student:	5	(£2,401)
Expected completion rate:	111	(70.0%)
Good honours:	91	(54.7%)
Graduate prospects:	=85	(55.5%)

London. Almost all of the British students are from state schools, just over 46 per cent of them from working-class homes. The dropout rate is high and rising, however, projected at 23 per cent in the latest survey – significantly worse than the national average for the university's subjects and entry qualifications.

A £200-million building programme will eventually concentrate the university on three sites in north London. There is a new art, design and media building, described by the Greater London Authority as "world class design" on the Hendon campus, catering for some 1,600 students. More than £50 million has been invested at Hendon on a library, learning resources centre and roofing in the main quadrangle to provide social space. New student facilities, including an entertainment venue, expanded nursery and refectory have been added to meet the demand from the extra students and staff. The campus, which boasts one of the country's few Real Tennis courts, also houses the business school and has a new teaching and learning centre that includes biomedical, psychology, sports and computing science laboratories.

The other locations include a picturesque country estate at Trent Park, which includes a gym and multipurpose sports hall, outdoor swimming pool, outdoor fitness trail and access to the on-site hockey training ground of Southgate hockey club. Nurses and other health students are based in four London teaching hospitals and on a campus at Archway which is shared with the University College and Royal Free Hospital medical schools. There is also a joint degree in veterinary nursing run with the Royal Veterinary College.

Previously disappointing results in the National Student Survey improved in 2011, but Middlesex remains close to the bottom 20. Dance and human resource management were the only areas to satisfy more than 90 per cent of final-year undergraduates. The number of residential places is planned to double in the next few years. Priority in their allocation is given to first years who live outside London and international students. Sports facilities have been improving and now include a "fitness pod" at Hendon with a gym and multipurpose outdoor courts.

Undergraduate Fees and Bursaries

» Fees for UK/EU students 2012–13 £9,000
» International student fees 2012–13 £10,400
» 1,095 NSP awards of £2,000 fee waiver and £1,000 cash; 675 awards of £1,000 fee waiver, all awarded on a points system.
» Academic, sports and other scholarships available..

Students

Undergraduates:	**14,400**	**(3,410)**
Postgraduates:	**2,775**	**(3,270)**
Mature students:	**33.0%**	
Overseas students:	**18.6%**	
Applications per place:	**6.8**	
From state-sector schools:	**98.7%**	
From working-class homes:	**46.4%**	

For detailed information about sports facilities:
www.mdx.ac.uk/sport

Accommodation

Number of places and costs refer to 2012–13
University-provided places: 940
Percentage catered: 0%
Self-catered costs: £111.30–£128.10 a week.
Full-year students have priority; residential restrictions apply.
International students are guaranteed a room provided they apply by the deadline.
Contact: accomm@mdx.ac.uk; www.mdx.ac.uk/accommodation

Newcastle University

For the last four years, Newcastle has been named as the best university city in the UK and there have been other accolades for its nightlife, picturesque streets and sustainability. The message appears to be getting through to sixth-formers, who applied in greater numbers than at most other Russell Group universities both in 2010 and 2011. Applications were down 6 per cent at the start of 2012, but this was still better than the sector average. The university will be charging undergraduate fees of £9,000 in 2012, but is proposing to spend £29 million on fee waivers and bursaries over the next five years.

Newcastle has almost completed the first phase of a £10-million-a-year programme of investment in its campus and facilities. The latest developments include an £8-million refurbishment of the students' union which opened in 2011, extra investment in library facilities, and a teaching and accommodation complex for international students taking pre-entry courses in English and academic skills. In addition, a £30-million research centre houses the Institute of Health and Society and the Centre for Bacterial Cell Biology.

The glass-fronted King's Gate building had already created a new "front door" to the university, as well as housing all the main student services and a visitor centre. New buildings have opened for music and medical sciences, and nearly 100 study bedrooms have been added. Science and engineering laboratories have been upgraded, disabled access improved and all students have now been provided with internet connections in university-owned flats and halls of residence.

The university has also been active overseas. A new campus in Johor, Malaysia, opened in 2011 and will add biomedical science to the existing medical degree in 2012. A second branch campus in Singapore offers degrees in naval architecture. For those who prefer to come to the UK, the university does well in i-graduate's International Student Barometer for overall student experience and ranks 8th in the world for its award-winning careers service.

Newcastle has also performed consistently in the 2011 National Student Survey, with 82 per cent of final-year undergraduates satisfied overall and 15 individual subjects coming in the top ten nationally. Media achieved the best results in the UK, medicine was joint first, while law, music, speech science and archaeology were all placed second. Newcastle is popular with students from independent schools, who take almost 30 per cent of the places, but the university was among the first in the UK that sought to attract students from a broader range of backgrounds. The dropout

---

King's Gate
Newcastle upon Tyne
NE1 7RU

0191 208 3333 (enquiries)
contact via website
www.ncl.ac.uk
www.nusu.co.uk
Affiliation: Russell Group

Edinburgh
Belfast
NEWCASTLE UPON TYNE
London
Cardiff

The Times **Rankings**
Overall Ranking: **23**

Student satisfaction:	=12	(82%)
Research quality:	=30	(0.65)
Entry standards:	22	(427)
Student–staff ratio:	=25	(15.3)
Services & facilities/student:	27	(£1,773)
Expected completion rate:	16	(93.8%)
Good honours:	23	(74.6%)
Graduate prospects:	13	(76.5%)

rate, at less than 6 per cent, is one of the lowest in the country.

The university's origins can be traced back to a school of medicine and surgery established in Newcastle in 1834, which later became part of Durham University before going its own way again in 1937. Its excellence in that area was confirmed by its selection as a national centre to disseminate best teaching practice in medicine. The Medical School has now formed a new partnership with Durham, with about a third of trainees spending their first two years at Durham's Stockton campus. Cancer research was the star performer in the latest Research Assessment Exercise, with 90 per cent of work considered world-leading or internationally excellent. Newcastle entered fewer academics than most members of Russell Group universities, but almost 60 per cent of its work reached the top two categories, with art and design, music, English, town planning and civil engineering all producing excellent results.

Recent additions to the portfolio of degrees have included food marketing and mechanical engineering with microsystems. Newcastle already had a number of unusual features for a traditional university, such as a fine art degree which attracts up to 15 applicants for each place. It also has a longstanding reputation for agriculture, which benefits from two farms in Northumberland. The award-winning NCL+

initiative encourages all students to develop employability skills through activities such as working as a student ambassador or writing for the university newspaper. On most courses, a career development module gives credit for work experience, volunteering or part-time employment.

The campus occupies 50 acres close to the main shopping area, civic centre and Newcastle United's ground. The university also boasts an expanded and refurbished independent theatre. Tyneside has plenty more culture to offer in the riverside Sage Gateshead music centre and the BALTIC Centre for Contemporary Art. The cost of living is reasonable and town–gown relations better than in many cities. Sport is a particular strength: a new £5.5-million sports centre supplements two older venues, which have been extensively refurbished. The main outdoor pitches are two miles away. Over £30,000 is awarded annually in sports bursaries for elite athletes.

Undergraduate Fees and Bursaries

» Fees for UK/EU students 2012–13   £9,000
» International student fees 2012–13   £11,500–£14,750
   Medicine and dentistry   £14,750–£27,305
» 455 NSP awards of £2,000 fee waiver, £1,000 cash year 1; £2,000 fee waiver year 2; £1,500 fee waive years 3 and 4.
» Household income below £42.6K and conditions, £1,000 fee waiver and £1,000 cash a year; 20 Promise Scholarships of £9,000 fee waiver each year.
» Other scholarships and bursaries available.

Students		
Undergraduates:	**14,775**	**(70)**
Postgraduates:	**4,440**	**(1,660)**
Mature students:	**8.0%**	
Overseas students:	**15.7%**	
Applications per place:	**6.8**	
From state-sector schools:	**70.9%**	
From working-class homes:	**20.1%**	

For detailed information about sports facilities:
www.ncl.ac.uk/cprs

Accommodation

Number of places and costs refer to 2012–13
University-provided places: 3,724
Percentage catered: 23%
Catered costs: £118.65 a week.
Self-catered costs: £73.99–£132.04 a week.
All single undergraduates are guaranteed a room in university-managed accommodation provided requirements are met. Local restrictions apply.
International students: as above.
Contact: web enquiry form at www.ncl.ac.uk/enquiries

University of Wales, Newport

The university's new £35-million City Campus opened in 2011 and won an award from the Royal Institute of British Architects for its striking design. It will be at the heart of Newport's new Cultural Quarter, designed to attract inward investment and strengthen the local economy. Student numbers have been expanding, but new controls since the switch to higher fees will deprive it of 20 per cent of the places for new undergraduates in 2012–13. The university reduced its planned fees for 2013–14 from £9,000 to an average of £7,500 when state funding was offered to make up the gap, but was allocated fewer places subsequently. Newport has been resisting official pressure for a merger with Cardiff Metropolitan and Glamorgan universities. The university was already pursuing closer links with both prospective merger partners, including a successful joint submission to 2008 Research Assessment Exercise (RAE) with Cardiff Met in art and design.

Applications fell by 10 per cent at the start of 2012, but this followed a string of increases. Students have been attracted by a range of new courses in areas such as photography for fashion and advertising, creative therapies in education, and applied drama. A poll of local employers was particularly positive about the university, and Estyn, the schools inspectorate, gave the best grades in Wales to the teacher-training courses. Newport achieved the highest possible rating in its last audit by the Quality Assurance Agency. However, student satisfaction levels have been disappointing in recent years. Despite considerable improvement in 2011, Newport remained on the verge of the bottom ten. Only business studies and initial teacher training reached 90 per cent satisfaction, although sports science came close.

The university, which was previously Gwent College of Higher Education, has over 8,000 students, including 500 from outside the EU. Virtually all the full-time undergraduates come from state schools and almost four in ten come from working-class homes. The projected dropout rate of 19 per cent is a little higher than the benchmark set according to the subject mix and entry qualifications. Newport operates a number of access schemes, and is a partner in the Universities Heads of the Valleys Institute, a community education initiative that was launched in 2010. It is expected to provide the equivalent of 4,000 places on courses up to Foundation degrees by 2015.

Newport describes itself as a "community university" and is actively involved with a range of local businesses. It was rated the number one university in Wales for enterprise education by the

---

Caerleon Campus
Lodge Road
Newport
South Wales NP18 3QT

01633 432030 (admissions)
admissions@newport.ac.uk
www.newport.ac.uk
www.newportunion.com
Affiliation: University
   Alliance

The Times **Rankings**
Overall Ranking: **108**

Student satisfaction:	=89	(75%)
Research quality:	=80	(0.10)
Entry standards:	102	(259)
Student–staff ratio:	115	(24.8)
Services & facilities/student:	106	(£1,012)
Expected completion rate:	=89	(78.0%)
Good honours:	103	(51.4%)
Graduate prospects:	108	(50.0%)

Knowledge Exploitation Fund for three years in a row, helping more than 70 new start-up businesses. Among its innovations were the Corus to Campus project for redundant steelworkers (previously employed by Corus). Newport is also well-known for photography and film, hosting the International Film School Wales, whose graduates include double-BAFTA winner Asif Kapadia, and Justin Kerrigan, director of the cult movie *Human Traffic*. Newport entered only 28 staff for the 2008 RAE, but their work was highly rated compared with most of their peers in similar institutions. More than half of it was considered world-leading or internationally excellent, with mechanical engineering and social work producing the best results.

The City Campus is now home to most courses in art and design, business and media. The building was designed to promote interdisciplinary activities, as well as to promote interaction with the business community. The Caerleon Campus, a few miles away, caters for humanities, education, health and social sciences and photography. This is also where the student village of 661 self-catered study bedrooms is located and where the Wales International Study Centre opened in 2008. Accommodation is guaranteed for students who commit to Newport by the end of August. The privately run Opal Student Halls are close to the City Campus, giving students the choice between the student village at Caerleon and the modern, purpose built block in the City Centre. A partnership with Newport Bus links the campuses, which are officially among the safest in Britain: Newport was the first educational establishment to pass an industry-standard security inspection.

A well-equipped sports centre at Caerleon has transformed facilities that previously compared unfavourably with those of other universities. The city of Newport is undergoing a £2-billion regeneration programme and has plenty of clubs and entertainment venues, but students in search of serious cultural or clubbing activity gravitate to nearby Cardiff. The university's transport links are good in terms of both road and rail. Newport sits 15 minutes from Cardiff, 30 minutes from Bristol and only 2 hours from London by train. The nearby M4 provides quick access to both the rest of Wales, and back into England.

Undergraduate Fees and Bursaries

» Fees for UK/EU students for 2012–13   £8,250–£9,000, with Welsh Assembly non-means-tested grant to pay fees above £3,465 for Welsh students.

» International student fees 2012–13   £8,700–£9,700

» Newport Bursary: household income below £25K, £4,000 over course; £25K–£50K, £2,000 over course.

» Academic enhancement bursaries and sports scholarships.

» Check the university's website for the latest information.

Students		
Undergraduates:	**3,800**	**(4,130)**
Postgraduates:	**820**	**(1,290)**
Mature students:	**36.9%**	
Overseas students:	**4.2%**	
Applications per place:	**4.2**	
From state-sector schools:	**97.7%**	
From working-class homes:	**37.5%**	

Accommodation
Number of places and costs refer to 2012–13
University-provided places: 661
Percentage catered: 0%
Self-catered costs: £79–£92 a week.
First years are guaranteed accommodation if requirements met.
International students: same as above.
Contact: accommodation@newport.ac.uk

For detailed information about sports facilities:
www.sports-centre.newport.ac.uk

University of Northampton

Northampton's aim is to be the number one university in the UK for social enterprise by 2015 and to make this its distinctive offer to students. The university intends that all degree courses should include some aspect of social enterprise, whether as a work placement, volunteering or building sustainable social and economic partnerships which would, in turn, be supported by the university. Podiatry, occupational therapy and events management degree programmes are already developing new social enterprises allowing students to earn money while they work and learn.

Fees for 2012–13 were set at £8,500, with Foundation degrees costing £6,000, but £2 million has been committed to bursaries for students from low-income families. Degree applications dropped by 10 per cent at the start of 2012, but this followed two years of record increases. A raft of new courses in leather technology, midwifery, nursing, and health and social care had helped to attract more students. Specialisms such as leather technology, fashion, and waste management have helped build overseas recruitment to more than 1,000 students from over 100 countries, while overall student numbers have risen to around 14,000. A new partnership with the London School of Business and Finance will also provide degrees in marketing and fashion marketing, initially at the school's London campus.

Although one of the newest universities, formed in 2005, Northampton can trace its history back to the 13th century. Henry III dissolved the original version, allegedly because his bishops thought it posed a threat to Oxford. The modern university originated in an amalgamation of the town's colleges of education, nursing, technology and art. It has a particular focus on training for public services in the region, with students combining their studies with work placements in the community. The police and criminal justice studies Foundation degree, delivered for Northamptonshire Police Authority, for example, has been designed to prepare students for a career in policing or the criminal justice system.

Business is the university's most popular area, but teacher training and health subjects are not far behind – the university is the region's largest provider of teachers and healthcare professionals. The School of Education was awarded the Training and Development Agency's highest grade for quality and was named an Outstanding Ofsted provider 2009–10. There have been good results in the National Student Survey, but Northampton found itself in the bottom half of the student satisfaction table in 2011. The best results were in complementary medicine, English, sociology and initial

---

Park Campus
Boughton Green Road
Northampton NN2 7AL

0800 358 2232 (courses freephone)
study@northampton.ac.uk
www.northampton.ac.uk
www.northampton
union.com
Affiliation: million+

The Times Rankings

Overall Ranking: **99**

Student satisfaction:	=77	(76%)
Research quality:	=106	(0.04)
Entry standards:	108	(240)
Student–staff ratio:	=93	(20.6)
Services & facilities/student:	48	(£1,489)
Expected completion rate:	78	(80.0%)
Good honours:	82	(57.2%)
Graduate prospects:	106	(50.4%)

teacher training.

Northampton was close to the bottom of the ranking for the 2008 Research Assessment Exercise, although there was some world-leading research in four of the ten subject areas, with history producing by far the best results. There are now 11 research centres, focusing on everything from contemporary fiction to anomalous psychological processes and transitional economics in China.

The university has two sites: Park Campus on the edge of Northampton and the smaller, but more central, Avenue Campus. They are linked by a regular and free weekday bus service. Park Campus is set in 80 acres of open green parkland, with accommodation, a sports hall, students' union centre and nightclub. A major expansion of the Sulgrave Building to provide new learning spaces for trainee teachers was completed in 2011, part of a £80-million programme of improvements. The Business School, which benefited from a £1.7-million extension in 2011, is also on the campus.

Avenue Campus, the centre for art, design, science and technology, and the performing arts, hosts frequent theatre performances, exhibitions, and its own art gallery. A £13-million investment saw the conversion of an adjacent Grade II listed former school into a technology and research centre with NVision and a 3D immersive technology and visualisation facility. Another university-backed development is the iCon building in Daventry, which opened at the end of 2011. The facility will offer a base for a diverse range of innovative, green businesses.

Northampton takes its mission to widen participation in higher education seriously: almost all the undergraduates attended state schools or colleges, while almost 40 per cent come from working-class homes. At 16 per cent, the projected dropout rate is slightly better than the national average for the university's courses and entry qualifications.

There are 1,699 residential places and another 500 planned for 2013. Sports enthusiasts are well catered for, with rugby union, football, first-class cricket and the Silverstone motor circuit on the doorstep. The university has also added a £100,000 gym to its sports facilities, which include a sports hall and outdoor pitches. The town has a number of student-oriented bars, but the two campuses' union bars remain the hub of the social scene. Both London and Birmingham are only an hour away by train,

Undergraduate Fees and Bursaries

- » Fees for UK/EU students 2012–13   £8,500
- » International student fees 2012–13   £9,100
- » Household income below £5K with conditions, 133 NSP awards of £2,500 fee waiver and £500 cash for years 1 and 2.
- » Household income below £25K, £1,000 bursary each year; £25K–£42.6K, £500 a year.

Students

Undergraduates:	**9,080**	**(3,245)**
Postgraduates:	**1,100**	**(1,435)**
Mature students:	**33.3%**	
Overseas students:	**8.8%**	
Applications per place:	**6.2**	
From state-sector schools:	**98.0%**	
From working-class homes:	**38.9%**	

For detailed information about sports facilities: www.northampton.ac.uk/info/20167/campus-facilities/384/sports-facilities

Accommodation

Number of places and costs refer to 2012–13
University-provided places: 1,699
Percentage catered: 0%
Self-catered costs: £48 (small twin) – £105 (en-suite single) a week (42-week contract)
New first years have priority, on first come, first served basis, provided requirements are met. Local restrictions apply.
International students: as above.
Contact: www.northampton.ac.uk/study/accommodation

Northumbria University

The demand for places at Northumbria has risen by more than a third in four years and remained steady at degree level at the start of 2012, despite the introduction of £8,500 fees. The university expects up to 40 per cent of undergraduates to qualify for financial support, with those from the poorest homes saving £4,000 in fee waivers and bursaries, while those achieving AAB at A level collect £1,000 scholarships. The university is also promising to improve staffing levels, building on an £18-million programme to recruit more academics. Seven of the current staff have won National Teaching Fellowships.

Northumbria has invested £160 million in its impressive city centre campus and remains among the leading post-1992 universities in *The Times* League Table. The first phase was completed in 2007, when design, law and business students moved into the new City Campus East development, which is linked to the existing main campus by an iconic new footbridge spanning Newcastle's central motorway. Extensive developments on the west side of the campus are now complete and include a £7-million refurbishment of the library, which is open 24 hours a day, and a £30-million sports centre which includes a swimming pool with an adjustable floor,

multiple laboratories and a climbing wall. The £7-millionn renovation of the students' union has seen immediate results as Northumbria won the 2011 "NUS Students' Union of the Year Award". An environmental chamber allows researchers to experience conditions equivalent to anywhere in the world, and there is a 3,000-seater indoor arena for professional sport and other events.

Northumbria is the largest university in the region, both at undergraduate and postgraduate level, and has more than 8,000 students from overseas. Three quarters of students are from the North East of England but numbers drawn from other parts of the UK have been rising year on year. A further 4,000 are studying Northumbria degrees in other countries.

Entry grades for those with A levels have been rising and are among the highest in the new universities, but half of the mature students enter through the Higher Education Foundation Certificate, an access course system with modules in more than 30 subjects. Free one-day taster courses run throughout the year to give local people an idea of what studying at Northumbria would be like. Almost a third of the students come from working-class homes, many from areas with little tradition of higher education. The projected dropout rate improved dramatically in the latest survey and, at only 10 per cent, is well

---

Ellison Terrace
Newcastle upon Tyne
NE1 8ST

0191 243 7420 (admissions)
er.admissions@northumbria..ac.uk
www.northumbria.ac.uk
http://mynsu.northumbria.
 ac.uk
Affiliation: University
 Alliance

The Times Rankings
Overall Ranking: **58**

Student satisfaction:	=55	(78%)
Research quality:	=91	(0.08)
Entry standards:	55	(318)
Student–staff ratio:	=51	(17.4)
Services & facilities/student:	65	(£1,329)
Expected completion rate:	=40	(87.7%)
Good honours:	72	(59.5%)
Graduate prospects:	57	(63.6%)

below average for Northumbria's courses and entry grades. Scores also improved in the 2011 National Student Survey, placing the university around mid table for satisfaction rates. Accounting, architecture, initial teacher training, human and social geography, Iberian studies, law, mathematics and statistics, social work and planning, all registered at least 90 per cent satisfaction.

Northumbria is one of only eight institutions to hold maximum Ofsted grades for its primary teacher training provision and one of five to reach this standard for secondary provision. Its PGCE training was second only to Cambridge's in a 2010 ranking. Many degrees are available as sandwich courses, with placements of up to a year in business or industry. Most subjects are based in the city centre, with health, education and community studies on the Coach Lane campus, on the outskirts of the city, where £18 million has been spent upgrading facilities. Coach Lane now incorporates a learning resources centre with a fully integrated library, a clinical skills centre, where students can learn in simulated hospital environments, and new sports facilities.

Northumbria's best-known feature is its School of Design, which has launched a new base in London. Its students won a string of awards in 2010, while the academics produced some of the university's best results in the 2008 Research Assessment Exercise. The university entered a comparatively low proportion of its academics, but more than a third of its submission was considered world-leading or internationally excellent. Architecture and the built environment, general engineering and nursing and midwifery were other high scorers. Northumbria intends to double its capacity in research and enterprise over the next five years.

Sport plays a growing role: Northumbria is consistently among the top 20 in the British Universities and Colleges Sport rankings. The sports scholarship programme has supported over 250 athletes from over 40 sports in the past ten years, some going on to success at the highest level. Most first years are offered places in university accommodation. Two large residential developments with en-suite rooms opened in 2011, bringing the total stock to 4,500 places, and there is a plentiful supply of privately rented flats and houses.

Undergraduate Fees and Bursaries

- » Fees for UK/EU students 2012–13 £8,500
- » International student fees 2012–13 £9,900–£10,600
  Physiotherapy £11,800
- » Household income below £16K, £3,000 fee waivers, £1,000 cash; £16K–£25K, £2,000 fee waiver, £1,000 cash; £25K–£40K, £1,000 cash.
- » Award of £1,000 a year for those with AAB at A Level or equivalent.

Students

Undergraduates:	**18,195**	**(5,980)**
Postgraduates:	**2,570**	**(2,680)**
Mature students:	**18.5%**	
Overseas students:	**9.7%**	
Applications per place:	**4.7**	
From state-sector schools:	**90.6%**	
From working-class homes:	**31.3%**	

For detailed information about sports facilities:
www.nusportcentral.com

Accommodation

Number of places and costs refer to 2012–13
University-provided places: 4,500
Percentage catered: 6%
Catered costs: £123.83 a week.
Self-catered costs: £84.49 (single) – £169.00 (studio) a week.
First years who need accommodation can be offered rooms. Local restrictions apply.
International students: first years are guaranteed accommodation if requirements met.
Contact: rc.accommodation@northumbria.ac.uk

University of Nottingham

Nottingham regained its status as the most popular university in Britain at the start of the 2012, when it bucked the national trend with a 9 per cent rise in degree applications. Coming as £9,000 fees were introduced, the latest figures represented the most impressive of a series of increases in the demand for places. The university was already one of the most selective, with more than seven applications per place in 2011, despite now having more than 40,000 students. It is seen as a prime alternative to Oxbridge and recently demonstrated its standing in research by attracting a £12-million grant from GlaxoSmithKline to establish a centre of excellence in sustainable chemistry.

Nottingham is the nearest Britain has to a truly global university, with campuses in China and Malaysia modelled on a headquarters that is among the most attractive in Britain. The university has been invited to establish a second Chinese campus in Shanghai. Despite dropping four places in this year's *Times* League Table, it remains in the top 20 and has broken into the top 75 in the QS World University Rankings. Nottingham has won two Nobel prizes since the millennium for work carried out at the university. Professor Sir Peter Mansfield, who won the medicine prize for research leading to the development of the MRI scanner, has spent almost all his academic career there.

About £70 million was spent on recruiting academics in advance of the last Research Assessment Exercise. The investment paid off with sharply improved results, which brought long-term increases in funding. Almost 60 per cent of a big submission was judged to be world-leading or internationally excellent, with pharmacy and Spanish, Portuguese and Latin American studies producing the best results in the UK, and chemistry and physics the second-best.

The university has succeeded in broadening its intake, but still has significantly more independent school students and fewer from working-class homes than the national average for the subjects it offers. There is a well-established programme of summer schools, masterclasses and support for teenagers from backgrounds without a history of progressing to selective universities. Once in, they tend to stay the course – the 4 per cent dropout rate is among the best in the country.

Consistently good results in the National Student Survey continued in 2011, when 87 per cent of final-year undergraduates were satisfied. Anatomy, physiology and pathology registered nearly 100 per cent satisfaction, while archaeology, biology, chemistry, classics, philosophy, veterinary sciences, initial teacher training and

---

University Park
Nottingham NG7 2RD

0115 951 5559 (enquiries)
undergraduate-enquiries@
   nottingham.ac.uk
www.nottingham.ac.uk
www.su.nottingham.ac.uk
Affiliation: Russell Group

The Times **Rankings**
Overall Ranking: **=20**

Student satisfaction:	=34	(80%)
Research quality:	=21	(0.72)
Entry standards:	20	(436)
Student–staff ratio:	16	(14.0)
Services & facilities/student:	34	(£1,656)
Expected completion rate:	11	(94.9%)
Good honours:	21	(74.9%)
Graduate prospects:	16	(76.0%)

drama produced outstanding scores after particular improvement in the grades for staff feedback – the most common cause for complaint nationally. The university has also stepped up its efforts to give students the best possible chance in the jobs market. The Nottingham Advantage Award offers extra-curricular modules, as well as providing scores of internships for graduates, who enjoy lifetime access to the careers service.

The original University Park campus has won eight consecutive Green Flag awards for excellent parkland and was named as the most sustainable campus in the world by the UI Greenmetric in 2011. A mile away is the 30-acre Jubilee campus, where futuristic buildings cluster around an artificial lake and house the schools of management and finance, computer science and education, as well as 750 residential places. A £90-million pound programme of new investment has seen the opening of new sports facilities, research laboratories and student accommodation, as well as adding high-quality teaching space in a range of subjects.

The Queen's Medical School is also close to University Park, although its graduate-entry outpost is in Derby. The biosciences and the new veterinary school are at Sutton Bonington, 12 miles south of the city in a rural setting. A third student services centre has opened there, so that there is now a centre on all three UK campuses.

Nottingham has long-standing links with the Far East, which provides the majority of its 8,000 overseas students in the UK. A Chinese physicist, Professor Fujia Yang, is the university's Chancellor. The two branch campuses outside Kuala Lumpur, in Malaysia, and at Ningbo, in China, now host another 8,000 students. The purpose-built campuses have echoes of Nottingham's distinctive clock tower. All students have the opportunity to move between the three countries.

The two main campuses are within three miles of the centre of Nottingham, with a good selection of student-friendly clubs. However, halls of residence and the students' union tend to be the centre of social life for students. New bars, café facilities and a nightclub were included in a £1-million student facilities. makeover Sports provision is excellent. A £1.6-million sports pavilion opened in 2010 at the university's playing fields adjoining the main campus.

Undergraduate Fees and Bursaries

» Fees for UK/EU students 2012–13 £9,000
» International student fees 2012–13 £11,990–£15,720
  Medicine £16,570–£28,800
  Veterinary medicine £15,720–£23,300
» Household income below £15K, £3,000 cash; sliding scale to £42.6K, £2,000–£750 each year.
» NSP award of £9,000 fee waiver for care leavers; £4,500 package for East Midlands students.
» Subject scholarships available.

Students

Undergraduates:	**23,025**	**(2,085)**
Postgraduates:	**7,345**	**(2,720)**
Mature students:	**8.4%**	
Overseas students:	**15.8%**	
Applications per place:	**7.3**	
From state-sector schools:	**71.3%**	
From working-class homes:	**17.5%**	

For detailed information about sports facilities:
www.nottingham.ac.uk/sport

Accommodation

Number of places and costs refer to 2011–12
University-provided places: 7,500
Percentage catered: 50%
Catered costs: £117.19–£189.32 a week (31 weeks).
Self-catered costs: £90.00–£161.34 a week (43–44 weeks).
First years are guaranteed accommodation if conditions are met.
International undergraduates: as above.
Contact: www.nottingham.ac.uk/accommodation

Nottingham Trent University

All three of Nottingham Trent's (NTU) campuses have benefited from a £130-million development programme that is transforming the facilities available to students. The latest phase of a six-year scheme saw £90 million spent on the regeneration of two listed buildings in the city centre. Other projects have added new lecture theatres, restaurants, student services areas and laboratories. Art and design facilities on the City site have been upgraded, as has the Boots Library, while £20 million has been spent on a new animal unit and veterinary nursing centre at the Brackenhurst campus, 14 miles outside Nottingham. But the developments have coincided with another fall in *The Times* League Table, making a drop of more than 20 places in two years. Student satisfaction has continued to decline, and graduate employment remains much lower than in the past.

NTU has over 26,000 students, 4,500 of whom are postgraduates and 4,500 part-time. International students make up more than 10 per cent of the student body in Nottingham and its partner colleges in the UK, while another 7,000 are studying overseas. Almost a third of the undergraduates come from working-class homes and over 90 per cent attended state schools or colleges, but the projected dropout rate of nearly 15 per cent is higher than average for the university's courses and entry grades. Best known for fashion and other creative arts, the university also boasts one of the UK's biggest law schools, offering legal practice courses for both solicitors and barristers, as well as degrees. A new three-year LLB (Hons) Law and Legal Practice course integrates an LLB law degree with the solicitors' Legal Practice Course.

An extensive research programme attracted a £7.65 million donation – thought to be the largest to a post-1992 university – to advance the university's work in cancer diagnosis and therapy. A new conference centre, opened in 2010, will also help to boost income and investment. The university held its own in the last Research Assessment Exercise, although it entered fewer academics than some of the other leading new universities. More than a third of its submission was rated world-leading or internationally excellent, with communication, culture and media studies, social policy, engineering and biomedical sciences producing the best results.

However, Nottingham Trent was in the bottom third of the table compiled from the 2011 National Student Survey. Chemistry, drama, history, and initial teacher training produced the best results. Applications were down by 17 per cent at the start of 2012, with the prospect of £8,500 fees for

Burton Street
Nottingham NG1 4BU

0115 848 4200 (admissions)
contact via website
www.ntu.ac.uk
www.trentstudents.org
Affiliation: University
Alliance

The Times Rankings

Overall Ranking: **=78**

Student satisfaction:	=102	(73%)
Research quality:	=71	(0.13)
Entry standards:	63	(302)
Student–staff ratio:	73	(19.0)
Services & facilities/student:	49	(£1,470)
Expected completion rate:	=61	(83.9%)
Good honours:	85	(55.9%)
Graduate prospects:	71	(59.6%)

degree courses and £6,000 for Foundation degrees. But this followed two years of substantial growth in the demand for places. The university has committed almost 30 per cent of its additional fee income to financial support for students and other measures designed to widen participation and improve student retention. Among the new academic developments are a number of sponsored degrees offered by the business school, where the students work full-time for a company whilst studying for their degree. Students have their fees paid by the sponsoring company and also receive a salary. A new management and finance degree will give students a degree and CIMA qualification in four years instead of the usual seven, also with fees and salary paid by a company.

The extensive City campus will soon include an expanded students' union building and 900 more residential places. Science and technology, education, and arts and humanities are taught five miles away on the Clifton campus, which has already seen the addition of six new blocks of high-quality student accommodation that will form part of a student village. The university runs a bus service linking Clifton and the city. The Brackenhurst campus is devoted to animal, rural and environmental studies. It includes one of the region's best-equipped equestrian centres, with a purpose-built indoor riding area. Another 300 residential places were added there in 2006, following a £3-million renewal of the teaching facilities. With private providers adding to the university's residential stock of more than 4,000 beds, all first years and overseas students can be housed.

NTU has a strong sporting reputation and always fares well in the BUCS leagues. The new Lee Westwood Sports Centre, opened by the golfer himself, is on the Clifton campus and boasts an array of top facilities, including sports halls, studios, fitness suites and a nutrition training centre. NTU alumni include England rugby player Nick Easter and Great Britain hockey players Crista Cullen, Adam Dixon and Alistair Wilson. Social life varies between campuses, but all have access to the city's lively cultural and clubbing scene. A late-night bus service links the main campuses and the city's new tram system serves the university.

Undergraduate Fees and Bursaries

» Fees for UK/EU students 2012–13   £8,500
    Foundation degree   £6,000
» International student fees 2012–13   £10,600–£11,300
» Household income less than £30K, fee waiver of £1,500 a year.
» 570 NSP awards of £3,000 fee waiver for three years.
» Check the university's website for the latest information.

Students

Undergraduates:	**20,380**	**(1,870)**
Postgraduates:	**1,820**	**(2,770)**
Mature students:	**13.3%**	
Overseas students:	**5.3%**	
Applications per place:	**6.3**	
From state-sector schools:	**93.2%**	
From working-class homes:	**31.0%**	

For detailed information about sports facilities: www.ntu.ac.uk/sport

Accommodation

Number of places and costs refer to 2011–12
University-provided places: 4,200
Percentage catered: 0%
Self-catered costs: £75–£137 (44–51 weeks).
First years and new students are guaranteed accommodation if conditions are met.
International students: guaranteed accommodation if conditions are met.
Contact: www.ntu.ac.uk/accommodation
accommodation@ntu.ac.uk

The Open University (OU)

The Open University (OU) is one of the great success stories of UK higher education and a model for open and distance learning institutions around the world. It does not appear in *The Times* League Table because the absence of on-campus undergraduates makes the OU unsuitable for comparison with other universities on some of the measures used. But fees of £5,000 a year for the equivalent of full-time study (120 credits) will be among the cheapest at any university in 2012–13.

The OU has ranked in the top three UK universities for student satisfaction in every National Student Survey since 2005. The university now has more than 260,000 students, making it one of the largest in the world, and more undergraduates alone than there are students at any of the UK's conventional universities. The average age of new undergraduates is 31, but the demand from school leavers has grown to the point where a quarter are under 25 years old. Over 60 per cent of undergraduates are female and most live in the UK, but there are now 18,000 students outside the country. The OU offers a wide range of support for disabled students and currently has around 12,500 students with disabilities.

The university's headquarters are at Milton Keynes, Buckinghamshire, but it has 350 study centres and regional centres in each of its 13 regions around the UK, as well as offices and exam centres in other countries. The open access principle that was a cornerstone of its foundation remains in place; no formal qualifications are required to study on most undergraduate programmes. Four out of ten undergraduates come with less than two A levels or their equivalent, while seven out of ten students remain in full-time or part-time employment, often working towards a qualification to progress or change their career. Over 50,000 students are sponsored by their employer. But the OU provides financial support for those from poor backgrounds and has expanded its efforts for 2012–13 with a new programme called Access to Success.

Almost 7,000 part-time associate lecturers (tutors) guide students through degrees. The OU's "Supported Open Learning" system allows students to work where they choose – at home, in the workplace or at a library or study centre. They can study full-time or part-time, at a pace to suit their circumstances. They have contact with fellow students at tutorials, day schools or through online conferencing and electronic forums, social networks and informal study groups. Degrees are modular. Learning materials are written specifically for each module and delivered in a variety of formats. An increasing

Walton Hall
Milton Keynes MK7 6AA

085 300 6090 (enquiries)
contact via website
www.open.ac.uk
www.open.ac.uk/ousa
Affiliation: University
 Alliance

Edinburgh
Belfast
MILTON KEYNES
Cardiff
London

The Times Rankings
The available data do not match the data used to rank the other full-time universities, so the Open University could not be included in the League Table this year.

amount of material is delivered online, and can be accessed on mobile devices as well as computers. OU learning materials are the result of years of experience and research into how to teach at undergraduate level, and are also used by other institutions.

Gone are the late-night BBC television programmes that were the mainstay of teaching until 2006. The OU now produces mainstream television and radio programming aimed at bringing learning to a wider audience. The university also leads the universities placing material on the iTunes U site and was one of the first in the world to make e-books available there. By the middle of 2011, there had been more than 42 million downloads and 422 free, interactive titles had been published. The content comes from the OU's OpenLearn website (**http://openlearn.open.ac.uk**), which contains almost 7,000 hours of free material taken from OU modules.

The 1,200 full-time academics have a proud research record: more than half of the work submitted for the 2008 Research Assessment Exercise was regarded as world-leading or internationally excellent. Art and design, computer science, geography and sociology produced the best results. The OU employs more than 500 people engaged in research and there are over 1,300 research students. The university spends approximately £20 million each year on research.

The OU covers all the main academic disciplines, and its business school produces more MBAs than the rest of the UK's business schools put together, as well as offering honours and Foundation degrees. In addition to degrees in a named subject, the OU also awards "Open" Bachelor degrees, where the syllabus is designed by the students by combining a number of modules. The OU has strong links to business and industry, and offers a range of professional and vocational qualifications, including more than 20 Foundation degrees. Modules worth 30 or 60 credits, typically run either from October to June, or from February to October. Assessment is by both continual assessment and examination or, for some modules, a major assignment. Except in fast moving areas such as computing, there is no limit on the time taken to complete a degree.

Undergraduate Fees and Bursaries

» Fees vary depending upon the type of course, on where you live and the number of credits you plan to study.
» In England a course of 120 credits of study (a year's full-time study) is £5,000.
» In Scotland, Wales and Northern Ireland, a course of 120 credits is £1,610.
» The costs of all courses are given in the OU prospectus: **www3.open.ac.uk/study/undergraduate/index.htm**
» Various forms of financial help are available. Details are given at: **www3.open.ac.uk/study/explained/financial-support.shtml**

Students

Undergraduates:	10	(195,010)
Postgraduates:	295	(13,390)

Accommodation

As the courses provided are part time, the university does not provide accommodation.

Contact: www3.open.ac.uk/contact/faq.aspx?t=S&cat=1-1SOVWF

University of Oxford

Oxford continues to top *The Times* League Table, as it has since 2002, when it wrested first place from Cambridge. But this year's scores could not be closer and the two ancient rivals have effectively repeated the dead-heat they experienced in the first edition of this *Guide* in 1993. Both are head and shoulders above the other institutions in *The Times* table and in the view of most experts. Oxford is the oldest and probably the most famous university in the English-speaking world. It is also among the top five universities in the world, according to the QS and *Times Higher Education* world rankings. By its own high standards, Oxford had a poor year for graduate employment, but still outscored Cambridge on staffing, completion rates and spending on student facilities.

The introduction of £9,000 fees had predictably little impact on the demand for places. There were still fewer than six applicants to the place – a much more favourable ratio than at some other leading universities – but 99 per cent of successful candidates achieve at least three As at A level, or their equivalent. Some subjects now demand two A* grades and another A at A level. Gradually, there may be more postgraduates and marginally fewer UK undergraduates, making the competition for places still more intense.

The university is still struggling to broaden its intake and shake off allegations of social elitism. The long-term growth in demand for places is due, at least partly, to more systematic attempts to get the message through to teenagers that Oxford is open to all who can meet the exacting entrance requirements. Student visits to comprehensive schools have been supplemented by summer schools, recruitment fairs and colleges' own initiatives, as well as tireless public statements of intent by the university.

For all the university's efforts to shed its *Brideshead Revisited* stereotype, however, official figures still show 45 per cent of Oxford's students coming from independent schools – the largest proportion at any university. Just one student in ten comes from a working-class home, despite the introduction of generous bursaries that will be extended for 2012–13. The university is planning to spend 70 per cent of the extra income on fee waivers and bursaries that will give those from the poorest homes support totalling nearly £10,000 in their first year and over £6,000 in every subsequent year. The projected dropout rate of less than 2 per cent is bettered only by Cambridge, and Oxford had among the most satisfied undergraduates in the 2011 National Student Survey. There was 100 per cent satisfaction in anatomy and close to it in medicine.

Applications must be made by mid

University Offices
Wellington Square
Oxford OX1 2JD

01865 288000 (admissions)
contact via website
www.ox.ac.uk
www.ousu.org
Affiliation: Russell Group

The Times Rankings

Overall Ranking: **1**

Student satisfaction:	=1	(87%)
Research quality:	2	(1.33)
Entry standards:	2	(574)
Student–staff ratio:	3	(11.1)
Services & facilities/student:	2	(£3,298)
Expected completion rate:	2	(98.1%)
Good honours:	1	(90.9%)
Graduate prospects:	5	(79.8%)

October – a month earlier if you wish to be interviewed overseas. There are written tests for some subjects and you may be asked to submit samples of work. Selection is in the hands of the 30 undergraduate colleges, which vary considerably in their approach to this issue and others. Sound advice on academic strengths and social factors is essential for applicants to give themselves the best chance of winning a place and finding a setting in which they can thrive. A minority of candidates opt to go straight into the admissions pool without expressing a preference for a particular college. The choice is particularly important for arts and social science students, whose world-famous individual or small group tuition is based in college. Science and technology are taught mainly in central facilities. All subjects operate on eight-week terms and assess students entirely on final examinations – a system some find too pressurised. Overall, however, Oxford is in the top two universities for student satisfaction.

The development of a new campus on the site of the Radcliffe Infirmary will be the first fruit of a £1.3-billion Oxford Thinking fundraising campaign. Oxford's biggest capital development for more than a century will provide more student accommodation for neighbouring Somerville College, a new Mathematical Institute building and a new building for the humanities. Recent developments include a £21-million social sciences library and animal research facilities that drew bitter (often illegal) protests from animal rights campaigners. The developments in the Science Area, in the centre of Oxford, will focus mainly on refurbishment and modernisation of existing buildings.

There was never much doubt about the strength of Oxford's research, but the 2008 Research Assessment Exercise found more than 70 per cent of it to be world-leading or internationally excellent. Oxford entered more academics for assessment than any other university – twice as many as some research-based universities of similar size. There were good results in all areas, but the university was pre-eminent in several medical specialisms, as well as statistics, development studies, education and French. Oxford also attracts the largest amount of research income among UK universities.

Undergraduate Fees and Bursaries

» Fees for UK/EU students 2012–13 £9,000
» International student fees 2012–13 £13,200–£18,550
  Medicine £15,150–£27,550
  College fees £6,157
» Household income below £16K, £5,500 fee waiver year 1, £3,000 other years; £16K–£25K, fee waiver £2,000–£1,000 a year.
» Household income below £16K, a bursary of £4,300 year 1, £3,300 other years; £16K–£42K, bursary on sliding scale £3,500–£500 a year.
» College scholarships and bursaries available.

Students

Undergraduates:	11,430	(4,960)
Postgraduates:	7,260	(1,265)
Mature students:	3.5%	
Overseas students:	11.1%	
Applications per place:	5.6	
From state-sector schools:	55.2%	
From working-class homes:	9.9%	

Accommodation

See chapter 13 for information about individual colleges.

For detailed information about sports facilities:
www.sport.ox.ac.uk

Oxford Brookes University

Even after a boom year for applications in 2011 and the subsequent introduction of £9,000 fees for degree courses, the demand for places at Oxford Brookes continued to grow at the start of 2012. There were already more than seven applications per place so, with the university proposing to cut its undergraduate entry by up to 15 per cent to increase the contact time with lecturers and improve the student experience, competition was set to become even more intense. Fees of £6,000 a year for Foundation degrees taught at further education colleges brought down the average for all the university's courses and much of the extra income from fees was committed to fund bursaries and fee waivers of up to £4,500 for the poorest students.

Oxford Brookes is firmly established as England's leading post-1992 university in *The Times* League Table, although it shares that title with Lincoln this year. Brookes is particularly popular with independent schools, which provide nearly a quarter of the undergraduates – by far the highest proportion among the new universities and twice the national average for the university's subjects and entry grades. However, the proportion from working-class homes, at 42 per cent, is also considerably ahead of the official benchmark. The university has been trying to attract more students from state schools and has targeted areas in Oxfordshire and the wider region.

The university's location has always been an advantage in student recruitment, but the quality of provision is the real draw. Its departments feature near the top of *The Times* rankings for several subjects. Ofsted rated primary teacher training outstanding, and the university has generally done well in the National Student Survey, although it dropped into the bottom half of the satisfaction table in 2011. Maths and statistics, biology, philosophy and health subjects produced the best results. The university is proud of its Brookes Virtual integrated e-learning network and has been chosen to pilot a national e-learning project to use new technologies and redesigned courses to expand the reach of education and lifelong learning. The university was previously awarded national centres for hospitality, leisure and tourism, and the teaching of business and undergraduate research, as well as one for teacher training in partnership with Westminster University.

Grades in the 2008 Research Assessment Exercise showed improvement, with more than a third of the work judged to be world-leading or internationally excellent. History, which made headlines in 2001 with a higher grade than its world-renowned neighbour, again produced the best results, but there were good performances, too, in history of art and computer science.

Headington Campus
Gypsy Lane
Oxford OX3 0BP

01865 484848 (enquiries)
query@brookes.ac.uk
www.brookes.ac.uk
www.thesu.com
Affiliation: University Alliance

The Times Rankings

Overall Ranking: =52

Student satisfaction:	=77	(76%)
Research quality:	61	(0.17)
Entry standards:	51	(333)
Student–staff ratio:	=45	(16.7)
Services & facilities/student:	64	(£1,332)
Expected completion rate:	45	(86.0%)
Good honours:	=45	(67.6%)
Graduate prospects:	56	(64.1%)

As a polytechnic, Brookes pioneered the modular degree system that has swept British higher education. After more than 20 years' experience, the scheme has now trimmed the 2,000 modules it once offered, but undergraduates can pair subjects as diverse as history and biology, or catering management and environmental management. Each subject has compulsory modules in the first year and a list of others that are acceptable later. Students are encouraged to take advantage of a range of placement and exchange opportunities as well as subjects outside their main area of study, such as additional language modules.

The extra income from fees will help to speed up planned improvements to the four campuses, two of which are only a mile from the city centre and linked to each other by a footbridge. Some £150 million has been earmarked for improvements to the Headington, Wheatley and Harcourt Hill campuses over the next few years. Before then, a £132-million library and teaching building is due to open at the original Gipsy Lane site in September 2013. This will provide social learning space that allows students to work together and engage with careers guidance, volunteering opportunities and student support services.

Maths and engineering have now joined computing and business five miles away at Wheatley. A new engineering building supports the university's status as a Government-designated regional centre for motorsport and high performance engineering. The Harcourt Hill campus, at Botley, focuses on teacher education, human development and learning. Oxford Brookes was in the top category in the People and Planet Green league of 2011, as it has been in all five years of the environmental assessments.

A 25-metre swimming pool and 9-hole golf course have been added to the already impressive sports facilities. The gym and climbing centre have been refurbished. Representative teams have a good record, with the rowers particularly successful, winning medals at three consecutive Olympic games, and the cricketers now combining with Oxford University to take on county teams. The students' union runs one of the biggest entertainment venues in Oxford, a city that can be expensive, but which offers enough to satisfy most students.

Undergraduate Fees and Bursaries

- » Fees for UK/EU students 2012–13   £9,000
  Foundation degrees at partner colleges   £6,000
- » International student fees 2013–14   £11,400–£12,640
  Physiotherapy   £12,640
- » Household income below £5K, fee waiver £2,500; £5K–£15K, £2,000; £15K–£40K, £1,000 each year.
- » Bursary of £2,000–£300 a year on sliding scale for household income £0–£30K.
- » Community scholarships for local students. Care leaver's bursaries.

Students		
Undergraduates:	**11,730**	**(2,405)**
Postgraduates:	**1,740**	**(2,505)**
Mature students:	**25.2%**	
Overseas students:	**15%**	
Applications per place:	**7.2**	
From state-sector schools:	**73.3%**	
From working-class homes:	**41.2%**	

For detailed information about sports facilities: www.brookes.ac.uk/sport

Accommodation

Number of places and costs refer to 2012–13
University-provided places: 4,400
Percentage catered: 3.5%
Catered cost: £132.46 a week (38 weeks).
Self-catered cost: £97.00–£147.50 (38 weeks).
All accommodation is allocated to first year who select Oxford Brookes as Firm choice through UCAS and meet all deadlines for application.
International students: as above.
Contact: accomm@brookes.ac.uk

University of Plymouth

Plymouth will become the only post-1992 university with its own medical school in 2013, having dissolved its partnership with Exeter University in the management of Peninsula School of Medicine. The new medical school will be small, with an annual entry of only 86 students, but Plymouth has kept all 64 of Peninsula's places in dentistry. As part of the plans, Plymouth has already invested £25 million to further medical and health research in the South West. The university is the largest provider of nursing, midwifery and health professional education and training in the region.

Plymouth is one of the UK's largest universities with nearly 30,000 students. The Vice-Chancellor, Professor Wendy Purcell, who graduated from the university in the 1980s, has declared a new mission to make it the top "enterprise university". Plymouth has dropped five places in the latest *Times* League Table, but it is the only university to have been awarded Regional Growth Fund money to promote economic development. It has also been chosen to lead the national Social Enterprise University Enterprise Network and is home to one of the country's top 10 business incubation facilities. Degree applications fell at the start of 2012, with the prospect of £9,000 fees for degree courses, but by less than the sector average.

Over £200 million has been spent on the main city campus in Plymouth. The library was extended and upgraded and the students' union refurbished, while a £35-million arts complex opened in 2007. A new building for the Faculty of Health and Social Work includes sports facilities and clinical skills laboratories as well as teaching space. Plymouth has also opened a £1-million Immersive Vision Theatre, thought to be the first of its kind at a UK university, which gives the feeling of being "in", rather than just observing, different types of image. The latest development will see the completion of a £19-million facility for the university's Marine Institute, containing the country's most advanced wave tanks and business incubation space for companies in the marine renewables sector. It is scheduled to open in September this year. The university's commitment to sustainability was also recognised through its ranking as the second greenest university in the People and Planet league and through the recent award of nearly £1 million to create the world's first IT integrated smart building management system.

The university is a partner in the Combined Universities in Cornwall, which is boosting further and higher education in one of the few counties without its own university. Plymouth has established a unique relationship with its 18 partner colleges, which have become a faculty of

---

Drake Circus
Plymouth
Devon PL4 8AA

01752 585858 (enquiries)
contact via website
www.plymouth.ac.uk
www.pcmd.ac.uk
www.upsu.com
Affiliation: University
Alliance

The Times Rankings
Overall Ranking: **64**

Student satisfaction:	=89	(75%)
Research quality:	59	(0.20)
Entry standards:	62	(303)
Student–staff ratio:	=40	(16.5)
Services & facilities/student:	72	(£1,301)
Expected completion rate:	=55	(84.5%)
Good honours:	=65	(61.1%)
Graduate prospects:	60	(62.4%)

the university, sharing £3.5 million in capital investment. They spread from Cornwall to Somerset, taking in Jersey, and have 10,000 students taking university courses.

The intake reflects Plymouth's position as the working-class hub of the southwest, with almost 95 per cent of students state-educated and almost a third from the poorest social classes. The projected dropout rate of less than 11 per cent is below average for the courses and entry grades. Some 12,000 students undertake work-based learning or placements with employability skills embedded throughout the curriculum from day one, while the new Plymouth Award recognises extra-curricular achievements.

Plymouth was chosen to house no fewer than four national teaching centres – in health and social care placements, experiential learning in environmental and natural sciences, institutional partnerships, and education for sustainable development – all of which have now been brought into the university's core activities. No university has exceeded the 14 National Teaching Fellowships won by its academics.

Plymouth entered by far the largest number of academics of any post-1992 university in the latest research assessments – twice the proportion entered by some of its peer group. More than a third of the submission was rated world-leading or internationally excellent. Computer science produced by far the best results, but civil engineering, geography and environmental science, and art and design also did well.

A 1,300-bed student village costing £15 million, has greatly improved the university's residential stock. There is a lively social scene as well as a thriving nightlife. With excellent and recently upgraded facilities for water sports as well as an £850,000 fitness centre, the sports facilities have improved, while a range of sports scholarships and bursaries will help support high-fliers. The university has a partnership with Plymouth Albion Rugby Club to promote and support sport in the city and it invested £2.5 million in the new £45-million Plymouth Life Centre. Students can benefit from exclusive sessions at the international-standard swimming and fitness facility which includes an Olympic-size swimming pool. Plymouth is also the only university in the UK to have its own diving and water sports centre.

Undergraduate Fees and Bursaries

» Fees for UK/EU students 2012–13	£9,000
» International student fees 2012–13	£10,500
Medicine (Peninsula, 2011–12)	£14,500–£22,000
» Household income below £16K, NSP awards of £1,000 cash, £1,000 university discounts, £1,000 placement assistance.	
» Care leaver and sports bursaries.	
» Check the university's website for the latest information.	

Students

Undergraduates:	**20,530**	**(6,750)**
Postgraduates:	**1,720**	**(3,500)**
Mature students:	**28.1%**	
Overseas students:	**6.6%**	
Applications per place:	**4.3**	
From state-sector schools:	**93.9%**	
From working-class homes:	**29.7%**	

For detailed information about sports facilities:
www/plymouth.ac.uk/recreation

Accommodation

Number of places and costs refer to 2012–13
University-provided places: 2,500
Percentage catered: 0%
Self-catered costs: £86–£140 a week.
First years are not guaranteed university provided accommodation.
International students: overseas students have priority for allocation.
Contact: accommodation@plymouth.ac.uk
www.plymouth.ac.uk/accommodation

University of Portsmouth

Portsmouth is back among the top ten post-1992 universities after a rise of four places in the latest *Times* League Table. There was a 9 per cent fall in applications as fees of £8,500 were introduced in 2012, but this followed a period of record demand for places. The university attracts double the numbers it received a decade ago, buoyed by a wider portfolio of courses, a modernised campus and new facilities in the city. Portsmouth has had the best record of its peer group in the National Student Survey. No former polytechnic produced better results in 2011, when languages, physical geography and environmental science, sports science and politics all satisfied more than 95 per cent of final-year undergraduates.

Languages are Portsmouth's traditional strength and the facilities rival those of many traditional universities. One of the largest departments of its kind teaches six languages to degree level (French, German, Italian, Mandarin, Spanish and English as a foreign language) and offers free language courses to all students. However, it is in health subjects that the university's reputation has been growing most obviously. The new £9-million Dental Academy trains student dentists in their final year at King's College London in a team-based primary care setting, working alongside other health professionals.

There is also a centre for molecular design and the UK's first dedicated brain tumour research centre. A new £1-million model pharmacy to help train pharmacists opened in 2009. Over 600 radiographers, paramedics, medical technologists, pharmacists, clinicians and social workers graduate from the university each year. Forty per cent of the work submitted for the 2008 Research Assessment Exercise was considered world-leading or internationally excellent. Applied mathematics and European studies achieved particularly good results, while biomedical and biomolecular sciences also did well.

The main city-centre Guildhall campus has undergone extensive redevelopment. A new £14-million building is due to open in September 2013, giving the Faculty of Creative and Cultural Industries more space for teaching, learning and exhibition facilities. Other plans include a major new building in the city centre with 598 student bedrooms and considerable extra teaching space. Earlier developments included the prize-winning green library complex and the aluminium-clad St Michael's Building, where £750,000 has been spent recently to refurbish laboratories. The business school is housed in a £12-million building on the main campus. Other recent additions include a sports science building with laboratories, a swimming flume and two British Olympic Medical Centre accredited climatic chambers. A new £9-million building for

---

University House
Winston Churchill Avenue
Portsmouth
Hampshire PO1 2UP

023 9284 8484
info.centre@port.ac.uk
www.port.ac.uk
www.upsu.net
Affiliation: University
  Alliance

The Times **Rankings**
Overall Ranking: **63**

Student satisfaction:	=42	(79%)
Research quality:	=62	(0.16)
Entry standards:	=76	(289)
Student–staff ratio:	=85	(19.8)
Services & facilities/student:	78	(£1,267)
Expected completion rate:	50	(85.1%)
Good honours:	95	(54.2%)
Graduate prospects:	=62	(61.9%)

the internationally recognised Institute of Cosmology and Gravitation opened in 2009. In addition, a £1.1-million nursery for the children of students and staff opened in 2010.

Many courses have direct input from business and the professions, around half of them leading to professional accreditation. Wherever possible, students are given opportunities for hands-on practice in their chosen career. Simulated learning environments include a mock court room, a journalism newsroom, a health simulation suite, a £1-million model pharmacy and a "forensic house" where criminologists work on simulated crime scenes. Teaching in all subjects is concentrated on the Guildhall campus, with most residential accommodation nearby. A £6.5-million student centre caters for the multicultural population of the university with alcohol-free areas and an international students' bar. There is also a new social learning space, with café, wireless internet and learning spaces for individuals and groups. Modernised sport, exercise and fitness facilities include gyms, dance studios and a sports hall.

The city of Portsmouth has a larger working-class population and more deprivation than some applicants may realise. Almost 30 per cent of the undergraduates come from working-class homes, although this is still below the national average for the subjects and entry qualifications. Efforts are being made to broaden the intake further through an award-winning membership club that introduces teenagers to higher education through workshops, holiday courses and access to university facilities. The projected dropout rate has improved considerably over the last decade and, at 12 per cent is now lower than the university's benchmark.

Many students live in Southsea, which has a vibrant social scene and quirky shops. In recent years the city has seen considerable regeneration, including the retail and entertainment complex at Gunwharf dominated by the 170-metre landmark Spinnaker Tower. The cost of living is not as high as at many southern universities, and the sea is close at hand. Hall places are offered to 90 per cent of first years and the university runs "secure a home" days at the beginning of September to help the remaining new arrivals with house-hunting. Hall students have access to a combined broadband, phone and TV service allowing them to call family and friends at no cost, using a PC.

Undergraduate Fees and Bursaries

» Fees for UK/EU students 2012–13 £8,500
» International student fees 2012–13 £10,000–£11,300
» Household income below £25K, £1,000 cash each year and fee waiver of £2,000 in year 1 only; £25K–£32K, £1,000 cash each year; £32K–£42.6K, £500 cash each year.
» Additional care leavers' support.
» Check the university's website for the latest information.

Students

Undergraduates:	**16,700**	**(2,330)**
Postgraduates:	**2,120**	**(2,250)**
Mature students:	**12.7%**	
Overseas students:	**12.7%**	
Applications per place:	**5.9**	
From state-sector schools:	**94.4%**	
From working-class homes:	**29.4%**	

For detailed information about sports facilities:
www.port.ac.uk/sport

Accommodation

Number of places and costs refer to 2011–12
University-provided places: 3,000
Percentage catered: 25%
Catered costs: £93–£120 a week (37 weeks).
Self-catered costs:£77–£121 a week (37 weeks).
Majority of first years offered university accommodation.
International, Channel Island and Isle of Man students guaranteed university accommodation subject to terms and conditions.
Contact: Student.housing@port.ac.uk
www.port.ac.uk/studentlife/accommodation

Queen Margaret University

Scotland's first new university of the 21st century saw stronger growth in the demand for places than any of its peer group at the start of 2012. A 5 per cent increase in applications followed even larger rises in the two previous years. Although it has dropped five places in the new *Times* League Table, Queen Margaret continues to outscore many former polytechnics.

Queen Margaret (QMU) moved into gleaming new premises in Musselburgh, to the southeast of Edinburgh, when university status arrived in 2007. The "campus in the park", as it has been dubbed, was designed in consultation with students, and is one of the most environmentally sustainable in the UK, exceeding current environmental standards. The university has made sustainability a top priority, in the curriculum as well as in the way it operates. The campus has won a string of awards, and in 2011 alone QMU won both a Green Gown and a Green Business Award, signifying the university's commitment to sustainable development and combating climate change.

Named after Saint Margaret, the 11th-century Queen of Scotland, the institution dates back to 1875 and was originally a school of cookery for women. The college had been awarding its own degrees for 15 years before it became a university. There are more than 6,000 students at all levels, three quarters of them female, although barely 1,000 began full-time degree courses in 2011. The university has established three flagship areas as a focus for future investment and development: health and rehabilitation, sustainable business, and culture and creativity.

Restructuring of the performing arts courses has consolidated four drama degrees into one interdisciplinary programme, under the title of drama and performance. The university no longer offers conservatoire training, but the new degree draws together the university's recognised strengths in acting, screen work, community theatre, contemporary performance, and playwriting to reflect the current needs of a changing profession. QMU also offers a degree in costume design, the only one of its kind in Scotland. Another new development saw the university go back to its roots with a partnership with the Edinburgh New Town Cookery School, run by a former graduate of QMU, to hone the practical skills of students on the international hospitality management degree. The university runs a food festival, which featured the leading chef Albert Roux as guest of honour in 2011.

Health is an area of particular strength: QMU has the broadest range of courses in Scotland, from dietetics, podiatry and audiology, to art therapy, music therapy

---

Queen Margaret University
  Drive
Musselburgh EH21 6UU

0131 474 0000
admissions@qmu.ac.uk
www.qmu.ac.uk
www.qmusu.org.uk
Affiliation: none

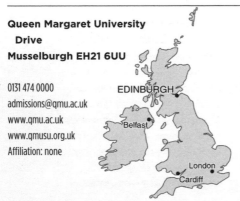

The Times **Rankings**
Overall Ranking: **83**

Student satisfaction:	=102	(73%)
Research quality:	=80	(0.10)
Entry standards:	49	(336)
Student–staff ratio:	=93	(20.6)
Services & facilities/student:	90	(£1,177)
Expected completion rate:	76	(80.3%)
Good honours:	=32	(71.7%)
Graduate prospects:	80	56.8%)

and health psychology. The university has an international reputation for its work in speech sciences, and launched a new CASL (Clinical Audiology, Speech and Language) Research Centre in 2011. Courses in international health attract students from all over the world, and there programmes in Angola, Guatemala, Uganda, Ethiopia, Gambia, India and Cuba. Almost a quarter of QMU students are from outside the UK, many studying in their home countries. Other international programmes run in Nepal, Egypt, Saudi Arabia, Greece and Switzerland. In 2008, the university opened the first UK university campus in Singapore: a joint venture with the East Asia Institute of Management, which already taught Queen Margaret degree courses.

All has not been plain sailing for the new university, however. Only one university had a lower average score in the 2008 Research Assessment Exercise and Queen Margaret has struggled with debts, although it has now reported a surplus a year ahead of the target date. The projected dropout rate of less than 14 per cent has improved for the last three years, but is still higher than average for the university's courses and entry qualifications. Three undergraduates in ten come from working-class homes and a similar proportion are over the age of 21 on entry.

An impressive learning resource centre, parts of which are open 24 hours a day,

offers a variety of study spaces. Specialist laboratories and clinics are well equipped. The nursing simulation lab, for example, is set out exactly like a hospital ward, helping to instil students with the confidence to move on easily to a work placement or career in the NHS or private practice. There are also specially equipped rooms for podiatry, radiography, occupational therapy, physiotherapy and art therapy.

The campus is located next to Musselburgh train station, from where Edinburgh city centre is only a six-minute journey. There is also a frequent bus service from the campus to the city centre. There are 800 residential places on the campus, 474 of them standard rooms and 326 premier, or double. Other features include a students' union building, indoor and outdoor sports facilities, a variety of catering outlets and landscaped gardens with a range of environmental features.

Undergraduate Fees and Bursaries

» Fees for Scottish and EU students 2012–13   No fee
» Fees for Non-Scottish UK (RUK) students 2012–13   £6,750
» Fees for international students 2012–13   £10,170–£11,790
» For RUK students, annual bursaries: household income up to £20K, £2,000 cash; sliding scale to £42.6K, £1,500–£500.
» Check the university's website for the latest information.

Students		
Undergraduates:	**2,780**	**(1,130)**
Postgraduates:	**505**	**(1,050)**
Mature students:	**31.2%**	
Overseas students:	**14.7%**	
Applications per place:	**6.3**	
From state-sector schools:	**92.7%**	
From working-class homes:	**30.0%**	

For detailed information about sports facilities:
www.qmu.ac.uk/sports

Accommodation
Number of places and costs refer to 2012–13
University-provided places: 800
Percentage catered: 0%
Self-catered costs: £104–£114 a week (either 40 or 50 week contract).
First years are guaranteed accommodation. Residential and age restrictions apply.
International students: guaranteed housing.
Contact: accommodation@qmu.ac.uk
www.qmu.ac.uk/accommodation/default.htm

Queen Mary, University of London

Queen Mary (QMUL) surprised many observers by joining the Russell Group of leading research universities early in 2012. But, with a big medical school contributing to a high volume of research, it fitted the profile of the group better than some of the other new entrants. QMUL is aiming to be among the top ten in the UK by 2015, although has set its own criteria, which give more weight to research than is the case in *The Times* League Table, where it remains 38th this year. QMUL opted for £9,000 fees for 2012–13 in order to meet the cost of delivering "research-informed" undergraduate degrees, as well as continuing to enhance the quality of its buildings and equipment. However, it estimates that about half of its undergraduates will benefit from bursaries and fee waivers, which will be more generous to first years.

More than £150 million has been spent developing the campus of the University of London's East End base for nearly 17,000 students and strengthening the academic staff. Some of the investment paid off in spectacularly improved grades in the 2008 Research Assessment Exercise, when almost two thirds of the work submitted was rated world-leading or internationally excellent.

Linguistics, geography and drama produced the best results in their fields, with dentistry, English and several medical specialisms in the top five, propelling Queen Mary into the top 25 UK universities for research in our table.

Queen Mary has the capital's most extensive self-contained campus. It includes a state-of-the-art learning resource centre with 24-hour access and an award-winning student village with 2,000 en-suite rooms. An arts quarter, containing research facilities, a conference centre, drama studio and teaching space, was completed in 2006. The £20-million Arts2 building was completed in 2011 and a BioEnterprise Innovation Centre for science companies has opened, next door to the £44-million Blizard Building – the striking home of Barts and the London School of Medicine and Dentistry, in Whitechapel. The Centre of the Cell is also located on the Whitechapel campus, the first such facility to be based within a working medical school research laboratory to give young people a glimpse of how scientists operate.

The modern setting is a far cry from the People's Palace, which first used the site to bring education to the Victorian masses, but there is still a community programme as well as conventional teaching and research. The arts-based Westfield College and scientific Queen Mary came together in 1989. The sale of Westfield's Hampstead

---

Mile End Road
London E1 4NS

020 7882 5511 (admissions)
admissions@qmul.ac.uk
www.qmul.ac.uk
www.qmsu.org
Affiliation: Russell Group

base released the necessary capital to begin to modernise the Mile End Road campus. Now the historic People's Palace building, which is still the college's most recognisable feature, is to be restored to host cultural events for the institution and the local community.

Queen Mary is best known for its strength in arts subjects, which boast a clutch of high-profile academics. But the medical school was rated in the top 30 in the world in 2011 and the college is also leading a national initiative to boost the number of maths graduates. Applications have risen at the rate of 7 per cent a year for most of the last decade, although they had dropped by a little more than the sector average at the beginning of 2012. There has been particular success in attracting overseas students, who make full use of a unit specialising in English as a foreign language and now fill about one place in six. Results have been consistently good in the National Student Survey and improved again in 2011, when overall satisfaction reached 88 per cent. Aerospace engineering, chemistry, French and law all satisfied at least 95 per cent of final-year undergraduates.

The majority of undergraduates take at least one course in departments other than their own, under the modular course system. Most degrees are organised in units to allow maximum flexibility. Interdisciplinary study has always been encouraged: for example,

medics can choose selected modules in English and drama. There is a flourishing exchange programme, which includes universities in the USA and Japan, as well as Europe.

Queen Mary attracts students from across the UK and over 120 countries around the world and has a socially diverse intake: more than a third of the undergraduates come from the two lowest socio-economic classes, many of them from London's minority ethnic groups. Social life centres on the campus, which features a refurbished students' union with a subsidised health and fitness centre and a new bar, and the West End is easily accessible by tube. Students welcome the relatively low prices (for the capital) in east London, which has more to offer than many expect when they apply.

Undergraduate Fees and Bursaries

» Fees for UK/EU students 2012–13   £9.000
» International student fees 2012–13   £12,250–£13,925
    Medicine   £18,500–£28,200
» Annual bursaries of £1,500 for those with household income below £25K; of £1,200 for household income £25K–£42.6K.
» Over 250 NSP awards of £1,500 fee waiver and £1,500 bursary in year 1 only.
» Other academic and targeted scholarships available.

Students

Undergraduates:	**11,100**	**(10)**
Postgraduates:	**2,725**	**(985)**
Mature students:	**16.5%**	
Overseas students:	**19.9%**	
Applications per place:	**7.1**	
From state-sector schools:	**85.4%**	
From working-class homes:	**34.4%**	

For detailed information about sports facilities: www.qmsu.org

Accommodation

Number of places and costs refer to 2011–12
University-provided places: 2,454
Percentage catered: 6%
Catered costs: £160 upwards a week.
Self-catered costs: £102–£138 a week.
First years giving Queen Mary as first choice get priority, if terms and conditions are met. Residential restrictions apply.
International students given priority if conditions are met.
Contact: residences@qmul.ac.uk

Queen's University, Belfast

Northern Ireland's premier university, Queen's has moved up three places in this year's *Times* League Table. It has been a member of the Russell Group of leading UK research institutions since 2006 and is now in the top 200 in the QS World University Rankings, with the stated aim of moving towards the top 100 in the next few years. The university has been recruiting high-calibre academics from around the world and is investing heavily in new and updated facilities to improve the student experience and enhance its research performance. The 2008 Research Assessment Exercise showed some progress, with more than half of the university's submission rated as world-leading or internationally excellent, and Queen's is ranked in the UK's top ten in 11 subject areas. Music, English and anthropology produced the highest grades and all branches of engineering were placed in the top ten in their respective disciplines. The university's reputation for research has been enhanced recently with a national award for innovation and degree applications were up 4 per cent at the start of 2012.

In recent years the Queen's campus has been transformed. The centrepiece is the £50-million McClay Library, said to be one of the most ambitious building projects in Northern Ireland, which opened in 2009. More teaching accommodation has been added, with better access for the disabled. A low-rise student village has replaced the previous tower block residences at a cost of £45 million, and a new centre for international students and postgraduates opened in 2010. Recent developments have included a £15-million Executive Education Centre for local and international business and plans are also well advanced for a £100-million Institute of Health Sciences. A new student guidance centre has brought services together at the heart of the campus and the students' union has had a £9-million refurbishment. It now includes Enterprise SU, an area for students to improve their enterprise and employability skills. Queen's offers Degree Plus – a qualification providing official recognition of extra-curricular activities and achievements to help graduates in the job market.

Scores have fluctuated in the National Student Survey. In 2011, they were close to the sector average, but satisfaction levels in pharmacy were the highest in the UK, while dentistry and agriculture were ranked second, and anthropology and chemical engineering in the top ten for their subjects. Enterprise teaching is embedded throughout the curriculum, and David Gibson, in Queen's University Management School, who pioneered the model, was named the *Times Higher Education* Most Innovative

University Road
Belfast BT7 1NN

028 9097 3838 (admissions)
admissions@qub.ac.uk
www.qub.ac.uk
www.qubsu.org
Affiliation: Russell Group

The Times Rankings		
Overall Ranking: **35**		
Student satisfaction:	**=42**	(79%)
Research quality:	**40**	(0.56)
Entry standards:	**35**	(387)
Student–staff ratio:	**=25**	(15.3)
Services & facilities/student:	**22**	(£1,933)
Expected completion rate:	**29**	(91.9%)
Good honours:	**=26**	(73.4%)
Graduate prospects:	**29**	(71.9%)

Teacher of the Year 2011.

Strictly non-denominational teaching is enshrined in a charter which has guaranteed student representation and equal rights for women since 1908. Theology is taught only at four associated colleges. Queen's was one of four university colleges for the whole of Ireland in the nineteenth century, and still draws students from all over the island. Interest in Queen's has been growing in Great Britain, too, with a 35 per cent rise in applications 2011, and overseas numbers have been boosted by a variety of agreements with universities in the USA, India, Malaysia and China. However, the majority of students still come from Northern Ireland and Queen's suffers in the comparison of entry grades in *The Times* League Table because relatively few sixth-formers in the Province take four A-levels.

Students are encouraged to take language programmes from a unique "virtual" language laboratory, which provides online tuition from any computer in the university. IT facilities are good: Queen's was the first institution to meet the national target of providing at least one computer workstation for every five undergraduate students. An unusually large proportion of graduates go on to further study, which does Queen's no harm in the employment stakes.

The city centre is not short of nightlife, but the social scene is still concentrated on the students' union and the surrounding area. Sports facilities, which include a university cottage in the Mourne mountains, are of a high standard. A £7-million extension to the physical education centre helped in Queen's selection as an official training camp for the 2012 Olympics, and a £13-million enhancement of the university's outdoor sports facilities has been completed. The university runs academies for football, rugby, rowing and Gaelic sports, which have strong external links. Numerous Queen's players are selected at club, provincial and national levels.

The university district is among the most attractive in Belfast, and is one of the city's main cultural and recreational areas. The university's highly successful international arts festival runs each autumn, and the university boasts the only full-time university cinema in the UK, as well as an art gallery and theatre, all of which are open to students and the wider community alike.

Undergraduate Fees and Bursaries

» Fees for Northern Irish/EU students 2012–13   £3,465
» Fees for English, Scottish, Welsh (RUK) students   £9,000
» International student fees 2012–13   £11,266–£14,460
   Medicine   £14,768–£27,860
   Dentistry   £22,624
» The top 50 NI students on STEM course, year 1 scholarship of £1,000.
» RUK students (excluding medical, dental and pharmacy) with AAB at A-Level or equivalent, £2,500 a year; with offer grades, £1,250 a year.

Students

Undergraduates:	**13,785**	**(4,570)**
Postgraduates:	**3,740**	**(2,105)**
Mature students:	**18.2%**	
Overseas students:	**4.9%**	
Applications per place:	**5.6**	
From state-sector schools:	**97.9%**	
From working-class homes:	**31.3%**	

For detailed information about sports facilities: www.qub.ac.uk/sport

Accommodation

Number of places and costs refer to 2012–13
University-provided places: around 2,000
Percentage catered: 0%
Self-catered costs: £69.80–£99.51 a week.
First-year students are guaranteed accommodation if conditions are met.
International students: as above.
Contact: accommodation@qub.ac.uk
www.stayatqueens.com

University of Reading

While other universities were struggling to attract students after the announcement of £9,000 fees, Reading was celebrating 10 per cent growth in the demand for places. Almost 20,000 applications by the official deadline for courses beginning in 2012 represented a record for the university, which already had more than six students chasing every place. In recent years, the university has invested over £400 million in new teaching and research facilities on campus, opened two new halls of residence and improved catering outlets and other student facilities.

Reading is one of the medium-sized campus universities that have demonstrated their appeal through the National Student Survey. Consistently in the top 20, it again satisfied almost 90 per cent of its final-year undergraduates in the results published in 2011. Classics and anatomy and physiology registered 100 per cent satisfaction among final-year undergraduates, while biology, chemistry and physics were all within three percentage points of that mark. Partly as a result of these successes, Reading is one of the biggest risers in the new *Times* League Table, moving up nine places to finish close to the top 20.

The university did well in the 2008 Research Assessment Exercise, despite entering a much higher proportion of its academics than many of its peers. More than half of their work was considered world-leading or internationally excellent, with archaeology and art and design doing particularly well. Reading was among the top 20 universities for the number of research grants awarded in 2010–11. There are international centres of research excellence in areas such as food security, agriculture, biological and physical sciences, meteorology, and European histories and cultures.

There are three main sites within Reading, including the original 320-acre parkland site, and the university also owns 2,000 acres of farmland at nearby Sonning and Shinfield, where the renowned Centre for Dairy Research (CEDAR) is located. To these has been added the former Henley Management College, which became the university's business school in 2008. The college's attractive site, on the banks of the river at Henley-on-Thames, houses postgraduate and executive programmes, while undergraduates are taught in the new £35-million business school on the main Whiteknights campus. An £11-million home for film, theatre and TV opened on the campus opened in the spring of 2011, while an Enterprise Centre brings together academic expertise with local and international technology-based businesses.

Reading was the only university established between the two world wars, having been Oxford's extension college for the first part of the last century, but the

---

Whiteknights
PO Box 217
Reading RG6 6AH

0118 378 8618/9
student.recruitment@
   reading.ac.uk
www.reading.ac.uk
www.rusu.co.uk
Affiliation: 1994 Group

The Times Rankings
Overall Ranking: =24

Student satisfaction:	=17	(81%)
Research quality:	=27	(0.68)
Entry standards:	40	(377)
Student–staff ratio:	23	(14.9)
Services & facilities/student:	50	(£1,454)
Expected completion rate:	=25	(92.3%)
Good honours:	=26	(73.4%)
Graduate prospects:	=40	(69.3%)

attractive main campus now has a modern feel. A multimillion-pound student services building provides a one-stop shop for student support and welfare, and sports facilities have been extended. Water sports are a strong focus, with off-campus boathouses on the Thames and a sailing and canoeing club nearby. Representative teams have a good record in inter-university competitions and the campus was chosen as a pre-Olympics training camp for basketball and fencing.

The university's location, a bus ride away from Heathrow Airport, and an international reputation in key areas for developing countries have always ensured a healthy flow of overseas students. About one undergraduate in six is from an independent school and just under a quarter come from working-class homes, below average for the university's subjects and entry qualifications. However, only 7 per cent of undergraduates are expected to leave without a qualification.

All undergraduates take career management skills modules that contribute five credits towards their degree classification. The online system, which has 200 web pages of advice, exercises and information, has been bought by 30 other universities and colleges. Sessions are delivered jointly by academics and careers advisors, with input from alumni and leading employers. Reading's latest graduate employment figures were the best for a decade and the university is hoping to improve them further by providing placement opportunities for all students regardless of degree.

The town – only a short walk from the campus – may not be the most fashionable, but it has plenty of nightlife and an award-winning shopping centre. It also offers temporary and part-time employment opportunities for students. London is easily accessible by train, but the cost of living is on a par with the capital. The university has spent £200 million on new student accommodation and there are plans for a private company to redevelop some of the older stock. The large students' union had a £500,000 refit in 2007, improving and extending its popular main venue. The union has been voted among the best in Britain, and has won numerous awards, including Best Bar None status for encouraging safe drinking. Students who live in town can make use of the free night bus service to take them back into Reading.

Undergraduate Fees and Bursaries

» Fees for UK/EU students 2012–13 £9,000
» International student fees 2012–13 £11,440–£13,645
» Household income up to £16K, £4,000 package, year 1; £2,500 package, other years; £16K–£25K, £3,000 package, year 1; £2,000 package, other years. £25K–£42K, £500 cash, all years.
» Other academic and targeted scholarships available.

Students

Undergraduates:	8,595	(120)
Postgraduates:	2,505	(1,970)
Mature students:	10.4%	
Overseas students:	13.9%	
Applications per place:	6.5	
From state-sector schools:	81.8%	
From working-class homes:	24.2%	

For detailed information about sports facilities:
www.sport.reading.ac.uk

Accommodation

Number of places and costs refer to 2012–13
University-provided places: about 4,300
Percentage catered: 20%
Catered costs: £119–£160 (40 weeks, catering during terms).
Self-catered costs: £98–£144 (40–51 weeks).
First-year undergraduate students are guaranteed a place if conditions are met.
International students: given priority if conditions are met.
Contact: www.reading.ac.uk/life/life-accommodation.aspx

Robert Gordon University

Robert Gordon University (RGU) has regained its status as the top post-1992 university in the UK and is on the verge of the top 50 in this year's *Times* League Table. Student satisfaction has risen and there has been further improvement in the university's strong suit of graduate employment, placing it in the top ten on this measure. With 100 per cent satisfaction in nutrition and high scores in accounting, anatomy, mechanical engineering, medical technology, pharmacy and social work, Robert Gordon was among the top 40 universities in the 2011 National Student Survey. The university had already improved its performance in the last Research Assessment Exercise. Almost a third of its submission was considered world-leading or internationally excellent, with library and information management the star performer. Three research institutes have since been launched to focus on the university's strengths in business and information; innovation, design and sustainability; and health and welfare.

So close are links with the North Sea oil and gas industries that RGU used to dub itself the Energy University. But with nursing and the health sciences now equally important, it has gone for the broader soubriquet of the Professional University.

The creative industries are a growth area and there is a full portfolio of courses in business, design and engineering. Flexible programmes, with credit accumulation and transfer, make for easy movement in and out of the university for an often mobile local workforce. Work placements, lasting up to a year, are the norm, helping to achieve an employment record that has been Scotland's best for several years and consistently one of the UK's leaders.

Like many new universities, RGU recruits most of its students locally, 60 per cent of them female. However, overseas student numbers have been growing sharply and the overall demand for places has been stronger than at most universities north of the border. There had been a 5 per cent increase in applications at the beginning of 2012, following even stronger growth in the previous year. Efforts to extend access beyond the normal higher education catchment have produced a diverse student population, with more than a third of the undergraduates coming from working-class homes and almost all attending state schools or colleges. The projected dropout rate of less than 14 per cent almost matches the UK average for RGU's subjects and entry qualifications.

Robert Gordon University has a pedigree in education that goes back 250 years. The university now offers about 150 degrees. Students from the city's two

---

Schoolhill
Aberdeen AB10 1FR

01224 262728 (enquiries)
ugoffice@rgu.ac.uk
www.rgu.ac.uk
www.rguunion.co.uk
Affiliation: none

The Times Rankings

Overall Ranking: **51**

Student satisfaction:	=34	(80%)
Research quality:	=62	(0.16)
Entry standards:	50	(335)
Student–staff ratio:	=74	(19.1)
Services & facilities/student:	80	(£1,252)
Expected completion rate:	=86	(78.3%)
Good honours:	=68	(60.6%)
Graduate prospects:	10	(78.4%)

universities mix easily, and there is healthy academic rivalry in some areas, despite the obvious differences. There is also a partnership with Aberdeen College, which has become an associate college of the university to encourage progression from school, to further education to higher education.

Named after an eighteenth-century philanthropist, RGU currently has two sites around the city. The historic Schoolhill site adjoins Aberdeen Art Gallery in the city centre, while Garthdee, where 70 per cent of undergraduates are taught, is located at the south side of the city, overlooking the River Dee. The university has spent £100 million on its buildings and facilities, including the Norman Foster designed Aberdeen Business School. Other recent developments have added specialist facilities for the Faculty of Health and Social Care. Another £170 million of improvements is planned for Garthdee over the next few years, providing new facilities for engineering, computing, art and architecture and the built environment. The first phase will be completed by 2013.

The university is pinning many of its hopes on new technology. An award-winning virtual campus was launched with an online course in e-business for postgraduates. It also enables management undergraduates to receive course materials via an intranet, and other degree and short courses are available. The new Moodle system is used across Robert Gordon courses for both on-campus and distance learning students.

Aberdeen is a long way to go for English students, but train and air links are excellent, and the city regularly features in the top ten for quality of life. A £12-million sports and leisure centre opened at the university in 2005, providing a centre of excellence for the region in hockey, as well as a 25-metre swimming pool, three gyms, a climbing wall and bouldering room, a café bar, three exercise studios and a large sports hall. Sport scholarships are available to budding athletes, with Olympic swimming hopeful Hannah Miley amongst the university's current recipients. Although accommodation can be expensive in the private sector, low prices in the students' union partially compensate, and there are enough residential places to guarantee housing to first years from outside the local area.

Undergraduate Fees and Bursaries

» Fees for Scottish and EU students 2012–13   No fee
» Fees for Scottish and EU students 2012–13   £5,000–£6,750
   Pharmacy   £8,500
» Fees for international students 2012–13   £9,500–£11,800
» Other academic and targeted scholarships available.
» Check the university's website for the latest information.

Students

Undergraduates:	**6,885**	**(2,220)**
Postgraduates:	**1,860**	**(2,160)**
Mature students:	**22.8%**	
Overseas students:	**12.2%**	
Applications per place:	**5.3**	
From state-sector schools:	**95.4%**	
From working-class homes:	**35.1%**	

For detailed information about sports facilities: www.rgu.ac.uk/rgusport

Accommodation

Number of places and costs refer to 2012–13
University-provided places: 1,563
Percentage catered: 0%
Self-catered costs: £62.50–£170.00 a week.
All first-year students are eligible to apply for student accommodation. Residential restrictions apply.
International students: given priority for accommodation.
Contact: accommodation@rgu.ac.uk
www.rgu.ac.uk/living/accommodation

Roehampton University

Roehampton suffered the biggest drop in applications of any university at the start of 2012 – scant reward for relatively low fees and a clear statement of the reasoning behind them. The university cut its own costs by 15 per cent and promised that 95 per cent of a student's fee would be spent on his or her education. But even though most degrees will cost less than £8,000 in 2012–13, applications still fell by 27 per cent. The only compensation for Roehampton was a healthy allocation from the pool of 20,000 places reserved for universities and colleges charging the lowest fees.

Roehampton has been fully independent since 2004, and the university has been making its mark in its own right, after four years in a federation with Surrey University. There have been record intakes, with applications growing consistently until now, despite rising entry requirements. Roehampton has a proud and distinguished history dating back to the 1840s, its colleges having been among the first in the country to open higher education to women. Today the university has a broad range of expertise across business, the arts and humanities, social sciences and the human and life sciences, while maintaining its historic strength in education.

Successes in the last Research Assessment Exercise, when Roehampton entered a much higher proportion of its academics than most of its peer group, added to the university's reputation. A third of the submission was judged to be world-leading or internationally excellent, with the university producing the best results in the country for dance and biological anthropology, and doing well in drama, theatre and performance studies, English literature and education.

Roehampton is a collegiate university with four distinctive colleges, which still maintain some of the traditional ethos of their religious foundations: the Anglican Whitelands, the Roman Catholic Digby Stuart, the Methodist Southlands, and the Froebel, which follows the humanist teachings of Frederick Froebel. Students need not follow any of these denominations to enrol in the colleges. The university also has a Jewish resource centre and Muslim prayer rooms.

All four colleges are based in a 64-acre campus, with stunning parkland and lakes, on or adjacent to Roehampton Lane. Whitelands is based in Parkstead House, the 18th-century mansion overlooking Richmond Park, which also houses the School of Human and Life Sciences. The buildings have been refurbished with IT facilities, student accommodation, laboratories and teaching space. The colleges all have their own bars and other

---

Erasmus House
Roehampton Lane
London SW15 5PU

020 8392 3232 (enquiries)
enquiries@roehampton.ac.uk
www.roehampton.ac.uk
www.roehampton
   student.com
Affiliations: Cathedral
   Group; million+

The Times Rankings

Overall Ranking: **86**

Student satisfaction:	=89	(75%)
Research quality:	58	(0.23)
Entry standards:	101	(260)
Student–staff ratio:	=95	(20.8)
Services & facilities/student:	59	(£1,372)
Expected completion rate:	95	(77.0%)
Good honours:	90	(54.8%)
Graduate prospects:	70	(60.1%)

leisure facilities, although they are open to all members of the university.

A £6-million building, mainly for dance and PE, opened on the main campus in 2005. More recent projects include a £4-million facility for the School of Arts and a new national centre of excellence for teaching on citizenship education, human rights and social justice. There is a fully functioning newsroom for journalism and media students at Roehampton and plans for online programmes in management and information systems to be delivered to thousands of students in other countries, in partnership with Laureate International Universities.

True to the university's origins, education remains the largest subject area, accounting for more than a quarter of the students. The Quality Assurance Agency complimented Roehampton on the accessibility of academic staff to students and the positive ways in which they responded to student needs. One example has been the provision of enhanced sports facilities on campus, with a new gym, two football pitches, running track and a multi-use games area. The sport performance and rehabilitation centre offers students, staff and local people physiotherapy, podiatry and sports massage, as well as access to physiological assessment, biomechanical analysis, sport psychology support and sports nutrition. The university is a high-performance centre for British

fencing and sitting volleyball. In 2010, the Roehampton tennis team was the British Universities Sports team of the year.

Like other London universities, however, Roehampton has struggled to reach national averages for student satisfaction. Only business studies, dance and philosophy satisfied more than 90 per cent of final-year undergraduates in the 2011 National Student Survey, when Roehampton was close to the bottom 20. More than 95 per cent of undergraduates were educated in state schools and 35 per cent come from working-class homes. The projected dropout rate improved dramatically in the latest survey. At only 8 per cent, it is barely half the average for Roehampton's courses and entry grades.

Most first years who want a hall place are offered one, with priority going to those living furthest away. While rents are not cheap for those who miss out on a place or prefer the private sector, students like the proximity of central London and the lively and attractive suburbs around Roehampton.

Undergraduate Fees and Bursaries

» Fees for UK/EU students 2012–13   £7,900–£8,250
» International student fees 2012–13   £10,400
» 75 NSP awards based on best UCAS tariff scores, of £3,000 year 1, £1,500 years 2 and 3, mainly as fee waiver.
» For those with 480 UCAS tariff points, £2,000 fee waiver each year; 340 UCAS tariff points, £1,500 fee waiver each year.
» Other scholarships available.

Students

Undergraduates:	**6,085**	**(575)**
Postgraduates:	**1,255**	**(1,225)**
Mature students:	**25.2%**	
Overseas students:	**5.6%**	
Applications per place:	**4.3**	
From state-sector schools:	**96.4%**	
From working-class homes:	**35.4%**	

For detailed information about sports facilities: www.roehampton.ac.uk/Sport-Roehampton

Accommodation

Number of places and costs refer to 2012–13
University-provided places: 1,500
Percentage catered: 0%
Self-catered costs: £96.95–£110.25 (standard) – £124.95 (en suite) a week.
First years are given priority if conditions met. Local restrictions apply.
International students: guaranteed for first year.
Contact: accommodation@roehampton.ac.uk

Royal Holloway, University of London

Royal Holloway is providing one of the three Olympic villages for the 2012 Games because of its proximity to Eton's Dorney Rowing Lake. The rowers will have access to one of Britain's most remarkable university buildings, the 600-bed Founder's Building, modelled on a French chateau and opened by Queen Victoria. It is the centrepiece of the University of London's "campus in the country", 135 acres of woodland between Windsor Castle and Heathrow. More than £100 million has been spent on the campus in the last five years, resulting in an impressive range of new and refurbished academic and social facilities.

Recent projects have included a major auditorium, extensions to the School of Management and other academic buildings, an extension to the main library and new student residences, which have been praised for their comfort and eco-friendly features. The students' union has been refurbished and the library and many teaching spaces are currently being upgraded. A new drama studio will open in 2012, supplementing the performance space that came with the conversion of a huge Victorian boiler house, and there are plans to extend the library and create a student services area.

Royal Holloway now has a record 9,000 students and buoyant demand for entry has withstood the introduction of £9,000 fees. Applications for degree courses were up by 1 per cent at the start of 2012, against the national trend. The university has promised a range of student support that, unusually, includes £1 million for postgraduates so that graduates with large debts are not deterred from continuing their studies. The extra fee income will also go towards an expansion of the academic staff and better student services.

Both Bedford College and Royal Holloway, which amalgamated to form the existing college 27 years ago, were founded for women only, their legacy commemorated in the Bedford Centre for the History of Women. However, the gender balance in the student population is now roughly equal and, although still best known for the arts, Royal Holloway has a broad portfolio of subjects, including a science foundation year for those wishing to change academic direction.

Of the work entered for the 2008 Research Assessment Exercise, 60 per cent was rated world-leading or internationally excellent, cementing Royal Holloway's place among the top 25 research universities. Music was ranked top in the UK, with 90 per cent of its research in the top two categories, while biology, drama, earth sciences, economics, geography, German, media arts and psychology were all in the top 10 in their fields.

The college has also had consistently good

University of London
Egham
Surrey TW20 0EX

01784 414944 (admissions)
admissions@rhul.ac.uk
www.rhul.ac.uk
www.su.rhul.co.uk
Affiliation: 1994 Group

The Times Rankings
Overall Ranking: **27**

Student satisfaction:	=55	(78%)
Research quality:	15	(0.83)
Entry standards:	=30	(399)
Student–staff ratio:	=32	(15.6)
Services & facilities/student:	45	(£1,512)
Expected completion rate:	28	(92.2%)
Good honours:	=30	(71.8%)
Graduate prospects:	50	(66.1%)

results in the National Student Survey, with another improvement in 2011 taking the proportion of satisfied students to 87 per cent. Human and social geography registered 100 per cent satisfaction, with physical geography and environmental science close behind and music, physics and psychology all producing good results.

Royal Holloway encourages interdisciplinary work, which is facilitated by a modular course structure with examinations at the end of every year. An Advanced Skills Programme, covering information technology, communication skills and foreign languages, further encourages breadth of study. The university offers a number of e-degrees and promotes numerous opportunities to study abroad, building on the international flavour of the campus and its links with institutions such as New York, Sydney and Yale universities.

Royal Holloway draws a fifth of its undergraduates from independent schools, although the proportion coming from working-class homes has been rising. The ethnic mix is above average and the projected dropout rate of 7.5 per cent is below the official benchmark. The new Royal Holloway Passport is intended to enhance graduates' employability. The scheme recognises the additional skills that students gain from many extracurricular activities and which future graduate employers greatly value.

Nearly 3,000 students are in halls of residence, many of them in the Founder's Building itself. The college's green belt location at Egham, Surrey, 35 minutes from the centre of London by rail, ensures that social life is concentrated on an extended students' union. However, the West End is close for those determined to seek the high life. Sports facilities are good and have been upgraded recently – Royal Holloway claims to be "the University of London's best sporting college". It has had considerable success with its "student talented athlete award scheme" (STARS).

Students enjoy an active cultural scene, and a thriving Community Action programme involves over 1,000 student volunteers working with various organisations and charities in the local area. A high proportion of students come from London and the Home Counties, so many go home at the weekend, but the lively students' union puts on entertainment and activities seven days a week.

Undergraduate Fees and Bursaries

» Fees for UK/EU students 2012–13 £9,000
» International student fees 2012–13 £12,220–£13,860
» 172 NSP awards of £2,000 fee waiver and £1,000 cash, year 1; £2,500 cash years 2 and 3.
» Household income below £25K, £2,500 package each year; £25K–£30K, £1,000; £30K–£42.6K, £750.
» Award of £1,000 a year for those with AAB at A Level or equivalent.
» Other scholarships and bursaries available.

Students

Undergraduates:	6,775	(660)
Postgraduates:	1,625	(460)
Mature students:	9.9%	
Overseas students:	25.2%	
Applications per place:	5.7	
From state-sector schools:	79.9%	
From working-class homes:	26.1%	

For detailed information about sports facilities: www.rhul.ac.uk/sports

Accommodation

Number of places and costs refer to 2012–13

University-provided places: 2,922

Percentage catered: 37%

Catered costs: £96–£140 a week (30–38 weeks).

Self-catered costs: £115–£142 a week (30–38 weeks).

First years are guaranteed accommodation provided conditions are met.

International students: non-EU students guaranteed accommodation.

Contact: studenthousing@rhul.ac.uk

University of St Andrews

St Andrews joined Edinburgh in setting the highest fees in the UK for undergraduates from England, Wales or Northern Ireland for 2012–13. They will pay £9,000 for the full four years of a degree, although there are bursaries for students whose family income is below £42,600. Scots and other EU students will continue to pay nothing. With almost 30 per cent of St Andrews students coming from south of the border, the new fees might have been expected to hit recruitment, but applications were up by 17 per cent at the start of 2012, with only a small decline from England.

St Andrews has been the leading Scottish university in *The Times* League Table for the last seven years, benefiting particularly from outstanding scores in the National Student Survey (NSS). It was in the top five in the UK for student satisfaction again in 2011, with 100 per cent ratings in Iberian studies and theology, close to that mark in physics and astronomy, and better than 95 per cent satisfaction also in history, business studies, other European languages, and maths and statistics. Nearly 60 per cent of the work submitted for the 2008 Research Assessment Exercise was rated as world-leading or internationally excellent. St Andrews was joint top in the UK for philosophy and top in Scotland for physics and astronomy, German, film studies, applied maths, French and psychology.

Scotland's oldest university and the third oldest in the English-speaking world will celebrate its 600th anniversary in 2013. St Andrews has long been fashionable among a mainly middle-class clientele – students from independent schools take 40 per cent of the places – but its appeal is far wider than that, with more than 7 applicants chasing each place. International students from over 100 countries account for more than a third of the intake and give the university a cosmopolitan feel. Fee concessions and exchange schemes have boosted applications, particularly from the USA, which provides nearly a fifth of first-year students on its own.

The town of St Andrews is steeped in history, as well as being the centre of the golfing world. The university at its heart accounts for nearly half of the 18,000 inhabitants. There are close cultural and social relations between town and gown. New students ("bejants" and "bejantines") acquire third or fourth-year "parents" to ease them into university life, and on Raisin Monday give their academic guardians a bottle of wine in return for a receipt in Latin, which can be written on anything. Another unusual feature is that all humanities students are awarded an MA rather than a BA.

Many of the main buildings date from

College Gate
St Andrews
Fife KY16 9AJ

01334 462150 (admissions)
student.recruitment@st-andrews.
ac.uk (pre-recruitment)
www.st-andrews.ac.uk
www.yourunion.net
Affiliation: 1994 Group

The Times Rankings
Overall Ranking: **6**

Student satisfaction:	=7	(83%)
Research quality:	=13	(0.84)
Entry standards:	5	(519)
Student–staff ratio:	12	(13.6)
Services & facilities/student:	6	(£2,308)
Expected completion rate:	3	(97.4%)
Good honours:	4	(82.9%)
Graduate prospects:	19	(74.1%)

the 15th and 16th centuries, but sciences are taught at the modern North Haugh site a few streets away. Everything is within walking distance, but bicycles are common. Although small, St Andrews offers a wide range of courses. The university's reputation has always rested on the humanities, which have a £1.3-million research centre. An £8-million headquarters for the School of International Relations opened in 2006, with Europe's first Centre for Syrian Studies, an Institute of Iranian Studies and a Centre for Peace and Conflict Studies. St Andrews has the largest mediaeval history department in Britain and has now added film studies and sustainable development. A full range of physical sciences is also on offer, with sophisticated lasers and the largest optical telescope in Britain.

A £45-million Medical and Biological Sciences Building opened in 2010, one of the first UK medical schools whose research facilities are fully integrated with the other sciences, offering an important new dimension to medical training and research. A £5-million Bio-medical Sciences Research complex, to lead the fight against superbugs and serious viral, bacterial and parasitic diseases, followed in 2011. The university is planning a Green Energy Centre and a Knowledge Exchange Centre for spin-out companies, new business and prototype testing on the site of the former paper mill five miles away at Guardbridge. Support

for scholarships and medical research are among the first targets of a £100-million fundraising campaign launched by Prince William and his then fiancée, both St Andrews graduates, to mark the university's 600th anniversary.

Students do not come to St Andrews for the nightclubs, but there is no shortage of parties in a tight-knit community. The sports facilities are excellent and more than half of all students live in halls. Self-catering accommodation for 920 students during term and three-star accommodation for golfers and other tourists in vacations was opened by Gordon Brown in 2007. Features such as the grass roof made it the first university residence to be awarded the Green Tourism Business Scheme's Gold Award. A further 250 residential places opened in 2010.

Undergraduate Fees and Bursaries

- » Fees for Scottish and EU students 2012–13   No fee
- » Fees for Non-Scottish UK (RUK) students 2012–13   £9,000
- » Fees for international students 2013–14   £15,500
     Medical science   £23,550
- » For Scottish students with household income below £42.6K, 50 bursaries of up to £2,000 a year.
- » For all students, top 100 at the end of year 1, £5,000 scholarship.
- » For RUK students, bursary to top up student's official funding to £7,500 a year.
- » Scholarships and bursaries are available.

Students		
Undergraduates:	**6,395**	**(975)**
Postgraduates:	**1,775**	**(395)**
Mature students:	**2.7%**	
Overseas students:	**36.2%**	
Applications per place:	**7**	
From state-sector schools:	**60.1%**	
From working-class homes:	**15.0%**	

For detailed information about sports facilities:
www.st-andrews.ac.uk/sport

Accommodation

Number of places and costs refer to 2012–13
University-provided places: 3,943
Percentage catered: 45%
Catered costs: £125.09–£204.88 a week (33 weeks).
Self-catered costs: £71.83–£157.08 a week (38 weeks).
Single first-year undergraduates are guaranteed accommodation if they apply by 31 May.
Policy for international students: as above.
Contact: accommodation@st-andrews.ac.uk
www.st-andrews.ac.uk/admissions/Accommodation

University of Salford

In recent years, Salford has slipped behind a number of new universities in *The Times* League Table. It is more than 20 places below the nearest pre-1992 institution. But a reputation for good graduate employment prospects, carefully targeted courses and an emphasis on the university's location close to the centre of Manchester have maintained its appeal to students. The demand for places had been buoyant for several years until the introduction of fees averaging £8,330 for 2012–13. Applications dropped by almost 15 per cent, in spite of a generous package of student support that will benefit up to 30 per cent of students.

The university is in the midst of a £500-million capital programme that will take 15 years to complete. It will include a £38-million Arts and Media Centre on campus, while a base at the MediaCityUK development in Salford Quays – home to five BBC departments – is already open. Over 1,500 students on 39 courses will enjoy exceptional opportunities to work with media professionals using the latest equipment, studios and laboratories. Salford Law School opened in 2007 in a £10-million building and £22 million was spent on a new home for the Faculty of Health and Social Care. New acoustic laboratories opened in 2008, with a reverberation room capable of transforming the quality of sound and an anechoic chamber, which is said to be the quietest place in the world. The world's first Energy House opened in 2011 – a full-size traditional terraced house built in a laboratory for students, researchers and industry to study domestic energy consumption.

Salford stresses its business links and modern portfolio of courses, including two-year Foundation degrees. The university does well on the Government's access measures: four in ten undergraduates come from working-class homes and there is a high proportion from areas sending few students to higher education. The projected dropout rate has fluctuated but a dramatic decline in the latest figures took it back above 20 per cent, well below the national average for the subjects and students' qualifications. The Student Life Directorate has been charged with improving every aspect of the student experience, even planning events for students staying at Salford over the Christmas holiday closure.

The university's growing involvement in health has seen the establishment of a national centre for prosthetics and orthotics, and Salford has a high reputation for the treatment of sports injuries. The School of Nursing and Midwifery, which received outstanding ratings from its regulatory body following a recent inspection, runs Europe's first nursing course for deaf students. There

---

The Crescent
Salford
Greater Manchester
M5 4WT

0161 295 4545 (enquiries)
contact via website
www.salford.ac.uk
www.salfordstudents.com
Affiliation: University
  Alliance

The Times Rankings		
Overall Ranking: **=91**		
Student satisfaction:	**=98**	(74%)
Research quality:	**56**	(0.28)
Entry standards:	**81**	(286)
Student–staff ratio:	**=37**	(16.2)
Services & facilities/student:	**109**	(£964)
Expected completion rate:	**102**	(75.1%)
Good honours:	**83**	(57.1%)
Graduate prospects:	**82**	(56.4%)

is also a BA in journalism and war studies – the only undergraduate degree in the UK to combine the two disciplines.

Engineering is the university's traditional strength, attracting many of the 3,000 overseas students. Two thirds of all courses offer work placements, half of them abroad and almost all counting towards degree classifications. The university has partnerships which provide research and work experience with the BBC, Adobe and Carnegie Mellon University, Pittsburgh among others. The Enterprise Academy scheme was commended by the EU after it helped 32 student businesses become established. Students are offered training in entrepreneurship and business skills, as well as a business mentor, while an innovative scheme also provides professional training and work experience for unemployed and under-employed graduates.

Online degrees have been introduced and the university has also made headlines with more unusual innovations, such as the appointment of Britain's first Professor of Pop Music. The university launched Salford Business School in 2006 and a new Centre for Applied Archaeology has been established. Salford led the way in formally recognising interaction with business and industry as of equal importance to teaching and research. The university entered a relatively low proportion of its academics for the 2008 Research Assessment Exercise, but still had among the lowest grades of the pre-1992 universities. Architecture and business produced the best results. The university has since established nine interdisciplinary research centres and a graduate school.

There has been some improvement in scores in the National Student Survey, although Salford is still close to the bottom 20 universities in 2011. The best results were in accounting, finance, physical geography and environmental science, physics and physiology. The modern landscaped campus, a haven of lawns and shrubberies along the River Irwell, is less than two miles from Manchester city centre and has a mainline railway station. University House, where students go for advice and support, has recently seen a £3-millon upgrade. Salford, which has been named one of the most gay-friendly universities, also has its own TV and radio studios. Another 2,000 residential places should be available on campus in 2013, while others are in a student village 15 minutes' walk away.

Undergraduate Fees and Bursaries

» Fees for UK/EU students 2012–13   £8,000–£9,000
» International student fees 2012–13   £9,790–£12,170
» For Greater Manchester residents with household income below £25K, 390 NSP awards of £2,000 fee waiver and £1,000 cash, year 1 only.

Students		
Undergraduates:	14,125	(2,630)
Postgraduates:	2,465	(2,355)
Mature students:	35.6%	
Overseas students:	12%	
Applications per place:	5.1	
From state-sector schools:	97.4%	
From working-class homes:	39.3%	

For detailed information about sports facilities:
www.sport.salford.ac.uk

Accommodation
Number of places and costs refer to 2012–13
University-provided places: 1,309 plus 1,930 managed by specialist providers
Percentage catered: 0%
Self-catered costs: £66.01–93.80 (standard); £91.07–£105.00 (en suite)
First years are guaranteed accommodation (terms and conditions apply).
International students: as above.
Contact: www.accommodation.salford.ac.uk

School of Oriental and African Studies, London

SOAS is the only higher education institution in the UK specialising in the study of Africa, Asia and the Middle East, and has a global reputation in subjects relating to two thirds of the world's population. Originally a specialist Oriental college, the school now covers a broad range of subjects. The library is one of just five National Research Libraries in the country, holding 1.5 million volumes, periodicals and audio-visual materials in 400 languages, and attracts scholars from around the world. Nevertheless, the prospect of £9,000 fees prompted a decline of 10 per cent in applications for degree places and SOAS has dropped out of the top 30 in the new *Times* League Table. Lower graduate employment was the biggest factor in a nine-place fall.

The 5,400 students on campus, plus over 3,000 studying distance learning programmes, come from over 130 countries. However, two-thirds are from Britain and the rest of the EU – and the proportion is higher still among the undergraduates. Independent school candidates account for almost a quarter of the British entrants to degree courses, while more than a fifth are from working-class homes. The school does well in the National Student Survey, remaining well above the national average in 2011. Politics and Asian studies produced by far the best results.

SOAS has a much wider portfolio of courses than its name would suggest, offering more than 350 degree combinations and 100 postgraduate programmes. Degrees are available in familiar subjects such as law, music, history and the social sciences, but with a different emphasis. There is also a more limited portfolio of Foundation programmes and language courses. Over 45 per cent of undergraduates take a language as part of their degree and the School has now introduced a Language Entitlement programme which offers one term of a non-accredited SOAS Language Centre course free of charge. The school was chosen to house a national teaching centre for languages and won a Queen's Anniversary Prize for the excellence, breadth and depth of its language teaching in 2010. The £6.5-million Library Transformation Project has added more language laboratories, music studios, discussion and research rooms, gallery space and other facilities. SOAS is in the top 50 in the QS World Rankings for the arts and humanities, and has been strengthening its academic staff in a variety of disciplines as it approaches its centenary in 2016.

The numbers taking distance learning courses, mainly outside the UK, have grown

---

Thornhaugh Street
Russell Square
London WC1H 0XG

020 7898 4034 (student recruitment)
study@soas.ac.uk
www.soas.ac.uk
www.soasunion.org
Affiliation: 1994 Group

The Times **Rankings**
Overall Ranking: **31**

Student satisfaction:	=108	(72%)
Research quality:	=30	(0.65)
Entry standards:	24	(419)
Student–staff ratio:	4	(11.3)
Services & facilities/student:	24	(£1,867)
Expected completion rate:	=53	(84.8%)
Good honours:	20	(75.4%)
Graduate prospects:	55	(64.5%)

considerably. The transfer of the University of London postgraduate programmes previously taught by Imperial College have made SOAS one of the world's largest providers of distance learning at this level. Postgraduates are attracted by a research record which saw more than half of the work submitted for the 2008 Research Assessment Exercise rated world-leading or internationally excellent. SOAS was ranked top in the UK for Asian studies and did well in anthropology, politics, history and music.

There is an option of spending one, two or three terms of a degree course in one of the school's many partner universities in Africa or Asia. The dropout rate has fluctuated over recent years. At 15 per cent in the latest statistics, it was significantly above the UK average for the subjects and entry qualifications at SOAS. The school will almost double its investment in student support with the switch to higher fees, as well as increasing its outreach activities, which include summer schools, masterclasses and academic buddying.

SOAS is located at the heart of the University of London in Bloomsbury. There is a second campus less than a mile away and adjacent to two of the three student residences, providing student-orientated facilities such as a Learning Resource Centre and an internet café. The centrepiece of the main campus is an airy, modern building with gallery space as well as teaching accommodation, a gift from the Sultan of Brunei. There is no separate students' union building, although the students do have their own recently refurbished bar, social space and catering facilities. The well-equipped and under-used University of London Union is close at hand, with swimming pool, gym and bars. The West End is also on the doorstep.

Nearly 1,000 residential places are available within 15 minutes' walk of the school. Another 101 places are available in flats at the second campus. However, the school has few of its own sports facilities and the outdoor pitches are remote, with no time set aside from lectures. Students tend to be highly committed and often politically active – not surprising since many will return to positions of influence in developing countries – and the variety of cultures makes for lively debate.

Undergraduate Fees and Bursaries
» Fees for UK/EU students 2012–13   £9,000
» International student fees 2012–13   £13,890
» Household income below £25K: 50% reduction in fees for those from low participation neighbourhoods; for academic achievers, £3,000 package a year; 30 NSP awards, year 1, for those on courses leading to a profession, £2,000 fee waiver, £1,000 cash.
» Check the university's website for the latest information.

Students		
Undergraduates:	2,860	(85)
Postgraduates:	1,710	(520)
Mature students:	26.6%	
Overseas students:	38.5%	
Applications per place:	5.4	
From state-sector schools:	73.6%	
From working-class homes:	22.5%	

For detailed information about sports facilities:
http://soasunion.org

Accommodation
Number of places and costs refer to 2012–13
University-provided places: 770 (Sanctuary Management Services); 170 (intercollegiate)
Percentage catered: 17%
Catered costs: £108.50–£276.50 a week.
Self-catered costs: £139.09–£241.71 a week.
Priority given to first years on first come basis. Residential restrictions apply.
International students: as above, although they are a high priority.
Contact: student@sanctuary-housing.co.uk

University of Sheffield

Sheffield was chosen as *Times Higher Education* magazine's 2011 University of the Year for combining a focus on its local community with high-quality, research-led academic activity. The university has just slipped out of the top 20 of *The Times* League Table but recorded high finishes in a number of subjects, largely as a result of a good performance in the last Research Assessment Exercise (RAE) and consistently high levels of satisfaction among the students. Sheffield has a more diverse student population than most of its fellow members of the Russell Group: more than 85 per cent of undergraduates come from state schools or colleges and almost one undergraduate in five comes from a working-class home. Although it is to charge £9,000 fees for 2012–13, the university expects more than a third of the undergraduates to benefit from a much-increased package of support.

Sheffield is in the top 75 universities in the world, according to the QS World University Rankings, and attracts more than 4,800 overseas students from 128 countries. Total student numbers have reached nearly 25,000, although applications were down by more than the sector average at the start of 2012, with the prospect of higher fees. Two new student villages and a high-tech library and learning centre have added to the feeling of a university on the move. The £23-million Information Commons, opened in 2007, operates 24 hours a day, providing 1,300 study spaces and 500 computers linked to the campus network, as well as 110,000 books and periodicals.

Sheffield was in the top 10 universities in the 2011 National Student Survey, with 90 per cent of final-year undergraduates satisfied overall. Business studies, microbiology and molecular biology, biophysics and biochemistry all registered 100 per cent satisfaction, while history, journalism, landscape design, physical geography and zoology all topped 95 per cent. More than 60 per cent of the work submitted for the RAE was judged to be world-leading or internationally excellent. Politics and information studies achieved the best results in the country, while town planning, philosophy, Russian, architecture, and mechanical and aeronautical engineering were near the top for their fields.

Academic buildings are concentrated in an area about a mile from the city centre on the affluent west side of Sheffield, with most university flats and halls of residence a little further into the suburbs. The main university precinct now stretches into an almost unbroken mile-long "campus". There has been sustained investment in new buildings and facilities over recent years –

Western Bank
Sheffield S10 2TN

0114 222 2000 (switchboard)
http://ask.sheffield.ac.uk/
www.sheffield.ac.uk
www.sheffield.ac.uk/union
Affiliation: Russell Group

The Times Rankings
Overall Ranking: **21**

Student satisfaction:	=12	(82%)
Research quality:	16	(0.82)
Entry standards:	16	(445)
Student–staff ratio:	=29	(15.4)
Services & facilities/student:	41	(£1,551)
Expected completion rate:	14	(94.0%)
Good honours:	25	(73.9%)
Graduate prospects:	24	(72.7%)

notably the conversion of the former Jessop Hospital into a new centre for the arts and humanities. The most recent developments have seen the renovation of the original University Library and the refurbishment of the Arts Tower. Despite economic constraints, the university is expanding its highly-rated Faculty of Engineering. New teaching laboratories are planned for the 4,000 engineers and a Graduate School is due to open in September 2013. Sheffield is the lead institution for systems engineering, smart materials and stem-cell technology in a research network of European, American and Chinese universities. There is a separate technology park centred on an advanced manufacturing research centre, in which Boeing is the senior partner.

The highly successful students' union has been redeveloped and is about to be extended further, creating more space and top-class facilities for students, staff and visitors in a single building. A famously lively social scene is based on the union – voted the best in Britain for the fourth time in 2011– but also takes full advantage of the city's burgeoning club life. In addition to its own popular facilities, the union owns a pub in the western suburb where most students live. Town–gown relations are much better and the crime rate lower than in most big cities.

Residential accommodation is plentiful, with most of the 5,689 university-owned places within walking distance of lectures, and private housing reasonably priced as well as being available very close to lectures. First-years from outside Sheffield are guaranteed accommodation. The Endcliffe Village caters for about 3,500 students in a mix of refurbished Victorian houses and new flats, while the new Ranmoor Village has over 1,000 students in en-suite self-catering apartments including some family apartments and studios.

The excellent sports facilities close to the main university precinct include five floodlit synthetic pitches, a large fitness centre with more than 150 pieces of equipment, swimming pool with sauna and steam rooms, sports hall, a fitness studio, multipurpose activity room, four squash courts and a bouldering wall. The 45 acres of grass playing fields for rugby, football and cricket are a bus ride away. Sheffield has one of the biggest programmes of internal leagues at any university.

Undergraduate Fees and Bursaries

» Fees for UK/EU students 2012–13 £9,000
» International student fees 2012–13 £12,160–£15,850
    Medicine £28,650
» Students from low income households in economically deprived areas, £9,000 fee waiver for year 1.
» Bursaries on sliding scale of £1,400–£500 for household income up to £42K.
» Other scholarships and bursaries available.

Students

Undergraduates:	**16,540**	**(1,470)**
Postgraduates:	**6,815**	**(2,135)**
Mature students:	**6.4%**	
Overseas students:	**14.1%**	
Applications per place:	**6.6**	
From state-sector schools:	**86.0%**	
From working-class homes:	**19.6%**	

For detailed information about sports facilities:
www.sport-sheffield.com

Accommodation

Number of places and costs refer to 2011–12
University-provided places: 5,689
Percentage catered: 10%
Catered costs: £4,674.60 – £5,765.34 (42 weeks; 31 weeks of catering).
Self-catered costs: £3,272.22 – £4,577.58 (42 weeks).
First years are guaranteed accommodation if conditions are met. International students: as above.
Contact: accommodationoffice@sheffield.ac.uk
www.sheffield.ac.uk/accommodation

Sheffield Hallam University

Sheffield Hallam has invested £100 million over the last ten years upgrading its facilities, and is planning to commit another £45 million to enhance the experience of its students and boost research. The university set fees of £8,500 for 2012–13, promising to spend much of the income on new academic appointments, personal support for students and a customised employability package. Hallam expects to spend £9 million a year by 2015 on bursaries and fee waivers worth up to £3,000 in the first year for students from the poorest homes. It is also establishing a joint outreach programme with Sheffield University that will focus on raising aspirations among those who might miss out on higher education.

The university currently exceeds most of its access benchmarks, although the nearly 35 per cent share of undergraduate places going to working-class entrants is just below average for the courses and entry qualifications. Almost 97 per cent of the intake is from state schools, while 18 per cent come from areas that send few students to higher education. The projected dropout rate of 11 per cent beats the benchmark set for the university.

Hallam has two campuses, one in the heart of the city centre, near the railway station, and the other not far away in a leafy inner suburb. Innovative library developments take pride of place on both campuses. Business and management courses, which account for easily the biggest share of places, have their own city-centre headquarters, as does the students' union, which took over the spectacular but ill-fated National Centre for Popular Music.

While most of the development has been on the main campus, the latest stage has seen the opening of a new social centre on the Collegiate Crescent site, which houses education, health and community studies. A £14-million development has allowed the Faculty of Health and Wellbeing to almost double in size, as extra provision is made for nursing, radiotherapy, physiotherapy and social work. The Centre for Sport and Exercise Science, with its £6-million research facility is one of the largest of its kind in Europe, with more than 2,000 students. The faculty is the biggest provider of health and social care training in the UK and offers the widest range of sports courses.

Another new development, combined with the refurbishment of existing city-centre buildings brought all the departments in the Faculty of Arts, Computing, Engineering and Sciences together on the main campus for the first time, placing them in the heart of Sheffield's thriving cultural industries quarter. The university also launched the Sheffield Business

---

City Campus
Howard Street
Sheffield S1 1WB

0114 225 5555 (enquiries)
enquiries@shu.ac.uk
www.shu.ac.uk
www.hallamunion.org
Affiliation: University
  Alliance

The Times **Rankings**

Overall Ranking: **=73**

Student satisfaction:	=77	(76%)
Research quality:	=75	(0.12)
Entry standards:	=59	(305)
Student–staff ratio:	=83	(19.6)
Services & facilities/student:	103	(£1,067)
Expected completion rate:	=55	(84.5%)
Good honours:	=61	(61.8%)
Graduate prospects:	78	(57.6%)

School in 2009, bringing together business, finance, management and languages, with the university's specialisms of facilities management, food and nutrition, tourism, hospitality and events management.

The 2011 National Student Survey left Sheffield Hallam close to the bottom 20 universities. Its best scores were in accounting, agriculture, maths and statistics, food studies and nutrition. The university did better in the latest International Student Barometer, where its overseas students proved to be the most satisfied in the UK with their learning experience and especially pleased with the standard of learning technology, laboratories and learning spaces. The university has a growing international dimension as well as bringing students to Sheffield: it celebrated its 5,000th Malaysian graduate in 2010 and has an office in India.

Hallam traces its origins in art and design back to the 1840s and celebrated the centenary of education and teacher training in 2005. It is now one of the largest of the new universities, with more than 36,000 students, including high proportions of part-time and mature students, and more than 1,000 taught on franchised courses in further education colleges. Business and industry are closely involved in the development hundreds of courses, with almost half of the students taking sandwich course placements with employers. More than 200 "specialist flexible courses" mix part-time study,

distance learning and work-based learning. The university claims to have the largest number of students at any university taking courses that include work placements of a year, and it offers a full fee waiver for that year out.

A "virtual campus" offers students email accounts and cheap equipment to access the growing volume of online courses, assignments and discussion groups provided by the university, even when they are at home or on work placements. Unlike many big post-1992 universities, Hallam now guarantees accommodation for first years, although the large local intake means that many live at home. Transport in the city is excellent, with both well-run bus and tram services. Sports facilities are supplemented by those provided by the city for the World Student Games. The impressive swimming complex, for example, is on the university's doorstep. Enthusiasm for sport produced the largest number of student volunteers for the 2012 Olympics at any UK university.

Undergraduate Fees and Bursaries

- » Fees for UK/EU students 2012–13 £8,500
- » International student fees 2012–13 £10,320–£13,520
- » 580 NSP awards of £2,000 fee waiver and £1,000 cash in year 1; £500 cash in years 2 and 3; for those not receiving NSP award, £500 bursary, years 1–3.
- » Award of £1,000 cash for those with AAB at A level or equivalent.
- » Check the university's website for the latest information.

Students		
Undergraduates:	**21,735**	**(6,085)**
Postgraduates:	**3,015**	**(5,670)**
Mature students:	**15.9%**	
Overseas students:	**7.5%**	
Applications per place:	**6.2**	
From state-sector schools:	**96.6%**	
From working-class homes:	**34.2%**	

For detailed information about sports facilities:
www.shu.ac.uk/sporthallam

Accommodation

Number of places and costs refer to 2012–13
University-provided places: 4,961
Percentage catered: 3.5%
Catered costs: £92.76 (39 weeks).
Self-catered costs: £72.52 (single standard) – £200.00 (large double self-contained flat) for 42–44 weeks.
All first years offered university allocated accommodation or private housing.
International students: as above, providing conditions are met.
Contact: www.shu.ac.uk/accommodation

Southampton University

Southampton promised "ground-breaking" reforms to its teaching and student support programmes in exchange for £9,000 fees for 2012–13. They included an academic adviser for every student to guide their independent learning and progress, and a more flexible curriculum. Fees will be reduced by £3,000 for students from the poorest backgrounds, while every undergraduate will receive the Southampton Entitlement of £300 a year to spend on services such as sports membership and access to campus arts venues. Applications still fell at the start of 2012, but by much less than the sector average. Until the switch to higher fees, the university had seen the demand for places grow steadily over several years, reflecting substantial investment in campus facilities and good results in the National Student Survey (NSS). The university is now in the final phase of a £250-million programme to upgrade its six sites in Southampton and Winchester.

More than 60 per cent of Southampton's submission to the 2008 Research Assessment Exercise was considered world-leading or internationally excellent, leaving the university firmly entrenched among the research elite. The best grades came in medicine, engineering, music, sociology and social policy, computer science and nursing.

Southampton is in the top 75 universities in the world, according to the QS World University Rankings and the proportion of income derived from research is among the highest in Britain.

Although the percentages of students from working-class homes and areas with little tradition of university education are lower than the national average for the subjects offered, the statistics agency considers this largely a matter of location. The university does exceed the benchmark set for the number of state school pupils, as it does for the proportion of students who have a disability. Students act as ambassadors, associates and mentors in local schools and colleges, as part of the university's existing efforts to broaden its intake.

Student satisfaction dipped slightly in 2011, but Southampton was still comfortably in the top half of the table. There was 100 per cent satisfaction in music, while chemistry, archaeology, biology, French and philosophy all topped 95 per cent. Research in chemistry is among the best in Europe, according to a specialist European ranking.

The main Highfield campus is in an attractive green location two miles from the city centre, adjoining Southampton Common, and has been the focus of recent development. The library has been greatly extended and a purpose-built student services centre provides learning support and other advisory facilities, most of which

---

University Road
Southampton SO17 1BJ

023 8059 2421 (enquiries)
admissns@soton.ac.uk
www.soton.ac.uk
www.susu.org
Affiliation: Russell Group

Edinburgh
Belfast
Cardiff London
SOUTHAMPTON

The Times Rankings

Overall Ranking: =18

Student satisfaction:	=42	(79%)
Research quality:	=25	(0.69)
Entry standards:	17	(441)
Student–staff ratio:	11	(13.4)
Services & facilities/student:	20	(£1,947)
Expected completion rate:	=21	(92.7%)
Good honours:	17	(76.4%)
Graduate prospects:	=27	(72.0%)

are backed up online for students in other areas of the university. A new social learning space, designed by students for students, opened in 2011 as part of the innovative "Create your Campus" competition, which gives students the opportunity to influence the development of their learning environment. The striking £55-million Mountbatten Building for electronics and computer science and the Optoelectronics Research Centre and the £50-million Life Sciences Building are recent additions. The uni-link transport interchange, which opened on the campus in 2010 is a major transport hub for the city, as well as for students.

The university has four sites in Southampton. The National Oceanography Centre Southampton is based in the city's revitalised dock area. A £50-million joint project with the Natural Environment Research Council, it is considered Europe's finest. The Avenue campus, near the main site, is home to most of the humanities departments. Clinical medicine is based at Southampton General Hospital.

Winchester School of Art, which has been part of the university since 1996, has also enjoyed significant recent investment in new facilities. The arts are well represented in Southampton, too, with three nationally renowned arts centres: the Turner Sims concert hall, the Nuffield Theatre and the John Hansard Gallery, all based at Highfield.

The university has also been expanding its international activities, opening a branch campus in Malaysia dedicated to engineering, where students will spend the first year of a degree before transferring to the UK. There are also joint degrees in graphic design and fashion design with Dalian Polytechnic University, in China. The Centre for Contemporary China links Southampton with a number of leading Chinese universities. In addition, medical students will be able to undertake a major part of their education in Europe for the first time in 2013. Trainee doctors in their final three years will have the opportunity to work in a German hospital.

Social facilities for students have been expanded and refurbished. Sports facilities are first class, with an indoor sports complex and a 25-metre swimming pool next to the students' union. The outdoor sports complex, just three miles from Highfield campus, has grass and synthetic pitches. Student housing is plentiful and first years are guaranteed an offer of accommodation.

Undergraduate Fees and Bursaries

- » Fees for UK/EU students 2012–13 £9,000
- » International student fees 2013–14 £12,420–£15,250
  Medicine £29,450
- » A tapered fee waiver scheme: from £3,000 fee waiver for household income below £25K to £200 at £42.6K; £300 annual credit for student services and transport.
- » Other scholarships and bursaries available.

Students

Undergraduates:	**15,635**	**(830)**
Postgraduates:	**5,070**	**(1,780)**
Mature students:	**11.0%**	
Overseas students:	**13.9%**	
Applications per place:	**7.2**	
From state-sector schools:	**83.7%**	
From working-class homes:	**20.8%**	

For detailed information about sports facilities:
www.sportrec.soton.ac.uk

Accommodation

Number of places and costs refer to 2012–13
University-provided places: more than 5,000
Percentage catered: 10%
Catered costs: £109.41–£152.39 a week.
Self-catered costs: £109.41–£152.39 a week (self-contained flat).
All first years are guaranteed an offer of accommodation. Conditions apply.
International students: All non-EU students are guaranteed accommodation. Conditions apply.
Contact: www.southampton.ac.uk/accommodation

Southampton Solent University

Southampton Solent will offer some of the lowest fees for England in 2012–13, having settled on £7,800 for all courses. The university said it was striking a fair balance between its commitment to social justice and the need to invest in improving the student experience. Solent secured one of the biggest allocations from the national pool of places reserved for universities and colleges charging the lowest fees, but applications were down 15 per cent at the start of 2012, and the university is only four places off the bottom of the latest *Times* League Table.

The largest of the nine universities created in 2005, Southampton Solent also has the broadest range of programmes, stretching from Foundation courses to doctorates. Over 12,000 higher education students embrace civil and mechanical engineering, as well as media, arts and business, with a separate maritime centre capitalising on the coastal location. The subject mix may be one reason that the former Southampton Institute is now one of the few universities with a majority of male students.

The rebranded Solent Curriculum plays to the university's strengths in "skills focused" courses. There is a strong representation of "non-traditional" disciplines, such as yacht and powercraft design, computer and video games, and comedy writing and performance. A Graduate Enterprise Centre provides advice and rent-free offices for those hoping to start their own businesses, while an internship scheme provides places for 100 recent graduates.

The university was in the bottom four for student satisfaction in 2011. Management produced some of the lowest scores anywhere in the National Student Survey, but sociology, publicity studies, naval architecture, English and modern foreign languages all satisfied more than 90 per cent of final-year undergraduates. Solent entered fewer academics for the 2008 Research Assessment Exercise than any university in England – fewer than one in ten of those eligible. But two of the three areas in which it made a submission contained some world-leading research, with art and design achieving much the best results.

Before the switch to higher fees, applications had risen by more than 50 per cent in five years and more were making Solent their first-choice university. Demand for places remains especially strong in marine-based courses, which benefit from an internationally renowned training and research facility for the shipping and offshore oil industries. The university is higher education's premier yachting institution, with a world champion student team that has won the national championships four times in

East Park Terrace
Southampton SO14 0YN

023 8031 9000 (main switchboard)
ask@solent.ac.uk
www.solent.ac.uk
www.solentsu.co.uk
Affiliation: million+

The Times Rankings
Overall Ranking: **113**

Student satisfaction:	=108	(72%)
Research quality:	=112	(0.02)
Entry standards:	=96	(268)
Student–staff ratio:	102	(21.2)
Services & facilities/student:	93	(£1,160)
Expected completion rate:	103	(74.9%)
Good honours:	112	(48.1%)
Graduate prospects:	115	(41.9%)

six years. Three new boats support courses at the purpose-built Watersports Centre, where some activities are targeted towards disadvantaged young people.

A quarter of the students come from Hampshire and there has been a substantial increase in the proportion with working-class roots, almost reaching the national average for the university's subjects and entry qualifications. Solent's projected dropout rate had been improving, but had slipped below the university's benchmark in the latest survey, at 17 per cent. There is a special link with Guernsey, which has no higher education of its own.

The main campus has few architectural pretensions, but is conveniently based in the city centre within walking distance of the station. Recent investment has included a new Centre for Professional Development in Broadcasting and Multimedia Production, which includes an online editing suite, digital television studio and gallery, for use by undergraduates as well as community groups and professionals. Creative Arts and Society courses now attract almost as many students as the consistently popular business school. There are new music studios with an industry-standard recording complex, as well as a performance space and dance studio.

Solent spent £18 million on capital projects during 2010–11, including £2.7 million on a ship handling centre, £3.2 million on new football facilities and £1.4 million on

a city centre site for the Southampton School of Art and Design. A new academic building and sports complex should be ready by 2014. Other recent additions include the Centre for Health, Exercise and Sports Science, which enables students to conduct the latest types of fitness testing. The new Centre for Football Research is expected to cement the university's position as a leader in football related academic study. Having assumed responsibility for sport development in the city, Solent has also become the country's largest provider of coaching education.

Students like the location, close to the city's growing complement of bars and nightclubs, as well as to the main shopping area. There are more than 2,300 hall places, most of which are allocated to first years and almost half of which are en suite. There is the usual range of sports facilities, with a sports hall and fitness suite on campus and outdoor pitches, tennis and netball courts four miles away.

Undergraduate Fees and Bursaries

» Fees for UK/EU students 2012–13 £7,800
» International student fees 2012–13 £9,500–£10,500
» NSP awards of £1,000 cash, £2,000 accommodation discount or fee waiver in year 1 only; complete fee waiver for Foundation year students.
» For UK students with household income below £25K, £400 cash a year.

Students		
Undergraduates:	**9,880**	**(1,730)**
Postgraduates:	**285**	**(390)**
Mature students:	**18.5%**	
Overseas students:	**14.3%**	
Applications per place:	**4.2**	
From state-sector schools:	**95.4%**	
From working-class homes:	**35.9%**	

Accommodation
Number of places and costs refer to 2012–13
University-provided places: 2,340.
Percentage catered: 0%
Self-catered costs: £89.95–£115.92 a week (41 weeks).
First years are allocated 90% of rooms.
International students: some accommodation is set aside.
Contact: Accommodation@solent.ac.uk
www.solent.ac.uk/accommodation/accommodation_home.aspx

For detailed information about sports facilities:
www.solent.ac.uk/sport

Staffordshire University

Staffordshire has fallen 11 places and almost out of the top 100 in the new *Times* League Table, following a drop of similar proportions last year. But only three university received a bigger allocation from the pool of 20,000 places reserved for universities and colleges charging the lowest fees. There will be plenty of demand for them after a 25 per cent growth in applications in 2011, even though there was a 12 per cent decline when fees of between £7,500 and £8,500 were introduced.

The university is based on two main sites: in Stoke-on-Trent and 16 miles away in Stafford. Both have modern halls of residence, sports centres and lively students' union venues. There are more than 9,000 students taking Staffordshire courses outside Britain, almost half of them located around the Pacific Rim. They now make up more than a third of the university's intake, in addition to a growing cohort of international students on the university's UK campuses.

Staffordshire is at the heart of Stoke's £287-million University Quarter project, where it is working with local further education colleges to transform the area of South Shelton with new facilities for students, encouraging more people to progress to higher education and helping the local economy. A new £30-million Science Centre will house the Faculty of Sciences, focusing on the university's strengths in forensics, biology and psychology. A further £12 million will be invested in the Stoke campus as part of a commitment to improve the student experience. There is even a 25-acre nature reserve – part of the university's sustained green commitment. The large Business School is based at Stoke, as are the Law School, the Faculty of Arts, Media and Design and the department of sport health and exercise. There is also a business village and a creative village offering affordable business start-up space.

Stafford is home to nursing and midwifery courses in the Faculty of Health, which also has bases in Telford and Shrewsbury. The Faculty of Computing, Engineering and Technology is also on the Stafford campus, where the Octagon Centre was once among the largest university computing facilities in Europe. The Ruxton New Technologies Centre boasts excellent facilities for its suite of entertainment technology courses, including a High Definition Television Centre. A footbridge links the campus with the university's technology park and business village. A third site in Lichfield houses an integrated further and higher education centre, developed in partnership with South Staffordshire College, as well as 26 business start-up units.

College Road
Stoke-on-Trent ST4 2DE

01782 292753 (admissions)
admissions@staffs.ac.uk
www.staffs.ac.uk
www.staffsunion.com
Affiliation: million+

The Times Rankings
Overall Ranking: **100**

Student satisfaction:	=55	(78%)
Research quality:	=108	(0.03)
Entry standards:	105	(248)
Student–staff ratio:	=106	(21.6)
Services & facilities/student:	92	(£1,161)
Expected completion rate:	99	(75.8%)
Good honours:	106	(50.6%)
Graduate prospects:	73	(58.9%)

The university is a pioneer of two-year fast-track degrees, which are now offered in accounting and finance, computing science, business, English and law. Staffordshire academics have also carried out the evaluation of the national programme of accelerated degrees. There already was an extensive portfolio of two-year Foundation degrees. The university's UK partners, which include the National Design Academy and local colleges in the Staffordshire University Regional Federation, are responsible for delivering a range of Staffordshire courses to a further 4,600 students.

Staffordshire is among the leading universities for secondary teacher training, but scores in the National Student Survey remained below the national average in 2011. Geography, nursing, physical geography and environmental sciences and subjects allied to medicine produced the best results. The university entered only a small proportion of its academics for the latest Research Assessment Exercise. Three of the ten subject areas had some world-leading research, with general engineering and education producing the best results. Applied research has led to the development of new products in markets as diverse as medical technology and recycling.

With 98 per cent of its undergraduates state-educated and almost four in ten coming from working-class homes, Staffordshire exceeds all the benchmarks set by the funding council for widening access to higher education. There is good provision for students with disabilities. The projected dropout rate had climbed further in the latest survey and, at 23 per cent, was well above the national average for the university's courses and entry qualifications.

Stoke is not the liveliest city of its size, but the University Quarter is attracting more social and leisure facilities. The campus, which is close to the railway station, is within easy reach of the city centre and has a buzzing students' union. Stafford is the more attractive setting and offers the best chance of a residential place, but the town is quiet and the campus is a mile and a half outside it. Sports facilities are good, especially in Stafford, where there is a modern £1.4-million sports centre and all-weather pitches. Good coaching has helped attract some outstanding athletes, who have access to a sports performance centre to help with training schedules, psychological support and dietary assessments.

Undergraduate Fees and Bursaries

- » Fees for UK/EU students 2012–13   £7,490–£8,490
  Two-year fast-track degrees   £8,890
- » International student fees 2012–13   £9,875
- » English students with AAB at A Level or equivalent, 204 NSP awards of £2,500 fee waiver and £500 cash, year 1; £1,250 fee waiver and £250 cash, years 2 and 3.
- » Household income below £43K, 1,000 bursaries of £500 a year and 1,000 bursaries of £1,000 fee waiver a year.

Students

Undergraduates:	**10,330**	**(8,110)**
Postgraduates:	**1,290**	**(2,270)**
Mature students:	**28.2%**	
Overseas students:	**5.5%**	
Applications per place:	**5.2**	
From state-sector schools:	**98.5%**	
From working-class homes:	**38.8%**	

For detailed information about sports facilities:
www.staffs.ac.uk/teamstaffs

Accommodation

Number of places and costs refer to 2012–13
University-provided places: 1,072 (Stoke); 605 (Stafford)
Percentage catered: 0%
Self-catered accommodation: £76–£103 a week (36 weeks).
First years have priority, if conditions are met.
International students: have priority, if conditions are met.
Contact: Accommodation_stoke@staffs.ac.uk
Accommodation_stafford@staffs.ac.uk
www.staffs.ac.uk/courses_and_study/student_services/
accommodation

University of Stirling

Stirling has dropped four places in this year's *Times* League Table and was one of only four Scottish institutions to see applications decline at the beginning of 2012. But the demand for places had risen more than 50 per cent over the two preceding years, far outweighing the latest 2 per cent drop. Stirling also remained in the top 30 in the 2011 National Student Survey, despite a slight dip in satisfaction levels. There was 100 per cent satisfaction in computer science and English, while biological sciences, French, philosophy, theology and psychology all satisfied more than 95 per cent of final-year undergraduates. Stirling was also named as the best in Britain for nurse education by the *Nursing Times*.

The university has one of the most beautiful campuses in Britain, nestling beneath the Ochil Hills in a loch-side setting. It is particularly well provided for sports facilities, having been designated Scotland's University for Sporting Excellence in 2008. Stirling is home to national swimming and tennis centres, as well as a golf course and a football academy. Stirling runs an international sports scholarship programme and manages Winning Students, the national sport scholarship programme for students in colleges and universities across Scotland.

The university remains relatively small, with only 12,300 students, and has a strong community feel. Five "core areas" have been nominated: health and well-being, culture and society, environment, enterprise and economy, and sport. Philosophy produced the best results in the 2008 Research Assessment Exercise, but nursing, film, media and journalism, economics, education and history all did well.

Stirling was the British pioneer of the semester system, which has now become so popular throughout higher education. The academic year is divided into two blocks of 15 weeks, with short mid-semester breaks. Students have the option of starting courses in February, rather than September, and can choose subjects from across all seven Schools. Degrees are built up of credits accumulated through modules taken and awarded each semester, rather than at the end of the academic year. Undergraduates can switch the whole direction of their studies, in consultation with their academic adviser, as their interests develop. They can also speed up their progress on a Summer Academic Programme, which squeezes a full semester's teaching into July and August. Full-time students are not allowed to use the programme to reduce the length of their course, but part-timers can use it to make rapid progress.

The intake is surprisingly diverse, with nearly 94 per cent of undergraduates state-educated and almost 30 per cent coming from working-class homes. Two-thirds are

Stirling Campus
Stirling FK9 4LA

01786 467044 (admissions)
admissions@stir.ac.uk
www.stir.ac.uk
www.stirlingstudentsunion.
  com
Affiliation: none

STIRLING
Edinburgh
Belfast
London
Cardiff

The Times Rankings

Overall Ranking: **50**

Student satisfaction:	=34	(80%)
Research quality:	49	(0.41)
Entry standards:	46	(342)
Student–staff ratio:	=91	(20.5)
Services & facilities/student:	85	(£1,209)
Expected completion rate:	=58	(84.3%)
Good honours:	53	(64.2%)
Graduate prospects:	68	(60.5%)

from Scotland. International exchanges are common, with many students going to American, Asian and European universities each year.

Stirling has started work on a £43-million project to expand and improve its student residential accommodation. This is the largest capital development undertaken by the university since the creation of the campus in the 1960s and follows an £11-million refurbishment of the library, completed in 2010.

The library was been completely reconfigured and redesigned, prompting an 80 per cent increase in usage. The School of Biological and Environmental Sciences has also been refurbished, as have the computer laboratories. The university has more than 700 computers for student use, many available 24 hours a day, and all rooms in halls are wired for internet use. Journalism students have the use of a high-tech newsroom. In 2009, the university launched the UK's first degree in financial journalism.

The sports facilities, which include a 50-metre pool and a golf centre with indoor facilities and a synthetic putting green, are used for teaching and research, as well as for training by elite athletes and recreation for the university community. Sports studies are particularly popular and 100 students in 2010 benefiting from sports scholarships that are available in golf, swimming, disability swimming, tennis, triathlon and football.

Students appreciate the individual attention that a small campus university can offer, although some find the atmosphere claustrophobic. Stirling is not the top choice of nightclubbers, but the students' union won "Best Bar None" status for three years in a row and there is a lively social scene. The MacRobert Arts Centre offers a full programme of cultural activities, while the surrounding countryside offers its own attractions for walkers and climbers. The campus has been described by police as one of the safest in Britain, but a community policeman is based there and available to students for extra advice.

Nurses and midwives can opt to study at the Highland campus, which is based in the modern Centre for Health Science, in Inverness. There is also a Western Isles campus, located in Stornoway, where the teaching accommodation is an integral part of the Western Isles Hospital.

Undergraduate Fees and Bursaries

» Fees for Scottish and EU students 2012–13   No fee
» Fees for Non-Scottish UK (RUK) students 2012–13   £6,750
» Fees for international students 2011–12   £10,200–£12,250
» For RUK students with AAA or AAB at A Level or equivalent, £1,000–£2,000 cash each year.
» 12 £2,000 RUK sports scholarships.
» Sports scholarships for Scottish students.

Students

Undergraduates:	**7,215**	**(1,260)**
Postgraduates:	**1,985**	**(1,165)**
Mature students:	**25.3%**	
Overseas students:	**10%**	
Applications per place:	**12.7**	
From state-sector schools:	**93.7%**	
From working-class homes:	**28.3%**	

For detailed information about sports facilities:
www.sportingexcellence.stir.ac.uk

Accommodation

Number of places and costs refer to 2012–13
University-provided places: 2,294
Percentage catered: 0%
Self-catered costs: £69.68–£110.32 a week (38 weeks).
All first years are guaranteed suitable housing arranged by the university.
International students: as above.
Contact: Accommodation@stir.ac.uk

University of Strathclyde

Strathclyde has set itself the target of becoming one of the world's leading technological universities. The Vice-Chancellor, Professor Jim McDonald, has called for improvements in research to achieve this goal, but has promised not to neglect the student experience. Even as Anderson's Institution in the 18th century, Strathclyde concentrated on "useful learning". The university promises courses that are both innovative and relevant to employers' needs – hence product design and innovation, energy systems or international business with modern languages. The university does well in the National Student Survey, finishing around the top 30 in 2011. Chemistry, computer science, economics, finance, marketing, maths and statistics, microbiology, physics and health subjects all satisfied more than 90 per cent of final-year undergraduates. However, Strathclyde suffered an 11 per cent fall in applications at the start of 2012, when most Scottish universities were enjoying increased demand for places.

Business and law were the main successes in the 2008 Research Assessment Exercise, (RAE), when almost 60 per cent of the university's submission was rated as world-leading or internationally excellent. Pharmacy and some branches of engineering also achieved good results. The business school, rated among the top 20 in Europe by *The Financial Times*, is normally considered Strathclyde's greatest strength. It is among the largest in Europe and one of only 55 in the world to be "triple accredited" by the main international bodies. The school has opened its own branch campus near Delhi. The engineering faculty is also the largest in Scotland and home to the biggest university electrical power engineering and energy research grouping in Europe.

The university is heavily involved in Scotland's "pooling" arrangement for research in potentially vulnerable science subjects. There were a number of joint submissions with neighbouring Glasgow University in the RAE. However, Strathclyde is not all about business and engineering. The faculties of Education, Law, Arts and Social Sciences were brought together in 2010 in order to maximise the potential for research collaboration and be more responsive to student needs. A £25-million hub for the faculty is under construction on the university's city-centre campus.

Mature students account for nearly a sixth of the places and have a special organisation to look after their interests. With nearly 22,000 students, including part-timers, Strathclyde is the third-largest university in Scotland. But its numbers swell to more than 60,000 when short courses and distance learning programmes are included. Strathclyde actively promotes wider access,

---

16 Richmond Street
Glasgow G1 1XQ

0141 548 2913 (enquiries)
ugenquiries@strath.ac.uk
www.strath.ac.uk
www.strathstudents.com
Affiliation: none

GLASGOW
Edinburgh
Belfast
London
Cardiff

The Times Rankings
Overall Ranking: **=36**

Student satisfaction:	**=42**	(79%)
Research quality:	**44**	(0.50)
Entry standards:	**18**	(440)
Student–staff ratio:	**=56**	(17.9)
Services & facilities/student:	**38**	(£1,635)
Expected completion rate:	**60**	(84.2%)
Good honours:	**19**	(76.0%)
Graduate prospects:	**=27**	(72.0%)

comfortably exceeding UK averages for state-educated students and the share of places going to applicants from working-class homes. The projected dropout rate had fallen below 10 per cent in the latest survey, but is still marginally higher than average for the university's subjects and entry qualifications.

The main John Anderson campus is in the centre of Glasgow, behind George Square and near Queen Street station. Apart from the Edwardian headquarters, the buildings are mostly modern. The university, which has taken to adding Glasgow to its name recently, has unveiled ambitious plans to invest £350 million over the next ten years to transform the city-centre campus. A range of new facilities will be added, including a Centre for Sport and Health. The Strathclyde Institute of Pharmacy and Biomedical Sciences – a centre for excellence in drug discovery and development research – opened in 2011. The £89-million Technology and Innovation Centre should be complete in 2014, enabling companies to work side-by-side with university researchers. In addition, the Advanced Forming Research Centre – a research partnership between the university and international engineering firms – has opened near Glasgow Airport.

Strathclyde's Jordanhill campus on the west side of the city was acquired from a merger with Jordanhill College of Education in 1993. The 67-acre parkland site houses the Faculty of Education, which is breaking new ground with Scotland's first part-time teacher training degree and also offers courses in speech and language pathology, community arts, social work, sport and outdoor education. The Jordanhill site is scheduled to close, its education students moving to the main campus, giving Strathclyde a unified, city-centre campus for the 2012–13 academic year.

There is a student village on the main campus with 1,400 places, all with network access. Another 500 residential places are nearby in the trendy Merchant City. The ten-floor union building attracts students from all over Glasgow with its reputation for revelry. There are over 40 sporting clubs and teams and another 40 social, cultural and political clubs and societies, plus a student newspaper and radio station. Proximity to Glasgow's vibrant and celebrated music scene is a plus, and for those with more sophisticated tastes, there are numerous theatres and arts organisations, as well as standout museums such as the Kelvingrove Gallery, one of Scotland's top attractions.

Undergraduate Fees and Bursaries

- » Fees for Scottish and EU students 2012–13   No fee
- » Fees for Non-Scottish UK (RUK) students 2012–13   £9,000 (capped at £27,000 for any course)
- » Fees for international students 2012–13   £10,200–£16,000
- » For RUK students, annual bursaries for household income below £21K, £4,250; sliding scale to £35K, £2,500–£500.
- » Other scholarships and bursaries are available.

Students

Undergraduates:	11,740	(2,585)
Postgraduates:	3,210	(2,690)
Mature students:	14.8%	
Overseas students:	6.6%	
Applications per place:	7.2	
From state-sector schools:	91.8%	
From working-class homes:	27.2%	

For detailed information about sports facilities:
www.strath.ac.uk/sport

Accommodation

Number of places and costs refer to 2012–13
University-provided places: 1,838
Percentage catered: 0%
Self-catered costs: £80–£112 a week.
First years are offered accommodation if they live further than 25 miles from the university.
International students: as above.
Contact: student.accommodation@strath.ac.uk
www.strath.ac.uk/accommodation/

University of Sunderland

Although some of Sunderland's laboratory-based science degrees will carry fees of £8,500 in 2012, the average for all courses after the various discounts on offer will be among the lowest in England, at £6,770. All home undergraduates at the university and some partner colleges will be entitled to free public transport throughout Tyne and Wear, or £500 off university rents. However, this still could not prevent a 15 per cent drop in applications at the start of 2012.

The university has a determinedly local focus, aiming to double the number of students coming from an area which has little tradition of sending students to higher education. No university recruits a higher proportion from "low participation neighbourhoods" than the 28 per cent at Sunderland – double the national average for the subjects on offer. A pioneering access scheme offers places to mature students without A levels, as long as they reach the required levels of literacy, numeracy and other basic skills. The Learning North East initiative, based on Sunderland's successful pilot for the University for Industry, even offers free taster courses to take at home.

Just less than 44 per cent of undergraduates have a working-class background, and the projected dropout rate has been reduced from more than 25 per cent to 15 per cent in recent years, almost matching the national average for the subjects and entry qualifications. Provision for disabled students is excellent, with award-winning information produced for those with disabilities, trained support staff in every academic school as well as in the libraries and special modules to help dyslexics. The campus also houses the North East Regional Access Centre, which assesses the learning support requirements of students with disabilities and specific learning difficulties. There is special provision at the five halls of residence.

Sunderland has two campuses, one of them among the UK's newest. The university has taken advantage of urban regeneration programmes to assist in the transformation of its facilities. The £75-million redevelopment of the original City Campus is well underway, after the opening of the £12-million CitySpace sports and social space and the new Sciences Complex and Quad. A £12-million student village is now fully open. The campus also boasts an outdoor performance area, a design centre, and the Gateway, a one-stop-shop for student services. The latest phase of the redevelopment plan will see the upgrading of facilities for fine art.

The university's other campus at St Peter's, an award-winning 24-acre site by the banks of the Wear, houses the business school and the faculties of applied sciences, law and arts, design and media. The Sir Tom Cowie

---

City Campus
Chester Road
Sunderland SR1 3SD

0191 515 3000 (course helpline)
student.helpline@
    sunderland.ac.uk
www.sunderland.ac.uk
www.sunderlandsu.co.uk
Affiliation: million+

The Times **Rankings**
Overall Ranking: **77**

Student satisfaction:	=42	(79%)
Research quality:	=68	(0.14)
Entry standards:	=89	(278)
Student–staff ratio:	47	(16.9)
Services & facilities/student:	74	(£1,294)
Expected completion rate:	80	(79.6%)
Good honours:	107	(50.5%)
Graduate prospects:	107	(50.2%)

campus is built around a 7th-century abbey described as one of Britain's first universities and incorporates a working heritage centre for the glass industry. A glass and ceramics design degree maintains a Sunderland tradition, while teaching and research in automotive design and manufacture serve the region's modern industrial base. The large pharmacy department is another strength and the well-equipped Faculty of Applied Sciences is one of the largest in the UK, with over 4,000 students. Sunderland now has more than 17,000 students in total, including 1,000 from outside the European Union.

Sunderland is making the most of the opportunity to link up with the multinational companies that have arrived on its doorstep. The Institute for Automotive and Manufacturing Advanced Practice has a team of 40 researchers and consultants working with local businesses, while nearby Nissan played an important role in designing a course in automotive product development. The media centre provides students with excellent television and video production facilities and is home to the student-run community radio station, 107 Spark FM. The popular media courses now include magazine, fashion and sports journalism.

The university is in mid-table for student satisfaction, outperforming most post-1992 universities. History almost managed 100 per cent satisfaction, but law and psychology were the only other subjects to top 90 per cent. The LLB degree includes space law, the first module of its kind in the UK. Sunderland had only moderate success in the 2008 Research Assessment Exercise, although more than half of the 16 subject areas contained at least some world-leading work. Communication, cultural and media studies produced by the far best grades, but history and English also did well.

Sunderland itself is fiercely proud of its identity and has the advantage of a coastal location. The leisure facilities are better than one might imagine: the city has the North East's only Olympic-sized swimming pool and dry ski slope, as well as Europe's biggest climbing wall and a theatre showing West End productions. Those in search of more cultural events or serious nightlife head for Newcastle, which is less than half an hour away by Metro.

Undergraduate Fees and Bursaries

» Fees for UK/EU students 2012–13   £7,800–£8,500
» International student fees 2011–12   £9,000
» NSP awards of £2,000 fee waiver and £1,000 cash in year 1 only; Access to Professions scholarship, £2,000 fee waiver, year 1, £500 cash, years 2 and 3.
» Award of £1,000 cash for those with AAB at A level or equivalent.
» One year's free transport in Tyne and Wear or £500 accommodation discount.
» Discretionary free accommodation scholarship for North East students with household income below £45K.

Students		
Undergraduates:	8,915	(6,005)
Postgraduates:	1,970	(890)
Mature students:	26.6%	
Overseas students:	14.9%	
Applications per place:	5.8	
From state-sector schools:	98.1%	
From working-class homes:	43.4%	

For detailed information about sports facilities:
www.unisportsunderland.com

Accommodation
Number of places and costs refer to 2012–13
University provided places: 1,462 beds in Halls, 548 (The Forge).
Percentage catered: 26%
Catered costs: £3,280 (standard) – £5,080 (1-bed flat) plus option to purchase meal vouchers.
Self-catered costs: £2,520.80 – £3,599.20 (en suite).
New first years are guaranteed accommodation in accordance with the university's allocation policy.
International students: as above.
Contact: www.sunderland.ac.uk/residentialservices

University of Surrey

Surrey has risen another three places in *The Times* League Table, repeating last year's success, due to a big rise in student satisfaction, higher entry grades and a further increase in spending on facilities. The university has remained true to its technological history while building a strong research base and a high degree of financial independence. Recent expansion in healthcare, human sciences and performing arts has added to the traditional strengths in science and engineering. Undergraduates in most subjects undertake work placements of one year (or two half years), often abroad. As a result, most degrees last four years. The format and the subject balance combine to keep Surrey near the top of the graduate employment league. Indeed, it has taken to describing itself as the "University for Jobs" to ram the point home.

The mix was proving popular before higher fees arrived: the demand for places doubled in six years, despite sharply increasing entry standards. But a 21 per cent decline in applications at the start of 2012 was among the biggest in its peer group. With almost eight applications to the place in 2011, competition remained intense, however. The university is also expanding its overseas activities, starting with an international institute in the Chinese city of Dalian, in partnership with Dongbei University. Nearer home, Surrey has taken in the Guildford School of Acting (GSA) and launched its first degree in English literature. The £4.5-million Ivy Arts Centre opened in 2011, with a 200-seat theatre and workshops for the GSA and students in dance, film and theatre.

All students are encouraged to enrol for a course at the European language centre, and a growing number of degrees, including a new range in engineering, have a language component. The cosmopolitan feel is enhanced by one of the largest proportions of overseas students at any university – more than a third – a feat which won Surrey a Queen's Award for Export Achievement. Students will have new international opportunities through the Universities Global Partnership Network, established in 2011, with North Carolina State University and the University of São Paulo.

More than half of the work submitted for the 2008 Research Assessment Exercise was considered world-leading or internationally excellent. Electrical and electronic engineering was ranked second in the country, while health and medical sciences, sociology and general engineering were in the top 10 in their fields. More recently, Surrey's chemical engineering received two awards for innovation and excellence from the Institution of Chemical Engineers.

Another indication of the university's

Guildford Surrey
GU2 7XH

0800 980 3200 (enquiries)
ug-enquiries@surrey.ac.uk
www.surrey.ac.uk
www.ussu.co.uk
Affiliation: 1994 Group

The Times Rankings
Overall Ranking: **26**

Student satisfaction:	=17	(81%)
Research quality:	=35	(0.61)
Entry standards:	=30	(399)
Student–staff ratio:	=56	(17.9)
Services & facilities/student:	11	(£2,081)
Expected completion rate:	33	(89.6%)
Good honours:	=45	(67.6%)
Graduate prospects:	25	(72.5%)

research strength lies in the growing proportion of income derived from sources other than Government grants: up from 10 per cent to about 70 per cent in little over a decade. The Surrey Research Park is one of only three science parks still owned, funded and managed by the university that opened it, helping Surrey to amass one of the highest proportions of private funding at any British university.

Scores in the 2011 National Student Survey rose by five percentage points, placing Surrey among the top 30 universities. The best results were in astronomy and physics, maths and statistics, chemistry and molecular biology, while satisfaction in travel and tourism was the highest in the country. The projected dropout rate of 8 per cent is better than average for the university's courses and entry grades.

The compact campus is a ten-minute walk from the centre of Guildford. Many of the buildings date from the late 1960s, but the new Business School, the newly refurbished and extended library and learning centre, and the gleaming European Institute of Health and Medical Sciences offer a striking contrast. The campus includes two lakes, playing fields and enough residential accommodation to enable all first years to live in. A new online network will allow students to work virtually with others on their courses through group work, discussions and blogs, as well as allowing lecturers to set coursework and interact virtually with students.

A second campus, under development adjacent to the Stag Hill headquarters, houses the new postgraduate medical school and over 1,500 new residential places for students and staff, as well as a new reception building with café, bar and lounge areas. The impressive Surrey Sports Park opened in 2010, with three multipurpose sports halls, tennis and squash courts, a 50-metre swimming pool, indoor climbing centre, extensive fitness suite and outdoor facilities.

The main campus is the centre of social life, and has seen recent improvements to leisure facilities including new dining and social areas. Guildford has plenty of retail, cultural and recreational facilities and the proximity of London (35 minutes by train) is an attraction to many students, although it also helps account for the high cost of living.

Undergraduate Fees and Bursaries

» Fees for UK/EU students 2012–13 £9,000
» International student fees 2012–13 £11,550–£14,440
» Household income below £25K, £2,000 fee waiver and £1,000 cash each year; £25K–£30K, £1,000 fee waiver and £500 cash each year.
» Award of £1,000 cash for those with A*AA at A level or equivalent.
» Sports and other scholarships available.

Students		
Undergraduates:	**9,570**	**(1,115)**
Postgraduates:	**4,005**	**(1,575)**
Mature students:	**16.5%**	
Overseas students:	**19.4%**	
Applications per place:	**7.7**	
From state-sector schools:	**90.7%**	
From working-class homes:	**28.8%**	

For detailed information about sports facilities: www.surreysportspark.co.uk

Accommodation

Number of places and costs refer to 2012–13
University-provided places: 4,851
Percentage catered: 0%
Self-catered costs: £65–£140 a week.
All first years are guaranteed a place.
International non-EU students are guaranteed accommodation for the whole of their course. Remaining places are allocated to final year students.
Contact: www.surrey.ac.uk/Accommodation

University of Sussex

Sussex has dropped four places in the new *Times* League Table, but remains in the top 20 and still 17 places higher than it was three years ago. The university, which is rated in the top 100 in the world by *Times Higher Education*, now generates more than a third of its income from private sources, largely in research contracts. Its reputation was enhanced by good results in the 2008 Research Assessment Exercise, when almost 60 per cent of an unusually large submission was rated as world-leading or internationally excellent.

There was a dip in Sussex's performance in the 2011 National Student Survey, but the university remained in the top 20 for satisfaction levels. There was 100 per cent satisfaction in philosophy and at least 95 per cent in biology, physics and astronomy, mechanical engineering and social work. Applications were down by 8 per cent at the start of 2012, with the prospect of £9,000 fees – slightly above the sector average. But large increases in the two preceding years ensured that the impact on the competition was limited.

Student support includes a work-study programme to help students earn money, funded work placements and three years' aftercare for graduates to help them into a career. The university was already aiming to improve the student experience with the Sussex Plus initiative, which provides recognition for students' voluntary work and other extracurricular activities. Other career-focused initiatives include an internship placement scheme and a leadership training programme. As part of a focus on flexible learning, the library, which has undergone a £6-million redevelopment, has introduced 24-hour opening during term. Careers and employability services are now based in the library building, adjacent to the new one-stop Student Life Centre, which houses other non-academic services.

The university has been celebrating its 50th anniversary with a year-long programme of events. The interdisciplinary approach that has always been Sussex's trademark has been re-examined to adapt this 1960s concept for the 21st century. Arts and social science students take the biggest share of places, but the life sciences are not far behind. The School of Business, Management and Economics, which opened in 2009, offers a portfolio of undergraduate and postgraduate business and management programmes. Dedicated student social space is to be created in each of the university's 12 schools to encourage staff and students to engage both academically and socially.

Sussex is committed to taking candidates with no family tradition of higher education and has much larger numbers of mature students than most of its peer group of

---

Sussex House
Brighton BN1 9RH

01273 876787 (enquiries)
ug.enquiries@sussex.ac.uk
www.sussex.ac.uk
www.bsms.ac.uk
www.ussu.info
Affiliation: 1994 Group

The Times **Rankings**
Overall Ranking: **=18**

Student satisfaction:	=17	(81%)
Research quality:	17	(0.77)
Entry standards:	36	(385)
Student–staff ratio:	=42	(16.6)
Services & facilities/student:	33	(£1,663)
Expected completion rate:	24	(92.4%)
Good honours:	13	(79.2%)
Graduate prospects:	=34	(71.1%)

institutions. The proportion of working-class students is significantly lower than the national average for the university's subjects and entry grades, but this is attributed to the university's south coast location. The projected dropout rate has been improving and, at 8 per cent, remains below the university's benchmark.

The campus is located within the newly created South Downs National Park, four miles from the centre of Brighton, with excellent transport links into town. The university is currently completing a £100-million campus development plan, which will refurbish Sir Basil Spence's original buildings and add new ones. A striking new teaching building has opened and work has since been completed on a £29-million academic building for business, management and economics, law, politics and sociology, which offers a mix of lecture theatres, study and teaching space, and a social centre. The Gardner Centre is being brought back to life as the Attenborough Centre for the Creative Arts, an interdisciplinary arts hub for the university and the wider community that will open during the 2012–13 academic year.

Student accommodation has also been both expanded and upgraded. A new residential complex opened in 2011, providing more than 4,000 bedspaces, including many en suite. Another 1,000 rooms are due to follow by the end of 2012. All first-year students are guaranteed a place in university-managed accommodation if they meet the deadline for applications. Sussex has always attracted overseas students in large numbers and has seen big increases recently. Three times in recent years it has been voted the best university experience in England in the International Student Barometer.

Relations with neighbouring Brighton University are good. The two institutions succeeded in a joint bid for a medical school, which opened in 2003 and recorded another 10 per cent increase in applications for courses beginning in 2012. The Brighton and Sussex Medical School is split between the Royal Sussex County Hospital and the two universities' Falmer campuses.

There is no shortage of social events on campus and Brighton has plenty to offer. Sports facilities are good enough to house pre-Olympic training. Sports scholarships are available to outstanding athletes, including four reserved for basketball and hockey players.

Undergraduate Fees and Bursaries

» Fees for UK/EU students 2012–13   £9,000
» International student fees 2012–13   £12,300–£15,400
    Medicine   £23,678
» Students whose parents did not go to university, or from families with household income below £42.6K, £1,000 cash a year plus £2,000 first-year fee waiver or accommodation discount, and academic and employability support.
» Check the university's website for the latest information.

Students

Undergraduates:	**8,595**	**(370)**
Postgraduates:	**2,310**	**(955)**
Mature students:	**15.2%**	
Overseas students:	**14.6%**	
Applications per place:	**6.4**	
From state-sector schools:	**86.8%**	
From working-class homes:	**20.8%**	

For detailed information about sports facilities:
www.sussexsport.com

Accommodation

Number of places and costs refer to 2012–13
University-provided places: 4,544
Percentage catered: 0%
Self-catered costs: £81.60–£131.50 (single) a week. Some shared rooms available.
First-year students are guaranteed accommodation if conditions are met.
International students: given priority providing conditions are met.
Contact: housing@sussex.ac.uk
www.sussex.ac.uk/study/ug/location/accommodation

Swansea University

Swansea has dropped five places and out of the top 50 in the latest *Times* League Table, leaving it below a post-1992 institution for the first time. Its attractive coastal location and easy access from outside Wales have helped to make it a popular choice for students. But the introduction of £9,000 fees for those from outside the Principality appear to have reduced its appeal in 2012, when applications dropped by more than 6 per cent, as they did at most universities in Wales.

Most of those who take up places seem to enjoy their time at Swansea: the university has done well in the National Student Survey, although a second successive decline in its scores left satisfaction rates below the UK average for its subjects and entry grades in 2011. American studies, biology, French, genetics, German and physical geography produced the best scores. Swansea became independent of the University of Wales in 2007. There are now about 500 degree courses in the modular scheme, and undergraduates are encouraged to stray outside their specialist area in their first year.

Established in 1920 as the UK's first campus university, Swansea has been outgrowing its parkland location overlooking the sea. Two miles from the city centre and offering easy access to the Gower Peninsula, the UK's first Area of Outstanding Natural Beauty, the Singleton campus is the smallest main site at any pre-1992 university. With more than 12,000 students and rapidly increasing research activities, the university is developing a second campus six miles away for science and innovation. The new base, which is due to open before the end of 2013, will focus on research and interaction with technology companies and also contains accommodation for 2,000 students, as well as retail facilities.

The new campus will relieve pressure on the current site and allow for new developments. It has already seen the opening of a £1.2-million facility in the university library to house the Richard Burton archives. Other recent additions have included the £4.3-million Digital Technium Building, which houses the media and communication studies department. A second Institute of Life Sciences building and a Centre for NanoHealth, based within it, opened in 2011 at a combined cost of more than £50 million.

The most important academic development of recent years came with the opening of the School of Medicine and the subsequent development of a full four-year graduate entry medical degree, launched in 2009. Previous entrants spent half of

---

Singleton Park
Swansea SA2 8PP

01792 295111 (admissions)
admissions@swansea.ac.uk
www.swansea.ac.uk
www.swansea-union.co.uk
Affiliation: none

their course in Cardiff, but the new degree is linked to a new NHS University Health Board and the Institute of Life Sciences. The institute is home to Blue C, one of the few supercomputers in the world dedicated to life science research. In addition, the physics department is involved with CERN's Large Hadron Collider.

The university has links to more than 100 partner institutions worldwide and offers many degrees that include opportunities to study abroad. Popular study abroad summer programmes allow students to experience living and studying in India, China, and the USA. The university has won more than £100 million in European funding for projects such as Graduate Opportunities Wales, which steers students towards small firms through industrial placements and vacation jobs. Closer to home, the department of adult and community education teaches mature students in locations throughout the Valleys and elsewhere in South Wales. Compacts with the region's schools encourage students in areas of economic disadvantage to aspire to higher education.

Swansea makes a particular effort to cater for disabled students, whose needs are coordinated through a £250,000 assessment and training centre. Other access measures have been only partially successful: the nearly 92 per cent share of places going to applicants from state schools and colleges is higher than the UK average for the university's courses and entry grades, but fewer than 8 per cent of the students come from areas of low participation in higher education. However, the projected dropout rate of less than 10 per cent is better than the benchmark figure.

The 1,800 computers available for student use represent one of the best ratios at any university. Swansea has recently opened two new halls of residence that take the total number of residential places to more than 3,000. The £20-million Sports Village includes a 50-metre pool, a warm-up pool, athletics track, all-weather pitches, indoor athletics training centre and gym, which attract top performers. The swimming pool is the Wales National Pool and is one of only five facilities in the UK to be awarded Intensive Training Centre status. The campus is the focal point of most students' leisure activities, but the city has a good range of leisure facilities.

Undergraduate Fees and Bursaries

» Fees 2012–13: £9,000, with Welsh Assembly paying fees above £3,465 for Welsh students.
» International student fees 2012–13   £10,100–£13,000
» Retention and priority subject bursaries on sliding scale for those with household income up to £30K.
» Award of £1,500 in years 1 and 2 for those with AAA at A level or equivalent; £1,000 in years 1 and 2 for AAB or equivalent.
» Sports scholarships and care leaver's bursaries available.

Students		
Undergraduates:	**10,380**	**(1,830)**
Postgraduates:	**1,690**	**(575)**
Mature students:	**18.8%**	
Overseas students:	**9%**	
Applications per place:	**3.9**	
From state-sector schools:	**91.8%**	
From working-class homes:	**26.5%**	

For detailed information about sports facilities: www.swan.ac.uk/sport

Accommodation

Number of places and costs refer to 2012–13
University-provided places: about 3,500
Percentage catered: 5%
Catered costs: £111.50–£116.50 a week.
Self-catered costs: £73 (standard) – £115 (en suite) a week.
First-year students holding a firm offer are guaranteed accommodation if conditions are met.
International students: offered up to 3 years.
Contact: www.swansea.ac.uk/accommodation/
accommodation@swansea.ac.uk

Swansea Metropolitan University

By the start of the academic year 2013–14, Swansea Metropolitan will have ceased to exist as an independent institution, making it possibly the shortest-lived university in the UK. But the university website says students will notice no difference when it merges with the University of Wales, Trinity St David. It will even keep its own branding, continuing to use the Swansea Met name and UCAS course codes. Unlike many mergers, this one was not prompted by financial concerns: the university's finances were named as the best in the UK in 2011.

Although university status arrived only in 2008, Swansea Met can trace its history back more than 150 years. However, it does not appear in the main *Times* League Table or in any of the subject tables because the university has again instructed the Higher Education Statistics Agency not to release data on its performance. The university believes that Government agencies should be the only assessors of higher education and considers external league tables "potentially unsound". Those figures that are available suggest that it would have appeared in the lower reaches of the table, but not right at the bottom.

Applications had fallen at the start of 2012, but by much less than the average for Wales or the rest of the UK. Only 18 universities out of 113 in our table registered lower scores for overall student satisfaction in the 2011 National Student Survey, but the university matched the UK average for its courses and entry grades at all types of institution. Only subjects allied to medicine satisfied 90 per cent of final-year undergraduates.

The 25 academics entered for the 2008 Research Assessment Exercise represented the smallest submission at any UK university. But there was some world-leading research in three of the four subject areas in which the university was assessed. Engineering produced the best results. Every faculty has a research director, and a series of research centres is planned.

Of just about 6,000 students, just over half are full-time undergraduates. Almost half of them are studying education or the humanities, and a third are over 21 on entry. Surprisingly, given the mix of subjects, more students are male than female. Two thirds of the undergraduates come from within 45 miles of Swansea, but there is also a long-established tradition of overseas recruitment, which accounts for almost 7 per cent of the places.

Based around the centre of Swansea, the new university is gradually developing an urban campus. There are five sites close to the city centre and another high above

---

Mount Pleasant
Swansea SA1 6ED

01792 481010 (admissions)
enquiry@smu.ac.uk
www.smu.ac.uk
www.metsu.org
Affiliation: none

***The Times* Rankings**

Swansea Metropolitan blocked the release of data from the Higher Education Statistics Agency and so we cannot give any ranking information.

the city, overlooking Swansea Bay, for education and the humanities. The main Mount Pleasant campus is the largest in terms of student numbers, hosting design and engineering, business and leisure courses. Its automotive engineering degrees – especially those focused on motorsport – are probably now the best-known feature of the university.

The nearby Dynevor site has seen the most recent development, with £12.5 million spent on such ventures as an impressive new building for art, design and media, which was rated excellent in the now-dated teaching quality assessments. All the faculty's students undertake an "external project" with a company or outside organisation, which has improved employment prospects in a notoriously difficult group of subjects. The former BBC building is the location for music technology, while the city's one-time Central Library is being redeveloped into an Institute for Sustainable Design, housing the schools of Industrial Design and Architectural Glass. The latest acquisition, on Swansea's High Street, will eventually house the business school and an innovation centre.

Employability and entrepreneurial skills are embedded into every programme and Swansea Met ranks as the best in Wales for producing successful graduate start-up businesses. It is also in the top category of the People and Planet Green League for environmental sustainability. Efforts to widen participation in higher education are high on the university's agenda. More than four undergraduates in ten have a working-class background and a high proportion come from areas with little tradition of higher education. Almost all the students are state educated. However, the projected dropout rate is by far the highest in Wales, at more than 27 per cent.

There are around 350 residential places – not enough for all first years – but private housing is plentiful and reasonably priced. The city has seen considerable development recently and has a good range of pubs and clubs. The university's sports facilities are not extensive, but the nearby Gower Peninsula, officially an Area of Outstanding Natural Beauty, is a prime location for surfers and walkers. A Swansea Met PGCE student from Mauritius will be part of the French sailing team's coaching staff for the 2012 Olympic Games.

Undergraduate Fees and Bursaries

» Fees 2012–13: £8,500–£8,750, with Welsh Assembly paying fees above £3,465 for Welsh students.
» International student fees 2012–13 £9,000
» Students living 45–69 miles from campus, £500 bursary a year; 70 miles and over, £1,000 a year.
» Check the university's website for the latest information.

Students

Undergraduates:	**3,485**	**(1,175)**
Postgraduates:	**755**	**(550)**
From state-sector schools:	**98.5%**	
From working-class homes:	**42.9%**	

For detailed information about sports facilities: www.metsu.org/content/740213/sports__ societies/sports

Accommodation

Number of places and costs refer to 2011–12
University-provided places: 350 (approx)
Percentage catered: 0%
Self-catered costs: £53 (twin) – £72 (en suite) a week (40 weeks).
First years cannot be guaranteed accommodation. Residential restrictions apply.
International students: guaranteed accommodation if conditions are met and application received by 22 August.
Contact: accommodation@smu.ac.uk; 01792 482082

Teesside University

Teesside reduced its planned fees for 2012–13 in order to be permitted to admit more students, leaving the average at less than £7,300 after allowing for discounts and student support. There will be almost 300 extra places as a result, at a time when degree applications had barely dropped from the record levels seen in the previous two years. Only the demand for Foundation degrees and other lower-level courses had fallen substantially at the start of 2012. Teesside has always had a diverse intake and Professor Graham Henderson, the Vice-Chancellor, said that for many students, the university's package of grants, scholarships, loans and other support measures would make higher education much more accessible and affordable in spite of higher fees.

The university has done better than many post-1992 universities in the National Student Survey. In 2011, there was 100 per cent satisfaction in history, while English, occupational therapy and physiotherapy all satisfied at least 90 per cent of final-year undergraduates. Teesside has also been a consistent performer in the International Student Barometer, which tests the views of overseas undergraduates. Middlesbrough has never been considered the most fashionable student destination, but in recent years the number of international applicants has soared.

Teesside also improved its grades in the 2008 Research Assessment Exercise, albeit with only a small proportion of its academics submitting work. Thirty per cent of the research was considered world-leading or internationally excellent, with computer science and history achieving the best results. Five research-led institutes will focus on digital innovation, health, culture, social science and technology.

The university has dropped seven places in the latest *Times* League Table, but official performance indicators also show it well ahead of the access benchmarks calculated by the Higher Education Statistics Agency. Only neighbouring Sunderland takes as many undergraduates (approaching three in ten) from areas of low participation in higher education, while more than 40 per cent of the intake comes from working-class homes. The projected dropout rate has improved enormously and, at 13 per cent, is now well below average for the courses and entry qualifications.

Five partner colleges in the Tees Valley, each with their own higher education centre, offer the university's Foundation degrees and other courses, and a new £13-million campus opened in Darlington in 2011. More than £130 million has been spent in recent years on the main campus in the centre of Middlesbrough. A £17-million sport and health sciences building, with dentistry training and hydrotherapy pool, opened

---

7 Borough Road
Middlesbrough TS1 3BA

01642 218121 (switchboard)
enquiries@tees.ac.uk
www.tees.ac.uk
www.tees-su.org.uk
Affiliation: University
  Alliance

The Times **Rankings**
Overall Ranking: **87**

Student satisfaction:	=42	(79%)
Research quality:	=101	(0.05)
Entry standards:	70	(295)
Student–staff ratio:	=81	(19.5)
Services & facilities/student:	67	(£1,315)
Expected completion rate:	108	(73.0%)
Good honours:	=98	(52.8%)
Graduate prospects:	74	(58.6%)

in 2010. The library is being refurbished in time for the 2012–13 academic year, adding social and interactive spaces as well as group learning areas and a café. Student satisfaction with the library is the highest in the North East.

Other recent developments include a centre for creative technologies for computing, media and design students, and an Institute of Digital Innovation, which supports Middlesbrough's bid to become a Digital City. Almost 100 new companies were created with university support in 2010–11, many incubated on campus as graduate business start-ups. Computer provision is generous, with 2,700 work-stations for student use. Specialist facilities for those studying computer games design, animation and digital media include a new digital sound and TV studio which can create special effects.

There are more than 25,000 undergraduates, two thirds of them taking part-time courses, and almost half of the full-timers are over 21 on entry. The 9,000 health students are by far the largest group in the university, but Teesside is also strong in niche markets such as computer games design and animation, sport and exercise, forensic science and health-related courses. Teesside supports the career development of its graduates for a minimum of two years after graduation and is expanding paid work placements as part of a student's

course. Over the past two years, more than 200 graduates have been placed with North East businesses, delivering a wide range of specialist support in projects lasting from three months to two years. That figure is set to rise as Teesside embarks on a three-year programme to deliver 550 graduate internships and knowledge exchange projects in the region.

Middlesbrough has more nightlife than sceptics might imagine, and the booming student population has attracted new pubs, cafés and student-orientated shops in and around the Southfield Road area. The cost of living is another attraction: university rents are reasonable and the lively students' union has twice won the title of Students' Union of the Year. Outdoor sports facilities include a water sports centre on the River Tees and elite athlete bursaries are available. The new Middlesbrough Institute of Modern Art (mima) is also putting the town on the cultural map and there is a full programme of "Culture on Campus" events during the year.

Undergraduate Fees and Bursaries

» Fees for UK/EU students 2012–13 £7,450–£8,450
» International student fees 2012–13 £10,450
» Household income below £16.2K and conditions, £3,000 fee waiver and £1,000 cash in year 1 only.
» Scholarship of £1,500 a year for those with household income below £42.6K and either showing high academic achievement or receiving Disabled Students' Allowance.

Students

Undergraduates:	9,565	(14,275)
Postgraduates:	1,540	(1,885)
Mature students:	28.7%	
Overseas students:	6.4%	
Applications per place:	4.4	
From state-sector schools:	97.8%	
From working-class homes:	42.1%	

For detailed information about sports facilities: www.tees.ac.uk/sport

Accommodation

Number of places and costs refer to 2011–12
University-provided places: 1,149
Percentage catered: 0%
Self-catered costs: £52.50–£90.00 a week (residences, 40 weeks); £60–£65 a week (managed housing, 40 weeks)
University managed residences are reserved exclusively for first years.
International students: as above.
Contact: 01642 342255; accommodation@tees.ac.uk; www.tees.ac.uk/accommodation

Trinity St David, University of Wales

The first students to apply to the new University of Wales Trinity Saint David will arrive in the autumn of 2012, just in time to see the institution merge again. This time the partner will be Swansea Metropolitan University, which was part of a "strategic alliance" with the university and three further education colleges for post-16 education in southwest Wales. Trinity has suffered a big drop in the latest *Times* League Table, mainly because of a decline in graduate employment prospects and a dip in entry standards at a time when they were rising in most universities.

In the whole of England and Wales, only Oxford and Cambridge were awarding degrees before St David's College Lampeter, which went on to be the smallest publicly funded university in Europe before merging with Trinity University College, 23 miles away in Carmarthen. Swansea is as far away again, but there is expected to be no impact on student life in either of the original bases under the new collegiate set-up. Swansea Met will even continue to use its own name in conjunction with the University of Wales Trinity Saint David title.

The former University of Wales Lampeter has continued to make a virtue of its size by stressing its friendly atmosphere and intimate teaching style. It remains a small, rural outpost that suits those who seek a quiet location. As an independent institution, it recorded high levels of satisfaction in every year of the National Student Survey (NSS), finishing in the top 20 in 2009. Based on an ancient castle and modelled on an Oxbridge college, St David's College was established to train young men for the Anglican ministry. The original quadrangle remains and the chapel is in daily use. There have been significant changes in recent few years – notably a big expansion in distance learning and the introduction of such subjects as Chinese studies, anthropology, IT, management, and film and media studies.

Lampeter is best known for theology, but archaeology produced the best results by far in the 2008 Research Assessment Exercise. The small campus includes a mosque for the growing number of Muslim students attracted by the well-endowed programme of Islamic studies. Media studies, which benefits from a well-equipped media centre for film and television students, has also been growing in popularity.

As a university college, Trinity did not qualify for inclusion in this *Guide*, although it was part of the University of Wales. With 2,200 students, including part-timers, it was hardly large, but still twice the size of Lampeter. Established in 1848, it is affiliated

---

Lampeter Campus
Lampeter
Ceredigion SA48 7ED

01570 422351 (switchboard)
contact via website
www.trinitysaintdavid.ac.uk
www.tsdsu.co.uk
Affiliation: Cathedral Group

The Times **Rankings**
Overall Ranking: **105**

Student satisfaction:	=89	(75%)
Research quality:	57	(0.27)
Entry standards:	106	(245)
Student–staff ratio:	=69	(18.8)
Services & facilities/student:	75	(£1,281)
Expected completion rate:	100	(75.6%)
Good honours:	111	(48.3%)
Graduate prospects:	104	(51.1%)

to the Church in Wales, but recruits students of all faiths and none. Trinity has a long history of teacher training, with arts and social studies the only other faculty. Results in the NSS were not as good as Lampeter's, but reached the average for Wales. The merged institution was close to mid-table in the 2011 survey, with initial teacher training the only area to satisfy more than 90 per cent of final-year undergraduates.

A new suite of art and design courses is being offered in association with Coleg Sir Gar, one of the partners in the new alliance. The subjects include digital illustration, ceramics and jewellery, graphic communication, photography and textiles. The Welsh Assembly and the Higher Education Funding Council for Wales invested £18 million in the original merger to produce a "distinctive and unique curriculum with a strong emphasis on Welsh cultural heritage and bilingualism". The aim is to serve the region, but also to attract students from all around the world through the Confucius Centre, the Islamic Studies Centre and the Welsh American Academy. However, a drop in applications of almost 15 per cent at the start of 2012 was (jointly) the biggest in Wales.

The university has strong bilingual policies and also takes Welsh to a wider audience, with the only university course teaching the language over the internet. Lampeter is deep in Welsh-speaking rural West Wales. Although only four hours from London and two from Cardiff, Lampeter's geographical position could be a problem for the unprepared. The town has just 4,000 inhabitants, with among the lowest crime rates in Britain, and the nearest station is more than 20 miles away.

Carmarthen is a county town of 18,000 people with reasonably-priced accommodation for the few first-year students who fail to secure a place in one of the halls of residence. Less remote as well as larger than Lampeter, it has a railway station and is not far from the end of the M4 for car drivers. Both locations are within reach of the sea and stunning countryside, as is Swansea.

Undergraduate Fees and Bursaries

» Fees 2012–13: £8,500–£9,000, with Welsh Assembly paying fees above £3,465 for Welsh students.
» International student fees 2011–12   £9,348
» Scholarships and bursaries available, including residential bursaries of up to £1,000 in year 1 and Welsh-medium scholarships up to £1,000 a year.
» Check the university's website for the latest information.

Students		
Undergraduates:	**3,065**	**(2,120)**
Postgraduates:	**915**	**(605)**
Mature students:	**29.4%**	
Overseas students:	**18.3%**	
Applications per place:	**2.2**	
From state-sector schools:	**96.8%**	
From working-class homes:	**39.1%**	

For detailed information about sports facilities: www.trinitysaintdavid.ac.uk/en/sport

Accommodation
Number of places and costs refer to 2012–13
L refers to Lampeter, CM to Carmarthen
University-provided places: 500 (L), 512 (CM)
Percentage catered: 0% (L), 44% (CM)
Catered costs: £109 a week; meals for 5 days (L & CM).
Self-catered costs: £68.00–£87.50 a week (L); £86.50 a week (CM).
First years can normally be placed in university accommodation.
International students: guaranteed housing for first year.
Contact: www.trinitysaintdavid.ac.uk/en/studentlife/accommodation

University of Ulster

Ulster is only just outside the top ten universities in terms of applications and saw no more than a small drop at the start of 2012, with new fee arrangements. Most students are from Northern Ireland and paying less than £3,500, while fees for the relatively small cohort from other parts of the UK are £6,000. The university's new corporate plan sets targets to lead in the provision of "professional education for professional life". One aim is for an increasing number of degrees to provide placement opportunities and professional accreditation.

There are four campuses – at Coleraine, Jordanstown (seven miles outside Belfast), Magee in Londonderry, and in Belfast city centre. Each campus has a distinct character and while some courses are offered at more than one campus, there is a degree of specialisation across the campuses. Belfast concentrates on art and design, architecture and hospitality; Jordanstown concentrates on business and management, the built environment, computing and engineering, health and sport sciences, and social sciences; Coleraine is focused on environmental and life sciences, humanities, modern languages and tourism management, whilst at Magee there is a concentration on creative and performing arts, nursing and social work,

computing, business and management, and social sciences. The Magee campus will be intimately involved in Derry/Londonderry activities as part of the UK City of Culture in 2013.

Ulster has over 25,000 students, including almost 9,000 part-timers. All undergraduates complete their studies on a single campus, each of which has well-equipped learning resource centres. Accommodation is guaranteed for first-years students at all four campuses. The university almost matched the UK average for satisfaction levels in the 2011 National Student Survey, with ophthalmics and sports science achieving 100 per cent satisfaction and biological sciences, food studies and sociology also achieving good scores.

The university's reputation was further enhanced by its strong performance in the 2008 Research Assessment Exercise. Nearly half of its submission was rated as world-leading or internationally excellent, with the university ranked in the top three for biomedical sciences, Celtic studies, and nursing and midwifery. Results improved in almost all areas, leaving Ulster within sight of neighbouring Queen's University in the research tables. Research at the university generates over £30 million for the Northern Ireland economy, emanating from each of Ulster's six faculties and across all four campuses.

In 2009, the university announced

Cromore Road
Coleraine
Co. Londonderry
BT52 1SA

028 701 23456
 (switchboard)
enquiry via website
www.ulster.ac.uk
www.uusu.org
Affiliation: none

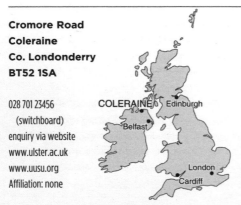

COLERAINE Edinburgh
Belfast
London
Cardiff

The Times Rankings
Overall Ranking: **=65**

Student satisfaction:	**=74**	(77%)
Research quality:	**=52**	(0.33)
Entry standards:	**=84**	(282)
Student–staff ratio:	**=40**	(16.5)
Services & facilities/student:	**47**	(£1,490)
Expected completion rate:	**85**	(78.5%)
Good honours:	**55**	(63.4%)
Graduate prospects:	**109**	(49.9%)

ambitious £250-million capital development plans which will see most of the activity currently based at Jordanstown transferred to the university's Belfast campus, where it has acquired a substantial additional site in the city's Cathedral Quarter. Jordanstown will be retained and developed further as Ireland's only dedicated sports campus. It is home to the Sports Institute of Northern Ireland. The university is well positioned in this regard having won 33 sporting titles across the island of Ireland in 2009–10. Over £20 million has already been invested here in a new high-performance sports centre. Facilities include an indoor sports hall, outdoor and indoor sprint tracks, a strength and conditioning suite, water recovery area, and sports science and sports medicine facilities.

A further expansion in student numbers is planned and will be concentrated at Magee where the university has recently signed an option agreement which will see Ulster almost double its footprint in the city. Plans for expansion at Magee include an Institute of Health and Wellbeing and an Institute of Sustainable Technologies. Magee also houses a Centre of Intelligent Systems and the historic Foyle Arts Centre. Further expansion is also planned in the schools of creative arts, computing and electronics as well as nursing.

Coleraine is home to the £11-million Centre for Molecular Biosciences. Building on its expertise, the university also introduced a new programme in pharmacy. Ulster has a strong commitment to widening access and is consistently among the top ten universities in terms of admitting students from the less advantaged socio-economic groups. The projected dropout rate had improved in the latest survey but, at nearly 16 per cent, was still higher than the benchmark calculated according to the university's subjects and entry grades. A range of scholarships is available including sports scholarships and others for high achievers in economically relevant subjects such as engineering, computing, science and economics.

There has never been a big representation from mainland Britain, but the university's contingent of international students includes many from the Republic of Ireland as well as further afield. The eLearning at Ulster programme provides an alternative mode of study, offering courses online to students all over the world. With more than half of Ulster's students home-based, the university is not always the focus of social life. The exception is the Coleraine campus, although many gravitate towards the nearby seaside towns of Portrush and Portstewart.

Undergraduate Fees and Bursaries

» Fees for NI/EU students 2012–13   £3,465
» Fees for English, Scottish and Welsh students   £6,000
» International student fees 2012–13   £9,500
» Check the university's website for the latest information.

Students

Undergraduates:	**15,305**	**(4,990)**
Postgraduates:	**1,905**	**(3,320)**
Mature students:	**22.7%**	
Overseas students:	**12.4%**	
Applications per place:	**6.3**	
From state-sector schools:	**99.9%**	
From working-class homes:	**46.5%**	

For detailed information about sports facilities:
www.sportsulster.com

Accommodation

Number of places and costs refer to 2012–13
University-provided places: 2,425 over three campuses.
Percentage catered: 0%
Self-catered costs: average £64 (standard) – £76 (en suite) a week (37 weeks).
First-year students are guaranteed accommodation if conditions are met.
International students: same as above.
Contact: accommodation@ulster.ac.uk
www.accommodation.ulster.ac.uk

University of the Arts London

The University of the Arts London has enjoyed the biggest rise of any institution in this year's *Times* League Table. Its extraordinary 22-place progress into the top 60 mainly reflects a big increase in student satisfaction, the university's Achilles heel in previous years. But staffing levels are also significantly improved and the university is up on almost every measure. The good news does not extend to applications, however. The demand for places had been growing by leaps and bounds before the introduction of £9,000 fees, but there was a 19 per cent decline at the start of 2012. The university had insisted that expensive courses, a central London location and the loss of virtually all its Government teaching grant left no alternative to the maximum fee.

The collection of world-famous art, design, fashion and media colleges that constituted the London Institute became a university in 2004. With over 20,000 further and higher education students spread through 14 sites around central London, it is Europe's largest arts university. The five component colleges became six when Wimbledon College of Art joined in 2006, bringing an international reputation in theatre design and the UK's largest school of theatre. The founding members, which continue to use their own names and enjoy considerable autonomy, were Camberwell College of Arts, Central Saint Martins College of Arts and Design, Chelsea College of Art and Design, London College of Fashion and London College of Communication (formerly the London College of Printing). The university is offering one Foundation course across Camberwell, Chelsea and Wimbledon.

Big changes were already under way before the change of title was agreed: a £70-million development programme next door to the Tate Gallery produced prestigious new premises for Chelsea College, with extensive workshop facilities, studios and a new library. Another £32 million was spent on new headquarters for the College of Communication at the Elephant and Castle, south of the Thames, where a Special Archives and Collections Centre includes the archives of the filmmaker Stanley Kubrick. The college has Film Academy status. London's largest open-air art gallery was launched in 2008 on the Parade Ground at the heart of the Chelsea College of Art and Design, and final-year students' work is also showcased online at a virtual degree show.

The biggest project of all has brought Central Saint Martins together on one site for the first time, moving to the new King's Cross development. The £200-million campus is based on a Grade II listed former granary, which accommodates a new School

---

272 High Holborn
London WC1V 7EY

0207 514 6197 (enquiries)
admissions@arts.ac.uk
www.arts.ac.uk
www.suarts.org
Affiliation: none

The Times **Rankings**

Overall Ranking: **60**

Student satisfaction:	113	(70%)
Research quality:	=35	(0.61)
Entry standards:	=57	(307)
Student–staff ratio:	=51	(17.4)
Services & facilities/student:	=81	(£1,216)
Expected completion rate:	=37	(88.3%)
Good honours:	50	(65.0%)
Graduate prospects:	=85	(55.5%)

of Performing Arts as well as the college's existing art, fashion and design courses. There is a 350-seat public theatre, studios and rehearsal spaces, as well as four levels of workshops, studios and exhibition space, with facilities for students from across the university.

Published assessments have barely done justice to the eminence of the colleges, although the 2008 Research Assessment Exercise saw half of the university's submission rated as world-leading or internationally excellent. The 2011 National Student Survey saw a rise of seven percentage points in overall satisfaction levels, but the 69 per cent average was still the lowest at any university. No subject satisfied 80 per cent of final-year undergraduates, fine art coming closest to this mark. All the colleges make good use of visiting lecturers, who keep students abreast of developments in their field, but the arts produce low satisfaction rates nationally.

The university has been running weekend classes and summer schools in an attempt to broaden the intake. The proportion of undergraduates from working-class homes is now close to 30 per cent. The projected dropout rate has been improving and, at 11 per cent, is better than average for the subjects on offer.

Students have access to the new Student Enterprise and Employability Service, the largest art and design specialist careers centre in the country, while the pioneering Emerging Artists Programme continues to support graduates in the early years of their careers. The university holds the only recruitment festival tailored to the needs of creative graduates, providing access to hundreds of industry professionals for networking opportunities and advice.

The colleges vary considerably in character and facilities, although a single students' union serves them all. The university's new student hub provides a central place for students to work, socialise and share ideas, as well as housing student services such as housing and careers.

The university is not overprovided with residential accommodation, although there are 13 residences spread around the colleges, providing more than 2,400 beds. House-hunting workshops help those who have to rely on an expensive private housing market. The university owns no sports facilities, although it has arranged student discounts with a number of providers.

Undergraduate Fees and Bursaries

» Fees for UK/EU students 2012–13 £9,000
» International student fees 2012–13 £13,300
» Priority to those with household income below £16K, 309 NSP awards of £2,000 fee waiver and £1,00 cash year 1 and £1,000 cash for other years; £1,000 a year for students from low-income groups who do not qualify for the NSP.
» Range of scholarships available.

Students

Undergraduates:	**12,930**	**(695)**
Postgraduates:	**2,495**	**(850)**
Mature students:	**23.8%**	
Overseas students:	**36.3%**	
Applications per place:	**7.2**	
From state-sector schools:	**95.6%**	
From working-class homes:	**27.1%**	

For detailed information about sports facilities: www.suarts.org

Accommodation

Number of places and costs refer to 2012–13
University-provided places: 2,507
Percentage catered: 0%
Self-catered costs: £92–£240 a week.
First-year students are offered accommodation if conditions are met. Priority for disabled students and those from outside London. International students: guaranteed if conditions met.
Contact: www.arts.ac.uk/housing/
accommodation@arts.ac.uk

University College London

The prospect of £9,000 fees had little impact on the demand for places at University College London. Applications were only marginally down at the start of 2012 and, with more than nine applications per place in 2011, entry was set to remain as competitive as anywhere in the country. UCL has dropped out of the top five in this year's *Times* League Table, but is rated among the top ten universities in the world in the QS rankings.

UCL's excellence is built on a history of pioneering subjects that have become commonplace in higher education: modern languages, geography and fine arts among them. From 2012, there will be a new requirement for a foreign language GCSE at grade C or above, although students will be allowed to reach this standard at UCL if they have not taken a language at school.

The 2008 Research Assessment Exercise provided further confirmation of UCL's academic power, with two thirds of its submission judged to be world-leading or internationally excellent. The top scorers were economics, which saw 95 per cent of its work rated in the top two categories, and computer science and informatics, immunology and infection, environmental sciences and history of art, all of which had at least 80 per cent at this level.

Architecture, chemical engineering, cancer studies, law, philosophy and psychology also produced outstanding results.

Already comfortably the largest of London University's colleges, UCL has grown rapidly in the past two decades and can now award its own degrees. It has more than 700 professors – the largest number in Britain – and includes a number of specialist schools and institutes. The School of Pharmacy was the latest to join, in 2012. UCL's medical school, with 11 associated teaching hospitals, is now a large and formidable unit. Its credentials were strengthened still further with the announcement that UCL will be a founding partner in the new Francis Crick Institute (formerly UK Centre for Medical Research and Innovation) being constructed adjacent to St Pancras Station. The centre will undertake cutting-edge research to advance understanding of health and disease.

The various acquisitions mean that there are now outposts in several parts of central and north London, as well as plans for an archaeology and conservation campus in Qatar, but the main activity remains centred on the original impressive Bloomsbury site. UCL is pioneering the idea of education for global citizenship, ensuring students are given opportunity and encouragement to explore academic ideas from different cultural perspectives and to work on problems of international

---

Gower Street
London WC1E 6BT

020 7679 2000 (main switchboard)
contact via website
www.ucl.ac.uk
www.uclu.org
Affiliation: Russell Group

The Times **Rankings**
Overall Ranking: **7**

Student satisfaction:	=42	(79%)
Research quality:	=4	(0.99)
Entry standards:	7	(498)
Student–staff ratio:	1	(10.1)
Services & facilities/student:	8	(£2,197)
Expected completion rate:	15	(93.9%)
Good honours:	10	(81.0%)
Graduate prospects:	4	(79.9%)

importance, as well as contributing to their local community and the university's social and cultural life.

UCL has done better than most London universities in the National Student Survey, with 88 per cent of final-year undergraduates expressing satisfaction in the results published in 2010. There was 100 per cent satisfaction for the second successive year in archaeological science, while anthropology, art and design, English, medicine and sociology all produced high scores. A growing number of degrees take four years, and most are organised on a modular basis.

More than 40 per cent of UCL's 25,000 students are postgraduates and about 9,000 are from overseas. Both categories are likely to become more numerous in the coming years. All first-year students are helped to make the academic and social adjustment to university life through UCL's Transition Programme, which includes a variety of activities such as peer mentoring and workshops. UCL stresses its commitment to teaching in small groups, especially in the second and subsequent years of degree courses. The projected dropout rate of 6 per cent is better than the national average for UCL's courses and entry grades.

UCL is conscious of its traditions as a college founded to expand access to higher education, but the 36 per cent share of places going to independent school students is one of the highest in Britain. Almost one undergraduate in five has a working-class background. Concerted attempts are being made to broaden the intake with summer schools for state-school students, outreach activities and campus-based programmes. UCL is sponsoring a new academy, which it sees as part of its contribution to the local community.

The academic pace can be frantic but, close to the West End and with its own theatre and recreational facilities, there is no shortage of leisure options. Students also have immediate access to London University's under-used central students' union facilities. Residential accommodation is plentiful and of a good standard. Indoor sports and fitness facilities are close at hand, but the main outdoor pitches, though good enough to attract professional football clubs, are a (free) coach ride away in Hertfordshire. Hockey players have access to Astroturf pitches at the Old Cranleighans ground, in Thames Ditton.

Undergraduate Fees and Bursaries

» Fees for UK/EU students 2012–13 £9,000
» International student fees 2012–13 £14,000–£18,500
  Medicine £27,500
» Household income below £25K, £1,500 cash and £2,000 accommodation discount if in UCL Residence (otherwise £3,500 cash) in year 1; following years, £3,500 cash; household income £25K–£42.6K, £1,000 cash, all years.
» Range of departmental and academic scholarships.

Students

Undergraduates:	**12,535**	**(870)**
Postgraduates:	**8,155**	**(3,125)**
Mature students:	**10.7%**	
Overseas students:	**34.5%**	
Applications per place:	**9.5**	
From state-sector schools:	**63.5%**	
From working-class homes:	**19.5%**	

For detailed information about sports facilities:
www.uclu.org/services/active-uclu

Accommodation

Number of places and costs refer to 2012–13
University-provided places: 4,545 (including 819 intercollegiate places)
Percentage catered: 30%
Catered costs: £159.25–£176.75 a week (39 weeks).
Self-catered costs: £94.50–£189.00 a week (39 weeks).
First years are guaranteed accommodation if conditions are met.
International students: as above.
Contact: Residences@ucl.ac.uk
www.ucl.ac.uk/admissions/accommodation

University for the Creative Arts (UCA)

England's newest university suffered the biggest drop in applications of any in the UK at the start of 2012. The prospect of £8,500 fees coincided with a decline of almost 30 per cent in the demand for places at the University of the Creative Arts (UCA). It will fall to Dr Simon Ofield-Kerr, the new Vice-Chancellor, to respond. He increased international recruitment at Kingston University's Faculty of Art, Design and Architecture, and expects to do the same at his new institution, while also maintaining its local roots.

With more than 7,000 students, UCA is sizeable by the standards of specialist institutions and applications had risen significantly before the switch to higher fees. The university is the product of a merger between two well-established arts institutes straddling Kent and Surrey. Indeed, the first version of its title was the unwieldy University for the Creative Arts at Canterbury, Epsom, Farnham, Maidstone and Rochester, although the multiple locations have since been dropped. The constituent colleges all date back to Victorian times, but university status arrived only in 2008. The location of each college is given in the map below: Canterbury (1), Epsom (2), Farnham (3), Maidstone (4) and Rochester (5).

By far the largest enrolment is at Farnham, in Surrey, where more than 2,000 students take courses in art, design, cinematics and communications. There is a purpose-built student village with 350 rooms in the centre of town and two galleries, as well as teaching space and a library and learning centre. The campus includes research centres in animation, crafts and sustainable design. Courses range from pre-degree Foundation courses in art and design to degrees in film production, motoring journalism and three-dimensional design.

The other four sites are of similar size in terms of student numbers. The second base in Surrey, at Epsom, specialises in fashion, graphics and new media, although it offers general art and design courses at further education level. Degrees include music journalism and fashion promotion and imaging. There is a modern library and learning resource centre for more than 1,200 students, a bar and café on campus and three halls of residence, the latest of which opened in 2010. A new £5.9-million teaching block includes learning and resource facilities, a 200-seat auditorium and a digital media centre. Photovoltaic cells on the roof and solar water heating will ensure that at least 20 per cent of the energy it uses is generated on site.

The largest of the three campuses in

UCA Canterbury
New Dover Road
Canterbury
Kent CT1 3AN

01252 892960 (enquiries)
admissions@ucreative.ac.uk
www.ucreative.ac.uk
www.ucasu.com
Affiliation: Guild HE

The Times **Rankings**
Overall Ranking: **103**

Student satisfaction:	=102	(73%)
Research quality:	=64	(0.15)
Entry standards:	100	(262)
Student–staff ratio:	79	(19.3)
Services & facilities/student:	42	(£1,539)
Expected completion rate:	74	(80.5%)
Good honours:	109	(48.9%)
Graduate prospects:	110	(49.5%)

Kent is at Rochester, which offers a full range of art and design, including fashion, photography and specialist design courses. The purpose-built campus is set on a hillside overlooking the city centre and River Medway. Halls of residence with 214 places are close to the campus, which has studio space, library and learning resource centre, and a gallery.

The Maidstone campus is in parkland, ten minutes from the centre of town, with another gallery and extensive library. The integrated teaching and research facilities include a multi-user video editing facility and video studio, printmaking area, animation resources and a specialist photography resource. Courses for more than 900 students encourage interdisciplinary study. So many aspiring students had to be rejected in 2010 that new broadcast media degree was launched in 2011 to accommodate some of the disappointed applicants.

At Canterbury, the accent is on architecture, but there are also degrees in fine art, interior design and more general art and design. The modern site is close to the city centre and contains purpose-built studios, workshops and lecture theatres. The Canterbury School of Architecture is the only such school to remain within a specialist art and design institution, encouraging collaboration between student architects, designers and fine artists.

The university offers four-year degrees, incorporating a Foundation year, as well as the three-year format, and two-year Foundation degrees, which can be topped up to produce honours. However, results in the National Student Survey have been poor in all five years of polling, as they have been for art and design generally. The 2011 scores saw the biggest improvement at any university, but still left UCA marooned in the bottom five. Only architecture and fine art satisfied more than 75 per cent of final-year undergraduates.

Many staff are practitioners as well as academics and the colleges have produced a string of famous graduates, such as Karen Millen and Zandra Rhodes, who has now become the university's Chancellor. There is also a strong research culture, although UCA had only limited success in the 2008 Research Assessment Exercise. Thirty per cent of the university's submission was considered world-leading or internationally excellent, but this left it well down the ranking for art and design.

Undergraduate Fees and Bursaries

» Fees for UK/EU students 2012–13   £8,500
» International student fees 2012–13   £10,870
» Household income up to £40K, annual bursary on sliding scale £900–£200.
» 186 NSP awards of £2,000 for university services, £1,000 cash.
» Range of creative scholarships and progression bursaries from UCA pre-degree courses.

Students		
Undergraduates:	**4,995**	**(200)**
Postgraduates:	**170**	**(100)**
Mature students:	**16.7%**	
Overseas students:	**9.9%**	
Applications per place:	**4.7**	
From state-sector schools:	**97.4%**	
From working-class homes:	**36.2%**	

For detailed information about sports facilities:
http://ucasu.com/clubs

Accommodation

Places and costs refer to 2011–12
University-provided places: 1,127
Percentage catered: 0%
Self catered costs: £54.70 (shared) – £122.20 (en suite) a week.
Priority is given to disabled students (new and returning) and new full-time students by distance.
International students: guaranteed housing if application received by mid June
Contact: accommodation@ucreative.ac.uk; www.ucreative.ac.uk

University of Warwick

The most successful of the "new" universities of the 1960s, Warwick has global ambitions. It has set itself the target of establishing itself among the world's top 50 universities, and has expanded its international activities that include a base in Venice, a programme for gifted teenagers around the world and the recruitment of more than 6,000 overseas students.

Warwick reached the top 50 in the QS World University Rankings for the first time in 2011 and has never been out of the top ten in *The Times* League Table. The university has reconfigured its research around its "Global Priorities Programme", which brings together expertise from different subjects to focus on key areas of international significance. Current themes include connecting cultures, food security, global governance, individual behaviour and innovative manufacturing. Warwick is the only European institution to be involved in a new Center for Urban Science and Progress, a consortium of leading universities established in New York.

The university does not neglect its locality, however. Its mission statement stresses community links and the extension of access to higher and continuing education. There is a smaller proportion of independent school students than at most of the leading universities – around a quarter – although this does not translate into large numbers of working-class undergraduates. The university has one of the lowest dropout rates in Britain at less than 4 per cent. Warwick is charging £9,000 undergraduate fees for 2012–13, but students from the poorest backgrounds will receive up to half of that amount in fee waivers and bursaries. Nevertheless, the prospect of higher fees still brought a 10 per cent drop in applications at the start of 2012.

Almost two thirds of the work submitted for the 2008 Research Assessment Exercise was considered world-leading or internationally excellent, placing Warwick among the top ten UK universities. Film and television studies, and horticultural research achieved two of the top scores for any subject at any university, while pure maths, French and Italian were in the top three. There were particularly high grades, too, for economics, applied maths, and theatre, performance and cultural studies. The science park is among the most successful in the UK.

Warwick was a late starter in the National Student Survey, due to opposition from the students' union, but is now in the top 20. Accounting, classics, drama, several European languages and finance all satisfied at least 95 per cent of final-year undergraduates. Warwick was awarded a national teaching centre in theatrical performance, in partnership with the Royal Shakespeare Company, and is collaborating

---

Coventry CV4 7AL

024 7652 3723 (admissions)
ugadmissions@warwick.ac.uk
www.warwick.ac.uk
www.warwicksu.com
Affiliation: Russell Group

The Times Rankings
Overall Ranking: **8**

Student satisfaction:	=17	(81%)
Research quality:	=9	(0.87)
Entry standards:	8	(496)
Student–staff ratio:	20	(14.5)
Services & facilities/student:	12	(£2,053)
Expected completion rate:	=4	(96.5%)
Good honours:	12	(80.8%)
Graduate prospects:	11	(77.6%)

with Oxford Brookes University on another centre to "reinvent" undergraduate research. It has also been funded to help devise a blueprint for improving the undergraduate curriculum in research-led universities.

The university invested shrewdly in business, science and engineering and there is now a thriving graduate entry medical school, with more than 2,000 students. Warwick is also one of the few leading universities to embrace two-year Foundation degrees, running courses in education and community enterprise, the latter taught at a local further education college. With over eight applicants for every place on conventional degree courses, many departments stick rigidly to offers averaging more than an A and two Bs at A level. The business school has grown rapidly, with a new £15-million extension, while chemistry and physics have also acquired new facilities recently.

Warwick's financial investment programme is set to continue to 2015 with another £150 million being spent on campus infrastructure. A second significant extension to students' union facilities opened in 2010 and an £8-million extension to the Warwick Arts Centre, which attracts over 250,000 visitors a year, has just been completed. A new Centre for Mechanochemical Cell Biology opened in April 2012 as part of the Medical School campus. The centre is part of the Science City Research Alliance, a strategic partnership of Birmingham and Warwick universities, focusing on advanced materials, energy futures and translational medicine. Also recently completed is an analytical science research facility for the physics and chemistry departments. A £12.5-million building houses a digital laboratory for manufacturing and engineering research, and a clinical trials unit. The university will also benefit from one of the largest donations ever from a member of staff, after Professor Lord Bhattacharyya made a £1-million commitment and has asked that it be put towards research.

The 750-acre campus is three miles south of Coventry, where many students choose to live, and three times as far from Warwick. University accommodation is plentiful, and more is in the pipeline, designed with environmental friendliness in mind. The latest development provides more than 500 rooms to add to the campus portfolio. The sports facilities are both extensive and conveniently placed on campus.

Undergraduate Fees and Bursaries

- » Fees for UK/EU students 2012–13 £9,000
- » International student fees 2012–13 £13,800–£17,600
- » English students from state schools, household income below £25K, £2,000 fee waiver and £2,500 cash a year; £25K–£36K, £1,500 cash a year; £36K–£42.6K, £500.
- » Range of other scholarships available.

Students

Undergraduates:	12,360	(5,610)
Postgraduates:	5,270	(4,925)
Mature students:	8.4%	
Overseas students:	23.1%	
Applications per place:	8.2	
From state-sector schools:	75.2%	
From working-class homes:	17.1%	

For detailed information about sports facilities:
http://warwicksport.warwick.ac.uk

Accommodation

Number of places and costs refer to 2012–13
University-provided places: 6,458 (on campus); 1,850 (head leasing)
Percentage catered: 0%
Self-catered costs: £78–£150 a week (30, 37, 39 and 50 week contracts).
First-year undergraduates are prioritised for campus accommodation (terms and conditions apply).
International students as above.
Contact: www.warwick.ac.uk/accommodation

University of West London

Like other universities to have changed their names in recent years, West London's decision to dispose of the tarnished title of Thames Valley University appears to have paid instant dividends. Degree applications were up 16 per cent at the start of 2012, as most other universities saw the demand for places fall. Professor Peter John, the Vice-Chancellor, said students recognised that the university had entered a "new dawn" and they were attracted by a guaranteed work placement, in-study financial support and a strong probability of getting a job once they graduate. Standard fees for 2012–13 were among the lowest in England, at £7,500, with specialist music and performance courses costing £8,200.

The university had already recovered from a traumatic period at the end of the 1990s, when barely 30 degrees were left, following official criticism of academic standards and a collapse in student demand. Helped particularly by changes in nursing education, which accounts for about a quarter of the places, there had been big increases in applications for two years before the change of title. The university's new name reflects a new, narrower geographical focus. Having tried the expansion route with little success, it is concentrating most activities on the university's original home in Ealing, where the main building has been refurbished. The Slough campus has closed. Its 1,000 full-time students, two thirds of whom are on pre-registration nursing courses, have moved to the Reading campus, leaving just part-time business courses and some post-registration nursing in Slough, at a different site. The restructuring will not alter the aim to become the country's leading university for employer engagement, with an accent on the creative industries and entrepreneurship.

The Reading campus, known as the Berkshire hub, is within walking distance of the mainline station and focuses entirely on nursing and midwifery. The Ealing campus has a more traditional university feel and has been refurbished and upgraded at a cost of almost £10 million. The landmark Paragon Building in Brentford, not far from the Ealing campus, will remain the headquarters of one of the largest healthcare faculties in Britain with top quality ratings for nursing and midwifery. The site contains 850 residential places, as well as teaching facilities.

Amid the reconstruction, new honours degrees have been launched in areas such as video production, 3D design, entrepreneurship, computing and information systems. The portfolio of two-year Foundation degrees is growing, with employers such as Compaq, Ealing Studios and the Savoy Hotel Group

St Mary's Road
Ealing
London W5 5RF

0800 036 8888 (admissions)
learning.advice@uwl.ac.uk
www.uwl.ac.uk
www.westlondonsu.com
Affiliation: million+

The Times Rankings
Overall Ranking: **110**

Student satisfaction:	**=102**	(73%)
Research quality:	**=95**	(0.06)
Entry standards:	**109**	(235)
Student–staff ratio:	**=98**	(21.0)
Services & facilities/student:	**46**	(£1,497)
Expected completion rate:	**113**	(68.2%)
Good honours:	**114**	(47.7%)
Graduate prospects:	**91**	(53.8%)

helping to provide courses. Some are run in conjunction with Stratford-upon-Avon College – one of several partner institutions.

The university did not appear in last year's tables, having instructed the Higher Education Statistics Agency not to release data on its performance during the transition to its new identity. It scores highly in the new edition for its spending on student facilities and has seen a sharp increase in student satisfaction, but still finds itself in the bottom ten overall. Computer science, finance and accounting were the only subjects to satisfy 90 per cent of final-year undergraduates. However, the School of Hospitality and Tourism is recognised by the Académie Culinaire de France for its culinary arts programmes, while the London College of Music, which is part of the university, has some of the longest-established music technology courses in the country.

West London improved its ratings considerably in the 2008 Research Assessment Exercise, but entered only a small proportion of its academics. Only nursing and midwifery was judged to have world-leading research. A policy of open access puts the university at a disadvantage on some measures in our ranking. It may also contribute to a projected dropout rate of almost 27 per cent in the latest survey, well above the norm for universities with similar entry requirements and curriculum.

Three quarters of the students are over 24, and about 60 per cent are female. Just more than 45 per cent of the undergraduates come from working-class homes. The university is also very ethnically diverse with only four in ten undergraduates of white, European origin.

The town-centre sites in Ealing and Brentford are linked by a free bus service. The busy Ealing base is within easy reach of central London without the metropolitan hassle that students encounter at some institutions in the capital. Almost half of the students are from London or Berkshire, and there is an unexpectedly large contingent of international students. Residential accommodation is growing and the Paragon building, in Brentford, won Building magazine's Major Housing Project of the Year award. However, students who rely on private housing find the cost of living high. There is a football ground and cricket pitch close to the Ealing campus, but otherwise sports facilities are limited.

Undergraduate Fees and Bursaries

» Fees for UK/EU students 2012–13   £7,500–£8,200
» International student fees 2011–12   £8,150–£9,540
» Students from London or Slough and studying STEM courses, 60 NSP awards and those with dependent children 178 NSP awards of a £3,000 support package.
» Range of other scholarships available.

Students

Undergraduates:	7,755	(4,855)
Postgraduates:	740	(725)
Mature students:	49.5%	
Overseas students:	16.2%	
Applications per place:	5.8	
From state-sector schools:	97.7%	
From working-class homes:	45.9%	

For detailed information about sports facilities: www.uwl.ac.uk/students.jsp

Accommodation

Number of places and costs refer to 2012–13
University-provided places: 839
Percentage catered: 0%
Self-catered costs: from £133.55 (en suite) – £181.00 (studio) a week (incl. utilities and internet).
First years are allocated housing on a first come, first served basis.
International students: same as above.
Contact: uas@uwl.ac.uk
www.uwl.ac.uk/students/student_life/Accommodation.jsp

University of the West of England, Bristol (UWE)

The University of the West of England, Bristol (UWE) is the largest provider of higher education in the southwest of England and one of the most popular post-1992 universities, both in terms of total applications and the proportion who subsequently choose to study there – one in four. But its applications had dropped by more than 13 per cent at the start of 2012, with the prospect of £9,000 fees for degree courses. UWE is implementing a £250-million extension and development of its main campus, eventually closing some outlying sites, but few of those admitted in 2013 will be affected by the changes.

The university has sometimes found itself in trouble for missing its benchmarks for widening access to higher education, but it has broadened its intake considerably in recent years. The proportion of independent school entrants has dropped to 9 per cent – still a figure exceeded by only one new university – while the share of places going to students from working-class homes is around 30 per cent. UWE has one of England's largest bursary and internship programmes. The dropout rate had been coming down but, at more than 21 per cent, the latest projection is well above the national average for the university's subjects and entry qualifications.

UWE's scores rose across all categories in the 2011 National Student Survey, matching the sector average for overall satisfaction. There were particularly high ratings in law, physical geography and environmental science, biology, medical technology and drama. The university is strongly committed to acting on student feedback and boasts one of the largest networks of student representatives in the country, supported by a comprehensive programme of training and personal development. The Graduate Development Programme helps new students settle in and supports them throughout their studies. More than half of the students come from the West Country and there are close links with business and industry. These provide guest lecturers, professors involved in practice, and thousands of part-time jobs and work placements for students, as well as helping to ensure that the curriculum is up-to-date and relevant. Recent links include CERN in Geneva, Hewlett Packard and the BBC, joining about 1,000 smaller organisations.

A tradition of vocational education regularly helps the university to a healthy graduate employment record. Law received a commendation from the Legal Practice Board and the degree in architecture and planning won a similar accolade from the

---

Frenchay Campus
Coldharbour Lane
Bristol BS16 1QY

0117 965 6261 (switchboard)
contact via website
www.uwe.ac.uk
www.uwesu.org
Affiliation: University
Alliance

The Times **Rankings**

Overall Ranking: **62**

Student satisfaction:	=55	(78%)
Research quality:	=68	(0.14)
Entry standards:	66	(299)
Student–staff ratio:	=95	(20.8)
Services & facilities/student:	54	(£1,409)
Expected completion rate:	93	(77.6%)
Good honours:	54	(63.9%)
Graduate prospects:	=52	(65.1%)

Royal Town Planning Institute for bringing together the two disciplines in one joint-honours course giving dual professional qualifications. UWE is one of just four universities recognised by the Forensic Science Society for the quality of courses in the subject. It has some 85 undergraduate and postgraduate courses with professional accreditation. Only two new universities entered more academics than UWE in the 2008 Research Assessment Exercise. More than a third of the work was judged to be world-leading or internationally excellent. Physiotherapy and other health subjects, media studies and general engineering produced the best results.

For the moment, there are four sites in Bristol itself, mainly around the north of the city. Only Bower Ashton, which has new studio space and media suites for its art, media and design students, is in the south. The main campus at Frenchay, four miles out of the city centre, has already doubled in size and is to expand again after the purchase of adjoining land. It includes the largest robotics laboratory in the UK and biggest exhibition and conference centre in the South West, allowing it to stage major careers fairs for its students and enhance links with employers. The St Matthias campus is to close, and its social sciences and humanities courses transfer to Frenchay over the next two years. Glenside campus is home to midwifery, nursing, occupational therapy, physiotherapy and radiography.

A network of 15 colleges stretches into Somerset and Wiltshire, offering UWE programmes. Hartpury College, near Gloucester, is an associate faculty of the university, specialising in agriculture, equine studies and other land-based courses, and there are university centres near hospitals in Gloucester and Bath that concentrate on nursing and allied health professions.

Bristol is a hugely popular student centre: an attractive and lively city, but not cheap. University accommodation has become more plentiful in recent years, with over 4,000 places available, including nearly 2,000 in a new £80-million student village on the Frenchay campus. Sports facilities were a bone of contention for students, but a new sports complex, opened in 2006 as part of a £300-million investment programme, is one of the largest in UK higher education. It was chosen as a pre-Olympics training site for badminton, fencing, table tennis, indoor volleyball and wrestling.

Undergraduate Fees and Bursaries
» Fees for UK/EU students 2012–13 £9,000
» International student fees 2012–13 £10,750
» 500 NSP awards of £1,000 cash and £2,000 accommodation bursary in year 1; £1,000 cash bursary thereafter. 500 awards of £1,000 cash for each year.
» Check the university's website for the latest information.

Students

Undergraduates:	**19,435**	**(4,800)**
Postgraduates:	**1,580**	**(4,715)**
Mature students:	**23.0%**	
Overseas students:	**7%**	
Applications per place:	**4.7**	
From state-sector schools:	**91.0%**	
From working-class homes:	**29.0%**	

For detailed information about sports facilities:
www.uwe.ac.uk/sport

Accommodation
Number of places and costs refer to 2012–13
University-provided places: about 4,000
Percentage catered: 0%
Self-catered costs: £3,945–£5,556 (40 or 45 weeks).
First-year students are guaranteed housing in university-approved accommodation provided requirements are met.
International students are offered accommodation where possible.
Contact: accommodation@uwe.ac.uk

University of the West of Scotland (UWS)

West of Scotland (UWS) continues to enjoy booming demand for its courses. Having registered the biggest increases in applications at any UK university in 2010 and 2011, it managed another 10 per cent increase at degree level in 2012. The achievement is particularly impressive in an area of relatively low participation in higher education at a time when the number of 18-year-old Scots is falling. Growth has been fuelled mainly by the move to an all-graduate nursing profession – the School of Health, Nursing and Midwifery is the largest north of the border – but degrees in subjects such as computer animation, commercial music, computer games technology, sports studies and music technology have all been popular.

Since the 2007 merger of Paisley University and Bell College, in Hamilton, UWS has become the largest of Scotland's seven modern universities. It returned to *The Times* League Table last year after blocking the release of data until all the statistics related to the new institution. The university has moved up three places this year, but still finds itself in the bottom ten.

Research grades improved in the last assessments, although UWS made only a small submission. A quarter of the work was rated as world-leading or internationally excellent, with biomedical sciences and social policy and social work producing the best results. The university made its debut in the National Student Survey in 2011 and recorded satisfaction levels close to the UK average. Music and performing arts scored well, but the primary teacher training degree was the star performer, achieving the best results in Scotland for initial teacher training.

UWS has continued its parent institutions' proud records in attracting under-represented groups onto courses. Almost all the students are state educated and 37 per cent are from working-class homes. Unfortunately, however, dropout rates have been high – the latest projection of 30 per cent non-completion is more than twice the benchmark set according to the subject mix and entry qualifications. Access measures are continuing, with hundreds of youngsters aged 14 and 15 attending the "University Experience" to sample a week of student life.

UWS's four bases are in Ayr, Dumfries, Hamilton and Paisley. Among the first developments were the £5.5-million library and student support services in Dumfries, a £2-million engineering centre at Hamilton and a £1-million employment centre for students across all campuses, which has its hub at the Paisley campus. The new Ayr campus, which is being developed in partnership with the Scottish Agricultural College (SAC), will create an innovative

Paisley Campus
Paisley
Renfrewshire PA1 2BE

0141 848 3000 (switchboard)
info@uws.ac.uk
contact via website
www.uws.ac.uk
www.sauws.org.uk
Affiliation: million+

The Times **Rankings**
Overall Ranking: **109**

Student satisfaction:	=77	(76%)
Research quality:	=68	(0.14)
Entry standards:	94	(271)
Student–staff ratio:	110	(22.2)
Services & facilities/student:	89	(£1,196)
Expected completion rate:	112	(69.3%)
Good honours:	113	(47.9%)
Graduate prospects:	75	(58.2%)

learning environment, one of the most environmentally sustainable in the UK, for around 3,500 students. The university's share of the project cost £80 million and is now complete, having added a highly energy-efficient new teaching building and a new student residence complex.

The university is planning improvements totalling £200 million on the four campuses, which are within reach of nearly 40 per cent of Scots. Another residential complex, costing more than £13 million, will open in Paisley in September 2012. Over £9 million was invested in student facilities in Paisley in the early years of UWS. The main campus, 20 acres in the town centre, has also benefited from a new library and learning resource centre, a £5-million students' union building, and recently upgraded indoor and outdoor sports facilities. The Dumfries campus, operated in partnership with Glasgow University, has over 500 students. The Hamilton campus contains teaching facilities, a students' union, an upgraded leisure centre and some accommodation. The Centre for Engineering Excellence is the newest addition.

Paisley is Scotland's largest town, while Hamilton ranks fifth. Both draw a high proportion of the students from the local area, many on part-time courses. Numbers at Paisley have grown particularly rapidly in recent years and there are around 1,400 international students, thanks to a growing number of Chinese and Indian nationals

and long-established links with over 50 EU institutions.

Courses are strongly vocational, with business, multimedia and health subjects by far the most popular choices. There are close links with business and industry and all students are offered hands-on computer training. Paisley was the first UK university approved by Microsoft, Macromedia and Cisco, and has the status of Microsoft Academic Professional Development Centre. A games development laboratory, supported by Sony, is part of a £300,000 package of investment in multimedia and games facilities.

Paisley pioneered credit transfer in Scotland, including credit for non-academic achievement, and the modular course system covers day, evening and weekend classes. Most students either take sandwich degrees or have work placements built into their courses, earning an average of £10,000 in the process, but the impact on graduate employment has not been as great as elsewhere.

Undergraduate Fees and Bursaries

» Fees for Scottish and EU students 2012–13   No fee
» Fees for Non-Scottish UK-domiciled students 2012–13   £7,250
» Fees for international students 2011–12   £10,000–£10,500
» For RUK students receiving maintenance grant, £500 bursary and £500 university accommodation discount in year 1.
» Check the university's website for the latest information.

Students

Undergraduates:	**9,895**	**(4,780)**
Postgraduates:	**785**	**(1,190)**
Mature students:	**41.1%**	
Overseas students:	**4.4%**	
Applications per place:	**3.2**	
From state-sector schools:	**98.0%**	
From working-class homes:	**37.2%**	

For detailed information about sports facilities:
http://sauws.org.uk/Sports

Accommodation

Number of places and costs refer to 2011–12
University-provided places: 1,088 (732 at Paisley; 200 at Ayr; 156 at Hamilton)
Percentage catered: 0%
Self-catered costs: £79 (single) – £134 (studio) a week (depending on location).
First-year students have priority (conditions apply).
International students: single students guaranteed accommodation if conditions are met and applications received by 27 July.
Contact: www.uws.ac.uk/accommodation

University of Westminster

The demand for places at Westminster rose by more than 25 per cent in two years before the switch to higher fees. Although applications had dropped by more than 6 per cent at the start of 2012 with the prospect of £9,000 fees for all degree courses, this was still better than the sector average. The university has promised that almost three quarters of UK degree students will receive partial fee waivers. It boasted the largest scholarship programme at any university before the fees went up, including more than 100 awards to international students.

Westminster has continued its slow progress up *The Times* League Table, with more satisfied students and better graduate employment figures. A new undergraduate academic model promotes deeper learning through year-long modules and weaves work-related skills into degree programmes. Theory and practice are integrated wherever possible and connections made between subjects. Undergraduates are also given research opportunities. The university is in the bottom ten for student satisfaction, however. Engineering and technology, pharmacy and other health subjects were the only ones to satisfy more than 90 per cent of final-year undergraduates in the 2011 National Student Survey.

Work is now well underway on the £38.5-million redevelopment of the university's greenfield Harrow campus, in the suburbs of northwest London, where the internationally recognised School of Media, Arts and Design enjoys some of the best facilities in Europe. There will be a new student centre with catering facilities and additional learning and social space. The School of Electronics and Computer Science has been consolidated onto a single site in London's West End, and the Harrow Business School merged with the Westminster Business School – also onto a single site in the West End. The School of Life Sciences, based at the New Cavendish Street site near the BT Tower, has recently invested £2 million in modernising its laboratories.

The university has launched a £5-million appeal to restore its main Regent Street building, which it claims as the birthplace of British cinema. It opened The Gallery, a new art and exhibition space, in the building in 2010. The historic headquarters building, near the BBC's Broadcasting House, houses social sciences, humanities and languages. Westminster offers one of the widest ranges of language teaching of any British university and partners the School of Oriental and African Studies in leading the Routes into Languages programme to encourage more people to learn a language. The West End sites provide the perfect catchment area for part-time

---

309 Regent Street
London W1B 2UW

020 7915 5511 (enquiries)
course-enquiries@
westminster.ac.uk
www.westminster.ac.uk
www.uwsu.com
Affiliation: none

The Times **Rankings**
Overall Ranking: **=95**

Student satisfaction:	**112**	(71%)
Research quality:	**=64**	(0.15)
Entry standards:	**=74**	(292)
Student–staff ratio:	**=62**	(18.4)
Services & facilities/student:	**71**	(£1,302)
Expected completion rate:	**=86**	(78.3%)
Good honours:	**81**	(58.3%)
Graduate prospects:	**72**	(59.3%)

Edinburgh
Belfast
Cardiff
LONDON

undergraduates, who account for over a fifth of nearly 16,500 undergraduate places. However, by no means all of Westminster's students are Londoners. Over 5,000 come from overseas – among the most at any post-1992 university – and Westminster also has the largest number of ethnic minority students in Britain. Westminster courses are also taught in nine overseas countries, from Sri Lanka to Uzbekistan, a characteristic which won the university a Queen's Award for Enterprise.

Westminster hit the headlines in the 2008 Research Assessment Exercise, when it was rated top in the UK for media studies with one of the highest proportions of world-leading research (60 per cent) in any subject. More than a third of all the work submitted by the university was rated in the top two categories, resulting a doubling of Westminster's research grants. Art and design, architecture and biomedical sciences all achieved good grades. The university has since been chosen to head a €1-million European research project to explore the relationship between scarcity and creativity in the built environment. Accolades for its teaching include fashionista.com ranking its fashion design degree second in the UK, and in the top 10 worldwide.

More than four out of ten undergraduates are from working-class homes – a much higher proportion than the national average for the subjects offered. The university also exceeds its benchmark for the admission of students from state schools and colleges. However, those from lower participation neighbourhoods are under-represented, while the projected dropout rate of more than 18 per cent practically matches the expectations for the university.

Westminster's students, like those at all the London universities, complain of the high cost of living, particularly for accommodation. The university has added considerably to its residential stock in recent years, with the opening of a £6-million block of halls in Harrow and the refurbishment of its Marylebone halls, but there is no way round the capital's inflated housing market at some stage. The Harrow campus is lively socially, but those based on the other campuses tend to be spread around the capital. Sports facilities are also dispersed, with playing fields and a boathouse in Chiswick, west London. Smoke Radio, Westminster's student radio station, has won several awards and has now spawned Smoke Television.

Undergraduate Fees and Bursaries

» Fees for UK/EU students 2012–13   £9,000
» International student fees 2012–13   £10,975
» Fee waivers given on a course by course basis to UK students.
» 222 NSP awards of a £3,000 support package for two years.
» Westminster Scholarship of £2,000 fee waiver for three years.
» Other scholarships available.

Students		
Undergraduates:	**12,670**	**(3,745)**
Postgraduates:	**3,220**	**(3,110)**
Mature students:	**28.8%**	
Overseas students:	**19.5%**	
Applications per place:	**5.4**	
From state-sector schools:	**95.4%**	
From working-class homes:	**44.3%**	

For detailed information about sports facilities:
www.westminster.ac.uk

Accommodation
Number of places and costs refer to 2012–13
University-provided places: 1,750
Percentage catered: 0%
Self-catered costs: £90 – £189 a week (36–51 week contracts).
First-year students have priority for 1,000 rooms. Residential restrictions apply.
International students: as above.
Contact: studentaccommodation@westminster.ac.uk
www.westminster.ac.uk/housing

University of Winchester

Winchester was one of about 20 universities to add to the discounts it planned to offer in 2012–13 in order to qualify for the extra places reserved for universities with the lowest average fees after allowing for student support. The switch paid off with a healthy allocation of additional places and only a small drop in the demand from applicants faced with headline fees of £8,500 for all courses. The university stresses its "human scale", with only 6,400 students and an emphasis on providing a supportive community for students to unlock their potential. The approach appears to have struck a chord: applications were up by significantly more than the national average for two years in a row, before the 3 per cent decline at the start of 2012. After successive finishes around the top 30 in the National Student Survey, however, the university has dropped to a mid-table position. Education, archaeology, English and history were the only areas to satisfy more than 90 per cent of final-year undergraduates in 2011, although journalism was in the top three nationally.

The university traces its history as an Anglican foundation back to 1840 and has occupied its King Alfred campus since 1862. The compact site is on a wooded hillside overlooking the cathedral city, a ten-minute walk away, with views of the surrounding countryside. Known as King Alfred's College until 2004, the university is still best-known for teacher training, which accounts for about a third of the places. Ofsted rates the teacher training courses as outstanding. It is one of the largest providers of primary school training in England, but courses on the main campus also span business, arts, humanities, health and social care, and social sciences. Degrees range from choreography and dance, through social work, business, accounting, law, media and teacher training to modern liberal arts. Fashion: media and marketing is a new degree planned for 2012 entry.

Winchester improved on already respectable grades in the 2008 Research Assessment Exercise, when it was ranked second among the new universities in history, with over half of its submission considered world-leading or internationally excellent. Overall, more than a third of the university's work reached the top two categories, and there was some world-leading research in four of the six subject areas.

The university is particularly proud of its low dropout rate, and the latest official projection of 12.4 per cent was marginally better than the national average for Winchester's courses and entry qualifications. Over 95 per cent of the British students are state-educated and very nearly three in ten are from working-class homes. Male undergraduates are heavily

---

Winchester

Hampshire SO22 4NR

01962 827234 (enquiries)
course.enquiries@winchester.ac.uk
www.winchester.ac.uk
www.winchester
students.co.uk
Affiliations: Cathedral Group,
Guild HE

The Times Rankings		
Overall Ranking: =75		
Student satisfaction:	=77	(76%)
Research quality:	=75	(0.12)
Entry standards:	=71	(293)
Student–staff ratio:	=64	(18.5)
Services & facilities/student:	102	(£1,070)
Expected completion rate:	49	(85.6%)
Good honours:	59	(62.4%)
Graduate prospects:	105	(51.0%)

outnumbered, and there are about 150 overseas students from a range of countries. Winchester students can take advantage of exchange schemes with American universities in New York, Maine, Oregon and Wisconsin, as well as with universities in Japan.

The main campus is well equipped, with its theatrical performance spaces, sports hall and fitness suite now supplemented by the £3.5-million Winchester Sports Stadium, which opened in 2008. Open to local people as well as students, the stadium has an Olympic standard 400-metre eight-lane athletics track with supporting facilities for field events and also a floodlit all-weather pitch. There are six performing arts studios in a new building that opened in 2010 on the King Alfred campus, offering the latest technology for student productions. A new Learning and Teaching Building currently under construction on the King Alfred campus will provide outstanding facilities for lectures and independent study. The building is due to open in September 2012.

An award-winning University Centre opened in 2007, transforming the students' union, adding a nightclub, cinema, catering facilities, a bookshop and a supermarket at a cost of £9 million. A "learning café" creates an informal working space with networked PCs and wireless internet access. An award-winning extension to the library made room for 200,000 books, 450 study spaces and 150 computers.

A £12-million student village, a short walk from the main campus, provides more than 700 residential places. The business school is also located on the West Downs campus. A second village, with en-suite rooms arranged in cluster flats with shared kitchen facilities, opened in 2010, and another new student village is under construction, due to open in the 2012–13 academic year. Winchester guarantees campus accommodation to first year full-time undergraduates, overseas students and students with medical needs as long they apply by the deadline. Students value the close-knit atmosphere and find the city is livelier than its staid image might suggest, with a number of bars catering to their tastes. Southampton is not far for those who hanker after the attractions of a bigger city, and London is only an hour away by train.

Undergraduate Fees and Bursaries

» Fees for UK/EU students 2012–13   £8,500
» International student fees 2012–13   £9,775
» Household income below £25K, fee waiver £1,750 year 1, £2,500 years 2 and 3, and £500 bursary a year; £25K–£42.6K, £1,000 fee waiver year 1; £1,500 years 2 and 3.
» 57 NSP awards of £3,000 fee waiver, year 1, £1,500 fee waiver years 2 and 3.
» Award of £2,000 cash or fee waiver a year for those with AAB at A level or equivalent.
» Sport and music awards available.

Students		
Undergraduates:	**4,435**	**(925)**
Postgraduates:	**205**	**(1,325)**
Mature students:	**16.4%**	
Overseas students:	**7.8%**	
Applications per place:	**4.5**	
From state-sector schools:	**96.1%**	
From working-class homes:	**29.9%**	

For detailed information about sports facilities:
www.winchester.ac.uk/campuscitylife/
Sportsfacilities

Accommodation
Number of places and costs refer to 2012–13
University-provided places: 1,220 on campus; 212 off campus
Percentage catered: 15%
Catered costs: £3,952.40 (term-time only).
Self-catered costs: £2,807.80 – £4,381.95 (37-40 weeks).
First years are guaranteed accommodation if conditions are met.
International students: non EU, as above.
Contact: housing@winchester.ac.uk
www.winchester.ac.uk/startinghere/Student%20accommodation/
Pages/Studentaccommodation.aspx

University of Wolverhampton

Wolverhampton bucked the national trend with 5 per cent growth in applications at the start of 2012, the biggest increase in the region and one of the largest in England. But Professor Geoff Layer, the Vice-Chancellor, said Government controls would leave record numbers of applicants competing for fewer places, even though the university was allocated extra places from the pool of 20,000 reserved for universities and colleges charging the lowest fees. Students will pay between £7,000 and £8,500 in 2012–13, depending on course and level.

The university is one of three that has refused to allow the Higher Education Statistics Agency to release data on their performance for league tables. Just outside the top 100 on its last appearance in *The Times* League Table, its student satisfaction and dropout rates have improved markedly since then, and it might have finished higher this time. A statement on the university's website says that tables such as ours disadvantage universities like Wolverhampton and do not represent a fair picture of their strengths. As a result, it is missing from both the main ranking and all the subject tables.

Wolverhampton's success in widening participation in higher education is such that it is one of only two universities in England where half of the undergraduates come from working-class homes. Almost all the students are from state schools and one in five comes from an area of low participation in higher education. The university draws two thirds of its 23,000 students from the West Midlands, although it has a growing contingent from overseas. A third of the places are filled by mature students and about the same proportion come from the region's ethnic minorities. Big outreach programmes take courses into the workplace.

The three West Midland campuses have their own learning centres and are linked by a free bus service. The original site is in Wolverhampton city centre, while sport and performance, education and part of the School of Health and Wellbeing are based in Walsall. A purpose-built campus at Telford in Shropshire focuses on business and engineering in a county with no higher education institution of its own. A branch campus in Mauritius will open in 2012, offering law degrees and an MA in education.

Wolverhampton has been investing millions of pounds in its "New Horizons" infrastructure programme. The project has seen £26 million spent on the City campus, notably on the flagship Millennium City Building and a teaching and administration building. A 350-bed student village has opened on the Walsall campus, together with

---

Wulfruna Street
Wolverhampton WV1 1LY

01902 321000 (enquiries)
enquiries@wlv.ac.uk
www.wlv.ac.uk
www.wolvesunion.org
Affiliation: million+

Edinburgh
Belfast
WOLVERHAMPTON
Cardiff
London

The Times **Rankings**
Wolverhampton blocked the release of data from the Higher Education Statistics Agency and so we cannot give any ranking information.

a Lottery-supported sports hall offering elite training facilities for judo and a Sports Science and Medicine Centre which are being used to train Olympic contenders. A £12-million building for the School of Education and the Institute for Learning Enhancement opened in 2008. At Telford the £7-million e-Innovation Centre has already won awards for the support it offers to e-businesses, while a new Performance Hub is opening at the Walsall campus.

The projected dropout rate is now well below the benchmark for a university with Wolverhampton's entry grades and subjects, at less than 13 per cent. Teacher-training courses are rated in the top four in the country by Ofsted, and Wolverhampton academics have been awarded six National Teaching Fellowships by the Higher Education Academy. Scores in the National Student Survey slipped slightly in 2011, leaving the university in the bottom 20. Only fine art, initial teacher training and nursing satisfied 90 per cent or more of the students.

The university pioneered interactive multimedia communication degrees, as well as offering one of the first degrees in British sign language and one of the first in virtual reality design and manufacturing. It was the first university to be registered under the British Standards for the quality of its all-round provision. Wolverhampton stresses innovation and enterprise in its work with students and businesses, encouraging student start-up companies and leading a project to develop student placements in these companies for those who wish to become entrepreneurs. The Flying Start Programme for Sports Business is the first of its kind in the UK, providing a series of specialist workshops.

Research is mainly applied, serving the needs of business and industry, as well as underpinning teaching at all levels. The university was ranked fourth in the UK for statistical cybermetrics and sixth for computational linguistics in the 2008 Research Assessment Exercise. A relatively low proportion of the academics were entered for assessment, but 30 per cent of their research was considered world-leading or internationally excellent.

Social facilities vary between sites. Wolverhampton has a growing nightlife and the university has been voted the friendliest in the West Midlands. The cost of living is reasonable and Birmingham is now only a metro tramride away.

Undergraduate Fees and Bursaries

» Fees for UK/EU students 2012–13   £8,000–£8,500
    Foundation degree   £7,000
» International student fees 2012–13   £9,925
» 420 NSP awards of £3,000 support package.
» Continuing achievement award of £1000 fee waiver after completion of each year.
» Award of £3,500 support in year 1 for those with AAB at A level or equivalent.

Students		
Undergraduates:	**13,020**	**(5,045)**
Postgraduates:	**1,845**	**(2,265)**
From state-sector schools:	**98.3%**	
From working-class homes:	**50.3%**	

For detailed information about sports facilities:
www.wlv.ac.uk/sport

Accommodation
Number of places and costs refer to 2012–13
University-provided places: 1,603
Percentage catered: 0%
Self-catered costs: £2,579 – £3,782.98 (37 weeks).
First-year students are offered accommodation provided requirements are met. Residential restrictions apply.
International students: same as above.
Contact: accommodationservices@wlv.ac.uk

University of Worcester

Worcester has the most ambitious development plans of all the new universities created in 2005. A second campus in the heart of the city opened in 2010 and a spectacular library and history centre – the first joint public and university library in Britain – opens in July 2012. On top of this, the university is investing in a state-of-the-art indoor sporting arena for the city, to open in early 2013. It will be one of only two specialist sports venues in the UK designed for wheelchair athletes.

The university is one of the fastest growing in Britain, with applications rising seven times faster than the national average in the last seven years. It was one of the few universities in England to see an increase in degree applications at the start of 2012, when fees of £8,100 were about to be introduced. Business courses have been particularly popular and there have been big increases, too, in physical education, sports studies, forensic science, marketing, pre-hospital and emergency care, journalism, social work and advertising. An emphasis on employability in the curriculum was commended in an audit by the Quality Assurance Agency in 2011 QAA institutional audit.

First as a post-war emergency teacher training college and later as a university college, the institution has always been the only provider of higher education in Herefordshire and Worcestershire. The university remains strong in education and also in nursing and midwifery – a mix that contributes to an overwhelmingly female student population. It received the best possible inspection report from the Nursing and Midwifery Council for its training of nurses, and one of the best Ofsted reports in the country for its teacher training, scoring "outstanding" in all sections. Worcester has also been selected as the partner university for the National Childbirth Trust and will deliver all of the UK's antenatal training. The six academic departments also cover applied sciences, geography and archaeology, a business school and arts, humanities and social sciences.

In the 2011 National Student Survey, 84 per cent of final-year undergraduates were satisfied overall – better than the sector average. There was 100 per cent satisfaction in sociology and very high scores in history and archaeology, nursing and social policy. The 23 academics entered for the 2008 Research Assessment Exercise represented the smallest contingent from any university in England. Only English had any world-leading research, although there are pockets of excellence such as the National Pollen and Aerobiology Research Unit, which produces all of Britain's pollen forecasts.

Henwick Grove
Worcester WR2 6AJ

01905 855111 (admissions)
admissions@worc.ac.uk
www.worc.ac.uk
www.worcsu.com
Affiliation: Guild HE

The Times Rankings

Overall Ranking: **=93**

Student satisfaction:	=55	(78%)
Research quality:	=115	(0.01)
Entry standards:	=78	(288)
Student–staff ratio:	105	(21.5)
Services & facilities/student:	107	(£1,006)
Expected completion rate:	66	(81.9%)
Good honours:	88	(55.3%)
Graduate prospects:	83	(56.2%)

More than a third of the undergraduates come from working-class homes. The projected dropout rate has declined to around 15 per cent, but is still slightly above average for the university's subjects and entry qualifications.

The St John's campus occupies a parkland site a 15-minute walk from the city centre. Recent developments there include a £7-million science facility which houses teaching laboratories and the National Pollen and Aerobiology Research Unit, a £1-million digital arts centre and drama studio, and a third-generation Astroturf pitch. Sport plays an important part in university life: a well-appointed sports centre also provides employment opportunities for students, while competitive teams are successful and the facilities for casual participants extensive. A mobile 3D motion analysis laboratory has been used by the England and Wales Cricket Board. Modest sports scholarships are offered in partnership with Worcestershire County Cricket Club, Worcester Wolves Basketball Club and Worcester Hockey Club. The basketball team have been national champions for three years in succession. The new Worcester Arena, opening in 2013, will build on the university's extensive work in disability sports, as well as providing a top class sporting venue for the region, capable of hosting major tournaments.

The new City campus occupies the site of the old Worcester Royal Infirmary. It includes teaching, residential and conference facilities and is home to the Worcester Business School. The Hive, the new library and history centre is next to the campus and will be open to all students and members of the public. It contains one of the largest children's libraries in the country, as well as the university's collections. An unusual feature of the university's widening participation work is extensive work with primary schoolchildren.

There are buses that run between the two campuses, as well as a cycle route. Halfway between the two sites are further new facilities, including specialist art rooms, dance studios, teaching spaces and the planned Worcester Arena. The university also has a number of partner colleges around the region offering Worcester courses. Social life revolves around the students' union. The cathedral city is not large, but is safer than many university locations, and has its share of pubs and clubs that cater for a growing student clientele.

Undergraduate Fees and Bursaries

» Fees for UK/EU students 2012–13 £8,100
   Foundation degrees at partner colleges £6,000
» International student fees 2012–13 £9,600
» 200 NSP awards of £3,000 fee waiver.
» Award of £1,000 fee waiver in year 1 for those with AAB at A level or equivalent.
» Other scholarships available.

Students		
Undergraduates:	**6,200**	**(1,895)**
Postgraduates:	**535**	**(1,460)**
Mature students:	**29.6%**	
Overseas students:	**6.2%**	
Applications per place:	**4.5**	
From state-sector schools:	**97.2%**	
From working-class homes:	**35.5%**	

For detailed information about sports facilities: www.worcsu.com/studentgroupscontent/ 782503/sports/

Accommodation

Number of places and costs refer to 2011–12
University-provided places: 970 university-owned; 200–230 university-managed
Percentage catered: 0%
Self-catered costs: £75–£127 a week.
First-year students are guaranteed accommodation, on a first come, first served basis, if conditions are met.
International students are accommodated if conditions are met.
Contact: accommodation@worc.ac.uk

University of York

York was one of four universities to join the Russell Group of leading research institutions at the start of 2012. Professor Brian Cantor, the Vice-Chancellor, said it was a mark of the great progress made by the university in its 50-year history. York remains just outside the top ten in *The Times* League Table, but is ranked among the top 100 universities in the world by QS and was *Times Higher Education* magazine's 2010 University of the Year. The university has been growing in popularity and the demand for places was unaffected by the introduction of fees of £9,000 for 2012–13.

York decided five years ago that it was too small to maximise its research capability, play a leading role in the economy of the region and satisfy the growing demand for its places. In an audacious move for a highly selective university, it has opened a second campus to accommodate up to 50 per cent more students and strengthen its research. A new residential college for 600 students and buildings for computer science, law, management, and theatre, film and television have already opened on the Heslington East site. The campus expansion will take 10 to 15 years to complete and eventually contain housing for an additional 3,300 students, as well as more academic buildings, sports facilities and a performing arts and community complex. A £21-million "hub" for the campus opened in 2010 and a second residential college for 650 students will follow in 2012. A £20-million refurbishment of the university library will also be completed in 2012, and a £16.5-million redevelopment of the department of chemistry is under way to provide new research and undergraduate laboratories.

The expansion has allowed York to introduce new subjects. The first intake of undergraduates in law and in writing, directing and performance in theatre, film and television graduated in 2011. Medicine was introduced in 2003 in partnership with Hull University. York also runs its own nursing and midwifery programmes. The university believes that, with more than six applicants for every place, other departments can grow at the same time as retaining or achieving a place in the top ten for their subject.

The university has done well in the National Student Survey, both in its own right and at the medical school, which is assessed separately. York has finished in the top 30 universities in all seven years of polling. In the 2011 survey, physical geography and environmental science, archaeology, biology and chemistry all satisfied more than 95 per cent of final-year undergraduates. In November 2011, the university won its fifth Queen's Anniversary

---

Heslington
York YO10 5DD

01904 324000 (admissions)
ug-admissions@york.ac.uk
www.york.ac.uk
www.hyms.ac.uk
www.yusu.org
Affiliation: Russell Group

The Times **Rankings**
Overall Ranking: **13**

Student satisfaction:	=17	(81%)
Research quality:	=9	(0.87)
Entry standards:	15	(453)
Student–staff ratio:	=32	(15.6)
Services & facilities/student:	15	(£2,025)
Expected completion rate:	12	(94.5%)
Good honours:	22	(74.7%)
Graduate prospects:	37	(70.6%)

Prize in 15 years, this time for its work in broadening the scope of archaeology.

Entrance requirements are high and the dropout rate of less than 5 per cent is among the lowest in the country. Every student has a supervisor responsible for their academic and personal welfare, and first-year undergraduates have access to free language tuition and a Mathematics Study Skills Centre. Undergraduates can also take the York Award, comprising a range of courses, work placements and voluntary activities which aim to prepare students for the world of work. Over 600 students work as volunteer teaching assistants in local schools.

York was among the top ten institutions in the 2008 Research Assessment Exercise, when more than 60 per cent of the work submitted was judged to be world-leading or internationally excellent. The university was ranked top in the UK for English and health services research, joint top for sociology, and among the leaders for linguistics, and nursing and midwifery. Nearly 30 per cent of the full-time students are postgraduates.

The original campus occupies 200 acres of landscaped parkland, a mile outside the historic, picturesque city centre. Students join one of eight colleges, which mix academic and social roles. Most departments have their headquarters in one of the colleges, but the student community is a deliberate mixture of disciplines, years and sexes. Nursing apart, only archaeology and medieval studies are located off campus, sharing a medieval building in the centre of the city.

Social life on campus is lively. There are television and radio stations, as well as several newspapers and magazines, to keep students abreast of campus issues. Sports facilities are good, and include a 50-station fitness suite, four sports halls and dance studio. The £9-million York Sports Village will open on campus in 2012, featuring a 25-metre pool, learner pool, 100-station gym, full-size 3G pitch and three further five-a-side pitches. Cultural events abound on campus and in the city, which is also famous for a high concentration of pubs. The club scene has improved, but students still head for Leeds for the top names.

Undergraduate Fees and Bursaries

» Fees for UK/EU students 2012–13   £9,000
» International student fees 2012–13   £12,720–£16,540
    Medicine   £24,080
» 171 NSP awards of £3,500 fee waiver and £1,000 accommodation discount.
» Household income less than £25K, £2,000 fee waiver and £1,000 accommodation discount year 1; £2,000 package other years.
» Other scholarships and bursaries available.

Students

Undergraduates:	**10,460**	**(1,170)**
Postgraduates:	**4,050**	**(995)**
Mature students:	**8.6%**	
Overseas students:	**12.4%**	
Applications per place:	**6.4**	
From state-sector schools:	**78.8%**	
From working-class homes:	**18.1%**	

For detailed information about sports facilities: www.york.as.uk/univ/sports

Accommodation

Number of places and costs refer to 2012–13

University-provided places: 5,196

Percentage catered: 20%

Catered costs: £115.43–£134.19 a week.

Self-catered costs: £90.09–£123.97 a week.

First-year single undergraduates are provided with accommodation if terms and conditions are met.

International students: as above.

Contact: accommodation@york.ac.uk

www.york.ac.uk/accommodation

York St John University

York St John set some of the lowest fees at any English university when it decided to charge only £3,500 for Foundation degrees in theology and education. But it was the honours degrees, costing £8,500, that attracted some of the biggest increases in applications in England. The demand for places was up almost 13 per cent at the start of 2012, following growth of almost 40 per cent over the previous two years. Continuing the theme of success, the university has gone up five places in the new *Times* League Table, benefiting from more satisfied students and better graduate employment. One of the four universities designated in 2006, York St John is a Church of England foundation that dates back almost 170 years. The eight-acre site faces York Minster across the city walls and is a five-minute walk from the city centre. Now serving over 6,000 students, the campus has seen £75 million of development in recent years and more is planned. The Fountains Learning Centre, which provides a striking entrance to the university, has just undergone a £1.1-million refurbishment programme. It now has 530 computer workstations, multimedia group-work facilities, 24-hour access to enhanced self-service facilities and an enlarged book stock, as well an internet café and lecture theatre.

Nearby, the prize-winning De Grey Court, which cost £15.5 million and serves the health and life sciences, links the university quarter with the city centre.

York Diocesan Training School opened in 1841 with one pupil on the register, in whose honour the current (and recently refurbished) students' union is named. Divided between York and Ripon for most of its existence, the institution diversified beyond teacher training in the 1980s and decided at the start of this decade to concentrate all its teaching on York. The university's mission statement says its provision is "shaped" by the York St John's church foundation, although it welcomes students of all beliefs.

Education and theology remains the biggest faculty, with 1,700 students taking programmes in teacher education, education studies, and theology and religious studies. Health and life sciences are not far behind in terms of size, with 1,600 full-time students and 200 part-timers studying courses such as physiotherapy and occupational therapy, as well as psychology and sport. The York St John Business School, launched in May 2008, engages with a range of local and regional small to medium-sized enterprises, as well as offering the normal range of undergraduate and postgraduate courses. The university has launched a number of successful enterprise initiatives. Its latest venture, the Phoenix Centre, a business

---

New Mayor's Walk
York YO31 7EX

01904 876598 (information hotline)
admissions@yorksj.ac.uk
www.yorksj.ac.uk
www.ysjsu.com
Affiliations: Cathedral Group,
  Guild HE

The Times **Rankings**
Overall Ranking: **80**

Student satisfaction:	=42	(79%)
Research quality:	=108	(0.03)
Entry standards:	=84	(282)
Student–staff ratio:	=103	(21.4)
Services & facilities/student:	95	(£1,150)
Expected completion rate:	=58	(84.3%)
Good honours:	=77	(58.7%)
Graduate prospects:	97	(53.1%)

incubation facility which it has taken over from Science City York, continues a focus on mentoring and support to both the university's graduates and new local businesses.

The Faculty of Arts, which was formed in 2001, has been one of the main points of expansion, especially in degree programmes such as film and television, media and American studies. The university was awarded a national centre for excellence in creativity, based on its work in English and theatre studies, although funding for such programmes has now ceased. Another music technology suite has been added and performance spaces include two dedicated TV studios, digital non-linear edit suites, digital imaging equipment and equipment for sound manipulation. There are also facilities available for set design and construction as well as prop and costume making.

Overall student satisfaction rose by three percentage points in 2011, taking the university into the top half of the table on this measure. Theology and religious studies, psychology and initial teacher training all produced among the best results in the country in the National Student Survey. Drama, dance and performing arts was the most successful field in the 2008 Research Assessment Exercise and the only one to contain world-leading research.

Seven out of ten students are female – one of the highest proportions in the university system. Almost 95 per cent of the students attended state schools or colleges, while 30 per cent are from working-class homes. The projected dropout rate of 9 per cent maintains the improvement of recent years and is well below the national average for the university's courses and entry qualifications.

Relatively high numbers of local mature students ease the pressure on residential accommodation. As a result, first years who want to live in university-owned accommodation are usually able to do so. More self-catering accommodation for 500 students, costing £10 million, opened in September 2009. Sports facilities are not extensive, but the Foss Building houses a sports hall, climbing wall, basketball, netball, indoor football and cricket nets. York is popular as a student city with a growing range of clubs as well as, supposedly, a pub for every day of the year.

Undergraduate Fees and Bursaries

» Fees for UK/EU students 2012–13 £8,500
  Foundation degrees £3,500
» International student fees 2012–13 £9,000–£11,500
» Fee waivers based on household income: below £10K, £2,000 a year; £10K–£20K, £1,250 a year; £20K–£30K, £750 a year.
» NSP awards of £3,000 fee waiver in year 1.
» Check the university's website for the latest information.

Students

Undergraduates:	**3,720**	**(1,350)**
Postgraduates:	**260**	**(620)**
Mature students:	**14.6%**	
Overseas students:	**4.1%**	
Applications per place:	**5.8**	
From state-sector schools:	**94.6%**	
From working-class homes:	**30.0%**	

For detailed information about sports facilities:
www.yorksj.ac.uk/ysjactive

Accommodation

Number of places and costs refer to 2012–13
University-provided places: 1,540
Percentage catered: 9.5%
Catered costs: £131.87 (semi-catered package) a week (33 weeks).
Self-catered costs: £61–£142 a week (44–48 weeks).
First years choosing university as first choice are guaranteed accommodation. Residential and age restrictions apply.
International students: guaranteed housing.
Contact: accommodation@yorksj.ac.uk

Colleges of Higher Education

This listing gives contact details for higher education institutions not mentioned elsewhere within the book. All the institutions listed below offer degree courses, some providing a wide range of courses while others are specialist colleges with a small intake. Those marked * are members of GuildHE (**www.guildhe.ac.uk**). Fees are given for UK/EU undergraduates for 2012–13.

Arts University College, Bournemouth*
Wallisdown, Poole, Dorset BH12 5HH
01202 533011　　　　　www.aucb.ac.uk
Fees 2012–13: £8,600

Bishop Grosseteste University College*
Lincoln LN1 3DY
01522 527347　　　　www.bishopg.ac.uk
Fees 2012–13: £7,500

BPP University College
BPP House, Aldine Place,
142-4 Uxbridge Road, London W12 8AW
0845 077 5566　　　　　www.bppuc.com
Fees 2012–13: £9,675 (two-year course)

College of Law
Birmingham, Bristol, Chester, Guildford,
London (Bloomsbury and Moorgate),
Manchester and York.
0800 289997　　　www.college-of-law.co.uk
Fees 2012–13: £9,000 (two-year course)

Conservatoire for Dance and Drama
Consists of 8 Schools, 6 in London, including RADA
Tavistock House, Tavistock Square
London WC1H 9JJ
020 7387 5101　　　　　www.cdd.ac.uk
Fees 2012–13: £9,000

Glasgow School of Art
167 Renfrew Street, Glasgow G3 6RQ
0141 353 4500　　　　　www.gsa.ac.uk
Fees 2012–13: Scotland/EU, no fee;
RUK £9,000

Guildhall School of Music and Drama
Silk Street, Barbican, London EC2Y 8DT
020 7628 2571　　　　　www.gsmd.ac.uk
Fees 2012–13: £9,000

Harper Adams University College*
Newport, Shropshire TF10 8NB
01952 820280　　　www.harper-adams.ac.uk
Fees 2012–13: £9,000

Leeds Trinity University College*
Brownberrie Lane, Leeds LS18 5HD
0113 283 7200　　　　www.leedstrinity.ac.uk
Fees 2012–13: £8,000

Liverpool Institute for Performing Arts*
Mount Street, Liverpool L1 9HF
0151 330 3000　　　　　www.lipa.ac.uk
Fees 2012–13: £9,000

New College of the Humanities
27 Old Gloucester Street, London WC1N 3AX
0207367 4550　　　　　www.nchum.org
Fees 2012–13: £18,000

Newman University College*
Genners Lane, Bartley Green,
Birmingham B32 3NT
0121 476 1181　　　　　www.newman.ac.uk
Fees 2012–13: £8,400

Norwich University College of the Arts*
Francis House, 3–7 Redwell Street
Norwich NR2 4SN
01603 610561　　　　　www.nuca.ac.uk
Fees 2012–13: £8,500

Ravensbourne*
6 Penrose Way, London SE10 0EW
020 3040 3500　　　　　www.rave.ac.uk
Fees 2012–13: £8,300–£8,500

Rose Bruford College of Theatre and Performance*
Burnt Oak Lane, Sidcup, Kent DA15 9DF
020 8308 2600　　　　　www.bruford.ac.uk
Fees 2012–13: £9,000

Royal Agricultural College*
Stroud Road, Cirencester
Gloucestershire GL7 6JS
01285 652531 www.rac.ac.uk
Fees 2012–13: £9,000

Royal College of Music
Prince Consort Road, London SW7 2BS
020 7591 4300 www.rcm.ac.uk
Fees 2012–13: £9,000

Royal Northern College of Music
124 Oxford Road, Manchester M13 9RD
0161 907 5200 www.rncm.ac.uk
Fees 2012–13: £9,000

Royal Conservatoire of Scotland
100 Renfrew Street, Glasgow G2 3DB
0141 332 4101 www.rcs.ac.uk
Fees 2012–13: Scotland/EU, no fee;
RUK £9,000

Royal Welsh College of Music and Drama
Cathays Park, Cardiff CF10 3ER
029 2034 2854 www.rwcmd.ac.uk
Fees 2012–13: £9,000

St Mary's University College*
Waldegrave Road, Strawberry Hill
Twickenham TW1 4SX
020 8240 4000 www.smuc.ac.uk
Fees 2012–13: £8,000

St Mary's University College*
191 Falls Road, Belfast BT12 6FE
028 9032 7678 www.stmarys-belfast.ac.uk
Fees 2012–13: £3,375

Stranmillis University College
Stranmillis Road, Belfast BT9 5DY
028 9038 1271 www.stran.ac.uk
Fees 2012–13: £3,375

Trinity Laban Conservatoire of Music and Dance
Music Faculty: King Charles Court
Old Royal Naval College,
Greenwich, London SE10 9JF
020 8305 4300
Dance Faculty: Creekside
London SE8 3DZ
020 8691 8600
www.trinitylaban.ac.uk
Fees 2012–13: £9,000

University Campus Suffolk
Waterfront Building, Neptune Quay
Ipswich IP4 1QJ
01473 338000 www.ucs.ac.uk
Fees 2012–13: £8,000

University College Birmingham*
Summer Row, Birmingham B3 1JB
0121 604 1000 www.ucb.ac.uk
Fees 2012–13: £7,800

University College Falmouth*
Woodlane, Falmouth, Cornwall TR11 4RH
01326 211077 www.falmouth.ac.uk
Fees 2012–13: £9,000

University College Plymouth St Mark and St John* (Marjon)
Derriford Road, Plymouth, Devon PL6 8BH
01752 636700 www.marjon.ac.uk
Fees 2012–13: £7,800

Writtle College*
Chelmsford, Essex CM1 3RR
01245 424200 www.writtle.ac.uk
Fees 2012–13: £8,000

Index